The Greater Middle East and the Cold War

The Greater Middle East and the Cold War

US Foreign Policy under Eisenhower and Kennedy

Roby C. Barrett

Paperback edition published in 2010 by I.B.Tauris & Co Ltd
6 Salem Road, London W2 4BU
175 Fifth Avenue, New York NY 10010
www.ibtauris.com

Distributed in the United States and Canada Exclusively by Palgrave Macmillan
175 Fifth Avenue, New York NY 10010

First published in 2007 by I.B.Tauris & Co Ltd

Copyright © 2007, 2010 Roby C. Barrett

The right of Roby C. Barrett to be identified as the author of this work has been asserted by him in accordance with the Copyright, Designs and Patents Act 1988.

All rights reserved. Except for brief quotations in a review, this book, or any part thereof, may not be reproduced, stored in or introduced into a retrieval system, or transmitted, in any form or by any means, electronic, mechanical, photocopying, recording or otherwise, without the prior written permission of the publisher.

ISBN: 978 1 84885 261 7

A full CIP record for this book is available from the British Library
A full CIP record is available from the Library of Congress

Library of Congress Catalog Card Number: available

Printed and bound in India by Replika Press Pvt. Ltd.

To Eli and Gus

In Memory of Roby Eli Barrett

Contents

List of Abbreviations	xi
List of Illustrations	xv
Acknowledgments	xvii
Preface	xix
Introduction	1
Chapter 1: The Greater Middle East 1953-1958	10

Preemption and Iran 1953; Defusing a crisis and sparking another – Egypt, 1953-1954; A peace for the Arab-Israeli conflict; Running afoul of non-alignment; Nehru and Bandung; Nasser and Bandung; Middle East policy: after six years, rethinking the paradigm

Part I: 1958 – The New Order and Reconsiderations	40
Chapter 2: The Wave of the Future	43

The Egyptian-Syrian Union, and saving the Middle East from Communism; A change in plans: fighting Communism with Nasser; A pro-Western alternative?; Britain's Middle East domino theory; Nasser at the pinnacle; Clouds on the horizon: the Lebanese and Jordan crises

Chapter 3: 'The Tempest'	64

The gathering storm: the Lebanese crisis; Macmillan's tempest: the Baghdad coup; Revolution in Iraq and a second honeymoon with Cairo; Coming to terms with revolutionary Iraq; Betting on the northern tier

Chapter 4: The 'Center of All Problems' – Iran and 1958   80

Containment through reform and economic development; Iran modernization: the race against time; Playing the Soviet card; The Baghdad coup and Iran; A new relationship with Tehran

Chapter 5: Controlled Democracy – Pakistan and 1958   93

Straddling the fence: the US, Pakistan and India 1956-1958; 1957 and the Kashmir dispute in the UN; Pakistan and the search for stability; The Baghdad coup and Ayub Khan

Part II: Revising Containment, 1959-1960   104

Chapter 6: The Arab Cold War and US Policy   107

Nasser and the revolution in Iraq; Conflict with the Soviet Union; Iraq and the Syrian connection; Washington's 'Red Scare' over Iraq; Coming to terms with Qasim; Soviet problems with their clients; Communist eclipse in Iraq; Nasser's Syrian labyrinth

Chapter 7: Jordan, Saudi Arabia, and Israel – the Bystanders   127

Jordan's premature obituary; Hussein dangles the Nasser card; Jordanian-UAR relations reach boiling point; Containment policy: Jordan and aid; Saudi Arabia: surviving Nasser's surge; Paranoids with real enemies: Israel and the Arab Cold War; US aid and relations with Israel; Israel's insurance policy: nuclear weapons

Chapter 8: Iran and Pakistan Cash In on Iraq   149

US aid and the Persian bazaar; Playing the Soviet card; US aid and complications; Political instability and increased Soviet pressure; The situation improves?; The future of Iranian-US relations; Pakistan's 'controlled democracy'; Paying the Pakistani bill; Ayub: faithful ally and voice of moderation; Difficulties for India: Pakistan and China; Developing the Soviet option; The non-Arab Middle East and the end of the Eisenhower era

Chapter 9: 1960 – JFK vs. Nixon, and the Greater Middle East   174

Campaign rhetoric and South Asia; Concerns about JFK in Tehran; 1953 reborn: JFK and peace in the Arab Middle East; JFK's campaign rhetoric: a fundamental difference?; Changing the guard with new – old ideas

Part III: Lessons from the Past – the Middle East 1961-1962   190

Chapter 10: Courting Nasser, 1961 – New Beginnings?   193

Nasser: the Kennedy view; Nasser fails in Jordan; Siding with feudalism and colonialism; The Syrians call it quits; Nasser's 'declaration of independence from advice'; Israeli complications; Revolutionary Arab nationalism reborn; The Israeli half of the peace equation; Repeating the past: the end of Kennedy's Middle East peace

Chapter 11: Iran at 'the Eleventh Hour' — 212

Soviet threats and Iran; The Shah's perspective on US-Iranian relations; Doing something about Iran; The eleventh hour arrives?; Support for Amini; Amini: 'the last hope'; Amini takes the reins; Amini, reform, and the reaction in Washington; Talbot chooses sides; Amini on the slippery slope

Chapter 12: The Shah Ascendant — 229

The Shah, military assistance, and Julius Holmes; Holmes: the Shah's ambassador; The Shah comes to Washington; The end of the Amini era; The aftermath of Amini; Kennedy and the Iranian reality; Crisis over – almost

Chapter 13: Pakistan, India, and Priorities — 246

Nothing new under the sun; The Harriman mission; The Johnson mission to South Asia; Mending fences with Ayub; Problems with India; Nehru: 'the worst official visit'; Menon and Goa; Pakistan reacts to Goa; Nehru's 'doubts and misgivings'; Nehru explores the Soviet option

Part IV: Frustrations of the Fall – JFK and 1963 — 264

Chapter 14: The Best Laid Plans — 267

September surprise: Egypt and the Yemen coup; The allies react; YAR-UAR diplomatic offensive; The advice of friends; Recognition of the YAR

Chapter 15: India, Pakistan, and China – Eastern Opportunities? — 278

Nehru's miscalculation; The Chinese teach Nehru a lesson; Washington attempts to take advantage; Problems with Pakistan; Another Harriman mission; New tactics for the pro-India faction; A solution to Kashmir

Chapter 16: 1963 – The New Frontier in Tatters — 293

Searching for a balance: Saudi Arabia, Yemen, and the UAR; A new dynamic: changes in Iraq and Syria; Soured relations with the UAR; Iran: another year, another crisis or two; India and Pakistan; The legacy of 1963

Conclusion: Reform and the Primacy of Containment   314

   Lessons in containment and economic development, 1953-1958; Containment revamped 1958-1960; Kennedy's Middle East and the Eisenhower legacy

Notes   329

Bibliography   459
   Archives and Collections   459
   Published Document Collections   459
   Interviews   461
   Published Works   461
   Dissertations   474

Index   475

List of Abbreviations

AAC	Asian-Africa Conference
AF	African Republics
AID	Agency for International Development
ANL	Australian National Library
APOC	Anglo-Persian Oil Company
ARAMCO	Arabian American Oil Company
AUC	American University at Cairo in Cairo
AUFS	American Universities Field Staff
AUFS-SAS	American Universities Field Staff – South Asia Series
AWD	Ann Whitman Diaries
AWF	Ann Whitman File
B.M.T.	Boston Metropolitan Transportation Authority
CAB	Cabinet Notes
CDF	Central Decimal File
CENTO	Central Treaty Organization
CFPF	Central Foreign Policy File
CIA	Central Intelligence Agency
CIA/FBIS	CIA/Foreign Broadcast Information Service
CO	Colonial Office
COF	Central Office File
CPO	Central Plan Organization
CRES	Central Intelligence Agency Resource Extraction System
CRO	Commonwealth Relations Office
DDE	Dwight David Eisenhower
DDEL	Dwight D. Eisenhower Library

DEA	Department of External Affairs
DMI	Department of Military Intelligence
DMK	*Dravida Munnetra Kazhagam* (Dravidian Progressive Federation)
DOD	Department of Defense
DOS	Department of State
EDC	European Defense Community
EEC	European Economic Community
FBIS	Foreign Broadcast Information Service
FO	Foreign Office
FRUS	Foreign Relations of the United States
GATT	General Agreement on Trade and Tariffs
GOI	Government of India
GOJ	Government of Jordan
GOP	Government of Pakistan
GRDOS-59	General Records of the Department of State – 59
GTI	Greek, Turkey, and Iranian Affairs
IAEA	International Atomic Energy Agency
IBRD	International Bank for Reconstruction and Development
ICBM	Intercontinental Ballistic Missile
ICC	International Control Commission
ICP	Iraqi Communist Party
IDF	Israeli Defense Forces
IMF	International Monetary Fund
INR	Bureau of Intelligence and Research
IPC	Iraqi Petroleum Company
JFKL	John F. Kennedy Library
JFK	John F. Kennedy
LBJ	Lyndon Baines Johnson
LBJL	Lyndon Baines Johnson Library
MAG	military assistance group
MAP	military assistance program
MAPAI	Israeli Labor Party
ME	Middle East
MEA	Ministry of External Affairs
MEDO	Middle East Defensive Organization
MI6	British foreign intelligence
MilAsst	Military Assistance
NAA	National Archives of Australia

NACPM	National Archives II – College Park, Maryland
NAI	National Archives of India
NATO	North Atlantic Treaty Organization
NE	Near East
NEA	Bureau of Near Eastern and South Asian Affairs
NEA/INC	Office of India, Ceylon, Nepal and Maldive Islands Affairs
NEA/SOA	NEA/South Asian Affairs
NF	National Front
NIACT	night action immediate
NIE	National Intelligence Estimate
NPIC	National Photographic Intelligence Center
NSAM	National Security Action Memorandum
NSC	National Security Council
NSF	National Security Files
NUC	National Unity Committee
NUP	Nationalist Union Party
NYT	New York Times
NZNA	New Zealand National Archives
OCB	Operations Coordinating Board
OPEC	Organization of Petroleum Exporting Countries
PDB	Presidential Daily Brief
PDP	Peoples' Democratic Party
POF	President's Office Files
POL	Political Affairs
PPDDE	Presidential Papers of Dwight D. Eisenhower
PPJFK	Presidential Papers of President John F. Kennedy
PPLBJ	Presidential Papers of Lyndon Baines Johnson
PRO	Public Records Office
PSD	Psychological Strategy Board
RCC	Revolutionary Command Council
SA	Saudi Arabia
SAG	Saudi Arabian Government
SAGF	Saudi Arabian General Files
SARG	Syrian Arab Republic Government
SAVAK police')	Sazman-e Ettelaat va Amniyat-e Keshvar ('Iranian secret
SEA	Southeast Asia
SEATO	Southeast Asia Treaty Organization

SHAPE	Supreme Headquarters NATO
SNIE	Special National Intelligence Estimate
SOA	Office of South Asian Affairs
UNO	United Nations Organization
UAR	United Arab Republic
UK	United Kingdom
UN	United Nations
UNGA	United Nations General Assembly
UNPCC	United Nations Palestine Control Commission
UNRWA	United Nations Relief and Works Agency for Palestine
US or USA	United States
USAID	United States Agency for International Development
USARMA	US Army Military Attaché
USG	United States Government
USSR	Union of Soviet Socialist Republics
WDC	Washington, DC
WHO	White House Office Files
YAR	Yemen Arab Republic

List of Illustrations

1 Eisenhower and Dulles discussing Suez, 1956	11
2 Nasser and Nehru Post-Bandung	32
3 Eisenhower and Nehru Official Visit, 1956	35
4 Nasser and Syrian President Quwatli	45
5 King Hussein and King Feisal, 1958	51
6 Eisenhower and King Saud	53
7 Raymond Hare	60
8 Dulles and Robert Murphy	71
9 Iraqi coup leaders Aref and Qasim	108
10 Meeting of British and Americans over Middle East, 1959	116
11 Eisenhower and King Hussein	130
12 Eisenhower and Nasser at UNGA, 1960	138
13 Eisenhower and Herter, 1959	145
14 Eisenhower and Shah of Iran, 1959	160
15 Kennedy with Myer Feldman	183
16 JFK and Prime Minister Macmillan	199
17 Kennedy with King Saud	208
18 Chester Bowles and Phillips Talbot	218
19 Chester Bowles and Julius Holmes	227
20 Shah of Iran Publicizing Land Reform	238
21 Ayub, Eisenhower, and Kennedy	252
22 Nehru and Kennedy	256

Acknowledgments

I owe the greatest debt of gratitude to my wife Cheryl for tolerating and even encouraging the original project, providing expert editing and advice on the paperback version and for tolerating my other academic adventures. I owe debt of gratitude to the memory of my father Roby E. Barrett for the storytelling that instilled a love of the past; to my mother Carol Ward Barrett for making education so important; to my daughter Tracy Barrett-Learn for lively scholarly exchanges, and entertaining research advice; to Michael Learn for rescuing me from my computer; to my friend Allen Keiswetter for comments and encouragement; to my friend Nancy Casey for her support, and to my colleague and friend Lisa Lacy for timely advice. My sincere thanks to Professor W. Roger Louis for his time and patient support; he provided counsel and encouragement that can only come from a true teacher and educator. Professor Louis also provided invaluable advice and encouragement during the publishing process. This effort might never have come to fruition without the early support, encouragement, and interest of Professor Margaret Omar Nydell and Professor John O. Voll of Georgetown University. Professor Nydell did her best to teach me Arabic at FSI. My thanks go to Professor Voll for his interest in the topic and investment of time and effort. His on-going investment of time and effort was fundamental to the success of this research project. I also want to thank Phillips Talbot, William 'Bill' Lakeland, the late General Andrew Goodpaster, Mohammad Hakki, Christopher Van Hollen, and the late Walt W. Rostow for their willingness to sit down and explain their view of events described in this work. Last, but certainly not least, I want to thank the Eisenhower Foundation for its generous award of the Dwight D. Eisenhower and Clifford Roberts Graduate Research Fellowship, which made much of the foreign archival research in this work possible.

Roby C. Barrett
30 April 2009

Preface

This second edition fundamentally reflects the original work with minor alterations. The changes tend to reflect editorial adjustments and to some tailoring of the narrative with regard to Iraq 1958 and its immeidate aftermath. Included are some additional comments by persons present in Iraq during and after the July Coup as well as some additional research related to subsequent articles that I have published. Overall, the genesis and thrust remains the same. Iraq 1958 significantly contributed to a foreign policy dynamic that not only influenced and in some cases dictated US foreign policy in the Arab world, but also created to a large extent the US approach to what we now refer to as southwest Asia, i.e., Iran, Pakistan, Afghanistan and India. The shock of the Baghdad coup led to the full embrace of the Shah, support for military rule in Pakistan, opposition to Soviet influence in Afghanistan, and the estrangement of Nehru's India. Arguably it laid the foundation in the 'Greater Middle East' for the challenges that we face in the 21st century. The study began with Keith Kyle's *Suez* which prompted me to consider the degree to which tactical decisions driven by 'immediate' pressures caused US administrations and the foreign policy apparatus too risk and at times sacrifice US strategic interests. The answer appeared to be – usually. The events of the last few years have tended to put an exclamation point on that conclusion. With this thought in mind, I began to think that a systematic study of a given period of time might be a rewarding and stimulating endeavor. A key consideration of such a study would be the degree to which narrow perspectives or preconceived ideas about immediate problems or crises prevented a greater awareness of the content in which problems occurred and thus undermined a prudent consideration of strategic interests.

This brought another observation, namely, that area studies and international relations tended to narrow the policy to the point that perspective on the broader context was lost. It also occurred to me that this had an effect on historical writing on the Middle East. Rarely did authors attempt to deal with the region within a context that reflected the fundamental organizational structure of the policy making and implementation organizations within the US government. That is to say that when John Foster Dulles described the Middle East as stretching form 'Morocco to India,' this statement reflected not only the reality and linkages on the ground but it also reflected the organizational structure within the US government that dealt with it. The Near East and South Asia Bureau and divisions within other government agencies reflected the connectivity across the region that I have chosen to describe here as the Greater Middle East. Historical writing on the topic tended to be broken into very focused monographs on bilateral relations, the Arab world, Iran, or South Asia. Few if any attempted to holistically deal with the region. The insistence by the Bush administration over the last six years that various issues across the region are unconnected and can be successfully dealt with on an independent basis, i.e., Palestine, Iran, Iraq, Lebanon, Pakistan, radical Islam, etc., also sparked a desire to explore the recent past and evaluate the experience of previous administrations in attempting to deal with tactical problems against a more strategic backdrop. How successful had they been at dealing with problems in the Greater Middle East as insolated rather than interrelated, coupled issues?

At the same time, I became increasingly interested in the 1950s and the struggles that accompanied the US's emergence as the dominant western power in the Greater Middle East. This interest brought me to the relationship between President Eisenhower and his two Secretaries of State, John Foster Dulles and Christian Herter. As my interest grew from casual reading to focused research, the idea came to me that a comparison between Eisenhower and Kennedy policy with regard to the Middle East might be worthwhile. Originally, I believed that the comparison would contrast the realist and, at times, ideological hard-line Cold War policies of Eisenhower against a broader, more flexible and open approach to the region under Kennedy. With a few exceptions, this was the view reflected in what scholarship existed. As I delved into the research materials, what I found was surprising. The administrations had far more in common than one would suppose. In fact, both were driven by very similar views of the best course for maintaining pro-western states and achieving modernization in the developing world. Both were committed to stability over political and economic reform. The real story lay not in the differences between the two administrations but in the similarities.

At this point, I concluded that only an in-depth research effort could adequately make the point. This effort would have to explain the policies of both administrations from the broader context of a Middle East that fundamentally covered the geographical area from North Africa to India. In addition to dealing with the region at the macro level, the study would have to delve into the details of the relationships and key events in order to glue the overall argument together. Beginning in 2001, that effort involved a global three-year research project to obtain a clearer understanding of what actually happened and to cast light on the real policy relationship between the administrations of Eisenhower and Kennedy. The research represented here is a broad selection of sources and materials. It includes multiple archives, collections, interviews, and libraries. It is an effort to interpret events and policy from a wide-angle perspective and support those views by telescoping in on key events, decision makers, and their motivations. Many of the topics discussed here have been dealt with within individual monographs, but their scope has been largely limited to single states or bilateral issues between two or three states; the dimension of the broader geo-political context is generally missing.

To accomplish this, the initial research effort focused on unpublished source materials. From the unpublished materials the research effort progressed to published collections, interviews, memoirs and first person accounts, and then secondary source materials. For example, rather than examining *The Foreign Relations of the United States (FRUS)* first and then working back into the archives, this effort took the opposite approach by examining archival materials first followed by a later examination of *FRUS*. The reader will find citations from the National Archives that are in *FRUS*, but those documents were first located in the files at the Archives. Where the document was found first in *FRUS*, then the citation is *FRUS*. Why do it this way? By going directly to the raw documents, I determined the historical significance uninfluenced by a previous judgment. It then became possible to compare a broader segment of documents to ascertain what actually happened and why. This methodology was also used at the Eisenhower, Johnson, and Kennedy presidential libraries. When combined with the research effort at the British, Egyptian, Indian, Australian, and New Zealand national archives, the historical shadow cast by published documentation sometimes took a different, and hopefully, more accurate form. With regard to referencing, I have also culled duplicate footnotes from the text. If there were three endnotes in succession from the same source and pages, I eliminated the first two and kept only the last reference. In practical terms this means that in some cases a notation might refer to the information in multiple preceding paragraphs within the same section. Transliterations reflected common usage, i.e., Nasser, not Nasir, and a simplification of Arab names, i.e., Abd-al-Karim al-Qasim to Qasim.

Despite the linkages and broadened geographical conceptualization, some regions and countries receive only passing mention. The North African states of Libya, Tunisia, Algeria, and Morocco are a case in point. This limited treatment results in part from the more peripheral role played by North Africa in the political action from 1958-1963. King Hassan II of Morocco and King Idris of Libya were included on Nasser's list of 'feudal states.' President Habib Bourgiba of Tunisia ranked almost as high as Nuri Sa'id in the Egyptian president's hierarchy of reactionary leaders, but these states were not central to the struggles of the late 1950s and early 1960s. They were central to the struggle for North African independence but that had its own much more European overtones. In Algeria, the liberation movement drove French participation in Suez in 1956 and later support for Israel but, by the late 1950s, there was growing acceptance that France would eventually have to seek an accommodation with local resistance leaders. Turkey also receives limited attention. This study takes the position that Ankara is a special case. Turkey's primary orientation was European. As a member of NATO, Turkey had special status and priority that dramatically differentiated it from even the other pro-western states of the Middle East despite its membership in both the Baghdad Pact and CENTO. Had Iran and Pakistan collapsed or joined the neutral camp Turkey would have stayed in the Western orbit of NATO and Europe. For this reason, Turkey is treated as more of a peripheral element.

In examining the historiography, there is no single historical work that compares in scope to this study, but the list of historical writings dealing with various aspects of this study is lengthy. My purpose is to create an historical mosaic as opposed to a narrow study. L. Carl Brown's *International Politics and the Middle East* to some degree introduces this idea of a mosaic and provides an overview of the 'Eastern Question' from the eighteenth century to the 1980s. Brown argues that the Middle East is a 'thoroughly penetrated society.' He goes on to state, 'The Middle East has been so continuously interlocked politically with the West as to have become almost an appendage of the Western power system.' Brown convincingly asserts that the Cold War competition in the Middle East constituted merely an extension of the Eastern Question that had plagued European powers since the beginning of Ottoman decline in the early 1700s, and that the United States is merely the latest new player. Assuming this is correct, the broader context of US involvement needs elucidation.

The current coverage of US policy in the Middle East during the formative years of the late 1950s and early 1960s comes in the form of limited treatments in articles or works on the Eisenhower and Kennedy years. None have dealt in depth with the late Eisenhower administration, and most tend to take the position that Kennedy brought in a completely new progressive approach. Warren Bass' *Support Any Friend* provides an interesting look at 'Kennedy's Middle East' from the perspective of the relationship with Israel, but consistently understates the impact of the pro-Israeli lobby on the administration. Bass also underestimates the understanding of Arab policy to be gleaned from memoirs, contemporary literature, and by triangulation through extensive multiple archival research. Douglas Little wrote several interesting articles on the Kennedy era including 'A Fool's Errand: American and the Middle East, 1961-1969,' 'The New Frontier on the Nile: JFK, Nasser, and Arab Nationalism,' and 'From Even-Handed to Empty-Handed: Seeking Order in the Middle East.' While insightful, these articles are very narrow in scope. In *American Presidents and the Middle East*, George Lenczowski provides a series of short policy summaries. He points out that Kennedy reaffirmed Eisenhower's policy along the 'northern tier' – Turkey, Iran, and Pakistan – with its obvious implications for India and Kennedy's efforts with the UAR. No comprehensive work exists.

On the Arab world, Malcolm Kerr's outstanding essay, *The Arab Cold War: A Study of Ideology in Politics* perhaps comes closest to offering a snapshot of the inter-Arab confrontation of 1958 to 1967. Kerr also produced the excellent article, 'The Emergence of a Socialist Ideology in Egypt,' in *The Middle Eastern Journal* in early 1962. This article is particularly interesting for its informed, ground level view of Nasser's attempt to establish an ideological basis for his regime. Kerr's article also meshes well with Mahmoud Hussein's work, *Class Conflict in Egypt: 1945-1970*. Hussein, an avowed Communist, argues that the Nasserist regime represented the triumph of a lower-middle class based 'state bourgeoisie.' Egypt adopted the ideological weapons of class struggle without the content.

Uriel Dann's *Iraq Under Qassem* and *King Hussein and the Challenge of Arab Radicalism: Jordan 1955-1967* are examples of the often solid works of limited scope that deal with the period targeted by this work. Published in 1969, the Qasim work is dated and lacks access to more recently declassified archival resources. Both the Iraqi and Jordanian works are useful and take advantage of published and periodical documentation from the period. The collection of essays by William Roger Louis and Roger Owen, *A Revolutionary Year: The Middle East in 1958,* offers interesting views of the emergence of the United States as the preeminent Western power in the Middle East, but limited references to Iran and Pakistan are the only ventures outside the Arab Middle East. Robert McNamara in *Britain, Nasser and the Balance of Power in the Middle East, 1952-1967* discusses the British relationship with Nasser but the chronological span leaves treatment of key issues at a cursory level and does not examine the impact across South Asia.

The various biographies of Nasser, Anthony Nutting's *Nasser*, Said K. Aburish's *Nasser, The Last Arab*, Robert Stephen's *Nasser*, and Jean Lacouture's *Nasser* provide insight into the Arab Middle East equation and some understanding of Nasser and non-alignment, but all suffer from the limitations imposed by narrow biographical focus. Wilton Wynn's *Nasser of Egypt* deserves mention because it is a sympathetic, contemporary account of the Egyptian leader by a journalist who knew him and Egypt in the 1950s. Wynn takes the view that handled correctly a Middle East peace could have come to fruition in 1955 following Anthony Eden's Guildhall speech that the Israelis scuttled. This and other sympathetic views of Nasser earned Wynn's work banishment from the political and journalistic mainstream. Nevertheless it is an interesting work that offers an informed alternative view of the Egyptian regime. Useful works target national history but these usually provide an overview of some of the specific issues affecting Israel, Jordan, Iraq, Saudi Arabia, Yemen, and Egypt; no work attempts to examine the period.

With respect to Iran, Jim Bill's work, *The Eagle and the Lion,* focuses primarily on the 1979 revolution. His treatment of the Eisenhower period is cliché in the sense that it borrows from generally accepted later interpretations of the Kennedy administration. Bill argues that Eisenhower coddled the Shah with military and security support and created the Iranian animosity and hatred of the regime that ultimately led to 1979. Bill's emphasis not only underscores the problems associated with interpretations of the relationship between the Eisenhower and Kennedy policies but also contributes to the idea that the United States might have brought about a different outcome. A recent article by April Summit in *The Middle Eastern Journal* entitled 'For a White Revolution: John F. Kennedy and the Shah of Iran,' comes much closer to the fundamentals of Kennedy policy toward Iran. The article does not adequately explain the struggle over policy formulation between the White House activists typified by Robert Komer and the State Department led by Ambassador Julius Holmes, nor does it explain how the resolution of that struggle pushed the US down the road to 1979.

In fact, M.E. Yapp's work, *Strategies of British India: Britain, Iran, and Afghanistan, 1798-1850*, offers a useful perspective on Persia in the nineteenth century that applies almost equally as well to the Iranian situation of the 1950s and 1960s. Writing about early nineteenth century British alliances with Iran to deflect Russian threats in the region, Yapp states, 'The Iranian alliance [was] an expensive and unwanted albatross which had been hung around their necks.' Both Eisenhower and Kennedy saw Iran as an albatross as well, but in the competition with the Soviet Union both were unwilling to risk potential consequences of aggressively pursuing an alternative to the Shah's rule. Much of the post-1979 writing on Iran suggests that the United States might have prevented 1979, an interesting 'salvationist' idea that seems to imply that the US was more responsible for Iran than the Iranians. Others take the less popular view that the Shah was actually in control and used the relationship with the US to his own ends. In 'Iran's Foreign Policy in the Pahlavi Era,' William Griffith writes that the Shah's 'positive nationalism' from 1953 to the early 1960s was 'quite successful in terms of the Shah's objectives.' He stabilized his personal rule, modernized his army, and assured himself of enough US support to allow him to undertake reforms to undercut his opposition. This included less reliance on Washington and land reform.

To the east, Pakistan and India were inseparable from the Middle East political and diplomatic dynamic of 1958-1963. Despite voluminous writing on India, Pakistan, and the conflict over Kashmir, there is little scholarship linking the escalation of the conflict to events in the Arab Middle East. The best existing historical writing on this period comes in the form of biographies of Nehru. The most recent, Judith Brown's *Nehru: A Political Life*, concludes that Nehru's insistence on personally conducting Indian foreign policy provided the innovation of the 'non-aligned' concept but ultimately impeded implementation because of poor management and the flow of new ideas in a shifting diplomatic environment. The author asserts that, unfortunately, Nehru was extremely difficult to deal with. Difficult or not, Brown's quote of Dean Acheson explains Western willingness to cultivate Nehru despite the difficulties: 'He was so important to India and India's survival so important to all of us, that if he did not exist – as Voltaire said of God – he would have had to be invented.' On the issue of connectivity with the Arab Middle East,

Brown argues that it was Nehru's relationship with Nasser that allowed him to attempt mediation at Suez and to work closely with Eisenhower who forced the British and French withdrawal. The author points out that as a result of Suez, Nehru came to believe that Eisenhower was actually 'flexible' with regard to non-alignment. The author also blames Nehru for V.K. Krishna Menon's gaffs and for the pathetic performance of the Indian defense establishment during the border war with China. Brown's treatment of foreign policy represents the best overview of Indian foreign policy of any of the biographies.

With regard to the border war with China, Neville Maxwell's *India's War with China* is superb, well balanced, and broad in its scope of inquiry. The 1970 publication date prevented Maxwell from accessing significant declassified research materials but interviews with participants more than compensate. Other works discuss Indian foreign policy and non-alignment but in a much less organized fashion. Sarvepalli Gopal's three-volume biography of Nehru explains Indian policy predominately in terms of Pakistan and China. Gopal's rationalizations of Nehru's shortcomings detract from an otherwise factually interesting work. In *Nehru: The Making of India*, Muhammad J. Akbar gives foreign policy a relatively low priority but he alludes to the issue of regional connectivity stating, 'It is an interesting point that India and the USA could not create a friendship that would have been eminently logical ... not because of any direct conflict of interest, but because of different perception of third-party problems: communism, Korea and from there, China, Indo-China, and, of course Pakistan.' Gopal's is the stronger work with regard to the Middle East and US foreign policy, but both Gopal and Akbar suffer from the limitation imposed by the biographical narrative.

In the case of Pakistan, several works discuss 1958 to 1963 within the context of its relations with India, the United States, and the members of the various western alliances to which Karachi adhered. Of these, most focus on the issue of military rule. These include Ayesha Jalal's *The State of Martial Rule,* Lawrence Ziring's *The Ayub Khan Era*, and Hasan Askari-Rizvi's *The Military & Politics in Pakistan*. Ayub Khan's autobiography, *Friends Not Masters,* is also an explanation for the military role in Pakistani politics from the former Pakistani president himself. As one would expect, Ayub is highly critical of Kennedy's 'betrayal' of Pakistan in 1962 and 1963. The best overall study of Pakistan that correlates with this study is *The United States and Pakistan, 1947-2000* by Dennis Kux. This work addresses the history of US-Pakistani relations paying particular attention to the Eisenhower and Kennedy years.

In a final comment on the formation of US policy, this work attempts to go beyond the normal historical analysis that focuses on the principals or 'decision-makers' in US foreign policy. 'Decision-makers' as we have learned of late often exhibit more the characteristics of a vacuous, empty vessel to be filled with information and ideas from the sources that they choose. This choice can make all the difference. In the Kennedy administration, Robert Komer exemplifies how a knowledgable, frenetic, and prolific fountain of memos and papers placed in a key position on the NSC can at times influence the policy process out of all proportion to his perceived position. For this reason, his oral history and files at the Kennedy Library are highly informative and instructive. Particularly, in the first two years of the Kennedy administration, Komer's voice often informs the policy-making apparatus to a degree that is disproportionate to the stature of his position and his overt political clout. Kennedy's distrust of the traditional foreign policy appartus and his desire to create a new policy paradigm magnified the influence of officials of Komer's ilk. This occurs to some degree in every administration but it was particularly pronounced in the early Kennedy years; thus a balanced, well informed policy depended on the mental acuity and intellectual rigor applied by senoir administration officials and particularly the one in the Oval Office. In the case of the Kennedy administration, the fundamental, pragmatic intelligence of the President allowed him to recognize policies gone awry and then to flexibly adjust. In late 1962 and 1963, Kennedy salvaged the US policies in the Middle East by shifting back to his predecessor's pragmatic model. It is an interesting process that this book attempts to describe. Kennedy grasped that world was not what he had conceived it to be in 1961. This is all the more interesting when viewed in light of other chief executives who have been hampered by the apparent inability to understand the difference between the world as they have conceived it to be, the reality that exists, the interests of the United States, and the necessity to adjust policies to avoid looming policy debacles. History may not repeat itself, but it certainly contains some interesting parallels and comparisons.

This review in no way represents a comprehensive discussion of all the scholarship related to this topic, but these works are typical of the current scholarship in the field in that period. This study is an attempt to provide a fundamentally different perspective. Its goal is to provide a breadth and depth in analysis that connects events, movements, and leaders across the Greater Middle East. It discusses the motivations that drove the complementary policies of Nasser and Nehru during the early 1950s. It includes an explanation of the profound impact that the Baghdad coup of 1958 had not only in the Arab world, but also in Iran, Pakistan, and India as well. It contains a careful examination of the similarity in the policies of the Eisenhower and Kennedy administrations, and the frustrations that faced the latter as he attempted, apparently in ignorance, to reinvent the policy initiatives that failed under Eisenhower between 1953 and 1956. This study takes all of these issues and places them in the larger regional context to which they belong. In doing so, *The Greater Middle East and the Cold War* offers new facts and a detailed re-examination of the events and key players from a fresh, more holistic perspective. Hopefully, the reader will find it useful and informative, but most of all, in light of the current myopic policies and unwillingness to see the connectivity between issues, the demonstrable historical interconnectivity of events across the region during the 1950s and 1960s will provide provocative perspective on the ideas and policies of the recent past.

Introduction

The Greater Middle East and the Cold War: US Foreign Policy under Eisenhower and Kennedy examines American foreign policy in the Middle East from 1958 to 1963. It also examines the Eisenhower experience between 1953 and 1955 as the basis for the more realistic approach to the region following Aswan decisions, Suez and mixed reaction to the Eisenhower Doctrine. This work's implicit lack of emphasis on the Suez war reflects the view that while certainly attention-getting, the flash and bang of 1956 represented an interlude, the exception rather than the rule in political, diplomatic, and even military interaction between the US, its Western allies, and the various states in the Greater Middle East. Much more typical and thus more central to an overall understanding of the policy interaction during the Eisenhower and Kennedy years were the periods before and after Suez. Both the Eisenhower and Kennedy administrations continuously searched for ways to sway countries of the Muslim Middle East to cooperate and participate in Washington's campaign to contain the Soviet Union and Communist influence. Both administrations promised rewards for countries that would come to either a formal arrangement or, in some cases, just a working arrangement with the United States, if it benefited containment. Initially, the 'promises' were most often heavily weighted toward economic aid and development assistance, but after 1958, security and military aid received increasing emphasis. This study of US foreign policy in the Greater Middle East examines the attempts, some successful and some not, to enlist the Muslim world in Eisenhower's and Kennedy's Cold War struggle to contain the Soviet and Communist expansion in the Greater Middle East.

It reevaluates and challenges many of the fundamental assumptions associated with the Eisenhower and Kennedy periods. By accessing a multiplicity of archival sources, it also places those policies within a broader, more complex regional context. At the same time, the work examines the political and diplomatic interaction behind this policy formulation at a level of significantly greater granularity, thus providing a more detailed view of the actual events and how policies related to those events developed. The ultimate aim of US global policy remained absolutely consistent for over 40 years: the containment of the Soviet Union, of Communist China, and of the spread of Communism. US policy in the Middle East, which, for the purposes of this study, includes the Arab Middle East, Iran, and the South Asia subcontinent, reflected this commitment. Containment in the region was the top priority of both administrations; Kennedy was no less a 'Cold Warrior' than Eisenhower. Despite these similarities, the Kennedy administration has consistently been given credit for more nuanced, sophisticated, reform-oriented policies. In contrast, Eisenhower and John Foster Dulles, his foreign policy confidant and lightning-rod, are often viewed as bumbling, coercive, and less astute than Kennedy and his team of policy experts. In reality, both administrations practiced containment in a remarkably similar manner. Both were uncomfortable with non-progressive, traditional regimes; both had a strong faith in and desire to see controlled reform in the region; and both, when faced by the possibility of anti-Western instability, supported anti-democratic elements and measures. As the most recent US administration is in the process of learning, liberal democractic notions of representative politics and economic development are much more easily talked about than realized throughout most of the region. In those cases where popular democracy did exist, it often ran counter to Western interests in general and US interests in particular. Eisenhower and Kennedy found the more democratic progressive regimes, Musaddiq's Iran and Nehru's India, at odds with Western interests, and exhibited a noted preference for authoritarian and even reactionary elements because of the stability they offered. Both administrations followed the mantra of imposed stability as the basis for 'controlled' political reform and economic development.

These reform-based policies and their faith in economic development as a buffer against Communism and Soviet influence owed a theoretical debt to early 'modernization theory'. Policymakers in both administrations borrowed eclectically from the precepts of 'modernization theory' to create a set of policies that supported economic development as a means to economic, social, and political reform. Military assistance, and in rare instances direct military support for a regime, covert and overt internal support for security organizations, and relentless political and diplomatic pressure supporting economic development and political reform comprised the major elements of American containment policy. In fact when all these elements are evaluated, economic development emerged as the preferred path to political, economic, and social reform, and thus pro-Western stability. Influential foreign policy advisors, including Walt W. Rostow, were intimately involved in both administrations and advocated policies that approached an almost absolute faith in the efficacy of economic development as a fundamental pillar of political stability and containment. This faith in economic reform also carried with it a steadfast belief that, when necessary, political stability had to be maintained by force in order to create a secure environment for development, but it was economic development that would provide the engine for long-term pro-Western social development and political liberalization. For example, Rostow had a glimpse of the future when he described 'the Amercan interest' as something that 'transcend(s) the problem of countering Communist aggressive objectives and techniques'. He added: 'It seems altogether possible that the United States could be confronted with a major danger even if communism should wither away as an effective force. The danger is that the underdeveloped countries develop along lines hostile to the West and Western tradition. Should their basic orientation be anti-Western and anti-American, the United States would confront a very grave set of problems as the presently underdeveloped societies were modernized and strengthened.'[1] This was an opinion expressed in 1957, the accuracy of which the West now can better appreciate.

Simply put, this theory described an approach to the developing world in which strategically placed economic aid could create the 'preconditions for economic growth', bringing countries to an economic 'take-off point'. While 'fluctuating' and 'sometimes painful', the theory held that this 'take-off point' would lead to prosperity in a final stage of 'self-sustaining growth'.[2] This growth constituted the path to social and political reform, fostering democratic political institutions and social justice. Spurred by the perceived success of post-war economic and development aid in thwarting Communist influence in Western Europe and Japan, these views became the Western democratic version of economic determinism, an answer to Marxist-Leninism.[3]

Both administrations adopted these arguments more or less as ground-truth. For both, economic aid was the preferred type of assistance in the Greater Middle East, accompanied, to varying degrees, by advocacy of political and social reform. Both administrations saw economic development and reform as the only way to establish stable societies and governments, the most effective bulwarks against Communist expansion. Both administrations pushed for political, economic, and, to some degree, social reform as the preferred means of preventing Communist expansion and of limiting Soviet, and to a lesser extent, Chinese influence. Economic development and reform became fundamental corollaries of Cold War containment. Whether the emphasis fell on economic modernization or political reform depended almost entirely on Washington's perception at any given point in time of the course that would best contribute to pro-Western stability. Eisenhower and Kennedy were also quick to drop calls for reform and to support repressive governments through military and security assistance when they perceived that reform would induce instability and threaten Western interests. Given these similarities, a question naturally arises: why have the historical interpretations of these two administrations diverged?

The Kennedy 'mystique' or 'myth' left an indelible imprint on outside perceptions. The understandable urge to canonize Kennedy and his policies as exceptional certainly had a major impact, but timing also played a significant role. In terms of the Middle East and Asia, Kennedy's tenure in office fell between the era of chaotic policy formulation in the mid-1950s and the realization in the late 1960s that his policies in Southeast Asia had been a fundamental mistake. If the relationship between Eisenhower's and Kennedy's policies is to be properly calibrated, understanding the chronological context is critical. In the early 1950s, Eisenhower faced the task of constructing a US policy in the developing world largely from scratch. This task was considerably more complex than that faced by the Kennedy administration. The initial learning curve in the Middle East was steep, and the Truman administration left no blueprint. In 1953, the United States was feeling its way through the Middle Eastern labyrinth. From Truman, Eisenhower, much to his chagrin, inherited Israel and an ill-defined set of policy ideas, including Middle East Defense Organization (MEDO) and 'northern-tier' concepts. Washington had largely relied upon the former colonial powers, principally the British and the French, to protect Western interests, and the US tended to follow their policy lead. The events of 1955 to 1958 increased the complexity of Washington's responsibilities in the Middle East. The period 1958 to 1963 witnessed the beginning of an even more profound change in the nature of British and French influence in the region. The British and French now made consultations and coordination with the United States a fundamental part of their policy formulation in the Middle East. Ironically, in the case of the British, these consultations tended to increase their influence in Washington, as US responsibilities in the region increased.

To adequately understand these developments and relationships, they must be examined within a chronological progression. Understanding Eisenhower's accomplishments in the 1958 to 1960 time frame requires a review of his early years, from 1953 to 1955. The dashed hopes for economic development and political and social reform during the early administration and the chaos of 1956 and 1957 resulted in the emergence of the pragmatic, workable US policies of 1958-1960. Thus, in 1961, Kennedy and his advisors inherited a largely functional set of policies and alliances. Try as they might to represent it in another light, Kennedy and his team essentially followed the course set by Eisenhower. Their attempts to deviate from the 1958-1960 models invariably failed, for one of two reasons. First, Kennedy's team failed to recognize that their policy initiatives were often replications of earlier, failed Eisenhower initiatives that ran fundamentally against the political grain in the region. Second, Kennedy often overestimated the impact of personal presidential diplomacy and his ability to use it to manage regional conflicts. Of these two problems, the most egregious was the unwillingness of Kennedy and his advisors to give credit where credit was due with respect to Eisenhower. As a result, the Kennedy administration dissipated much of its strength and influence in the Middle East trying to resurrect long-dead policy initiatives. Under both Eisenhower and Kennedy, regional issues, leaders, and forces determined the agenda, and for these, parochial regional interests took precedence over Washington's fixation on containment.

The shift toward regional influences reinforces the need for an examination of events within a significantly broader geographical setting. This geographical context exceeds the limitations imposed by traditional area studies. It reflects Dulles' repeated references to the Middle East as the region stretching 'from Morocco to Pakistan', thus drawing India into the equation. This expanded geographical view of the 'Middle East' is a particularly effective vantage point for viewing the 1950s and 1960s. The advent of non-alignment and positive neutralism overlaid an often ignored historical connectivity with a loose ideological and political framework. At the same time, Washington's global commitment to containment and its support for political and economic modernization further reinforced this more holistic conceptualization of the region. In 1958, events in Iraq affected relations with Egypt and India, as well as with neighboring Iran and Jordan. In like manner, problems between India and Pakistan complicated US relations with Egypt. Colonial control had tended to isolate problems, whereas its removal resulted in a reemergence of historical regional connectivity. As a result, policymakers in Washington had to adjust to a situation in which decisions in one area of the Greater Middle East often had immediate and pronounced repercussions in another.

The Anglo-American alliance added an additional level of complexity. Beyond a shadow of a doubt, the British, of all the Allies, exerted the greatest influence on Washington's practice of containment. Policy differences, sometimes major, existed, but each recognized that they needed the other. In the Persian Gulf and Arab Middle East, where British interests were paramount, London's influence created a series of fluctuations in US policy. The confusion, disagreements, and sometimes cross-purpose policies, as well as the areas of cooperation between Washington and London, are central to any evaluation of the evolution of the Anglo-American relationship. Fundamental changes in their abilities to project power brought on the confounding and always perplexing task of rethinking long-held assumptions. As Britain's unilateral ability to protect its interests collapsed, the British adjusted their tactics and began to use their influence with Washington to achieve many of those same goals. Eisenhower and Kennedy often found themselves modifying policy because of British influence. Good relations with London constituted the bedrock of US Cold War strategy, and global containment depended on it; therefore, British interests in the Greater Middle East had to be considered, even when they ran counter to US plans and views.

With Winston Churchill as its initial practitioner, the British learned early on that US concerns over Communist inroads could be exploited in a way that directly benefited the interests of Her Majesty's Government. The Suez crisis in 1956 taught London that the failure to manage Washington could have serious and humiliating consequences. To this end, Prime Minister Harold Macmillan used his relationship with Eisenhower to reestablish British influence in Washington. This influence most often aggravated US relations with revolutionary nationalist regimes and resulted in a clear US tilt toward the traditional rulers of the region.[4] British policy also influenced indigenous regional dynamics. In general, the British saw aid not in terms of political and economic modernization, but as a means of influence and maintaining the status quo. Thus, they consistently urged the US to desist from providing aid to revolutionary regimes, or what Washington often viewed as the more progressive states in the region, and urged an aid policy that fostered traditional regimes and British interests. The British focus on influencing Washington became particularly acute following the 1958 debacle in Iraq. The British had their pet regimes and interests, and they were adept at using their influence in Washington to protect them.

In addition to Anglo-American relations, Israel and oil also influenced the practice of US foreign policy and containment. Israel and Zionism constituted the only issues upon which all of the Arab states and Muslim populations in the region could agree. Even Hindu-dominated India shunned Israeli participation in the non-aligned movement because of the potential political and diplomatic fallout. The Jewish state was a clear liability for US hopes in the region. Both Washington and London viewed Israel as a policy albatross, an obstacle to a successful policy in the Middle East. Despite this problem, the Eisenhower and Kennedy administrations clearly supported Israel's survival. Both administrations attempted to orchestrate peace settlements and both failed. Beyond the generalities, Eisenhower contrasted sharply in his Arab-Israeli policies with Kennedy. The Republican administration attempted to pursue a balanced policy between the Arabs and Israel. Kennedy, after considerable internal debate, succumbed to domestic political pressure and increasingly pursued pro-Israeli policies for domestic political reasons. From 1958 to 1963, the so-called Arab Cold War had sublimated the Arab-Israeli dispute to a degree; however, the Palestinian refugees and the Arab-Israeli conflict remained a fundamental regional issue. The revolutionary regimes in the Arab Middle East had all achieved power in part as a result of the inability of their predecessors to deal successfully with the Zionist issue. Across the region, being a good Arab, a good Muslim, or, for that matter, a non-aligned, anti-colonial regime in good standing, required opposition to Zionism as a colonial creation. Fundamental to the struggle for power, influence, and leadership in the Arab and Muslim worlds was the question of who would best confront expansionist Zionism. Israel as an issue existed at or near the surface of any US attempt to further its influence in the Middle East. As a further complication, Tel Aviv pursued its own interests regardless of the consequences to the US, and the Israelis consistently undermined any US attempts to bring about a more pro-Western stance on the part of the secular, more 'progressive', revolutionary Arab regimes.

Oil constituted the other background influence on US policy. Oil definitely contributed to the US obsession with containing the Soviet Union in the Middle East. The Eisenhower and Kennedy administrations not only grasped the immediate, critical petroleum requirements of their European and Asian allies, but they also understood the long-term implications of growing oil consumption in the United States. The British played the more immediate and significant role in the equation. British oil interests in the region provided petroleum products to European markets and, at the same time, propped up the British economy. European, Japanese, and British willingness to partner with the United States in the global containment of the Soviet Union depended on oil. With the exception of post-1958 Iraq, states ruled by traditional regimes possessed most of the petroleum resources of the region. Advocating reform-oriented modernization as the corollary of containment in those oil-producing states carried risks. Reform could bring instability and even collapse; therefore, while theoretically committed to reform, both the Eisenhower and Kennedy administrations were reluctant to push reforms that might threaten the flow of crude. Oil was a thread periodically pushed to the forefront as Washington attempted to deal with crises in Iran, Iraq, and Saudi Arabia. It explained US support for British interests in the Gulf, and it underscored Washington's increasing support for 'white revolutions' and 'controlled democracy'.

These themes, taken in aggregate, underscore the fundamental connectivity between the Eisenhower and Kennedy policies of containment and modernization in the Greater Middle East. They also demonstrate US susceptibility at any given time to the influences of indigenous forces, the British, oil, and Israel. By taking an initial short digression, we will see how Kennedy's administration attempted to reinvent Eisenhower's failed policies of 1953-1954 and found itself limping back to what remained of Eisenhower's bequest. In the mid-1950s, Eisenhower and Dulles learned the pitfalls of an ideologically motivated activist policy. Failing to appreciate adequately the experience of his predecessors, Kennedy repeated many of those same mistakes in the early 1960s. In these two experiences, we will hear a warning echoed against well-intentioned policy activism that presumes to impose simplistic foreign solutions on very complex, well-established political, economic, and social structures. From the US perspective, the end results of such policies in the Middle East have rarely been predictable, with the exception that they have almost always created unpleasant situations that complicated relations.

While this study focuses on the period from 1958 to 1963, the seeds of these events were sown between 1953 and 1955. In 1953, Joseph Stalin died, the Korean War ended, the French were preparing a knockout blow against the Viet Minh in Indochina, the situation in Europe was improving, and a new administration took office. In 1953, events in Iran seemed to offer a reassuring model for dealing with regional nationalism run amuck. In Iran, Muhammad Musaddiq, *Time* magazine's Man of the Year in 1951 and the man who nationalized British oil interests, symbolized the threat that secular nationalism posed to Western interests if it was not managed correctly. Although he was thoroughly Westernized and a reformer, Musaddiq's nationalism threatened the British-dominated status quo in Iran and encouraged other potentially anti-Western nationalist elements in the region. More problematically, Musaddiq's tolerance of leftist political groups seemed to promise increased Soviet influence, or the potential for a neutral Iran.[5] As will be seen, this increased

Iranian political ferment and instability initially provoked distinctly different reactions from Whitehall and the White House.

In Egypt, agitation over the Suez Canal, while a nuisance, appeared to be nothing more than a new version of historical frictions that had always afflicted Egyptian society and official Egypt's love-hate relationship with the West. In 1952, the collapse of the regime of King Farouk I at the hands of a group of largely British-trained military officers was hardly a national tragedy. The emergence of General Muhammad Neguib and the Revolutionary Command Council under the control of Colonel Gamal Abd-al-Nasser held both risks and promise. It looked as though American influence and aid might protect British interests, and at the same time enlist Egypt in a pro-Western mutual security arrangement. Washington hoped that the withdrawal of British forces from Suez would dampen political unrest and anti-Western, if not anti-British, agitation. In South Asia, Pandit Jawaharlal Nehru continued to preach his brand of 'neutralism', while he struggled to maintain the central government's control over fractious Congress Party associates and over the impoverished polyglot state inherited from the British. Despite periodically tense relations with the West, Nehru understood that the economic development of India depended on Western aid and his relationship with the United States and Britain. To that end, India continued its participation in the British Commonwealth. In Iraq, the situation actually appeared to improve. The Baghdad government began various projects designed to raise the standard of living for the general population. Problems in the region appeared manageable, and while there were clouds on the horizon, most expected that the Western allies would maintain their ascendancy. In 1945, future Prime Minister Harold Macmillan had made two observations: 'In the Middle East, Britain was still a Great Power', and the United States supported the 'strength and prestige' of Britain in the region. Given that only the Suez Canal treaty negotiations with Egypt were a serious point of contention, it appeared that Macmillan's observation would hold true in the 1950s as well.[6]

Against this backdrop, the freshly-minted Eisenhower administration was determined to show its superiority over the outgoing Truman establishment. Eisenhower wanted to create a new paradigm for relationships with emerging nations, particularly in the Middle East and Asia. He also wanted the British to change their posture outside of Europe. Eisenhower viewed Truman's close association with the British as a major mistake. The new president was absolutely certain that he could better manage the mess created by Truman. Eight years later, Kennedy and his set of advisors held the same negative view of Eisenhower. In fact, both Eisenhower and Kennedy were acting well within the policy parameters of containment and economic development. To understand this parallel experience, this study first looks at how the Middle East dynamic, complicated by the necessity of cooperation with London, unstrung the policy plans of the Eisenhower administration between 1953 and 1955. Then, in the series of chapters that follow, the study will explore Eisenhower's 1958-1960 accommodation with the new Middle Eastern political reality, as well as Britain's deft adjustment to its own receding power and influence. Subsequent sections will examine Kennedy's policies and highlight the remarkable similarities and nuanced differences that existed between the policies pursued by the two presidents. By tracing and examining the similarities and differences between their two administrations during this critical period in the context of the dynamics created by regional leaders, revolution, non-alignment, the British, Israel, and oil, the study will analyze the degree to which Eisenhower and Kennedy operated within the same fundamental set of policy parameters.

Chapter 1: The Greater Middle East 1953-1958

Placing US policy in the late 1950s and early 1960s in historical context requires an analysis of the policy initiatives and attitudes in the early Eisenhower administration. Eisenhower and Dulles, whose nomination as Secretary of State had been opposed in London, arrived in office with decidedly anti-colonial attitudes and predispositions.[1] This anti-colonial bent put them at cross-purposes with long-established British interests. Despite the realities of post-war empire, London had intended to preserve its system of political influence and economic interests, and no one was more committed to the preservation of this system than Winston Churchill. In 1951, after six years of Labour rule, Churchill once again resurrected the Conservative Party's political fortunes, and cobbled together a government after six years of Labor rule. The economic benefits of the remnants of empire provided Churchill with all the incentive necessary to press Eisenhower to acquiesce to British policies and interests in the Middle East.

The critical first meeting between the President-elect and Prime Minister proved a harbinger of things to come. Wasting no time, Churchill used the excuse of visiting a friend, Bernard Baruch, and traveled to New York in early January 1953 for pre-inauguration talks with Eisenhower.[2] The discussions covered a range of topics – the Communist threat, European economic and defense issues, and trade with the Communist bloc. Eventually, the conversation turned to the situation in the Middle East. Eisenhower raised the issue of a defensive alliance modeled on the North Atlantic Treaty Organization (NATO) and designed to contain Soviet expansion and Communist inroads into what Dulles defined as the Middle East, the region from Morocco to Pakistan.[3] The Labor government of Clement Atlee had attempted to create a MEDO but the stench of colonial domination had effectively undermined every attempt. Given the Arab states' lack of

Courtesy of National Archives
Eisenhower and Dulles discussing Suez, 1956
Eisenhower with John Foster Dulles discussing the Suez Crisis. The British opposed Dulles' appointment as Secretary of State, but Eisenhower saw Dulles as a loyal instrument whom he could use to execute his foreign policy and a lightning-rod to divert criticism from the Oval Office. Despite rumors to the contrary, Dulles was Eisenhower's creature, not the reverse.

enthusiasm and Egypt's outright hostility, an alternative that would become known as the 'northern tier' emerged.[4] The Truman administration had toyed with the idea, but Secretary of State Dean Acheson left it to the incoming administration to decide how to proceed. In his talks with Churchill on 6 January 1953, Eisenhower broached the subject of the 'northern tier' as an alternative should MEDO 'prove unfeasible'.[5] Unlike London, Eisenhower and Dulles retained some hope that, with US sponsorship, a regional defensive pact which included Egypt might be feasible. The mere fact that the new administration in Washington might attempt to directly insert itself into the region was disquieting enough, but the lectures on the necessity of respecting regional nationalisms were nothing short of alarming.

During the campaign, both Eisenhower and Dulles had made numerous pronouncements on the passing of empire and the rise of nationalism in the developing world. In the meeting with Churchill, Eisenhower made it clear that they were very serious about supporting the emerging states and their national aspirations. When Churchill raised the issue of joint action in the Middle East, Eisenhower reacted negatively and quickly pointed out to the Prime Minister that his joint proposals with Truman on Iran had backfired and only served to taint Washington with British colonialism. The President-elect told Churchill:

'All that [Churchill] did was to get Mossadegh to accuse [the United States] of being a partner of the British in "brow-beating a weak nation".' Eisenhower elaborated: 'Nationalism is on the march and world Communism is taking advantage of that spirit of nationalism to cause dissention [sic] in the free world. Moscow leads many misguided people to believe that they can count on Communist help to achieve and sustain nationalistic ambitions.' With regard to Churchill's concerns, Eisenhower allowed, '[I]n some instances immediate independence would result in suffering for people and even anarchy.'[6] Despite his concern about 'immediate independence', the message was clear. The new administration intended to chart its own course, and clearly viewed British opposition to emerging national movements and association with London's colonial past as a liability.

Eisenhower also told Churchill that he viewed persuasion and the more aggressive use of US economic and military aid as the basic levers of foreign policy in the region. The heavy emphasis on economic aid reflected the influence of advisors, including Walt Rostow and other technocrats, who believed that through economic aid the United States could bring developing nations to the point of economic self-sufficiency and thereby foster pro-Western democratic institutions and societies. Advisors like Rostow would later migrate to the Kennedy and Johnson administrations and effectively promote similar policies there.[7] The meeting also heightened Eisenhower's concerns about the British and his old comrade-in-arms, Churchill. He believed that Churchill was 'trying to relive the days of World War II ... sitting on some rather Olympian platform with respect to the rest of world, and directing world affairs' with another American president. Eisenhower added:

> Winston does not by any means propose to resort to power politics and to disregard legitimate aspirations among weaker peoples. But he does take the rather old-fashioned, paternalistic, approach that since we, with our experience and power, will be required to support and carry the heavy burdens of decent international plans, as well as to aid infant nations towards self-dependence, other nations should recognize the wisdom of our suggestions, and follow them.

Eisenhower commented that while Churchill's view might be 'true – in the abstract', the reality of the situation dictated the use of 'persuasion and example', 'patient negotiation, understanding and equality of treatment', and not a 'take it or leave it' approach. Strategic cooperation with London was critical, but Washington had every intention of avoiding the baggage of British colonialism, while promoting a 'slower and more orderly progress towards independence' for the developing world.[8]

The new administration believed that immediate, or what Eisenhower referred to as 'momentary independence', brought the threat of instability and potential Communist takeovers, but it clearly supported an 'orderly' transition to full independence and an appropriate expression of constructive nationalism for developing nations.⁹ On 10 January 1953, Eisenhower and Dulles confirmed that the priorities for US policy in the Middle East would be containment of the Soviet Union and of Communist influence through economic development, covert assistance to pro-Western elements, and, if necessary, military assistance. Resolving the 'critical' problem of Iran was second on the list. Next came a solution to the Anglo-Egyptian impasse over basing rights in the Suez Canal, followed by a solution to the Arab-Israeli dispute.¹⁰ In each case, economic and development aid were to be the fundamental incentives. The similarities, in terms of both policy planning and practical application, between Eisenhower's intended policies in 1953 and those of the Kennedy administration in 1961 were uncanny. In 1953, the Suez Crisis (1956) and the Iraq Coup (1958) had yet to undermine the aura of London's expertise and dominance in the Middle East; yet the new administration was leery of Britain's colonial baggage and particularly reluctant to support Churchill in the disputes with Iran and Egypt. In February 1953, Eisenhower told British Foreign Secretary Anthony Eden that the 'somewhat frightening phraseology' of Churchill's private correspondence left concerns that London would 'tie our hands in advance' in Egypt.¹¹ Egypt was the centerpiece of US policy plans for supporting progressive regimes and for the potential revival of MEDO. In contrast, Churchill viewed the Middle East as traditionally a British sphere of influence, and its oil as a necessity for continued British influence in the world and for prosperity at home. The thought of a concerted Yankee intrusion on behalf of emerging progressive regimes and the potential threat that such a move posed to British interests was to say the least distressing.

Preemption and Iran 1953

In early 1953, and ironically again in 1961, Iran constituted a serious immediate concern. The policy of containment required the maintenance of a pro-Western Iran tied to the US through Western security arrangements. In 1953, the Iranian crisis drove a series of US policy decisions that made a Middle East collective security arrangement based on the 'northern tier' increasingly attractive. Musaddiq's political roller-coaster and his confrontation with London over the Anglo-Persian Oil Company (APOC) substantially increased Iranian instability. While the administration lamented the inability of the Shah, Muhammad Reza Shah Pahlavi, to hold his own against Musaddiq and the National Front, Dulles stated: 'Prime Minister Mossadegh could not afford to reach <u>any</u> agreement with the British lest it cost him his political life.'¹² Dulles underlined the word 'any' indicating that he clearly understood the Iranian prime minister's lack of political options. The Secretary of State flatly stated that Musaddiq was not a Communist and, in doing so, cited 'secret radio' attacks on him by the Communists for being 'a vile servant of the Shah'. Nevertheless, with British whispers about the Communist threat and prodding, Washington began increasingly to fear that a dictatorship under Musaddiq could bring the Communists to power through his assassination or a coup. The administration's proposed solution was to strengthen Musaddiq's position through additional economic assistance.[13] The British used the 1951 assassination of the moderate Prime Minister, General Sephabod Haj Ali Razmara, by purported elements of the Tudeh, the Iranian Communist Party, to increase anxiety in Washington about what might happen to Musaddiq; nevertheless Eisenhower continued to resist British calls for intervention.[14] The role of oil in propping up the pound sterling drove British anxiety over Iran. In contrast, Eisenhower's cabinet, and in particular Secretary Dulles, believed that the oil issue could be managed with the Musaddiq government in power. Despite rising concern about what might happen, the Eisenhower administration preferred an alternative to intervention.

The British took a dim view of any US plans to strengthen Musaddiq. London vociferously complained that US support would result in an irreparable loss of British face.[15] Still, attempting to avoid intervention, Washington instigated an anti-Communist 'psychological strategy program' as a part of a broader anti-Soviet campaign designed to stir up anti-Tudeh sentiment.[16] Nothing quieted the unrest. With the pro-Western propaganda campaign failing, direct aid blocked by British protests, increasing instability, and the exaggerated specter of a Communist takeover, London's arguments that the Musaddiq government had to be replaced gained traction with Eisenhower. The fear of what might happen drove the decision to take preemptive action.[17] What resulted was the confused, circus-like coup of 16-20 August 1953. With the support of most of the Shi'a religious establishment, military elements led by General Fazlullah Zahedi overthrew the Musaddiq government. Zahedi restored the Shah to the throne, crushed the Communist Tudeh, suppressed the National Front, and handed Iranian petroleum to an Anglo-American consortium. From the perspective of the Eisenhower administration, the coup may have defused the immediate crisis, but it hardly solved the problem of Iranian stability. The administration continued to view economic development and social and political reform as the only real insurance against instability and Communist subversion. At the 30 December 1953 NSC meeting, Dulles' comments continued to reflect the administration's desire for fundamental reform in Iran. The Secretary complained that the Shah and Zahedi had accomplished little in the way of 'critical' economic and social reform. While a solution to the dispute over oil appeared to be in the offing, none of the problems that brought on the instability had been addressed. Dulles went on to say that the only bright spot was the suppression of the opposition. Most of the Tudeh leadership was in jail, the National Front ceased to be an immediate factor, and British-Iranian relations had resumed with 'no serious domestic repercussions'.[18]

The success of the Iranian coup established a mindset in Washington. The reform policies of nationalist politicians in the Middle East tended to create political instability, which, in turn, opened the door for Communist and Soviet inroads. Regimes that relied on conservative military officers appeared to provide a lower-risk path to economic development and political and social reform. Despite later protestations to the contrary, the administration's faith lay in General Zahedi, not the Shah. As a result, the Eisenhower administration pointedly maintained a degree of separation between its policies and personal support for the Shah. For good reason, the administration supported the territorial integrity of a pro-Western independent Iran, not the Pahlavi dynasty. There were serious questions about the Shah's ability to rule. Real faith lay in the conservative military and security services, not only as the foundation for stability, but also as the potential instrument for controlled reform. Finally, Islam and the religious establishment across the region constituted a natural enemy of Communism, and thus another potential ally in the Cold War. This support for religious conservatives served the US well for almost four decades in combating Soviet influence and hostile nationalist regimes.[19] The Iranian coup also moved Washington toward a view of Western interests in the region that was more closely aligned with British views. Eisenhower and Secretary Dulles now had confidence that, when necessary, the US had the capability to control the political situation through covert action.

Defusing a crisis and sparking another – Egypt, 1953-1954

Unfortunately for Churchill and the British government, Egypt was not Iran. In January 1953, when Eisenhower arrived in the White House, the new revolutionary government in Egypt stood at the center of two pressing problems in the Middle East: the Anglo-Egyptian dispute over Suez and the Arab-Israeli conflict. Initially, Eisenhower considered the Anglo-Egyptian dispute over the presence of British troops in the Suez Canal zone as a more acute problem than either the Arab-Israeli dispute or Musaddiq's rogue government in Iran. The new revolutionary government was under the official leadership of General Muhammad Neguib, but was dominated from behind the scenes by Nasser and the Revolutionary Command Council (RCC). The Egyptians demanded British withdrawal from the Canal zone and threatened guerrilla war if London refused. Given the administration view that Egypt was the key to Western fortunes in the Middle East, Washington made it clear that the British presence was an impediment to US interests. Eisenhower and Dulles wanted to pursue a policy of economic assistance, including support for the Egyptian plans to dam the Nile at Aswan. They believed that economic aid would make the new Egyptian government look inward toward economic and social reform, and resolve the 'failure of successive governments to deal with the dangerous internal economic and social situation'. Eisenhower held that Egypt was 'obviously the key' to the issues of Sudan, the Suez Canal, MEDO, the Arab-Israeli dispute, and the Palestinian refugee problem.[20] In 1961, Kennedy's assessment and plans with regard to Egypt were virtually identical to those of Eisenhower. Egypt was the 'key' to US policy goals.

In May 1953, Eisenhower characterized the Anglo-Egyptian crisis over the Suez Canal as the 'most dangerous' situation in the Middle East and dispatched Dulles to assess the situation. For the British, the thought of John Foster Dulles loose in their sand box was maddening. Now, in addition to the US

Ambassador to Egypt Jefferson Caffery giving 'aid and comfort' to the Egyptians, Harold Macmillan groused, 'No doubt the Egyptians (who already rely on the American Ambassador Caffery) ... are hoping to get something out of Dulles, who is due to arrive in a day or two. ... Dulles is sure to make a "gaffe" if it is possible to do so.'[21] Churchill's government fumed over pressure to come to terms with the Egyptians. Undeterred, Dulles reported: 'if unsolved situation [between Britain and Egypt] will find Arab world in open and united hostility to West and in some cases receptive to Soviet aid.'[22] US pressure sparked a row with London. In a bid to moderate this pressure, Churchill threatened an Anglo-Israeli alliance to intimidate Egypt. A skeptical but cautious Dulles reported that such a British move would undermine 'any hope of extending United States influence over the Near East and building at least a minimum of strength here', and would lead to the 'accomplishment of one of primary aims of Soviet Russia'. To appease the British, Dulles pressed Neguib, Nasser, and the RCC to postpone alleged plans for a guerilla war and promised that the US would press to 'moderate the British position'. This is exactly what Churchill had feared and Macmillan had prophesied.[23]

Following a meeting with Neguib, Dulles met separately with Nasser on 11 May. Both the US embassy and the CIA had consistently reported that Nasser was the real power in the RCC and thus, the *de facto* leader of Egypt. Hoping to gain a new hearing for MEDO, Dulles promised additional pressure on the British and more economic aid. Dulles broached the idea of MEDO, and Nasser asked against whom the defense pact was aimed. Dulles replied: 'Against the Soviet Union'. Nasser asked Dulles: 'How can I go to my people and tell them I am disregarding a killer with a pistol sixty miles from me at the Suez Canal to worry about somebody who is holding a knife 5,000 miles away? They would tell me first things first.'[24] By the end of the meeting, Nasser believed that Dulles clearly understood Egypt's rationale for declining to enter a defense pact. Nasser also believed that despite his refusal on MEDO, the US would provide modern arms for the Egyptian army, allowing unofficial cooperation between Washington and Cairo.[25] Dulles reported that while the Egyptians were 'most agreeable, it does not (repeat not) correct deep basic distrust of British which is dominant consideration overriding any fear of Soviets.' The Secretary then concluded that MEDO as envisioned was 'impracticable' due to 'recurrent' tensions and British pressure against economic and political aid.[26] This did not change the view that Egypt was central to US policy interests. On the next leg of his trip, Dulles reported from Damascus that the instability of the regime of Adib Shishakli underscored that there was 'no adequate substitute for Egypt' as a partner in the Arab world.[27] Concluding that an Egyptian-based MEDO might constitute a 'future rather than an immediate possibility', Dulles stated 'the northern tier of nations shows awareness of the danger' of Soviet expansion and thus, the Secretary breathed new life into the an idea first floated during the Truman administration, namely a defensive alliance based on the 'northern tier'.[28] He also concluded that Arab participation in a Western military alliance would create problems in the Arab world that ran directly counter to US interests.[29] Dulles correctly concluded that 'the Arabs were more fearful of Zionism than of Communists.'[30]

Dulles' view that the British constituted the main obstacle to the success of US policy in the Middle East brought increased pressure from Washington on London over the Canal. Anglo-American relations worsened proportionally. In late May 1953, the State Department reported that relations with Britain were 'worse than at any time since Pearl Harbor'. Warning that US pressure threatened his government, Churchill hinted that a Labor government might suspend US basing rights in Britain. At the boiling point, Churchill muttered about setting up high-level talks with the Soviets on the Egyptian situation, and blamed Dulles and Ambassador Caffery for the lack of progress on the new Canal treaty. Few took the threats seriously, but the administration unhappily concluded: 'We have to play along with the British for the time being, and take the beating, which would inevitably result through our association with an ally whom the Egyptians and other Arab states hated as imperialists.'[31] The Eisenhower administration walked a tightrope in attempting to avoid a break with London or with Egypt that would benefit the Soviets. In December 1953, Churchill sent a thinly-veiled, alarmist warning to Eisenhower:

> I am very much worried at the idea of the grant of American economic aid to Egypt at a time when our differences with them are so acute. It would, I am sure, have a grave effect in this country on Anglo-American relations. The Socialist opposition would use it to urge us to press for the inclusion of Red China in U.N.O. and might class it with trade to that country upon which subject [Joseph] McCarthy's unjust charges are already much resented. The frontier of the Suez Canal zone shows very much the same conditions of unrest and potential warfare, as does the frontier in Korea. So much for the opposition. On our Conservative side too we have a disturbed and increasingly angered section who could at any time cancel our modest majority. ... Whether in your policies and immense responsibilities you would get much help from a Socialist Government, I shall not attempt to predict. ... What I fear, however, is that the offended Conservatives might add their voices to that section of the Socialist Party who criticize the United States.[32]

Just for good measure, Churchill added that a Socialist government would likely recognize Communist China as well. Annoyed by the 'somber tone' of Churchill's letter, Eisenhower responded that recognizing 'Red China' was hardly a threat since the British were already trading with them.[33] Still, London's alarm and Churchill's growing aggravation gave Washington pause.

The President wanted Churchill to commit that if the US withheld aid and Egypt agreed to the terms discussed by the Prime Minister and President at their earlier meeting in Bermuda, Britain would then settle its differences with Egypt.[34] The Prime Minister reassured Eisenhower: 'If the Egyptians accept our present terms we shall certainly abide by them. But we do not think you ought to give them moral and material support while they threaten and assault our troops and conduct a campaign of hatred against us.'[35] In 1954, the Anglo-Egyptian treaty over the Canal allowed a British military presence until 1956, and the right of reoccupation if the Canal were threatened. In reality, the British, no longer able to to maintain large forces in Egypt, were willing to settle for the right of reentry. The problem revolved around defining what constituted an emergency. Eventually, the Egyptians grudgingly accepted the right of reentry in the event of a war that included an attack on Turkey.[36] Although unforeseen at the time, the inclusion of Turkey would provide a flashpoint that ultimately unraveled the British position in Iraq and accelerated the collapse of British prestige in the region. On 27 July 1954, the Egyptians and the British signed an agreement that provided for the phased withdrawal of British forces.[37] Finalized in October 1954, the treaty seemed to resolve the Anglo-Egyptian impasse and cleared the way for closer Egyptian ties with the West. In November 1954, Nasser removed Neguib and took direct control of the government.

In reality, the treaty, coupled with Dulles' alternate strategy for containment along the 'northern tier' unintentionally undermined the administration's early hopes for Western gains. Nasser and the RCC had needed US help in getting an agreement with Britain; thus the completion of the treaty reduced Cairo's dependence on Washington. The treaty also provoked a revolt by the Muslim Brotherhood, forcing Nasser to take a public anti-Western stance. The fact that the propaganda campaign was largely orchestrated with CIA assistance was beside the point; Nasser could no more openly pursue pro-Western policies after the treaty than before it.[38] Relations between Cairo and Washington were further complicated by dashed Egyptian expectations. Nasser believed that Dulles had promised massive US economic and military aid in return for compromises with the British.[39] During the winter of 1954, it became increasingly evident that any aid would have strings attached, a situation that Nasser, politically could not afford.[40] From Nasser's point of view, the utility of a relationship with Washington was rapidly decreasing. Washington alluded to economic aid, and military aid was limited to security assistance for internal purposes, not modern arms for the Egyptian army.

At this point, Dulles' 'northern tier' substitute for the Egyptian-based MEDO crashed head-on into US-Egyptian relations. With Washington acting as the mid-wife, on 2 April 1954 Pakistan and Turkey had announced their 'Agreement of Friendly Cooperation'. Rumors had circulated for months about the potential for an alliance. At the eastern end of the region, the arming of Pakistan would galvanize Nehru into a frenzy of opposition to US policies, but the response in the Arab Middle East was muted on the condition of non-participation by Arab states. On 1 August, at Egyptian prodding, the Arab League issued a statement opposing the inclusion of any Arab states in a non-Arab defensive alliance. Iraq adhered to the Arab League declaration only when speculation about membership in the Turkish-Pakistani pact resulted in nationalist rioting in Baghdad, and the British supported the Iraqi decision. The

British government feared that US influence in Iraq would increase as it had in post-coup Iran and post-revolutionary Egypt.[41] At this juncture, the terms of the Anglo-Egyptian treaty altered the course of events in the Arab Middle East. The treaty linked Egypt to Turkey and the British defense of the Canal by stating that British forces could reenter the Suez Canal zone in the event of an attack on Turkey. The fact that the Egyptians had strongly opposed this clause was lost on the Iraqis. Nuri Sa'id interpreted the treaty as a tripartite defensive arrangement between Turkey, Egypt, and Britain, with Iraq effectively out in the cold. To recoup Iraq's position, he moved to form his own alliance with Turkey. In early January, Iraq and Turkey announced their intention to enter into a defensive alliance.

The Egyptian reaction was swift and decidedly negative. Nasser called for a ministerial-level Arab conference in Cairo. Viewing the Iraqi move as a direct challenge to Egypt's leadership and an indication of the continued British divide-and-conquer policy, Nasser moved to form an Arab defense arrangement that isolated Iraq. The Cairo Conference of 22 January was a humiliating failure. Only Yemen and Saudi Arabia supported Egypt, while Syria, Jordan, and Lebanon refused to condemn Iraq. The failure of the conference brought a vitriolic propaganda campaign aimed at Nuri Sa'id, Iraq, and anyone else that supported the 'Anglo-American stooge'. It caused Washington to reconsider support for Iraq's inclusion in any Western defense scheme.[42] Having specifically warned the US about the inclusion of Arab states in its defensive alliances, Cairo began to view the US role with greater suspicion. Nuri Pasha had managed to place the Eisenhower administration's security plan on a collision course with the very country that Washington viewed as the 'key' to the region.

Recognizing an opportunity to separate the US from Egypt, the British now supported the inclusion of Iraq and other Arab states into the defense alliance. London threw caution to the winds in its Iraqi policy by undermining the Arab nationalist credentials of the Hashemite regime. Still hoping for US economic aid, support for the Aswan project, and US arms, Nasser wanted to preserve his relationship with Washington; however, the potential for Iraq's inclusion in a Western military alliance raised serious questions about the potential threat that Eisenhower's containment policy posed to Egyptian interests in the region. In Washington, Eisenhower and his advisors were beginning to grasp the limitations that the political realities of the Middle East placed on the influence to be gained through economic assistance and on local participation in its plans to contain the Soviet Union. Largely in deference to Cairo's negative reaction to Iraq's inclusion in what became the Baghdad Pact, Washington provided support but refused to join, while still hoping to gain something positive from its courtship of Nasser.

A peace for the Arab-Israeli conflict

Eisenhower and Dulles, in essence, agreed with Secretary of State George C. Marshall's assessment that the recognition of Israel had fundamentally been a policy made for emotional and political reasons during the presidential campaign of 1948. By 1953, the creation of Israel was so much spilt milk, but it threatened to sour relations with the Arab and Muslim worlds. The problem now centered on how to neutralize Israel as a stumbling block to US-Arab relations. Eisenhower clearly understood the problems associated with any attempt to foster improved Arab-Israeli relations:

> There is no doubt that American initiative in the establishment of the Israeli State and the resulting Arab refugee problem has led to increased anti-Western feeling throughout the Arab countries and has embittered, in particular, Arab-American relations. It may be, too, that the aid which Israel has received from the United States has delayed the possibility of a settlement by enabling Israel to avoid facing the issue that, unless she trades with the Arab countries, she cannot be a viable State.

With regard to the situation in Egypt, the President viewed the Arab-Israeli dispute as a distraction from the proper focus on economic progress. He stated: 'It is doubtful, therefore, if any Egyptian Government could risk settling these international questions without ... at least having made a start with economic policies designed to raise the miserable standard of living of the bulk of the Egyptian people.'[43] Eisenhower, like Kennedy in 1961, believed that economic development coupled with a settlement of the Arab-Israeli dispute was not just desirable, but mandatory in order to protect the long-term interests of the US.

With this in mind, on his Middle East mission in May 1953 Dulles stated: 'We had come here with belief Egypt afforded best opportunity for Arab leadership toward better relations with Israel and the West.'[44] Eisenhower believed that an Arab-Israeli peace was possible as long as the US could maintain a relatively neutral stance and could induce both the Arabs and Israelis to focus on economic development. Against the backdrop of the Anglo-Egyptian negotiations over the Suez Canal, the administration attempted to leverage the Egyptian regime into breaking the impasse over an Arab-Israeli peace settlement. Eisenhower had repeatedly stated that his administration intended to 'do what it thought was right' and not, as Vice President Richard M. Nixon put it, 'kowtow' to domestic Jewish political pressure. Washington believed that it could use economic leverage and manipulate the valve on foreign aid to control Israel. Secretary of Defense Charles E. Wilson suggested: 'when a horse gets too frisky you should cut down on his oats.'[45] The administration believed that it could use economic leverage to drive the Israelis to the bargaining table and to force them to compromise with the Arabs.

A solution to the refugee problem was to be the first step.[46] The plan also called for guarantees on the part of Israel 'against any further expansion at the expense of neighboring nations'. It included compensation for Palestinian refugees and the right of return for refugees. Lastly, it called for a settlement of the Jordan River water-usage issues and a joint program to develop water resources in the region. Washington clearly linked an agreement on the development of the Jordan waters, the settlement of the refugee problem, and just for good measure, the internationalization of Jerusalem as the basis for peace in the region.[47] During his Middle East trip in May 1953, Dulles broached the topic of refugees with Israeli Prime Minister David Ben-Gurion. Ben-Gurion quickly disabused Dulles of any hopes of Israeli cooperation. Rejecting a comprehensive peace settlement, Ben-Gurion wanted a 'de facto' peace with an end to 'economic hostilities'. In addition, he made it clear that Israel had no intention of allowing the 'right of return'. Dulles quickly drew the only conclusion possible, namely that any hope for peace rested on the success of a step-by-step approach.[48]

Wanting to scuttle compromise and knowing full well that the Arabs would reject it, Ben-Gurion wanted to offer an Israeli proposal. His goal was to place the Arabs at a 'moral disadvantage and thereby neutralizing growing American interest in Arab friendship'.[49] The administration recognized the ploy for what it was and pressured the Israelis to withhold any initiative. Concluding that the refugee problem was a dead issue, Washington then focused on the Jordan waters issue as a first step in getting an agreement between the two sides.[50] The administration understood that the Arabs would not sign an agreement that recognized Israel's right to exist, and Eric Johnston, the chief negotiator, worked diligently on a plan to circumvent this issue.[51] The British had warned that in pressing too hard for the water-sharing agreement, the United States would 'risk a major loss of prestige and position'.[52] Johnston reported that he believed that he could get the Israelis to agree but would have problems with the Arabs. In point of fact, Johnston obtained an agreement from the Arabs, but the Israelis changed their position, jeopardizing the entire negotiation.[53] Johnston fell back on entreating the Israelis to review his proposals so 'that your painstaking and serious consideration will bring us closer to the end we are seeking'.[54] At this point, the Israelis effectively removed the potential for any settlement with Egypt and undercut the possibility of participation by any Arab state in any agreement with Israel through military action. On 28 February, Israeli forces mounted a raid into Gaza in retaliation for minor border incidents. Dozens of Egyptian soldiers and police were killed.[55] Not only did this make an agreement with Israel unthinkable, but it also brought to a head the issue of modern arms for the Egyptian army. From Nasser's perspective, the Iraqi issue and the Gaza raid made it appear that the West intended to strengthen Egypt's enemies and undermine his prestige throughout the region. Nuri Sa'id and Ben Gurion had succeeded in undermining the lynchpin in Washington's Arab policy.[56]

Although efforts related to the refugee problem and the Jordan waters lingered, by 1956 it was apparent that no agreement would be forthcoming.[57] Despite the Eisenhower administration's good intentions, it simply underestimated the complexity and intractability of the problem. None of the parties involved were interested in a compromise settlement. The Israelis in particular viewed any compromise as a threat to their goal of creating a Jewish state and excluding the Arab population. In a note of cynicism about the prospects for the plan, an anonymous bard penned the following for the State Department file:

> Flow Gently Sweet Afton
>
> Come quickly Sweet Arabs
> Let's meet while we can
> We've something enticing
> 'Tis Johnston's own Plan
> We only entreat you
> Be ready to sign
> We'll furnish the paper
> And the dotted line.
> Now all that we ask you
> Is simple and sweet
> Just have full authority
> Whenever we meet
> So you all may sign up
> And then we will tell
> Those waters of Jordan
> To steam heat all Hell.[58]

The Jordan-waters plan collapsed; domestic political concerns outweighed any economic benefit. The British had never the liked the project, US officials ascribing this to London's 'pique' at not being 'sufficiently' consulted before Johnston undertook his mission. Washington believed that the British were 'loathe to take an action which they [felt] would put all their eggs in one basket'. London only got on board at the end because they feared a loss of prestige if the American plan worked.[59] British reluctance turned out to be justified. Eisenhower and Dulles had a plan, but no one was willing to participate in it. With the failure of the Jordan- waters effort, the Eisenhower administration's efforts to establish a peace process effectively ground to a halt. Economic incentives were simply insufficient inducements to outweigh the associated political risks. This was not only true in the Arab world, but in Israel as well, where the Arab 'threat' became the critical internal political issue. Fear politics and exaggerating that threat became the political bread-and-butter that paid off in Knesset seats. Thus, Arab and Israeli fear of a settlement trumped any gain that might accrue from increased economic aid. This clearly demonstrated the limitations that economic aid could play as an inducement to an Arab-Israeli settlement.

Running afoul of non-alignment

In late 1954, the Eisenhower administration looked with justifiable satisfaction on its overall Middle East policies. The situation in Iran, while leaving much to be desired in the way of political reform and economic development, was stable. However grudgingly, Egypt and Britain had signed a new treaty that would remove British forces from the Suez Canal zone. Economic pressure and incentives showed promise as the first steps toward a possible Arab-Israeli peace. At the same time, a rudimentary alliance system to contain the Soviet Union seemed to be emerging. Issues and problems remained, but on the whole, the marriage of containment and economic development appeared to be working. In reality, these tactical successes had begun the process that would turn US relations with the 'progressive' regimes in the Middle East on their ear.

Just as the linkage between Turkey and Egypt in the Anglo-Egyptian treaty of 1954 had unintended consequences, the inclusion of Pakistan in the Western defense structure alienated India. At the same time, it made New Delhi an integral part of the Middle Eastern power struggle. Ironically, Nehru's marriage of political democracy and economic development in India largely followed the model that Eisenhower and his advisors saw as so central to pro-Western development in Asia, and yet the requirements of containment would foster an increasingly problematic relationship between the world's two largest democracies. These problems also contributed to growing political and diplomatic synergy between India and Egypt; neither Nehru nor Nasser were willing to trade national interests for arms or economic assistance from the West.[60] Given their deep-seated distrust of Great Power machinations stemming from their colonial experiences, India and Egypt absolutely refused to enter a Western military alliance.

Nehru had made it clear that he envisioned a new political order for Asia that rejected the traditions of *Realpolitik*. At the 1947 Asian Conference, Nehru stated: 'Asia far too long had been petitioners in western courts and chancelleries. That story must now belong to the past. We propose to stand on our own feet.'[61] In India during the early 1950s, Nehru began to reverse the trend toward diffusion of political power following independence. He was consolidating power at the 'Center'. The power of regional political chiefs threatened to fracture the unity of the republic. Nehru believed that external alliances would provide ammunition to his internal political opponents and undermine Congress Party rule. Just as important, he was ideologically committed to non-alignment. Non-alignment, or 'neutrality' in Washington's parlance, had a clear anti-American, almost pro-Communist tint. It flew in the face of the 'with us or against us' attitudes that framed the Cold War diplomatic and security mentality. Despite this, Nehru's India was too important to ignore or totally alienate. The Eisenhower administration had pronounced concerns with respect to non-alignment, but in the case of India, Washington had prudently announced a policy of 'respect for, but non-acceptance of, neutralist policy'.[62] India was the largest democracy in the world, a potential Asian counterbalance to Communist China, and Nehru had innumerable admirers, including key members of the US Congress. Eisenhower and his advisors recognized the necessity of a working relationship with New Delhi. In addition, India had played a key role in Korea, and chaired the International Control Commission on Indochina. Having carefully monitored US-Pakistani bilateral developments, New Delhi expressed immediate concern when Dulles, following his Middle East tour in May 1953, referred to an alternative defensive alliance on the northern tier and explained that this meant Turkey, Iran, and Pakistan.[63]

No one in Washington had any illusions about the desirability of avoiding involvement in the Kashmir dispute. The Eisenhower administration viewed it as an issue for British management because it 'involve[d] two members of the British Commonwealth'. This was more or less consistent with the British view that the Commonwealth provided a potential venue for quiet mediation away from the glare of the United Nations (UN) and public posturing.[64] Officially, the US based its policy on two conditions: first, India and Pakistan should only employ peaceful means in settling their disputes; and second, a plebiscite in Kashmir, preceded by demilitarization, should determine the final disposition of the disputed area. New Delhi adamantly opposed the second condition. In January 1953, the State Department reported the following to the White House: 'There [is] no present indication that Nehru and the Indian Government are prepared to reach [an] agreement' on demilitarization or a political solution 'except on their own terms.'[65] Thus, Nehru's commitment to non-alignment and his hard position on Kashmir offered Washington little room to maneuver in building its containment of the Soviet Union or in removing Kashmir as a potential regional flashpoint.

In December 1953, concerned that the administration lacked a real option in dealing with Nehru's position, Eisenhower wrote to a friend that he saw a looming clash between US policy and non-alignment:

> In between these two extremes (Left and Right) is a vast center group, which in basic beliefs has much in common, and, for this reason, should be a closely-knit organization. In point of fact this vast center or 'Middle of the Road' group prefers to shut its eyes to the dangers represented in the extremes – in the current state of affairs, the only threatening extreme is Communism. The group of nations of which this center is constituted constantly indulges in all kinds of divisive arguments and name-calling that grow so important in their cumulative effect as to nullify any attempt toward unity in working against the common enemy.

Pakistan was a case in point. Eisenhower pointed out: 'India would rather see Pakistan weak and helpless in front of a Russian threat than to see that country grow strong enough to give substance to its hope of annexing Kashmir.'[66] The White House decided that despite the potential fallout with India, US security required a defensive military arrangement with Pakistan. Anticipating New Delhi's reaction, the administration pinned its hopes of managing India on the importance of massive US aid. The US was the largest contributor of economic assistance, by a wide margin, and Nehru's plans for economic development were totally dependent on that aid.

Viewing this economic leverage as insurance against a radical Indian reaction, the Eisenhower administration encouraged the formation of a defensive alliance between Turkey and Pakistan. In December 1953, Nehru expressed his opposition to arms for Pakistan to Vice President Richard Nixon during the latter's visit to India. On his return to Washington, Nixon argued strongly that the US could not afford to 'back down on this program solely because of Nehru's objections. ... Because such a retreat would cost us our hold on Pakistan and on many other areas in the Near East and Africa.'[67] Arguably, Nixon's assessment tipped the balance in favor of providing arms to Pakistan.[68] On 16 February 1954, the administration welcomed Pakistan and Turkey's decision to 'study' defense collaboration. President Eisenhower called it 'a constructive step towards better ensuring the security of the whole area of the Middle East'. Eisenhower approved Karachi's simultaneous request for military aid, stating that he was 'gravely concerned over the weakness of defensive capabilities in the Middle East'. In hopes of mollifying India, the President pointed out that the weapons were for 'defensive' purposes only and not 'in any act of aggression toward any other country'.[69]

The White House interpreted Nehru's professed fear of Pakistani aggression as a stalking-horse for Indian leader's real motivation – namely to increase his own power and prestige by attracting more countries to the Afro-Asian 'neutralist bloc'. The administration understood that New Delhi would be unhappy with arms for Pakistan, but Nixon's somewhat naïve and oversimplified view of managing Nehru resonated with the administration: 'The best way to handle [Nehru] would be for a special envoy to the President to go to New Delhi and explain to Nehru firmly and forthrightly just why we thought it desirable to give military assistance to Pakistan, and to offer reassurances as to our intentions vis-à-vis India.' Dulles hoped to hide behind the collective security agreement of what the State Department termed the 'so-called northern tier' in order to claim that military assistance to Pakistan was not bilateral.[70]

By March 1954, Eisenhower had tired of trying to mollify India and made it clear that the security requirements of the US would determine the status of military aid to Pakistan. Eisenhower sent a personal letter to Prime Minister Nehru stating that 'improving Pakistan's defensive capability' served the interests of regional security and assured him, 'What we are proposing to do, and what Pakistan is agreeing to, is not directed in any way against India.' The President pointedly reminded Nehru that India received 'substantial economic and technical aid' from the US and dangled military aid 'of a type contemplated by our mutual security legislation,' meaning, of course, aid to allied partners, should India desire it.[71] Again, he reassured New Delhi that the US would take 'appropriate action' in the event that Pakistan attempted to direct this military aid toward India. Washington implicitly understood how this news would play in Delhi. In an effort to 'counteract some of the ... irritation in India at the prospect of US military aid to Pakistan', Washington commended the Indian government and military for its 'exemplary performance' in handling disengagement operations in Korea.[72] Rostow's evaluation of containment and Communist China underscored the consensus existing in Cold War Washington. No matter how problematic relations might be, the success of India's 'democratically engineered rural revolution' and the 'evolution of solid military, political, and economic policies in Free Asia' were vital if the West was to deny Beijing 'military and ideological primacy in Asia.'[73] Rostow's analysis underscores the segued strategic view of Asia held by both the Eisenhower and Kennedy administrations.

Nehru reacted with a vehemence that surprised all but the most experienced India hands in the foreign policy community. The Indian Prime Minister claimed that the US had completely altered the 'roots and foundations' of any proposed settlement on Kashmir. With broad public support in India, Nehru argued that the US had taken Pakistan's side in the dispute and was now assisting Karachi in its 'encirclement' of India.[74] Nehru attacked both the Americans and the Pakistanis for bringing the Cold War into South Asia and creating the very instability that the alliance purportedly sought to prevent.[75] Nehru chastised Washington for attempting to pressure India into a military alliance with the US by arming Pakistan and making it 'practically a colony of the United States'.[76] Nehru threatened an 'agonizing reappraisal' of US-India relations and hinted at acquiring arms from the Soviet Union.[77] Taken aback, Washington attempted to minimize the Indian reaction. In India, senior officials termed Eisenhower's letter of explanation 'condescending' and praised the Prime Minister's 'dignified response'.[78] Nehru pointedly demanded that US observers in Kashmir leave because 'the US had ceased to be neutral as a result of [its] military assistance to Pakistan.'[79] He then publicly and contemptuously dismissed Eisenhower's personal letter of explanation.[80] From Eisenhower's perspective, Indian neutrality had become 'neutrality against the West', as Nehru increasingly refused to differentiate between the Soviet and US political systems. To further harass Washington, India became stridently critical of the US refusal to allow UN membership for Beijing, with Nehru publicly claiming that the US had 'little understanding of Asian nationalism'.[81] Despite his pique, Nehru resisted more radical action against US interests. He understood that the loss of US economic aid would have disastrous consequences for Indian economic growth.[82] This situation left Washington with policy schizophrenia. Pakistan, where no amount of economic aid provided stability, was vital to Western defense, and in contrast, India, which refused all entreaties to join a Western alliance, represented the test case of 'whether underdeveloped economies can achieve progress by Western liberal means'. Nehru's 'socialist' leanings notwithstanding, his vision appealed to Washington's belief in economic prosperity and reform as the surest counterbalance to Communist expansionism.[83]

The situation frustrated Nehru as well, but US aid prevented a head-on confrontation with Washignton. He would find other ways to vent his unhappiness with US policy. The arming of Pakistan contributed directly to a vigorous Indian campaign to assert its prerogatives and emphasize its independence from Washington, and to show its overall displeasure with Western military alliances. Coincidentally, Nehru had at his disposal the perfect instrument for harassing the Americans. This instrument left no doubt as to the origin of the message but provided Nehru with a fig leaf of deniability.[84] Nehru had appointed Vengali Krishnan Krishna Menon to the Indian delegation at the United Nations, following his controversial tenure as head of the Indian High Commission in London. An avowed leftist, inspired by the Hindu radical Lokmanaya Bal Gangadhar Tilak and the Bolshevik Revolution, Menon had served as Nehru's friend, publicist, and personal representative in Britain during the 1930s and 1940s, where he became the self-styled 'Ambassador of St. Pancreas'.[85] Menon described himself well when he stated: 'I never chase controversies, controversies chase me.'[86] Arriving in New York almost simultaneously with Eisenhower's arrival in Washington, Menon's high-profile attacks on the West coupled with his pro-Soviet leftist views served as a lightning rod for criticism and friction. Opponents of aid for India and critics of 'non-alignment' transformed Menon into India's American face.[87] By claiming that he had authored the term 'non-aligned' and by his uncompromising hostility to the West, he managed to further taint non-alignment as pro-Soviet.[88]

Concurrently, the Geneva Convention on Indochina was convened, with India as the chair of the International Control Commission. Understanding full well the implications and probable outcome, Nehru placed Menon in the Indian delegation at the conference, where he managed to severely antagonize Washington.[89] Chester L. Cooper, a member of the US delegation in Geneva, described Menon's contribution thus: 'Krishna Menon, who blew in and out of Geneva on short notice, was clearly the Super Star of the Geneva Follies and relished his role. He consciously and conspicuously played to audiences well beyond the confines of the Palais des Nations. He was wordy, windy, and exasperatingly oratorical.'[90] Menon made it clear that he was implementing Nehru's policies.[91] Despite differences in style, Menon was, in fact, the more radical and strident expression of Nehru's positions. US assistance to Pakistan aside, Nehru abhorred Eisenhower's commitment to Asian leaders like Chiang Kai-Shek and Sygmund Rhee. In non-policy areas, Nehru increasingly resented what he viewed as the attitude of 'American superiority', and pushed for limiting US influence. 'I dislike more and more this business of exchange of persons between American and India. The fewer persons that go from India to America and from America to India, the better.'[92] Widely despised in the US, Menon became a symbol of India's and Nehru's leftist tendencies, and of the danger posed by the non-aligned movement.[93]

Nehru and Bandung

Nehru's commitment to non-alignment accelerated and intensified the deterioration of Indian relations with the West. The geopolitical and military aspects of US containment policy began to overshadow the initial commitment to economic development as the initial central theme in combating Soviet, Chinese, and indigenous Communist influence. In much of the developing world, Washington's linkage of military and economic policies under the containment umbrella transformed perceptions of the US from the champion of emerging nationalism to a neo-colonialist interloper tied to a very British-like policy of indirect colonialism. In January 1954, Shri Morarji Desai noted the growing British influence on US policy in the region and commented to Nehru: 'There is smug satisfaction in Britain at the US dropping its anti-colonialism.'[94] Comments from senior British officials encouraged this perception. On 14 January, British Deputy Labor Leader Herbert Morrison told D.N. Chatterjee, the Indian High Commissioner in London that: 'It is sad but if India keeps out of all essential defense arrangements then I suppose facilities in Pakistan will have to be used.'[95] The Indians also understood that the issue of arms for Pakistan had created a new political dynamic. In another dispatch, Chatterjee stated: 'Pakistan has moved somewhat into the American orbit of influence' and 'India [had] broken with America,' which put London in a difficult situation given that 'the menace of Russia against interests in the Middle East is such that only with American help can Britain hope to counteract it.'[96] As Nehru described it: 'Somehow the exigencies of the cold war [led] the US to indirectly encourage colonialism.'[97] Non-alignment not only came to symbolize independence and freedom of action to Nehru, but it also provided a means to indirectly tweak the Eisenhower administration for its policies. Nehru's unhappiness also placed a greater emphasis on pressing forward with a major non-aligned initiative.

The 1954 Colombo and 1955 Bandung conferences were directly stimulated by Nehru's objections to the system of Western alliances. The 28 April to 2 May 1954 Colombo conference was a relatively limited affair; however, it quickly took on broader overtones. Key participants quickly recognized it as a path to greater stature and independence of action. Krishna Menon's attendance with Nehru became a major divisive note. Menon urged Nehru to take extreme positions and, at one point, rudely interrupted the Pakistani Prime Minister Muhammad Ali telling him: 'We are sick and tired of your submissions.'[98] Nehru also lost his temper with the Pakistani Prime Minister, stating that further discussion was useless 'with America represented here'. Not to be outdone, Ali shouted back, calling Nehru and Menon 'stooges of Chinese and Russian imperialism'. The Indians and Pakistanis disagreed on everything, from condemnations of Communism and anti-Communist movements to the order in which the 'US, the UK, China, and USSR,' (the Indian version) or 'China, the UK, the US, and USSR' (the alphabetic Pakistani version) were to be listed in the call for non-intervention in Indochina. Apparently, Nehru's experience at the Colombo conference created something of a quandary for him. Pakistani Prime Minister Muhammad Ali acquitted himself well, holding his own against an overconfident Nehru: 'Nehru underrated his young but dynamic opposite number in Pakistan and overrated his own ability to hustle the other Prime Ministers into meek compliance.'⁹⁹ Already leery of a follow-on Afro-Asian conference the next year, Nehru set about finding additional international support to counteract Pakistan before he committed to attend.

Nehru's lukewarm support for an Afro-Asian conference in 1955 raised doubts that it would occur. Initially, the Eisenhower administration believed that the effort would likely collapse; however, by late 1954, it had become apparent that Nehru intended to proceed and on a clearly anti-American note. He stated: 'I do not like either Communism or colonialism. Communism is only a threat. Colonialism is a fact.' Nehru made it clear that the principle agenda at Bandung would be colonialism.¹⁰⁰ While public pronouncements were somewhat muted, the press, particularly the Indian press, carried the undiluted themes of the conference: 'From championing the cause of freedom in Asia, [the five] Colombo powers [were] slowly moving toward [an] ideological crusade against colonialism.' The commentary went on to bemoan the American 'vested interest in ... decaying empires and, despite her anti-imperialist record in past, has now put herself in the false position of defending these anachronisms in name of fighting Communism.'¹⁰¹ Taking the diplomatic initiative by inviting Beijing to attend, Nehru sent Britain and the United States scrambling for a response. In fact, the potential diplomatic and political ramifications were so broad that the Eisenhower administration had great difficulty in formulating a strategy at all.

On 14 January 1955, Dulles called a meeting of key State Department and CIA officials in an attempt to come to some resolution concerning the proper course of action for Washington. His younger brother, Allen Dulles, Director of the CIA, expressed serious concern about the purpose of the Bandung meetings. Director Dulles argued that given the combination of Chou En-lai and Nehru many of 'the relatively inexperienced Asian diplomats' would be 'ensnared' into supporting anti-colonial resolution 'seemingly in favor of goodness, beauty and truth'. In addition, Washington feared that 'the Bandung meeting would provide Chou En-Lai with an excellent forum to broadcast Communist ideology to a naïve audience in the guise of anti-colonialism.' Suggestions for dealing with the 'rigged conference' ran the gamut from delaying it to organizing a boycott to supporting the attendance of solidly pro-Western nations in the region. The sole point of agreement was the necessity of undermining the Indian and Chinese positions and of achieving this by working 'hand-in-hand with the British', given that three of the five sponsoring nations were in the Commonwealth.¹⁰²

Washington worried about the potential for an anti-Western tone and increased acceptability for Communist China in the world community. The conference also highlighted the differences between the non-aligned and pro-Western camps in Asia and the Middle East. Burmese Prime Minister U Nu denied that it would be 'anti-Western per se', but allowed that in the context of discussions about colonialism there would undoubtedly be 'disparaging remarks about colonial powers and those are mostly Western powers.' In Washington, the Dulles brothers, with the White House's blessing, searched for a way to encourage the 'development of Sino-Indian rivalry at Bandung'. In a hand-written comment on the intelligence report, an official stated: 'On the other side of coin, U.S. has not been idle. For several months a working group chaired by State has been active preparing specific counter-actions.'[103] The administration feared that the conference might turn into a 'regular affair' dominated by India and China with the 'likely by-product [of] a very solid block of anti-western votes in the United Nations'. Secretary Dulles concluded that, given the exclusion of Israel from the conference, Arab attendance would determine its success or failure. He reluctantly discussed using US 'influence' in Cairo to prevent Egyptian attendance: 'If, without using strong-arm methods we can prevent the Conference from taking place we would welcome this outcome; but we are not prepared openly to oppose it or to threaten lest such a posture elicit an unwanted counter-reaction.' Instead, Dulles proposed that should the conference actually take place, the United States, working with Britain, should use attending friendly states to 'propose courses of action which would embarrass Communist China' and minimize the possibility of the formation of an Asian-African bloc.

The Secretary's first priority was to determine the British position toward Bandung and to coordinate strategies with London.[104] From London, the administration received mixed signals. On 15 January, the British Ambassador in Washington, Sir Roger Makins, was quoted in the *Indian Express* as stating that there was 'nothing sinister in forthcoming conferences in Asia'.[105] At the same time, the Foreign Office had instructed its embassies to 'discourage attendance'.[106] The Eisenhower administration took the public view that Bandung was an 'opportunity' for the US to use surrogates to make the 'Chinese Communists prisoners of their own pious professions. Resolutions opposing aggression, intervention, subversion, and so on will tend to strengthen, for what it is worth, the "moral containment" of Peiping.'[107] When the Bandung conference actually convened on 18 April 1955, the US and Britain had already lobbied friendly nations intensely, and now believed that it might 'result in a more peaceful attitude on the part of the Chinese Communists'.[108] The administration also concluded that Afro-Asian unity and cooperation could work to the US's advantage. The overt outcome was more or less benign, with the predictable statements on colonialism and recognition of various liberation movements, including the FLN in Algeria.[109] Despite some hopes for the contrary, Washington concluded that the conference had tended to reaffirm his leadership role in the non-aligned world, particularly in Africa and Asia.[110]

Nasser and Bandung

The Colombo Powers committed relatively early on to an Afro-Asian conference at Bandung; however, in late 1954 and early 1955 it was unclear how successful the conference would actually be. Washington viewed the participation of the countries in the Arab Middle East as the litmus test of success. Initially, the US subjected Egypt to the 'strongest pressure' not to attend. The Indians believed that Washington wanted to use an Egyptian refusal to attend as the springboard from which to convince most of the Arab states to boycott the conference.[111] Unfortunately for the Eisenhower administration, US influence in Cairo had taken a downward turn, and Nehru's courtship of Nasser seemed to pay off. On 21 January 1955, Kermit Roosevelt, the CIA conduit to Nasser, informed Washington that not only had the Egyptians definitely decided to attend the conference, but also that Nasser himself would probably head the delegation.[112] It was no accident that Nasser decided to attend Bandung on the eve of the Cairo conference on the Turkey-Iraq agreement. Left with no alternative, the State Department urged the British 'to revise their position' and support the conference as well.[113] Then, on 28 February, an Israeli raid on Gaza effectively pushed Nasser into the same political boat as Nehru. In Nasser's mind, Western aid for Israel and Iraq created a similar reaction to that of Nehru's with regard to weapons for Pakistan. In addition, Nasser needed modern arms for the Egyptian army. In an attempt to compromise with Nasser's opposition to Arab participation in Western political alliances, the British promised a 'moratorium' on the entry of other Arab states, with the exception of Iraq. By the eve of the Bandung conference, Nasser had concluded that he had to challenge the British, Iraq, and Israel to survive politically.[114]

Nehru found the Western alliance system equally intolerable. Pakistan had become the eastern pillar of the Baghdad Pact and the western pillar of the Southeast Asia Treaty Organization (SEATO). India and Egypt now faced a British-led, American-sponsored and -financed anti-Soviet alliance that was arming their principal regional adversaries. Nasser's acceptance of Nehru's invitation to attend the Bandung Conference of Non-Aligned Nations, held on 18-24 April 1955, became a foregone conclusion. Realizing that the conference would, in fact, occur, the Eisenhower administration encouraged pro-Western states in Africa and Asia to attend in an attempt to transform the conference into a pro-Western display of solidarity. Fearing that Pakistan would attempt to assume 'the self appointed role of spokesman of the Arab countries – or rather the Muslim World,' the Indian government needed the presence of a staunchly neutral Egypt. In return, Nehru was prepared to give Egypt's leader equal billing with other prominent non-aligned leaders, elevating his stature over that of the other pro-Western attendees.[115] By enticing Nasser to Bandung and engineering Communist Chinese representation in the form of Chou En-lai, Nehru demonstrated his displeasure with the Western alliance system in general and US policy in particular.

At Bandung, Nasser found himself feted and flattered by Nehru and by Achmad Sukarno of Indonesia. After the conference, Nasser announced from New Delhi that: 'the only wise policy for us [Egypt and the Arabs] consisted in adopting positive neutralism and nonalignment.'[116] From an Egyptian perspective, Nasser 'went to Bandung an Egyptian and returned a world figure and revolutionary'.[117] Initially, Eisenhower and Dulles were not overly

Nasser and Nehru Post-Bandung
Nasser and Nehru following the Bandung conference in April 1955. The caption read 'Please You First' referring to their decision to simultaneously recognize Communist China, much to the chargin of the Eisenhower administration. This relationship would come to symbolize 'positive neutrality' and non-alignment in the Greater Middle East.

concerned with the results of Bandung; it appeared that the pro-Western states had held their own. Others were less sanguine. Charles Habib Malik, who attended as a member of the Lebanese delegation and later became Lebanese foreign minister, warned the Dulles brothers' special envoy, Wilbur Eveland, that Tito, Sukarno, and Nehru would unite the developing nations of Africa and Asia to oppose the Western alliance systems and create a potentially anti-Western bloc in the United Nations. Malik also described Nasser as 'mesmerized' by non-alignment and beguiled by the attention showered on him. To the annoyance of the White House, Malik's concern took concrete form when Nasser proclaimed Egyptian adherence to non-alignment. The aggravation caused by this move paled in comparison to the announcement that would follow.

At the conference, Chou En-lai appeared totally reasonable to the delegates, someone 'with whom one could do business'.[118] In secret discussions with Nasser, Chou offered to raise the issue of arms for Egypt with Moscow. Shortly after Nasser's return from Indonesia, the Soviet Ambassador to Egypt, Daniel Solod, offered not only modern weapons on generous payment terms but also help with the Aswan Dam project. Initially suspicious, Nasser held back, hoping for an American counteroffer. When none was forthcoming, he negotiated the so-called Czech arms deal, signing the agreement on 27 September 1955.[119] Nasser told Miles Copeland, his CIA contact, that the Arab world understood that the Baghdad Pact did not offer freedom of action for defense against Israel: 'Any regional military agreement which did not take this attitude into account would be a fraud.'[120] Nasser was correct, and the fact that the US only offered arms to support internal security merely served to confirm this.[121]

The Czech arms dealt a double shock to the Eisenhower administration. In the minds of many in Washington, it irretrievably linked 'non-aligned' and pro-Communist policies, but perhaps more importantly, it directly affected US-Soviet relations. Eisenhower believed that at the Geneva conference 1955, he had achieved an 'understanding' and 'basis for a working relationship' with the Soviet Union with regard to spheres of influence. This 'understanding' included the Middle East in the Western sphere. The Czech Arms agreement amounted to a Soviet double-cross and demonstrated that the new leadership in Moscow could not be trusted to abide by its agreements.[122] Understanding or not, the Soviets armed Nasser. Perhaps Nasser would have found his way to Moscow without Nehru's help, but Nehru certainly paved the way. He provided Nasser with an ideological justification and international support for his actions. The Indian Prime Minister also facilitated a diplomatic imbroglio between the US and the Soviet Union. Together, they sent the US and Britain scrambling for new approaches to the region and a new policy paradigm.[123]

The Soviet arms agreement with Cairo had other troubling repercussions. The Shah and his 'pro-Western' advisors revised their assessment of Iran's value to American interests in the region. They found the threat of neutralism or non-alignment to be an effective shield against pressure to reform and useful leverage for additional economic and military aid. On 13 September 1955, John D. Jernegan, Deputy Secretary of State for NEA, and Norman B. Hannah, Desk Officer for Iranian Affairs, met with Sir Robert Scott and Willie Morris of the British Embassy in Washington. In a 'gloomy' summary of affairs, they discussed the 'internal drift' in Iranian domestic programs. More ominously, the British informed the Americans that the Shah was making 'exorbitant demands ... as the price for adherence to the Baghdad Pact'. The British wanted the US to intervene with additional aid and pressure on the

Shah to reform his government. Jernegan demurred, stating that pressure on Iran to join the Baghdad Pact might result in even greater demands for aid.[124] The Iranians finally joined, but the situation in Tehran showed little improvement. By early 1956, the US assessment of the Shah's government stated:

> It would be a mistake to think that this Government, unless it drastically changes its character, can or will provide the firm leadership for the successful execution of important reforms – political, economic or administrative. At one time it appeared that the Shah was moving directly toward the establishment of a clanking military dictatorship which would soak the rich and attempt to break up the land-owning aristocracy in order to win the favor of the 'people'. But from all reports and from a study of his moves, the Shah does not have the capacity to make a sustained effort in the direction of basic social reforms, and an attempt by him to embark on such a program would probably have chaotic results.

The British Embassy in Tehran observed that while the Shah would 'use every means short of open blackmail to obtain money from the United States Government … it is unlikely that he would in the conceivable future openly flirt with the Soviets.'[125]

The Embassy underestimated the Shah's alacrity in adjusting to the Nehru-Nasser model. Two months later, news of a Soviet 'good neighborly' visit by the Shah to the Soviet Union filtered in from Tehran. In addition, the Soviets were now openly supporting historic Iranian claims to Bahrain, and comparing it to Nikita Khrushchev's support for India over Kashmir and the Afghan Pushtuns in their territorial disputes with Pakistan. The Soviets billed the Shah's planned visit as 'the prelude to a new phase in the friendly and peaceful relations between Iran and Russia'. Alarmed, the US Embassy opined: 'The Embassy fears the Russian campaign may prove to be pretty heady stuff to a people who are almost pathetically grateful for any gesture inflating their national prestige and to a Shah who is notoriously vulnerable to flattery.'[126] At the same time, Iranian officials sought assurances that events like the Nehru visit to Washington did not portend lessening of US support for the Baghdad Pact.[127] The Shah warned that Iranian support for US initiatives and the Baghdad Pact would wane 'if the neutral or doubtful countries in the Middle East fare better than Iran and the other … Baghdad Pact members in the new aid program.'[128] In typical Pahlavi fashion, the Shah vacillated between challenging the United States by improving relations with the Soviet Union and worrying that the arguments of neutralists like Nehru might undermine Iran's principal source of military support, the Baghdad Pact. With the memory of Nasser's accommodation with the Soviet Union painfully fresh, Washington worried that Iran might also seek its own version of an arrangement with Moscow.

Eisenhower and Nehru Official Visit, 1956

Eisenhower welcoming Nehru to the White House for his 1956 official visit. Despite differences over policy matters, at a personal level both leaders seemed to share great respect for each other, in contrast to the icy relationship between Nehru and Kennedy. Nehru saw Eisenhower as an equal. He did not view Kennedy in the same light.

Middle East policy: after six years, rethinking the paradigm

The experience of the Eisenhower administration between January 1953 and the consummation of the Egyptian-Czech deal for Soviet arms in September 1955, followed by the chaos and frustrations of 1956 and 1957, forced a broad reassessment of US policy across the Middle East. In pursuing a policy of containment, the Eisenhower administration had linked economic development, political reform, and military assistance to prevent Soviet expansion and Communist influence in the region. Economic development was the key to bringing long-term, pro-Western stability to the region. In 1953, Eisenhower and his advisors borrowed the ideas and terminology from the progressive economic development theories of American academia that would dominate a generation of US policy makers. They believed in creating 'take-off points' and in the ability of the US to use economic and development aid to make emerging national states, even those with revolutionary regimes, 'look inward' and focus on domestic development instead of regional rivalries. The Eisenhower foreign policy establishment was niggardly in its provision of military assistance, attempting to limit military aid to security assistance and to support internal security without providing offensive capabilities. While Washington viewed economic development as the best means of assuring pro-Western stability and preventing Communist expansion, economic reform merely represented the preferred path to containment. Eisenhower's administration, like that of Truman before and of Kennedy after, was committed to containment by any means necessary. When Washington believed that the tactical situation dictated short-term methods, then the administration was absolutely willing to use military aid, security assistance, covert assistance, and, in rare cases, direct intervention to maintain repressive regimes. To the policy makers, political expediency demanded the immediate maintenance of pro-Western political reliability, even at the expense of long-term stability.

Eisenhower came to Washington believing that colonialism was dead and that the West had to make accommodations with growing nationalism in the developing world. On the one hand, the US recognized the importance of good relations with their traditional European allies, but on the other wanted to distance themselves from the heritage of colonialism in the developing world. From the very beginning, Eisenhower made it clear to Churchill and the British that he believed their focus should be on European affairs and that they should give up the trappings of empire in places like Egypt and Iran. The administration initially resisted British calls for intervention in both Iran and Egypt. The intervention in Iran came only after Washington concluded that Musaddiq's continued rule had the real potential to result in a pro-Soviet coup.[129] In the case of Egypt, the administration infuriated London by consistently taking the Egyptian side and pressuring Britain to compromise with the new revolutionary regime. Eisenhower and Dulles viewed the traditional regimes supported by the British as anachronisms soon to succumb to the rising tide of nationalism. Despite this preference for progressive regimes, Eisenhower's lack of success in using economic incentives and the promise of future military aid to induce key states, like Egypt and India, to enter Western defensive alliances created frictions that over time boded well for increased British influence in Washington. Eisenhower found that the traditional regimes and a British presence provided the only real basis for Western alliance systems in the region. It also provided a screen behind which the US could support pro-Western elements and avoid overt participation. Obviously, this system fooled no one, and increased US friction with various nationalist movements. It appeared that the US had abandoned support for nationalism and opted for neo-colonialist policies that followed a basically British model.[130] The Eisenhower administration's obsession with containment of the Soviet Union through defensive alliances and selective economic aid created a series of conflicts that placed the most influential leaders in the region, Nehru and Nasser, and many emerging nationalists at odds with US policies.

For Eisenhower, it had been a calculated risk from the beginning. The White House understood that US support for the 1954 Turkish-Pakistani defense arrangements would evoke a negative reaction in New Delhi, but they failed to gage the intensity. They believed that economic aid to India would mute Nehru's criticism, and to some degree they were correct; Nehru did not break off relations. Even had they predicted the extent of Nehru's unhappiness, they most likely would have proceeded with arms for Pakistan anyway. Later that year, the move by Hashemite Iraq to join, and British support for Iraq's inclusion in the defensive alliance with Turkey surprised and annoyed Washington. It further strained the relationship between Washington and Cairo, but friction or not, Washington supported the combining of the various bilateral agreements and the enticement of Iran into a defense alliance. At the same time, the administration did not back away from supporting the British lead in the alliance, thus firmly identifying ever-increasing American involvement in the region with Britain's colonial past. The creation of the 'northern tier' alliance, known as the Baghdad Pact, firmly attached the very neo-colonial label that Eisenhower and Dulles had so assiduously attempted to avoid, and it alienated Nehru and Nasser.

This alienation of Nehru and Nasser also undermined, in the minds of policy makers in Washington, one of the levers on which the early Eisenhower administration had constructed containment: the efficacy of economic aid as a means of controlling or channeling the policies of developing national states. From the very beginning, in words to be echoed eight years later when the Kennedy administration took office, Eisenhower and Dulles had believed in the seemingly irresistible logic that economic development and the benefits of improved standards of living would entice the states of the Greater Middle East to abandon their internecine disputes and focus inwardly on creating prosperity for their people. The Holy Grail of economic development would bring pro-Western, political stability. Having reduced regional tensions, this inward turn would eliminate the need for massive arms buildups, allowing member states to rely on the US defense umbrella for protection against the Soviets and for security assistance to protect against Communist subversion. This long-term strategy for pro-Western stability in the region ran counter to short-term political reality. Political self-preservation tended to be a short-term issue. The experiences of 1953-1955 basically turned the administration's containment policy on its head, and shattered Eisenhower's faith in economic development as the cure-all for Western influence.

Increasingly, political stability rested on the loyalty and pro-Western orientation of the military and security forces. Even in the case of traditional monarchies, the loyalty of the military became the primary issue associated with pro-Western governments. Stability had become the watchword, and the military was the key. Eisenhower had not abandoned his support for other reform policies. To the contrary, political and economic reform remained highly desirable, but rather than being the lead elements of containment policy, political reform and economic development would now only be pursued within the context of a stable, pro-Western environment. When economic or political reform threatened to destabilize a Western ally, the focus immediately returned to the loyalty of the security forces, the maintenance of order, and the suppression of threats to the particular regime. Controlled, top-down reform became the only acceptable model for the region.

In addition, consummation of the Czech arms deal in late 1955 undermined confidence in US policy in the Middle East, and led to broad criticism of Eisenhower and Dulles. It also underscored the limitations of economic aid as a primary bargaining tool. Nasser's discussion with Chou En-lai at Bandung and the subsequent Czech arms deal happened as a result of internal Egyptian political requirements, even with US support for the massive Aswan Dam project hanging in the balance. Nasser determined, and correctly, that the Gaza raid and repeated provocations by Israel required the acquisition of modern arms for the Egyptian army. At the other end of the Greater Middle East, economic aid for non-aligned India had not prevented Nehru's attacks on US policy or Indian acceptance of Soviet economic assistance. Nehru's clear support for the Egyptian position emphasized the potent political synergy between Egypt and India, and impressed on the Eisenhower administration the necessity for the US to chart a course of action independent from that of the colonial powers.[131] Despite Nasser's nationalization of the Suez Canal, Washington made it clear to London that the United States would not be a party to any coup attempt against Nasser.[132] When the British, with their French and Israeli allies, launched the Suez war to unseat Nasser, Nehru played a key role in inciting world opinion against British, French, and Israeli intervention.[133] When the war ended in disaster for Britain and France, not only was Nasser's stature elevated to mythic proportions, but it also made the United States the principle arbiter of Western policy in the Middle East.[134] Never again would either Britain or France take major unilateral action in the region without clear US agreement. The British Ambassador to Egypt at the time, Sir Humphrey Trevelyan, concluded: 'The basic cause of our failure was that what we could do in 1882, we could not do in 1956. We no longer had the same power in the world.'[135]

After Suez, the White House understood that it faced a difficult new reality in which long-term economic development and stability had to give way to short-term reality. Containment of the Soviet Union and its fellow traveler, Nasser, now rested on the survival of pro-Western regimes, no matter what their internal political system, state of economic development, or social structure. On 23 November 1956, the OCB concluded: 'It is likely that for the time being Nasser will remain the leader in Egypt.' The report observed that relations with Egypt 'seem to indicate that the United States cannot successfully deal with President Nasser'.[136] Eisenhower and Dulles believed that to protect Western interests, the United States would have to become directly involved. In January 1957, the President made a speech that became known as the 'Eisenhower Doctrine'. He referred to a 'power vacuum' in the Middle East. Intended as a holding action to discourage Soviet adventures, the speech brought a sharp reaction.[137] Nasser warned: 'If there is any power vacuum in the Middle East, it will be filled by Arab nationalism.'[138] The year

1957 also witnessed a parallel development that further aggravated relations with India. Pakistan insisted on dragging up the issue of Kashmir in the United Nations, against US and British wishes. The resulting marathon speech by Krishna Menon attacking Pakistan and its colonial backers, Britain and the United States, created another low point in relations with India. Positive US contributions, including successful US pressure on the British and French to withdraw from Suez and on Israel to withdraw from the Sinai, received little or no credit in the non-aligned Middle East.[139]

1957 stood as the low point in US relations in the Middle East. A constant barrage of negative propaganda from Arab nationalists, the non-aligned states, and the Communist bloc on the one hand, combined on the other with attacks by domestic right-wing critics, Israel and the Jewish lobby, and the British and French sent the Eisenhower Administration searching for a new policy paradigm through which to promote containment and recoup lost US influence.[140]

Part I: 1958 – The New Order and Reconsiderations

The events of 1958 confirmed the validity of John Foster Dulles' more holistic view of the Greater Middle East as the region stretching from Morocco to Pakistan. Developments in Cairo and Damascus sent shock waves across the Arab world, ultimately bringing down the Hashemite monarchy in Baghdad. The collapse of the pro-Western regime in Iraq in turn rippled through Tehran, Karachi, and New Delhi, as well as the Arab Middle East, causing a series of reactions and counter-reactions that laid the foundation for more than four decades of friction and conflict. For that reason, 1958 stands as the pivotal year in American foreign policy across the Greater Middle East. Nasser and Nehru stood at the apogee of non-alignment and positive neutrality, representing a 'third way' between competing superpowers. Their policies demonstrated that charting an independent course had political and material benefits. Increasingly, non-aligned and aligned states borrowed their tactics to extract aid and support from their power-bloc sponsors. In addition, 1958, more than 1956, heralded the end of colonial power and the beginning of the contemporary era. British attempts to indirectly control the Arab Middle East following World War II had failed. The Arab League as an instrument of British foreign policy had backfired and, as feared, turned into 'Dr. Frankenstein's monster'. The idea of a Middle East Defense Organization under British leadership was a non-starter.[1] The Canal treaty of 1954, a shotgun wedding with Uncle Sam presiding, further demonstrated the inability of Britain to control events. The flash and bang of Suez merely confirmed an existing reality. Regardless of the success or failure of Anthony Eden's adventure with his friends in France and Israel, the British were going to have to get out of Egypt. Suez also affirmed the close connection between the political and regional aspirations of the primary non-aligned powers, Egypt and India. The political institutions of Nehru's India and Nasser's Egypt diverged widely, but their style of charismatic leadership, the jealous protection of independence, the obsession with national honor, and the shared colonial experience created a synergy that was real. Despite their very different temperaments and backgrounds, Nehru and Nasser were pragmatic politicians, motivated by revolutionary idealism and a belief in their leadership roles in the Greater Middle East. At the time, many blamed the failure of the Suez on Washington; 1958 exposed for all to see Britain's weakened stature and circumscribed options in the Middle East.

By 1958, both Nehru and Nasser had amply demonstrated their determination to pursue policies tailored to what they saw as their own political priorities. Nehru's expulsion of US observers attached to the United Nations contingent in Kashmir, the harangues of Krishna Menon against Pakistan and the West, and Nehru's sponsorship of Communist China left little doubt about Indian willingness or ability to act independently. Nevertheless, Nehru's position on everything from Indochina to military alliances in Asia and Africa may have been problematic to the West, but he opposed the Communist party in India and led the largest democracy in the world. In short, he was a useful window on the non-aligned and developing world and a Western-educated leader to be cultivated and tolerated. Nasser was another matter. Far more impatient and insecure, Nasser demonstrated his independence and non-alignment in his reaction to the 'northern tier', to Western support for Israel, and in attending the Bandung conference. He turned to the Soviet Union for arms, and when the United States refused to support the Aswan Dam project, he nationalized the Canal, sparking the Suez imbroglio. Nasser demonstrated that he had to be taken seriously, because failure to do so invited unanticipated and often unpleasant developments. Thus, it was Nasser who set the tone for the pivotal year of 1958. Since Eisenhower's declaration of January 1957, relations with Egypt had been particularly strained; however, at a fundamental level, the Eisenhower administration continued to view Egypt as the key to the Arab Middle East and desired a working relationship with the Egyptian leader.

The developments of early 1958 forced the Eisenhower administration to accelerate plans for a new formula for US policy in the Greater Middle East. Containment required the preservation of pro-Western states and the encouragement of truly neutralist policies on the part of the non-aligned. In dealing with the latter, Eisenhower and his advisors turned again to economic assistance as the most effective lever for maintaining some semblance of normal relations with the radical nationalist states of the region and as a vehicle to find an accommodation with Nasser. To some extent, long-standing US policies toward Nehru and India served as the model for this accommodation. Despite problems, the relationship with New Delhi had proven useful, and a tactical case-by-case approach to issues had maintained ties and influence in New Delhi. Economic aid had also prevented a total breach with India over military aid to their neighboring rival, Pakistan. A similar approach to Egypt, based on renewed economic incentives, appeared to hold the potential for like results. Decreased tensions with Egypt also might to some degree undermine

Soviet influence and perhaps alleviate Nasserist pressure on the 'northern tier' alliance, particularly on Iraq and other pro-Western Arab states and Iran.

US policy evolved in a less ambitious, less ideological, and more pragmatic approach. Between 1953 and 1955, Washington had set its goals high, too high, hoping to solve long-standing Middle East disputes over Kashmir and Palestine while coaxing Egypt and India into defensive alliances against the Soviet Union and China. The policy approach of 1958 was more modest and aimed at reducing Egyptian and Indian opposition to the Baghdad Pact and SEATO and at undermining Soviet influence. As this policy adjustment got underway events in Baghdad struck Cairo, Tehran, Karachi, New Delhi, London, and Washington like a bolt from the blue. The varying reactions would have repercussions that would carry into the 21st century.

Chapter 2: The Wave of the Future

By the end of 1957, the situation in the Arab Middle East had reached a revolutionary 'watershed'. Nasser and Nasserism appeared to be the 'wave of the future'. Having assailed the Eisenhower Doctrine for its assumption that the departure of Britain had created a 'vacuum', Nasser now appeared poised to thwart Washington's plans to use its 'agents' in the region to 'split and enslave the Arabs'. These 'agents' included the monarchies, the Gulf emirates, and Israel.[1] Nasser probably recognized that the Eisenhower Doctrine was not *per se* a plot to 'get' him or undermine 'positive neutralism' by force, but bashing Washington was a useful vehicle for rallying regional support.[2] In addition, despite this hostility, policy makers continued to view Nasser as the key to US influence in the region. His 'victory' at Suez had made him the standard by which Arabs judged their leaders. The confluence of Nasser's simplistic ideas on revolutionary Arab nationalism and his pronouncements on non-alignment and positive neutralism formed an ill-defined ideological potpourri. This very lack of definition and systematic ideological structure worked in Nasser's favor.[3] Nasserism promised something to everyone, while challenging the traditional ruling elites, many of whom were aligned with the West. By 1958, Nasser had not only navigated Egypt into the post-colonial period, but had also become the symbol of radical change in the Arab world. Now, the central question was how to proceed.

In one sense, Nasser's success confirmed the accuracy of State Department and CIA assessments. Both had predicted that Egypt was the most important Arab state and that Nasser alone determined the course of Egyptian policy. Eisenhower and Dulles subscribed to this assessment. Unfortunately, the relationship with Nasser and thus Egypt had not gone well. In Washington, ideological prejudices had made the relationship virtually unworkable. The White House believed that Nasser had become a Soviet proxy during the preceding five years. Still, Washington faced the conundrum of coming up with a policy for the future. Any improvement in relations, given the political bent of the Republican Party's right wing, required an ideological justification. Given Nasser's arms relationship with the Soviet Union, Eisenhower reverted to economic aid and financial incentives as the basis for regenerating normalized contacts with Cairo.

In London, the Macmillan government also wanted an accommodation with Nasser and a settlement of claims resulting from the Suez crisis that would allow for the reopening of the Canal. Wary, London believed that the West would have to confront and thwart Nasser's more aggressive policies, but wanted to see the chapter on Suez closed. Improved relations or not, neither Britain nor the United States had any illusions about Nasser's intentions to undermine Iraq, Jordan, the Gulf emirates, and the Aden Protectorate. For the British, their oil concessions in Iraq and the Gulf were critical. London believed that any further erosion of its position and prestige in the Arab Middle East, whether in oil-barren Jordan or in Aden, would threaten its position in the Gulf states, but the British also understood that in the post-1956 order any action against Nasser required the clear agreement of the United States. Thus, British confrontations with the Egyptian leader became indirect affairs carried out by proxies and colored by the cynical British view of Nasser's intentions.

1958 witnessed an unusual situation in which Nasser, Eisenhower, and Macmillan were all attempting to define Nasserism. Nasser wanted to chart a course for the future of the Arab world. In the face of right-wing Republican opposition, Eisenhower needed a definition that would justify a working relationship with Cairo. London wanted a definition that would, when necessary, garner American support in containing revolutionary Arab nationalism. Given that so much rode on this exercise, a brief examination of Nasser's accumulated ideological baggage as of 1958 is in order. Nasser may have lacked a structured, clearly articulated framework for ruling, but he possessed a crude set of ideologically-based principles. These simplistic ideas, expressed in his 1952 manifesto, resonated with the Egyptian people, radical Arab nationalists, and with many emerging nation states. He called for destroying imperialism and its 'stooges'; ending feudalism; ending monopoly and capitalist domination of government; bringing social justice to the masses; creating a strong national army; and creating a 'sound democratic life'.[4] In 1953, Nasser contributed his own ideas on a revolutionary creed. He published *Philosophy of Revolution*, a rambling polemic about the nature of 'permanent revolutionary struggle'.[5] Nasser's successes between 1955 and 1958 meant that the serious pursuit of these goals resulted in varying degrees of trouble for the Western powers. For the United States, Nasser's successes were largely an annoyance; for the British, Nasser's success could mean catastrophe. Nasser's success confirmed the US administration's long-held assumption that Egypt and its leader were the barometer of the Arab world for the foreseeable future. For two years, US policy in the Middle East had gone into free fall; the 'vacuum' that resulted in the Eisenhower Doctrine now resembled a policy 'black hole' stretching from North Africa to Pakistan.[6] Nasser's success,

Corbis

Nasser and Syrian President Quwatli

Nasser and Syrian President Shukry Quwatli in February 1958, celebrating the Egyptian-Syrian Union and the formation of the United Arab Republic. Although not apparent until much later, this would mark the hightide of Nasser's pan-Arab ambitions. The union added a sense of urgency to US plans to reconstruct a working relationship with Nasser.

largely at the expense of the West, now pushed Washington toward an accommodation.

The Egyptian-Syrian Union, and saving the Middle East from Communism

In early 1958, Nasser's growing influence combined with US domestic criticism of the administration forced Eisenhower to reexamine its policies toward Nasser. Looking for areas of potential cooperation, Eisenhower and Dulles focused on Nasser's shared antipathy for Arab Communism. This initiative received a boost when talk of Arab unification under Egyptian leadership began to take concrete form. Syria's call for unification with Egypt surprised policy makers. Popular agitation in other Arab capitals added weight to the view that Nasserist influence might actually culminate in some form of a broadly unified Arab state. In addition, the weakness of pro-Western Arab regimes lent an air of inevitability to the Nasserist triumph and placed additional pressure on the administration to come up with new policies.

This reevaluation of US policy also required an assessment of the problem presented by US-Israeli ties. In a January 1958 review of US policy, Secretary Dulles pointed out that both the State and Defense Departments had opposed the establishment of Israel because they had envisioned the very situation that now confronted the United States. Dulles bluntly stated that because of the 'potency of international Jewry', not even the Soviet Union advocated an end to the Jewish state. He concluded that 'no greater danger to US security' existed than that posed by the Arab-Israeli dispute, viewing it as the means by which the Soviet Union might eventually gain control of the Middle East. With evident exasperation, Dulles commented: 'We are confronted with a clear threat to the security of the United States, and we cannot present a clean-cut practical solution. Accordingly, we are in fact reduced to following the old British formula of "muddling through."' He grudgingly added that this policy had worked 'thus far with Saudi Arabia, Iraq, Jordan and Lebanon'. In evaluating Arab unity, the administration saw some benefits, including an increased sense of security among the Arabs, but feared that true unity might result in an outright attempt to destroy Israel, or even worse, a 'uniform' regional oil policy that threatened the 'vital oil supply of Western Europe'. To protect Western interests, the administration concluded that the US had little choice but to increase economic and military assistance to states in the region, including neutrals, 'in order to develop local strength against Communist subversion and control and to reduce excessive military and economic dependence on the Soviet bloc'.[7]

Washington concluded that it needed an arrangement with Nasser.[8] Thus, moves toward improved relations were already under consideration when, in January 1958, the Syrians agreed to unification on Nasser's terms. In fact, the details of the agreement surprised even the Syrian Ba'thists, army officers, politicians, and also Egyptian officials.[9] Skeptics pointed out the inherent conflicts between Egyptian and Syrian political practice. Syrian President Shukri al-Quwatli allegedly warned Nasser: 'You have acquired a nation of politicians; fifty percent believe themselves to be national leaders, twenty-five percent to be prophets, and at least ten percent to be gods.'[10] Nasser believed that Syrian acquiescence to his demands for a centralized state on the Egyptian model, including the dissolution of all political parties, would overcome the potential for problems.

In Syria, the Ba'th Party agreed, but its leadership had the clear expectation of becoming Nasser's political partners and the ideological arbiters for the new state.[11] Michel Aflaq, the key Ba'th party official, argued: 'We will be officially dissolved but we will be present in the new unified party, the National Union. Born of the Union of the two countries, this movement cannot be animated by principles other than those of the Ba'th.'[12] Of course, Nasser had no intention of sharing power with the fractious Syrian politicians. Nevertheless, on 1 February 1958, from the balcony of the Abdin Palace, Nasser and Quwatli, the President of the Syrian Republic, proclaimed the creation of the United Arab Republic, announcing that Nasser would be its first president. Rejecting a federal system, Nasser believed that centralized control would eliminate the possibility of collapse, and in fact make the 'ungovernable' Syrians governable.[13] Events in Cairo sparked widespread popular agitation for union, economic and political change, and the removal of traditional leaders across the Arab world.[14] Nasser was proclaimed the 'new Saladin'.[15] To the suspicious West, Nasser presented the union as a move by Syrian Ba'thists to forestall a Communist coup. He argued that the abolition of political parties reduced instability and leftist influence by shifting the focus to 'Arab unity'.[16] Union also gave the Egyptian president a leg-up on his rival, Nuri Sa'id, in Baghdad. Thus Nasser agreed to a union with Syria, a country in which 'he had never set foot'.[17]

Seeing the handwriting on the wall, Washington took a positive position to avoid being criticized for opposing the sacred cow of Arab unity. The administration also viewed Nasser as more palatable than the chaotic political situation and the threat posed by the Syrian Communist Party. The secret US position held: '[T]he question of Arab unity [was] a matter to be determined by Arabs themselves and the US would support unity or any form thereof which results from freely expressed wishes of Arab peoples concerned.'[18] Dulles successfully opposed any public statement reflecting this view, because it might have facilitated Egyptian domination of the Arab world and spread positive neutralism. It also had the potential to undermine pro-Western Arab regimes and discourage possible anti-union moves by pro-Western Arab regimes.[19] In the confusion, Iraq, Jordan, Lebanon, and Saudi Arabia publicly welcomed the union despite that they might create an opposition group. Although pessimistic, the Eisenhower administration wanted to keep its options open.

> While these four countries may privately oppose union, it is doubtful whether they will be able to adopt any common line of action concerning the formation of effective opposition to the union. ... Jordan's efforts to interest Iraq and Saudi Arabia in a closer association of the three Kings to which Lebanon could adhere have so far fallen on barren ground. However, in order to be ready in the unlikely event that the four Arab states come up with a common position of opposition, which is feasible and acceptable to us, we are giving urgent consideration to appropriate ways in which we could assist those states in the implementation of their common action.

In reality, Washington was in no position to openly oppose or deny recognition to the UAR. 'The long-term risks of our being openly identified with opposition to the United Arab Republic or with its possible collapse are ... greater than the short-term risks of establishing correct diplomatic relations with it at the outset.' On 7 February 1958, the Egyptian desk at the State Department recommended that the US explore the potential for improved relations with Cairo, stating: 'Although the Egyptian attitude could not be called particularly friendly, ... it is certainly less unfriendly than previously.'[20]

A change in plans: fighting Communism with Nasser

To belay any potential opposition, Nasser dangled a tempting carrot in front of Eisenhower. Playing the reluctant suitor, he argued that he had been forced to accept union to prevent a Communist takeover. He asked Washington for a three-month moratorium on criticism in order to allow him a free hand in dealing with the Communist threat. Much to the US's pleasure, Nasser promptly declared the Communist Party, along with other parties, illegal, and launched a campaign in both Syria and Egypt to suppress Communist elements.[21] Suppression of the Communists resurrected, albeit in more modest form, plans in Washington to provide Egypt with economic aid and financial incentives. In response to the 'more neutral' international stance from the 'new republic', Secretary Dulles recommended that 'a schedule could be drawn up in which certain actions by us could be taken without delay in response to positive actions by Nasser'. This list included trade, cultural exchanges, economic assistance, military training, CARE programs, and grain under Public Law 480.[22] Only a matter of weeks before, Nasser had been reviled as a Soviet agent in the Middle East; now he was to be the recipient of US economic aid. Using the thin veil of the 'schedule', the United States moved quickly to take advantage of Nasser's promise to do something about the Communists in Syria. The administration began immediate preparations to ease relations, provide him with aid, and normalize the relationship, even as a crisis in Lebanon loomed on the horizon. Ironically, the administration had so thoroughly vilified Nasser that some saw the anti-Communist campaign as a ruse approved by Moscow to further Soviet interests. As the *The Nation* put it, 'Officials in Washington are straining their eyes to find advantages for the United States in the fusion of Egypt and Syria into a single nation. It's a strenuous exercise and may afflict its practitioners with a permanent squint.'[23] *Newsweek* stated: 'As long as Syria and Egypt continued to accept massive Soviet aid, they can hardly claim to be stemming Communist influence.' The display of Arab unity in Damascus and Cairo upstaged talks between Jordan, Iraq, and Saudi Arabia. At the Baghdad Pact conference in Ankara, the US again refused to join, and offered only $10 million in military aid, a miserly sum in comparison with the military aid from the Soviet Union to Syria and Egypt.[24]

In the Arab world, both supporters and opponents of the Egyptian-Syrian union criticized Dulles and the administration for their 'negative, unimaginative and contradictory' policies.[25] 'Communists and radical nationalists' described Dulles as 'senile', 'bloodthirsty', and an 'Arab baiter'. Pro-Western Arabs bitterly blamed Dulles' handling of the Aswan Dam project, the denial of arms to the Egyptians, and US support for Israel for causing Nasser's turn toward the Soviet Union. There was also considerable criticism for pressuring countries into defensive pacts. The generally pro-Western Beirut newspaper *Le Jour* stated: 'Arab relations with Dulles have been like a dialogue with the deaf.'[26] As Washington and Cairo prepared to embark on another courtship, Lebanon, or so it appeared, would become the test case for US-Egyptian cooperation. The administration hoped that contacts in Beirut, via the Egyptian ambassador to Lebanon, Abd-al-Hamid al-Galib, with Abd-al-Hamid al-Sarraj, Nasser's Syrian intelligence chief, might prevent a confrontation in Lebanon.[27] Observers on the scene were not that optimistic. As one diplomat put it: 'What else can we expect? To hope that the Lebanese won't resort to violence is like hoping dogs won't chase cats.'[28] Egyptian Ambassador Ghalib became an important conduit for extra-official contacts with Cairo. Dulles instructed US officials in Beirut on 'the importance of not giving Ghalib any reason to believe that he is being used as a channel in connection with US-Egyptian relations'. The Secretary then provided a detailed list of policy positions to be given to Ghalib, knowing full well that he would immediately forward them to Cairo, and probably to Sarraj. The Beirut channel attended to the negative policy chores vis-à-vis Nasser so that embassy contacts in Cairo could be more positive.

Dulles' 'instructions' to the US Embassy in Beirut laid out the US position in detail. As an olive-branch offer, Ghalib was told: 'The door to improved relations with Egypt is open.' The instructions expressed a desire to focus on the 'broader issues' in the relationship and argued that the real US position on 'neutrality and nationalism' had been either misrepresented or misunderstood in Egypt. Dulles expressed support for 'association with other free nations for collective security' but made it clear that 'the US does judge nations by their acts.' Ghalib was told that Egypt had not been neutral and had attacked independent countries which had merely banded together to protect themselves from Communism. 'Whatever their intent, these Egyptian actions and propaganda have benefited International Communism and, in this sense, Egypt has not, in practice, been neutral.' The instruction singled out Nasser's insistence that countries opt for 'positive neutralism' in lieu of 'collective defense' against Communism, and stated that when Egypt accepted the right of others to determine their own method of self-defense, 'one of the principle causes of current difficulties with the US will be removed.' The instructions asserted that the Eisenhower Doctrine merely supported the 'very integrity and independence, which Egypt has sought and treasured', and denied plans for US economic dominance in the region. Washington then offered to unblock Egyptian assets in return for a settlement of the Suez Canal Company's claims. It ceased calling for accommodation on the 'broader' issues to focus on specific problems.[29]

In a creative reaction to the formation of the UAR, the British managed to agree with Washington's position and simultaneously take a potshot at Dulles. Preditably, they had considerably more misgivings about the union than Washington. First, they feared increased pressure on Hashemite Iraq and Jordan, and second, they questioned the competence of the Secretary of State by expressing concern that he would be hoodwinked by Nasser's anti-Communist rhetoric. The British agreed with the US position that the current position should be neither support nor condemnation.[30] As to the Egyptian claim that they were saving Syria from the Communists, the British pointed out that General Afif al-Bizri, a well-known associate of the Communists, supported the agreement. Concerned about any US accommodation with Nasser, the Foreign Office commented: 'The line that Nasser is saving Syria from Communism will doubtless be pushed hard with King Saud [ibn Abd-al-Aziz al-Saud], as well as with the Americans.'[31]

The union created other problems for the British. At the Baghdad Pact meeting, Nuri Sa'id, the Prime Minister of Iraq, suggested that the majority of the Syrian people in a 'free election' would elect for union with Iraq and not Egypt. He then sounded out the council about support for Iraq's claims to the districts in the 'Mosul vilayet' ceded to Syria but belonging historically to Iraq. At first, Dulles seemed to encourage such an Iraqi initiative, with US backing if 'some part of Syria might wish to secede and join Iraq.'[32] The prospect of the United States, and particularly Dulles, embroiling Hashemite Iraq and its British oil concession in a perilous adventure struck a nerve in London. British attendees reported to London: 'We are disturbed by Mr. Dulles's ready response to Nuri's hint that the opportunity might be taken to incorporate parts of north-eastern Syria into Iraq.' In London, the FO rejected the idea of any support for Iraqi expansion, arguing that it would serve to consolidate the union with Egypt and provide opportunities for expanded Soviet influence. Iraq was simply too weak, even with Jordanian help, to challenge Syria and Egypt. The British believed that, left to its own devices, the union would generate its own set of disruptive forces in Syria and create serious problems for the Egyptians and their Syrian supporters.[33] From London's perspective, the principal aim was containment of the union.

A pro-Western alternative?

With Iraq discouraged from adventures, Lebanon came to center stage as the most immediate crisis confronting the West. Lebanese President Camille Nimur Chamoun, a Maronite Christian, had, with Western assistance, rigged the election of 1957, paving the way for his reelection to the presidency in 1958. Under the National Pact of 1943, a president could not succeed himself, and the next president had to be a Sunni Muslim. Frightened by the Egyptian-Syrian union, Chamoun plotted to retain power, and at the same time to embroil the West in supporting him with troops, if need be. In the name of 'stability', he decided to disregard the conditions of the National Pact of 1943

King Hussein and King Feisal, 1958

King Hussein I of Jordan and King Feisal II of Iraq in early 1958, discussing the creation of the Arab Union to counter Nasser and the UAR. Their youth underscores Western fears that they were no match for Nasser and the rising tide of revolutionary Arab nationalism. Feisal's death in the Baghdad coup of July 1958 put an exclamation point on those fears.

and retain the presidency for another term.[34] Chamoun's Foreign Minister, Charles Malik, believed that unification between Syria and Egypt meant the end of Lebanese independence unless the West, meaning principally the United States, actively opposed Nasser. He argued that the union would increase anti-Western Arab nationalist 'intransigence', and create a new balance of power in the Middle East that favored the Soviet Union and increased pressure on Jordan, Lebanon, and Iraq. He warned that without outside help, Lebanon would not survive.[35]

London's attitude to the union continued to be partially colored by their immediate unwillingness to believe that it was 'real'. The British recognized the threat posed by a true union, but realistically, they also saw an upside.

> While the whole thing is still so fluid we feel that there is no need to be unduly alarmed at the prospects. ... A union, which resulted in any real

unification of Egyptian/Syrian administrative and diplomatic services etc., would leave a good many Syrians out of a job. Resentment in Syria is likely to be exacerbated by the Egyptian tendency to treat their smaller allies in a cavalier fashion, and Syrians find it hard to work harmoniously for any length of time with other Syrians let alone Egyptians.

The FO predicted an 'initial honeymoon period' followed by 'disillusion and dissension'. London dismissed Malik and the Lebanese as unduly alarmist, but sought out American views on the Lebanese request for 'military assistance' just the same.[36] Consultations between London and Washington concluded that the Lebanese were overreacting, and that verbal reassurances to the Lebanese government were sufficient for the time being.[37] Chamoun and his supporters would have to wait for outside support.

After some discussions, the British finally agreed with the fundamentals of the American position laid down by Dulles in Ankara. The Western powers would not directly intervene. Only another Arab state could initiate intervention, which precluded moves by Turkey, Iran, and Pakistan. Finally, the United States would buttress any Arab initiative, but if that failed, Washington would take no action.[38] On 30 January 1958, members of the Baghdad Pact and the US finally agreed on the 'restrained' response. They would neither support or openly oppose the union. While Syrian resistance should be discreetly encouraged, neither the British nor the Americans would take the lead. In addition, at London's urging, Washington agreed that it would encourage Baghdad to refrain from unilateral opposition. The preferred course of action would be for Iraq, Jordan, Saudi Arabia, and Lebanon to actively pursue an 'alternative expression of Arab unity', with Baghdad Pact support. The agreement encouraged member states, a euphemism for Iraq, to approach other states and 'urge upon them the desirability of the earliest and most effective action they are willing and able to take'.[39] In very short order, Washington realized that no effective opposition to the union existed in Syria and that only King Saud of Saudi Arabia showed any inclination to oppose it.[40] Even Saud's opposition would be short-lived.

The reaction of other Arab leaders to the union underscored the potency of Nasser's message. While publicly supporting the union and discussing the possibility of an alliance with Nasser, the Saudis plotted to permanently curtail Nasser's activities. At King Saud's urging, Saudi officials attempted to bribe Sarraj, the Syrian intelligence chief, to assassinate Nasser and stop the union. Sarraj accepted the money, but unfortunately for Riyadh, King Saud had misjudged his man.[41] Sarraj could not be bought. Nasser had made Sarraj and his associates in the security apparatus the basis for centralized control in Syria because of their loyalty.[42] Nasser used the attempted compromise of Sarraj to embarrass Saud and his advisors. The UAR propaganda attacks on Saud sparked pro-Nasser unrest in the Kingdom, placing Saudi vulnerability on public display. There was also unrest in Tunisia. Habib Bourgiba, President of

Courtesy of National Archives
Eisenhower and King Saud
Eisenhower with King Saud during the King's official visit to the US.

Tunisia, claimed that his security services had uncovered a Nasserist plot to assassinate Bourgiba and take over the government. In Iraq, an alarmed King Feisal II reappointed Nuri Sa'id as Prime Minister and announced the federation, with British backing, of Jordan and Iraq in an Arab Union.[43] Embarrassed by the Sarraj affair and facing significant internal Nasserist pressure, Saudi Arabia refused to join.[44] Nasser labeled the Union as nothing more than a belated attempt to shore up feudal regimes.

In Saudi Arabia, Crown Prince Feisal Ibn-Abd-Al-Aziz forced King Saud to give up responsibility for defense, foreign affairs, and finance. Nothing if not shrewd, Feisal placated domestic unrest by supporting an accommodation with Nasser while he sought to 'clean up the Augean stables of Saudi finances' and save the monarchy. Because the educated classes viewed Nasser as the 'only Arab leader worth following', Feisal charted a policy that followed Nasser's lead in non-Arab affairs while avoiding confrontations on Arab matters.[45] Feisal embraced 'positive neutrality' and promised cooperation with both the Iraqi-Jordanian Arab Union and the UAR.[46] To broaden support for the Kingdom, Feisal conditionally offered to reestablish relations, broken off over territorial disputes and the Suez War, with France and Britain. As a gesture to Nasser, Feisal criticized the US position on free passage for Israel in the Gulf of Aqaba, calling it 'aggression against Egypt' and contrary to international law. In the face of Egyptian demands that Saudi Arabia end US 'basing rights' at

Dhahran, Feisal demurred, stating the status of US 'transit rights' would not be changed.[47]

The exposure, on 6 March 1958, of the Saudi plot against Nasser and the resulting crisis in Riyadh sent tremors through Washington. The administration considered King Saud a pro-Western stalwart, and President Eisenhower had hoped that Saud's influence might one day rival that of Nasser. Instability in Riyadh was disturbing.[48] In a meeting with Eisenhower, Secretary of the Treasury Robert B. Anderson urged a declaration that NATO and the US 'would not tolerate the prospect of the loss of Middle Eastern oil to the West'. Describing the situation as 'very grave indeed', Dulles lamented that instability in Riyadh also undermined the Iraqi and Jordanian regimes. He added: 'It was plain that Nasser had caught the imagination of the masses throughout the entire area.'[49] On 13 March 1958, the weekly NSC meeting reflected an ominous foreboding with regard to the Saudi regime. The administration feared a collapse, or perhaps a formal alliance with Cairo on the Syrian model. Citing the presence of over 10,000 Egyptians in the Kingdom, Eisenhower questioned the Secretary of State about the legalities of invoking the Eisenhower Doctrine, and Dulles, the lawyer and this time the voice of reason, commented that the Doctrine pertained only to the direct threat of 'International Communism'. Obviously frustrated, but taking the hint that the Saudi situation looked like an internal Arab matter, Eisenhower unhappily groused: 'Even so, we simply could not stand around and do nothing and see the whole area fall into the hands of Communism.'[50] The administration continued to have difficulties making the mental adjustment from Nasser, the Communist agent, to Nasser, the Arab nationalist. Misunderstanding the situation, Eisenhower also expressed his concern about Saud's replacement by his 'pro-Nasserist' brother, Feisal.[51] Trepidation about weakness and instability in Saudi Arabia, Iraq, Jordan, and Lebanon, coming on the heels of the formation of the UAR, caused the White House to forge ahead with a cautiously pragmatic 'live and let-live' policy toward the UAR. Nasser was officially out of the 'deep-freeze'.[52] Washington moved to counter Moscow's influence and regain its own lost influence in Cairo, perhaps limiting Nasser's own expansionist plans.[53] US policy refocused on containment in a manner fundamentally consistent with that of Eisenhower's early administration.

Britain's Middle East domino theory

In his memoirs, Harold Macmillan aptly described 1958 as 'More Arabian Nights.' Now, two years after Suez, the British government was attempting to conclude negotiations with the UAR to settle outstanding claims from the Suez crisis and resume diplomatic relations with Cairo. Nevertheless, Macmillan and his advisors still viewed Nasser as a real threat to Iraq and Kuwait. British oil interests in these two states determined to a great extent the economic health of Britain itself. Aden, Jordan, and the Gulf emirates also played an important role for British interests. Whitehall believed that should any of these states succumb to Nasser's Arab nationalist agitation, the damage to British prestige would encourage nationalist elements in Iraq and Kuwait and might well presage a collapse of the entire British position in the Middle East. Although less acutely, the British also feared Nasserist agitation in Lebanon and Sudan.[54] If Lebanon collapsed, Nasser and the Syrians would concentrate their subversive talents on Iraq and Jordan. The inclusion of Sudan in Arab the Union might very well reverse hard-won Egyptian recognition of Sudanese independence, and further enhance Nasser's prestige. Fearing any increased stature for their nemesis on the Nile, the British lamented the US decision to resume aid and worked assiduously to minimize it.

As noted in the immediate aftermath of the formation of the UAR, the first British priority was to prevent Nuri Sa'id, encouraged by promises of US support, from leading Iraq into a military debacle by opposing Nasser. Macmillan commented that Nuri was 'full of plans – some of them rather dangerously vague – for detaching Syria from Egypt'. Macmillan summed it up thus: 'The problem we have is to head Nuri off impossible or dangerous schemes, which are bound to fail, without losing his confidence or injuring his will to resist Egypt and Russia.'[55] At the Baghdad Pact conference, Dulles' off-hand remarks on detaching parts of Syria were alarming because the Iraqi government viewed them as US support for Nuri's schemes. Suez was obviously fresh in Macmillan's mind. Fearing that Dulles would court disaster and leave the Iraqis out on a limb, London cautioned Sa'id in the strongest possible terms not to follow Dulles' lead. As if things were not complicated emough, the Iraqi Prime Minister chose this moment to raise the issue of Kuwait, long claimed by Iraq, in the context of forming an Arab union to counter the UAR. Sa'id wanted London to pressure the Kuwaitis to join the proposed Iraq-Jordan union. The British, for a number of reasons, were horrified by any Iraqi mention of a union with Kuwait, and moved to quash that idea. By the spring of 1958, it appeared that London had managed to get the Iraqi situation in hand.

In contrast to Iraq, Yemeni scheming and UAR-sponsored subversion directly threatened British control in Aden. Yemen and Egypt enjoyed an on-again off-again relationship since 1955, based on various treaties of friendship and cooperation. Yemen's ruler, Imam Ahmad, and his heir apparent, Crown Prince Muhammad al-Badr, saw Arab nationalism as a vehicle to press Yemeni claims over Aden and the Protectorate. Borrowing rhetoric from Radio Cairo and using an Egyptian-supplied transmitter, Radio Sanaa began to broadcast colorful nationalist slogans, including: 'The Arab giant will drive imperialism into the pit', and the more evocative: 'The claws of death have clutched at the imperialists.'[56] Using Badr as the catalyst, Nasser engineered a Yemen-UAR alliance and brokered military and economic support from the Communist bloc. In return for 'federating' with the UAR, Nasser ended the 'vitriolic' attacks from the Cairo-based Voice of the Arabs Radio, and curbed Muhammad Mahmud al-Zubayri's anti-Imamate Free Yemeni movement.[57] In December 1957, the Imam's unhappiness with the American-sponsored Yemeni Development Corporation caused him to decline American agricultural experts, road-construction assistance, and an aerial survey of Yemen.

The British were of two minds about this down-turn in US-Yemeni relations. Seeing an opportunity to enlist US support against the Imam and Crown Prince, British Colonial Office officials in Aden and diplomats in Yemen wanted the US to participate in an 'anti-Communist' propaganda campaign. Unwilling or unable to provide its own aid, the Foreign Office wanted the US to increase economic and development assistance to Yemen as leverage to force the Yemenis to moderate their policies toward Aden. The British took exception to US indifference to the prospect of a long-term Egyptian-style economic and military relationship with the Soviets and Chinese.[58] The British wanted Washington to establish a consulate in Ta'iz and to provide additional economic aid to the Yemenis. They were extremely concerned that Soviet and Egyptian penetration of southern Arabia would bring increasing pressure on Aden and the Protectorate.[59] When on 25 January 1958 Zaidi tribesmen allegedly attempted to overthrow the Imam, the British became the scapegoat. Oliver Kemp, the British Consul, dejectedly wrote to London saying: 'It now seems probably that the Imam will accept the Soviet loan and open a Soviet legation.'[60] London chimed in with the observation: 'Whatever the truth about the origin of the plot the effect will be detrimental to the efforts of the US to establish any sort of position in the Yemen.'[61] The lack of American alarm was enormously frustrating. In fact, resigned to chronic problems in Yemen and a long-term Soviet and Chinese presence, the Eisenhower administration preferred to use aid to gain some influence at the source of the problem, in Cairo.[62] At the British Foreign Office, D.M.H. Riches groused about the Yemeni situation: 'The US attitude is rather strange. They are almost making way for the Russians.'[63]

As if to heighten London's concerns, on 28 January 1958, the eve of the Egyptian-Syrian union, Badr, speaking from Damascus, declared Yemeni solidarity with Nasser: 'Yemen's fate is tied to Syria and Egypt, and Yemen will fight imperialist pacts with all her power.'[64] Thoroughly alarmed, the Colonial Office lobbied intensely for military operations to stop border incursions. In London, key Foreign Office officials, Sir Frederick Hoyer-Millar and D.M.H. Riches, explained to Sir William Hayter that it was no longer that simple. The days of unilaterally bashing the natives were past. Commonwealth countries had to be kept informed. The Canadians, who chaired the UN Security Council, had to be on board.[65] As Sir H.J.B. Lintcott put it:

> There is some tendency in Canada to think that it is no longer necessary or possible for us to maintain our special position in the Middle East, and this is not less true when it comes to defending a colonial position in Aden by means of attacks (however provoked) on foreign soil, than in defending the kind of arrangement we have with the Persian Gulf states and Muscat. We are engaged in an exercise to try to bring Canada round

towards our point of view on Middle East policy generally; but it will take time.[66]

Of course, Washington also needed to be apprised of the situation. These tasks completed, the British launched a vigorous spring campaign against rebellious tribes and military units along the border with Yemen.

By late spring 1958, the Yemenis began to shelter artillery in populated areas along the border, increasing the possibility of escalation, civilian casualties, and serious political fallout. London told Washington: 'Another success for Nasser in this area would have serious consequences for Western prestige throughout the Middle East. All of this increases the need for coordinated action by Britain and America.'[67] At this point, Macmillan got some unwelcome advice. Believing that the Imam wanted a way out, that Badr was in disgrace, and that Soviet influence was waning, Washington told the British to bring in the UN and negotiate.[68] If Whitehall was skeptical, the Colonial Office was apoplectic; they believed that 'the tide in the Yemen over the last 18 months flowed steadily in the direction of more Soviet and Egyptian influence' and adamantly opposed UN involvement or bilateral talks with Yemen.[69] Nevertheless, in June, both sides agreed to limited talks concerning the border demarcation, but not the status of Aden or the Protectorate.[70] London hoped to 'satisfy the Americans and Mr. [Dag] Hammerskjold [UN Secretary General] and ease the pressure in Parliament for a time. We shall give the appearance of doing something. ... The only danger would be a refusal to accept a proposal, which the Yemenis could subsequently quote against us.'[71] The results were better than expected. Horace Phillips, the leader of the British delegation, reported that the discussions had 'yielded no less, and perhaps a little more, than I expected them to'. Ever wary, Phillips assumed that the Imam might not want a settlement, but rather a 'breather' so that he could 'gather his strength for a bigger and better effort to sabotage the federation'.[72] Just as the US had predicted, the Yemenis wanted to reach an accommodation.[73] Issues like Yemen combined with other British setbacks encouraged Washington's view that London's policies were often outmoded and created unnecessary problems for the West.[74]

Nasser at the pinnacle

Problems in the Arab Middle East aside, the Soviet threat to containment provided the final push for a new policy toward Nasser. The Soviets had followed up their military and economic aid by inviting Nasser to visit Moscow; he accepted. Although the US Ambassador in Cairo, Raymond A. Hare, prophetically pointed out that Nasser's greatest successes had come while he was 'the irresponsible champion of Arab nationalism', and that 'disenchantment' in Syria might result in the 'possible deflation of Nasser's ego', the White House was less certain.[75] On 21 February 1958, Washington informed members of the Baghdad Pact that the US intended to recognize the UAR because 'withholding recognition would be politically disadvantageous'.[76]

During March, Washington sought to engage Cairo on a number of questions, including Suez Canal claims, hostility toward Iraq and Jordan, and Yemen issues.[77] On 20 March, in a meeting with Ambassador Hare, Nasser stated that he intended to concentrate on 'domestic matters' and had no intention of interfering with states like Jordan and Iraq.[78]

Five days later, the administration began its second attempt in five years to use economic incentives to gain leverage in Cairo. Requesting Embassy comments, Washington suggested a staged plan that included cultural exchanges, unfreezing Egyptian assets, Public Law 480 grain, capital investment projects, and even the possible of military training for Egyptian officers. The goal was clearly stated:

> We would not contemplate adoption of policies proposed in this stage in absence of basis for significant improvement in our relations with UAR. While we would not expect Nasser to turn pro-West, we would wish convincing signs that he had become alive to danger of international Communism and evidence that he had abandoned efforts to undermine pro-Western Arab regimes.[79]

The administration attempted to enlist West Germany in a plan to offer *ad hoc* economic development aid.[80] At a press conference on April 8, 1958, a reporter pointedly asked Secretary of State Dulles to comment on the US choices vis-à-vis Nasser, i.e., either 'to block the further spread of his influence ... or to try to get along with him'. Dulles responded: 'I think that we are getting along with him as far as I am aware.' For added emphasis, Dulles denied that the US opposed Arab unity, asserting only that it opposed unity by force.[81] This statement was the first public acknowledgement that something 'new' was afoot between the United States and Egypt.

Not to be outdone, the following day Senator Hubert Humphrey, Chairman of the Senate Foreign Relations Committee, wrote to William M. Rountree, Assistant Secretary of State for Near Eastern, South Asian and African Affairs:

> It appears that the time may be at hand for a re-evaluation of our relationships with Egypt. ... In light of the growing power of Egypt since the formation of the United Arab Republic, I am sure that our country is giving the utmost thought and consideration to what should be our future relationships. Are we considering the reestablishment of the CARE program in Egypt? I think we should. Are we considering releasing the impounded Egyptian funds? I believe that this should be done. Are we considering extending technical aid to Egypt? I feel that this should be given favorable consideration. And, finally, has Egypt made any request for the purchase of agricultural products under the terms of Public Law 480? If so, I hope that such a request will be honored. I will welcome your advice and counsel on these matters.[82]

The Democrats saw an opportunity to emphasize Republican foreign policy setbacks in the fall elections. On 17 April, Rountree responded to Humphrey, saying that all options were under review, including PL 480 grain and the CARE program. He pointed out that the release of frozen assets awaited only the formal acceptance of the Suez Canal settlement. Rountree reassured the Senator that the United States sought better relations with the UAR as a means 'to strengthen the stability and security of the Near East'.[83] The rapprochement with Nasser was under way. Reacting to the surprise announcement, the media, particularly in the Middle East, linked the new US policy to Nasser's upcoming Moscow visit. Pro-Western newspapers, like *Al-Nahar* in Beirut, 'criticized Washington for engaging in [an] "auction with Moscow" over Nasser's friendship', and called the new policy 'Nasser's victory over the United States'. They labeled Dulles' attempt to economically isolate Nasser a failure. Others were cautiously optimistic: 'The US can, if really willing, turn a new page in [the] history of [the] Middle East.' Many Middle East observers argued that the Eisenhower administration lacked the key ingredients for success, namely a respect for 'neutrality' and non-interference in the region. The skeptics argued that concessions from Israel were mandatory: 'If not, what can [Dulles] hope to get out of his friendly overture to President Nasser?'[84] *The New York Times* described US-Egyptian relations as in the 'deep freeze', stating: 'Whether a genuine rapprochement was in the offing or not, …[t]he Egyptians are particularly eager to get their financial assets in the United States, frozen since President Nasser nationalized the Suez Canal Company, released.' The article also pointed out: 'This let-up may be merely a pause between rounds.'[85]

The situation now had to be explained to the British. On 9 April 1958, Washington had approached London about its planned first stage to free frozen funds and resume limited aid programs.[86] The British responded with a resounding lack of enthusiasm. The Foreign Office informed the State Department that while they did not mind the licensing of quasi-military items and other items like radios and civilian aircraft, they objected to $400,000 worth of road building and communications equipment. They reasoned that a resumption of the US aid program to Egypt would have an 'adverse' effect on the Iraqi-Jordanian Arab Union. In the interest of cooperation, the Americans dropped the bulldozers and offered Fulbright student scholarships and folk dancers instead.[87] Experience tempered the administration's hopes for better relations with Cairo:

> We have decided that effort should be made to place US-UAR relations on more normal basis. Although under no illusion that Nasser's basic philosophy or objectives can thereby be effectively altered to reflect pro-Western orientation, we nonetheless believe that removal of certain points of friction and minor irritants might help achieve this purpose and that it might place us in position to exert more effective influence over UAR policies.

Fearing a backlash from pro-Western states in the region, Dulles warned US missions against 'magnifying' the significance of the new policy: 'The steps we are taking are relatively minor and are not repeat not to be viewed as a major policy shift.'

As a result of British concerns, Dulles instructed the US embassies in Baghdad and Amman thus: 'You should reaffirm to Iraq and Jordan Governments our support for the maintenance [of] their independence and integrity and our willingness [to] provide appropriate assistance to them in their efforts [to] build [a] strong and lasting union.' The embassies were to stress that Nasser's behavior toward Iraq and Jordan would be a major factor in determining the course of Egypt's future relationship with Washington.[88] After the US released Egypt's frozen assets, on 26 April, Ambassador Hare again met

Courtesy of National Archives
Raymond Hare
Raymond Hare, US Ambassador to Egypt during the rehabilitation of relations with Nasser in 1958.

with Nasser. The Egyptian President wanted assurances that the US would not attempt to remove his regime. As Nasser put it: 'I want to feel that my back is safe.'[89] He blamed Egyptian-Iraqi hostility on the Hashemites, and stated that he foresaw no specific US-UAR problems in the future and that he was not opposed 'in principle to American objectives'. Nasser pointedly told Hare that the Soviets had always been more receptive to non-alignment, and that therefore he did not anticipate any problems with Moscow. Hare reported to Washington that Nasser's confidence during the meeting made him uneasy. The Ambassador wanted to respond to Nasser's question about US intentions vis-à-vis the UAR before the Moscow trip, but could think of no way to accomplish that without 'undue and perhaps undignified haste'.[90]

Delayed because of Suez, Nasser's official visit to the Soviet Union was an impressive event. Nasser was the first non-Communist to receive the 'guest of honor' salute in Red Square. He announced: 'The Arab people intend to get rid of every foreign domination. They believe in non-alignment.' Rivaling the welcome accorded Tito and Nehru, Nasser listened to students chant from Lenin's tomb: 'Hail to the leader of the Arab world.' Perhaps more telling was the total lack of official criticism from the West. As one commentator put it: 'Swallowing hard, the U.S. tried to act as if it did not mind – so as Nasser did not go too far.'[91] Although well aware of Egypt's weaknesses, in May 1958 Nasser undoubtedly felt that he controlled his destiny and the destiny of the Arab world. Many in the Arab world shared his vision and enthusiastically embraced it, while the leaders of traditional regimes feared its effect on their restive populations.

Clouds on the horizon: the Lebanese and Jordan crises

Even as Nasser was being feted in Moscow, UAR pressure on Lebanon and Jordan intensified. Both the Chamoun government and the Hashemite monarchy faced growing instability. The building crisis in Lebanon pitted pro-Nasserist, pan-Arab elements against the pro-Western Chamoun, who now faced Nasserist Arab nationalism in addition to age-old Syrian ambitions toward Lebanon.[92] Both Radio Cairo and Radio Damascus broadcast open invitations to revolt. Egyptian arms shipments to the rebels, and the participation of Syrian military personnel as instigators in Lebanese riots, fueled the instability.[93] As late as 7 May 1958, Chamoun minimized the threat posed by Nasser and the unrest generated by his attempt to succeed himself as President. Noting Egyptian-inspired attacks in the 'venal press of Beirut' and on Damascus Radio, as well as Syrian arms-smuggling, he stated that he saw 'no evidence of a concerted UAR plan' to topple his regime.[94] As events spiraled out of control, Chamoun became increasingly alarmist about Syrian involvement.[95] With the crisis mounting, Washington faced some unpleasant choices. Wary of intervention given the lack of a viable exit strategy, Dulles pointed out to Eisenhower: 'Once our forces were in, it would not be easy to establish a basis upon which they could retire and leave behind an acceptable situation; that might create a wave of anti-Western feeling in the Arab world comparable to that associated with the British and French military operation against Egypt, even though the circumstances were quite different.'[96] At some levels, the Foreign Office expressed similar views: 'In fact we hope just as much as they do that no military intervention will be necessary. It is fraught with all sorts of problems and dangers for us, for example, if a Syrian pipeline was blown up again.'[97] Intervention had to be a last resort.

As if Lebanon were not enough, the situation in Jordan took an unexpected turn for the worst. There was widespread unrest, and Jordanian security arrested a number of officers and enlisted men for plotting to overthrow the monarchy by assassinating both the King and Samir al-Rifai, the Prime Minister. The regime in Amman made a compelling case that the plot originated with UAR agents in Syria, and emphasized the similarities between UAR subversion in Jordan and in Lebanon. King Hussein hammered home the view that if Chamoun fell, Nasser would 'emerge in the eyes of the Arab world as the victor'. Such an eventuality would encourage every 'malcontent' in the region 'with [the] definite probability [that the] entire Middle East will be lost [to the] free world.'[98] The Lebanese and Jordanian arguments were steadily gaining traction in London and Washington.

On 17 May, following his return from Moscow, Nasser met with Ambassador Hare in one of their now regular exchanges of views. Claiming that he had been 'out of touch', Nasser stated that he had instructed UAR officials in Cairo and Damascus to take no action regarding Lebanon during his absence. At the same time, he argued that Washington was 'ignoring the facts' in Lebanon. Whether or not 'out of touch', Nasser was remarkably well-informed. He pointed out that well-known pro-Western Christians opposed Chamoun and his constitutional gambit, and contended that this fact underscored the existence of 'genuine internal opposition'. He argued that every former Lebanese Prime Minister opposed Chamoun and his plan, stating: 'It was pure nonsense to imply that the U.A.R. was in any way responsible for the revolution, which had spontaneously broken out. It was high time the West realized that Arabs everywhere, whether Christian or Moslem, were tired of being exploited.' He added: 'The U.A.R. had always respected, and would continue to respect, the independence of the Lebanon.'[99] Blaming Chamoun, Nasser wanted Lebanese General Fuad Chehab as a compromise replacement for Chamoun, and no reprisals against the rebels.[100] Miles Copeland, who was working for the Dulles brothers, believed that even Nasser feared that his Lebanese adventure was getting out of hand: 'Setting off such an operation is like starting a forest fire, it is easy to start but difficult to stop.'[101] Nasser wanted turmoil, but not Western intervention; it was a fine line. In preventing intervention, he hoped once again to take credit for saving the Arab world from imperialism. Nasser complained to Hare that Western policies in Lebanon unfairly targeted the UAR and its supporters.[102] Nasser accused the US and Britain of trying to 'humiliate' the UAR, and decried the conspiracy to undermine his 'new prestige' and 'neutralize him in order [to] stab him in [the] back'. Hare responded by telling Nasser the US had the records of organizational and financial plans to prove direct Syrian military involvement. Nasser's only response was to look at the ceiling and drop the subject.[103]

Washington and London concluded that, at a minimum, Nasser wanted a temporary truce and amnesty for the rebels 'to have their hands free to start all over again when the time seems propitious'. Nasser also sought to forestall any plans for Western intervention. His instincts told him that if the West refused to intervene and the UAR mediated the dispute, his Lebanese opposition would be severely weakened and eventually collapse.[104] He had neutralized King Saud, and left Iraq and Jordan dangerously isolated.[105] The trick now was to isolate Lebanon and Jordan from foreign support. Nasser believed that without such support, Lebanon, Jordan, and even Iraq would succumb. Dulles agreed with Nasser's assessment. He argued that intervention was a high-risk proposition but concluded that the United States could not allow anti-Western forces 'to take control of Lebanon by force without our intervention, this will in any case be the prelude to a series of further coups, the political death of Nuri and Hussein, and the final collapse of any Western position in the area.'[106] In a vacuum, Nasser's faith in Arab unity, Arab nationalism, non-alignment, the will of the Arab people, and the inevitable collapse of traditional regimes was justified, but events were not occurring in a vacuum.

Chapter 3: 'The Tempest'

During the first half of 1958, Nasser's power and influence achieved its pinnacle. The positive shift in US policy and his trip to Moscow convinced him that he was immune from outside intervention.[1] His prominence in the non-aligned movement provided him with a legitimacy unthinkable only three years before. The Syrian union, coupled with pro-Nasserist agitation against his Arab opponents, appeared to portend the inevitable collapse of traditional Arab regimes and the continued spread of his influence. It was understandable that Eisenhower and Dulles would conclude that Nasserism, or some similar form of radical Arab nationalism, was the 'wave of the future'. It was in this atmosphere that Washington dusted off its policies of 1953-1955, modified them, and basing them on carrot-and-stick economics attempted to build a realistic working relationship with Nasser. This renewed effort to improve relations with Cairo reaffirmed Washington's long-held view that Egypt, for better or worse, was indeed the most important country in the Arab Middle East, and that the tottering traditional regimes would likely come under the influence of Cairo or fall to pro-Nasserist elements. Given the Cold War paradigm that viewed Communism, albeit incorrectly, as monolithic, the White House tendency to view revolutionary Arab nationalism and Nasserism as also monolithic was consistent, if similarly flawed. In 1958, events would reveal a more complicated reality.

Despite rapprochement with Nasser, US concerns about Lebanon and the potential for UAR expansion left the impression in London that Eisenhower actually regretted his decision not to back the British at Suez in 1956.[2] Eisenhower no doubt had second thoughts from time to time but fundamentally believed that the British had mishandled the crisis from start to finish; this reality was lost on Whitehall. London convinced itself that the US now clearly recognized Britain's superior Middle East expertise. In this regard, in late May 1958, the Foreign Office telegraphed the British Embassy in Washington:

In connexion with possible action in the Lebanon, various plans must be made in the closest cooperation with the United States. Because of our greater experience in the Middle East, the suggestions must often come from us. I am, however, particularly anxious that we should avoid giving the impression that we are trying to push the American's into an operation.[3]

The British believed that the Eisenhower Doctrine and the US reaction to the Lebanese situation represented the precise policies that they had advocated at the time of Suez. Prime Minister Macmillan stated: 'The new American policy could hardly be reconciled with the Administration's almost hysterical outbursts over Suez.'[4] On 14 May, Macmillan chaired a cabinet meeting to discuss American preparations to deploy troops and preserve 'the integrity and independence of the Lebanon'.[5] Heartened by the belief that Washington actually intended to move to curtail Nasserist activities, Macmillan stated: 'If the Eisenhower doctrine of 1957 represented a marked change from the attitude of the American Administration in 1956, the interpretation now to be given to it in 1958 was not merely in worlds but in deeds, a recantation – an act of penitence – unparalleled in history.'[6] London concluded that Eisenhower and Dulles had recognized their Suez blunder and had no intention of repeating it. The British clearly missed the point: Eisenhower wanted to avoid intervention at almost any cost, and had little faith in London's influence in the Middle East.[7]

The gathering storm: the Lebanese crisis

While London worked on gaining Commonwealth support, Washington contemplated the next step and how to avoid intervention.[8] Eisenhower viewed a military operation as very high-risk. As mentioned, there was the issue of an exit strategy. At the same time, having just initiated a new policy based on economic incentives with Nasser, the possibility of Cairo engineering the collapse of an independent Lebanon through their Syrian partners presented an equally unappealing and embarrassing possibility. Dulles wanted Chamoun to compromise. He told the Foreign Office that given the dangers associated with military action, 'Chamoun should do everything possible to maintain control without it.' The British government was split, with some supporting and others opposing intervention. Those in London wanting action against Nasser groused: '[US] eyes are fixed too much on the hope that intervention will be avoided and too little on the measures necessary to ensure its success. They want to avoid a direct clash with Nasser.'[9] In Washington, Dulles painted a gloomy picture for the NSC. Beirut was quiet but the standoff between government troops and rebels continued around Tripoli. Infiltration continued unabated across the 'wide open' Syrian border. Worse still, Dulles saw a Nasserist takeover as the only real alternative to Chamoun.[10] By early June, unrest in the countryside threatened to engulf Beirut. On 10 June, Macmillan met in Washington with Eisenhower. In addition to possible courses of action in Lebanon, they discussed ways to assist Iraq and Jordan.[11] They agreed that a successor to Chamoun had to be found, given that Chamoun himself had sparked the current crisis.[12]

On 14 June, Chamoun and Lebanese Foreign Minister Malik asked the Eisenhower administration if it would intervene militarily should the Lebanese government request it. Washington equivocated, stating that any intervention would be to protect American lives and property and to preserve the independence of Lebanon, not to support any particular faction. Given the presence of UN observers, Washington sought to avoid the appearance of conflict with UN Security Council peace initiatives. In contrast, the British, wanting intervention, offered a counter-proposal:

> Our idea is that the Lebanese should ask for an emergency meeting of the Security Council at which they would appeal for the despatch of a U.N. military force. We and the U.S. would support this suggestion and offer contingents. Once it was vetoed, we should be free to go to the direct assistance of the Lebanon on our own account, at the same time taking the Lebanese case to the Assembly under the 'Uniting for Peace' procedure.[13]

The British now seemed to push for intervention and, needing US concurrence, scrutinized every cable from Washington and crafted every response in an effort to create an environment that would increase the odds on US action.

In a reversal of policy, the British now attempted to arrange quietly for Jordanian and Iraqi participation in any potential Lebanese intervention. Perpetually annoyed with Dulles, London became increasingly frustrated with the Secretary's desire for French participation. London was certain that a French 'gate-crash' as they put it, meant that neither Iraq nor Jordan would participate. As things would turn out, London would have been far better off had the Hashemites stayed out of it. London also opposed Dulles' near-fixation on 'extending' Chamoun's tenure beyond the 24 July date for new elections. The British Embassy in Washington complained: 'Mr. Dulles is rather obstinate about this, and I find his reasoning unconvincing and in places alarming.' London wanted Chamoun's political career expeditiously buried. Finally, Whitehall and the Foreign Office became increasingly concerned that Eisenhower was waffling on intervention.[14] Dag Hammerskjold warned Dulles against intervention, arguing that a UN solution was far preferable, but the UN Secretary General conceded that should the UN or Lebanese fail to resolve the matter, Western intervention at the request of the Lebanese government would be 'legal'.[15] In a news conference on 25 June, Chamoun added weight to Hammerskjold's argument. He stated that the Lebanon would provide time for the UN observers to carry out their mission, but added: 'We will not accept this U.A.R. attempt to lay its hand on Lebanon.'[16]

On that same day, the eve of his departure for a non-aligned conference in Yugoslavia, Nasser received a pointed message from Washington via Ambassador Hare. Hare's instructions from Dulles were clear: 'US attitude toward UAR cannot but be affected by attitude of UAR toward other independent states of area ... leave no doubt of this in his mind.' To make certain that Hare understood, Dulles added an additional sentence under his personal signature: 'Essential thing at moment is to bring end to Lebanese crisis.'[17] By early July, little had changed. The White House vacillated between apprehensive optimism about Chamoun's chances for survival and the hope that Nasser, heeding US warnings, would end support to the rebels. At the same time, Washington apprehensively coordinated a contingency strategy for intervention with its allies.[18]

On 1 July, in a meeting with Chamoun, the US, British, and French ambassadors told him that only a political solution held any chance of ending the civil war. They pressured him to drop attempts to succeed himself as President. When asked about Washington's position, US Ambassador Robert Mills McClintock informed Chamoun that the US was committed to the preservation of Lebanon's integrity predicated upon Chamoun's earlier statements that he would not seek a second term. Angrily pointing out that his current difficulties resulted from his steadfast support of the West, Chamoun warned that a Nasserist triumph in Lebanon would encourage rebellions and the overthrow of the regimes in both Jordan and Iraq.[19] Once notified, Washington was unhappy that the American Ambassador had been associated with the Anglo-French démarche. Apparently the representations made at the meeting had exceeded a previous agreement. Rountree complained to Viscount Samuel Hood (Lord Hood) at the British Embassy in Washington, who agreed that it was an 'unfortunate incident'. Hood then relayed the British Foreign Secretary's concern over the 'lack of concrete evidence of UAR interference in Lebanon'.[20] The US, France, and Britain may have been somewhat at odds over the meeting, but there were indications that Chamoun had gotten the message and was lining up his replacement, General Fuad Chehab, the Chief of Staff of the Lebanese Army. Fortunately, Chehab was Nasser's compromise candidate as well.[21] It appeared that the crisis might dissipate and the intervention could be avoided.

Macmillan's tempest: the Baghdad coup

During the first six months of 1958, the situation in Baghdad appeared to improve. In March 1958, the US Embassy there had reported that Hashemite opposition in Iraq, while having dabbled in various forms of 'neutralism, leftism and nationalism', was 'at the moment enthralled by only one important commodity – Nasserism', but that it was 'neither particularly significant nor effective'.[22] The British had maintained their position in Iraq, come what may, for over 30 years. Iraq stood as the bulwark of the British political, economic, and military position in the Middle East. When Nasser announced the creation of the UAR, the British assessed the situation in Baghdad, dividing the Iraqis into three groups. First, the Embassy described the opposition as the 'unthinking public', 'students', and 'some politicians' who saw Nasser as an Arab hero and welcomed the announcement 'uncritically'. Second, there were the 'active politicians' who were largely suspicious and resented his claims to Arab leadership. Then: 'Finally, the Palace, the members of the Government and the many officials and professional men who have a broader understanding of the situation see the Union as a threat to Iraq, to its oil revenues, to its development programme, to its monarchial regime and all that it stands for.'[23] London subscribed to this latter view.

To provide an alternative to Nasser's vision for Arab unity, the Iraqi government immediately began to explore a union with Jordan, Kuwait, and Saudi Arabia. Nuri Sa'id expected King Saud to 'sit on the fence'.[24] London quickly blocked Kuwait's participation, fearing that it would 'probably backfire' and make Kuwait a target for Nasserist agitation. The Foreign Office observed that the Ruler of Kuwait, by maintaining 'a delicate balance', had prevented a 'collision with Arab nationalists' and the younger generation in Kuwait. Adherence to the Baghdad Pact would probably be 'repugnant' to Kuwaiti progressives and bring calls for unity with the UAR. This would be a disaster, since Kuwait provided the British with a petroleum safety net and price leverage against other oil producers.[25] Nuri Sa'id also had his eye on incorporating Kuwait into Iraq, and in conversations with the US Ambassador to Iraq he demanded 'money and Kuwait', threatening to resign if he did not get both. When Macmillan learned of the demand, he compared Sa'id to Nasser, stating: 'Nuri [has] been difficult for some time and was now attempting a Nasser-type operation against Kuwait.' The Prime Minister found it a 'great shock ... to learn that Nuri has out and out threatened Kuwait.'[26] There was considerable apprehension at the British Embassy in Baghdad. In February 1958, wanting more US economic and military aid for Baghdad, Sir Michael Wright warned London that the long-term prognosis was problematic.

> The Iraqis, with far too few exceptions, are not natural leaders and, conscious that Iraq is a small and new state without much international experience, they are all to inclined to look to others for inspiration: hence much of the appeal of Colonel Nasser. This means that the Government and the many in Iraq who believe in the Western alliance look to Britain and America for leadership and help. ... if the West cannot give at least some of the help that is needed, it will be extremely difficult in the long term for the present regime to maintain itself in the face of the challenge I have described.

The British and the Iraqi governments saw the Egyptian-Syrian union as a direct threat to oil exports, given the pipeline stretching from Kirkuk across Syria to the Mediterranean.[27] London wanted more support from Washington, both financially and militarily, in propping up the Baghdad regime. Ironically, the British and Iraqi fixation on the UAR would prove their undoing.

On 14 July 1958, the long-anticipated coup against Hashemite Iraq finally occurred. Oddly enough, it came as a total surprise. As Christian Herter, the Under Secretary of State, put it, the coup caught everyone 'absolutely flat-footed'.[28] It was the long-feared event that the British and Americans tried to convince themselves would not happen. Iraq had experienced so much unrest, so many rumors of revolt and actual revolts, all of which had failed to dislodge either the Hashemites or the British, that the ease and success of the Bastille Day conspirators astonished even the most pessimistic.[29] It was swift, violent, and conclusive. Brigadier Abd-al-Karim al-Qasim and his cohorts had learned from the short-lived Rashid Ali coup of 1941. Taking no chances, the plotters decapitated the regime, removing any figure around which a cohesive opposition might coalesce.[30] Iraq put an exclamation point on Suez; British power and influence in Iraq had vanished and Albion was clearly on the defensive in the Persian Gulf. In Washington, the coup merely confirmed Eisenhower's and Dulles' conviction that the imperial British system in the Middle East was at best outmoded, at worst detrimental to Western interests, and now a thing of the past.[31]

Adding insult to injury, the British had arguably shot themselves in the foot. They had encouraged the Iraqi government to move military formations to the Syrian border in an attempt to divert UAR attention from Lebanon. Unfortunately, the Iraqi high command issued ammunition and arranged for brigades commanded by rebel plotters to pass through, rather than around, the capital. Proper security precautions were not taken, and no other loyal army units were in the city. The rebel 19th Brigade's detour on the night of July 13th to besiege the palace, occupy the Radio Baghdad station, and take over the telephone exchange were the first signs that something was amiss. The ease of the takeover, the liquidation of government officials, and the murder of the royal family also surprised the conspirators. They had expected a protracted struggle, and when rioting broke out, they lacked an immediate plan to deal with the situation. Phebe Marr, the widely respected historian of Iraq, stated that in the immediate aftermath of the coup senior army officers hestitated waiting to see what the British and others might do, and when no action was forthcoming they moved to support the plotters.[32] Quickly recovering, Iraq's new leader Qasim declared martial law on 15 July, issued shoot-on-sight orders, and restored order.[33] The new regime realized that excessive rioting and damage to foreign interests would damage its credibility, bring a departure of foreign technicians and invite intervention. No. 10 Downing Street concluded that a 'small body of troops ... ran amok', murdering Nuri Sa'id, the King, the Crown Prince and other key officials. In Macmillan's words: 'when the full account reached us it was clear that the tragedy was complete.' There had been no inkling of a real nature of the threat from the military.[34] Macmillan expressed Whitehall's shock: 'All this was devastating news destroying at a blow a whole system of security which successive British Governments had built up.'[35] Washington agreed that the British 'system of security' in the Middle East had largely collapsed, and that Nasser was behind it.

Following news of the coup, Eisenhower said, speaking to Dulles by telephone: 'It looks as if you have a solid Arab world against us because Jordan can't stick.' The president did not say 'we'. Dulles agreed and then added: 'The main problem is our relations with Turkey, Iran, and Pakistan. We always felt we would lose the Arab world but did not want to [do so] under circumstances that would lose the confidence of these countries [Turkey, Iran, and Pakistan].'[36] In Washington, the complete surprise and the lack of information about the new regime created a flood of criticism. Senator J. William Fulbright complained: 'It is possible that there might be some legitimate excuse for being surprised about the rebellion. I do not think there is any excuse to come in and say, "We do not know anything about this government". They have had several days. They ought to know a lot about it if they have any kind of organization at all. ... Here we are just fumbling in the dark.'[37]

Facing harsh criticism from all quarters, the administration was under pressure to act. Just as the failure to form MEDO in 1954 had provided the impetus for the formation of a defense alliance based on the 'northern tier', the Iraqi coup revitalized and inextricably linked containment policy to the survival of that alliance. It was with Turkey, Iran, and Pakistan in mind that Washington considered taking action in Lebanon. Both the State Department and the CIA concluded that inaction would result in three probable outcomes; these conclusions went far beyond the Arab Middle East. First, Nasser, who they believed was behind the coup, would take over the entire region. Second, the United States would lose influence and probably critical bases, including Wheelus Air Force Base in Libya and last, the US could lose some particularly sensitive intelligence sites in Iran and Pakistan that directly affected the strategic defense of the continental United States. This assessment directly linked the outcome of the situation in Lebanon to US global credibility.[38]

In some quarters, there had been the initial assumption that the British would intervene immediately to redress the situation; when it became apparent that this would not be the case, the paranoia intensified. On 14 July, at a tense and hastily convened NSC meeting, Allen Dulles briefed the CIA's sketchy intelligence on the situation in Iraq. Director Dulles confirmed that the Crown Prince was dead and a 'Leftist government' headed by pro-Nasserist army elements had taken over.[39] He told those present that the situation in Jordan was 'extremely critical'. There were fears of another Nasserist coup, and concerns that an 'extremely alarmed' Israel might occupy all of 'Trans-Jordan' in the event of 'disorder'. As the briefing continued, the Director became more alarmist, stating: 'The fate of Kuwait is presently in the balance.' Dulles reported that King Saud demanded 'action at once, stating that if the United States and United Kingdom do not act now they are finished as powers in the Mid-East'. As for Lebanon, he stated that Chamoun had frantically asked for US, British, and French intervention in Lebanon within 48 hours. Unwilling to be outdone by his younger brother, the Secretary of State, participating by telephone, became even shriller: 'If we do not respond to the call from

Chamoun, we will suffer the decline and indeed the elimination of our influence – from Indonesia to Morocco.'⁴⁰

Despite mushrooming alarm in Washington, the US Embassy in Beirut calmly reported: 'As for hard evidence of an increased military threat to Lebanon, it is difficult to find this morning.'⁴¹ The cacophony of concern

Courtesy of National Archives
Dulles and Robert Murphy
Robert Murphy, Special Envoy to the Middle East following the Lebanese crisis and the Iraqi coup. Murphy's association with Eisenhower dated back to the North African campaign in World War II; he was a trusted trouble-shooter.

drowned out the Embassy's even-keeled evaluation, and Eisenhower ordered troops into Lebanon.[42] He later stated that when he went into the meeting, his 'mind was practically made up.' After the decision was made, Eisenhower telephoned Macmillan, who offered his complete agreement and cooperation. Macmillan informed Eisenhower: 'We have a request from the two little chaps.' King Hussein had requested British troops as well.[43] In a follow-up telegram, Macmillan promised Britain's support and called for 'urgent action', but he quickly made a point of London's main concern. The Prime Minister warned the president that attacks on British oil installations would surely result: 'all of which will inflict great loss upon the international companies and particularly upon us who depend on sterling oil.' Having pushed Washington to act, Macmillan now urged caution because of the complexity of the situation.[44] The message was not lost on the White House. On 18 July, Eisenhower cabled Macmillan with a review of the situation, including his thoughts on the situations in Lebanon, Jordan, Iraq, Turkey, Iran, Pakistan, the Persian Gulf, and Saudi Arabia. The President assured Macmillan: 'We shall seek ways to help them be sturdy allies, first in quality and second in quantity, insofar as that quantity can be usefully provided and maintained.'[45] Clearly, Eisenhower and Dulles were entertaining more aggressive assistance to pro-Western regimes in the region. In addition, both agreed that the United States and Britain had to mount coordinated and effective propaganda campaigns at the UN and against the Communists in the Middle East who had appropriated Arab nationalism.[46]

Revolution in Iraq and a second honeymoon with Cairo

Ironically, Nasser, who had worked diligently for the overthrow of the Hashemite regime and Nuri Sa'id in Iraq, knew little more about what had actually happened than Washington or London. Naturally, he assumed that the coup was good news, and Egypt immediately recognized the new regime in Baghdad. He then optimistically awaited an announcement from Baghdad of solidarity with the UAR. In Yugoslavia, when the revolution occurred and the British and Americans announced their interventions in Jordan and Lebanon, Nasser believed that Iraq was next. On 17 July, he secretly traveled to Moscow, seeking assistance. He was disappointed. The Soviets offered unlimited bluster and moral support, but risking a nuclear war with the United States over some Arab revolution in Iraq was not on their agenda. On 18 July, he flew to Damascus and met with Sarraj, the UAR Syrian security chief, and an emissary from Baghdad, Abd-al-Salam al-Aref, Qasim's pro-Egyptian deputy. Qasim had dispatched Aref to enlist Nasser's aid. The meeting resulted in a pact of mutual support and friendship. It would prove to be the first and last agreement between Nasser and the new Iraqi regime. Convinced that Nasser was behind the coup in Baghdad and having little insight into the political dynamic between Baghdad and Cairo, Robert Murphy, Eisenhower's special envoy, went to the Middle East on a fact-finding mission shortly after the Iraqi coup. Murphy met with Nasser, who denied rumors of an impending UAR move against Amman. When Murphy told Nasser that King Hussein had faith in the loyalty of his army, Nasser laughed and said: 'I overthrew the King of Egypt after plotting for five years, and nobody suspected anything. How can Hussein be sure what is going on in his Army? You know what happened last month to his cousin, King Faisal of Iraq!'[47]

Washington did not yet understand that the Iraqi revolution, as Nasser would begin to ascertain, was just that – an Iraqi revolution. Qasim had no intention of joining Egypt and Syria, primarily because he had every intention of preserving Iraq's oil wealth for Iraq.[48] In Baghdad, an internal debate erupted over the nature of the relationship between Baghdad and the UAR. While Qasim paid lip service to Arab unity, Kurdish groups in the north and the large Shi'a population in southern Iraq opposed submersion in a super state dominated by Sunni Arabs. In addition, the well-organized Iraqi Communist Party (ICP), having witnessed Nasser's dissolution and suppression of Communist elements in Egypt and Syria, had no desire to suffer the same fate. Also, Qasim had no intention of living in Nasser's shadow. As a result, Nasserists, like Qasim's deputy, Colonel Abd-al-Salaam al-Aref, found themselves increasingly isolated and alienated from the new regime.[49]

During the fall of 1958, UAR-Iraq relations deteriorated as Qasim suppressed pro-UAR elements. The arrest of Aref was a clear 'slap in the face', and placed Nasser in uncharted territory. Attacking the 'feudal' Hashemites or Saudis was one thing, but dealing with an Arab nationalist rival with solid revolutionary credentials was another.[50] In addition, to counter Nasserist and Ba'thist influence, Qasim opted for greater reliance on Communist support. From Washington's perspective, this reliance made Qasim vulnerable to a Communist coup, the very reasoning that had prompted Eisenhower to take action in Iran in 1953.[51] From Nasser's perspective, Qasim's alliance with the Communists not only deprived him of Iraq's potential membership in the UAR, but it also raised concerns about the geographical and ideological proximity of the Syrian and the Iraqi Communists and their mutual loathing of the UAR President. This situation did not bode well for stability in an already restive Syria. The Eisenhower administration concluded that Nasser's revolutionary activities would most likely moderate as he attempted to deal with Iraq, and speculated that Qasim and his Communist allies 'would strengthen those Syrians who would prefer looser ties with Egypt and possibly closer relations with Iraq'.[52] Qasim's courtship of the ICP also enhanced his standing in Moscow, cooling the Kremlin's relationship with Cairo. In reaction, the Egyptian press and other Nasserist outlets began to focus editorials and articles on the 'dangers of Communism' in the Arab world.[53] This growing coziness between Iraq and the Soviet Union created friction between the Egyptians and their Russian benefactors.[54] Success was breeding dissension among the Arab Middle East's 'happy band of brothers in revolution'.[55]

Thus, by the fall 1958, the Egyptians found their problems multiplying. Iraq exhibited more hostility and all was not well in Syria. Nasser's Ba'th Party allies had grown more disillusioned with Egyptian rule. Jordan no longer appeared to be easy pickings, since Israeli Prime Minister David Ben-Gurion had made it ominously clear that any change of regime in Amman would result in decisive Israeli action to occupy the West Bank and to 'make provision' for the Palestinian population there.[56] The Israelis ratcheted up the pressure by openly shopping for support for just such a move in the event of a Jordanian collapse.[57] The level of speculation over potential Israeli action against the West Bank and even for possible moves east of the Jordan had a predictable 'deterrent effect'.[58] Nasser found his options limited to covert undermining of the Hashemite government in Jordan. By December 1958, Nasser's year of revolution was over. With the less desirable 'revolutionary' outcome in Iraq and the Soviet tilt toward Baghdad, he, like Washington, needed a new ally.

Coming to terms with revolutionary Iraq

As for Lebanon and intervention, Washington, by now, was beginning to understand what had really happened in Baghdad and how Lebanon fit into the picture. The shrill voices of 14 July had receded. At the 18 July Cabinet meeting, Secretary Dulles pointed out that the United States had opposed the British folly of including Iraq in the Baghdad Pact. With some justification, he stated that the strain placed on the Hashemite regime by its membership of the Pact brought about its collapse. He concluded that oil supplies would be stable so long as threats to Kuwait, Iran, and Saudi Arabia were quashed. A calmer and more collected Secretary explained that the President's decision to send in troops was based on the 'frightened' appeals of Chamoun and Hussein. He stated that it would maintain US credibility with 'smaller nations' but solve nothing. Dulles stated: 'We have no illusions that this response will solve the problems of that area – in fact it may make them worse. It is not a popular action and in fact it is pregnant with difficulties: To send in armed forces to try to stem the tides of rabid nationalism. ... But failure to act would have shaken the foundations of the free world – from Morocco to the Western Pacific.' In something of a soul-searching self-indictment, Eisenhower concluded that the US had not done enough to protect and aid their friends in the region or to combat their enemies. Eisenhower stated that the US position had to be 'rehabilitated' in the region and that would require money.[59] In an article headed 'What Now?', *The Nation* hit the nail squarely on the head: 'The news from Baghdad sent us barging into Lebanon before we had received a second report from the observers – before, indeed, we even know exactly what was happening in Iraq.' Facing a storm of criticism, the United States and Britain now attempted to sort out what had actually happened.[60]

On 16 July, John Hay 'Jock' Whitney, the US Ambassador to London, reported that the landings in Lebanon had heartened Prime Minister Macmillan. He hinted that the British had a much wider agenda. 'British are convinced US-UK must be prepared to follow through in Jordan and Iraq as necessary to restore western position in entire area. In other words, British believe that now we have started, we must see the job to a finish or we will be in worse shape than before marines landed at Beirut.'[61] In fact, Foreign Secretary Selwyn Lloyd's trip to Washington following the coup was based in part upon the premise that the US and Britain must act quickly in both Iraq and Jordan or 'it would be too late.'[62] At an 18 July dinner with the ambassadors of the 'Old' Commonwealth, Lloyd tried to put the best face on the situation and deflect Dulles' criticism of British policy. He argued that 'if Britain had not gone in the Baghdad Pact would have collapsed, and Iran, Sudan, Pakistan and perhaps even Turkey would have despaired and reinsured with Russia.' Lloyd also pointed out that Eisenhower had made the decision to intervene in Lebanon on an *ad hoc* basis.[63] On 14 July, at the Foreign Office, despite the hand wringing and flailing about, D.M.H. Riches, the Chief of the Arabian Department, minuted his superior, Sir William Hayter, with a note of reason.

> If the revolution in Iraq succeeds, when the smoke clears we shall presumably be left with a military dictatorship on the Nasser model. This government will certainly express emotional solidarity with pan-Arabism and therefore with Egypt; but it is likely to wish to preserve Iraqi oil revenues for itself and therefore to maintain its separate identity. It seems unlikely that it would even join the United Arab States – except perhaps as a desperate last fling if it felt its position severely threatened.

Riches predicted that the new revolutionary government would 'prosecute the Iraqi claim to Kuwait with greater vigour than the previous Iraqi Government.' With considerable prescience, he argued that in such a case, Egypt would likely support a Kuwait free of Iraqi control, either as an independent state or as a part of the UAR, and he predicted that Saudi Arabia would have the same goal. Riches stated that his views were based on a 'rational attitude on the part of Arab governments'. He cautioned that intervention might result in 'Arab policies, which on the face of it are contrary to the individual interests of the countries concerned' and 'certainly contrary to Western interests.'[64]

The Colonial Office and British authorities in Aden took a narrow, hard line, and a thoroughly alarmist view of events. Sir William Henry Tucker Luce, Governor General in Aden, 'fully' endorsed the views of Arab notables in the Aden Federation:

> The events in Iraq, Lebanon and Jordan constitute a crisis of the greatest magnitude both for the future of the Arab world and for the West's relations with it. Unless there is swift and effective intervention by Western powers to contain the expansion of Russian influence and to curb Nasser's ambitions, the Arabs would soon be united in bondage and not in freedom as so many of them desire. They clearly regarded suppression of the Iraq rebellion as an essential part of intervention.[65]

The Colonial Office requested that the contents of the telegram be presented in the situation briefing to the Foreign Secretary and brought to the attention of the Joint Intelligence Committee. The responsible Foreign Office officials commented that no one 'need attribute very great importance to this particular reaction' and that the request to make it a part of Selwyn Lloyd's briefing was 'absurd.'[66]

With Qasim's 'junta' in control and expressing a desire for 'friendly relations' with the United States, Washington adopted a wait-and-see attitude.[67] Still trying to understand the situation and offer some constructive observations, Dulles concluded that Iraq needed to maintain good relations with the West because of oil revenue and Nasser. In something of a contradiction, he stated that he still believed that Nasser was the real 'authority' behind the Qasim regime and that the authority behind Nasser was the Soviet Union. In contrast, the CIA believed that the Iraqi regime had no effective opposition but would probably disappear within six months in a Nasserist coup. The Agency also made it clear that they thought the long-term British position in Jordan and Iraq was untenable, thus contributing to the view that Jordan was a bad bet for US support.[68]

Betting on the northern tier

Pointing out the advantages of his original 1953 concept of a 'northern tier' alliance, Dulles suggested that Iraq leaving the Baghdad Pact would remove the Arab element, thereby opening the way for US participation in an alliance with Turkey, Iran, and Pakistan. Washington could then take a direct role in protecting its regional interests.[69] In late July 1958, Dulles told an emergency meeting of the Baghdad Pact that the US would join the Pact and significantly increase assistance to Turkey, Iran, and Pakistan.[70] The meeting also reinforced the Secretary's view that time might take care of Nasser's prestige if the UAR's energy could be 'channeled' and allowed to dissipate. This view followed Allen Dulles' argument that the differences existing between types of Arab nationalism and approaches to Arab unity spelled trouble for Nasser: 'Many Arab countries give lip-service to close relations with Nasser, but when it comes to dividing up oil revenues or the waters of the Nile, it is a different story.'[71] The British understood US policy in only one dimension – that of the damage that a US rapprochement could potentially do to Britain's remaining interests in the region. In fact, London's decision to drop plans for intervention and to recognize the Qasim regime, which Washington expected to come under Nasser's direct control, contributed to the US view that the Arab world was an inevitable loss.[72]

Disenchantment with the Eisenhower administration's UAR tilt also affected British views of the situation in Jordan. Angered by US policy toward Jordan, Sir Charles Johnston, the British Ambassador in Amman, wrote to the Foreign Office complaining that:

The State Department view ... reflects that defeatist 'Rountreeist' philosophy, which has always seemed to me unworthy of a great country like the U.S. It assumes what I call the double standard. Nasser is against us, therefore we must kowtow to him and regard his triumph as inevitable. Jordan is for us, therefore the task of preserving it is utterly hopeless and we must see how we can hand it over to Nasser as gracefully as possible. This theory blandly overlooks the fact that Nasser's regime is now at least as unpopular in Syria, and perhaps also in Egypt itself, as Samir Rifai's is in Jordan.

Johnston argued that: 'The Americans should not allow any infantile anti-Monarchist prejudices to blind them to this fact. Monarchy is a very ancient and tenacious principle, in the Arab world.' He went to say: 'It would be naïve to think that, after living with it for millennia, the Arab world is suddenly going to drop it because one Colonel and one Brigadier have shown themselves successful military conspirators in 1952 and 1958 respectively.'[73]

Johnston could have given Washington a little more credit. The administration had no illusions about Nasser, but it simply did not think Jordan's survival was worth the cost. Dulles believed that the West had to 'sandbag' its positions in Lebanon, Israel, and the oil-rich Persian Gulf against an Arab nationalist 'flood which is running strong'. Accepting Arab nationalism and anti-Western policies as a fact of life, Dulles intended to buy time until the flood subsided. Choices had to be made, and the administration believed that Jordan, in the direct path of the flood, had little chance of survival. Dulles also wanted Jordan to make a soft landing because of Israel. Washington feared that a violent collapse in Jordan would bring the calamitous consequences of Israeli intervention. For this reason, Washington wanted the British to leave voluntarily, believing that failure to do so invited another Iraq and Israeli intervention. With the British gone, a transition could occur that would avoid Israeli intervention, with its potential for regional conflict and a possible nuclear confrontation with the Soviet Union.[74]

While London and Washington struggled with the situation, it become more apparent that unification with the UAR did not fit Qasim's agenda, and triangular friction developed between Cairo, Baghdad, and Moscow. This rift caused Anglo-American policy goals to diverge. Even in the worst of times, Eisenhower's policies reflected a conflicted relationship with Nasser. Washington erred in ideologically linking Nasser's Arab nationalism and need for arms from the Soviet Union to pro-Communist sympathies, but Nasser's suppression of the Communists in Egypt and Syria brought a more sophisticated White House view. In addition, Iraqi opposition to Nasser relieved many of the concerns about UAR regional hegemony. When pro-Nasserist elements, led by Colonel Aref, prominent Ba'thists, and Rashid Ali al-Gaylani, fell from power in Baghdad, US concern about Nasserism receded even more.[75] An old fear took its place as Qasim turned to the Iraqi Communists for support.[76] The situation in Iraq provided a situation in which real Communists appeared to be on the road to political control.

Compared to the ICP in Iraq, Nasserism looked ideologically benign. The developing ties between Washington and Cairo and growing US concern about ICP influence in Iraq complicated the British campaign to normalize relations with Baghdad and protect their interests in Iraqi oil. The US clearly intended to use Nasser to counterbalance increasing Communist influence. NSC 5820 reflected this intention, stating that the US would 'normalize' relations with the UAR: 'Recognizing that U.S. accommodation with Nasser would contain elements contrary to U.S. interests, deal with Nasser as head of the UAR on specific problems and issues, area-wide as well as local, affecting the UAR's legitimate interests, but not as leader of the Arab world.'[77] As for Jordan, the directive proposed to 'encourage such peaceful political adjustment by Jordan, including partition, absorption, or internal political realignment, as appears desirable to the people of Jordan'. In short, Sir Charles Johnston was correct: Washington believed that the 'controlled' dismantlement of the Hashemite kingdom constituted the only real option.[78] After literally years of soul-searching, the administration came to a realistic policy toward Nasser: 'The main problem facing the U.S. in the area is not Arab nationalism, but Soviet influence and activities.'[79] It was a return to the fundamental policies of containing Communism rather than nationalism.

With regard to Iraq, the administration concluded that while Qasim might want to curtail Communist influence in Iraq, he was unable or unwilling to do so because of the Ba'thist-Nasserist threat. Concern existed that Communist influence might have already reached the point where Qasim could not control it.[80] The less charitable views were positively alarming: 'The Qasim regime has shown no disposition to part company with the Communists even though it is now relatively free to do so. ... The Qasim regime's inertia in the face of this Communist aggressiveness appears to have convinced most Iraqis that Qasim has wholly surrendered to the Communists and must be removed.' This clear focus on the Qasim regime and its Communist supporters promised nothing but complications for British attempts to keep the lid on its relationship with the Baghdad regime.

As for Nasser, the report states that: '(Nasser) at last realizes that he cannot divorce local Communist movements from the USSR and deal separately with each on different bases. Circumstances are driving him to attack Qasim – and at least indirectly the Soviet Union – as enemies of Arab Union, or risk losing control of the union movement. ... Refusal to face this issue carries the risk of appearing weak or over-obligated, with a commensurate loss of stature.'[81] The Qasim regime lumped anti-Nasser and anti-US themes together. They pervaded the Communist-inspired riot that greeted Assistant Secretary Rountree on his December 1958 visit to Baghdad. The riot also provided additional impetus to the increasingly pro-Nasserist US tilt. In Cairo, Rountree found the Egyptians as concerned as Washington about Communist influence in Iraq because of its implications for Syria.[82] For Eisenhower, Nasser's shift was a long-delayed gift. Finally, Washington and Cairo saw eye to eye on Communism. For Washington, Communism posed a global problem; for Nasser, the revolutionary apostates in Baghdad threatened his view of Arab nationalism and unity. For very different reasons, Nasser and Eisenhower agreed on Qasim's Iraq.[83]

Cooperation with Nasser put the US in bad stead in Baghdad, and complicated relations with the Macmillan government on issues ranging from Yemen to Jordan to Iraqi oil. By December 1958, the British concluded that, despite Communist influence, Qasim represented the best guarantee against an overt Communist takeover.[84] Qasim had followed through on his commitments vis-à-vis the British-controlled IPC, an important if not 'vital' British interest.[85] The Macmillan government concluded that: 'It is essential in the interests of the maintenance of our economy and standard of living to maintain our control of British oil interests in the Gulf, more particularly Kuwait.' For London, this interest included 'occupying and running Kuwait as a colony. ... So long as the Iraqis know that we can do without Iraqi oil if necessary, by relying on Kuwait, they have a strong inducement to come to terms with us.'[86] Wanting to avoid this extremity, the British sought to keep US-Iraqi relations on even keel. London attempted to soften Washington's 'very gloomy' view that Iraq had taken a 'straight Soviet line'.[87] The British pushed their own 'philosophy ... namely that Qasim is our best bet and that we can't take any action which would make life difficult for him or provoke him into taking an anti-Western line.'[88] Despite the Macmillan government's best efforts, containment and not British economic interests would be Eisenhower's first priority. Eisenhower intended to take Macmillan's concerns into consideration and coordinate with London to the extent possible, but the President's perception of US interests would be the driving force. The Baghdad coup meant that the Qasim regime with its Communist supporters would face US hostility and encouragement to Nasser. It also meant that the Eisenhower administration intended to revitalize its Soviet and Communist containment policy with increased for military, security, and economic support Iran and Pakistan.

Chapter 4: The 'Center of All Problems' – Iran and 1958

The coup in Iraq not only confirmed the fractious uncertainties of Arab politics and the downward slide of British influence in the Middle East, but it clearly demonstrated the interconnectivity of Cold War politics across the Greater Middle East. The Iraqi coup had far-reaching consequences for US policy in the region. Nowhere were these consequences more obvious than in US relations with Iran and Pakistan. Qasim's coup set in motion a series of changes in US policy that complicated US relations for almost five decades. While policies toward Pakistan and Iran had similarities, each had its own unique characteristics. In some ways, the impact on Iran was the most dramatic. To understand these changes, one must examine the pre-1958 political context, the immediate reaction to the Baghdad coup, and how the coup fundamentally altered the relationship between Washington and Tehran. Washington had always viewed Iran as geopolitically critical to US interests in the Middle East, but by the mid-1950s sites in Iran had become strategic assets in the Cold War directly affecting US security. In the mountains of northeastern Iran, US installations literally overlooked the Soviet missile development and test facilities at Turatom and Baiknour. These sites provided direct signals and telemetry intelligence on Soviet missile tests and capabilities.[1] Given the technologies of the 1950s and 1960s, they were irreplaceable.

This situation dictated that the US had to do everything in its power to maintain a pro-Western government in Tehran. Prior to 1958, this meant that the Shah received military assistance and economic aid, and was put under considerable pressure to enact fundamental reforms designed to stabilize and broaden the base of his regime. The Eisenhower administration emphasized economic development and reform while resolutely resisting the Shah's demands for massive military aid. Washington adhered to the premise that only economic development could lay the foundation for the fundamental political, social, and economic reform which would produce long-term stability in Iran.

This dictated limited military and security assistance to provide the Shah's regime with the ability to maintain internal order and suppress any indigenous Communist or anti-Western threats to the regime. It did not entail making Iran into a real military power.[2] Eisenhower's White House was just as convinced of the efficacy of aid and development as an antidote to Communist influence as the Kennedy administration, despite the fact that the latter received far more credit for pushing economic development and reform. Walt Rostow's views on the efficacy of economic development, political reform, and the potential for economic 'take-off points' fostering political democracy were just as in vogue with Eisenhower as they were under Kennedy and Johnson.[3] This policy ran directly counter to the Shah's priority of making Iran the dominant military power in the Persian Gulf and the military equal of Turkey. The history of the Shah's relationship with the Eisenhower administration is one of Iranian demands for more military aid and Washington's attempts to push the Peacock Throne toward economic growth and reform.

Containment through reform and economic development

From the Shah's 1953 restoration, the Eisenhower administration pressed and chided the regime repeatedly about the lack of progress toward political, economic, and social reform. This is not to say that Iranian military and security services did not receive their share of funding and aid. Containment strategy in its Iranian context required the maintenance of a stable political and civil environment and sufficient military capability to maintain the border and deter internal threats. Stability also required an efficient security apparatus to protect the regime. The US plan never envisioned an Iranian military capable of stopping, or even significantly delaying, a full-scale Soviet invasion. Unfortunately, the Shah convinced himself that the latter was possible and that the Eisenhower administration had promised exactly that as a *quid pro quo* for joining the Baghdad Pact. This differing view between Washington and Tehran spawned a periodically contentious relationship.

Early on, the US desire for reform focused on land reform and redistribution as a method of solidifying the Shah's rule. What seemed like a good idea on the Potomac was a two-edged sword in Persia. Land reform attacked the prerogatives and livelihoods of the large landowners who supported the Shah against nationalist groups like the National Front and Musaddiqists, and potentially undermined that support. Despite the risks, land reform held other attractions for the Shah. At some level, he wanted to free himself from reliance on the traditional landowners and their influence. The Shah believed that this traditional source of political support also curbed his ability to create a new, modern Iran in the image of Atatürk's Turkey. Stubbornly opposed to reform, the conservative landowners, who tended to be linked by blood and marriage ties to the bazarri and cherical classes, blamed US pressure on the Shah for his attempts to liberalize. They argued, and with some justification, that rapid land reform would lead to chaos, which would lead to drastically reduced production and the political instability associated with 'problems feeding the cities'. All of this would open the door to the Communist Tudeh. In addition, the landowners saw no practical difference between US-backed liberal land reform and a Communist revolution and collectivization.[4] The Shah's ability to balance American pressure to reform, his own desire to undercut the landowning classes, and the desirability of political support from the traditional power centers determined the stability of the regime.

In 1954 and 1955, with the encouragement of the Eisenhower administration, the Shah supported land reform and an anti-corruption campaign. This created a state of near political war between the Iranian parliament, the Majlis, and the throne. In September 1955, to avoid a crisis, the Shah abruptly moved to improve relations with the 'conservative political elements'. Observers, depending on their viewpoint, called it a 'shrewd political maneuver' or 'another indication of his unstable and emotional character'. More likely, this political maneuvering reflected growing self-confidence, and new-found leverage in resisting calls for reform by his foreign benefactors, Britain and America. Whatever the reason, the Shah dropped the 'talk of widespread new reforms'.[5] He also placated secular elements in Iran, paving the way for the repression of increasingly dissident conservative Shi'a clergy and their anti-government activities.[6] The Shah's move coincided with the Soviet arms deal for Egypt, and with entreaties by the US and Britain for Iran to join the Baghdad Pact. Here, a clear axiom of the West's relationship with Pahlavi Iran imerged: the more the West needed Iran, the more latitude the Shah exercised on the domestic front and the more leverage for aid. Having no illusions about the fate of the monarchy should reformists or Communists come to power, the Shah threw his political lot in with the West; however, the Shah used the tactics employed by neutralists like Nasser and Nehru to improve his situation. Pointing out that he had options, the Shah mixed professions of loyalty and friendship with the West with grousing about the paucity of US aid and comments about the rewards of neutralism.

As for Iranian participation in the Baghdad Pact, the Shah had his price, harping on his point that the pro-Western Middle East could not be defended without Iran. He argued that: 'A militarily strong Iran was therefore essential. Iran would not become partner in regional pact until its armed forces had been strengthened to point where it could take its place in the line on basis of at least comparative equality.' The Shah wanted additional economic aid as well, which Iranian officials creatively justified by pointing out that Baghdad Pact membership had a 'serious effect on Iranian economy which depended to considerable extent on its exports to Soviet Union.' Knowing that London considered Iranian participation in the Baghdad Pact critical, the Shah exerted pressure to gain British assistance in acquiring the maximum American aid. After a conversation with the Shah, the British Chargé in Tehran commented: 'It would appear that chief purpose of Shah's summoning us was to put himself in favorable light on both domestic and foreign issue and then appeal again for Western, i.e., US, military and also budgetary aid in order that he might go ahead and adhere to Baghdad pact. It is possible, moreover, that Shah felt that bringing in British on his appeal, he believed this might increase pressure on U.S.'[7] Using the specter of the Soviet threat and membership in the Baghdad Pact as leverage, the Shah believed he would get the aid he demanded.[8] Despite hints of massive aid, the Shah actually received relatively little, and most of that was directed toward internal security. However, he did receive copious amounts of free advice from Washington about how funds for direct budgetary and economic development should be employed.

There were even key disagreements on the economic front. In 1956, against the advice of the Eisenhower administration, the Shah centralized economic development in a Central Plan Organization (CPO) under a Shah loyalist, Abol Hassan Ebtehaj. Rejecting US advice to pursue broad economic development objectives aimed at raising the standard of living of the Iranian people, he used the CPO to concentrate on infrastructure. Tehran presented the CPO as a means to avoid graft and inefficiency by fostering foreign investment and development in Iran. In effect, Ebtehaj became the father of what would become massive foreign involvement in Iranian development. CPO policies, coupled with foreign oil concessions and membership in the Baghdad Pact, intensified xenophobic Iranian nationalism and magnified public perceptions that the Shah had perpetrated a 'sell out' to Western interests. For the Shah's opposition, it was a propaganda gold mine. They argued that the Shah gave the West cheap oil, supported the Baghdad Pact, and then handed more than 60 per cent of Iran's oil revenues back to Western firms by favoring them for large-scale development projects.[9]

By 1956, the Shah faced three major centers of domestic opposition: the large landowners and merchants; the Shi'a clergy; and the various nationalist groups nominally lumped together under the National Front. These groups felt betrayed by the lack of opportunities for Iranians to participate in the new economy, but fortunately for the Shah, the opposition groups distrusted each other more than the regime. By electing to build a 'heavy economic base' in a program that resembled Japan's industrialization efforts of the late nineteenth century, the Shah's program under Ebtehaj largely ignored the rising expectations of the people, creating widespread discontent.[10] In these circumstances, the army and the newly created security agency, SAVAK (Sazman-e Ettelaat va Amniyat-e Keshvar), constituted not only pillars of the Shah's personal rule, but also a prerequisite for the very economic modernization and reforms sought by Washington.[11] The Eisenhower administration preferred a different approach, but the Iranian monarch made it clear that he had his own ideas about the approach to modernization.

Iran modernization: the race against time

Could the desire for economic betterment on the part of the Iranian people be ignored without threatening the very existence of the Pahlavi dynasty? Washington had its doubts. American officials believed that something had to be done to improve the lot of the common Iranian, or 'demagogues' would fan Iranian xenophobia into a 'political storm alongside which the Mosadeq era would appear a gentle breeze'.[12] This focus on a 'heavy base' also created budgetary problems and chronic shortfalls that were aggravated by the Iranian government's inability to deal with fiscal hard choices, particularly when they involved the military. As a result, foreign aid became the routine anticipated source for making the budget work.[13] These trends alarmed the Eisenhower administration. Decisions about Iranian aid did not center solely upon a simple binary question of support for the military versus support for economic development; they became a more complex equation in which support for the military translated into the stability needed for economic development. Pursuit of the 'heavy model' for industrial development generated a need to strengthen the coercive power of the state. In the administration's view, the pay-off from the 'heavy base' approach would not come soon enough to prevent destabilization in Iran. Rising concern about the Shah's ability to survive resulted in discussions about alternatives: 'The United States should then review its policy towards Iran, taking into consideration whatever steps may be possible to disassociate its own prestige from the prestige of the Shah and to open better channels of communication and influence to opposition groups than now exist.' Thus, fearing that 'the Shah's position as a ruler may be in jeopardy', the Eisenhower administration continued to encourage more reform and projects that directly benefited the people, while attempting to maintain some distance from the Shah in the event he fell.[14]

As chronic economic and budgetary problems generated a perpetual state of crisis, the Shah careened from optimism to despair about the regime's floundering economy and security situation. The Shah's 'despair', no doubt sometimes real, also developed into an art form for extracting more military and economic aid. Politically, the US pressured the Shah to 'broaden' his base through controlled initiatives designed to foster political pluralism. To relieve the pressure, the Shah, citing Reza Shah's lament that his political legacy had not been institutionalized, announced his decision to create political parties 'whose politics stopped at the frontier'. The goal was to 'canalize [the] energies [of the] younger generation and to lead [the] people out [of] political illiteracy'. The initiative was an embarrassing failure. Political projects *du jour*, coupled with increasingly exorbitant demands for aid, raised questions about the Shah's political sophistication and, periodically, his hold on reality. As a result, serious questions arose concerning the viability of the regime. In July 1957, the US Embassy in Tehran reported:

> In a certain sense, the Shah lies at the center of all problems in Iran and certainly is an extremely important factor in their solution. Most Iranians recognize that the Shah has decided to rule personally as well as reign. This giving up of a mere constitutional role in favor of the exercise of power to make policy decisions for Iran has rather far reaching effects for the Shah as a national symbol. His is the credit for success and his the

onus of failure. He has deliberately removed himself from the apolitical role of the constitutional monarch and put himself in the scales of political survival in this country. As of now, his prospects for success (survival) do not seem too sanguine.[15]

The Iranian people had nothing to show for the Shah's rule. No increased feeling of security or justice had emerged. The Iranian government had produced no visible results for the common people and economically most Iranians did not see any improvement in their lot.[16]

This lack of progress and general lack of confidence in the Shah's ability to rule meant that 'the Government, i.e., the Shah, the Crown, as a national symbol and institution, could be seriously damaged'.[17] The Shah's attempts at Western-style education reform were having the opposite effect: 'The grass roots xenophobia of the average Iranian [is] perhaps the most sinister aspect of Iranian life today. What is most disturbing, at least from the viewpoint of the United States policy goals here, is that latent xenophobia flourishes among just those groups, which have had the most contact with Westernization.' Observers in Tehran believed that urban middle-class xenophobia resulted from the superficial adoption of Western values without the underlying acceptance of 'community cooperation', 'individual freedom', and 'toleration'. The US embassy reported: 'If westernization proceeds in the same pattern as it has up to now (and this seems not unlikely) it is not unreasonable to expect that xenophobia will increase – and, frighteningly enough, precisely in those groups in which one would normally place the hope of Iran's salvation from all forms of extremism.' The Shah's non-Iranian origins and close association with the US and Britain fueled this xenophobia. It was strongest among the educated elite, who believed that in a meritocracy they would rule in place of the Shah's entourage of sycophants. By 1957, predictions of chaos and severe damage to US policy interests were the order of the day. The survival of both the Shah and the pro-Western orientation of Iran were very much in doubt.[18] As a result of this pessimism, the Eisenhower administration quietly worked to keep its options open. Washington guaranteed the survival of an independent Iran and its territorial integrity, but pointedly refused to extend that promise to the Pahlavi dynasty, a point not lost on the Shah.

Seeing the potential for the Shah's collapse, Washington viewed the Iranian military as the most reliable pro-Western center of power. The military became the guarantor of the Shah's rule and the alternative to it. As for the Shah, he had no illusions about his ability to rule without a loyal, coercive military, and security apparatus at his disposal. Requests for military aid had as much to do with ensuring loyalthy as with actual need. Believing that the Shah's regime faced a growing and perhaps insurmountable crisis, the Eisenhower administration pressed for reform, even reform that incurred potentially serious risks to what remained of the Shah's popularity. In referring to the Shah's speech on land reform, agricultural improvements, housing to meet population growth, industrialization, consumer goods, and corruption, the administration argued that:

> Actions along the lines of his remarks will certainly be unpopular in Iran, but they will be good for Iran. Since the Shah is already unpopular among his people, it is most advisable for him to stop worrying about temporary political reactions, carry on as a strong man with military support, and give the nation the bitter medicine it needs. If he is to fall, this line might hasten his fall, but it also opens up the possibility that if he lasts a few years more, he will not fall at all.

Given this kind of support, it is little wonder that the Shah wanted more weapons for the army and worried about US commitment to his regime. The Shah expected criticism from 'positive neutralists' like Nehru and Nasser, but the paucity of US aid and negative views of his regime were galling.[19] Aligning with the West and pursuing pro-Western policies had netted the Shah disappointing amounts of aid, growing domestic criticism, threatening foreign criticism, and the increasingly negative evaluation of his allies. Despite the Shah's predisposition to paranoia and his inability to accept responsibility for his own actions, he had real problems.

Playing the Soviet card

In December 1957, concerns about 'growing' Soviet influence in Tehran came to the fore. Coming at the same time as rumors concerning a union between Egypt and Syria, it placed additional pressure on Eisenhower and Dulles. The British Ambassador to Iran, Sir Roger Bentham Stevens, reported to both the Foreign Office and his American counterpart in Tehran on 'excellent progress' by the new Soviet Ambassador, Nikolai Mikhailovitch Pegov, in improving Iranian-Soviet relations. Labeling it a Soviet 'good neighbor policy', the British ambassador pointed to increased exchanges in trade and cultural delegations and in discussions about Soviet technical assistance. The British argued that given the 'sensitive and suspicious' nature of the Iranian people and the perceived lack of tangible results from Iran's relationship with the West, significant Soviet gains were a real possibility. The Soviet propaganda machine compared social and economic gains in the Soviet Central Asian republics to the relative lack thereof in Iran. Stevens commented: 'If the disparity is too great an explosive situation will build up.'

While the Soviets were making inroads, Sir Roger and the British had an ulterior motive. They were pressing the US to either join the Baghdad Pact or significantly increase military and economic aid to its members. Moscow, of course, wanted Iran to withdraw from the Pact, to support Soviet policies in the Middle East, and to declare neutrality. To achieve these goals, the Soviets had altered their tactics from the stick to the carrot, with what the British termed 'impressive' results.[20] Given the chronic concerns about the Shah and Iranian stability, this report further alarmed Washington. Although contesting some of the details, the US Embassy in Tehran grudgingly agreed that the Soviets had indeed been making headway.[21]

In late January 1958, on the eve of the formation of the UAR, a concerned Dulles visited Tehran for talks with the Shah. US aid had resulted in little real economic improvement. The land tenancy and ownership system perpetuated the enrichment of landowners at the expense of the peasantry.[22] Dulles hoped to 'pacify the Shah' on the subject of aid before the Baghdad Pact meeting in Ankara.[23] In meetings with Dulles, Prime Minister Manuchehr Eqbal and Minister of Court Husain Ala raised the Soviet offers of aid and better relations. The Iranian leadership pointed out that Soviet largesse in Syria, Egypt, and Afghanistan had created a public, negative comparison with US aid to Iran. They complained that the US had given $250 million to non-aligned India and wondered aloud why Washington could not help its ally. Eqbal told Dulles that the Soviets had offered to assist Iran in meeting its budget crisis. He then argued that given the Soviet danger, the United States needed to join and actively participate in the Baghdad Pact. On the defensive, Dulles blamed Congress for limiting aid to Iran and for barring US entry into the Baghdad Pact.[24] Some of the meetings were explosively contentious. At one point, in a meeting with CPO Director Ebtehaj, Dulles point-blank refused to provide $100 million to balance the Iranian budget and $100 million in loans. Ebtehaj became angry and stated that he 'did not mind whether he remained in his job or not, to which Mr. Dulles replied that Mr. Ebtehaj must not suppose that he himself or the U.S. Government minded either!'[25]

Through Pakistani Prime Minister Malik Firoz Khan Noon, the Iranians let it be known that they were considering withdrawing altogether from the Baghdad Pact. Noon, of course, claimed that only his personal intervention had prevented it. While Dulles conceded that the 'psychology' of increased military aid to Iran in the form of tanks, artillery, and training programs might have some positive effect, the Secretary told the Iranians that: 'a new world war would start with a Soviet attack on the United States, not on Iran. He did not, therefore, consider that it was necessary for Iran to have a large army which would only deflect her energies from economic development.'[26] For economic development, he offered the Iranians an additional $30 to $40 million in US Development Bank loans to help with budget deficits over the next few years.[27] Relieved, Dulles reported to Washington that he 'hoped' the new aid would take 'a good deal of the heat off the [Baghdad Pact] Ankara meeting.'[28] The Secretary sweetened the offer of additional US aid by asking the Shah to make an 'informal visit' to Washington for conversations with President Eisenhower.[29] Despite the threats and pressure, Dulles steadfastly pushed economic development as the primary means of maintaining Iranian stability and containing the Soviet Union.

Despite his best intentions, Eisenhower felt obliged to put together another 'limited' military aid package in an attempt to appease the Shah and hopefully get him to focus on economic development; the risks of cutting the Shah off from military aid were too great. In April 1958, British Foreign Secretary

Selwyn Lloyd, an advocate of more US aid, accurately described the importance that the West attached to maintaining the Shah's regime, stating that it was 'largely benevolent and ... more beneficial to Iran and to Western interests than that of any conceivable alternative'.[30] During this period, the Shah took a proactive hand in his quest for additional military aid. Just prior to his July 1958 trip to Washington, rumors began to appear that the formation of a new Iranian cabinet, more friendly to the Soviet Union, might be in the offing. The palace would neither confirm nor deny the rumors.[31] Although a transparent threat, any mention of improved relations between Iran and the Soviet Union caused concern.

Dulles warned Eisenhower that the Shah, unhappy with repeated rejections for military aid, might attempt to get a commitment in their one-on-one meetings.[32] The fundamental objective was to convince the Shah that regional security rested not on Iranian military power but on the US military deterrent.[33] In the meetings with the President, the Shah asked the US to 'take a broader view (of) his defense needs'.[34] He argued that a military buildup in Turkey, Pakistan, and Iran would emphasize the US support for 'constructive nationalism', as opposed to the 'positive neutralism' espoused by the non-aligned camp.[35] He made it clear that he believed his support for the West and participation in the Baghdad Pact had earned him better consideration. Shrewdly, the Shah addressed military matters only in generalities, allowing officials in his entourage to badger the State and Defense departments about specific Iranian requirements.[36] On Arab issues, the Shah expressed his opposition to US aid for Nasser and argued for programs to counter Nasserist influence. He recommended that King Saud be 'built up' as the center for Arab opposition to Nasser.[37] Had he been clairvoyant, the Shah could not have better timed his visit or his requests for additional military aid.

The Baghdad coup and Iran

Iranians of all political persuasions had accepted the possibility, if not the probability, of a coup in Baghdad. These views of Iraqi instability and rumors of plots against the Baghdad regime had mirrored similar rumblings in Iran. Nevertheless, the ferocity and rapidity of the coup in Baghdad stunned everyone. Though truly frightened, the Shah recognized opportunity when it knocked. Wasting no time, on 15 July 1958, the Shah informed the US Embassy that: 'Arms are life or death now.' Arguing that the Egyptians and the Russians now had Baghdad Pact defense plans, the Shah predicted its collapse, leaving Iran 'alone' to face the Soviets and their allies.[38] Also taken aback by the reversal in Baghdad, Eisenhower wrote the Shah on 19 July, promising that the United States now intended to bring the Iranian military up to 'agreed operational strength and to a high level of operational efficiency', including stepped-up deliveries of equipment and intensified training schedules.[39] On 20 July, the Shah cited the 'changed situation' and pressed the US Ambassador, Edward T. Wailes, for a reassessment of the requests for military aid made in Washington in the preceding week. The ambassador reassured the Shah, but emphasized the need for additional support in the field of internal security.[40] Eisenhower and his advisors had already discussed the fact that the Shah apparently failed to comprehend that it had been the Iraqi army which had overthrown the Hashemite regime; and it was the Iranian amy that the Shah wanted to strengthen. In Washington, the administration authorized an additional $50 million in assistance to Iran, and, fearing disaffection in the army, placed the highest priority on promoting internal security.[41]

The coup in Iraq also brought disturbing reactions on the street in Iran. The coup shook what little shaky confidence existed in the Pahlavi regime. Middle-class elements opposed to the regime were buoyed by the collapse of the Hashemites, while pro-Western supporters of the Shah feared the worst. All expected 'something' to happen in Iran as well. On the news of American and British intervention in Lebanon and Jordan, pro-Western elements optimistically awaited Western action to 'reverse the situation in Iraq'.[42] When it became apparent that there would no moves against the Baghdad regime, political supporters of the Shah predicted worsened relations with Iraq, in the expectation of a Nasserist- or an increasingly Communist-dominated, pro-Soviet regime. Opponents of the Shah's rule, classified as 'Mosadeqist intellectuals and other representatives of the militant side of the urban middle class', agreed that relations with Iraq would worsen significantly, but they welcomed such increased hostility. Discounting the Communist and Soviet threat, the Shah's opponents believed that hostility from Baghdad would hasten the fall of the Shah and his 'corrupt regime'. Sophisticated observers in official Iranian circles had expected the Hashemite regime's collapse for some time, and despite some private misgivings, they recognized the new Iraqi government in relatively short order – much to the consternation of many Iranian conservatives.[43]

Time seemed to increase the 'concern and uncertainty' of pro-Shah elements, while anti-Shah groups appeared increasingly confident. Comments about the assassination of the Shah could be heard in street conversations. Rumors spread that the Shah was more and more 'depressed'. Palace security had been strengthened and arrests of army officers heightened tensions.[44] The US Embassy warned that a move to force the Shah into a constitutional role could be in the offing, and speculated that in that event the Shah would flee, as he had in 1953. Although it seemed unlikely in the 'immediate future', the Embassy also reported that: 'The possibility of coup to overthrow the monarchy cannot be disregarded.' The lack of immediate substantive reforms made 'the overthrow of the monarchy likely'.[45] Washington redoubled its efforts to force the Shah to enact reforms.[46] As the situation worsened, Iranian requests became even more outlandish. In December 1958, Ebtehaj, the Director of the CPO, began to argue for more economic and budgetary assistance because of the 'U.S. military's pressing upon the Shah's armed forces in excess of Iran's needs'.[47] The Iranians had obtained the military assistance that the Shah had sought for over five years, and now blamed it for Iranian budgetary problems and demanded increased economic aid. Washington was trapped in the labyrinth of a Persian bazaar.

The British analysis of the post-Baghdad coup situation in Iran did nothing to alleviate the general alarm. London compared the situation in Tehran to that in Iraq. British Ambassador Sir Roger Stevens' report that compared the Hashemites' long and 'holy' lineage, traceable to the 'grandfather of the Prophet himself', to that of the Shah, the son of an 'upstart and illiterate soldier', prompted derision at the State Department. Stevens made the interesting observation that the Shah had less in common with King Feisal II than with the hated Crown Prince, Abd-al-'Ilah, the *de facto* Iraqi ruler. Abd-al-'Ilah's lack of contact with the people of Iraq and corruption made him an unsympathetic figure. Stevens concluded:

> There is every reason why what happened in Iraq should also happen in Iran. In practical terms the Iranian regime is more oppressive, less enlightened, and less efficient than its Iraqi counterpart. If this regime does survive, it will not be due to its merits but to defects in the organization of the opposition, to the absence of any explosive force quite corresponding to Arab nationalism, and perhaps to greater vigilance on the part of the authorities induced to some extent by the Iraqi example.

The Embassy stated that the events in Iraq had 'palpably increased' the danger to the Shah's regime and encouraged more radical opposition to his rule.[48] Sir Roger added that if he were 'an ostrich', he could paint a 'rosy' picture of progress under the Shah, but 'the extent to which the overt expression of public dissatisfaction has grown in the last few weeks is truly remarkable.' Stevens called 14 July 1958 'a watershed in Iranian thinking about their own future'.[49]

It quickly became apparent that any competition for influence between Tehran and the new regime in Baghdad would occur in Kurdistan. The turmoil in Baghdad generated intensified interest in the Kurdish areas along the Iranian-Iraqi frontier. With an estimated 1.5 million Kurds in Iran, two million in Turkey, and another 800,000 in Iraq, the Kurds became a source of concern. On the positive side, Kurdish unrest in Iraq constituted a potential lever to pressure good behavior from the Qasim government; on the negative, Soviet support and the strong leftist influence among Kurdish groups potentially threatened Iranian territorial integrity. Fortunately for Washington and Tehran, the Kurds in Iraq and Syria were far more affected by events than those in Iran. Despite leftist tendencies among some Kurdish groups, they generally viewed pan-Arab nationalism as a threat to Kurdish autonomy, making Kurdistan a more potent lever against Baghdad than Tehran. That said, the Eisenhower administration discouraged Tehran from attempting to use Kurdish nationalism against Baghdad, fearing that such a policy might backfire in both Iran and Turkey.[50] While the Iranians wished to exploit the Kurdish view that they were 'distinct from and superior to their Arab neighbors', the new regime in Baghdad also grasped its potential vulnerability and promised to promote 'Kurdish national rights within Iraqi unity'.[51] To counter Iraqi efforts to co-opt the Kurds, the Iranian government sent General Timur Bakhtiar, Director of SAVAK, to Kurdistan. He invited all Kurds in Syria and Iraq to consider Iran their 'motherland'. Predictably, the move to co-opt the Kurds provoked more requests for Western aid to support infrastructure improvements, roads and bridges in the Kurdish regions of Iran.[52] The palace argued that these improvements served the dual purpose of providing tangible benefits to the local population while allowing better access to the region for Iranian security forces. The Iranians held the short-term advantage in Kurdistan, but fearing a pro-Soviet Kurdish tilt, the British and Americans intensified monitoring of 'leftist' Kurdish elements, particularly those residing in the Soviet Union.[53] In Iraq, Washington's Kurdish efforts resulted in the closing of the US Consulate in Kirkuk. Fearing an Iraqi and Soviet reaction, the administration announced: 'The United States can have no part in encouraging any disloyal action by the Kurds in Iraq.' Washington pressed the point with the Shah that inciting Kurdish 'dissidence ... would be a dangerous game'.[54] Eisenhower intended to avoid any actions that might destabilize the Shah's regime.

A new relationship with Tehran

Late 1958 found the Shah more dependent than ever on Western support, but ironically more in control of the relationship than at any previous point. The 'Bastille Day coup' in Baghdad, as Sir Roger Stevens called it, created new realities in the Shah's relationship with the West. No matter how problematic, the Shah had to be placated and supported. Ever manipulative, the Shah had learned that utterances about withdrawing from defensive agreements and proposed trips to Moscow netted much more than quiet cooperation. Thanks to Qasim, from 1958 onwards the Shah's leverage in his relationship with the US would steadily increase. Iraq irrevocably changed the nature of the Anglo-American relationship with and over Iran. The Gulf had been something of a British lake for 150 years but now the British found themselves in a defensive posture, hanging on with Washington's support. As a result, British diplomatic efforts focused heavily on influencing Washington's Iranian policy. US political and military support for the Pahlavi regime became the guarantor of British commercial and economic interests, not only in Iran but throughout the Gulf as well. A symbiotic relationship developed between British policy recommendations to Washington and the Shah's requests for economic and military aid. London wanted to keep the Shah happy and in power, and they wanted Washington to pay for it. With regard to the Shah, the Foreign Office believed that Britain could not afford to 'return to our old practices of active benevolence and unsolicited advice', believing that Britain's strength since 1953 lay in 'non-intervention'. In contrast, the American Chargé, John W. Russell, got a two-minute audience in which the Shah asked: 'Had the Iranian

Ambassador in Washington lately been advising President Eisenhower on how to run the United States of America?' The Shah made it clear that he resented US advice. In criticism, Russell commented to the British Ambassador: 'After all, who loves a governess?' Apparently someone at the FO was more sympathetic to the US's predicament and penned in a marginal comment: 'Most children!' The British took the attitude that pushing reform in Persia was a waste of time and usually counter-productive as well.[55]

In contrast, Washington would not give up pursuit of a long-term solution to Iran's problems through reform and some form of political liberalization. The Eisenhower administration truly believed that it not only had an obligation to push reform, but that reform would work in the long run to stabilize Iran. Shaken by Iraq and fearing the same in Iran, London encouraged Washington to desist from its reform campaigns and to focus instead on specific policies that affected Iranian relations with the West.[56] London viewed the internal situation in Iran as irreparable, and reforms as a likely destabilizing factor. 'The shah remains the most important piece on the board. If he falls, the game is over.' London could not envisage any subsequent regime that would be 'remotely tolerable'. The shaken British believed that, just as liberalization may have played a role in the collapse in Iraq, in Iran liberalization would let the 'Djinn ... out of the bottle' and invite a Bastille Day in Tehran.[57]

Chapter 5: Controlled Democracy – Pakistan and 1958

As in Iran, the Baghdad coup altered the US relationship with Pakistan. Pakistan formed the lynchpin connecting Western defense organizations in Southeast Asia to those in the Middle East. A member of both SEATO and the Baghdad Pact, Pakistan's adherence to a pro-Western orientation constituted a critical element in containment policy. As in Iran, US intelligence sites, located near Peshawar, provided critical data on Soviet military activities, including missile development and deployment. It also served as a base for U-2 flight operations over the Soviet Union. This reliance on Pakistan had grown steadily during the 1950s to the point where the Eisenhower administration could not, under any circumstances, contemplate the loss of Pakistan, either as a member of the Western containment structure or as a physical platform for intelligence operations targeted against the Soviet Union.

To a considerable degree, Pakistan's policies vis-à-vis the United States mirrored those of Iran. Karachi's primary bartering chip was its willingness to support Western strategic interests vis-à-vis the Soviet Union in return for military and economic aid. Karachi then used US aid to compete with non-aligned India, its real regional rival. Using its leverage, Pakistan extracted not only aid but also Western political and diplomatic support in its struggle with India over Kashmir. As in Iran, Pakistan government officials speculated and debated the benefits and drawbacks of non-alignment or improved relations with Beijing or Moscow. There were also differences. Where Iran was a relatively isolated issue, US support for Pakistan complicated relations with India. As the interdependency of the US and Pakistan grew, Nehru became increasingly antagonistic toward both. Short of placing US economic aid for India at risk, Nehru strongly advocated non-alignment and UN membership for Beijing to goad the Eisenhower administration. During 1956 and 1957, increasing tensions between New Delhi and Karachi placed Washington in the increasingly difficult position of maintaining good relations with the world's largest democracy on the one hand, and with an ally critical to containing Communism on the other. The events of 14 July 1958 would push the value of Pakistan as a Western ally to the fore and ultimately send India in search of alternative partners to counterbalance the increasingly close ties between Pakistan and the US.

Straddling the fence: the US, Pakistan and India 1956-1958

As pointed out earlier, US military assistance to Karachi and its adherence to SEATO and the Baghdad Pact caused US-Indian relations to take a sharp downturn in 1954 and 1955. These frictions not withstanding, relations improved somewhat in 1956 as a result of the Suez crisis. The Eisenhower administration sought Nehru's assistance in attempting to settle the Suez controversy, and although this assistance was unsuccessful due in large part to Krishna Menon's diplomatic shortcomings, Eisenhower and Nehru both opposed Israeli, British, and French intervention. Hoping to exploit the temporary confluence in US and Indian policy, Eisenhower invited Nehru to Washington.[1] The administration wanted to explore future areas of cooperation in the Middle East and Asia with Nehru. On 17-18 December 1956, Nehru and Eisenhower met and discussed the situation in the Middle East, among other topics.[2] Nehru was clearly concerned about the safety of the canal, given its importance as the principle trade route from India to Europe. He downplayed concerns about Arab nationalists 'responding to the whims of a Nasser' and the need for a counterbalance like King Saud. Nehru argued that Nasser actually represented the lesser evil and served as a 'brake' on the more radical elements in the Egyptian military. He also proposed the idea that the US should consider supporting the Egyptian ruler, with the goal of strengthening his internal position. At the same time, Nehru deflected attempts to get him to influence Nasser to compromise with the West, saying: 'We must make an earnest attempt to settle the underlying grievances in the region.'[3] Raising the issue of the Baghdad Pact, Nehru underscored Indian concerns about the potential for a Pakistani attack using US supplied weapons. He cited Pakistan as the principal cause of Indian 'resentment' toward the US.[4]

When Eisenhower initiated a discussion of Kashmir, Nehru provided a detailed summary of the dispute and offered the Indian view that the United Nations need only accept the status quo, and Pakistan would follow suit, albeit with some 'grumbling'. Arguing that Pakistan and its stability were critical to the Western defensive posture in the Middle East, Eisenhower attempted to find some basis for a mutually acceptable settlement of the issue. Nehru simply refused to discuss any solution except the status quo;[5] this unwillingness to entertain any compromise did not bode well for the future. For internal political reasons, neither Pakistan nor India could afford to compromise. For Nehru, the risk of surrendering any Indian territory in a plebiscite invited demands from untold numbers of groups wanting to assert their own regional prerogatives. Nehru and the Congress Party could blame the British for the creation of Pakistan, but would have only themselves to blame if a Kashmiri plebiscite favored Pakistan and opened the Pandora's box of Indian regional nationalisms.

1957 and the Kashmir dispute in the UN

The US position on Kashmir reflected Washington's assessment that only bilateral talks at the prime-minister level could possibly achieve a settlement; the administration correctly believed that referral to the UN would simply result in a Soviet veto, on behalf of India, of any constructive resolutions.[6] In 1957, the Indian parliament declared Kashmir an 'integral part of India', sparking demands from Pakistan for the long-delayed plebiscite and questioning the legality of the accession of Kashmir to India. The Pakistanis wanted the Security Council to pass a resolution against the integration of Kashmir into India, dispatch UN troops to Kashmir to replace Indian and Pakistani units, and immediately begin to set up a plebiscite.[7] The Indians interpreted the Pakistani move as a British-inspired attempt to embarrass the Indian government in retaliation for India's support of Nasser during the Suez crisis in 1956. Wanting to avoid a fight at the UN, the US and Britain obtained a temporary compromise by getting Security Council support for sending the President of the Security Council, Gunar V. Jarring, on a fact-finding mission to the region. Jarring had been the Swedish ambassador in New Delhi and knew Nehru well. Arriving on 14 March 1957, he shuttled between New Delhi and Karachi for four weeks; he returned to New York and submitted his initial report on 29 April 1957. The report called on Pakistan and India to adhere to the decisions of August 1948 and January 1949. It criticized the lack of progress and called for a plebiscite. It stated that both India and Pakistan should 'refrain' from statements or acts that might 'aggravate the situation'.[8] The plan called for a five-step process leading to a plebiscite. A 'no war declaration' by both governments was to be followed by a UN force in Pakistani Kashmir and the withdrawal of all but 6,000 of Azad Kashmir militia from the region. An administrator would then oversee the plebiscite.[9]

The Pakistanis now wanted a Security Council resolution. Knowing that the outcome would be a Soviet veto, Washington and London delayed. Pakistan's Huseyn Shaheed Suhrawardy vociferously complained that despite Pakistan's bilateral defense agreements with the US and the fact that 'there was no question about the action which should be taken on the Kashmir question', the Eisenhower administration was more concerned about its relations with India.[10] US officials in Washington and New Delhi had hoped, to no avail, that the Jarring mission would provide a respite from Indian criticism of the US and an opening for some new approaches.[11] Now, as Pakistan made veiled threats about its relations with the US, India rejected calls for a plebiscite and labeled the Jarring report a pro-Pakistani document created by the British, Americans, and their allies. As one observer put it, the Indians had no intention of pursuing a course that 'might lead anywhere'.[12] London viewed the outlook for avoiding a confrontation with India as 'bleak'.[13] As US Ambassador Ellsworth Bunker put it: 'India will not agree to a plebiscite, principally for the reason they can least afford to talk about, i.e., fear that this would give rise to communal strife which might develop to uncontrollable proportions affecting ... the foundations of the secular state which they are trying to establish.'[14] Knowing they would be the 'biggest losers' diplomatically, London and Washington searched for an alternative despite the fact that a solution acceptable to one party would, by definition, be unacceptable to the other.[15]

On 10 July 1957, Pakistani Prime Minister Suhrawardy visited Washington and made an all-out effort to obtain US support for a plebiscite in Kashmir. Eisenhower told Suhrawardy that the US would support Pakistan's call for a plebiscite in the UN 'so long as no other solution is mutually agreed on by both parties'. The president pointed out the likelihood of a Soviet veto, and counseled patience on taking the UN route.[16] In a meeting with Suhrawardy, Secretary Dulles told the Prime Minister that countries in the Middle East were focusing on military aid to the detriment of economic development.[17] In the end, Pakistan agreed to delay until Jarring submitted his final report. In October 1957, Jarring formally reported to the UN, stating that he had made no progress on a settlement over Kashmir because of the Indian argument that Pakistan was in violation of the 'cease-fire' agreement. Pakistani Foreign Minister Firoz Khan Noon then presented the Pakistani position, and a proposed compromise resolution.

In response, Krishna Menon launched into a five-and-a-half hour speech that 'reiterated probably more intransigently than ever India's stand'.[18] Menon rejected a plebiscite because it inferred that Kashmir was neither a part of India nor of Pakistan, declaring that 'Kashmir was an integral part of the Indian Union, separable only by an act of the sovereign Parliament of India.'[19] Menon delighted in categorically rejecting the Jarring report, stating: 'We are open to settle any matter peacefully and by negotiation. But the security of integrity and unity of the nation are not matters for argument.'[20] Knowing that US animosity toward Menon made him the wrong messenger, the Indian government, on 9 October 1957, sent Tiruvallur Thattai Krishnamachari, the Indian Minister of Finance, to 'explain' its position to Eisenhower, while seeking more economic aid. When asked about Kashmir, Krishnamachari explained that the current government in Pakistan was not 'strong enough to assume responsibility for a decision on Kashmir'. He then expressed the real fear in Delhi: 'If Kashmir should be lost to India the Congress party would fall from power.' Krishnamachari then restated his request for additional US economic aid, citing India's defense requirement to counter the threat of US and other Western arms shipped to Pakistan.[21]

During 1956 and 1957, the Indian central government faced an increasingly strong challenge from separatist groups, particularly in the south of the country. In a report to the American Universities Field Staff in May 1957, Executive Director Phillips Talbot discussed Indian issues in a state-by-state format. While commending the Congress and Nehru on India's progress toward 'unity in diversity', he stated that the 'politically fissiparous tendencies in free India' showed just how far India and Nehru had to go. In an article entitled *Raising A Cry for Secession*, he analyzed the 'Ambitions of the Political Dravidians' in South India. Because of its unclear 'ultimate' goals and localized political support, the *Dravida Munnetra Kazhagam* or Dravidian Progressive Federation (DMK) and its separatist message 'portends to many thoughtful persons the possibility of a future threat to a Indian unity'. While noting the differences in context, Talbot compared the Tamil DMK to the Muslim League of the 1930s. His article included a DMK cartoon depicting Mohandas Karamchand Gandhi saying that Muhammad Ali Jinnah would give up his demand for Pakistan and equating that with the Congress position on the DMK.[22]

The Tamil cultural identity traced its royal origins back to the Chola kings (907-1310 CE). The political platform, a potential political bombshell, included 'full freedom to secede from the Indian Union', nationalization of industry, readjustment of the five-year plans to industrialize South India, reductions in defense spending, and the inclusion of all Tamil-speaking areas under the same political organization, to be renamed Tamilnad. The DMK made other demands as well. As a Madrasi Brahman commented: 'That's the one trouble with India, each part of the country not only has its separate language and literature but also its great royal tradition. These help feed the fire of regionalism under our new democratic system. Each group wants to recreate its past greatness.'[23] Talbot clearly viewed regionalism based on language, culture, and/or religion as a real threat to the Indian national polity. This simultaneous threat from the DMK merely reinforced the determination of Congress and its leadership to resist any notion of a plebiscite on Kashmir and Jammu. Viewing compromise on Kashmir as a threat to the political existence of the Congress Party and national unity, Nehru and India rejected calls for compromise and relied on the Soviet veto. Under pressure from Pakistan, the US and Britain supported the Pakistani position on the plebiscite only to see it fall as predicted to Indian intransigence and the Soviet veto.

Pakistan and the search for stability

In October 1957, Suhrawardy's government fell, in part because of the machinations of Pakistani President Iskander Mirza, a major-general, who had never been particularly happy with Suhrawardy and his policies. The collapse of Suhrawardy's government created a chaotic political situation as a multitude of political parties vied for advantage. The economy also stagnated, undermined by rampant corruption. In this environment, Foreign Minister Firoz Khan Noon became Prime Minister, leading what the US Embassy described as a 'wobbly' ruling coalition with 'yet another political crisis' in the wings.[24] Pakistani instability increased, along with concerns in Washington about its defensive alliances and the threat posed to containment. In Washington and London, a consensus existed on at least one aspect of Pakistan's future, namely that the only real unifying factor was Pakistani fear of India. Pakistanis by and large blamed the British and Lord Louis Mountbatten, who they believed were in collusion with Nehru and had attempted 'to undercut the foundations of Pakistan at its inception by gerrymandering the border and by preventing Pakistan from obtaining its allotted share of the partitioned assets'.[25] Street opinion followed consistent themes: first politicians had little creditability because they changed parties and programs on a regular basis for personal political gain; second, a general frustration with political instability permeated civil life; and third, corruption permeated all levels of society. As one frustrated businessman put it: 'We need a Hitler to get out of the mess we are in.' In addition, Pakistan had its own secessionist problems. The split between East Pakistan, the Pashtun-Afghan areas, and West Pakistan created a significant hurdle for the government in Karachi. On the positive side, the 'government's writ' controlled most of the country, the civil service worked well enough to prevent collapse, the judiciary had maintained its independence, and the army was 'first class'.[26] This assessment of the military and its British-trained officer corps would turn out to be the critical issue for the future.

London also worried that all the historical good will between Pakistan and Britain was potentially at risk due to instability and a lack of progress on Kashmir. In April 1958, the CRO official in Karachi, Sir Alexander Symon, stated that the perceived lack of clear-cut Anglo-American support for Pakistani with regard to Kashmir undermined relations. He worried that faltering economic development would combine with estrangement from the Muslim world and further aggravate these problems. Symon called for more US aid, viewing it as the primary prop that maintained Pakistan's loyalty to the West.[27] The fact that India was viewed as 'non-aligned' and more successful than Pakistan, which had 'chosen to identify itself with … the free-world in military alliances that Indian policy makers abhor', raised questions in Karachi about the benefits of partnering with the West.[28] Pakistani doubts intensified when in April 1958 Nehru rejected a meeting with Pakistani Prime Minister Noon to discuss Kashmir. Nehru stated: 'The kind of meeting suggested by Dr. Frank Graham, the proposed UN mediator, would place the aggressor and the aggrieved party on an equal footing.' Nehru welcomed bilateral talks but stated that the presence of a third party gave the appearance of mediation when there was, in fact, nothing to mediate.[29]

This rejection of UN efforts led directly to the personal involvement of President Eisenhower. On 17 April, Dulles sent a memorandum to Eisenhower suggesting that the United States attempt to facilitate a solution to the problem of Kashmir. The Secretary recognized that friction between Pakistan and India over Kashmir undermined the US and opened the door for Soviet advances. Dulles proposed to link disputes over the Indus waters, Kashmir, and arms, so that a 'wider field for compromise will exist'. He told Eisenhower: 'This approach, I am convinced, could best be initiated by a personal appeal from you to the leaders of both countries. In this we would, in strict secrecy and without prejudice to our present position if the new approach were unsuccessful, offer our good offices to assist them to reach agreement on all three questions.'[30] The president reacted enthusiastically, stating that he was 'all for the approach' but that it must be undertaken in the 'utmost secrecy'. He offered direct involvement if the moment were right; 'In fact, if there should ever be realized sufficient progress in negotiations to warrant the hope that a personal gesture might help assure success, there is no inconvenience at which I would balk.'[31] Eisenhower believed that a solution to Kashmir would put US relations with India and Pakistan on a sound footing, bring a focus to economic development, maintain Pakistan in the Western defense alliances, and, most of all, preserve US intelligence bases in Pakistan.

On 14 May 1958, Eisenhower wrote to Nehru, proposing that the United States send a 'special representative' to facilitate talks on Kashmir. The President argued that perhaps the US might be well-placed to provide 'good offices' because of its extensive aid and its good relations with both New Delhi and Karachi.[32] The Pakistanis welcomed the offer, while Nehru stalled. He stated that while he had problems with certain aspects of the proposal, it was interesting and that he would discuss it with his cabinet. Nehru countered that the presence of a third party, while perhaps helpful, might result in leaks, which, given the upcoming elections in Pakistan, could increase its 'unpredictability and uncooperativeness'.[33] On 8 June, Ambassador Ellsworth Bunker reported from Delhi that Desai, acting on behalf of Nehru, told him that Nehru wanted to continue US involvement through normal diplomatic channels – meaning Bunker in New Delhi and Ambassador James M. Langley in Karachi. Bunker believed that the Indians saw that the 'negotiations would be a long-range operation' and wanted to wait for the outcome of the Pakistani elections. Recognizing the difficulties, Bunker added: 'It may take a year or two years or even more to reach desired solution but I think that patience, perseverance and the logic of events will ultimately bring us to success.'[34] In reality, Nehru's 'leaving the door open' was a stalling tactic pure and simple. He did not want to tell Eisenhower no.[35]

In Pakistan, time was running out for the parliamentary politicians. As early as May 1958, General Mirza indicated to US Ambassador Langley that the military were discussing a takeover to deal with the political instability. The generals wanted to suspend parliamentary elections scheduled for the fall. Officially, Langley informed the generals that such a step should only be taken as a last resort, but that ultimately it was a Pakistani decision.[36] By summer, Langley's visits to President Mirza's office had become so frequent that his name was removed from the daily log of visitors. Pakistani newspapers routinely published the list of visitors and Langley's visits were drawing attention. Langley's access also became a conduit for Pakistani politicians to deliver messages to Mirza. Aware of what was coming, Washington warned the Ambassador that in the event of a coup, the US could not be seen as having orchestrated it.[37] Clearly, the military had lost all patience with the politicians. In May 1958, the US Consul in Dacca, the capital of East Pakistan, commented that Mirza had created a stir with talk of postponing the elections and cautioned strongly against supporting a coup. He argued that a 'Mirza dictatorship' would strengthen the hand of the Communists and provide a pretext for Indian agitation in Bengal, while destroying the US's reputation.[38] Ideally, Eisenhower and Dulles preferred to avoid a coup, but should Noon be defeated, Pakistan would continue to face political instability, economic deterioration, and international problems, including, in the administration's mind, possible Communist penetration.[39] The fear of Communist gains in staunchly Muslim Pakistan seemed overblown, but the fear of a weak government opting for some form of non-aligned neutrality was a serious possibility. By July 1958, the prospects for stability in Pakistan appeared remote. Washington concluded that Pakistan needed at least temporary political stability as a basis for economic development, the key to long-term stability. The internal political situation, coupled with the Kashmir dispute, undermined both.[40]

The Baghdad coup and Ayub Khan

Washington was already on edge over stability in Pakistan when the Iraqi coup pushed the administration over the brink. There was also talk that the Karachi government might negotiate with the Soviet Union for economic assistance in the form of a steel mill. This combination of events created enormous alarm on the Potomac that Soviet economic aid, combined with the collapse of Iraq, might undermine the commitment of the Pakistani government to the Western defense alliances and thus threaten containment. Fearing the 'gravest injury' to US interests, Eisenhower and his advisors edged toward the position that democracy and economic development might be the key to long-term stability, but without some short-term fix for the political chaos, Pakistan might be lost to the West.[41] The inability of the Pakistani political parties to act responsibly and work together to alleviate the economic crisis and political chaos heightened concerns in Washington. Rather than increasing stability, the upcoming Pakistani elections loomed as a source of even greater political instability.[42] Eisenhower and his advisors concluded that the benefits of a stable, pro-Western Pakistan took precedence over other considerations, including political democracy.

In early October, President Mirza informed Ambassador Langley that the Pakistani military had decided to take over the government. Mirza wanted Langley to give him an idea of the US reaction. Having had more than enough of Pakistan's chronic instability, Washington instructed Langley to tell Mirza that countries had the right to determine their own form of government based on what was best for the welfare of its peoples. Undoubtedly, given the intelligence interests related to the Peshawar facility, Washington knew full well from other sources about the intentions of the military, but there is no evidence that the Eisenhower administration did more than give Mirza and Ayub a nod; the Pakistani generals did not need any US support to take control. In early October 1958, Mirza and the Army Chief of Staff, General Muhammad Ayub Khan, took over the government and canceled parliamentary elections. Mirza told Ambassador Langley that the military had waited until the situation had become severe enough and the politicians had made big enough 'asses of themselves', so that the move would have widespread support.[43] An audible sigh of relief was heard in Washington following the Mirza-Ayub 7 October takeover. In private, administration officials believed that the coup had produced Pakistan's first 'stable, strong, unified government'. The lack of violence, the few arrests, and a crack-down on corruption boded well for the military regime.[44] In a further political consolidation, Ayub Khan took complete control on 27 October, and sent Mirza into retirement. In Washington, the administration believed that this move would be 'likely to improve the situation generally in the country'.[45]

The apparent contradiction between supporting a military dictatorship under General Ayub and official support for democracy and representative government created a real dilemma for the Eisenhower administration. Viewed in the context of Iraq, no one in Washington wanted to take a chance with Pakistani instability. Still, officials at the State Department and the White House had hoped for a better option. In essence, security issues had dictated a compromise of fundamental principles. In this regard, Fred Bartlett, the South Asian desk officer, wrote:

> When the takeover [in Pakistan] took place so soon after the Iraq and Burmese 'incidents', I was very dispirited. It seemed to me that the takeover meant that in one more country, and a country which was a good friend of the United States, the light of the democratic ideal had been snuffed out. What made it worse, in my personal opinion, was that because of the larger issue of national freedom versus Kremlin hegemony, we were not in any position to protest.

Because the Indians viewed the Communist threat to Pakistani as a 'hoax' to acquire arms for its confrontation with India, New Delhi saw US support for a military dictatorship as the height of hypocrisy. The irony was not lost on the US government. In New Delhi, Ambassador Bunker questioned the efficacy of new aid to the Pakistani regime shortly after Mirza and Ayub overthrew the parliamentary system. Bunker argued: 'The consequences in the long run for the moral standing and reputation of the US in India, and indeed elsewhere may be serious.' Bunker also feared that support for Ayub's dictatorship might strengthen the hand of Communists and leftists who were arguing for a non-democratic solution to India's political problems.[46] Regardless of its concerns about the reaction in India, Washington informed Ayub that 'whenever appropriate and within its available resources [the] USG desires [to] assist GOP in future as it has in past.'[47]

The Indian Embassy in Washington reported to New Delhi: 'The abrogation of constitutional government in Pakistan and assumption of full powers by a military junta failed to cause any serious concern in the USA.' The Indians viewed US support of a military dictatorship as a continuing trend to preserve authoritarian regimes that supported containment. They argued that the 'assurances' given by the 'military dictators of Pakistan of continued support for military alliance' guaranteed continued US support for the Pakistani regime. The Indian Foreign Ministry took a particularly negative view, arguing that Karachi's participation in the Baghdad Pact, coupled with the increased military aid to Pakistan, was a clear attempt 'to browbeat India'. These developments also served to underscore the lack of importance Washington placed on the 'hard earned Indo-US good will of recent years'. The embrace of Ayub and military rule in Pakistan increased Indian disappointment that improved US-Indian relations lacked a higher priority. In addition, the fact that Pakistan now had a priority over India in the immediate aftermath of the Baghdad coup increased Indian frustration with the US.[48]

The split between supporters of a pro-Indian and a pro-Pakistani policy intensified within the US government. This competition had existed from the moment India and Pakistan emerged as independent nations. Cold War imperatives and Indian insistence on non-alignment forced trade-offs between what the Eisenhower administration viewed as its immediate security interests and its long-term goal of economic development and stable, pro-Western, democratic governments in the region. In New Delhi, Ambassador Bunker stressed accommodation and economic development, the cornerstone of democratic development, a view shared by both Eisenhower and Dulles. Bunker stated:

> In many of the newly independent countries where political freedom has come before economic freedom, the roots of democracy are shallow and the plant itself withers quickly when subject to adverse [political or economic conditions]. ... [W]e must constantly keep the long-term battle for men's minds ... in the forefront of our thinking. ... Massive military aid to countries with a weak economic base is not in the long run a genuinely effective course of action, even from a military point of view. It is building on sand.[49]

The tone of the exchanges between the Indian and US governments was that of political equals. While acknowledging the efforts of President Eisenhower on behalf of world peace, Nehru made it clear that he believed the US misread the events in Iraq and Lebanon, and reacted in a manner that threatened the gains made by Washington since the Suez crisis of 1956. Just as he disagreed with US actions in Lebanon and the evaluation of Nasser and Iraq, Nehru saw no linkage between the coup in Iraq and any necessity to arm or support a Pakistani military dictatorship.[50]

Ambassador Bunker clearly viewed Washington's position on Ayub's October 1958 coup as a factor further damaging US credibility. No doubt disturbed by having to justify the US position to Nehru, he argued:

> One of the strengths of the United States throughout the world and also here in India has been that, while many question our judgment, on the whole they have not questioned our motives or our basic principles. This

is a priceless asset and it disturbs me greatly to see us getting into a position where we can be thought to be departing from our fundamental convictions to serve expediency.[51]

Eisenhower viewed support for the military government in Pakistan as an expediency necessitated by containment. As for India, the administration pursued its preferred long-term strategy for stability, namely economic development and support for political democracy as a bulwark against Communism. To counter the negative propaganda related to supporting the Ayub coup, the US initiated a campaign to 'make [the] Indian people conscious of [the] magnitude [of] US assistance, both absolutely and in relations to the Soviet effort'. Washington wanted 'steady progress in India's economic development under democratic institution'.[52] As Ambassador Bunker put it: 'it is not in the United States' interest to see India's economy collapse, notwithstanding divergences' in political policies. 'India is the key to the direction things will take in this part of the world.'[53] There were debates in Washington over the amount of aid and financial policies for India, but the focus remained on economic development. This contrasted sharply with the situation in Pakistan, highlighting the fundamental contradiction between support for economic development through democratic means in India and that for the expediency of stability through military rule in Pakistan.

Washington had to make an exception for Pakistan, the 'cornerstone of US policy in this part of the world' and the 'anchor of the Baghdad Pact and of SEATO', particularly when this system was 'in real danger of being wiped out if something is not done to arrest the deterioration in many aspects of Pakistani life'. Pakistan's 'Byzantine' political milieu threatened vital US interests; therefore, the pragmatic requirement for pro-Western stability took precedence.[54] Eisenhower and Dulles needed a new policy to rationalize their support for military rule in Pakistan. Ambassador Bunker suggested that the US take 'practical steps' to mitigate the contradiction between supporting a military dictatorship and 'our proclaimed devotion to democracy'. He called for the adoption of a policy that 'emphasized economic aid and play[ed] down military support'. Washington argued that it focused aid on the 'people rather than the military dictatorship'. The administration rationalized that the Ayub interlude constituted a 'temporary bridge' on Pakistan's road to permanent representative government, and was consistent with Washington's 'ultimate support' for democracy.[55] Nehru had always been uneasy with what he believed to be the US tendency to emphasize the military aspect of its alliances in order to contain the Soviet Union and China; now, with a military government in control of Pakistan, these concerns escalated.[56] The Eisenhower administration was discomfited by the necessity to support Ayub, but it concluded that the successful containment of the Soviet Union required stable, pro-Western governments and an atmosphere conducive to economic development. If it required 'temporary' military rule to deliver these preconditions for success, then so be it.

Part II: Revising Containment, 1959-1960

1959 marked the beginning of a significant shift in emphasis for US foreign policy in the Greater Middle East. The Eisenhower administration moved toward more pragmatic policies driven by situational requirements. The goal was still containment, aimed at undermining Soviet influence and the potential for Communist gains in the region. US policy continued to utilize military assistance, economic aid, and support for controlled reform, but the application became significantly more sophisticated. The change reflected the Eisenhower administration's improved apprehension of the regional situation. The Baghdad coup also served to simplify, and to focus Washington on, its pragmatic interests in the region. To prevent a repetition of the Iraq disaster, Eisenhower and his advisors were far more willing to provide military and security assistance than they had been prior to July 1958. Security aid had now become a prerequisite for economic development and reform. At the same time, Washington had become more cautious in advocating reform.

Other factors were in play as well. John Foster Dulles, the implementer of and lightning rod for Eisenhower's foreign policy, was increasingly incapacitated by cancer and would die by early spring. Eisenhower understood Dulles, as he put it, 'Until I thought I understood the inside of that man's mind as I knew my own.'[1] With Dulles' passing, Eisenhower decided to enter the Cold War fray with his own brand of personal diplomacy. In addition, the picture in the Middle East had altered radically for the British. With pretensions of imperial prerogatives now gone, the British, girding to defend what was left of their influence and economic interests in the region, played second fiddle to Washington and always sought Washington's concurrence on important policy issues. On the fringes of the Middle East, increasing competition and conflict between China and India placed Nehru on the diplomatic and ideological defensive. Indian denunciations of Western defensive alliances and regional policies moderated as New Delhi became more aware not only that it needed Western economic aid, but also that it might need friends in a potential confrontation with Beijing.

The emergence of an alternate center for Arab revolutionary agitation in Baghdad, backed by Iraqi Communists, renewed the old courtship between Washington and Cairo. At the same time, Nasser's attempts to reassert his authority as a revolutionary leader created strains between the UAR and much of the Arab world. Washington no longer feared monolithic Nasserism because it had encountered something worse – Communist-backed Iraq. Qasim's regime in Baghdad and its dependence on the Communist Party of Iraq (CPI) for support represented the worst of Washington's fears for the region. For Nasser, Qasim's dependence on the Communists created a different sort of aggravation. Communist support allowed Qasim to curb pro-Nasserist and pro-Ba'thist elements and effectively rejected Nasser's leadership. In a nutshell, Washington and Cairo now had a common problem, which overshadowed their chronic conflicts.

The negative reverberations of Washington's anti-Iraqi, anti-Communist, and pro-Nasser stance were particularly strong in London and New Delhi. Lubricated by Iraqi oil, the British government, with some alacrity, put the unpleasantness of July 1958 behind it and came to a working agreement with the Qasim government. Qasim's Communist connection, although problematic, was secondary to securing the future of British oil interests in Iraq. In this regard, the US had become a liability, as growing hostility from Cairo, with the appearance of American backing, threatened the British arrangement. The British, with some justification, viewed strengthening ties between Washington and Cairo as the latest round in the Eisenhower administration's aggravating infatuation with Nasser. Just as in 1954 and 1956, what the British viewed as a misbegotten relationship again reared its ugly head and threatened important interests in the region. The British argued vehemently that Qasim was not a Communist and that pro-Nasserist and pro-Ba'thist pressure merely increased his reliance on CPI support. Again aggravating, the Americans appeared willing to accept the inevitability of the collapse of traditionally pro-Western Arab regimes with ones headed by more radical nationalists or by Nasserists.

The Hashemite collapse in Baghdad made the survival of the Pahlavi regime in Iran critical to US interests in the region – a reality not lost on the Shah. The demands from Tehran escalated, accompanied by the Shah's comments about the benefits of neutrality. Although the administration's push for reform continued, placating the Shah and enlisting his support became the priority. The size of the military assistance group (MAG) in Tehran increased dramatically, as did US support for internal Iranian security organs. At the same time, the Eisenhower administration intermittently urged the Shah to give up direct rule, hoping to broaden his political support. Washington continued to view the government in Tehran as critically unstable, and began a systematic program to shore it up. In contrast, the British argued that Iran was simply unfixable, and that no matter how bad the situation became, there was no alternative to the Shah. To the British, Iran was simply Iran; any change in government in Tehran would be detrimental to Western interests. The British consistently warned Washington that attempts to tinker with reforming the Iranian system had the potential to bring about its collapse.

The post-1958 situation also had important implications for India. In Washington, the 'Communist threat' made maintenance of the Baghdad Pact, which became CENTO, a critical priority. India was important, but Pakistan constituted the eastern anchor of the Western defensive posture in the Middle East and the western anchor of SEATO. In addition, the United States had to maintain its intelligence facilities at Peshawar. Thus, Pakistan, with its new military government under General Ayub Khan, had to be courted, even at the expense of relations with India. To deal with the aggravation that was sure to follow in New Delhi, the administration proposed to offer additional economic aid to encourage an 'inward focus' away from the rivalry with Pakistan. Washington worked with India in policy areas on which they agreed, but anticipated areas of sharp disagreement and minimal Indian support for US diplomatic initiatives. Unable to solve the problems in the region, the Eisenhower administration now focused on core US interests: containment of the Soviet Union and its potential allies.

Chapter 6: The Arab Cold War and US Policy

Rather than ushering in a new age of Arab unity and solidarity, the Iraq coup signaled the beginning of what Macolm Kerr so aptly described as the 'Arab Cold War'. This period constitutes one of the most important and least examined periods of the history of the Arab Middle East. In addition, the implications of the Arab Cold War for the rest of the Greater Middle East have also been largely ignored.[1] The United States, Britain, and the Soviet Union found their regional interests and strategic goals subordinated and often frustrated by the parochial interests of political leaders and states in the region. They also discovered that the more their policies took regional issues into account, the greater their potential for some success. During this period, the Eisenhower administration displayed, comparatively speaking, a great deal of flexibility in adjusting containment policy to this reality. In terms of pro-Western allied states, containment policy continued to focus on military assistance, economic aid, and reform, but in dealing with non-aligned and at times hostile neutrals, it added a new dimension. US policy took an increasingly pragmatic view of the regional political situation and then calibrated how to employ aid or pressure to moderate anti-Western policies. US-UAR relations were a case in point. Eisenhower and his advisors learned that small amounts of economic aid, coupled with US political support for Cairo in the Arab Cold War, netted more for US containment strategy and influence in Cairo than all the threats and boycotts of the past. Nasser could not be bought, but to some degree he could be temporarily leased or enlisted for tactical political gain. It was not a strategic solution to US problems in the region, but it was far superior to what had transpired between 1955 and 1958.

Iraqi coup leaders Aref and Qasim
Abd-al-Salaam al-Aref and Abd-al-Karim al-Qasim shortly after their successful 14 July 1958 coup in Baghdad. Within months, Aref would be in prison, sentenced to death for plotting with Nasser against Qasim. Ironically, his sentence commuted, Aref would lead the February 1963 coup against Qasim, who was captured, tried and executed within the first 48 hours.

Nasser and the revolution in Iraq

In late 1958, Nasser's stature in the Greater Middle East and the non-aligned world symbolized and, to a large extent, defined the dynamic for change in the Middle East; however, the emergence of an alternate revolutionary power center in Iraq forced a policy reevaluation in Cairo. Initially, Nasser worked cautiously and patiently to maintain the façade of Arab unity and civility as the Qasim regime adjusted to its new responsibilities. Nasser's patience stemmed at least in part from the confidence generated by his phenomenal run of political good fortune. Like the Eisenhower administration, Nasser really believed that he was 'the wave of the future'.[2] Undoubtedly, Nasser had jumped to the same conclusion as everyone else, namely that the strong pro-Nasserist elements in the Qasim regime and broad support for Nasser in Iraq would translate into an alliance, or perhaps union. Qasim's intentions were unclear but nevertheless, the Egyptian leader, his advisors, and his Syrian allies believed that Qasim would ultimately embrace the Nasserist formula or succumb to those who did.

This confidence colored Cairo's initial dealings with Baghdad. It reflected what would turn out to be a misplaced confidence that the ultimate outcome was a foregone conclusion. Nasser believed that he could afford to wait, and thus focused on his more immediate concern with Lebanon. By December 1958, disturbances in Iraq between the Ba'thists and Communists demonstrated the ability of the Communists to mobilize the masses against any movement toward union with Egypt. That same month, Qasim claimed that his security forces had uncovered a conspiracy against the revolutionary government instigated by Rashid Ali al-Gaylani. Gaylani was the former Iraqi colonel who had led the 1941 coup against the monarchy and British. Gaylani was arrested, tried, and sentenced to death. Qasim commuted the sentence to life in prison. Simultaneously, the pro-Nasserist Abd-al-Salaam Aref, who had been shipped off to Bonn as Iraqi Ambassador because of his Nasserist leanings, returned to Baghdad without permission. He was summarily thrown into prison, and after a brief trial received a death sentence as well. Aref's detention brought widespread arrests of Ba'thist and Nasserists.[3]

The reaction in Cairo was predictable. Nasser began to have second thoughts about his theory that patience with Qasim would pay off. Qasim clearly had his own ideas about the future of Iraq, and the discipline and organizational skills of his Communist allies now appeared to be a real threat to Nasser's brand of Arab unity. The US Embassy shared Nasser's concern about Communist discipline. Decribing the ability of the ICP to take advantage of the death of one its 'Popular Militia Force' in a clash with 'Ba'thist Arab Nationalists', the embassy reported:

> Communist Arabs cannot be fit into the molds, which have become the clichés to describe Arabs. They (the Communists) are not lazy, are not lacking in ability to cooperate, coordinate, and they obviously are willing to follow directions. Their performance in action on an increasing number of newsworthy occasions is timely, doctrinaire and impressive. Public attention is drawn to their rallies, parades, speeches and petitions whenever they occur. They demand, and get, the ear and eye of Iraqis.[4]

In Washington, officials became increasingly convinced that Qasim, in order to maintain power, had grown too reliant on the Iraqi Communists and was now unable to control them. The Communists became the focus of Egyptian ire and Western concern for two somewhat different reasons. The US had a straightforward fear of a Communist takeover. Nasser's hostility stemmed from the fact that ICP support for Qasim allowed him to pursue a course independent of the UAR, and encouraged Communist and anti-UAR elements in Syria.

This clash between Cairo and Baghdad produced another festering issue as well. Nasser's neutralism and relations with the Soviet Union had made Egypt the center of diplomatic and non-aligned activity in Africa and the Arab Middle East. It had in fact propelled his meteoric rise in world affairs. All roads in the Arab and non-aligned world seemed to wind their way through Cairo. As one observer put it: 'There were hardly enough palaces in Cairo to house all of the dignitaries who came on visits in January 1959.' Be that as it may, the situation between Nasser and Qasim complicated UAR relations with Moscow. As the Ba'thists and Nasserists struggled with Qasim and his Communist supporters for control of Iraq, Nasser found himself stuck between his need for Soviet military and economic assistance and his profound antipathy toward the ideological competition from Iraq and the Communists.

Qasim's refusal to come to terms with Nasser threatened Cairo's newfound political and diplomatic prominence, and potentially undermined Nasser's position with his Soviet benefactors. The Baghdad press heightened the acrimony by accusing Nasser of plotting against the new regime in Iraq 'just as he previously plotted against the Iraqi monarchy'. Worse still, the Soviet Union sided with Qasim.[5] The Soviet Union wanted the Iraqi republic to remain independent of Egypt for two reasons. First, the Kremlin believed that a large, unified Arab and largely Muslim super-state in the Middle East might excite similar aspirations among the Soviet Union's Muslim minorities. Second, Qasim relied on the ICP for his grip on power, and the ICP had close ties with Moscow. For the Russians, this situation translated into more potential influence in Baghdad than in Cairo. In addition, Nasser's crackdown on Egyptian and Syrian Communists aggravated Moscow, and their relationship with Qasim had potential as a counterweight against growing anti-Communist-based rapprochement between the US and the UAR.[6]

Conflict with the Soviet Union

On 23 December 1958, the simmering disagreements between Nasser and Qasim developed into an open conflict with the Soviet Union. In a speech at Port Said, Nasser charged that the Syrian Communists had 'rejected Arab nationalism and Arab unity' and 'called for separation' of Syria from Egypt. He labeled separation as 'the call of the Zionist ... and reactionaries'.[7] Nasser also pointed out that the Arabs had resisted not only the crusaders from the West, but also the 'Tartars' from the East – a comparison not lost on the Soviets.[8] In January 1959, Nasser sent Khrushchev a letter, via the Soviet Ambassador in Cairo, Evgeny Kiselev. The letter, something of an ultimatum, stated: 'We consider that the fate of Iraq affects us and we are not going to leave it under the Communists. But we do not want this to be the cause of a quarrel with the Soviet Union. You must decide whether you want to deal with the Arab people or only a few isolated Communist parties.'[9] On 27 January 1959, in the opening address at the 21st Communist Party Congress in Moscow, Khrushchev predictably lashed back at the 'campaign being conducted against progressive forces in some countries under the spurious slogans of anti-Communism'. To add insult to injury, he also spoke highly of Qasim. The Soviet leader then pointedly named the UAR as the principle culprit, stating: 'The struggle against Communists and other progressive parties is a reactionary undertaking' that served the interests of 'imperialist' forces.[10]

The Egyptian leader had made a pointed reference to Egyptian independence and Soviet support for building the High Dam at Aswan, stating: 'We are ready for cooperation with the Soviet Union, but we shall no more sell our freedom for roubles [*sic*] than for dollars.' Khrushchev responded: 'They say they don't want to sell their independence for roubles. Let me remind them that we didn't impose our aid on them.'[11] Replying from Damascus, Nasser accused the Soviet Union of reneging on its official position, that the suppression of the Communist Party was an internal Egyptian affair, and on its professed commitment to *pancha sheela*, the 'five principles' of the 1954 Colombo Conference. These included non-interference in the internal affairs of other nations.[12] In a strongly-worded letter to Khrushchev, Nasser demanded that Moscow declare its 'exact intentions toward the U.A.R.'. For added emphasis, Muhammad Husayn Heikal launched a broadside in *Al-Ahram* the next day. Under the 'large red headline' of 'Frankly', the article explained that Egypt and the Soviet Union were friendly 'despite, and not because of, the local Communists'.[13]

Taken on balance, the view that the 'entire Iraqi affair had the magical power of spellbinding the Egyptian leader' may not be far from the truth.[14] Since Bandung, no other leader in the Arab world had come close to Nasser's stature.[15] In addition, his credentials in the non-aligned movement and his relationship with the Soviet Union had further enhanced his clout. Now Qasim threatened it all. In addition, Qasim had oil, and an economic alliance with his old enemy, the British; he had the support of the ICP and increasingly of the Soviet Union. Qasim was positioned to threaten Cairo's Syrian adventure with Moscow's apparent blessing. Nasser also personally disliked Qasim, a man that he never met. Qasim was a crude affront to Nasser's image of Arab nationalism.[16] On 20 February, Moscow, now alarmed with the escalating rhetoric coming from Cairo, responded to Nasser's letter with a letter of flattery and goodwill, blaming the rift on the 'evil agents of imperialism'.[17] Those evil agents on the Potomac were increasingly pleased with the developments.

Iraq and the Syrian connection

In retaliation for UAR propaganda attacks, Qasim encouraged anti-Nasser agitation in Syria. He provided moral and material support to the Syrian Communists and fanned anti-UAR sentiment. Baghdad called for Syria to sever its ties with Cairo and enter into a union with Iraq. This agitation took advantage of the rising discontent in Syria over Egyptian domination of the UAR governing apparatus. Nasser became increasingly dependent on the services of Colonel Sarraj, the head of Syrian internal security, and the most steadfast of the UAR supporters in Syria.[18] By 1959, disillusionment with the union was growing as the Syrians found themselves marginalized in a centralized Egyptian system that had little in common with the traditional political and economic structure of Syria. Dissatisfied Syrian groups became progressively more than receptive to anti-Egyptian machinations. The Ba'thists, disappointed in Nasser's refusal to adopt their Arab socialist principles, had a final falling-out with the Egyptian leader, and were eliminated from power. The fact that Nasser's quarrel with Qasim had damaged that part of the Syrian economy associated with Iraqi trade complicated matters for Cairo.[19] Additionally, Egyptian-style bureaucracy and corruption transformed Syria into a colonial market for Egyptian goods. Finally, Nasser's attempt to gain support through land reform and nationalization backfired. He failed to understand that a strong, stubborn middle class, tied to every facet of Syrian life, including the military, existed in Syria. In addition, the Syrian military were discontented because Egyptians received the key posts and promotions.[20]

Like his boss in Cairo, Sarraj had enjoyed a string of good luck, and had now set his sights on an even bigger prize – the regime in Baghdad. Sarraj, undoubtedly with Nasser's strategic if not tactical approval, set about planning the overthrow of Qasim's regime. He recruited pro-Nasserist and pro-Ba'thist elements within the Iraqi military and government.[21] Whether or not Sarraj exceeded his mandate from Cairo, he certainly had clearance from Nasser for a destabilization campaign against Qasim. Fearing just such a coup, Qasim spent February and March removing nationalist and pro-Nasserist ministers and officers from the government and army. In their place, he elevated personal supporters and Communists. It was obvious that serious trouble was brewing. In late February, Allen Dulles reported to the NSC: 'In Iraq, rumors circulating of action being organized in the north against Qasim regime, with "cue" to be given by Nasir.' The same report expressed concern over the growing influence of the ICP in the press and government.[22]

The trouble came on 6 March 1959. Communists called for a rally in Mosul, which sparked the premature revolt; fighting broke out between Communists and local nationalists on 7 March. On 8 March, prominent leftists and pro-Qasim elements in Mosul were arrested, and the coup was underway. A lack of coordination with plotters in Baghdad doomed the revolt from the beginning.[23] Sarraj had not only supplied the Mosul coup leadership, headed by Iraqi Colonel Abd-al-Wahhab al-Shawwaf, with material support, but also with Syrian and UAR manpower. The Iraqi plotters had radio equipment that still bore their Syrian markings and some of the infiltrators wore their Syrian uniforms. UAR complicity in the coup was undeniable.[24] Qasim's security forces rounded up the opposition in Baghdad and then counterattacked the rebels in Mosul. Shawwaf was killed and resistance rapidly collapsed. Upon recapturing Mosul, troops loyal to Qasim, along with the Communists, many freed from jail, ran wild: 'By the time it was suppressed, naked mutilated bodies hung from lampposts.'[25] For a week, the wealthy, Ba'thists, nationalists, and Nasser's supporters faced the frenzy of semi-judicial tribunals and summary executions. Already paranoid, Qasim now used special courts to destroy his internal opposition, while Radio Baghdad and the Iraqi press pilloried the UAR and thoroughly embarrassed its leader.[26]

Nationalists and pan-Arabists were eliminated from the government, while the confidence of the Iraqi Communists and Soviet hopes surged.[27] The Communist organizations in Baghdad published a list of eight demands following the failed coup. These demands called on the government to purge the army and state of conspiratorial elements; withdraw immediately from the

Baghdad Pact; carry out all death sentences immediately, including those against Aref and Gaylani; arm the People's Militias; arrest elements of 'doubtful' loyalty; entrust key positions only to those of proven loyalty to the 'present democratic republic'; take a clear stand on all elements opposed to the republic; and finally, demand that the UAR 'stop encouraging internal and foreign plots nourished by imperialism against our dear republic, fortress of Arab nationalism'.28 Qasim also declared most of the Egyptian embassy staff in Baghdad *personae non gratae*, and charged that Nasser had planned the coup attempt 'down to the smallest detail'. The Baghdad press blasted Nasser: 'Abdel Nasser is revealed as the great plotter, enemy, shedder of blood. Those who proclaim pan-Arabism and raise Abdel Nasser to the rank of prophet have been exposed. Nasser sent arms to Mosul because he wanted to annex Iraq to his kingdom.'29 Baghdad called Nasser the 'foster son of American imperialism'.30 To forestall UAR propaganda attacks related to Iraq's continued membership in the Baghdad Pact, on 24 March Qasim formally withdrew. Foreign Minister Hashim Jawad told British Ambassador Sir Humphrey Trevelyan that the move would allow Iraqis to assume a 'neutralist policy which membership in the Pact did not allow'. The Iraqis asserted that they wanted to maintain 'the most friendly relations' with the members of the Pact, but without participation.31

Privately holding Sarraj responsible for the failed coup, Nasser launched a violent campaign in the UAR press and radio against Qasim and redoubled his efforts to overthrow the Iraqi leader. He accused Qasim of delivering Iraq into the hands of the Communists. The Egyptian leader also saw the hand of the British at work in Baghdad. By attacking Qasim for his Communist support and the Russians for providing it, Nasser put the British in the position of having to maintain its position in Iraq with the IPC without coming into conflict with the anti-Communist positions of the United States. Cairo partially succeeded in portraying the British as lukewarm anti-Communists.32 The British preferred Qasim to Nasser and made little secret of it. London even continued to supply the Iraqi army with weaponry and support.33 Nasser also saw the British hand in warming relations between Iraq and Jordan. In response, he lashed out first at the Communists and then at the enemies of Arab unity, while simultaneously seeking more support from the United States.34

Washington's 'Red Scare' over Iraq

Concern in Washington about Iraq had returned to its July 1958 levels. This was driven to a large degree by the steady flow in intelligence reports about growing Communist influence. Some government circles, particularly those around Vice President Richard Nixon, were openly discussing and advocating either overt or covert military intervention. On 17 February 1959, a Special National Intelligence Estimate (SNIE) concluded that Qasim lacked the 'ability to stem the movement toward a Communist takeover'. The report cast doubt on Qasim himself being a Communist, but offered a bleak picture of continued

Communist successes. It noted that, fortunately, the security services and Ministry of the Interior had remained in the hands of non-Communists.[35] The aftermath of the failed Mosul revolt further aggravated Washington's concerns. John D. Jernegan, the US Ambassador, reported that: 'Overt signs point sharply Left.' He stated that the 'Basic question remaining is whether Qassim and GOI [Government of Iraq] are too along road to Communism to turn back and whether Iraq consequently is fated to be first Soviet Satellite in Arab World.' Seeing a 'grave danger' that in 'the short run' Iraq would 'come under preponderantly Communist control', Washington searched for a stopgap solution.[36]

The State Department wanted to reduce Communist influence, and queried the Embassy in Baghdad on a number of options. These included: offering continued military aid despite Iraqi withdrawal from the Baghdad Pact; a direct warning about the dangers of Communism; an orchestrated warning about Communist subversion from Turkey or Pakistan; or the possibility of providing discreet but 'direct encouragement or assistance' for Nasser's efforts to 'reverse [the] tide of events in Iraq' by direct intervention or by cutting the oil pipeline through Syria.[37] The prospect of working with Nasser also received a boost in Washington; William Lakeland, the same person who had served as liaison between Nasser and the British in 1954, had become the head of the Iraqi desk at the State Department. Lakeland had had a close relationship with Nasser and Heikal in the early 1950s and he strongly believed Nasser to be far preferable to Qasim. As a result, he was receptive and supportive of policy based on fears of a Communist takeover in Iraq.[38]

In Cairo, Nasser had no intention of putting up with Qasim or the Communists. He fed US fears of a Communist coup. On 5 March, Allen Dulles told the NSC: 'Events seem to be moving in the direction of ultimate Communist control.' The CIA Director underscored his interpretation of events by pointing out that Qasim had just appointed his brother-in-law, Colonel Fadhil Abbas al-Mahdawi, to the post of Minister of the Interior. The Director added: 'This individual is either an out-and-out Communist or very nearly one.' Secretary Dulles stated that the situation in Iraq 'perhaps dictates some U.S. contact with Nasser' because 'we seem to be confronted ... with a choice between Communism and Nasserism and the latter seems to be the lesser of two evils.'[39] Eisenhower grumbled at one point that making a choice between Qasim and Nasser was like a 'choice between Al Capone and John Dillinger'.[40]

The consistent reports supporting the position that a Communist takeover likely sprang, at least in part, from three other issues that had arisen in the intelligence community. The failure to predict the Iraqi coup in July 1958 and the subsequent criticism of the intelligence agencies created an impetus at the CIA not to be wrong again. To report that a Communist coup was possible or even probable and have it not occur was far more acceptable than to report the opposite and then witness a Communist takeover. The intelligence community was taking no chances in its reporting. Also there was a very high degree of interest in the Iraq situation among policy-makers. This translated into a desire for as much information as possible on the situation there. As a result, priority given to reporting on Iraq gave an added, if inadvertent, emphasis to the administration's concerns. Lastly, and this is more difficult to assess, there was the issue of John Foster Dulles' illness and the personal and professional effect that this had on his brother, CIA Director Allen Dulles. As Senate Foreign Relations Committee testimony and the reaction of the press to the Iraqi coup showed, Allen Dulles faced considerable criticism for the 'intelligence failure'. In early 1959, his brother Foster was dying of cancer and would resign his position as Secretary of State. In addition to the personal loss, Allen Dulles faced the professional uncertainty of a world without Foster as Eisenhower's principal foreign policy advisor. Reporting on Iraq that emphasized the threat of a Communist takeover served two purposes. First, it protected the Director from the charge of an intelligence failure, and second, it made him a useful ally for those within the administration, particularly Vice President Nixon, who advocated a more aggressive response to the Iraqi situation. In short, the message that key administration officials wanted to hear also offered political protection to the Director. These influences undoubtedly added urgency to the growing alarm. Fortunately, an experienced President would choose the ultimate course of action.

Initially Washington believed that London shared a similar concern about the situation. In reality, the British were more concerned about US and UAR actions undermining the British IPC or the interruption of Iraqi oil flowing through UAR-controlled pipelines. US mutterings about intervention in Iraq made London very nervous. On 22 March 1959, Macmillan and Eisenhower met and discussed the Iraqi situation. Eisenhower pushed for the formation of a joint working group to study contingencies for Iraq in the event of a civil war or a Communist takeover. London actually welcomed the working group because it provided a window on US plans and an opportunity to influence US policy. The British believed that they could make US intervention 'doubtful' but wanted Washington to come to that conclusion 'independently'. The British cabinet concluded: 'We should avoid appearing to push them into a decision one way or the other.' In the event that Wasington decided to intervene, London would then decide whether or not to try to dissuade them. In a cabinet paper, with the notation that the contents had already been discussed with the Prime Minister and Foreign Secretary, the British laid out their position, under the heading 'The status quo':

> It has always been our appreciation that our interests are best likely to be served by Qasim's maintaining himself in a position dependent neither on the Communists nor on the pro-Nasserites and able to pursue a central and neutralist line of policy. ... So long as Qasim remains in power and continues to give evidence of his intention to maintain the independence of Iraq we should not countenance, still less encourage, any designs against him from any quarter.

Courtesy of National Archives
Meeting of British and Americans over Middle East, 1959
British Foreign Secretary Selwyn Lloyd, President Eisenhower, Prime Minister Harold Macmillan, and Secretary of State John Foster Dulles meeting in February 1959 on the Middle East situation in general and Iraq in particular. Dulles was to die of cancer in May.

The Eisenhower administration had not categorically endorsed non-intervention; however, it now agreed that under the present circumstances 'non-intervention' was 'the right policy'. The cabinet recommended that the British and US 'clandestine services' develop 'contingency plans' in the event of a civil war. The paper directed that Israel, Iran, Turkey, and Jordan be warned not to act against Iraq or the UAR without consulting the US and Britain.[41]

The British also believed that they had managed to convince the Americans that doing nothing was the best course: no arms, no warnings, and absolutely no conniving with Nasser. The British warned Washington that the 'Iraqi charge that Nasser [was] acting as [the] cat's-paw for imperialist[s]' had gained wide acceptance in the Arab world. Selwyn Lloyd had already met with the Acting Secretary of State Christian A. Herter at the British Embassy in Washington and requested US pressure on Nasser to restrain his current attacks on Qasim. Herter demurred, stating that Nasser might misinterpret such action as siding with Qasim, thus undermining the UAR's current anti-Communist campaign. Herter added that there was no indication that US intervention with Nasser would have the desired effect anyway, and expressed his reluctance to take any direct action in that regard.[42] Noting that the situation in Iraq 'presented a very dark picture', the State Department cited the 'rapprochement' with Nasser and his 'effective campaign' against Communists and the Soviet Union. Herter and Rountree did not want to take any drastic action in the region that might undermine US gains with the UAR. They urged covert encouragement to Nasser's anti-Communist campaign, stating: 'We have already taken steps to make clear to Nasser that we approve of what he is doing and that we support him in this battle.'[43] In short, Nasser's anti-Communist campaign, with its fall-out for Qasim, was too important to US policy goals to risk sending the wrong message to Cairo and 'any assistance to Iraq would be greeted by both press and congressional hostility.'[44]

The British were apparently having more success at influencing US views in Baghdad. Ambassador Jernegan supported the 'cessation of Nasser's personal attacks on Qasim'. Desk officers in Washington noted that: 'In fact, however, it has been clear for some time that the State Department suspects Jernegan of sharing to some extent the undue optimism – if one can call it that – about Qasim's position and prospects that they, and to an increasing degree the American press attribute to H.M.G.' London's influence was also reflected in Jernegan's message to Washington on the pipeline issue:

> We think it would be serious error if UAR cut oil pipelines at this time. Step would immeasurably exacerbate UAR/Iraq feud and would strengthen rather than weaken Qassim [*sic*] regime. West would inevitably be blamed along with UAR, whereas Soviet bloc would have good opportunity tighten hold on country by extending increased aid to cushion shock of 'imperialist' squeeze on oil revenues. Iraq would no doubt demand large loan from IPC to tide it over fiscal emergency, under threat of nationalization.

Jernegan was getting a reputation for being too much under British influence. Aware that his recommendations might not sit well, he apologized that his 'cogitation' resulted in a 'generally negative reaction' to Washington's queries about what proactive action could be taken. Aware of the proximity of his position to that of the British, Jernegan acknowledged London's 'deep aversion to Nasser', and tried to distance himself from their views by commenting that the British 'declare somewhat greater confidence' in Qasim than was warranted. Jernegan added: 'We recognize they [the British] may yet be proven right. In any case, we see no present alternative to support of Qassim [*sic*].'[45]

At the same time, the Eisenhower administration sought to maintain a 'correct but friendly attitude' toward the Iraqi government, while making 'energetic efforts to persuade' allies that they were underestimating the danger of a Communist takeover. The policy statement concluded that the United States should coordinate closely with the British and jointly examine the steps that might be required, if military intervention became unavoidable.[46] There were those in the administration, including Vice President Richard Nixon, who took a more aggressive stance. Nixon believed that the State Department position was too passive and that Iraq could not be allowed to go Communist. He felt that the US had to be prepared to replace the Qasim government before the Communists could take control.[47] Nixon wanted a 'Mossadegh type operation' to overthrow Qasim and put pro-Western military officers in power.[48] No doubt Nixon was influenced by the consistent reporting, since the failed Mosul coup, of Communist gains, and privy to the information that Director Dulles reported to the Senate Foreign Relations Committee on 27 April that the Communists had moved from a position of 'negligible influence' under the old regime 'toward a position where they will exercise outright control, be it from the façade of a "national front", or as an outright "people's democracy".' The failure of the Mosul coup and the resulting Communist gains had markedly increased fears of a Communist takeover.[49]

On 17 April, Nixon chaired the NSC meeting. He questioned Assistant Secretary Rountree at length on the State Department suggestion that the United States wait and see what would happen in Iraq before taking any aggressive action of a military nature in that country. At this point, Rountree argued that the United States would have to wait until the Communists actually came to power, so that Arab opinion would swing in favor of intervention or of US incitement of the Iraqi military to overthrow the regime:

> The revulsion against any government set up under [US] aegis would be so great that it would probably be swept away and its replacement would in all likelihood be a Communist government. Thus for this reason alone we cannot advocate this course, apart from the long standing United States principles which would be violated by what would in effect be unprovoked United States aggression and apart from the catastrophic psychological reaction throughout Africa and Asia which would inevitably portray us as being worse aggressors than the Communists.[50]

Fearing a Communist takeover, Nixon was no doubt trying to assert himself and lay claim to a substantive role in foreign policy. The 1960 election was only 16 months away and he was trying to build his image as a substantive decision maker in the administration. John Foster Dulles was terminally ill with cancer and had just resigned, and Eisenhower was in Georgia playing golf. Allen Dulles, not wanting to be 'wrong again' on Iraq offered assessments of the Communist threat that played to Nixon's fears. Nixon also made it clear that he believed the traditional foreign policy apparatus would never recommend military or covert action, no matter how grave the situation. As a result, he made it plain to those present that he wanted to see more aggressive options, both covert and overt, to potentially deal with the problem in Baghdad. Nixon's effort to assert himself notwithstanding, the majority of those present at the meeting would only agree that plans might be necessary but that the situation required no immediate action.[51] On his return to Washington, Eisenhower sided with Rountree's assessment, which reasoned that intervention would undermine other US relationships in the region and that when US forces departed from Iraq the government it had put in place would be shortlived.[52]

Coming to terms with Qasim

Concerns about a more aggressive US posture on Iraq did not preclude encouraging Nasser. In a policy assessment in April 1959, the State Department acknowledged that: 'While we have not directly linked with Nasser's present campaign against communism [and] the steps we have recently taken to aid Egypt, there is no doubt that Nasser knows that we have taken these steps as a sign of approval of his current campaign and that they have emboldened him in his anti-Communist efforts.'[53] Washington approached Nasser 'to explore parallel measures which the US and the UAR might take' with regard to Baghdad, and expressed support for his anti-Communist campaign. Nasser responded with a predictable request for more aid to enable his program to continue. While the US and UAR attempted to undermine Qasim, London pursued an accommodation with him, lubricated by the flow of Iraqi oil. To justify this policy, London took the position that 'Iraq will preserve an attitude of independence and neutrality', and offered to continue arms shipments to Baghdad. Although agreed to by Eisenhower, British arms sales raised eyebrows in the US and NATO. At an NSC meeting, Nixon now groused that apparently 'the British thought they could make a deal with the Iraqi Communists [because] they considered Nasser a greater danger than the Communists to the Near East.' Eisenhower added that fundamentally the British felt that 'Nasser cannot be trusted.'[54]

British Ambassador Sir Humphrey Trevelyan applauded Macmillan's decision to provide arms, stating that it would 'encourage ... some vestige of independence' from the Qasim regime. London explained that arms for Qasim and the army made both less dependent on the Communists and their Soviet sponsors. Trevelyan stated: 'Conversely a refusal would be profoundly depressing and demoralizing to Qasim's anti-communist supporters who want to retain links with the West. It might indeed have the effect of just pushing Qasim himself over the communist brink. Her Majesty's government therefore believes that the action they are taking is in the best interests of the Middle East as a whole.'[55] The Ambassador also pressed London for assistance in reducing the level of UAR attacks on Qasim by having a third party, perhaps Tito, go to Nasser with the suggestion. The British were absolutely convinced that the UAR attacks, coupled with internal agitation, were in fact dangerously increasing the leverage of the Communists over the regime.[56]

Sir Humphrey wanted London to help 'the Americans find it possible to take a more positive line with Qasim in spite of the unfavourable features of the situation'.[57] Trevelyan argued: 'One of our main problems is how to improve relations between the Americans and Qasim.' This obsession with improving US-Iraqi relations constituted an on-going project for the British in Baghdad. It spawned all manner of novel ideas. Deciding that the Eisenhower administration and Qasim regime lacked 'practical issues to deal with' together,

Sir Humphrey seized upon dates. He suggested the following to London: 'I think that the key may be dates, and have suggested to my American colleague that by some means or other they should buy a vast quantity of bad Iraqi dates and give them away somewhere or sell them at a loss. It might have quite a considerable effect. He thinks that it will horrify the AID people in Washington, but has noted it down as a possible idea.'[58] Sir Humphrey was either really thinking outside the box, in desperation, or suffering from too much Iraqi sun.

Soviet problems with their clients

The failed coup in Mosul also reignited UAR-Soviet disagreements. From Cairo, Nasser continued his attack on the threat that Communism presented to Arab unity, reopening the row with the Soviet Union. The Cairo press called Qasim and his followers the 'Communist agents of a foreign power' and stated in print: 'Iraq is ruled by a Red butcher.'[59] On 15 March 1959, from Damascus, Nasser delivered a speech accusing Qasim of handing Iraq over to Communists. Arguing that Communism threatened Arab nationalism and Islam, Nasser used a play on Qasim's name, 'Kassim' as opposed to Qasim, meaning 'divider'. His allusion to the 'subservience' of Qasim to the Communists in Iraq got a quick reaction from Moscow.[60] On 16 March, Khrushchev responded, describing himself as 'chagrined' by Nasser's use of the 'language of imperialists' in his attacks on Iraq. Khrushchev stated that the Soviet Union would not be 'indifferent' to the 'situation emerging' in Iraq, and he chided Nasser for having put his personal view of Arab unity and the interests of the UAR above those of the people. The Egyptian press responded, referring to the 'showdown' between 'Arab nationalism' and 'Communist imperialism'. Then, on 19 March, Khrushchev delivered his most stinging rebuke yet: he called Nasser 'a rather hotheaded young man' and stated that the Egyptian leader had undertaken 'more than his stature permitted'.[61]

Never one to shrink from an escalating war of words, Nasser responded the next day: 'If today the Soviet Premier supports a small group of our countrymen against the unanimity of our people, in no circumstances can we accept this.'[62] He added: 'Had it not been for this passion and hot-headedness, our country would have been turned into rocket bases against the Soviet Union and into Western bases against the Socialist and Communist world.' Nasser then declared: 'If a Communist State is established, the Communists will smite down all patriotic and nationalist elements – or eliminate them, as we say – by inventing incidents until they get rid of all these elements and will then establish a Red terrorist dictatorship in which subservience prevails.' Nasser also accused the Communists in Iraq of allying themselves with British agents.[63] As the exchanges escalated, Nasser denigrated the Soviet contribution to Egypt in 1956 and credited the United States and the United Nations with the key roles in stopping the fighting.[64] In April, Nasser gave an interview to a visiting Indian journalist. He stated: 'Our quarrel is really with communist conspiracy against Iraq and the whole Arab World. ... We are fighting the plot of a communist minority in Iraq which functions as a tool of Russia and international communism in the same way as the pre-revolutionary regime there executed orders of British and American imperialism.' In the same interview, Nasser's analysis colorfully lumped the British and their policies toward Iraq in with the Soviets:

> British policy is conditioned by two factors. First of all, they still suffer from Suez sickness. They are like wounded wolves out for revenge against me for having taken Suez away from them. They will use any instrument – Kassem, communists, anything that comes their way to destroy [me]. That is why they are helping Iraq and conducting press and radio propaganda against me. ... Additionally, [the] British want to continue flow of their petroleum company in Iraq and influence Kassem in favor of their vested interests.[65]

Nasser's emphasis may have been slightly off, but he certainly grasped the basics of Russian and British policy. Thus, the spring of 1959 found Moscow pressuring its erstwhile client in Cairo to cease and desist from its attacks on the Qasim regime, and it found London attempting to convince Washington to do the same thing. Nixon was on the mark when he commented that the British seemed to prefer working with Iraqi Communists to dealing with Nasser.[66]

Communist eclipse in Iraq

Given Nasser's problems with Moscow, British attempts to undermine his influence, and the conflict with Damascus, it was only natural for Nasser to turn to his former 'friends' in Washington. Nasser understood the Eisenhower administration's fixation on Communism. The UAR position on Iraq, Communism, and, at that moment, Soviet influence in the Middle East, complemented US containment policy. Nasser's suppression of Communists in Egypt and Syria resonated positively in Washington. While the administration did not believe that Nasser had had a total change of heart, the friction between Cairo, on the one hand, and Baghdad and Moscow on the other was the first positive news for the US out of the Arab Middle East in years. In a document entitled 'Nasser Steps Up Anti-Communist Drive', INR at the State Department commented:

> The conclusion is difficult to avoid that Nasser has made a decision to carry on his fight with Iraq regardless of the consequences for his relations with the USSR. In the final passages of the speech, reaffirming the determination of Arabs to resist communist as they did imperialist control, Nasser recalled the earlier struggle of Arab nationalism in Iraq 'when Hulagu conquered Baghdad and the Tartars occupied Iraq' and expressed confidence in the victory of Arab nationalism just as in the past when 'Hulagu was defeated and the Tartars crushed.' The next important

question is whether Mr. Khrushchev is willing to acknowledge the challenge implied in Nasser's recent speeches and if so how he will respond.[67]

Nasser played his retooled relationship with the Americans to the hilt. It provided leverage against the Soviet Union, in his dealings with the British and with various Arab states, particularly Jordan and Saudi Arabia. In Iraq, improved US-Egyptian relations made the US a prime target for media attacks charging Washington 'with collaborating with Nasser against Iraq'.[68]

In the summer and fall of 1960, the situation in Iraq offered some encouraging signs that Qasim had begun to recognize the potential threat from the Communists. He probably recognized them all along, leaving control of the security services and army in the hands of non-Communist nationalists who were loyal to him. On 1 May 1959, massive Communist rallies in Baghdad called for the appointment of Communists to the government and for an elected representative assembly.[69] Qasim responded on 2 May with a speech that many viewed as a 'slap in the face of the Communist Party'. He flatly stated that: 'groupings, parties and party politics were not at that moment beneficial to the country.' Then, he directly attacked the Communists for demanding positions in the government. Although cautious, London was hopeful that Qasim's speech signaled a 'real determination by Qasim to govern the country and not be pushed around by the Communists'.[70] When a Communist rally in Kirkuk, on 14 May 1959, exploded into two days of ethnic and class violence, Qasim arrested Communists and removed them from key positions in the peasants' and trade unions.

Returning from Baghdad, Anthony H. Nutting reported that the situation in Iraq was 'very dicey indeed'.[71] Nutting stated that Qasim's suspension of all political activity was a real attempt to curb the power of the Communists. He argued: 'In this way, they put the Communists in the dilemma of either having to oppose the government or accept the suspension of their own political activists.' Nutting also reported that the Iraqi regime was highly suspicious of American activity. Ambassador Trevelyan bolstered this view, and had repeatedly reassured the Iraqi leadership that Washington was not attempting to create a 'Moslem front' to undermine the regime.[72] The British believed that neither Qasim nor the army would readily relinquish power to the Communists, but that if Qasim disappeared in a 'palace revolution', the next leader 'would be more a prisoner of the Communists than Qasim'. Nutting concluded: 'The politics of Baghdad, like the traffic, were in a state of indescribable confusion.'[73]

In June 1959, Qasim and the Communist leadership clashed over a decision to allow 'exiles' to return home to celebrate the *Eid* and reduce prison sentences for 'feudalists and reactionaries'. The Iraqi Communists found their power curbed in other ways as well. Organizers of Communist demonstrations found themselves the targets of 'truncheon-wielding police'. Communist demands for a purge of the foreign ministry had failed in the face of determined resistance by Foreign Minister Jawad. Perhaps most significantly the rumors of a split in the Communist party over tactics and support for Qasim promised more problems for the leftists. In Washington, the CIA predicted 'a real show-down' between Qasim and the Communists, but stated that Qasim's preference for maneuvering and for a more cautious approach to his rivals would probably delay the confrontation. Coupled with an expected new long-term contract between the IPC and the Qasim government, these modestly encouraging signs effectively precluded any serious thoughts of intervention in Washington.[74]

Just as the situation in Iraq seemed to be calming somewhat, the Ba'thists who had escaped prison attempted a sudden change in leadership; on 7 October 1959, they attempted to assassinate Qasim. Although wounded, he survived.[75] The attempt resulted in the usual flurry of rumors in Baghdad about invasions from Jordan, Syria, and other Nasserist plots. The Communists were predictably vocal, hoping to recapture their lost political momentum. Communist influence had been clearly on the decline since its height at the time of the March coup attempt in Mosul. They also faced a better-organized, more active anti-Communist movement. Qasim encouraged this development as a counter-weight to surging Communist power earlier in the year.[76] As further evidence of slipping Communist fortunes, the Baghdad newspaper *Al-Thawra* had called for the establishment of a new political party headed by Qasim himself. At the State Department, Lakeland described the rumors as 'kite flying', but the Communists were concerned enough to come out strongly against such a move.[77] It smacked too closely of Nasser's abolition of political parties.

In late December a military court headed by Colonel Mahdawi began a series of televised 'show trials'. Described as 'one of the most gross perversion of justice yet witnessed', the trials became a platform for pro-Qasim demagoguery with the verdicts 'a foregone conclusion'. The logic of the trial was that because some Ba'thists had plotted against the regime, then all Ba'thists were guilty of plotting against the regime. Disaffection with the trials and the regime spread, but there was no outspoken opposition. The US embassy reported: 'No one dares, however to argue the point publicly lest he become a guest of Mahdawi and Majid Amin on their popular evening quiz show.'[78] Mahdawi, the most notorious of the judges, accused US Ambassador Jernegan of being in league with Nasser and of paying the Ba'thist plotters to overthrow the Qasim regime.[79]

By early January 1960, the Communist influence and ministers in the Iraqi government brought open concern. The Shah of Iran stated that he did not believe that Qasim was a Communist but that Communist influence was certainly on the rise. He counseled that anti-Communist forces in Iraq were much stronger than anyone realized, and lamented that no one seemed to have a plan to assist them.'[80] No one seemed able to adequately analyze the situation or provide accurate analysis of the future. For example, in January 1960 the Indian Embassy reported: 'Qassim [*sic*] is a transitional phenomenon corresponding to the state of Iraq now. ... Qassim's failings are the failings of Iraq. ... If Qassim is a split personality, so is Iraq and it is difficult to decide which affects the other more in the present circumstances. As was said long ago, the times produce the leader and every people gets the ruler it deserves.'[81] Non-Communist Iraqi parties were increasingly concerned that Qasim 'underestimated (the) danger (that the) Communists could become'. Qasim's pronounced tilt to the left reflected his consuming fear of 'pro-Nasser nationalists'.[82] The Indians were obviously operating slightly behind the actual course of events.

On 1 January 1960, Qasim ended the ban on political parties, giving the appearance of making good on his promise to allow the resumption of political-party life in Iraq.[83] In February, unfortunately for the Communists, Qasim decided that they had become too powerful and set about redressing the situation. For months, two rival wings of the Communist party had struggled for control. Now, both groups applied for licenses to operate as the sole Communist political party in Iraq.[84] In early February 1960, the regime announced its intention to grant a license to the minority, splinter group under Daoud al-Sayegh as the Communist Party of Iraq. This move diluted the power of the Communists in Iraq by creating a leadership crisis within its ranks. The Iraqi Foreign Minister Jawad had presaged this move when he stated that despite the power of the larger ICP there were 'ways of clipping its wings'.[85]

With no choice but to support Qasim, the mainstream Communists now lacked a party vehicle.[86] In addition to the political emasculation of the mainstream group, the conclusion of the conspiracy trials also indicated a loss of Communist influence. In sentencing 76 of the 78 defendants, the court showed surprising leniency. Some of the accused were actually acquitted, and the court only sentenced a handful of the 'ring leaders' to be hung.[87] The Qasim government presented itself as having curbed Communist influence.[88] Economic problems also brought friendlier attitudes toward Washington. More Iraqi students were attending US universities and technical schools, and there seemed to an increase in attempts to acquire Western technical assistance. While the regime, bolstered by oil revenue, looked stable in the short term, the longer view was an entirely different matter. Many began to question Qasim's competence to run the country.[89] Industrial output had fallen sharply from pre-revolutionary levels. Qasim was increasingly isolated and unable to deal with Iraq's mounting economic and political difficulties. His only salvation appeared to be the weakness of any opposition and the lack of an alternative leadership.[90] As a result, the Qasim regime found itself, in the words of *The Guardian*, 'losing its grip' on the political and economic levers of power. Observers saw the lack of direction and focus of the once infamous Baghdad mobs as another indication of the malaise in the government.[91] By 14 July 1960, the second anniversary of the revolution, the 'continuing revolution in Iraq had come to a halt.'[92] Now Qasim's sole goal had become survival.

Nasser's Syrian labyrinth

Any *Schadenfreude* Nasser may have felt with regard to Qasim's predicament was no doubt tempered by his own problems in Syria. In October 1959, Nasser sent his old confidant Marshal Amer to Damascus to function as viceroy. Amer was to use the 'carrot and not the stick'. Nasser simply failed to grasp that the arrival of an Egyptian field marshal in the role of viceroy would only increase disaffection among Syrian politicians and the military.[93] Salah al-Din al-Bitar and Akram Hourani, two leading Syrian Ba'thist politicians, made a trip to Cairo to voice their opposition, but Nasser intimidated them. In December 1959, after returning to Damascus, they resigned in protest from the government. Nasser saw the resignation as disloyalty. He concluded that Syrian politicians could not be trusted and removed them from key positions in the UAR government, further undermining the UAR administration in Syria.[94] Sarraj remained to support what increasingly appeared to be an Egyptian occupation. There were now only three Syrians, 'political nonentities', in the higher echelons of the UAR government.[95]

At this juncture, Nasser appointed Sarraj, his chosen head of the *muhabbarat* (or security service), to head the Syrian executive. Sarraj understood that Syrian resentment of Egyptian rule had risen to dangerous levels and that the only way to prevent a revolt in the military was through arrests and interrogations.[96] In his zeal to preserve the union, Sarraj ran afoul of Amer. The very Syrians who were planning a revolt against the Egyptians began to complain to Amer about Sarraj and his programs of suppression. Annoyed with Sarraj, Amer sought to quell the unrest by ordering an end to the arrests and interrogations. When Sarraj protested, Amer, with Nasser's blessing, ignored him. Amer, in effect, blinded the security apparatus and acquiesced to the very Syrian military officers who would lead a coup against UAR rule.[97] In London and Washington, most observers doubted, despite the 'mounting wave of discontent', that the Syrians would either significantly assist or rise up to expel the Egyptians.[98]

For the US, patience was paying off. Having resisted the temptation to intervene in Iraq, the Eisenhower administration had allowed the fractious nature of Iraqi politics to take its toll on the Qasim regime. Concerns about Communist influence were mitigated to a significant degree by Qasim's astute maneuver that split the party. In addition, Nasser's problems in Syria now seemed to portend limitations on UAR expansion. The fundamental conservatism of the Eisenhower administration's approach to the region was netting the same results that Vice President Nixon and the more radical advocates of a more aggressive policy had touted as the benefits of intervention, and Eisenhower had done so without the potential expense in lives and dollars or the immeasurable damage to the US reputation in the region. In addition, increased aid to Cairo had temporarily improved US influence with Nasser and encouraged him to pursue the blatantly anti-Communist policies long sought by the Eisenhower administration.

Despite the fact that the fear of monolithic Nasserism had subsided, Washington continued to worry about the survivability of traditional regimes in the region, but now it appeared that whatever nationalist regime might replace the Hashemites in Jordan or the Saudis would most likely pursue a course on the Iraqi mode of independence from Cairo. After the difficult learning curve of 1955 to 1958, the Eisenhower administration had come up with a set of pragmatic policies that worked, albeit with a constant need for adjustments. Washington had also come to the realization that the United States government lacked the ability to engineer or impose a 'strategic' solution to the problems in the region or for that matter to implement a 'strategic plan' to protect its own interests there; however, it could, and at times very effectively, take advantage of the inherent regional conflicts and political dynamics to further and protect the longer-term interests of the US government.

Chapter 7: Jordan, Saudi Arabia, and Israel – the Bystanders

The Arab Cold War held clear benefits for three relative bystanders in the Arab Middle East. Nasser's frustration and obsession with Qasim's Iraq and the resulting fall-out in the Syrian UAR and with the Soviet Union diluted the Egyptian leader's ability to focus on other revolutionary opportunities. For Jordan, Saudi Arabia, and Israel, the Arab Cold War brought a relative respite from political and subversive pressure that would further serve to ensure their survival. From 1958 through 1960, the two Arab monarchies, Jordan and Saudi Arabia, faced increasing political instability and financial problems which, coupled with focused subversion from the UAR, might have toppled both regimes. Because of the hostile relations between the UAR and Iraq, Jordan and Saudi Arabia were able to navigate this critical period of internal crisis and emerge stronger and more stable than at any time in the past. This did not mean that anyone in Washington, or for that matter London, would describe either monarchy as stable, but in a relative sense the regimes in Amman and Riyadh were clearly less vulnerable and better led than they had been in a decade. Even more critical, by the early 1960s the United States was committed to their survival. For Israelis, the Arab Cold War provided a diversion behind which they developed what Ben Gurion believed would be the ultimate assurance of survival – nuclear weapons. Each of the bystanders took advantage of the conflict between the UAR and Iraq in their own way, and in the end they would find their positions enhanced and those of Nasser and Qasim significantly diminished.

In terms of vulnerability, in early 1958 most in Washington believed that the Hashemite regime in Jordan would succumb to the Nasserist 'wave'. King Hussein faced Palestinian and pro-Nasserist plots in the government and military. There was little enthusiasm in the Eisenhower administration for supporting Jordan, which was not even a part of the US scheme for containment in the region. Nevertheless, despite objections from key elements in the US foreign policy community, Amman found itself the recipient of significant amounts of US military and economic aid. This aid did in fact represent an investment in containment, but only an indirect and somewhat unwilling one. US support for King Hussein was, in large part, a contribution to relations with London. The Eisenhower administration supported Jordan because the British viewed the collapse of the Amman regime as potentially disastrous to their remaining position in the Middle East. Wanting to avoid further damage to the British position and needing London's cooperation on a variety of other issues, Washington supported a regime that it believed would soon succumb to radical Arab nationalism. How this arrangement matured is instructive in understanding the British approach to protecting its regional interests by enlisting US financial and political support. Nasser's overconfidence also contributed to Jordan's survival. He viewed a collapse of the Hashemites as a foregone conclusion. As the conflict with Qasim intensified, Nasser's frustration with King Hussein increased, and Jordan became a major test of Nasser's influence and a major affront to his prestige. Only the loyalty of Bedouin units in the army, British backing, Israeli preference for the Hashemite monarchy, and lukewarm American support kept the last Hashemite regime afloat.[1]

Jordan's struggle to survive also highlighted a new level of complexity in relations between the Atlantic cousins. Eisenhower's pro-Nasserist tilt and Macmillan's continued antipathy toward the Egyptian leader created debate over Anglo-American policy toward Jordan. Clear disagreements, often expressed in a most entertaining manner, existed between Britain's Kipling-esque Ambassador, Sir Charles Johnston, and the US Embassy in Amman, the NEA Bureau at the State Department, and the CIA in Washington.[2] Without a doubt, Johnston was the most colorful participant in this policy tug-of-war. Fighting to preserve Britain's commitment to the last Hashemite, Sir Charles had an unabashed admiration for desert royalty and absolute disdain for Arab nationalists and their supporters.[3] He derisively dismissed US views of Nasser and other revolutionaries as the 'wave of the future' and engaged in all manner of chicanery to undermine policies that smelled of accommodation with revolutionary regimes. Jordan became something of a test case for Anglo-American cooperation and compromise in the post-1958 Arab world.

The Arab Cold War also benefited the Middle East odd couple – Saudi Arabia and Israel. Nasser's feud with Qasim, his problems with the Soviet Union, his difficulties in Syria, and the war of words with King Hussein necessitated good relations with other key Arab states in the region. One could argue that the conflict with Qasim caused Nasser to miss his best opportunity of undermining the Saudi regime. In the middle of a dynastic crisis, Saudi Arabia found an anti-Communist alliance with Nasser useful as well. The alliance reduced the potential for Nasserist agitation and increased the Kingdom's influence with Washington. Shrewdly, Crown Prince Feisal used the respite to improve relations with the UAR, while introducing reforms and undermining revolutionary groups at home. In addition, Feisal impressed upon

US officials the progress being made in modernizing the Kingdom, particularly in the realm of financial reform. Economic aid was less an issue with the Saudis, but reform constituted a major issue, if Saudi Arabia were to develop a stable economy and society.

As for Israel, with Nasser finally involved in an anti-Communist crusade, Washington avoided actions that might stir up the Arab-Israeli conflict and damage its anti-Communist campaign. The Eisenhower administration used economic aid as leverage to prevent Israeli schemes that might derail Nasser's anti-Communist campaign, but as a by-product of minimizing potential disagreements with Israel, the administration failed to confront signs of a growing nuclear weapons program. As a result, the distractions of the Arab Cold War and US preoccupation with maintaining UAR pressure on Iraq allowed the Israelis to divert aid into a nuclear weapons program. Ironically, the weakest monarchy, Hashemite Jordan, and the two most ideologically hostile regimes, Zionist Israel and Wahhabist Saudi Arabia, benefited the most from the 'Arab Cold War'. These issues and circumstances converged in 1959 and 1960 to form a critical chapter in the Cold War politics of the Greater Middle East.

Jordan's premature obituary

Predictably, Nasser's attempt to bring Jordan to heel involved the operational skullduggery of the Syrian intelligence service and its chief, Colonel Sarraj. The collapse of Hashemite Iraq, in July 1958, raised expectations that King Hussein was next. Although the young King had survived riots, plots, and assassination attempts, it appeared that his luck had run out. Hussein seemed to have two choices: toe the UAR line or be overthrown. After the crisis-ridden 1958, New Year in Jordan began on a shaky note. To bolster King Hussein's confidence, the Eisenhower administration approved a February 1959 'private visit' to Washington for informal talks with President Eisenhower. Still, expecting a Hashemite collapse, the administration was careful not to classify the trip as an 'official visit'. The Jordanian government expected significant new military aid and perhaps even a 'mutual defense guarantee'. The Eisenhower administration quickly dashed these hopes. The White House agreed to increased military aid, but took the position that the United States had 'consistently refused to give mutual defense guarantees to any Middle East country, and [did] not propose to start with Jordan.'[4] It was a polite but firm vote of no confidence from Washington.

US officials in both Washington and Amman pointedly pressed the Jordanians to come to terms with the UAR.[5] In Amman, the Embassy stressed Washington's 'interest in the independence and integrity of Jordan', but offered a stern warning: Jordan needed to mend its political fences with its neighbors. The warning added that US aid should not be interpreted as an endorsement of a defiant Jordanian policy toward its more powerful neighbors. Under prodding from the White House, the State Department made it clear that US

Courtesy of National Archives
Eisenhower and King Hussein
Eisenhower at the White House with Jordan's King Hussein. Although convinced that Hussein's regime would most likely fall, Eisenhower met with the King to offer his encouragement if not the material support that the King wanted. During this visit, the Jordanian security service uncovered a plot to overthrow the Hashemite regime.

aid was to allow 'Jordan under the King's wise leadership, ... to expand and improve her own connections with other Arab States'. Additionally, US officials pointed out to King Hussein and Prime Minister Rifai' that they did not believe that 'Nasser is at present interested in working for the overthrow of the regime in Jordan.' Eisenhower encouraged and offered to assist Jordan in improving its relations with Cairo.[6]

London received American matchmaking between Nasser and King Hussein badly. Whitehall strongly opposed any suggestion of 'détente' between King Hussein and Nasser. The subject gave Sir Charles Johnston, British Ambassador in Amman, near apoplectic seizures. Fearing that Washington might push King Hussein into an alliance with Nasser in a US-sponsored joint quest 'to resist Communist encroachment', the British worked behind the scenes to undermine US plans.[7] Given what the British viewed as their interests, London had reason for concern. In an NIE dated 10 March 1959, the Eisenhower administration made its assessment clear: 'Over the long run, we have little confidence in Hussein's ability to hold his throne or, indeed, in the viability of Jordan as a state.' The estimate went on to suggest that it was impossible for us [the US] to satisfy the desires and ambition of the King and

Rifai', and stated that the US should discourage Jordan from further reliance on Anglo-American largesse for survival. It also called for Jordan to seek at least a partial accommodation with Arab nationalists and the UAR.[8]

On edge about US intentions and the King's visit to Washington, Sir Charles Johnston complained to London: 'We are clearly in for another period of instability which will last as long as the King's absence and will be intensified while Samir is away as well.' Sir Charles cited the 'financial and military disadvantages of [Nasser] adding Jordan to his empire', but quickly added that a success in Jordan might offset Nasser's problems with the Iraqis. Fearing Sarraj's entrepreneurial streak, Johnston warned that Nasser's Jordanian and Syrian supporters might initiate action without his authority in 'an attempt to force his hand'.[9] Johnston worried about the army, stating: 'In this country, however, we must always be prepared for the worst.'[10] The Ambassador also fretted about what he called Lakeland's 'pet scheme' to induce the former Jordanian Chief of Staff, Major General Sadiq Shara, to defect while in Washington, because it 'would, no doubt, greatly strengthen the forces in the United States Government which would like to see (its) Jordanian commitment dropped.'[11] As events turned out, Shara should have adopted Lakeland's 'pet scheme'. While King Hussein was away, the Jordanian security service uncovered a plot against him that implicated Shara. Traveling with the King, Jordanian Prime Minister Rifai' scoffed at rumors that al-Shara would be arrested upon his return to Jordan, stating that 'if General Shara goes the Jordan Army will cease to exist and only a Bedouin mob will be left.'[12] In fact, Shara was arrested on his return and served 12 years in prison for his role in the plot. The plot in large part had been foiled because of the vigilance and loyalty of General Habis al-Majali, the Jordanian Chief of Staff and his intelligence organization.[13]

The results of the Washington meetings of 24-26 March 1959 were predictable. The Jordanians requested more aid and emphasized the Nasserist threat. At one point, Rifai' even argued that a Nasserist takeover in Iraq was more serious than a Communist one. Exhibiting an uncompromising hatred for Nasser, Rifai' criticized US aid to the UAR stating: 'Nasser should not be saved at the very moment when he had weakened himself in his battle against the Soviets.'[14] These views did little to enhance Washington's opinion of the Jordanian regime. Putting the best face on things, Washington called the visit a 'success'.[15] As predicted, upon his return Rifai' resigned as Prime Minister and took a parting shot at Nasser, stating that the trip's purpose had been to 'show up Nasser in his true light as a false leader [of] Arab nationalism who had single-handedly opened [the] Middle East to Communists.' When prodded by questions of Nasser's anti-Communist utility, Rifai' exploded, criticizing 'what he called the pro-Nasser clique among [US] policy making officials' and stated that he had 'warned everyone he talked to in Washington against giving this "Egyptian Dog" a third chance, explaining the first one was U.S. support for Nasser against Naguib, the second our action during the Suez Crisis.' Rifai' ranted that if the US government 'raised one finger to help Nasser it might as well pack up and leave Middle East … [because] it will earn the hatred of all Arabs, particularly the Syrians and Saudi Arabians.' Rifai' also stated that Jordan was encouraging elements in Syria to oppose the UAR. In response to a question about a united front of Nasser and King Hussein against the Communists, Rifai' bluntly made no bones about it: 'I know only too well how you Americans hate communism, well we hate Nasser even more.'[16]

When word of US encouragement for a UAR-Jordanian rapprochement reached Amman, Sir Charles erupted in what could only be described as a vesuvian expression of displeasure. Johnston snarled that the US intended to offer up 'any "small potatoes" like Jordan which might stand in the way' of Nasser pursuing an anti-Communist campaign.[17] In a cable to London, Johnston howled that US policy 'seemed to mean' that Jordan would keep its independence for a while but under a 'Nasserist prime minister', and then at some point King Hussein would oversee the transition of Jordan into a republic. Never shy about expressing his views, Johnston lambasted American Chargé Edwin M. Wright, and blasted anyone in London who might be thinking about acquiescing to what he viewed as the American scheme. He stated:

> Unlike Mr. Wright, I had seen a pro-Nasserite Prime Minister [Nabulsi] in operation here. His regime had simply opened the door to chaos and Communism, and I saw no reason to think that the result would be different if the experiment was repeated again now. Whatever might be Nasser's own attitude towards Communism, his Jordanian supporters (particularly those now in exile) had played the Communist game for all they were worth and would no doubt do so again. … If the Americans are in effect, letting Nasser take over Jordan while trying to build him up as an anti-Communist champion, they will have to pay <u>him</u> a subsidy comparable to what they pay the present Jordan Government, if they want to prevent him from being sunk by the Jordanian millstone. That being so, it seemed far more sensible to pay the subsidy directly to a regime which, whatever its shortcomings, is at least robustly pro-western, rather than to an untrustworthy opportunist like Nasser.

Johnston informed London that after expressing his views to the US Chargé, 'Mr. Wright expressed general agreement.' 'Mr. Wright' was more likely afraid to disagree. To make absolutely certain that no one in London missed his point, Sir Charles added: 'I trust that, if there is any danger of Mr. Hare's policy being adopted, its risks as regards Jordan can be pointed out with force to the State Department.'[18]

After some reflection, the Foreign Office reassured Johnston that they were certain that Washington would discuss any radical changes in policy prior to making them. At the same time, the FO made it clear that Whitehall was not unhappy with the idea of a US-UAR sponsored anti-Communist front, and believed that Jordan needed to broaden her contacts in the Arab world and participate in the Arab community rather than try to exist in isolation. London also stated that a 'live and let live' arrangement with Nasser, if handled properly, might be both desirable and achievable.[19] This exchange also indicated a growing difference of opinion between the Foreign Office and old-line Colonial officers like Johnston; the latter were having difficulty coming to terms with a changed environment, where American financial resources and interests were displacing traditional British approaches to the Middle East. Although still grousing, Johnston was somewhat mollified by this response, and the fact that his close relations with the new Jordanian Prime Minister, Hazza al-Majali, guaranteed him the leverage of political access in both Jordan and London, and vis-à-vis the Americans.

Hussein dangles the Nasser card

In September 1959, Nasser and Saud met in Cairo and announced a decision to put past differences aside and form a united Arab front against Zionism and Communism. Saud then suggested another meeting in Riyadh or Jidda, and wanted to include King Hussein. Relating to Hussein the gist of his recent visit to Cairo, Saud invited Hussein to participate. Seeing an opportunity for additional leverage, Hussein approached the British and American Ambassadors separately with his 'quandary'. Speaking to Johnston first, Hussein stated that, given his history with Nasser, he would not consider a trip to Cairo, but that a meeting in Saudi Arabia was a different matter. Hussein knew exactly how Sir Charles would react. Johnston made the obligatory statement that it was a Jordanian matter and then listed the negatives. Johnston told the King that his attendance would place him in the anti-Qasim camp, and Jordan should seek neutrality in the Iraqi-UAR dispute. Johnston also cited the personal risk, stating that 'Nasser's need for further successes' and Jordan's 'undue dependence' on Hussein's survival raised serious questions. Johnston pointed out that Nasser had managed to 'plant a bomb in Saudi's palace last year'. He suggested that the King 'temporize and avoid meeting Nasser for the time being'.[20] While British concerns about King Hussein's safety might have been real, a Jordanian alliance with Saudi Arabia and Egypt, with which latter London lacked diplomatic relations, would have damaged British influence. It also had the potential to lead to a breach with Iraq, and thus threatened petroleum revenues. Given these possibilities, London quickly agreed that Hussein should be discouraged from attending.[21]

Then on 18 September, to his chagrin, Johnston learned that King Hussein had asked the US Ambassador Sheldon T. Mills for advice on the meeting with Saud and Nasser. Mills told Hussein that he saw no threat of assassination and that Washington viewed cooperation between Saudi Arabia, Jordan, and the UAR as a positive counterbalance to the 'unfavorable trend in Iraq'. Unhappy with the US advice, Johnston planned to discreetly discourage Jordanian participation, emphasizing possible repercussions with Iraq.[22] At this point, the State Department approached the Foreign Office directly in the 'hope' that they would encourage the meeting.[23] Concerned about a confrontation with

Washington, the British formulated a strategy designed to gently nudge the Jordanians to forego the meeting with Nasser, without running afoul of the US. The British approach worked, and Hussein informed Saud that he could not attend.[24] Johnston wanted to inform the Americans of the King's decision in what was a clear game of diplomatic 'one upmanship', but London advised caution: '(We) still attach the greatest importance to avoiding any appearance of stage management on our part.'[25] Sir Charles's preference for putting a sharp stick in the State Department's eye had the potential for upsetting the trans-Atlantic relationship.

The Iraqi reaction to the mere rumor of Hussein's participation in a meeting with Saud and Nasser underscored the importance that the British attached to preventing the meeting. The British Embassy in Baghdad pointed out that Qasim's Communist supporters were already talking of a 'Nasser-Hussein-Saud bloc formed under the guise of combating Communists in the Arab states'.[26] The British were further upset by an article that appeared in the *New York Times* on 25 September captioned: 'Hussein to Meet Nasser and Saud'. The article cited 'reports that King Hussein is preparing to renew his claim to the Baghdad throne and that if he does so Cairo and Riyadh are ready to give him at least tacit support.' In the covering letter, the British Embassy in Washington commented that this article 'may not help matters'. The embassy stated: 'The implication that Cairo and Riyadh are calling the tune for Hussain [sic] will not enhance his prestige, but then the Iraqis are unlikely to be very worried.'[27]

Domestic perceptions of the political situation in Jordan did not help matters. Squabbling between key political figures reinforced the impression that the King could not keep his house in order. In public comments, former Prime Minister Rifai' stated that the Jordanian attacks on the UAR were a sign of weakness. These outbursts from influential Jordanians indicated the existence of an ongoing power struggle between Rifai' and Prime Minister Majali, and they undermined perceptions of the King's authority.[28] Prime Minister Majali hoped to smooth over the differences plaguing Jordanian society and to steer a middle road with Nasser. In January 1960, he convened a 'secret parliamentary session' to discuss whether or not Nasser was serious in his expressed desire to have better relations with Jordan. Majali believed that conflicts between UAR officials in Syria and the remaining Ba'thist ministers and politicians there had alienated the Ba'th in Jordan to the point that their cooperation in a conspiracy against King Hussein was highly unlikely. The Prime Minister argued that Cairo's problems in Syria reduced the Nasserist threat and might open the way to better relations with the UAR.[29]

The possibility of better relations with the UAR predictably came to naught. In the spring of 1960, the frustrated Jordanian regime embarked yet again on an anti-Nasser propaganda campaign. This time Jordan's attempt to match UAR's vitriolic insults greatly alarmed both the US and the British; London in particular cringed at Majali's statement that 'normal relations' meant 'subservience and obedience' to the UAR. The irrepressible Ambassador

Johnston in Amman saw little chance for the situation to improve, and noted that the Egyptians treated the Jordanians like 'wogs'.[30] As the propaganda attacks gained in intensity, Radio Amman blasted 'Nasser and his retinue' for their 'immoral plots, impudent policies and disdain of Arab public opinion'.[31] Fearing that the situation would get out of control, London cautioned: 'It is very short sighted of the Jordanians to imagine that they can compete with Cairo in a propaganda war. They have neither the technical resources nor the flair.'[32]

Exasperation at the British diplomatic mission in Cairo showed as well. Charged with normalizing relations with the UAR, Sir Roger Stevens complained: 'The Egyptians continue to persuade themselves that the British run Jordan and have forces stationed there, they will continue to believe that we are behind Jordan's anti-U.A.R. propaganda.'[33] Most likely pleased by the prospect of trouble in Cairo, and perhaps encouraging it, Sir Charles Johnston enjoined that he saw little to indicate that the Jordanians were willing 'even to tone down their hostile broadcasts and we are therefore unable to suggest a way out of this difficulty.'[34] By July 1960, Sir Roger Stevens in Cairo had become so frustrated that he asked to invoke 'American advice'. London raised the issue in Washington, but reported that the US 'showed no special enthusiasm' about getting involved.[35] London wanted US intervention on Jordan's behalf with Nasser. Instead, Washington instructed the Amman Embassy to tell King Hussein: 'In this connection we continue to hope His Majesty's government will resist, as it has on occasions in the past, frequent temptations to indulge in heated propaganda exchanges or to give encouragement to untrustworthy adventurers seeking its support for activities aimed at undermining Jordan's neighbors.'[36] Then the Jordanians actively began to foment trouble in Syria. Willie Morris, at the British Embassy in Amman, lamented: 'It is the conceit that the Hashemite Kingdom is a force to be reckoned with, which is so distressing.' He concluded that Jordanian meddling in Syria would only convince Nasser that Hussein had to go. He urged: 'This was an occasion on which we should use our influence to restrain the King and Government from what could be suicidal folly.'[37]

Jordanian-UAR relations reach boiling point

Any hope for restraint collapsed in the whirlwind that followed the assassination of Jordanian Prime Minister Majali on 29 August 1960.[38] Quite logically, the Jordanians assumed that Nasser and his Syrian henchman, Sarraj, were to blame. King Hussein threatened a propaganda war with Nasser that would reach 'new heights'. Hussein named Bahjat Talhouni to replace Majali, paving the way for the security forces and the army to increase their role in Jordanian political life. The assassination also highlighted the differences in US and British political preferences for Jordan. Majali had been a British favorite, while Washington felt far more comfortable with Rifai'. Prime Minister Talhouni was viewed as being in the Rifai' camp. In Amman, citing Talhouni's lack of popularity with the 'West Bankers', Willie Morris stated: 'British feel

Majali's loss deeply and despite his faults he will be "irreplaceable".' The British Embassy interpreted the assassination as the accomplishment of a key UAR goal, namely 'weakening local and national government in Jordan for some time to come'.[39] Considerably less upset, American officials surmised that the British lament reflected the fact that Talhouni was close to Rifai', an American favorite. Talhouni was also more 'closed mouthed' and less friendly toward the British. Thus Talhouni would 'probably be less satisfactory as source information' for the British in Amman.[40]

Showing a studied lack of concern, Washington viewed the Jordanian situation as an expensive aggravation and Majali as London's man. Additionally, the Eisenhower administration had tired of King Hussein and his political entourage contributing to their own troubles by baiting Nasser and then crying wolf. The cries of distress were so frequent that NEA developed its own inter-office code for dealing with the alarmist requests from Hussein, also known as the 'PLK' or 'plucky little king'. Senior officials at State would routinely instruct the Iraq-Jordan Desk to send the 'PLK' a 'BOGHAKYPU [see note] message and calm him down.'[41] Many believed that the Jordanians had gotten what they should have expected, if not deserved. To support this view, they cited Jordan's anti-UAR campaign, including Radio Amman's propaganda calling Nasser 'a Red agent' and 'a small Farouk', and issuing threats about the 'dark fate awaiting all dictators'. In October 1960, to further goad Nasser, Hussein decided to ignore the elimination of his Hashemite relatives in Iraq and recognize the Qasim regime in Baghdad.[42]

In Washington, there was an additional incentive to downplay any UAR responsibility for the assassination. Nasser planned to attend the UNGA at the end of September, and efforts were underway to arrange a meeting between Nasser and President Eisenhower. Jordan had become a nuisance that threatened to get in the way of the United States' real goal, namely using Cairo as a counterbalance to Communist influence in the region, thereby enhancing the effectiveness of containment policy. As a result, US officials argued that Majali's assassination was a tragic 'act of terrorism' with only limited tactical consequences.[43] The Eisenhower administration expressed concern about Jordanian stability but coolly concluded that, outside of the government and Majali's clan and tribe, no one in Jordan seemed to care very much about the assassination. In point of fact, Washington was more apprehensive that increased influence of the military would bring demands for more aid. In that regard, the Embassy in Amman took a preemptive hardline with Talhouni about military aid requests.[44]

The Americans seemed almost pleased with Majali's abrupt departure from the Jordanian political scene, because it held the promise of better American access to and influence with the Jordanian government.[45] London and Washington agreed on one thing, namely that the Jordanians could not afford to overreact. The British feared that Jordanian demands for the extradition from Syria of the two Jordanians involved in the assassination might spark an open conflict. London got both the UN and Washington on board for a coordinated effort to prevent precipitous action on the part of the Jordanians. All were 'strongly urging restraint', while the Majali family demanded immediate action against the UAR.[46] Perversely, Jordanian attempts to reassure the British that they planned no such action only increased British concerns. King Hussein stated that he had no intention of sending Jordanian forces into Syria unless the UN failed to 'obtain any redress' or if they were invited in by Syria to 'support an appropriately constituted new regime'.[47] Since no one expected the UN to achieve 'redress' and the Jordanians had convinced themselves that 'Syria [was] ripe for revolt', the possibility that Bedouin elements in the Jordanian army might take direct action against Syria presented a sobering, if not terrifying, prospect to the British. Worse yet, the King actually seemed convinced that Jordan could win a war with the UAR. The cousin of the slain Prime Minister was General Habis al-Majali, who happened to be Commander-in-Chief of the Jordanian armed forces. General Majali had convinced himself that Jordan could take on the UAR militarily, despite the deficiencies of the Jordanian air force and the limited capability of the army. He believed that Jordan would win any war within 24 hours, through surprise coupled with an 'imminent revolt' in Syria. Majali had by-passed key officers who held more 'realistic' views of military operations to push his aggressive plans with the King.[48]

King Hussein would not accept the fact that action against Syria could destabilize the internal Jordanian security situation, leading to chaos and collapse. Johnston clearly understood and informed London: 'We must, of course, continue our all-out attempts to prevent the King from taking this or any other form of military action.'[49] Prime Minister Macmillan reacted to Johnston's message by sending a message to King Hussein advising caution. Macmillan made it clear that the British government would not intervene as it had in 1958, except to provide for the safety of British citizens and to evacuate the King and his family on 'humanitarian grounds'.[50] The letter had the proper effect. Two days later, Johnston reported: 'Our impression is today that the temperature has dropped but that the crisis is far from over', and stated that he 'would not be happy until [he] saw them [the Jordanian Army on the Syrian border] beginning to return to their normal quarters.'[51] The British were skeptical of the US contention that even if UAR agents had assassinated Majali, Nasser may not have had any direct knowledge of either the planning or execution.[52] Nevertheless, the Foreign Office advised that while Washington was being 'cautious in asserting direct UAR Government responsibility in Majali assassination', Johnston was not being critical enough of the information coming from the Jordanians. In London, the Foreign Office told the US Embassy: 'Reports both from King Hussein and Ambassador Johnston are ... being treated with some reserve.'[53]

The fact that the Cairo press and *Sawt al-Arab* ('Voice of the Arabs') radio continued a 'violent campaign' against Jordan did little to convince anyone that Nasser was not directly involved in Majali's demise. In the period immediately

Courtesy of National Archives
Eisenhower and Nasser at UNGA, 1960
Eisenhower with Nasser at the September 1960 UNGA. Despite pronouncements about a more open policy toward the non-aligned, and Nasser in particular, Kennedy refused to meet with Nasser for fear of losing Jewish and pro-Zionist votes.

following the assassination, Cairo Radio welcomed the death of Majali, calling him 'an agent of imperialism' and advised King Hussein to 'commit suicide'. The local Egyptian press ran articles stating that 'the son of Talal' was mad and listed British officers serving in Jordan by name on Cairo Radio and *Sawt al-Arab*. Damascus Radio warned Hussein that the people of Jordan would kill him, and called for an uprising. In Amman, Johnston complained that the 'tone of UAR Press and broadcasting ... have reached a peak of violence never achieved in 1958.'[54] Although certain that the UAR government was involved, accusing Nasser of arranging the assassination would only damage Britain's efforts at rapprochement with the UAR, further inflame the Jordanians, and perhaps provoke a border war between Syria and Jordan. At this point, London just wanted the problem to go away.

Containment policy: Jordan and aid

President Eisenhower's meetings at the UNGA underscored the fact that the administration viewed Jordan as adding an unwanted complication to higher priority objectives in the Middle East. Secretary of State Herter had recommended that Eisenhower take the opportunity to meet with key Afro-Asian leaders. Nasser was at the top of the list. On 26 September, Eisenhower met with Nasser in New York and discussed a wide range of issues, including the conflict with Israel, the Congo situation, and Communist influence in the region.[55] On 7 October Eisenhower had a half-hour meeting with King Hussein at the White House. The President explained that he had raised the assassination of Majali with Nasser and that Nasser had denied any role. The President also told Hussein that Nasser had taken the position that if Israel wanted free passage through Suez, then they would have to recognize the right of return for all Palestinian refugees. Hussein expressed hope for more UN involvement and enhanced 'peace prospects' in the region and, with that, the meeting ended.[56] At the UNGA, Hussein publically denounced the UAR as a 'pro-Communist' threat to the 'basic aims of the Arab nation'. In Amman, the US Embassy viewed the speech as unfortunate: 'This denunciation is certain to be considered by UAR as full scale attack on part of Jordan and as such is likely to lead to UAR reaction which may be far from pleasant to GOJ.'[57]

During the UNGA, British and US diplomats asked India to weigh in to defuse the situation. The Indians saw nothing to be gained by getting involved and said as much. At the Ministry of External Affairs, F.S. Dutt commented that in the interest of 'keeping Jordan alive' Washington and London were probably discouraging 'any adventures on the part of King Husain [*sic*]'. The Indians surmised that more pressing problems in other parts of the world, including the fact that 'the British government wants to go nearer Nasser', had created a strong desire to see 'détente' between Amman and Cairo. Officials in the MEA questioned whether or not London and Washington had really exercised any 'restraining influence' over the Jordanians. The Indians saw no advantage in getting involved. R.K. Nehru stated: 'I agree with F.S. [Dutt] that the British and the American[s] would probably like to see a detente between the U.A.R. and Jordan', but 'I agree that it is not desirable for us to meddle in this matter. We should keep aloof.'[58] There would be no non-aligned help in settling this dispute.

The issue of political support for the Hashemite regime constituted only one of the Anglo-American difficulties over Jordan: the other was paying for it. While the British certainly did not want the Jordanian government to collapse, it simply could not afford the bill associated with maintaining its stability. As noted, many in Washington viewed aid to Jordan as a waste. The US had confronted the British on the issue, stating that a 50-50 split on Jordan appeared more realistic to Washington.[59] They saw the regime as unstable, and the current aid bill, an 85-15 split, had London getting the better bargain. In addition, the United States provided 70 per cent of the funding for UNRWA to support the Palestinian refugees. There was a feeling in Washington that, if the British saw Jordan as strategically important, then they should be willing to foot more of the bill. American concerns finally came to head in the fall of 1960. In London, Under Secretary of State Douglas Dillon told Selwyn Lloyd, now Chancellor of the Exchequer, that the US would only provide budgetary support for Jordan through March 1961. Dillon then flatly informed the British that they would have to increase their contribution. Selwyn Lloyd responded by saying that the 'UK had not much direct interest in Jordan.' He added that

London had been 'rather relieved when they had been "kicked out"' because their 'concerns lay more with the Commonwealth.'[60] In short, Britain did not want to see Jordan collapse, and they now believed that Washington was on the hook to prevent it. London argued that because of commitments in Oman, parts of Africa, and the sub-continent, no additional money was available for Jordan. At that point, Dillon stated that as of 1 April 1961 direct budgetary aid to Jordan would have a shortfall of $6.5 million and that Washington expected London to pick up the tab or to come up with another source of funding, whereupon the West Germans became the focus of that alternate source of funding.[61]

As the Eisenhower administration came to a close, the Jordanian situation remained very much up in the air. Luck had favored King Hussein, and he had survived. Neither London nor Washington wanted to pay the bill to float the Hashemite regime. The US favored a Jordanian policy of working with Egypt and Nasser against Communist inroads in the region. In effect, Nasser had become the more desirable active partner in Washington's containment strategy. Only British allusions to the negative effect of a Jordanian collapse on their position in the Gulf prevented the Eisenhower administration from leaving the Hashemites to their own devices. In effect, London had made the case that further damage to its position in the Middle East would hurt its ability to support the US in other areas. From London's point of view, the logic followed that the US should pay the lion's share of aid support to Jordan in order to protect broader Western interests in the region. What Selwyn Lloyd apparently meant when he referred to Jordan was that the 'UK had not much direct interest in Jordan' as long as the US footed the bill for Hussein's survival.'[62] Under Eisenhower, the US had provided just enough aid to allow Jordan's survival; it remained to be seen what would happen after April 1961.

Saudi Arabia: surviving Nasser's surge

At the same time that the Hashemites in Jordan were struggling to survive Nasser's maschinations, Saudi Arabia faced a critical test as Nasser's influence grew in the Kingdom. Nasser viewed Saudi Arabia as the epitomy of a feudal state, and he was, in fact, not far from the mark. Slavery was still legal there, and the traditional Saudi institutions could not manage a modern state. King Saud was at best incompetent and, at worst, dangerously unstable. From Nasser's perch in Cairo, the Saudi Kingdom looked like a rotten apple about to fall. King Saud, who had voiced his support for the Eisenhower Doctrine in early 1957, brought the full-brunt of UAR propaganda down on the Kingdom in March 1958 by bungling an attempt to subvert Colonel Sarraj, the Syrian security chief. Led by Crown Prince Feisal, members of the royal family pressured Saud to step down as ruler and to embrace a program of fundamental reforms. Knowing that he needed time, the shrewd Feisal moved to neutralize Nasser. The Egyptian leader viewed the announcement on 22 March 1958 that Feisal would now head the Saudi government and reassert the Kingdom's adherence to 'positive neutrality' as a significant political and diplomatic victory.⁶³ Nasser no doubt believed that this development, at the least, neutralized Saudi Arabia, and perhaps constituted the first step toward the end of the monarchy. The Kingdom sat on an ocean of oil but was virtually bankrupt due to the mismanagement, corruption, and incompetence of King Saud. Feisal understood that if the dynasty was to survive, he needed to buy time by following Nasser's lead in pan-Arab affairs. Given the 'street' popularity of Nasser, the ruling family had little hope of winning a propaganda campaign or a war of subversion with the UAR. In addition, attempting to regain power, King Saud waged a dynastic and bureaucratic battle with Feisal, when the latter refused to recognize King Saud's debts. As the struggle intensified, the almost total lack of visibility into the inner workings of the royal family, and Feisal's poor health, created rumors that sent shudders through the Washington foreign policy establishment. As one observer put it: 'Faisal [sic] appears to be the only member of the royal family who understands modern processes of government. The resumption of power by the King might be disastrous to Saudi Arabia.'⁶⁴ This murky internal sparring was a constant source of concern.

Chafing under Feisal's fiscal restraints, Saud cast about for political allies, temporarily embracing a discontented group of young princes that had formed around Tallal ibn Abd-al-Aziz. Tallal was ostensibly the leader of the *Nejd al-Fattah* or 'Young Nejd'. He and his compatriots were disillusioned reformers. They believed that Feisal's assumption of power in 1958 would bring constitutional government to the Kingdom. Feisal soon proved that he had no intention of creating a constitutional monarchy, and Tallal's group went into open opposition. Historically, King Saud had opposed Tallal and his reformers, but now, with Feisal controlling the purse strings, Saud courted the reformist opposition.⁶⁵ In December 1960, the reformers supported Saud's successful bid to retake control of the Council of Ministers. Radio Riyadh announced on 25 December 1960 that a new constitution for Saudi Arabia would be written and accompanied by other liberalizing reforms. Four days later, the King ordered Radio Riyadh to announce that a constitution would not in fact be forthcoming. When Saud returned to his old ways, clashes ensued between him and the reformers. Eventually, the King forced Tallal from office, leaving the Kingdom more vulnerable and divided than ever before.⁶⁶

Between 1958 and 1961, a serious attempt by Nasser to topple the regime might well have succeeded, but Saudi Arabia's window of vulnerability, like that of Jordan's, coincided with Nasser's attempts to deal with problems in Syria and with Qasim in Iraq. Nasser simply lacked the ability to focus on the Kingdom. In the mean time, more perceptive members of the royal family recognized that Feisal had to retake control of the government and manage the relationship with the UAR. In Washington, Feisal gained a reputation as a proto-Nasserist, not by making pronouncements, but by spreading rumors about his adherence to the Nasserist line.⁶⁷ Feisal's former alignment with the *Nejd al-Fattah* and rumored support for constitutional government enhanced his image as a progressive Arab nationalist. Feisal also possessed solid anti-

British credentials, having refused oil supplies for Jordan at the time of the British intervention in 1958.[68] Saudi Arabia also had no diplomatic relations with Britain because of the Buraimi Oasis dispute.[69] Serious negotiations about renewing British-Saudi relations only occurred after the UAR announced in December 1959 that it would renew relations with London.[70]

As the Buraimi dispute simmered on, the Saudis began to make claims vis-à-vis Oman, which the Egyptians and even the Iraqis supported. The British were not happy: 'The Omani nationalist movement is a pure invention of U.A.R./Saudi and Iraqi propaganda.'[71] The Saudis followed Nasser's lead on the question of the French and Algeria.[72] In September 1959, Feisal engineered King Saud's attempt to arrange an anti-Communist summit in Saudi Arabia with Nasser and King Hussein of Jordan, scoring points in both Cairo and Washington.[73] Not all Saudi initiatives with Nasser were just to buy time for reform. The Saudis sincerely sided with Nasser in his anti-Communist campaigns in Egypt and Syria, and against Iraq. While obviously wary of the ultimate intentions of Cairo, the Saudis actively opposed the Communists. Feisal's pro-Nasser policies, coupled with improved US relations with Cairo, opened the way to even better relations between Riyadh and Washington. As one observer put it: 'With Britain and France away from the field, the USA entrenches herself in this country more and more.'[74]

On 19 April 1959, the United States issued an intelligence estimate for Saudi Arabia. It seemed to confirm at least the partial success of Feisal's policies: 'The 1958 Iraqi revolt and its aftermath, including fears of increased Communist influence, have diverted the interest of Arab Nationalists in general, and of Nasser in particular, away from the traditional states. ... As a result, Feisal has been able to devote much of his time and effort to internal matters.' The report went on to state that Feisal had stabilized the currency, established the 'first real national budget', and managed modest improvements in the administration.[75] For the future of the Saudi monarchy, Crown Prince Feisal's arrival on the scene in 1958 was an extraordinary stroke of good fortune, but the simultaneous outbreak of the Cold War between Qasim and Nasser was a blessing from Allah himself.

Paranoids with real enemies:
Israel and the Arab Cold War

Ironically, the other great beneficiary of the Arab Cold War was Israel. In 1956, Eisenhower's opposition to the Anglo-French-Israeli invasion of Egypt had preserved Nasser's rule and, in 1957, the administration had demanded and gotten Israeli withdrawal from the Sinai Peninsula over the strenuous objections of Israel's Ben-Gurion and despite pressure from the American Jewish community.[76] Eisenhower had demonstrated his willingness to put real pressure on Israel. Recognizing that there would be a political price to pay because of Zionists groups pressuring a Democratic Congress, the administration relaxed its pressure on Israel, when it might have forced a comprehensive peace plan for the region. In addition to domestic political considerations, the primacy of containment policy placed a premium on Nasser's anti-Communist activities. This essentially precluded pressuring Egypt as well, and diverted Washington's attention away from the issue of an Arab-Israeli peace. The Israelis argued: 'As long as the West cannot consent to its [Israel's] complete disappearance from the region, and to cede its positions to Nasser, there is no basis at all for a common language between the West and Nasser.' Admitting that for the 'time being' Nasser had left Israel alone and put the 'Arab countries at the head of his list', the Israelis warned that any attempt to work with Nasser and 'providing him the benefit of a truce' was folly. Playing on old fears, the Israelis stated: 'Appeasement in the long run necessarily means undermining the whole structure of Western interests in the region and serving [sic] Soviet efforts at penetration.'[77]

While useful at times, there was always a high price associated with relations with Israel. During the Lebanese and Jordanian crises, overflights of Israel, by US aircraft moving British troops and supplies to Jordan, had been critical in maintaining the Hashemites on the throne. In return, the Israelis obtained something approaching a security guarantee from the Eisenhower administration. When the press picked up the story, which the Israeli government may have planted, the Soviets felt that they had to react.[78] Moscow demanded that Israel stop the flights immediately. Ben-Gurion, feigning fear of a Soviet attack, stopped the overflights. When Dulles charged that Israel was caving in to Soviet blackmail, the Israelis pointed out that a long list of countries had received US guarantees in the event of an attack by Moscow. Abba Eban informed Dulles: 'We are not defended by an American guarantee and the Soviet Union is able to wipe us out in five minutes.' Dulles replied that after discussions at the White House, President Eisenhower had decided that the Eisenhower Doctrine for the Middle East covered Israel as well. America would come to Israel's aid if the Soviets were to attack.[79]

In early 1959, the British began one of their periodic evaluations of the pros and cons of good relations between Jordan and Israel. The British Embassies in Tel Aviv and Amman argued that good relations between Jordan and Israel served to dampen down problems in the region in general and on their borders in particular. The Foreign Office predictably concluded that influence and good relations with Israel were useful, despite Israel being a 'largely negative factor'. London decided that the best course was to 'keep carefully in step with the Americans; avoid action which will exacerbate Arab opinion; [and] not allow ourselves to be led by the nose by Israel importunity.'[80] In an attached minute, Sir Frederick Hoyer-Millar scribbled a warning: 'I think the moral is that we must go slow with the Israelis ... with our steady improving Anglo-Israeli relations, be careful not to give the Israeli's too much rope.'[81]

US aid and relations with Israel

No matter what London's position, Israel's fortunes were tied to the United States. Almost every Israeli policy decision included a discussion of how the US would react. Every potential new regional development found its way into cabinet discussions and often the press. Strangely enough, in the early months of 1959, John Foster Dulles' illness, resignation, and death highlighted the trepidation with which the Israeli government viewed changes in Washington. The Israeli government and press were reassured by the appointment of Christian Herter as Secretary of State, but it appeared that Richard Hare, the US Ambassador in Cairo and the architect of 'détente' with Nasser, would replace Rountree at NEA. This increased the Israeli 'tendency to see an Arab behind every desk at the State Department', or 'Byroadism': Byroade attempted to make Egypt the principal US partner in the region. As the uproar grew, British Ambassador Francis Rundall wryly commented:

> The Israeli press is showing its usual tendency to cry before it is hurt, but it would be unwise to discount entirely the effect, which recent developments in the apparent attitude of the United States towards Israel have had here. ... The United States is not always popular here, but whatever happens it remains the rich uncle, and the imagined prospect of Israel's worst enemy becoming the new favourite nephew is not, from any point of view, a welcome one.

This turmoil occurred simultaneously with negotiations to end its grant-in-aid program for Israel.[82] Washington made it clear that any consequent loss would be made up in some other way, but the situation had become an internal Israeli political issue. Golda Meir stood up in the Knesset and criticized the 'insanity' of the State Department's pro-Nasser policies. This speech resulted in a routine rebuke from Washington and copious amounts of hand-wringing in Israel. The State Department viewed the commotion as the price for doing business with Israel. From a State Department perspective, relations with Israel were proceeding much more smoothly than they had for some time.[83]

Israel's insurance policy: nuclear weapons

Despite the occasional heated exchange over aid or Nasser, Israel benefited from the fact that, distracted by the Arab Cold War, the Eisenhower administration missed early signs of Israel's nuclear weapons program. In 1955, David Ben-Gurion made the secret acquisition of nuclear weapons an absolute priority. US intelligence resources focused on France and other industrialized states, placing Israel in the 'Third Category Priority' list of those countries not considered a proliferation risk. In 1957, Israel shifted from a pool-type research reactor to a 'real' production reactor. This triggered no alarms, and Washington approved technology transfers and monetary grants for research. Hiding behind what seemed to be a sensible move toward nuclear power, the Israelis quietly proceeded with a baseline weapons program. Israeli shifts in priorities appeared to reflect inexperience and budgetary concerns more than an ulterior motive. Additionally, US approval of the construction of a 10-megawatt reactor at Nachal Soreq by American Machines and Foundry

Courtesy of National Archives
Eisenhower and Herter, 1959
Eisenhower with Secretary of State Christian Herter in 1959. Herter became Secretary of State after Dulles' death on 24 May 1959. Herter's relationship with Chester Bowles, both of whom were Connecticut polticians, eased the transition from the Eisenhower to the Kennedy administration.

provided the Israeli government with the perfect screen for its weapons program.

There were other indicators as well. In early 1958, at the time of the Soreq deal, the National Photographic Intelligence Center (NPIC) discovered large-scale construction in the Negev desert during a routine U-2 flight. The CIA Program Director, Arthur C. Lundahl, and his deputy, Dino A. Brugioni, briefed President Eisenhower and Atomic Energy Commission Chairman Lewis Strauss on the facility. Both believed that it was probably a nuclear weapons facility. The lack of questions from either Eisenhower or Strauss led Lundahl and Brugioni to conclude that the administration wanted Israel to acquire nuclear weapons. In fact, Eisenhower immediately sent a list of specific questions to the Ambassador in Tel Aviv who, in turn, presented them to Ernst David Bergmann, the head of Israel's nuclear program. Somewhat disconcerted, Bergmann admitted that Israel had decided to build a reactor but no firm decision had been taken on exactly what kind it would be. Evidence of French-Israeli cooperation in the nuclear weapons field led to the May 1959 resignation of Dan Tolkovsky as head of the Development Department in Israeli defense. In June, there were rumored heavy-water agreements with Norway, indicating that something beyond research and peaceful development might be going on.[84] In addition, the Israeli embassy in Washington indicated that Israel wanted an exemption from the inspection regulations of the International Atomic Energy Agency (IAEA).

The Eisenhower administration had shown a particular commitment to the creation of an international agency dedicated to non-proliferation of nuclear weapons. The IAEA was slated to take over monitoring and safeguarding functions. The United States wanted to change its nuclear agreements such that non-compliance with IAEA regulations would be grounds for terminating cooperation with that nation on nuclear energy. The administration had no intention of undermining, through making an exception of Israel, the very agency whose creation it had sponsored. The Israelis began to offer justifications for the exception. They argued that if the IAEA center were in Cairo then the Israelis would not be allowed access. In addition, the IAEA might give the Egyptians access to the Israeli reactors. Israel provided another hint about their real objective, stating that they could not comply with the IAEA strictures because they wanted 90 percent-enriched uranium-235 as opposed to the 20 percent-enriched allowed under IAEA guidelines. Israel wanted reassurances that the US would not terminate bilateral agreements based on IAEA findings.[85]

The Eisenhower administration refused, but stated that the United States would not terminate its agreements and cooperation 'without full prior consultation and consideration' with Israel. Washington also insisted that the agreements be modified to include the termination clause, but offered to study the matter further.[86] On 27 June 1959, Washington responded that while Article V, the offending termination clause, would be in the agreements, 'the proposed amendment is not intended to mean that the Government of the United States would feel the need to terminate the Agreement in the event the Government of Israel is not ready to accept the administration of safeguards and controls by the International agency at a time when there has not been a widespread transfer to administration by the International Agency of bilateral safeguards.'[87] In other words, the United States would continue to monitor Israel's nuclear program as it had in the past and Tel Aviv had bought some more time for its efforts.[88]

With the nuclear issue buried for the time being, the Israeli government immediately returned to the pursuit of conventional weapons. Whether intentional or inadvertent, this resumption of the business as usual requests for aid and arms further screened the nuclear program. In a meeting with Secretary Herter, Golda Meir, the Israeli Foreign Minister, introduced a new request for conventional weapons. Citing recent shipments of Soviet arms to Nasser as the justification, the Israelis argued that they had to keep up, in 'quality if not in quantity', with Cairo. In the same breath, she mentioned to Herter that Israel was out of money. Officials at the State Department called the new weapons requests 'depressing to face', since another round of Israeli security demands had been completed only four months before.[89] In London, the Foreign Office commented: 'The Israelis' arguments to us were different. ... But it is interesting that after a year of comparative peace (except for an occasional push for guided weapons) we too have begun to hear that old request again.' London speculated that the 'younger and wilder MAPAI men' were the source because of 'genuine alarm caused by reports of the rate of absorption of arms by the UAR'.[90]

During the summer of 1960 another debate erupted over the Dayan Plan, which called for removal of the Bedouin population from certain sensitive areas in the Negev. As one journalist close to the MAPAI put it: 'The transfer of a certain number of Bedouin to permanent settlement in a more northerly area will ... [make it] possible to establish on this strip [non-Arab] security settlements, which are extremely vital for a certain area.'[91] Why was this area vital? In June 1960, the US Embassy in Tel Aviv reported rumors that the French were assisting the Israelis in the construction of a major nuclear facility near Beersheba in the Negev. In August, French participation was confirmed. Under renewed pressure, the Israelis called it a metallurgical research facility and offered no additional information. Then in October 1960, the British informed Washington that the Beersheba site was indeed a nuclear installation. Both British and American Military Attachés got pictures of it, and confirmed that it was a nuclear reactor site. When confronted, the French denied assisting the Israelis with the reactor or even knowing anything about it. The ultimate confirmation came from a nuclear scientist from the University of Michigan, Henry Gomberg, who was visiting Israel. In late November 1960, after talking with Israeli nuclear engineers, he concluded that Israel had a dual track nuclear program: the American reactor at Nachal Soreq for research, and the French reactor at Beersheba for nuclear weapons production.

Two weeks after John Kennedy won the presidential election, the Eisenhower administration concluded that Israel was building a nuclear reactor capable of producing weapons-grade plutonium. Despite Ben-Gurion's claims to the contrary, the Atomic Energy Commission and the CIA concluded that the 'nuclear complex cannot be solely for peaceful purposes.' In an effort to save face, the outgoing Eisenhower administration told the Congressional Joint Committee on Atomic Energy: 'We [the United States] have been assured categorically at the highest level of the Israeli government that Israel has no plans for the production of atomic weapons.'[92] On 21 December 1960, Ben-Gurion publicly announced that Israel was completing a large nuclear reactor of 24-megawatts to be used 'exclusively for peaceful purposes' and called rumors to the contrary 'deliberate or unwitting untruth'.[93] In Washington, Israeli Ambassador Avrahm Harman argued that the facility would take three years to complete and that 'this allows ample time to discuss any implications [of] Israel's atomic program.' The State Department reported that Harman stated that he 'personally had not understood urgency USG attached to subject when it first brought to his attention and expressed hope that with assurances GOI has now RPT now given there would be no QTE nagging doubt UNQTE.' US intelligence sources now believed that the site was definitely a nuclear weapons facility and that it would be operational within a year.[94]

The State Department reminded Harman of the 'sense of urgency' that Washington attached to proliferation issues 'anywhere', and particularly in a volatile region like the Middle East. The US strongly suggested that, in addition to Ben-Gurion's promise not to develop nuclear weapons, Israel should open the facility to IAEA inspection. On 29 December, Washington forwarded a list of questions to Tel Aviv for presentation to the Israeli government, including: 'Can Israel state categorically that it has no plans for producing nuclear weapons?'[95] On 6 January 1961, Washington issued public affairs guidance to posts and military installations stating that Washington requested information from Israel, over and above Israel's denial that they intended to build nuclear weapons, but received no response.'[96]

On 12 January 1961, President Eisenhower held a senior level conference to discuss the Isreali nuclear issue. In an apparent attempt to put the best, if not the most candid, face on the situation, Secretary Herter proposed that the State Department issue a statement that the Israeli plutonium production plant at Dimona was for 'peaceful purposes'. Secretary Thomas S. Gates, Jr. countered: 'Our information is that the plant is not for peaceful uses.' John A. McCone, the Deputy Director of the CIA, stated that his analysts believed that a 'chemical separation plant' existed at the site and that 'the Israelis would not build such a plant just to do part of the job.' His next statement surely made everyone in the room uncomfortable: 'The plant had probably been financed from U.S. support for Israel.' The outgoing administration decided to take the position that the US government did not know the source of the funding for the facility and to issue a statement calling for complete IAEA inspection and monitoring of the facility.[97] The Israelis had won the race. It would take the new administration time to organize itself to deal with the nuclear issue, and John Kennedy had been heavily dependent on the Jewish votes to get elected. Israel expected some questioning, but, quite correctly, did not expect any action from Washington on this issue.

Chapter 8: Iran and Pakistan Cash in on Iraq

In 1959 and 1960, Iran and Pakistan adjusted to new reality in the Greater Middle East by first recognizing and then utilizing their new-found leverage with the United States. The collapse of the Baghdad regime had severely shaken Washington and London and placed a premium on preventing the fall of more allied regimes in the region. In fact, as Secretary Dulles pointed out in the days immediately following the Baghdad coup, Iraq was not even a part of his original concept of the 'northern tier', but Iran and Pakistan were keys. Be that as it may, the collapse in Baghdad frightened the Eisenhower administration because a repeat in either Iran or Pakistan would undo its containment or encirclement of the Soviet Union. Only five years early, a nationalist leader in Iran, Musaddiq, had forced the Shah to flee the country, and the US and Britain by the narrowest of margins had overthrown Musaddiq and placed the Shah back on the throne. In the intervening time, the Shah had not led Iran's government, economy, or society to anything that approached the level of stability that Washington desired. At the beginning of 1959, Eisenhower feared, and with justification, that the situation in Iran might bring about a repeat of that in Iraq the year before. Unstable perhaps, but the Shah recognized the opportunity presented by Washington's concern, and he pressed for aid, particularly military aid, arguing that had the US been less niggardly prior to July 1958, the coup in Baghdad might never have happened. With regard to Pakistan, the administration believed that instability and possible collapse had only been averted in October 1958 by the military takeover led by General Ayub Khan. Because of Ayub's firm grip on power and personal aura of no-nonsense competence, Washington was concerned about Pakistan, but not on edge as it was about Iran.

Always a source of concern, Iran's stability following the Baghdad coup emerged as a major preoccupation in Washington. US-Iranian relations now had a new problematic twist. Between 1959 and 1960, the Shah learned to use

US concerns, and even perceptions of his own personal stability, as leverage to demand increased economic and military support. With increasing sophistication, the Shah employed Washington's fears of a neutral Iran and an accommodation with the Soviet Union to transform demands for aid into tangible results. At the same time, the Shah blunted attempts by the Eisenhower administration to pressure his regime toward political and economic reform. The Eisenhower administration consistently pressed for reform and economic development as the only sure path to Iranian stability, but after the Baghdad coup, Washington feared that rapid reform could destabilize the regime. Reform could not be undertaken at the risk of a Pahlavi collapse; therefore, it had to be controlled reform. The stability and survival of a friendly regime in Tehran was the first priority.

Pakistan found itself in a very similar position, and undoubtedly General Ayub Khan, the President of Pakistan, and the Shah of Iran frequently compared notes on the status of aid and support coming from the United States. The impact of developments in Iraq on Pakistan and India were as dramatic and, in many ways, more far-reaching than in Iran.[1] Just as Nasser's 1953 rebuff of MEDO led to US-sponsored defense alliances in the 'northern tier', the Iraqi coup and the prominent Communist influence in Baghdad brought renewed efforts to ensure the containment of the Soviet Union. In Pakistan, this led to US support for military rule, which in turn further strained ties with India. By early 1959, the Eisenhower administration came to view Pakistan's government as the most stable since independence. General Ayub Khan, now President, had Washington's confidence and particularly that of President Eisenhower. Ayub's government had transformed a chaotic political and economic situation into something that was reasonably stable and efficient. Ayub also exuded confidence and a sense of purpose. By curbing corruption and instilling order, Ayub impressed the White House. This translated into increased military and economic aid. Pakistan was the lone bright spot in the Western alliance system in the entire Greater Middle East.

Now, with the United States reeling from Iraq, Ayub renewed his demands for modern weapons. He argued that they were necessary for Pakistan to fulfill its obligations to both CENTO and SEATO. To demonstrate his options, Ayub began to explore the possibility of better relations with Beijing. As in the case of Iran, apprehension over events in Iraq, coupled with irreplaceable US strategic intelligence assets in Pakistan that directly affected the continental security of the United States, made Washington receptive to Ayub's requests.[2] Nehru could not appear to back down in the face of Pakistani military aid from the US. With Krishna Menon at the helm in the Ministry of Defense, the answer was obvious – call Moscow – and so began India's efforts to establish an indigenous, modern, weapons program. Menon was convinced that a military relationship with the Soviet Union was more advantageous than one with the West in terms of ideology, costs, and creating an indigenous manufacturing base.[3] While Washington tried to explain the benign nature of its agreement with Karachi, Nehru pondered the potential threat posed by

Pakistan. Ironically, neutral India pursued the focus on economic development and reform most advocated by the Eisenhower administration, but US military aid to Pakistan, in reaction to the Iraqi coup, forced a reappraisal. In the 1959 to 1960 time frame, Washington viewed Iran as more unstable than Pakistan; therefore, its role is examined first.

US aid and the Persian bazaar

Appropriately, this new period in US-Iranian relations began with Iranian requests for more military and security aid to combat growing threats from the Soviet Union. The annual budgetary cycle for Tehran began in March; therefore, pleas for additional military and economic aid started appearing in November and December. These aid requests usually touched off a series of US national security assessments of Iran and the Shah. The 1959 budget cycle differed only because of an increased sense of urgency generated by the Iraqi coup. Intelligence estimates and cable traffic after July 1958 overflowed with ominous warnings about the 'precarious' situation in Iran and the Shah 'as an individual of very uncertain quality'. In addition, Iran was the only non-Communist country in the world which shared a long border with the Soviet Union but with which the United States had no defensive alliance.[4] The Eisenhower administration recognized that the problems of corruption, incompetence, and the personal instability of the Shah contributed to the instability in Iran, but saw no alternative to continued support for his regime. Washington would have preferred an alternative to the Shah, but no acceptable option existed.[5]

Eisenhower and his advisors wanted fundamental reforms in Iran to improve the Shah's chances of survival, but the instability of the Shah's government and the monarch's idiosyncrasies made the administration cautious. Washington feared that under pressure the Shah might lose control of the 'precarious' political situation or stampede into an accommodation with the Soviet Union. They believed that 'meaningful political, social, and economic reforms designed to increase popular support' were in the best interests of the Shah and the West, but that possibilities for reform were tied to the Shah's personal sense of security. Aware of 'latent Iranian xenophobia' toward the US, the administration also recognized that it needed an effective 'informational and cultural program.'[6] Despite misgivings, Eisenhower concluded that military aid was required to get the Shah to reform his regime. The Shah assumed, and probably correctly so, that he understood Iran better than experts in Washington. Making this assumption, the progression of events in 1959 and 1960 takes on a significantly different interpretation. From his reinstatement in 1953, the Shah had a set of reasonably clearly-defined goals. He wanted to transform Iran into the primary strategic partner for the West in the region, thus attaining regional political, military, and economic preeminence. Turkey was his model. The Shah believed that with US assistance, he could emulate Mustafa Kemal – Atatürk – and transform Iran into a modern, secular society. None of this seemed remotely possible prior to

1958, until the collapse of Iraq thrust Iran to the forefront of Western security concerns. The Shah immediately understood and acted on his newly-acquired leverage.

On 6 December 1958, Washington got its first real taste of what the future would hold for Iranian-American relations. Citing the threat to Iran from the Soviet Union and Soviet-supplied Afghanistan, Abol Hassan Ebtehaj, CPO Director, appealed for dramatically-expanded military aid. Then on 9 December, displaying amazing cheek, Ebtehaj complained that new military requirements levied by the United States had resulted in financial difficulties and that Iran required additional economic aid to compensate. Seeing a looming financial pit, the administration tried to defer the Iranian requests. Washington explained that Tehran needed better accounting practices and a better distribution of oil revenues. The administration also shifted the issue to the IBRD.[7] Undetered, the Shah continued to press. He had Washington over the proverbial barrel, and he knew it.

During December 1958 and January 1959, the Shah now began to demand enough military assistance to bring 'existing' military units up to 'full strength'. Tehran also attempted to enlist the help of General Nathan F. Twining, Chairman of the Joint Chiefs of Staff, who visited Tehran and then sent a letter to the Secretary of Defense Neil McElroy on 23 December 1958, strongly recommending that the US join the Baghdad Pact and shift aid programs to support Pact members.[8] To emphasize his requests, the Shah, with increasing frequency, complained that the lack of US support might well oblige him to seek an accommodation with Moscow. The Shah wanted 'satisfaction' on his budgetary requirements, support for his military-assistance goals, and a bilateral security agreement with the United States.[9] The Shah argued that Washington had not lived up to its Baghdad Pact commitments and had shown a decided insensitivity to Iran's security situation. Malcolm E. Yapp described the Iranian alliance with Britain in the early nineteenth century as follows: '(L)ike many a marriage. After a breathless courtship and whirlwind ceremony the groom had begun to examine his situation.' The groom 'complained about the bride-price' and 'sickened of the union', but 'was alarmed by the appearance of a new suitor' and began to 'discover attractions' that he had 'previously despised'. 'It was a question of whether the future held a second honeymoon or a divorce.'[10] This description fit the US-Iranian relationship perfectly. Neither was particularly happy with the situation, but neither could afford the consequences of a messy divorce.

The Shah's December 1958 demands roiled Washington for weeks. On 16 January, the State Department informed the Department of Defense that, while it supported the military-assistance goals of Iran, military support for the Baghdad Pact could not undermine aid to other critical nations in the region. The report also singled out India, stating that the United States could not refuse aid to 'our other friends in the Middle East or even to certain sensitive countries such as India, whose "neutralism" we may deplore but whose loss through neglect would be an even greater blow to the free world cause.'[11]

Rountree at NEA told US Ambassador Wailes to call on the Shah and remind him of the following:

> It seems evident that in his frustration as to how to strengthen his position he has grossly underestimated US contribution to Iranian security and indeed to stability of his own regime. While we realize that Shah no doubt has taken this line in belief it would precipitate greater US willingness to accede to his desires, we cannot discount possibility that in his present apparent frame of mind he might take some action, which he and we would later deeply regret.

Rountree described the scale of the US commitment to Iran and pointed to the London Declaration of July 1958 and the US Congress's Joint Resolution on the Middle East as examples of security commitments. Playing on the Shah's antipathy toward the Soviet Union, Rountree told Wailes to remind the monarch that Soviet 'multi-lateral guarantees', based on the adoption of a 'neutralist foreign policy', had proven unreliable in the past.[12] Wailes met with the Shah, but came away with the understanding that the Shah felt that he got 'little out of the (Baghdad) Pact'.[13]

Facing the Shah's spiraling demands, Secretary Dulles told the NSC on 22 January that the Shah's demand for a bilateral agreement that promised US intervention against all enemies, including domestic ones, was simply unacceptable to the administration and certainly to the United States Senate. The ailing Secretary of State warned that the Shah, in frustration, might actually resort to a 'flirtation' with the Soviet Union. George Allen, Director of USIA, supported Dulles, stating that he was glad that 'Dulles had decided to hold the line', because 'the Shah was best blackmailer that he knew of'.[14]

Playing the Soviet card

Predictably, the US Embassy in Tehran reported that the British, Pakistanis, and Turks reported that the Shah would improve relations with the Soviet Union in retaliation for the lack of a US 'blank check' for joining the Baghdad Pact.[15] Wailes suggested that a letter from the President might delay any rapprochement. The Ambassador reiterated that the Shah's problems were internal, not external, and that emphasis on military aid merely exacerbated the domestic situation. In an attempt to further mollify the Shah, President Eisenhower wrote him on 30 January 1959, reciting the instances of Soviet perfidy and pointing out that 'regardless of the actual terms of any new treaty with the Soviet Union, the impact on your friends would be unhappy.' The President then addressed the issue of the bilateral agreement with the US, pointing out that the United States' 'strong determination to support Iran's independence and integrity has not in the past depended upon, and need not in the future depend upon, any particular provision of formal agreements between us.'[16]

Despite reassurances, Iranian negotiations with the Soviets in January and February 1959 left the Western allies holding their collective breaths. The situation in Iran had begun to affect other sensitive relationships as well. The British wanted to complete the sale of arms to Qasim's Iraqi regime in an effort to strengthen the hand of the Iraqi army against the rising influence of the Communists.[17] For Iraq, the move made sense. In Iran, the US Embassy believed that it might push the Shah over the brink in his negotiations with the Soviets. Wailes 'most strongly' urged that 'no indication' of a possible arms sale to Iraq be given: 'Even a hint in that direction right now might prove catastrophic at present, driving the Shah into the arms of the Soviets out of resentment and exasperation.'[18] In Tehran for a visit, the British Minister of Defense, Duncan Sandys, effectively pressured the Shah and his advisors to wait.

In less than a week, the Soviet negotiations ceased to be an issue. Talks on the non-aggression pact failed. Despite the failure, the fact that the Shah would have signed the agreements had the Soviets immediately agreed to his terms before Western pressure could be brought to bear was of serious concern in Washington.[19] The collapse of the negotiations was so acrimonious that warning flags once again surfaced vis-à-vis the possibility of Soviet retaliation against Iran. Foy D. Kohler, in the European Bureau at State, warned Rountree in NEA that the Soviets were doubly chagrined because not only did the talks go badly, but also the Shah almost immediately announced his intention to sign a bilateral security agreement with the United States. The London Embassy reported that Moscow's reaction would be 'surcharged by their indignation and resentment of the Iranian conduct of the talks with them. They will consider that they have been deliberately gulled by the Shah and can be expected to concentrate their attack on him personally.' The Soviet experts at the State Department believed that the Soviets saw the potential for a repeat of the Iraqi coup, only this time in Iran, as the natural progression following a Communist consolidation of power in Iraq. They also predicted new personal attacks on the Shah and trouble in Kurdistan and Azerbaijan.[20] In addition, the Soviets initiated over-flights of the Iranian border areas.[21]

Over the next week, concern mounted. A special memorandum for President Eisenhower apprised him of the situation, and briefly recapitulated the events surrounding the failure of the Soviet-Iranian negotiations, adding that it had been a 'personal affront to Khrushchev'. Because the Soviet Premier had authorized the negotiations at the personal instigation of the Shah, the report expressed concern that the Soviet reaction might include a Soviet occupation of Azerbaijan. It ended by stating that Iran, despite the pressure, intended to go ahead with the agreement, but that the United States:

> must recognize that there are dangerous potentialities in the present situation. We cannot know the extent to which the Soviet statements are bluff, and thus cannot be certain that they will not take action vis-à-vis Iran which would pose a serious dilemma for us. We do know that the

Soviets are endeavoring by all means at their disposal to prevent the signature of the bilateral agreements and that their signing, in the light of the history of the recent Soviet-Iranian negotiations, would be viewed with great seriousness by the Soviet Union, even though the agreements in fact do not contain any new commitments on our part.

Herter went on to state that despite the dangers, the failure to consummate the bilateral agreements would constitute a major setback for the United States. He stated the signing had to proceed but that Washington should be prepared for any contingency.[22] Fears of the worst proved unfounded, but the incessant attacks of the Soviet propaganda machine on the Shah had their effect. The Shah could now point to his sacrifice for the Western alliance and complain that he had not been properly rewarded.

The Shah had made progress. He now had a bilateral security agreement, albeit one not totally to his satisfaction. Iranian military and economic aid had increased, although not to the levels that the Shah desired. Perhaps more important, the United States continued to be seriously concerned about the stability of his regime: 'We remain pessimistic as to the longer term outlook for the Shah's regime.'[23] Reflecting an uneasy intelligence community, Allen Dulles summed it up: 'The Shah ... as of now does not seem sure where he is going.'[24] In reality, the Shah may not have known exactly how to get where he was going, but he knew exactly where he wanted to go. Within a matter of months, he would renew, more forcefully than ever, the battle for dramatically-increased military and economic aid.

US aid and complications

Despite increases, the Shah's dissatisfaction with the amount of US aid mounted over the summer and fall of 1959. Since the collapse of the talks with the Soviet Union early in the year, the Soviets had brought considerable propaganda and economic pressure to bear on the regime. By clamping down on cross-border transit and stopping trade in foodstuffs to border regions in Iran, the Soviets forced Tehran to make up the difference.[25] The propaganda campaign was aggressive, and pointedly directed at Pahlavi rule. Soviet radio stations beamed into Iran more than 70 hours per week of Persian-language broadcasts. These broadcasts called for the overthrow of the Shah's rule and an end to American influence.[26] For example, on 12 April the Shah and his regime were labeled 'the betrayers of the Iranian people'. On 5 June, the broadcasts labeled the Shah's policies 'anti-nationalist and treacherous'. On 8 July, Moscow radio called for 'power in the hands of a real national government'. Additional broadcasts alluded to the fate of the 'tyrant' and 'traitor'.[27] From the Shah's point of view, he had maintained his relationship with the West despite the considerable risk that it entailed. He had rejected an opportunity to come to terms with the Soviets and, in return for his loyalty, the Eisenhower administration refused to meet Iran's minimum requirements for military and economic aid, while leaving him to face the brunt of Soviet propaganda and economic pressure. The Shah believed that Washington was simply ungrateful.

As the Shah exerted more pressure, Washington received all manner of advice. Pakistani President Ayub told American Ambassador Langley that the Shah was 'a good chap' but lacked the ability to delegate authority: 'Why don't you fellows get him to adopt the president set-up so that he will be an executive with good men about him, and get things done?'[28] On the issue of the Baghdad Pact, Ayub agreed with the Shah. He stated that without a command structure and more economic aid the Pact would wither on the vine. In the past Ayub had ridiculed the Shah, but now the collapse of Iraq and the instability in Iran bolstered Pakistan's importance to US containment policy, and he wanted to take full advantage. In reporting the meeting, Ambassador Langley commented: 'Ayub obviously thinks he is sitting on top of heap, that US is in position from which it can not extricate itself and he doesn't propose to help it do so.' In the near term, Ayub was absolutely correct.[29]

Always ready with an opinion, Israeli Prime Minister Ben-Gurion argued that the US had let the Shah down following the bilateral accords: '[The] US "appeared" to be doing more for Nasser than for Iran which [was a] clear friend.' Ben-Gurion suggested that more military assistance and 'psychological' support to Iran might also influence the government of Afghanistan to 'turn away more from Russia, more toward the West'.[30] Even Dag Hammerskjold, UN Secretary General, expressed concern about the situation in Iran. He informed Washington that Khrushchev and Andrei Gromyko had both made it clear that propaganda attacks on Iran would not cease unless the Shah concluded a non-aggression treaty with the Soviets and renounced its bilateral defense agreement with the United States. Hammserskjold added that the Shah really felt that both the United States and Britain had let Iran down in the propaganda war. These gloomy predictions had an effect in Washington. The State Department concluded: 'There is the clear danger that the Shah might be persuaded by the faint-hearted and the neutralists around him that he should take one of these steps to relieve the immediate pressure.'[31]

To make certain that the Eisenhower administration got the message, the Shah sent Minister at Court Alaa to meet with the British Chargé J.W. Russell on 23 July. Alaa bombarded Russell with a long list of complaints about everything from Britain's 'pro-Iraqi policies' to the lack of substantive support for the Tehran regime.[32] Two days later the Shah summoned Russell to the palace for a discussion. The Shah exuded confidence and requested that the British and Americans provide more open-handed support to his regime.[33] With regard to London, the Shah stated that he believed that they 'not only were not supporting Iran over the Shatt [al-Arab] dispute, but actively encouraging the Iraqi in their encroachment on Iranian rights.' The Shah pointedly asked: 'Why are you British always so keen on helping your enemies at the expense of your friends?'[34]

When British Ambassador Sir Geoffrey Harrison returned to Tehran, he requested an audience with the Shah. His purpose was to brief him on the recent talks with the Soviets in Geneva and to allay what he described as 'the pathological fear common to all Iranians' that in the spirit of compromise the Great Powers 'sacrifice the interests of smaller nations'. The Shah thanked the British Ambassador for the 'moral and diplomatic support', but then inquired directly about 'what practical support' would be forthcoming. The Shah raised his concerns about the lack of a clear statement on the defense of Iran in the event of a Soviet attack, the lack of a real command structure within the Baghdad Pact, and the paucity of military assistance to Iran. The Shah confidently added that he 'attached not the slightest importance to the Soviet propaganda campaign' against him. In the area of reform, he stated that he was carefully studying the issue of land reform and, despite its unpopularity with many of his 'friends', he intended to pursue it.[35] The Shah obviously intended land reform as an example of good-faith efforts to modernize Iran, but his primary concern was military and security assistance.

Political instability and increased Soviet pressure

Facing upcoming Majlis (parliamentary) elections, Iranian politicians repeated their gloomy views on the political situation. Sardar Fakher Hekmat, the Speaker of the Majlis, complained about rampant corruption in the government and army and noted rising dissatisfaction among the population. Inflation put enormous pressure on the working classes, and the government had refused to invoke price controls. Inflation also drove corruption, as government officials, the police, and the military turned to graft to maintain their standard of living. Hekmat argued that the Shah hesitated to deal with the problem because of the fear induced by the current Soviet propaganda campaign. With regard to the army, the speaker stated: 'The Shah has lost his nerve. ... The SHAH ONLY THINKS HE HAS THE CONTROL OF THE ARMY.'[36] With Iraq fresh on their minds, Washington feared that the Shah might lose control of the armed forces. Although not very comforting, the increased military funding provided new weapons and created an additional source of graft that tied the key army officers more closely to the regime.

To get some relief, on 2 September 1959 the Iranian Ambassador in Moscow, Masud Ansari, met with Chairman Khrushchev to discuss the propaganda campaign. Not in a charitable mood, Khrushchev bluntly stated that propaganda attacks on the Shah would cease only when Iran embarked on a neutralist foreign policy and sharply reduced its cooperation with the United States. The Soviet leader went on to say that, given his personal involvement, the Shah should not anticipate any changes until these conditions were met. Khrushchev then pointed out the benefits of neutralism, citing the UAR, Afghanistan, and India as examples. Khrushchev argued that 'a weak nation like Iran cannot rebuff the powerful Soviet Union with impunity', and he reminded the Shah that Iran had received little substantive reward from the West for its loyalty, a point on which both the Shah and Khrushchev could agree.[37]

Given the aggressive Soviet position, the Shah wanted the Soviet campaign against his government to be a priority item on President Eisenhower's agenda in his talks with Khrushchev, scheduled for Camp David from 25 to 27 September. Although on the agenda, the two leaders never got around to Iran.[38] Not wanting to insult the Shah, the administration informed him that several important issues, including Laos and bilateral US-Soviet relations, were displaced by the Russian preoccupation with Berlin, but that US officials had made US support of Iran clear to Gromyko.[39] To further assuage the Iranians, on 9 October President Eisenhower met with Iranian Prime Minister Manuchehr Eqbal, congratulating him on Iranian courage in withstanding the Soviet propaganda campaign.[40] In an interesting twist, Soviet Ambassador Pegov, with 'all sweetness and light', met with the Shah prior to the Camp David meeting and expressed his hope that Iran would see that the advantages of 'neutralism', convincing the Shah that the worst had passed.[41] As a result, the Shah took the lack of a discussion at Camp David with surprising equanimity.

To further mollify the Shah, President Eisenhower scheduled a December 1959 visit to Tehran on his world peace tour. The visit boosted the Shah's morale, but it had a downside. On 14 December, in a meeting with President Eisenhower, the Shah launched into his plans for a major military buildup. This included five new air bases, one a medium-bomber base, and a Nike missile system to defend Iran against a Soviet-inspired invasion from Afghanistan and Iraq. The President told the Iranian ruler that he would have his people look at the issue. Eisenhower focused on economic concerns, and suggested that a better relationship with Afghanistan might be in the offing if a solution to the Helman River issue could be found. The Shah agreed, and promised to have the Iranian Foreign Minister look into it.[42] After Eisenhower's departure, the Shah tasked the American military assistance group to begin formalizing the planning for the bases. To head off a real problem, Secretary of State Herter requested that the President write a letter to the Shah to 'make clear' that local wars, i.e., with Afghanistan and Iraq, were not included under the mutual defense agreement. Herter also suggested that the letter point out that Iran's real problems lay in economic development, not the military field.[43] Eisenhower's letter emphasized the US commitment in the event of a Soviet attack and stressed the need for reform in the finances and the administration. It pointed out that while the goal of modernizing Iran's forces was laudable, excessive spending on the military could be catastrophic for the country's economy.[44]

The situation improves?

Early 1960 brought some encouraging signs. The Iranian government had more revenues than expected to meet its budgetary requirements. The US administration hoped that this would reduce demands from Tehran for assistance.[45] Despite this bright spot, the overall stability of the regime had not appreciably improved; and the improved revenue picture was a temporary respite, with the long-term trend being downward.[46] In June, the Shah announced that Iran would hold elections under a two-party, majority-rule system. If either the government or the parliament failed to carry out its duties, it would be dismissed and the Shah would resume direct rule.[47] On the surface, the formation of political parties and elections looked like political reform. The reality was another matter. The approved parties, Mardom and Melliyun, had little popular support. While the Mardom party made real attempts to attract dissatisfied elements in society, neither party really reflected the 'actual spectrum of political opinion in Iran'. The parties were designed to function as safety valves, not political institutions. The actual possibility that the parties might survive as popular, independent political entities was remote; however, the Shah now pointed to them as examples of political liberalization and representative government.[48]

Many experienced, reform-oriented politicians argued that no real political liberalization would occur since all of the candidates were personally approved by the Shah and vetted by the security apparatus. Dr. Amini, the former Ambassador to Washington, stated that until the parties, the Majlis, and the Shah dealt with inflation and corruption, all would lack credibility. He argued that the population required immediate relief from 'economic pressure'.[49] In addition, the Shah's land reform, in its final form, was meaningless, due to concessions to the large landowners; its only value was as propaganda.[50] Intelligence reports became increasingly alarmist, expressing fear that any major disturbances could bring the overthrow of the Shah. The CIA believed that army and security forces might join an uprising if there were election irregularities. The agency warned that the security forces might take advantage of disturbances to depose the Shah and stated: 'Our purpose ... is to reiterate our judgment that ... there is a chance that the present regime may not be able to survive [the elections] and their repercussions.'[51]

The 'fiasco' of the 1960 Majlis elections dealt political liberalization a critical blow. Corruption and vote-rigging were endemic. The entire exercise resembled a bad comedy. The situation was so severe that the Shah intervened and voided the election; this action bought some time to reassess the situation and come up with an alternate plan, but there was little hope that a real solution to the situation could be found.[52] In addition, both of the approved political parties, the Mardom and the Melliyn, had participated in the political shenanigans and were discredited.[53] The Shah publicly blamed Prime Minister Manuchehr Eqbal for the election mess, and Eqbal resigned with his cabinet on 29 August 1960. Jafar Sharif Emami replaced Eqbal and formed a new cabinet on 31 August. The Shah instructed the new cabinet to conduct new 'free' Majlis elections, improve relations with the Soviet Union, and implement an economic stabilization program. Despite the removal of all of the recognized pro-American ministers, the Emami government looked much like that of Eqbal. A weak Foreign Minister, Yadollah Azodi, ensured that the Shah would maintain personal control of foreign affairs, while Medi Qoli

Courtesy of National Archives
Eisenhower and Shah of Iran, 1959
Eisenhower with the Shah of Iran in December 1959. Despite increased military and security aid, Eisenhower continued to press the Shah on the issue of political, economic, and social reform. The President was firmly convinced that only real reform could bring stability to Iran.

Alavi-Moghadam, the new Interior Minister and member of the Shah's inner circle, maintained palace control of the police. Timur Bakhtiar stayed as

Undersecretary for Security and Information, or SAVAK. The Shah made certain that the security apparatus reported directly to him.[54]

In Washington, the chaos associated with the election of the 20th Majlis accelerated concerns about the stability of the Shah's regime. On 6 July 1960, the NSC issued an official statement of policy toward Iran: 'Since 1953, Iran has been regarded in the area as a symbol of U.S. influence, and its reversion to neutralism or its subjection to Soviet control would represent major psychological setbacks, with repercussions for U.S. prestige throughout the Middle East and Asia.' The report cited the vulnerabilities of the Shah's regime, and stated that Washington needed to foster an environment in which the Shah would eliminate corruption, enact social and economic reforms, and allow political liberalization. Washington recognized that social and economic reform attacked the privileges of the principal supporters of the Shah's regime: 'Thus the problem confronting the United States is how best to influence the Shah to move constructively. A problem confronting the Shah, however, is the extent to which his regime can move in the direction of satisfying popular demands without alienating conservative elements on which traditional support of the regime rests.' In addition, the NSC report pointed out that the Shah tended to react badly to criticism. If pressured too strongly, he might seek an accommodation with the Soviet Union. Washington concluded that if the regime appeared to face problems of serious instability, the United States would have to 'dissociate itself to the extent feasible'.[55]

The Shah may have lacked Reza Shah's forcefulness and perhaps intelligence, but he certainly understood his situation and Iran better than Washington. Any precipitous move toward reform would alienate his supporters and place his rule in jeopardy. In a policy assessment, the US concluded that most Iranians probably did not aspire to a truly democratic political system based on a Western model. Instead, they wanted their economic and social grievances addressed by the government. Once in power, the 'reformers' themselves would not permit political freedom because in the fractured cultural and ethnic environment of Iran, true political freedom constituted a recipe for chaos. The question was 'if not the Shah, then who?' No clear alternatives existed, and the Shah's departure would create a huge unknown. Political discontent was rising. In addition, the second Seven-Year Plan (now in its fifth year) projected a deficit of over $130 million by 1962. The dual problem of an increased deficit, coupled with the balance of payments problems, raised the possibility of economic collapse. In Washington, analysts determined that by delaying IMF loan repayments and providing a $70 million US loan, both the economic and potential political crisis could 'probably' be averted.[56] The Shah argued that without US support he would have to turn to the Soviets for aid.

On 19 July, Chairman Khrushchev sent a letter to the Shah, outlining Soviet attempts to improve relations with Iran and listing examples of US penetration of the Iranian military and security services.[57] The Soviet move offered the Shah another opportunity to use Soviet leverage. During the course of the summer and early fall 1960, the Shah had annulled the Majlis election, and Washington had turned down the military build-up that the Shah had discussed with Eisenhower the year before. In September, the Iranian monarch let it be known that he was once again reexamining his relations with the Soviet Union, due to the lack of material support from his allies.[58] To make certain that both Washington and London were acutely aware of his 'growing insecurity', the Iranian Foreign Ministry requested assistance from both the American and British Embassies in Tehran in 'drafting terms' for an agreement with the Soviets that would be acceptable to the Western allies.[59]

In responding to the Iranian request, the US and British argued: 'Any agreement of the kind proposed by Mr. Gromyko would be open to Soviet exploitation for propaganda purposes in the outside world. It seems particularly important to avoid giving the Russians an opening of this kind at this time when they seem bent during the next six months on exploiting of opportunity of mischief-making and wedge-driving in the free world.'[60] The Western allies were so concerned about the Shah's reaction that they chose not to present him with assessments of Iran's military needs that ran counter to his views. As John W. Bowling on the Iran Desk put it: 'What president would be willing to send the Shah into a seething rage by being brutally frank with him re our military program. ... He only has to beckon and Pegov will be there. Who wants to risk being remembered as "the man who lost Iran"?'[61] No doubt someone in Washington noticed the correlation between the Shah's bouts of insecurity and his pique at not getting what he wanted, but no one wanted to challenge him either. Washington restated its support for the regime, and amended the military arms package with regard to specific requests from Tehran.[62] To what degree the Shah's perceived insecurity and instability were real is impossible to tell, but clearly the perception alone paid off.

By November and December 1960, the situation had changed little. The Soviets continued to pressure the Shah, and he complained that the United States had not lived up to its side of the bargain that brought Iran into CENTO. In fact, the Eisenhower administration had allowed the Shah to believe that he would receive massive amounts of military aid. A key factor in his decision to join the Baghdad Pact had been Turkish persuasion that membership would mean military parity between Turkey and Iran. Washington knew about the 'misunderstanding' and had not bothered to correct it. Following the Iraqi coup, President Eisenhower himself had offered to bring 95 per cent of the units in the Iranian Army up to full strength, to consider the activation of additional units, and to compensate for the strain on the economy with more financial aid.[63] The Shah's complaints about the gap between expectations and reality were understandable. This resulted in continued commitments to the military and security services totaling 55 per cent of Iranian oil revenues. As a result, the rising educated middle class felt woefully short-changed. In addition, discontent had spread through the landowning classes as the Shah toyed with land reform in an effort to placate the US's calls for reform; there appeared to be no solution in sight.[64]

The future of Iranian-US relations

By the end of the Eisenhower administration, the US was moving toward the view that it needed a new approach to Iran. Several memoranda from the Iran Desk circulated on the eve of the Kennedy administration taking power. These revisionist views stated that US policy to date had made it possible for the Shah to 'resist Soviet pressures', but that any relief was temporary. The United States now faced the challenges of Soviet influence, the Shah's resentment over his alleged lack of Western support, and Washington's growing identification with the increasingly unpopular Pahlavi regime.[65] There was also the conflict between the kind of military that the Shah wanted, a large army like that of Turkey, and the Pentagon's view of what Iran really needed, namely mobile light forces, stronger police, and security units.[66] Before Eisenhower left office, these issues resulted in the bureaucracy preparing to recommend to the new administration that it invite the Shah to Washington on a state visit and 're-argue the whole thing', meaning military assistance. The proposal stated that if the new administration did not give into to the 'importuning' by the Iranians, they could probably get the 'Shah's grumbling' agreement on the fundamental points. These points included a commitment to the 'trip line' defensive approach, increased internal security assistance, and 'improved morale and reliability' in the military. The theory was that the Kennedy administration could then obtain an agreement on the strategies to improve the political and economic situations. Iran Desk Officer Bowling articulated one drawback: 'One would have to take a sizable but still acceptable risk that the Shah would either turn to the Russians or abdicate.'[67] Apparently, Bowling mistakenly believed that Kennedy would be less concerned than Eisenhower about being remembered as 'the man who lost Iran'.

Pakistan's 'controlled democracy'

In contrast to the continued instability in Tehran, Ayub Khan appeared to have found an approach that worked so efficiently that the system imposed in Karachi emerged as Washington's preferred model for the region. Although the Eisenhower administration supported democracy in theory, the practical exigencies of the security situation in Pakistan made strong pro-Western military rule a very attractive 'temporary' option. The White House came to view a period of authoritarian rule as the only realistic path to stable, responsible, pro-Western democracy. From independence, Pakistan survived as a result of economic aid and its important strategic position within the US concept of containment. Washington believed that Pakistan had become the 'cornerstone of US policy in [that] part of the world, … [an] anchor of the Baghdad Pact and of SEATO'. American Ambassador Langley's contradictory description illustrated Washington's conflicted attitude. He stated that Pakistan was a 'bulwark of strength' which was 'in real danger of being wiped out if something is not done to arrest the deterioration in many aspects of Pakistani life.' By 1957, chronic political instability and corruption had undermined confidence in civilian democratic rule. The latest in a long line of failed politicians, Prime Minister Noon proved to be a 'weakling'. Despite significant economic and military support, political and economic paralysis threatened total collapse. While Communism was not a real threat (Pakistan was 98 per cent Muslim), Washington feared non-alignment and an accommodation with the Soviet Union or China.

US officials characterized the political climate as 'increasingly Byzantine and sterile'. Military spending approached 65 per cent of the budget. Key US officials privately recognized that requests for arms were in fact a 'hoax' to acquire arms to control the Pashtun tribes and to confront India, but the need for a continued pro-Western political stance in Karachi forced them to look the other way. To provide additional justification for its 'wink and nod' toward Ayub's coup, Washington employed some creative logic.[68] The administration reasoned that because economic improvement and stability required reduced defense spending, only a military leader could affect the changes necessary to free up funding for economic development. Through the ascendancy of Ayub, the military would feel politically secure enough to reduce its budgetary share.[69] Military rule also offered protection against the wrong kind of military coup, as in Iraq. Ayub was acceptable to Washington – a progressive, pro-Western leader, committed to paying lip service to 'controlled democracy'.[70] One fundamental problem remained, namely squaring a military coup and thinly veiled dictatorship, albeit benevolent, with traditional US principles of support for democracy and economic development.

Blending various elements of containment theory, the Eisenhower administration constructed a model in which stability, rather than a chaotic democracy, created the conditions for economic development, social progress, and finally stable democratic political reform. It became a choice between evils. It was a question of whether Washington wanted to deal with hostile or friendly authoritarian governments. Stable democratic governments aligned with the West did not appear to be viable; therefore, if there was a choice between authoritarian regimes, Washington naturally preferred pro-Western ones. In the Middle East, the military appeared to have on average less political and ideological baggage and be a more stable and progressive vehicle for change.[71] Ayub effectively argued that economic development required political stability and an end to corruption: 'History would never have forgiven us if the ... chaotic condition were allowed to go on.' He had supporters: many in Pakistan agreed. As one Karachi businessman put it: 'Now we know where we stand and can plan ahead.' Many began to view the Ayub experiment as the preferred model for economic development.[72] Ayub's 'temporary bridge' on Pakistan's road to democracy provided a realistic way to avoid chaos.[73] In effect, the Eisenhower administration adopted just that posture, and proceeded to transform Ayub into a champion of stable 'controlled democracy' – the key words being 'stable' and 'controlled'.

Paying the Pakistani bill

In the 1959-1960 time frame, the Eisenhower administration hoped, illogically, to reduce military aid and increase economic development in Pakistan through military rule. In February 1959 Muhammad Khurshid chaired a meeting of the Pakistani general staff and senior US military and State Department officials. Economic assistance, military aid, and budgetary expenditures were at issue. First, the Pakistanis wanted new weapons to replace the 'old junk' from World War II, some of which was still in the US inventory. For example, the Pakistanis wanted '395 jet airplanes', but mentioned that they would settle for '35 high performance fighters' armed with advanced missiles. When Ridgeway B. Knight, the US Chargé d'Affaires, emphasized the need for economic aid, Khurshid stated: 'Pakistan wishes it could devote more of its resources to economic development and less to defense; however, Pakistan's defense requirements must take into account the security and geography of the nation and its obligations to its allies.'[74] This was almost the same argument used by the Iranians. Containment and US intelligence installations provided Pakistan with a trump card. The balance between civilian economic development and military spending notwithstanding, the military were in charge, and they wanted new weapons.[75]

The Pakistanis developed a transparent but effective approach. First, they hit US officials over Kashmir, knowing that Washington wanted to stay out of the Pakistani-Indian dispute. Eisenhower had hoped that Ayub would be inclined to let the Kashmir issue with India go 'dormant', but Karachi continued to press at every opportunity.[76] Knowing US officials' hands were tied on that issue, the Pakistanis argued that the alliance with the US netted nothing on the critical issue of Kashmir; therefore, at least, Washington could provide more aid. The rough symmetry between this approach and that of the Iranians was no accident: 'If you cannot help us with India, you have to assist us in confronting the Soviet Union and Afghanistan.'

Charmed by General Ayub's personality, Sandhurst education, and manners, the Eisenhower administration campaigned to make the Pakistani dictator democratically presentable. The astute Ayub billed the coup as a 'revolution away from Communism' and stated that he would 'restore workable constitutional government in Pakistan' at the earliest possible date.[77] Washington parlayed these statements into a rehabilitation program for Ayub, which included press and academic coverage of the new regime in Karachi. Leading experts on South Asia viewed Ayub's 'martial law' as 'harsh only to those who have been destroying Pakistan's moral fiber'.[78] The first intelligence estimate published after the coup stated that the political and economic situation in Pakistan had improved and, for the next year or two, no threat to military rule appeared likely. In addition, it commented that Pakistan would remain staunchly pro-Western and, other than 'modest' trade, there would be no expansion of ties with either the Soviets or the Chinese.[79] Given this positive assessment, the administration argued that since military expenditures resulted largely from 'our encouraging that country [Pakistan] to join the

Baghdad Pact', military aid should be maintained and economic aid increased. The Embassy cited 'promising steps in the fields of fiscal, administrative and agrarian reform, which merit our support and encouragement'.[80]

One year after the takeover, the Embassy assessment credited Pakistan with a 'strong stable government' in Karachi, and Ayub with a 'benevolent dictatorship' that professed its intention to 'return to a more democratic form as soon as conditions permit'. This assessment bluntly stated that a 'too-early and ill-planned return to democracy might not be in Pakistan's best interest, or our own.'[81] Washington continued to push for more economic development and reduced tensions with India. Ayub could hardly minimize calls for military hardware since this would undermine the support of the military who put him in power.[82] To preserve an air of reasonableness, Ayub stated that he only wanted to modernize the forces currently under arms; he was well aware that this clever position echoed the very advice being giving to Iran. He also offered to make these troops available for joint duty with the US in the region. Knowing what Washington wanted, Ayub accompanied every request for weapons with an emphasis on the need for Pakistan's economic development.[83]

Ayub: faithful ally and voice of moderation

Pakistan's newfound stability and Ayub's 'reasonableness' appeared to offer an opportunity for improved Indo-Pakistani relations as well. In May 1959, Ayub proposed that India and Pakistan create a common defensive policy. Nehru flatly rejected the proposal, calling the Pakistani government a 'naked military dictatorship'.[84] In September 1959, Ayub and Nehru met briefly at the airport in New Delhi, giving the impression that the potential for improved relations was in the offing. Ayub in particular seemed to believe that some common ground might be found with Nehru. The Pakistani leader attempted to enlist the Australians to broach the topic of bilateral talks. Declining the honor, the Australians felt that: 'At the present time, Mr. Nehru is extremely 'touchy' as to outside suggestions regarding his policies with other countries, ... With respect, ... the relations between India and Pakistan touch upon interests and emotions altogether too sensitive for there to be room for any useful Australian intervention, however benign our intentions.' In part, Nehru's sensitivity stemmed from an 'extraordinarily stupid and apparently quite incorrect' article written by Ayub's personal secretary, Qudratullah Shahab, concerning the Ayub-Nehru meeting in New Delhi. The article indicated that Nehru wanted to compromise on Kashmir, and it drew harsh criticism in Nehru's speech on 12 September in the Indian Parliament. This article, coupled with the 'considerable strain' resulting from the failure of Nehru's goodwill policy toward China, left the Indian Prime Minister in no mood for compromise with anyone, much less Ayub.[85]

Betting that Nehru's 'touchy' state might be used to advantage, Ayub told Washington that Pakistan was open to any reasonable settlement and actually wanted an 'outside party' to 'adjudicate' the Kashmir problem. The Pakistanis informed the State Department that Ayub had initiated the meeting with Nehru in September and was willing to enter comprehensive discussions on Indus waters, border alignments, and Kashmir. In response, Nehru only indicated an interest in the Indus waters issue.[86] By appearing proactive on the peace front, Ayub hoped to garner US sympathy, additional aid, and even support on the Kashmir issue. Ayub knew that if he played his cards correctly military aid, perhaps including advanced fighters, would be forthcoming.

In a sweeping effort at personal diplomacy focused on developing countries, President Eisenhower embarked on a world 'peace mission' in December 1959. The trip included a four-day visit to India, the 'leading non-committed country of the world', and 36 hours in Pakistan, 'a stalwart ally' of the US.[87] The trip also provided an opportunity to stress to both nations the importance of economic development and the need for a Kashmir settlement. In the face of aggressive Chinese moves on India's northern border, the president pledged his support for Indian democracy and, in Pakistan, he encouraged the building of 'representative institutions' that would not 'succumb to either external aggression or internal subversion'. Eisenhower wanted both Pakistan and India to turn away from their confrontation over Kashmir and focus on economic development, social reform, and the Communist threat.[88]

In meetings with Eisenhower, Ayub underscored Soviet inroads into Afghanistan and Pakistan's role as a 'strong bulwark against Communism'. He also reiterated that until the Kashmir issue was resolved, relations with India would continue to fester. Ayub complained about US Congressional support for India and opposition to military aid to Pakistan, pointedly naming Senator Kennedy, Senator J. William Fulbright, and Congressman Chester Bowles as culprits. When Eisenhower pressed Ayub over Indo-Pakistani relations, Ayub repeatedly redirected the conversation to new military hardware for Pakistan – F-104 Starfighters, Sidewinder missiles, and Nike-Hercules anti-aircraft missiles. Eisenhower promised to review the military aid. Ayub relegated discussions of economic development to Minister of Finance Muhammad Shoaib in another meeting. Ayub's anti-Communist stance impressed the President, and he accepted Ayub's view that 'in some decades' the improvement in education would allow the Pakistani people to vote for their leaders.[89] Ayub had made an important friend in Washington.

Upon returning to Washington, Eisenhower summoned Walt Rostow to the White House to discuss the need for greater US efforts in the developing world.[90] The trip solidified a policy direction that emphasized the Communist Chinese threat against India and the need for both India and Pakistan to focus on economic development, as opposed to their long-simmering territorial disputes. Ayub obtained much of what he wanted, including an extension of military aid beyond the levels of the 1954 agreement. The package included Sidewinder missiles, B-57 aircraft, and an evaluation of an F-104 purchase.[91] On 3 March 1960, Eisenhower's personal intervention gained approval for the Starfighter sale. Washington asked the Pakistanis to hold the details 'tightly' for the 'time being'.[92] The Pakistanis responded by asking Washington not to inform the Indians of the fighter-aircraft shipment at all. Washington agreed to consult with Karachi should it decide to notify New Delhi.[93] Eisenhower had concluded that no real alternative existed but to provide Ayub with the weapons he had requested. Pakistan was a key member of CENTO and SEATO, and hosted critical US intelligence sites. At the Badaber site, Pakistan monitored Soviet missile tests in Central Asia, while Peshawar supported U-2 operations.[94] Both were considered critical to the strategic defense of the United States itself. That is all the leverage Ayub really needed.

Ayub had played the situation well. He had new arms for his military. He had avoided political compromise over Kashmir on Nehru's terms without angering Eisenhower.[95] Ayub had increased his value to the US as well, and yet he continued to support Arab issues, like Algeria and Palestine, in return for Arab support on Kashmir. In turn, he became something of a roving ambassador to Saudi Arabia and the UAR, supporting Muslim solidarity against Communism.[96] At the same time, Ayub's nationalist and Muslim credentials also allowed him to maintain strong relations with nationalist elements in Iraq, providing a useful window on the Qasim regime.[97] Ayub also appeared to be on the way to a successful implementation of land reform, something long advocated by Washington. Ayub wanted to move land ownership from the large land-owning families to mid-sized landowners made up largely of bureaucrats and army officers, who were the principal support for the regime.[98] These reforms further enhanced the Pakistani leader's reputation as a model progressive ruler. The collapse of Iraq, the weaknesses of Iran, and Soviet influence in Afghanistan had played into his hands, and Washington happily embraced him.[99]

Following the US presidential election in November 1960, the only question that remained was whether or not a new administration would honor the Eisenhower commitments. For this reason, Ayub and the Pakistani leadership preferred the election of Vice President Nixon. Following Kennedy's November victory, Ayub summoned Ambassador Rountree to his office. He wanted reassurance that the defense arrangements with the United States would continue under the new administration, and he took the opportunity to impress upon Washington that his rule had brought stability to Pakistan. He had been a loyal ally and, in return, he expected preferential treatment if Pakistan were to continue to meet its alliance and security commitments.[100]

Difficulties for India: Pakistan and China

When President Eisenhower arrived in New Delhi on his good-will trip, he received a hero's welcome. Beset by chronic domestic political and economic problems and the nagging dispute over Kashmir, the Indian Prime Minister now faced a direct military and diplomatic challenge from the Chinese. He needed friends. None of this was lost on Eisenhower. In his first meeting with Nehru on 10 December, discussions focused on Pakistan. Nehru was circumspect in his criticisms of Pakistan, but he wanted US assurances that they would control Ayub. Nehru used vaguely optimist words like 'progress' and 'they were essentially the same people' in describing Pakistan. Nehru complained that despite progress on refugee compensation and Indus waters, Pakistan 'would interject something which tended to impede matters'. Nehru's main concern was security. He told Eisenhower that he feared a Pakistani 'stab in the back' while India confronted the Chinese on the border. On 13 December, after touring India, Eisenhower returned to New Delhi and held additional meetings with Nehru. In an effort to secure the Pakistani front, the Prime Minister wanted Eisenhower to pressure Ayub into an agreement renouncing military force. Nehru argued that it would reduce Indian fears of Pakistani military modernization. In that situation, Nehru stated: '[India] would simply not take note of it or make an issue of it.' The President wanted to mute Indian reaction to the arms program for Ayub, and stated that he thought the Indian suggestion had merit.[101]

Hoping that an agreement might be possible, he instructed the US Embassy in Karachi to explore the possibility with Ayub. The President told Ambassador Rountree to inform the Pakistanis that: 'Our purpose would be to make sure that President Ayub understands the great opportunity this could give him in modernization of his army.'[102] Rountree warned that Nehru had proposed this approach in the past, beginning with Pakistani Prime Minister Liaquat Ali Khan in New Delhi on 22 December 1949, and gave little chance for it to succeed. Predictably, when presented with the suggestion, Ayub stated that this was an old Indian ploy that would commit New Delhi to nothing and allow them to consolidate their position in Kashmir. Ayub stated that Pakistan could only agree to such a proposition if the process for a Kashmir agreement were firmly established and adhered to by both parties. He argued that such an initiative would be fatal to his regime and the US position in Pakistan unless the Indians made a significant compromise.[103] Nehru had no intention of compromising; thus Eisenhower would have to settle for the satisfaction that concern in New Delhi was mounting with regard to Chinese intentions.[104]

Through early 1959, India pursued a non-aligned foreign policy as it had in the past. New Delhi believed that the US would continue to be India's principal economic partner, and treated aid as a virtual entitlement. The Indians saw it as an obligation of a rich country like the United States, and thus the aid failed to garner much pro-US sentiment in India. Washington was reluctant to pressure India by using aid, out of concern that any decease might send Nehru to Moscow for assistance or create instability and political extremism.[105] Despite some optimism that internal Communist political gains and the border issue with China might result in a harder Indian line toward Communism, the nature of the relationship remained unchanged.[106] Surprisingly, Washington did not want an Asian competition between India and China; Eisenhower himself argued against using India as a 'counterweight' in 'competition' with China. The President stated: 'It was best not to take a black and white position on the counterweight issue. On the other hand, it was very important to give India a chance to grow as a free and democratic country.' He added that at some point in the future India might well become a 'counterweight', but at this point it was premature and dangerous. Indian democracy and independence were vitally important to the West, and should not be risked in an escalating competition with China.[107]

China had become the flaw in Nehru's policy of non-alignment. The lack of a clearly-agreed-upon border between China and India had been a potential problem for some time. The area was so remote that the Indians ignored it, and neither the Chinese nor Indians pushed their conflicting claims.[108] Then, in 1956, reports of Chinese road-building prompted Indian patrolling on the border. These patrols found Chinese survey parties penetrating deep into the disputed areas. Additional patrols in 1957 confirmed a Chinese presence as much as 70 miles inside the disputed zone. In March 1958, an intelligence report from Bhola Nath Mullik to Nehru recommended a formal 'protest' to the Chinese.[109]

In addition, the border issue coincided with growing Indo-Chinese difficulties over Tibet. From November 1956 to February 1957, the Dalai Lama, Tenzin Gyatso, visited India. Apparently encouraged by the visit, Dalai Lama 'showed some independence' vis-à-vis the Chinese on his return. Tibet reached a flashpoint, and the angry Chinese cancelled a visit Nehru had planned to make there. Beijing feared that Nehru would encourage calls for greater independence. In March 1959, Tibet broke into open revolt against the Chinese.[110] The Dalai Lama escaped from Lhasa, seeking sanctuary in India, where public opinion and the press strongly condemned the Chinese actions. *The Hindustani Times* remarked: 'We may go on saying that we want to be friends with China. The Chinese don't seem to value our friendship much and this must in the end compel us away from what has seemed for a long time to be an unnatural orientation of our foreign policy.'[111] Nehru was in a 'no win' situation.[112] Nehru wanted good relations with China, but he could not ignore the popularity of the Dalai Lama's cause among the Indian electorate. The Chinese saw India as a haven for fleeing rebels and the spiritual leader of the rebellion, and in trying to straddle the issue, Nehru 'pleased no one'.[113]

At this point, Nehru decided to act. Additional patrols in 1959 resulted in a border skirmish and several Indian border police were killed or captured by the Chinese.[114] In October 1959, just as the situation in Tibet reached boiling point, Nehru pressed the Chinese for recognition of the McMahon Line. On 10 November, Chou En-lai replied with a courteous but solid rebuff. The British Foreign Office described it as a 'very clever move' that would be unacceptable to New Delhi but make Beijing 'appear conciliatory and reasonable'.[115] Chou replied that the Sino-Indian border had never been delineated, that no agreement or treaty existed between China and India in that regard, and that China could hardly accept a 'product of the British policy of aggression' as a legal demarcation.[116] The Chinese were negotiating, but the Indians had painted themselves into a psychological and political corner. Given its territorial insecurity and paranoia, India saw territorial issues in terms of Pakistan and Kashmir.[117] In a statement in the *Lok Sabha* (Indian Parliament), Nehru said, 'The McMahon Line is the firm frontier, firm by treaty, firm by right, firm by usage and firm by geography.'[118] This rigidity would ultimately prove costly, as would Nehru's loyalty to his friend, Krishna Menon, the Minister of Defense.[119]

Despite rising tensions, Nehru could not believe that armed conflict with China was possible. Why fight over a sparsely populated, largely worthless piece of land? A conflict with China also ran counter to the spirit of his commitment to bring China into the world community. Finally, acceptance of the possibility of war with China stood juxtaposed to the 'intellectual and ideological' framework on which Nehru had based Indian foreign policy.[120] The idea that the two most prominent members of the Asian brotherhood of nations would actually come to blows undermined the entire concept of *pancha sheela*, and the spirit of the Bogor and Bandung conferences. Worse, it would prove the Americans right and justify the Pakistani adherence to defensive military pacts. Nehru ignored growing warnings from the West and rejected Ayub's call for a joint India-Pakistan approach to defense in facing the Chinese. Nehru would cling to non-alignment, while seeking new support.[121]

Developing the Soviet option

Following the meetings with Eisenhower, Nehru began to cultivate a Soviet relationship. In February 1960, Khrushchev stopped in New Delhi twice on his trip to Indonesia. Although the Soviet leader did not specifically mention the dispute with China, he assured India of support. Perhaps encouraged by Khrushchev's presence, Nehru gave a speech in the *Lok Sabha* flatly rejecting any compromise with China. The Chinese had been busy. Under pressure, Burma agreed to a new border demarcation with China, and a Nepalese delegation in Beijing had taken positions 'manifestly aimed at India'. In April, Chou and Nehru met to discuss the issues. There was no compromise on either side. At this point, the Indians decided to establish permanent military posts in the border region to prevent further Chinese encroachments. Nehru simply could not bring himself to believe that China would fight, given the unforeseen consequences of such an eventuality.[122]

As the situation with China grew more intractable, New Delhi learned that the United States had indeed included advanced supersonic aircraft in its modernization of the Pakistani armed forces. Nehru had believed that the shipment of supersonic aircraft to Pakistan would not materialize. As a result, the actual announcement of the agreement came as more of a shock than it should have. The Indians responded with an immediate request for US transport aircraft, which was approved.[123] They quickly followed this with a request to purchase Sidewinders and F-104 aircraft. Washington dodged the request and referred the Indians to the British for a 'similar' weapon. Fulfilling the Indian request would cause a major breach with Pakistan.[124] Krishna Menon had been the source of both requests.[125] Menon believed that only Pakistan constituted a real potential military threat to India.[126] His argument that the aircraft and missiles were to counter the Chinese threat represented a ploy to expose the pro-Pakistani tilt in US foreign policy. Menon used the situation to discredit the United States and create an opening for military cooperation with the Soviet Union. The predictable US rejection gave Menon what he wanted: Nehru's blessing to initiate arms talks with Moscow. In August 1960, India began to negotiate not only for the purchase of transport aircraft and helicopters from the Soviet Union, but also for a manufacturing agreement. This development alarmed Eisenhower. The Pentagon told the White House: 'Once the Soviets establish themselves in the eyes of the Indians as a dependable and economical source of aircraft, their opportunity to conclude other deals for military equipment would be enhanced, thereby increasing Indian dependence on the Soviet Union.'[127] In a 26 September 1960 meeting with Eisenhower at the UNGA, Nehru stated that he saw little hope for resolution of the border issue with China. Soviet arms for India never came up.[128] The new administration would have to deal with Pakistan, India, and the future.

The non-Arab Middle East and the end of the Eisenhower era

By the end of the Eisenhower administration, US foreign policy in Iran and Pakistan retained a decided preference for economic development as the basis for creating stable pro-Western states and potentially lasting democratic institutions, but the realities of the security situation dictated support for authoritarian or military regimes and the aid programs necessary to support them. Washington feared that a failure to act in this way or too much pressure to reform would result in the adoption of neutralist policies that would undermine the strategic interests of the United States. Those interests included intelligence assets in Iran and Pakistan that were of increasing importance to the strategic defense of the United States. In the case of Pakistan, these sites had to be maintained, at the risk of alienating India. Fundamentally, military aid programs ran counter to Eisenhower's own best judgment about how to serve the long-term interests of their allies, but immediate strategic security interests took precedence. In the case of Iran, the administraton saw little option but to placate the Shah with military assistance while pressing for economic and political reform. At the end of the Eisenhower administration, containment strategy and Iran's role in it resembled the situation of December 1954. The Pahlavi regime faced serious economic problems and social unrest. The Shah was still obsessed with acquiring military hardware at the expense of economic development and modernization. Washington continued to fear the Shah's moods and his vacillating leadership. In addition, opposition to his rule appeared to be mounting. Eisenhower was convinced that only economic development and social and political reform could ultimately save Iran for the West, but he and his advisors feared that pressure to reform and almost certainly rapid reform might very well set in motion events that would mirror Baghdad in 1958. Eisenhower wanted a stable alternative to the Shah's regime, but one simply did not exist. In Pakistan, the situation looked brighter. Ayub Khan had stabilized the regime and appeared to be making headway in pursuing controlled reform. The decision to provide Pakistan with modern arms intensified a fierce debate within the United States government between those who believed that India, not Pakistan, should be the focus of US policy. The fact remained that India had refused to commit to Western defense arrangements and was pursuing a new military-assistance relationship with the Soviet Union. Ayub gave every appearance of being a stable, solid ally and, as such, had to be valued. The Eisenhower administration, quite simply, saw no real alternative to supporting the Shah and Ayub and their demands. The experience of Iraq and the fragility and instability of democratic and pro-Western regimes in the region dictated a decided preference for authoritarian control and, if necessary, iron-fisted stability. The Kennedy administration now had to decide if it would follow Eisenhower's lead. Chester Bowles, former Ambassador to India and a critic of both the Shah and Ayub, was a Kennedy advisor. He was also a realist who told Kennedy 'that on foreign policy there was not much difference between the democratic and republican parties' – a harbinger of things to come.[129] Kennedy could now try his hand.

Chapter 9: 1960 – JFK vs. Nixon, and the Greater Middle East

Predictably, the events in the Middle East and South Asia found their way into domestic US politics. The candidates in the 1960 presidential election used the turmoil in the region in an attempt to gain political advantage in what would turn out to be a very close election. The Democrats pointed to the gains that the Soviet Union had made in the region, and the Republicans argued that because of their experience they had been able to manage a complex, difficult situation, and the country could not risk the inexperienced leadership of the junior senator from Massachusetts. These events were invariably cast in terms of the Cold War and the effectiveness of the containment policy under Eisenhower. The Kennedy campaign played on the uncertainty and chaos of the 1955-1958 period, and attempted to define Eisenhower foreign policy in those terms. The Democratic challenger made Dulles' foreign policy a major negative campaign issue. The idea that Communist influence was growing in Africa and Asia became a part of the same campaign tactic that created the non-existent 'missile gap'.[1] The Suez crisis, problems with Nasser, strained ties with India, the coup in Iraq, and Soviet regional influence contributed to the view that the Eisenhower administration represented the moribund policies of the past. It added to a growing sense that the US had fallen behind the Communist bloc in the contest for world influence. It also provided a rallying point for much of the intellectual and academic community. The Democrats gained valuable and articulate allies among those with whom Dulles had had a long and prickly relationship. Kennedy tapped into both the hostility toward policies and the personal animosity of those who had viewed Eisenhower's policy under Dulles as simplistic and moralizing.[2] There was plenty of both.

Additionally, the election appeared to have the potential to become a political watershed. The consensus view assumed that the election of Vice President Nixon would see the continuation of conservative, anti-Communist policies that favored traditional Western allies in the Middle East. Nixon's statements during the campaign were clear enough: on 23 April 1960, he told the American Society of Newspaper Editors, 'We can and will make clear that the moral difference between our system and the Soviet system is fundamental and cannot be narrowed in any way by the dialogue of peaceful competition.'[3] In June, he stated: 'We will maintain the military strength we need to defend freedom. We will use our economic resources, public and private, to assist others in their quest for progress with freedom and for national self-determination, free of all outside domination. And we put the enemies of freedom on warning, world-wide, that we will tolerate neither subversion nor overt aggression against the integrity of free nations.'[4] Nixon steadfastly believed that nations like Iran, Pakistan, Tunisia, Saudi Arabia, Morocco, and other conservative states should continue to be the backbone of US policy and receive the lion's share of economic and military aid. The Vice President's advisors, like Attorney General William P. Rogers, reinforced the conservative, anti-Communist bent of his campaign. Rogers advised Nixon to take a hard line on his visit to the Soviet Union 'and not to let Russian lies about the U.S. go unanswered'.[5]

In contrast, it appeared that a Kennedy administration might offer something new. Countries like India and Egypt saw signs that fundamental change might result from a Democratic administration. The 1960 presidential campaign began in earnest for the Kennedy camp in 1958. Kennedy and his advisors focused on the series of setbacks associated with Soviet gains in the developing and non-aligned world, and systematically created 'facts' to differentiate his party from the Republicans.[6] Influenced by the economic evangelism of advisors like Walt Rostow, the Senator borrowed the 1953 views of Eisenhower and turned them against Nixon. He argued that in the developing world the United States could 'join with our allies in channeling enough aid to close the ever-widening gap between our living standards and theirs [and] encourage their economies to grow faster than their population and stabilize their infant government against the chaos on which Communism feasts.'[7] Kennedy and his advisors insisted that the Republicans had allowed Communist inroads in the developing world through their unsophisticated approach to emerging nationalisms. They accused the Eisenhower administration of ignoring the necessity of economic development, despite the fact that Eisenhower had repeatedly tried to pursue modernization policies recommended by advisors like Walt Rostow. This nuance was totally lost on the American public.[8] Wanting to set himself apart from the Eisenhower administration and Nixon's campaign, the Senator argued that the State Department policies of the Eisenhower administration were staid and out-of-date.[9] In fact, the campaign rhetoric created a false sense of optimism in the Kennedy organization that economic development would result in developing countries sharing the same values and priorities as the West.[10]

Campaign rhetoric and South Asia

Kennedy focused on India, not Pakistan. He charged that the Eisenhower administration 'in a changing time, [had] not changed; in a time that required foresight and innovation, they have relied on the old policies, some of which are long outdated.'[11] Kennedy argued that 'the fundamental task of our foreign aid program in the 1960s is not negatively to fight communism: its fundamental task is to help make a historical demonstration that in the twentieth century, as in the nineteenth – in the southern half of the globe as in the north – economic growth and political democracy can develop hand in hand.'[12] The Senator accused the Republicans of blocking economic aid to India, calling it 'the most critical area [of] the so-called undeveloped world'. He linked the survival of democracy in India to economic competition with the Communist Chinese: 'If India fails and China succeeds, then of course the balance of power moves against us. This in the 1960's will be the great area of competition.'[13] The Democrats took every opportunity to emphasize the forward-looking nature of their programs and Moscow's successes. They stated that while the US did nothing, the Russians were training their students in languages and foreign cultures in order to effectively spread Communism throughout 'Africa and India'.[14]

In accusing Eisenhower of being 'indifferent' to international ideological and economic competition, Kennedy compared India and China repeatedly: 'Ten years ago China and India started from the same economic base, with the same economic problems, and yet China, by methods repugnant to us has begun to move its industrial growth forward at a faster rate than that of India through freedom.'[15]

Kennedy hammered the Republicans for failing to address the need for massive Western support for the Indian government's Third Five-Year Plan. He argued that with 35 per cent of the underdeveloped world's population, the failure of their economy and democratic system would shift the balance of power decidedly against the United States: 'I believe that four years of Mr. Nixon would be a government frozen in the ice of its own indifference, and I don't think the world can afford it.'[16] India became the focal point for dire predictions about the battle with Communism. Kennedy stated: 'We face … a difficult situation in India, as India attempts to finance its third five-year plan. If India fails, Asia will fall. If India fails, Africa will fall. … Has this Administration spoken at all about what we and the Western Powers are going to do about India…?'[17] In effect, the Kennedy campaign transformed the Eisenhower administration's own focus on Communism into a political opportunity. Wedded to anti-Communist rhetoric, Kennedy found himself using the domino theory to attack Republican policy.

Kennedy's pronouncements, particularly those in the fall of 1960, reflected a growing sense of urgency in the campaign. His polling numbers were sliding, and the opposition attacked his lack of experience in foreign affairs. He was doing everything possible to distance himself from Eisenhower policies and present his candidacy as something fresh and with new ideas. Kennedy and his advisors worked to hide the direct relationship that existed between his ideas and the policies already pursued by the Eisenhower administration in India and Pakistan. First, almost all the issues and ideas concerning aid and economic development focused on the competition between the US and the Communist bloc. Kennedy exaggerated the level of neglect on the part of Eisenhower, and ignored the fact that the Democrats' arguments had been the basis for Eisenhower's policies in India since 1953. Pakistan received little or no attention from Kennedy during the campaign. He ignored the coup in Pakistan, and did not criticize Eisenhower over Ayub because he, like Eisenhower and Dulles, saw no alternative to supporting the Pakistani regime. Lastly, the presence of Rostow, Bowles, and John K. Galbraith on the Kennedy foreign policy team made economic development the focus of Kennedy campaign rhetoric. The press and others viewed this as new policy when, in reality, the Eisenhower administration had consistently pursued this type of effort, not only in India and Pakistan but also in Iran and Egypt, since 1953.

The Kennedy team also had another subtle advantage in playing the India card. Prior to 1958, maintaining economic funding for India had been a difficult task because of India's non-aligned stance. The right wing of the Republican Party viewed Nehru's non-alignment as something between outright Communism and political naiveté that, in either case, contributed to Communist expansion. Then Nehru appointed Krishna Menon as his deputy over the Indian delegation at the UN. This left US-Indian relations in a lurch.[18] Menon was Nehru's friend; nevertheless, powerful factions in the Indian political structure roundly detested him. He also preferred the lifestyle of London and New York to that of New Delhi. Nehru found it politically more useful to assign Menon abroad rather than have him create political problems for the Prime Minister in New Delhi. Unfortunately, Menon went out of his way to antagonize the United States and to praise the Soviet Union and Communist bloc. In addition, he insisted on high-profile, often inexplicable, votes or abstentions in the United Nations.[19] Moscow could not have hoped for more consistent support had Menon been an agent of influence. His attacks on the West and his obvious pro-Soviet leanings, coupled with a love of the limelight, made Krishna Menon 'Mr. India' in the eyes of the media and conservative political groups in the US.[20] His close and well-publicized relationship with Nehru tainted the India Prime Minister. As a result, every aid bill for India between 1956 and 1958 brought a pitched political battle between the administration and the Republican right wing in Congress.[21]

With respect to US domestic politics, this process had two salient effects on the Eisenhower administration, both of which made their way into the presidential campaign. First, the Eisenhower administration found it difficult to maintain the current level of aid to India, let alone to increase it. Menon and non-alignment effectively poisoned the well. Second, the considerable aid that was forthcoming served as a lightning rod for right-wing criticism of 'foreign aid' in general, and of India in particular. As a result, the administration tried to keep its support of India out of the newspapers and political sight as much as possible; thus the Kennedy campaign could use the perception that Washington was doing nothing to support democratic India.

Belatedly, Nehru recognized the liability that Krishna Menon posed at the UN and, in 1957, brought him home as Defense Minister.[22] Menon himself had apparently asked to resign, telling Nehru: 'I am the wrong kind and create more conflicts and difficulties – so it is best for me to "go".' The *New York Times* agreed, stating that Menon had a 'talent' for making 'a few devoted friends and many devoted enemies'.[23] Nehru rejected Menon's resignation, but realized that his usefulness in New York had ended. By bringing Menon back to India, Nehru might as well have sent him to the moon; Menon had no understanding of or real backing within the Indian political structure. As an adult, he had never lived in India; however, his departure did create slightly improved political prospects for India in the US.[24] Menon's presence in New York might have precluded the use of aid to India as a campaign issue, but circumstances had changed. With Menon gone and aid to India understated, the Kennedy campaign pounced on the political opportunity.

Kennedy's apparent campaign preferences had a downside. Pakistan was more important than ever to US interests in the Middle East and to containment. Ayub had scored a major victory in obtaining new advanced weapons from the Eisenhower administration. Basking in his new-found importance in Washington, President Ayub had serious misgivings about the possibility of a Kennedy victory. Judging from campaign rhetoric, the Pakistanis concluded that a Kennedy win might reverse their gains and jeopardize both their economic and military-aid packages. Prestige and legitimacy were also issues. Pakistani politics, both foreign and domestic, had always reflected the insecurity of being viewed as an Indian Muslim 'rump state'. Eisenhower had reversed much of that. Pakistan was a key US ally and, perhaps with Ayub in control, the most stable in the region. Membership of CENTO and SEATO aside, it was Pakistan, and not non-aligned India, that supported Washington diplomatically in international forums like the UN. Averell Harriman, a key Kennedy advisor, exacerbated concerns when he told *The Times of India*: 'Unhappily U.S. policies have aggravated rather than eased the situation, and contributed to an arms race detrimental to both countries. In emphasizing the military, the Eisenhower Administration has failed to appreciate the urgency of economic progress as democracy's best defense against communist subversion in this area.'[25] Ayub saw Kennedy's campaign attacks on Eisenhower's India policies as a clear threat to Pakistan. As a military man, he understood Pakistan's importance to the United States' strategic position, and he made it clear that a Kennedy victory could endanger US-Pakistani relations and certain critical security and intelligence agreements between the two countries.[26]

Concerns about JFK in Tehran

By 1960, Iran had received over $1 billion in US economic and foreign aid, with a major surge following the Iraqi coup of 1958. The Shah watched the presidential campaign with great interest. He, like Ayub, secretly supported the candidacy of Nixon over Kennedy. The coup in Iraq and rising Communist influence had shifted the nature of Iranian-US relations, and placed Tehran in a much stronger position. Fear of a coup in Tehran or a declaration of neutrality from the Shah had their desired effect on Washington. The growing US association with the Shah and his authoritarian regime was unfortunate but, at least for now, unavoidable. Containment took precedence. With the loss of Iraq, stabilizing and strengthening the Shah's regime had become a priority. Reduced pressure from Washington for political and economic reform in turn reduced internal pressure on the Shah's regime. Risky substantive changes were now unacceptable. The Eisenhower administration shared those same fears. The Iraqi regime had fallen during a period when reform and economic development appeared to be transforming Iraq into a more open, pluralistic society. As for the Shah, he enjoyed more leverage in Washington than at any previous time. Understandably, the Shah supported the status quo in the form of a Nixon victory.

Iran never emerged as an election issue for the Kennedy campaign. The fundamental reasons for this were two-fold. The situation in Iran was considered so volatile that, like the Arab-Israeli dispute, both campaigns adopted a virtual hands-off policy. Iran was not a topic for public debate. Such a debate could well have encouraged the Shah's opponents and further threatened the regime. It might also have pushed the Shah toward an arrangement with the Soviet Union. In addition, the Eisenhower administration and the foreign policy experts of the Kennedy campaign were united in their desire to see a program of controlled reform from above, backed by a strong, loyal military and security apparatus. The Shah need not have worried. Only by splitting hairs could any observer discern a real difference between the policies of the Eisenhower administration and those proposed by Kennedy toward Iran. High-value intelligence sites overlooking Soviet missile development centers and silos in Central Asia made support for the Shah a necessity.[27]

1953 reborn: JFK and peace in the Arab Middle East

With regard to the Arab Middle East, Kennedy also developed a campaign to differentiate himself from the Eisenhower administration, by employing a thoroughly jaundiced interpretation of the events of 1956-1960. Between 1955 and 1958, President Eisenhower and his Secretary of State, John Foster Dulles, faced a series of foreign policy crises in the Middle East unlike anything experienced before by an American administration. Even the Iranian crisis of 1953 paled in comparison with the turbulence and fluidity of the Arab world during those years, whose ups and downs gave the impression that the West had completely lost the initiative in the region. Democrats in Congress quickly seized the opportunity to make political mileage in the 1958 and 1960 elections. Eisenhower's demand that the British and French withdraw from Suez caused a serious rift with America's closest allies, just as forcing the Israelis to withdraw from the Sinai infuriated Israel and the Zionist lobby. Arguably, the Eisenhower administration performed decently in dealing with this series of changes, but political reality and perception diverged more significantly than usual. As a result, the Aswan imbroglio, the Suez crisis, the Iraqi coup, problems in Syria, and the intervention in Lebanon gave the appearance of a rudderless policy, benefiting the Soviet Union and radical Arab regimes.[28] To further complicate Eisenhower's woes, the serious illnesses faced by both the President and the Secretary of State, a major heart attack and cancer respectively, reinforced the popular view of a tired, old, and moribund administration tied to ineffectual, outmoded policies.

The ensuing cacophony of criticism from the Democrats, the Zionist community, Israel, and allies reinforced the notion that US policy was badly mismanaged. Political and media criticism further reinforced this image by portraying the Soviets as controlling the initiative through their radical Arab clients. In a 'what went wrong' environment, the Arab Middle East became a campaign issue in which Kennedy's style triumphed over both substance and reality. Kennedy's confident manner served him well, as he depicted himself as having the ability to control Middle East events through a new policy. This begs the question – did the Kennedy administration really believe its own rhetoric? The evidence suggests that Kennedy and his advisors actually managed to convince themselves that they could control and influence events by applying hardheaded policy planning and by focusing on economic development and personal presidential diplomatic approaches.

The Arab Cold War of 1959-1960 also assisted Kennedy by ushering in a lull in the Arab-Israeli dispute. Ironically, Eisenhower's and Dulles' initiatives to improve relations with Nasser allowed Kennedy to advocate economic aid without fear of political backlash. The manner in which the Kennedy campaign employed the situation in the Arab Middle East is a lesson in style and communication skills. Before 1959, the Democrats, including Senator Kennedy, basically followed the administration lead on policy toward the UAR. Reassessments now criticized Eisenhower for having a simplistic view of Communism and Arab nationalism. Kennedy had begun to build this cause in closed sessions of the Senate Foreign Relations Committee in 1957, when he grilled Admiral Arthur W. Radford, Chairman of the Joint Chiefs of Staff, on the issue of Nasser. In countering Radford's view of Nasser's Communist leanings, Kennedy pointed out that it was likely that Egypt's relationship was simply a 'matter of convenience' 'when he could not receive arms from us [the US]' after the Gaza raid of 1955. In the debate over the Eisenhower Doctrine, Kennedy stated: 'My only concern has been that this guarantee is liable to influence the Syrians and the Egyptians to even closer ties with the Russians and that it will break the Arab unity, which has been one of the sources of at least Nasser's strength, if it is at least our policy to break this unity, making the

Egyptians and Syrian more isolated from the West, and cause them to develop even closer ties with the Communists.' After Admiral Radford's statement that the Russians were 'much more apt to take Iraq by internal coup than by … overt military action,' Kennedy raised questions about Iraq, stating that in fact the guarantee proposed by the President had the potential to make Iraq more vulnerable. While asserting that the guarantee was a positive move, in a preview of things to come, the admiral admitted the small amounts of military aid to Iraq might cause junior officers to 'think [about the Soviets] maybe that is the side we should be on'.[29] Of course, by the following year, the Eisenhower administration had come to this conclusion about Nasser and Communism, and had understood the risks and vulnerabilities in Iraq, but the Kennedy campaign ignored these aggravating details. Kennedy claimed that the unenlightened policies of the Eisenhower administration had driven the non-aligned world, including Nasser, toward the Soviet Union. In a deft political maneuver, Kennedy and a handful of Democrats supported the Eisenhower Doctrine, not because they thought it was a good idea, but because, as Senator Humphrey put it, President Eisenhower's unilateral announcement had put the Senate in 'sort of a box'. A vote against it would have undermined the US position abroad. Kennedy got credit for supporting the President, and put himself in a position to criticize the administration if things did not go well.[30]

With Rostow, an early Eisenhower advisor on his foreign policy team, Kennedy bought into the idea of economic development as the answer to problems in the Middle East. Thus Kennedy's policies reflected the same optimism as Eisenhower's had in the 1953-1955 period, and ignored the hard-learned lessons of 1955-1958. Kennedy's ideas were a reversion to the economically-driven policies in which Eisenhower and Dulles originally had so much faith and of which Rostow had been a part. These views hardened into a tailor-made approach for the economic and social engineering popular with the 'best and brightest.' It also cleared the way for the application of the developmental principles espoused by the Charles River school of economists, who believed that the timely application of strategic economic aid would bring developing countries to a self-sustaining stage, or 'take-off point.' At this juncture, economic development would replace militarism and confrontation, reducing Soviet influence and enhancing that of the West.[31] The fact that this policy substantially mirrored the early policies of Eisenhower, Dulles, and Herter was ignored.

In addition, Chester Bowles, Averell Harriman, and Rostow believed that John Foster Dulles had mishandled foreign policy in general and that he had been particularly inept in dealing with the issue of non-alignment. In the case of Nasser, they argued that the Egyptian government turned to the Soviet Union only after being rebuffed by the West – Nasser's favorite refrain.[32] They managed to conveniently overlook the fact that Israel and the American Zionists, Kennedy's steadfast supporters, had more than a little to do with the Egyptian request for arms and with the subsequent US rebuff. By 1960, as a result of improved relations engineered by Eisenhower, Egypt appeared to be the perfect laboratory in which to reverse the Soviet tide and reestablish Western influence. These ideas also meshed well with Kennedy's view of himself and of what kind of an administration he would head. He wanted modern, progressive ideas and policies. He wanted to shake up the foreign policy community with new blood and ideas.[33] Kennedy also wanted better relations with progressive regimes. Nasser cut a much more progressive and impressive figure than the Jordanian or Saudi monarchies. The message of secular nationalism and social and economic development roughly paralleled Kennedy's view of himself. Finally, and most importantly, Kennedy believed that these elements, combined with the ideas of economic development, offered the promise of a comprehensive settlement of the Arab-Israeli dispute.

On the one hand, the Kennedy campaign attacked the Eisenhower administration for its poor handling of the situation with Egypt; on the other, it assiduously sought and received support from Jewish and pro-Zionist groups. During the 1960 presidential campaign, these policy elements appeared repeatedly in Kennedy speeches, particularly those addressed to Jewish groups.[34] Kennedy focused on the Israeli and Zionist unhappiness with Eisenhower over his even-handed policy in the Middle East. Myer Feldman, a Washington lawyer, became Kennedy's 'de facto ambassador to American Jewry', a position that did not exist in Eisenhower's White House.[35] Ted Sorenson, Myer 'Mike' Feldman's direct supervisor in the White House, later commented that Feldman's influence paid off handsomely in domestic politics but his involvement in foreign policy served to undermine a balanced Arab-Israeli policy.[36] One can only guess at the substance of the private discussions with Jewish leaders, but the pronouncements paid off in overwhelming Jewish support for Kennedy in the election. Despite a tacit agreement with the Nixon campaign to avoid the Arab-Israeli dispute as a campaign issue, Kennedy pressed the boundaries by focusing on the Cold War and the issue of Soviet influence.[37]

The Kennedy campaign also attacked Eisenhower policy on two general issues that had Middle East implications – 'flexible response' to nationalist movements, and increasing Soviet influence. Concerning the issue of flexible response, Kennedy argued that Dulles's vaunted 'brinksmanship' had placed the United States in a position where it had to choose between 'world devastation and submission'.[38] Kennedy attacked the 'so-called Eisenhower Doctrine' for allowing Soviet influence to become 'immeasurably greater', and wisecracked that countries in the Middle East believed that 'the shortest route to Washington was through Moscow'.[39] Ironically, in March 1957 Senator Kennedy had led seven defecting Democratic senators in support of the administration on this very issue. This vote not only funded the Eisenhower plan, but also allowed significant discretion to the administration on how the money would be used. At that time, Kennedy had stated: 'An administration defeat on the Middle East resolution' would mean 'repudiation of our Government on a major foreign policy issue before the eyes of the world.'[40] In Alexandria, Virginia, Kennedy stated that: 'never before have the tentacles of communism sunk so deeply into a previously friendly area – in Iraq and the Middle East …', and further that: 'Eisenhower Middle East Doctrine was a farce and the Baghdad Pact was a failure.'[41] Obviously, these were campaign

Courtesy of National Archives
Kennedy with Myer Feldman

Kennedy with Myer Feldman who was Special Conselor to President Kennedy for issues on domestic Zionist issues and Israel. Feldman was disliked by some senior administration officials who felt that advocacy of Israeli interests and warnings about electoral consequences of pursuing pro-Arab policies prevented a balanced Middle East policy.

speeches, but they gave the impression that Kennedy had a new policy for the region. He outlined a plan that called for the United States to reaffirm its friendship to nations in the region regardless of race, religion, or politics.[42]

Kennedy carefully cultivated Zionist organizations. On 10 August 1960, in a letter to Rabbi Israel Goldstein of New York, the candidate stated that he would urge 'continued economic assistance to Israel and the Arab peoples to help them raise their living standards' and 'direct Arab-Israeli peace negotiations and the resettlement of Arab refugees'. He then stated his personal belief that: 'the central and overriding problem in the Middle East is the problem of achieving peace in the area.' He went on to say that his administration would focus American diplomacy on ending the 'state of war' between Israel and the Arab states. In his letter to Goldstein, Kennedy suggested a conference of the 'contending states' to settle the issue, and ended by saying that: 'this will be our firm objective.'[43] On 26 August, he spelled out his administration's planned Middle East policy in a speech to the Zionists of America Convention in New York, based on US friendship for all peoples and religious groups in the Middle East, willingness to 'halt any aggression by any nation', and finally his promise that:

> All the authority and prestige of the White House be used to call into conference the leaders of Israel and the Arab States to consider privately their common problems, assuring them that we support in full their aspirations for peace, unity, independence, and a better life – and that we are prepared to back up this moral support with economic and technical assistance. He went on to say that the region needed 'water, not war; tractors, not tanks; bread, not bombs'.

The speech presented an overview of his goal for his administration – a comprehensive peace and the use of economic development to achieve it.[44]

JFK's campaign rhetoric: a fundamental difference?

What differentiated the Kennedy administration policy from the late Dulles-Herter-Eisenhower administration with respect to the Middle East? The only substantial difference existed in attitudes about the potential for what Kennedy termed a 'comprehensive peace'. He believed it was possible.[45] Given that his policy tools were identical to those of Eisenhower, what drove this conclusion? Both the British and Americans had failed since 1918 to achieve an Arab-Israeli settlement, and now Kennedy not only believed that he could make it happen but also made this aspiration the centerpiece of his policies for the region. Despite all the similarities, including the advisors in some cases, the Kennedy foreign policy team believed that their approach was different from that of Eisenhower.

In the Arab Middle East, Kennedy believed that personal diplomacy, in effect his charm and style, would allay Nasser's concerns about US intentions and remove the personal animosities that had poisoned Egyptian-American relations. As NSC staffer Robert Komer, also known as 'Blowtorch Bob', stated: 'The President was his own Secretary of State in dealing with ... Middle East affairs.' Phillips Talbot, head of the NEA Bureau, shared this view to some degree. In effect, the primacy of Nasser and the ultimate goal of a comprehensive peace created a policy troika, with Komer, Talbot, and Ambassador Badeau working together, coordinating information for the President. Kennedy did this to control and carry out the policies that he had in mind.[46] He believed that by focusing on Nasser's self esteem, he could improve the chances for US-UAR cooperation, undermine the Soviets, and advance the cause of a peace settlement with Israel.[47] This was a tall order. Second, like the previous administration, Kennedy intended to use economic aid as a lever to influence Egyptian policy. He believed that the technocrats in his administration were more sophisticated than those in Eisenhower's, and would be able to place aid more precisely in order to bring Egypt to the 'take-off' point. Interestingly enough, there was relatively little additional funding, and yet the new administration believed that it would succeed where Eisenhower had failed. Finally, Kennedy brought specialists from outside the government into the policy-making tent. This gave the White House the option of excluding all but a few professional Foreign Service officers from the process when desired.

These two appointments go a long way towards explaining Kennedy's thought processes in relation to the Greater Middle East in general and to the UAR and the Arab-Israeli dispute in particular. Talbot had been the executive director of the American Universities Field Staff for ten years. AUFS consisted of a loose collection of academics who were expected to spend about half their time in a particular region and half in the US, teaching or lecturing. Although Talbot's field had been India and Pakistan, under his direction AUFS had produced a number of studies of Arab nationalism and the non-aligned movement. He understood the issues, but was not tainted by either the pro-Zionist or the Arabist label. Given the state of relations between India and Pakistan, and Nasser's connections with the non-aligned movement and with India, Talbot possessed solid academic-type expertise in the region. In addition, many of the opinions expressed in the various AUFS reports agreed with notions that Kennedy held about the situation in the Middle East. For example, statements like 'the theme [since 1956] is a tragic one of the decline of the West in the Middle East and the rise of the Soviet Union', or the contention that Nasser was not a 'power mad dictator' but 'a prisoner as well as the leader of the nationalist upsurge', resonated with views held by Kennedy.[48]

With regard to the US embassy in Cairo, administration officials thought that John Badeau's appointment would send a message of sensitivity to Nasser. Badeau was a *bona fide* Arabist. In addition, he was well known to the AUFS primarily as the former President of the American University in Cairo. Chester Bowles, who helped set up the Kennedy foreign policy team, would later complain that the Middle East team was 'terribly closed, very closed'.[49] The fact that Badeau had no diplomatic experience, lacked stature as a political player in the US, had only briefly met Nasser, and had never met President Kennedy before his appointment did not alarm anyone in the administration.[50] By sending Badeau, Kennedy solidified his ability to conduct personal diplomacy. It represented another manifestation of this idea that US-UAR difficulties were rooted in an unfortunate misunderstanding and that once it had been rectified, partially through personal contacts between Kennedy and Nasser, there would follow numerous possibilities, including an Arab-Israeli peace. The President had stated his policy priorities, the economic experts were in place, and he had taken control of the diplomatic process by placing appointees like Talbot and Badeau, who depended on his patronage, in key positions.

Viewed through the Middle Eastern prism, Kennedy's plan to engage the UAR appeared ill-conceived at best. The idea that Nasser and the UAR leadership were merely expressing nationalist sentiments in terms of revolutionary ideology constituted a basic tenet of the Kennedy Middle East plan, whose proponents believed that Nasser's commitment to revolutionary ideals was largely rhetorical, and that his actions rarely matched his words. In reality, Nasser had for decades been a revolutionary driven by ideas of class struggle and anti-colonialism in any form. It was not a theoretically structured, clearly articulated approach; instead, he believed in a loose collection of ideas and theories. Viewed in terms of a longer chronological frame of reference, Nasser's early attempts to express this ideological bent would have alerted Kennedy to the more revolutionary aspects of his thought and to the Egyptian leader's tendency to pursue less than well-conceived policies, which made him somewhat unpredictable. In 1953, Nasser published *Philosophy of Revolution*, a vague, metaphysical rambling about the 'permanent revolutionary struggle.' It nevertheless gives an insight into Nasser's attempt to express an ideological basis for his views and actions.[51] Nasser, the military officer turned politician, acquired ideas and coupled them with his own. The result was an eclectic Egyptian political, social, and economic ideology.[52] He consistently expressed three ideological themes: 'elimination of imperialism', 'eradication of feudalism', and 'eradication of monopoly and the domination of capital'.[53] Even Nasser's insistence that all political parties disband at the time of the Syrian-Egyptian unification in 1958 constituted an ideological motivation to create a society with one creed and no organized political parties.

Nasser's ideas were crude and lacked clear articulation, but they were real. The Kennedy administration missed the significance of this component in the situation for two basic reasons. First, the new administration understood ideological motivations largely in terms of materialist economic factors. Kennedy's view of economic development followed virtually the same paradigm as that of Eisenhower and Dulles when they arrived in office in 1953. Second, key Kennedy advisors who were dealing with Nasser, particularly Badeau, believed that apparent ideological differences expressed frustration with the West and nationalist rhetoric, and not differences of substance. The idea that Nasser held some fundamental revolutionary views was foreign to the Kennedy establishment.[54] Third, pragmatically, Nasser intended to benefit no matter which party won the election. He maintained his non-aligned, Arab-nationalist credentials, and his absolute opposition to Arab Communism. Nixon would identify with these policies.[55]

Nasser was anti-Communist and a nationalist, but he was a revolutionary nationalist whose more radical tendencies periodically ran afoul of US policies and interests in the region. The Eisenhower administration understood and applauded Nasser's consistent anti-Communist stand, but they also understood that he was a revolutionary with his own vision for the Middle East.[56] Despite these warning signs, Kennedy downplayed the ideological content of Nasserism. The degree of revolutionary and ideological motivations within the Egyptian regime would only become undeniably apparent well after the new administration had taken office.'[57] The Eisenhower State Department had learned to limit their ambitions and hedge their policy bets with the UAR; caution was the guiding principle. Kennedy equated caution with a lack of imagination. He had a superficial grasp of the dynamics at work in the region. Kennedy and his advisors believed that the region had stabilized and that the Arab-Israeli situation had improved. They failed to understand that the union with Syria and the conflict with Iraq had monopolized Nasser's attention. He was simply too busy to take on other revolutionary adventures. The basic revolutionary nature of the Egyptian regime, with its hostility toward Israel, had not changed, to say nothing of Israeli hostility toward the UAR. It was a complete misunderstanding of the Arab-Israeli context.

From Nasser's point of view, the misunderstanding served an important purpose. Closer ties with the United States proved useful; he projected himself as a nationalist and anti-Communist by suppressing the Communist parties in the UAR and by working with the US on Iraq. His efforts paid off in the form of PL 480 grain and discussions of more aid. Also, his improved relationship with the US gave him added respectability with the conservative Arab states. The messages coning out of the US presidential election sounded positive on the subject of 'North-South' divisions and the efficacy of non-alignment.[58] Improved relations in his efforts to deal with regional problems did not represent a basic policy or ideological shift. When considering the chase for Arab-Israeli peace, Kennedy failed to consider the broader context.

The leverage of economic aid constituted another area in which the Kennedy administration appeared threadbare. This is perhaps the most amazing element in Kennedy policy, because it is difficult to understand how the administration could offer anything to Egypt on a scale that would modify its behavior or have a realistic chance of bringing Egypt to the 'take-off point'. The United States had attempted to use economic leverage to influence Nasser from as early as 1954. With a little more reflection, the Kennedy advisors would have realized that funding for the Aswan Dam, a huge sum, did not deflect Nasser from arms deals with the Soviets or attacks on those Western policies with which he disagreed. PL 480 wheat or other aid anticipated in the

1960s paled in comparison with Aswan, so it is almost incomprehensible that anyone would conclude that US aid could buy influence. As a serious component of any effort to get Nasser to the bargaining table with Israel or to obtain a significant compromise on almost any important issue, economic aid was a non-starter.

Finally, the prospects for an Arab-Israeli peace as laid out in the campaign appeared to lack any basis in reality. Had Nasser been personally predisposed to such a possibility, and in 1960 he was not, he would not have survived the preliminary discussions. US aid, political support, and goodwill counted for very little in the internecine wars for leadership in the Arab world. The single issue that the Arabs agreed upon was Israel. Nasser understood that he had come to power at least in part because of the preceding regime's total impotence during the 1948 war. More fundamentally, Nasser had become the embodiment of Arab nationalism and unity for most of the Arab world – he believed that Israel represented the last physical vestige of colonialism in the region. Any economic aid and political accommodation was better than none, but to actually participate in a peace discussion was not possible. At the highest levels, the administration failed to view the issue from Nasser's perspective, and, more importantly, failed to draw on the experience and caution of the Eisenhower State Department.

Changing the guard with new – old ideas

Issues related to the Middle East perhaps played an important role in the outcome of a very close election contest. In a way, it was Eisenhower's success in weathering the events of the mid-1950s that enabled Kennedy to selectively use those issues to advantage. It contributed to the view that the Eisenhower administration had unnecessarily alienated the leaders of the non-aligned world, Nehru and Nasser.[59] Kennedy was assured of the Jewish and Zionist vote because Eisenhower had forced the withdrawal of Israeli forces from the Sinai in 1957.[60] With India, Menon's departure from New York in 1957 removed a major irritant. At the same time, Indian complaints about arms for Pakistan, coupled with the lack of publicity for pre-1958 economic aid to New Delhi, served to lend credibility to Democratic assertions that Eisenhower had done nothing in India's capitalist competition with its Communist neighbors. These issues allowed Kennedy to 'muddy the water' with regard to Eisenhower foreign policy. They also united change-oriented elements in the American foreign policy community on the side of the Democratic challenger. They brought the support of key media elements, many of which had long criticized the Eisenhower-Dulles foreign policy goals and tactics.

This combination contributed to the perception that something was fundamentally wrong with the direction in which the United States was headed. Perception is the key in politics. By focusing on the trials and tribulations of 1955-1958, Kennedy managed to get the public to overlook the overwhelming consistencies between his proposed policies and those of Eisenhower. As one astute observer reported: 'Senator Kennedy has given no indication that he sees the necessity for a fundamental rethinking on international approaches. His assessment of problems has been, in most instances, moderate; his criticisms have concerned American methods and diplomatic inadequacies rather than basic aims and objectives.'[61] As the new Kennedy administration relearned the lessons taught to Eisenhower and Dulles during the early and mid-1950s, we will see just how accurate this observation was.

Part III: Lessons from the Past – the Middle East 1961-1962

As 1961 began, one interpretation of the situation in the Middle East appeared to bode well for the non-aligned states; however, another perspective indicated that traditional and authoritarian regimes were holding their own, or in some cases learning to manage the revolutionary climate of the region. In particular, conservative military elements were taking an increasing proactive role in the political life of the Greater Middle East. Turkey underwent a coup in 1960, and although the military stated that they had no desire for a permanent governing role, the generals made it clear that they intended to be the guardians of political stability. Iran seemed to be headed for another of its periodic convulsions, with unforeseeable results. Whatever stability existed in Pakistan was due to a military dictatorship. India refused to deal with Pakistan on Kashmir, and faced a growing Chinese threat in the north. In the Arab Middle East, Jordan and Saudi Arabia had survived the deluge of 1958, and, while their respective situations had improved, the prognosis for both regimes remained uncertain. Sudan and Yemen had maintained their independence but charted courses decidedly accommodating to Nasser. Israel appeared unwilling to make any real compromises with the Arabs, even in return for security guarantees and sophisticated arms. Then there was the problem of Tel Aviv's 'peaceful' nuclear program, which the CIA believed was a weapons facility. Despite all of this, Kennedy and his advisors sincerely believed that they were poised to make great diplomatic gains where Eisenhower, Dulles, and Herter had failed.

Given the fact that leaders like Nasser, Nehru, and Qasim, with more to lose, had problems assessing future developments, it is little wonder that the incoming Kennedy administration had difficulty in calibrating the political climate and coming up with a more progressive strategy for US foreign policy. In Washington, several contradictory views existed concerning the potential for US and Western gains in the Middle East. The widespread view among the more politicized of Kennedy's advisors was that the Eisenhower administration had badly bungled US relations in the Middle East and had alienated the progressive non-aligned regimes, particularly the UAR and India. This group focused on the events of 1954 to 1957 - the Czech arms deal, Suez, and hostility toward the Eisenhower Doctrine. They argued that by treating emerging nationalist regimes with respect and by providing non-military aid, revolutionary fervor would continue to diminish as they increasingly focused on economic development. They failed to grasp, or ignored, the simple fact that their proposed solution reflected not only the spirit but also the exact wording of the policy pronouncements of the incoming Eisenhower administration in 1953. It was precisely the policy that Eisenhower and Dulles had pursued from 1953 to 1954 in their quest to correct what they viewed as the bungling of the Truman administration. The Kennedy policy goals made it appear that the election of 1960 had erased the institutional memory of the government[1]

The policy myopia that afflicted Kennedy and his advisors when it came to the Greater Middle East resulted from the fact that these more proactive policy advisors, who wanted to see dramatic change, initially held the upper hand in the administration. Because of this, the Kennedy administration would take a somewhat contradictory position on the legacy of the Eisenhower administration. On the one hand, they would argue that Eisenhower and his team had bungled policy from 1954 through 1957, and on the other, they viewed administration policy as having 'improved situation' in the region since 1958. They also used their often skewed perceptions of Eisenhower to heavily influence their projections of what new policy initiatives might work in the future. Strikingly, they believed that US-UAR cooperation heralded the end of the UAR's revolutionary phase and portended progress toward better relations in the future. The UAR, as it had in the Eisenhower administration, remained the centerpiece of US policy, including renewed optimism with respect to a possible settlement of the Arab-Israeli conflict. In South Asia, increasing problems between India and China appeared to promise progress on multiple fronts. Kennedy believed that the Chinese threat could mutate into Indian support for US policies in Southeast Asia, and held out hope of a major pro-Western reorientation of Indian foreign policy. Washington hoped that India would reconsider its neutralist stance and move into a pro-Western and anti-Communist alignment. The new administration believed that friction with China would shift the focus of Indian foreign policy concerns away from Pakistan and allow a compromise settlement on Kashmir.

In parallel, Kennedy and his more proactive advisors hoped to push traditional regimes toward more liberal, if not democratic, policies. They believed that the gradual introduction of reforms would result in a pro-Western political stance. These reforms were intended to co-opt dissident elements and broaden the base of popular support for the regimes. In theory, this process would allow traditional regimes to develop more representative political institutions. The idea was to prevent revolutionary explosions and the potential for the ascendance of anti-Western regimes. An important part of encouraging and providing an atmosphere conducive to reform was to reinforce the progressive but non-revolutionary model in those regimes that had already dispatched, in one way or another, traditional rule. By incentivizing moderate policies in states like the UAR and solving key regional conflicts over Palestine and Kashmir, Kennedy and his advisors believed that they could reduce the threat posed to the traditional regimes, making political reform a significantly less risky proposition. A move to the political center would also increase the influence of the West and lessen the opportunity for Soviet meddling in the region. The new President concluded that the only way to achieve these goals was through aggressive activism and his own personal involvement in diplomacy. During 1961 and 1962, a series of situations unfolded that completely undermined these plans. Nasser's Damascene adventure suffered an unambiguous collapse. What emerged in 1961 and 1962 was the education of the Kennedy administration about the limitations of US power and influence in the Greater Middle East.

Chapter 10: Courting Nasser, 1961 – New Beginnings?

In January 1961, the new administration made improving relations with Nasser an immediate priority. Like Eisenhower before him, Kennedy and his advisors believed that the UAR lay at the heart of almost every issue in the Arab Middle East. It threatened the traditional and pro-Western regimes across the region, played an increasingly important role in Africa, was a ranking member of the non-aligned movement, and confronted Israel. There was also the belief that Nasser had entered a post-revolutionary stage and was progressing toward a more conservative stance on several key issues. Unfortunately, the new US administration could not have been more mistaken. Nasser was still the revolutionary who believed in the principles of the Egyptian revolution: the destruction of imperialism and its 'stooges'; the ending of feudalism; and the ending of monopoly and capitalist domination.[1] These views were more than rhetoric. He still believed in the 'permanent revolutionary struggle' described in *Philosophy of Revolution*.[2] Nasser still thought that Egypt belonged to, and had an obligation to bring revolutionary progress to, 'three circles' – the Arab, the African and the Islamic.[3] As stated at Bandung, he continued to oppose 'imperialism', 'feudalism', and 'capital monopoly'.[4] By 1955, the Eisenhower administration had become very familiar with the troubling ideological element in Nasserist thought and actions and recognized that the US could only successfully work with Nasser on a case-by-case basis.[5]

The incoming Kennedy administration failed to comprehend that a fundamental ideological change had not in fact occurred in Cairo. In reality, Nasser was simply busy, consumed by problems with Iraq and in Syria, as well as the continuing confrontation with Israel and disputes with traditional Arab regimes. Initially, for Nasser, Kennedy's misunderstanding served a useful purpose. He could use closer ties with the United States to his advantage. By projecting himself as a nationalist and an anti-Communist, he gained US support, muted his opposition, and managed to keep the Israelis somewhat in line. The UAR also received PL 480 grain and the promise of more aid. His stature in Washington made him respectable in the view of some conservative Arab states, mainly Saudi Arabia, and provided leverage against others.

By 1961, political, economic, and regional problems brought new pressures to bear on Nasser's regime. As one observer put it: 'For nearly two years there have been no revolutionary "victories" in the Arab World, and it has begun to look as though President Nasser is stuck.'[6] This situation directly affected domestic Egyptian politics. Nasser relied on the lower middle classes for support. The army officers who formed the backbone of the regime were largely from those classes, and their continued support of his nationalist ideology was critical.[7] The successes of 1954-1959 had focused these groups on the great Arab revolutionary cause: 'They kept their eyes fixed on distant horizons and paid little attention to what was going on at home.' The failure to subdue Iraq, Habib Bourgiba's defiance in Tunisia, and King Hussein's survival in Jordan had tarnished Nasser's revolutionary vision for the Arab world. Many believed that Nasser's focus on Africa and the Congo conflict reflected the failure of his Arab policies, an attempt to maintain Egypt's revolutionary impetus.[8] In addition, the thinly veiled nuclear weapons program in Israel and other forms of Western military support raised serious doubts about the utility of a pro-Western stance, domestically or in foreign policy. Perceptive observers concluded that the UAR was about to enter into 'a new period of revolutionary thrust, [in which] the future lies in a forward movement of anti-Western extremism'. The stage appeared set for a radicalization of UAR foreign policy and greater cooperation with the Soviet Union.

Simultaneously, the Egyptian lower middle classes began to examine the benefits of Nasser's revolution, creating additional pressure for internal change. Nasser's program to reduce the dependence of the UAR economy on foreign investment fit well with his political program based on the Arab nationalist ideal of 'Arabia for the Arabs'. This trend was particularly pronounced in economic areas long dominated by the minorities. The Egyptian government nationalized the National Bank of Egypt and the pharmaceutical industry; both moves were a blow to foreign and traditional Egyptian commercial interests. With their foreign commercial ties, minorities felt more economic pressure, backed up by the ever-present security services. In addition, the UAR government used the Congo situation as a pretext for the expropriation of Belgian property and commercial interests. Nasser made it clear that he expected to transform the UAR into a 'socialist cooperative'. Nationalization provided some short-term political gains and relief from acute economic problems, but it created long-term problems. Capital flight further constricted the availability of foreign exchange. UAR foreign exchange, already low, faced further depletion from the economic situation in Syria. Three years of drought and crop failure had drained the coffers in Damascus and left Syria unable to feed itself. This necessitated a shift of a significant amount of Egyptian foreign exchange to prop up the Syrian half of the UAR.[9] The combined effect of

Egypt's foreign, political, and economic policies placed political stress on the revolutionary credentials of the regime, setting the stage for a radicalization of policies.

Nasser: the Kennedy view

The technocratic bent of the Kennedy administration approached problems from the standpoint that they could be properly managed through a combination of sensitivity to nationalist ideals, high-level personal diplomacy, and economic aid; the White House believed that Nasser would then abandon revolutionary agitation and opt for a closer working relationship with the West. This, in turn, would open the door to a peace treaty with Israel, closer US economic ties, the further development of an anti-Communist front, and perhaps an end to Soviet influence. In the State Department, the Middle East experts took note of Kennedy's ideas. On 9 February 1961, G. Lewis Jones, Assistant Secretary of State for NEA, circulated a memo entitled, 'President Kennedy on the Middle East'. He used excerpts from *A Strategy for Peace*, in which Kennedy had written: 'American (and Western) Middle East policy over the past eight years has been a failure', advocating 'a solution to the Arab-Israeli dispute as a whole, not on a piecemeal basis'. Jones underlined that Kennedy intended to focus on 'helping people instead of regimes' in the region. Kennedy emphasized 'revitalizing the Development Loan Fund' and developing a 'Middle East Nuclear Center' in Israel – something that actually happened, but not as Kennedy had conceived it.[10] The memo put the State Department on notice that the new administration had its own ideas about what was possible. Whether those ideas were realistic or not remained to be seen.

The memo also signaled the beginning of the traditional dance between a new administration, with its own foreign policy agenda, and the professionals in the foreign policy establishment. The latter almost always had a better grasp of the feasible. This accounted for the note of skepticism in Jone's memo. On 11 May 1961, Kennedy addressed a series of letters to Arab leaders. To a significant degree, this bulk mailing was a screen for sending a very focused letter to Nasser. After commenting on the 'rich contributions' of the Middle East and invoking the 'concepts' of independence and non-interference expressed by Americans from George Washington to Franklin Roosevelt, Kennedy listed American contributions to Egypt. Ironically, all were attributable to the Eisenhower administration, including support during the Suez crisis of 1956, the Food for Peace Program, and other forms of assistance. He promised more aid for 'Middle East states that are determined to control their own destiny, to enhance the prosperity of their people, and to allow their neighbors to pursue the same fundamental aims'. The message talked of a settlement to the Palestinian refugee problem through 'repatriation or compensation' and offered US assistance in brokering a solution.[11] The Kennedy message evoked memories of 1953 and 1954 and of Eisenhower and Dulles; 'cooperate with Washington and we will reward you'.

The messenger had changed, but the message remained the same – with one large problematic difference. Kennedy needed pro-Zionist votes to stay in power.[12] Muhammad Heikal, Nasser's confidant and the editor of *Al-Ahram*, stated that Nasser's early 'admiration' for Kennedy changed to 'doubts' and 'hesitation' on reports of Israeli and Zionist influence in the administration. According to Heikal, Chancellor Konrad Adenauer told Nasser that West Germany had come under pressure from the Kennedy administration to sell arms to Israel so that the US could avoid the stigma of doing so. Whether it was the Adenauer visit or rumors of secret arms deals, concern existed in Cairo that Kennedy might not follow Eisenhower's practice of refusing to supply sophisticated weapons to Israel.[13] Fluent in English, Nasser was a voracious reader of newspapers and political commentary. Without a doubt, he knew more about Kennedy than Kennedy knew about him. Nasser believed that Eisenhower had a stature and political independence that Kennedy did not, and his cautious response reflected that belief. Nasser reviewed the history of US-UAR relations and pointed to the improvement since 1958. But the Egyptian President also made his position plain on the Palestinian issue. He cited chapter and verse on all the Israelis' transgressions and on their unwillingness to compromise on a just solution for the Palestinians. Nasser made it apparent that his options in dealing with the Palestinian issue were limited, and that only real Israeli concessions could break the deadlock.[14]

Nasser had also launched a domestic radicalization program. The Kennedy administration missed the significance of this trend for two basic reasons. First, administration experts believed that Nasser had become more nationalistic in outlook and would focus on UAR economic matters instead of revolutionary activity.[15] Second, Kennedy and his Middle East team of Komer, Talbot, and Badeau believed that apparent ideological differences with Nasser were expressions of frustration with Western hostility toward regional nationalisms. Badeau, for example, recognized the 'schizophrenic fears of neocolonialism', but he thought that this was manageable. He correctly argued that Israel pursued policies that 'served Israel's ends, but not American interests'.[16] Talbot believed that problems with Nasser were rooted in Dulles' insensitivity and fundamental ideological differences. What differentiated Kennedy from Eisenhower in the Arab Middle East? Both wanted improved relations and cooperation on issues of mutual agreement. The only substantial difference related to the potential for what Kennedy termed a 'comprehensive peace'. He had learned nothing from Eisenhower's and Dulles' failures.[17]

Talbot, Komer, and Badeau worked to control and coordinate information that would place much of the tactical decision-making in President Kennedy's hands. Kennedy believed that his own personal touch would significantly contribute to a settlement.[18] In effect, focusing on Nasser's self-esteem would improve the chances for his cooperation vis-à-vis relations with the Soviets and for a peace settlement with Israel.[19] Next, just as the Eisenhower administration had, Kennedy believed that economic development aid would bring Egypt to an economic 'take-off' point and thus spawn pro-Western policies and potentially more liberal institutions. With relatively little additional funding, the new administration believed that it would succeed where Eisenhower had failed. Last, Kennedy believed that the traditional Foreign Service was an obstacle to progress, and that he could avoid the bureaucracy by bringing specialists and technocrats from outside the government into the policy-making tent.

Nasser fails in Jordan

Just as Kennedy began the process of courting Nasser, the situation became more complicated. Ironically, because of his anti-Communist campaign and Iraqi propaganda, Nasser found himself being closely identified with the US; as a result, he found his revolutionary credentials coming into question. Jordan provided a case in point. In April 1961, the US and Britain had to make some critical decisions about the extent to which they would continue to prop up the Hashemite monarchy. Reduced aid and support would weaken King Hussein and likely lead to collapse. The majority of any aid for Jordan would have to come from Washington. The Kennedy administration would therefore make the decision that determined whether or not Jordan could continue its current anti-Nasserist course or come to an accommodation with the UAR. Washington had either to support King Hussein or to allow events to take their course. Both courses of actions had supporters but the pro-Hussein element had gained an edge. Even the financially-strapped British came up with additional funding.[20] After some debate, the Kennedy administration decided that the 'continued integrity, stability and pro-West orientation of Jordan' was in US interests.[21] In effect, Washington had dealt a serious blow to Nasserist ambitions in Jordan. From this point on, every spring the British and Americans would negotiate a new aid arrangement for Jordan. The British now had Washington firmly on the hook to support Hussein. With Jordan more or less secure, British interests in Jordan had waned as London focused on the Gulf. The British assessment of the situation was confirmed when Washington proposed to cut budget support in early 1962.[22] Wafsi al-Tal formed a new government on 28 January 1962, replacing the Talhouni government.[23] As a result, on 3 February, King Hussein and the new Prime Minister called US Ambassador Macomber to the palace to make an 'urgent appeal for full restoration' of US budget support.[24] King Hussein hinted that the combined Anglo-American subsidy cuts would put him under great pressure from 'many elements in Jordan' to accept aid from places other than his 'Western friends'. Threatening relations with the Soviet Union, he argued that he could hardly 'deny' the Jordanian people the 'benefits' that might accrue 'from taking aid from both sides in the cold war'.[25]

On 6 March, Macomber learned that the British would not reverse their decision about support for Jordan. Alarmed, he wrote to Washington:

> Soon after my arrival, I concluded that Jordan was, internally, on a descending spiral which, if not arrested, would in time almost inevitably

lead (to) the reemergence of conditions here comparable to those of 1958 and 1956. If one considers what happened in Baghdad in 1958 as a 12th-hour situation and what is going on in Iran at this time as an 11th-hour effort to stave off such a situation, I have felt we were roughly at the 8th or 9th hour of a similar trend in Jordan.

Jordan's supporters in the administration argued that King Hussein had responded to calls for reform by installing Prime Minister Tal, and now his reward appeared to be a reduction in aid.[26] Tal's selection as Prime Minister had been an attempt by Hussein to shore up his sagging popularity among Palestinians and some East Bank Jordanians, but his lack of political experience and 'alleged association with the British' made him vulnerable.[27] Reforms in the various ministries and the civil service reduced corruption but seriously alienated many of his supporters, including to some degree the army.[28] Tal wanted to include the army, led by Lt. General Habis Majali, the Jordanian Chief of Staff and brother of slain Prime Minister Hazza Majali, in the 'cleansing' program. This brought strong opposition, not only from Majali, but also from members of the royal family who believed that Majali and the army were too important to the regime to risk alienation.[29] Ultimately, King Hussein had little choice but to support Majali, underscoring the limitations facing reformist politicians.

In Cairo, Nasser understood that the lack of an appropriate accommodation from Hussein was linked directly to US policy.[30] Hiding behind a British skirt paid for with American dollars, an emboldened Hussein let Nasser know that he wanted improved relations with Cairo, but on his own terms. In correspondence with the Egyptian leader, Hussein stated that improved relations were his goal, but Hussein dismissed 'real unity' with the UAR as 'not practical'.[31] Thus the UAR propaganda campaign against Jordan continued unabated, and Amman retaliated in a way that undermined Kennedy's initiatives with Nasser. Amman radio called Nasser's cooperation with the UN peacekeeping force, among other things, a 'liquidation of the Palestinian cause'.[32] This placed Nasser in a position where accommodation on any peace plan was impossible.

Siding with feudalism and colonialism

In 1961 the UAR feud with Iraq took an unusual turn. Facing escalating political and economic difficulties, Qasim revived Nuri Sa'id's claim to Kuwait. Iraq's IPC negotiations with the British had become increasingly difficult. The British used their oil interests in Kuwait to leverage new concessions from Baghdad. Qasim had made periodic threats that he would launch an anti-imperialist campaign over Oman, Palestine, and Arab oil. In fact, on 1 May 1961, Humphrey Trevelyan, British Ambassador in Baghdad, reported: 'we would not read anything immediately sinister' into Qasim's comments about 'blood ties' and 'no frontier' between Iraq and Kuwait, but as

Courtesy of National Archives
JFK and Prime Minister Macmillan
Kennedy at Key West, Florida, in his first meeting as President with British Prime Minister Harold Macmillan. From left to right, Charles Bohlen, Kennedy, McGeorge Bundy, Harold Caccia, British Ambassador, and Macmillan.

May and June progressed, the war of words escalated.[33] By using the crisis to distract Iraqis from the problems at home, Qasim managed to back himself into a corner. Although the exact decision-making process remains a mystery, in late June Qasim began moving troops and tanks to the Kuwaiti border.[34] Whether this was an attempt to intimidate Kuwait into concessions or a serious move to occupy its oil-rich neighbor, the outcome proved disastrous for Qasim. Following a request for support from the Kuwaiti ruling family, the British immediately dispatched marines and air units from Bahrain.[35]

Prior to doing so, Prime Minister Macmillan made sure that the Americans were on board 'on this occasion' and then asked the 'Old Dominions' for their diplomatic support.[36] In March 1961, Macmillan had met with Kennedy to solidify the relationship with the new administration in order to make certain that there would be minimal policy disconnects. From Baghdad, Ambassador Trevelyan warned that the Iraqis might use the situation 'to convert an inter-Arab quarrel into a first-class anti-British issue'.[37] The British further insisted that the Kuwaiti ruler, Sheikh Jabir al-Ahmad al-Sabah, make a public request for assistance and 'send a telegram through commercial channels' to the UN Security Council.[38] The British also quietly contacted the UAR government to explain its position and to express its intention of immediately withdrawing its troops after the crisis had passed. Once again, Qasim's unpredictability placed Nasser in a very difficult position.

As the self-appointed leader of Arab nationalism and unity, Nasser could either support the 'feudal' Kuwaiti regime, or stand by and allow the colonial British to do it. On 27 June, the UAR government perfunctorily stated: 'Arab problems should be settled by Arabs.' He also acknowledged that Iraq was clearly in the wrong.[39] Nasser simply could not countenance his Iraqi nemesis taking control of Kuwait, be it through occupation or intimidation. Rather than see that happen, Cairo made a major policy shift. The UAR had systematically opposed the admission of Kuwait to the Arab League, arguing that it was a British colonial possession. Now, not only had Qasim threatened Kuwait, but the British, followed closely by Saudi Arabia, had also moved troops to the Kuwaiti-Iraqi border. If the Egyptian leader wanted to have any pretense of leadership in the Arab world, a quick response was in order.

Cairo now feared that 'feudal' Saudi Arabia might actually grab part of the mantel of Arab leadership. On 2 July, Muhammad Heikal published an article in *Al-Ahram* entitled 'A Bad Day for All Arabs.' He stated that the motives behind Qasim's threat against Kuwait constituted one of 'the great enigmas of the Middle East'. He labeled it: 'Suez in reverse'. In what can only be regarded as an officially approved policy statement, Heikal argued: 'The original Suez symbolized the victorious struggle for Arab rights but Qasim had, by threatening a small Arab country which had just become independent, produced the incredible situation wherein Saudi and Kuwaiti troops were standing shoulder to shoulder with British Imperialists who had returned with no bloodshed and no shots fired facing an Arab army.'[40] Attacking Qasim for returning the British imperialists to Kuwait proved too much of a temptation for Nasser.[41] Nasser cast his lot with 'feudalism' and 'colonialism' to protect another 'feudal' Arab state against revolutionary Iraq. As a by-product, on 20 July Cairo found itself diplomatically cornered, and agreed to Kuwait's admission into the Arab League.[42] The irony was complete. Nasser, of course, made every effort to give the appearance of having a key role in the defense of Kuwait and of making the defense an Arab affair. To this end, Cairo blustered and made threats about UAR moves from Syria against Qasim. Nasser also improved the UAR relationship with Saudi Arabia and even acquired Riyadh's contingency approval to base fighter aircraft at Dhahran in the event of another Iraqi move toward Kuwait.[43] The Iraqi feint toward Kuwait did uncomplicated damage to US-British relations with Iraq: now, British support for Kuwait effectively removed British economic interests in Iraq and London's stake in the survival of Qasim;[44] this in turn removed London's economic incentive to moderate US policies toward Baghdad. The British predicted the long-term reliance of the Kuwaiti ruling family on British arms, a dependency that protected British oil interests in Kuwait and counterbalanced IPC problems in Iraq.[45]

As for Nasser, Kuwait did nothing for his declining revolutionary Arab-nationalist prestige. He now needed a distraction and new successes. In no small measure, this explains Cairo's shift in focus from the Middle East to Africa. Nasser believed that Africa, the last bastion of colonialism, presented an alternative to the stalemate on the Arab front. Nasser supported the Algerian liberation movement, but in places like Guinea, Mali, Somalia, and the Congo, the Egyptian leader saw the potential for political and economic gain in supporting anti-Western nationalist elements. Israel had made steady commercial gains, with the clear intent of compensating for the Arab boycott in Africa; therefore, Nasser argued that he was challenging Zionism. The UAR also needed markets for the manufactured goods of its developing industry.[46] With the support of revolutionary African rulers like President Nkrumah of Ghana, Nasser began to push policies that clashed with Western interests. Then, in the Congo, the assassination of leftist Prime Minister Patrice Lumumba by pro-Western elements became a specific rallying point. Nasser's interests and those of the Soviet Union coincided once again.[47] Nasser's African thrust may have been ideologically consistent, but it carried little domestic weight, increasing his need for an Arab success. At the same time, the Kennedy administration was becoming more aware that its obligation to pro-Zionist voting blocs made improved relations with the UAR problematic.[48]

The Syrians call it quits

The creation of the United Arab Republic had been the catalyst behind Eisenhower's rapprochement with Nasser. The new potential political reality that it represented was part of the Eisenhower legacy, and formed a key element in Kennedy's perception of and policy toward the region. It drove the President's personal focus on the relationship with Nasser. The UAR meant that Nasser controlled two of the three confrontation states, and the third, Jordan, was expected to fall under UAR direct or indirect control. Viewed from the prospective of 1956-1960, Nasser appeared to have transformed Arab unity and nationalism into 'the wave of the future'. Then, on 28 September 1961, the Syrian military mounted a coup, arrested Egyptian Field Marshal Amer, Nasser's viceroy in Damascus, and announced withdrawal from the UAR. Nasser's reaction was swift and emotional. He attacked the Syrian 'reactionaries' for restoring the power of 'feudalism and capitalism'. He reserved special attention for the Ba'th Party, stating: 'We would not allow them to divide the Syrian people through discrimination similar to racial discrimination with Ba'thists getting all the privileges and other Syrians being deprived of everything.' He accused the Ba'th command structure of plotting secession for personal gain.[49] Given the competition with Qasim in Iraq and his uneasy relationships with the more conservative Arab states, the Syrian coup was a bitter disappointment. The Syrians and Ba'thists countered, stating Nasser had caused the split by threatening Arab unity, nationalism, and socialism.[50] These bitter exchanges, added to those with Iraq and Jordan, further radicalized Nasserist policy.

Nasser correctly identified the principal opposition to his socialization of Syria as the entrenched middle class and the wealthy. He believed that they had organized and financed the coup, and that he should have dealt harshly with them from the beginning. He concluded that the only way to preserve the revolution in Egypt was to follow a policy of 'no appeasement' in dealing with reactionary elements. He ordered the 'socialist measures' passed during the previous summer to be put into full effect. On the night of 16 October 1961, police and security units arrested scores of wealthy individuals with links to the old regime. The various newspapers began printing lists of wealthy individuals, along with editorials describing the impact that these 'parasitic' elements had on society. On 22 October, Zakariya Mohieddin, Vice President and Minister of the Interior, made additional arrests and initiated the sequestration of property and assets belonging to the wealthy. The attacks on the wealthy served to deflect popular attention from the failure in Syria.[51] In a statement issued on 4 November, Nasser argued that the arrests and confiscations were to 'clear the way' for the 'people' to take control of the 'social revolution'. The people would realize this control through three new popular government organs: the National Congress of Popular Forces; the Constituent Councils for the National Union; and the General Congress of the National Union. In *Al-Ahram*, Heikal wrote: 'the revolution now requires genuine representatives of the people and their aspirations' but 'these representatives must share a "unity of thought".'[52] While the internal radicalization had no doubt been long considered by Nasser, the Syrian situation made it serve the dual purposes of neutralizing the rich and diverting the attention of the masses.

The British took some delight in Nasser's Syrian come-uppance but could not fully savor the moment. London fretted that any attempt by the Egyptians to recoup their position in Syria might involve Jordanian intervention. Such a move would create great risks for King Hussein, and would necessitate the removal of Jordanian troops from Kuwait, where they were serving as a deterrent to possible Iraqi adventures.[53] In Washington, this Arab eruption came as a surprise, and presented the Kennedy administration with a problem.[54] Kennedy hoped that by refraining from taking advantage of Nasser's situation, the resulting goodwill might encourage Cairo to make some accommodations. The administration faced the delicate problem of preserving the 'personal relationship' with Nasser while dealing with the new government of Syria. Komer quoted Kennedy as saying: 'Look, I'm going to have to tell this guy we're going to have to recognize the new government because it is the government that's in power, but let's explain our policy.' To soften the blow, Badeau met with Nasser, prior to US recognition of Syria, to deliver a personal message from the President and to explain the US position.[55]

In Cairo, Ambassador Badeau feared that Syrian attacks on Egypt for conspiring with the US against the Arab cause would compel Cairo to demonstrate its anti-imperialist credentials. Badeau prepared Washington for Egyptian 'attacks on the US'.[56] Nasser would have to demonstrate that he was not the US' 'chosen instrument in the Middle East'.[57] The US Embassy in Amman refuted rumors that they were 'working with opposition elements' in Jordan in an effort to replace the current regime and install another with 'pro-UAR policies'.[58] On 16 October 1961, McGeorge Bundy queried Secretary of State Rusk on behalf of the President: 'The President is greatly interested in what policy we should pursue, in the post-coup situation, toward both Egypt and the new Syrian regime. Is the at least temporary loss Nasser has sustained likely to lead him to turn his energies more inward and to create opportunities for bettering US-Egyptian relations via US development assistance?'[59] The

President still lacked a firm handle on the situation. In response, INR at State warned that Nasser would continue 'building up his own position' vis-à-vis East and West and providing little or no *quid pro quo*.[60]

On 16 November, in a formal NSAM, Kennedy's foreign policy advisors recommended: 'While we are not enchanted by what Nasser appears to have in mind with regard to both internal and external affairs, the current psychological setting would appear to be more favorable than at any time since Suez for sympathetic attention to the UAR's aid requirements.' NEA cited the fact that the US 'did not kick him when he was down' and that a 'promising personal relationship between President Kennedy and Nasser had been developed through exchanges of letters.'[61] Meetings in October with Senator Hubert Humphrey offered some encouragement to this view. Nasser told Humphrey: 'I am not a Communist, I am a leftist' and 'I am not a Marxist in the true sense.' He also strongly defended African socialist leaders whom the US had branded as Communist.[62] In reporting, the US Embassy in Cairo emphasized Nasser's views on Communism, repeating his statement describing 'Arab Communists as traitors'. Nasser commented that he was aware that Communists directed and backed by Moscow were 'reviving popular front technique in Near East and Africa'.[63]

Nasser's 'declaration of independence from advice'

A follow-up memorandum signed by Dean Rusk on 10 January 1962 further illustrated Washington's optimism. Borrowed almost in its entirety from Talbot's memorandum of 3 January, it argued that systematic aid to the UAR should continue in order to 'encourage orderly economic development' and to 'provide [Egypt with] significant Western alternatives' to prevent the UAR's economic and political dependence on the Soviet bloc. This memorandum recommended an official visit by Nasser to Washington. It pointed out that UAR representatives had played a 'restraining influence' during the Palestinian refugee debate in the UNGA.[64] Referring to the Rusk memo, George Ball attempted to advance a potential Nasser visit from November to April 1962. Among other points, Ball believed that the visit would modify Nasser's 'radical domestic policies directed toward "social justice"' and his belief that the Zionist lobby directed US policy. It would also advance 'the personal relationship between you and President Nasser for future exploitation'.[65] Komer added: 'It is the Arab/Israeli issue which makes a visit difficult; paradoxical as it may seem, however, better relations with Nasser might give us more leverage toward promoting an ultimate Arab/Israeli settlement than any other course.'[66]

Almost simultaneously, the Kennedy administration received another warning that it had misjudged the fundamentally revolutionary nature of Nasserist politics. Following a five-day visit to Egypt, Chester Bowles, an advocate of better relations with Nasser, wrote an assessment of the UAR. On 21 February 1962, after meeting with Nasser and key members of the UAR government, Bowles described the leadership as functioning with the backdrop of a 'colonial past, scarred by deep-seated suspicions, frustrations, and plagued by a sense of weakness and inferiority'. Bowles added: 'All this leads me to believe that the current US view of Nasser and his colleagues is oversimplified and defective. We have underestimated the basically revolutionary character of the regime.'[67] The White House was not yet ready to acknowledge the ideological warning implicit in Bowles' telegram.[68]

Events soon validated Bowles' warning. On 22 February, the day after the cable was sent, Nasser delivered a speech accusing the US of 'improper activities in Syria and attacking Jordan over the Johnson Plan'.[69] Surprised, the administration placed Nasser's visit on hold.[70] In explaining the decision, Talbot revealed that the administration was catching on: 'Following so closely on Nasser's talk with you, his speech makes it apparent that he has present priorities higher than that of creating an atmosphere that will permit him to deal normally with us and with more limited repercussions.' Referring to Nasser's outburst as 'a declaration of independence from advice', Talbot hoped that the visit could be rescheduled for December.[71] The trip ultimately fell through, as a result of political concerns that it could do Kennedy domestic political damage with the Zionist lobby and Jewish voters, and cause problems with Congress.[72] At a conference in June 1962, Talbot stated that it was 'important to remember that the White House was staffed by people who do not as yet have full perspective' on the problems in the region.[73] He supported the Nasser visit and agreed with the chiefs of missions from around the Arab world, but as a political appointee, he discreetly put the best face on an embarrassing situation.

Nasser was also weighing the pros and cons of the situation. The Algerians had just succeeded in winning their independence from France; thus US support for a settlement was no longer of value, and perceptions of cooperation were hurting the Egyptian leader's revolutionary credentials.[74] The US had undermined his plans in the Congo. Seeing little to be lost, Nasser decided to use President Kennedy's correspondence to counter Arab criticism over his cooperation with Washington. On 10 September 1962, Muhammad Heikal informed Ambassador Badeau that Nasser had decided to publish portions of his letters to President Kennedy in the newspaper the following day. Heikal explained that this resulted from attempts by Jordan, Saudi Arabia, and Syria to undermine Egypt by claiming that Nasser had sold out the Palestinians in return for US aid.[75] The abuse heaped upon Kennedy in late September made what Talbot had earlier called 'Nasser's declaration of independence from advice' look tame. On 22 September 'The Voice of the Arab Nation', a clandestine UAR radio station, used parts of the Kennedy correspondence, not previously published in *Al-Ahram*, to criticize Kennedy personally. The broadcast specifically called US economic aid a 'method of enticement' and a 'foolish' attempt by President Kennedy to 'find a basic solution to Middle East problems'. The article and the broadcast created a major stir. The White House reacted by telling Talbot and Badeau to call it to the attention of their UAR counterparts, but not to make a formal protest.[76]

The public rejection of Kennedy overtures and use of the correspondence revealed for the first time the real value that Nasser placed on his personal relationship with President Kennedy. It was not reassuring. Nasser would shortly make the independence of his policies even more apparent.

Israeli complications

Nasser's frustrations with the Kennedy administration increased in other areas. During the later years of the Eisenhower administration, Israel had attempted to obtain Hawk anti-aircraft missiles. Tel Aviv always received the standard answer that the US government did not want to contribute to an arms race in the region by supplying advanced weapons to anyone. In the spring of 1962, Kennedy offered, via Shimon Peres, to provide the Hawks to Israel. In this case, Kennedy's offer was to demonstrate support for Israel with one eye on the upcoming presidential campaign in 1964. In the election of 1960, the Jewish vote had made the difference, and Kennedy knew it.[77] George Ball stated that the Hawk decision was a 'gesture toward Israel', pure and simple, and it was hailed by Israeli propaganda as a 'first step toward a tacit US alliance with Israel'.[78] In commenting on Kennedy, Golda Meir stated that the US was 'in effect, Israel's "ally"', and the Hawk sale confirmed it.[79]

The meandering path of the Hawk sale provides additional illumination. On 9 July 1962 Talbot, in NEA, specifically recommended that the sale should not take place, citing the lack of a credible threat from the UAR. In addition, Secretary Rusk argued that the US should not be the first to introduce such sophisticated weaponry into the region. Rusk also made it clear that the State Department did not feel that Israel's recalcitrance with regard to the Johnson Mission and its retaliatory raids into Arab territory should be rewarded.[80] A week later, Bill Bundy at Defense undermined State by taking the position that the Hawk would not 'shift the balance of military power' in the region.[81] In August, Secretary of State Rusk changed his position and recommended that the Hawks be sold to Israel after getting Nasser's reaction, with the intention of increasing Israel's security and thus its flexibility in its current policies. That same day Rusk submitted the Johnson Plan for an Arab-Israeli peace to Kennedy. The Hawks were to provide a *quid pro quo* for acceptance of the Johnson initiative.[82] On 9 August, writing to Myer Feldman, Kennedy's counselor for Israeli and Jewish affairs, Talbot argued that the Hawk offer should only be made with the proviso that Ben-Gurion made progress on disarmament issues with Nasser and supported the Johnson Plan.[83]

Fearing a 'most violent opposition' reaction from Ben-Gurion, Feldman suggested that he deliver the letter to the Israeli Prime Minister.[84] Kennedy agreed.[85] Given the marked distrust and insinuations from other Kennedy administration officials concerning Feldman's relations with the Israelis, it is not inconceivable that Feldman warned Ben-Gurion not to react to the Johnson initiative but to wait for an Arab rejection. Ben-Gurion undoubtedly knew the specifics of the Feldman mission well before the latter arrived in Tel Aviv, given Feldman's contacts at the Israeli Embassy.[86] Ben-Gurion immediately began to put conditions on Israeli acceptance of the Johnson Plan. Rusk saw the power-play coming and on 20 August he cabled Feldman: 'I hardly need stress that it would be most unfortunate if Israelis were to end up with the Hawks and strengthened security assurances while being responsible for derailing the Johnson Plan before it could even be given a good try.'[87] Nasser pointed out that his acceptance of the Hawk transfer and the Johnson plan would open the UAR up to the charge that he had sold out the Arab cause for US aid. Citing the propaganda war against the UAR over Israel, he argued that a departure from Eisenhower's negative position on modern weapons would create an arms race.[88] From Nasser's perspective, the US decision to supply Hawks showed growing Israeli influence with Kennedy and served to remove yet another inhibition on the part of the UAR leadership to resume its export of revolutionary Arab nationalism.

Revolutionary Arab nationalism reborn

Egyptian ties to Yemen dated from the 19th century and Muhammad Ali's campaign. By the mid-20th century, various Yemeni Imams had made some half-hearted attempts to modernize their country. One of these efforts was to introduce new educational opportunities, and most of the teachers were Egyptian. The Egyptians were providing military advisors and training, and the Soviet Union had also begun to supply arms and some advisors.[89] In April 1961, the Egyptian Consul in Ta'iz reported an assassination attempt on Imam Ahmad: 'more Yemenis wish Imam Ahmad dead than wish him to remain alive.' He described Yemen as disorganized and so 'steeped in corruption and treachery' that everything could collapse, leaving the Soviet bloc 'with its fingers deep in the Yemeni pie'.[90] Soviet aid programs had 'earned much greater good will' in the Imamate than American aid, and Nasserist support for Yemeni claims to Aden and the Protectorate was popular. Nervous about Aden, London believed that: 'If [Yemen] cannot be induced to be actively friendly, every effort should be made to keep it neutral.'[91] Geopolitically, close ties to Egypt made sense to the Imam. At odds with Saudi Arabia and the British in Aden, the Mutawakkalites needed friends. Recognizing the tie, the Eisenhower administration even changed representational responsibility for Yemen from the Embassy in Saudi Arabia to that in Cairo.[92]

The Kennedy administration believed that Nasser and Egypt represented a progressive, anti-Communist middle way between the 'feudal' despotism of the Imam and Communist penetration. Kennedy's policies closely followed those of Eisenhower. Both administrations came down squarely on the side of reform and change. Neither wanted significant commitments in southern Arabia, nor direct involvement. Badeau summed up this policy, stating that US policy support for monarchies has 'played into the Russian hands as they … depict [the US] to the Middle East as the supporters of the vanishing order' while they support revolution. He then added that he believed 'that the traditional order is doomed' and that 'radical change' was probably the 'wave of the future'.[93] In December 1961, while doing his ideological house-cleaning,

Nasser renewed his commitment to revolutionary nationalism, and added his former ally the Imam of Yemen to the list of obstacles to Arab unity and social reform.[94]

When Nasser talked about feudalist states supported by Western imperialism, the Saudis undoubtedly ranked highest on the list. Komer stated that Kennedy 'got pretty bored with his correspondence with Faisal ... one of those conservative Arabs of the old puritanical Wahhabi sect'. Most correspondence with Feisal was left to the White House staff, while JFK handled Nasser's personally.[95] Badeau's view of Saudi Arabia typified the administration's evaluation: 'Faisal, coming to power, will seize eleventh hour chance to introduce needed reforms and thus assist in securing Saudi stability for at least immediate future.'[96] By 1961, the power struggle between King Saud, who was supported by his sons; Crown Prince Feisal, who was supported by his half brothers, also known as the 'Sudayri Seven'; and a group of young reformers aligned with Prince Tallal ibn Abd-al-Aziz al-Saud was nearing its conclusion.[97] During an official visit by King Saud to Washington, on 13 February 1962, President Kennedy discussed a list of issues with the King, including internal reform and support for Kuwait against Iraqi claims.[98] King Saud predictably raised the issue of US support for Nasser. He also stated that the US needed to force the implementation of various UN resolutions on the Palestinian problem and to oppose more openly British and French colonialism in Aden and Algeria.[99] In contrast, Talbot and Ambassador Hart met with Crown Prince Feisal in Riyadh on 17 February and discussed in detail the relationship between Nasser's destabilizing effect and the need for reform in the Kingdom. Feisal understood and focused on the critical issues.[100]

During this period, US unhappiness with King Saud grew. Saud complained constantly about the status of US military assistance to the Kingdom.[101] He also pushed for attacks on Nasser, accusing the Egyptian President of selling out to Israel in return for US aid. Then he complained bitterly about the US failure to provide radio transmitters to counteract Cairo Radio's attacks on the Kingdom.[102] This served to underscore the US position vis-à-vis the inter-Arab struggles. The US gave aid to Nasser to leverage a peace settlement with Israel. Nasser attempted to undermine the Saudis, who complained to the US about aid to Nasser. The US reassured the Saudis, who attacked Nasser for trading the interests of Palestine and the Palestinians to the US for aid. This made it impossible for Nasser to seriously consider a settlement with Israel even if he had been inclined to do so. The new administration was slowly beginning to appreciate the lack of any real desire on the part of the Arab states to find a solution to their differences with Israel or, for that matter, each other.

The Israeli half of the peace equation

Israel's nuclear program, coupled with its intransigence on regional issues like the role of the United Nations, Jordan water, and Palestinian refugees, undermined any attempts by the White House to find solutions to the

Courtesy of National Archives
Kennedy with King Saud
Kennedy with Saudi Arabian King Saud ibn Abd-al-Aziz at Palm Beach, Florida during the King's 1961 official visit to the US. At the time, Saud was in a power struggle with Crown Prince Feisal for control, and Kennedy, uncertain of the outcome, was attempting to maintain good relations with both.

problems in the Middle East. Politically, the Kennedy administration could not push for concessions from Israel. The British view was blunt: 'In any event Israel will remain the albatross of western policy in this region.'[103] Political and economic instability also contributed to Israeli intransigence. A political crisis developed over the 1954 Lavon Affair.[104] In the winter of 1960-1961, the Israeli economy experienced a sharp downturn, with price rises and inflation not being matched by increased 'receipts'. Concern over its growing isolation fostered more intensive efforts to apply political pressure on the White House for support. Myer Feldman arranged regular meetings between the President, senior administration officials, and the leadership of various pro-Zionist organizations.[105]

On 4 January 1961, Ben-Gurion promised the Eisenhower administration that the US would be allowed access to Dimona. On 30 March, President Kennedy inquired about the status of the visit to Dimona and was told that the Lavon Affair crisis had delayed the visit. After discussions with the Israeli ambassador, the State Department concluded: 'Having given his word, [Ben-Gurion] does not like being pushed by the United States' and that given his political difficulties, he could not afford to add a 'Dimona Affair' to the list.[106] On 30 May 1961, both the Palestinian refugee problem and the Dimona reactor came up in a meeting between Ben-Gurion and President Kennedy in New York, during the UNGA. The two leaders agreed that American nuclear experts would be allowed a cursory 'inspection' of the Dimona facility. The US could then confidentially reassure the Arab states of the peaceful nature of the facility. When informed of the arrangement, the British were less than impressed, stating: 'We doubt whether reassurances from the Americans will in practice reassure the Arab states that Israel is not preparing for nuclear weapons development; publicly, at least, it will be difficult for the UAR to accept on this question the word of a country consistently represented as a main prop of Israel. We therefore regard some form of international or failing that, neutral inspection as essential.' When provided with a summary of the US 'inspection' of the Dimona facility, the British concluded: 'The U.S. scientists were not as persistent and thorough in their enquiries as they might have been.' The Foreign Office pointed out that the US had 'no evidence' that would convince the Arabs that the facility was anything other than a nuclear weapons center. London's suspicions were further aroused when they learned from the Canadian government that Israel was attempting to find alternate sources of uranium.[107] Taking heed of British and Arab skepticism, the US pressed Israel to allow 'free-world' access to the Dimona reactor. Having 'accepted at face value Israel's assurances that its development was peaceful', the White House actively sought to convince the rest of the much more skeptical world that it was not being duped.[108]

On the refugee issue, the Israeli government clearly understood that the Eisenhower administration had supported the repatriation of or compensation to the Palestinians who had lost property in 1948-1949. Support in the new administration for the Johnson Plan created serious concern in Israel. Ben-Gurion had vehemently stated his opposition to any repatriation in June 1948 – 'no Arab refugee should be admitted back' – and his position had not changed.[109] Naively, Kennedy appeared to believe that the Israelis sincerely wanted a reasonable settlement with the Arabs, and would compromise. The White House failed to understand that Israeli opposition to Arab repatriation was absolute. At their May meeting, Ben-Gurion told Kennedy that the UN Palestinian Conciliation Commission would fail because the Arab states merely wanted to use the Palestinian refugees to destroy Israel. The President nevertheless pressed ahead, asking Ben-Gurion to consider options for a solution. Washington was mildly encouraged by signs that the Israelis were actively considering the issue, when in reality the American focus on the refugee problem had set off alarms in Tel Aviv.[110] The Israelis viewed any compromise on the refugee issue as 'the slippery slope'.[111] Even when offered the sweetener of Hawk anti-aircraft missiles, long denied to Israel by Washington, Ben-Gurion greeted repatriation with 'a severely skeptical response'. Ben-Gurion then proposed preconditions to the Johnson Plan that he knew were unrealistic and that Nasser would reject.[112] Just to make certain that all involved understood the official Israeli position on refugees, on 6 November 1961 the Knesset passed a resolution against repatriation of refugees, while making vague promises about compensation.[113]

Ben-Gurion and other Israeli officials had not given the Kennedy administration any consideration on a single key issue, not the nuclear program, nor Jordan water, nor the Johnson refugee plan. In contrast, Kennedy had significantly compromised Washington's position. US government contacts with the Israelis would bring a predictable list of military and economic aid requests, accompanied by a litany of complaints about American aid to Nasser. During much of 1961, the Israelis complained of 'cooling' relations with the US. It was a 'deliberate' pattern of behavior. To support their argument, the Israelis would then list the military items that the US had refused to provide. US officials would in turn bring up Israel's lack of support for plans to rectify the Palestinian refugee situation and the need for additional substantiation of the peaceful purposes of Israel's nuclear development program.[114]

Repeating the past: the end of Kennedy's Middle East peace

In 1962, the Kennedy administration again focused on the Johnson Plan for refugees, and resurrected the Johnston Plan for the Jordan river valley. The Arabs were showing a decided reluctance to agree to the refugee plan, and Dr. Johnson himself believed that only an extraordinary level of involvement on the part of the President had any hope of bringing results. He was also concerned that the Kennedy had lost interest in the effort.[115] This was a repeat of the Eisenhower administration's plans that had failed in 1953-1955; nevertheless, the Kennedy administration, looking for some means of fostering Israeli-Arab cooperation, issued a policy directive on 26 February 1962, calling for US support for water projects 'consonant with the Johnston Plan'.[116] Johnson's own apprehension about the potential for the success of the refugee plan and the Administration's attempt to unofficially revive the Johnston plan clearly indicated that Kennedy policy with regard to the Arab-Israeli dispute had returned to its Eisenhower roots. Kennedy, unlike Eisenhower, could not point to a single concrete issue where he had supported an Arab cause vis-à-vis Israel. The Israelis had successfully blunted all efforts to wring concessions from them, and now they focused on making certain that Nasser did not gain additional influence in Washington.[117]

Between January 1961 and September 1962, the Kennedy administration relearned the lessons taught to Eisenhower between 1955 and 1958. Neither the Arabs nor the Israelis were interested in realistic compromise. The Israelis had newfound political leverage in Washington, via a narrowly-elected Democratic president who needed Jewish votes. They had no reason to compromise, because ultimately the resident at 1600 Pennsylvania Avenue was in no position to keep them honest. The Arabs still saw little to be gained from an administration that desperately needed domestic Jewish political support. Nasser saw less reason to pursue strengthening his ties with Washington. The US and Britain were also moving more into line on policy issues. The imbroglio over Kuwait eliminated disagreements with the US over how to deal with Iraq. In addition, the Kuwaiti crisis served to underscore the fact that

Britain refused to act unilaterally without specific US agreement. Now largely out of Iraq, tied by treaty to an independent Kuwait, lacking substantial relations with Egypt and Saudi Arabia, British influence clearly rode US coattails in the Arab world.

For the Arabs, the Syrian secession increased Jordan's chances of survival. The two most powerful Arab states and their respective revolutionary regimes were struggling. From the US perspective, the situation in Iraq had improved with the decline in influence of the Communist Party, but the Kennedy administration's hopes for its relationship with Nasser seemed to be in trouble as Egypt spiraled toward potentially more aggressive internal and external policies. In Saudi Arabia, the struggle for power between Crown Prince Feisal and King Saud continued, but there were indications that Feisal might be gaining the upper hand. In addition, Washington had once again been sensitized to the US interests in Saudi oil. As the fall of 1962 approached, most of the tendencies pointed to the return of the Kennedy administration to the fundamentals of past policies, but a catalyst for making them coalesce was lacking. That catalyst would shortly appear.

Chapter 11: Iran at 'the Eleventh Hour'

The situation in Iran best illustrated the degree to which Kennedy's White House inherited the policies of Eisenhower, and conversely how subsequent historical interpretations have focused on minor differences in order to build a case that Kennedy policy was more progressive and reform-minded. For both administrations, Iran was a critical, if problematic, part of their commitment to confront and contain the Soviet Union through defense alliances. Both wanted to eliminate the sources of instability through economic development and social and political reform. While the short-term results of these policies were almost identical, Kennedy's divergence from Eisenhower on the key issue of support for the Pahlavi dynasty had significant long-term repercussions. The Kennedy administration, in seeking to free itself from the Shah and find an alternative to his rule, miscalculated and ultimately bound itself and the United States even more tightly to the fortunes of the Pahlavi dynasty. In a series of decisions driven by a combination of 'hyper-activism', inexperience, hubris, and distrust, Kennedy and his closest advisors temporarily succeeded in excluding the traditional foreign policy apparatus from the decision-making process.[1] This temporary situation resulted in a misunderstanding of the nature of Iranian political instability in May 1961, which ultimately led to the situation where US fortunes and those of the Shah were one and the same. After a brief flirtation with an alternative political power center, Kennedy would find, as had Eisenhower's administration before him, that no real alternative to the Shah existed.[2]

Kennedy's direct support for and endorsement of Prime Minister Ali Amini, followed by a belated realization that Amini had no real political backing, left Kennedy no option but to offer the same level of support to the Shah. By overestimating the potential of the National Front opposition, by misunderstanding the political crisis in Iran, and by underestimating the ability of the Shah to manipulate the situation to his advantage, the Kennedy administration tied the United States to personal support of the Shah that only ended in 1979. The fear of an Iranian collapse drove this well-intentioned but ultimately ill-conceived policy.³ Ambassador Macomber in Amman expressed the administration's view most clearly when he described Iran as being at the '11th hour'.⁴ Just as Eisenhower had worked assiduously not to become 'the man who lost Iran', Kennedy was, if anything, even more determined to avoid that distinction.⁵ The new administration believed that it faced an imminent crisis requiring special focus. To that end, Kennedy ordered Phillips Talbot to set up and chair an 'Iranian Task Force'. In the administration's view, the Shah was 'weak', 'insecure', and driven by 'a huge megalomania', making him 'very difficult to deal with'.⁶ Because of the Shah's apparent instability, Kennedy and his advisors concluded that the Pahlavi rule and a pro-Western Iran were on the verge of collapse.

Soviet threats and Iran

Was the situation in Iran that serious? Probably not, but in defense of Kennedy's foreign policy team, the situation was frightening. In a 10 April 1961 meeting on the Black Sea, Khrushchev told Walter Lippmann that despite weaknesses in the Communist Party, Iran was ripe for revolution. The Soviet Premier stated: 'You will assert that the Shah has been overthrown by the Communists, and we shall be very glad to have it thought in the world that all the progressive people in Iran recognize that we are the leaders of the progress of mankind.'⁷ Taking an alarmist view, the Kennedy administration believed that only immediate and extensive reform could save the regime. Instead of viewing the latest Kremlin pronouncement in the context of Khrushchev's 1959 diplomatic embarrassment in Iran, the White House took the Soviet leader's statement as a direct challenge to its 'pay any price, bear any burden' pronouncements. Kennedy also believed that Iran could become the model for the growth of democracy and Western economic ideals in the Middle East and the Islamic world, a case study in economic development and reform.⁸ However, in January 1961, Iran appeared to be the next Iraq, and the new administration was convinced that only 'reform' could save it.⁹ With regard to reform, Eisenhower's and Kennedy's tactics were similar, as was the Shah's reaction. Kennedy should have been in a stronger bargaining position. Three years had passed since the turmoil of 1958, and yet the ability to influence the Shah's rule proved as elusive for Kennedy as it had for Eisenhower. Like the previous administration, Kennedy and his advisors recognized that the US needed Iranian telemetry sites and an anti-Communist Iran. The question centered on what was the best Iranian political vehicle to support US interests.

The Shah's perspective on US-Iranian relations

Immediately after the inauguration, the Shah sent Kennedy a letter addressing Iran's potentially 'bright future' and citing its natural resources and lack of overpopulation. The Shah argued that his rule had replaced one of 'martial law', 'tenure of power', 'intimidation', 'blackmail', 'mob rule', and 'surrender to the domination of communism'. He stated: 'Iran is the one country that enjoys a democratic regime with all the freedoms except the freedom to commit treason and to betray the interests of the Fatherland.' He then pointed out that this 'bright future', to which Iran was 'entitled', required military assistance that 'only America can furnish'. Playing the neutralist card, the Shah stated: 'These times are fraught with danger and the question is not whether any one country is to remain more or less within the committed group of nations.' The Shah pointedly declared that Iran was 'the key to the region', and thus the 'key to Asia'. The Iranian monarch then offered a rhetorical question: 'Would it be too much to hope that you will bear this in mind when you decide upon the assistance which you are willing to extend to Iran for her economic development as well as for her military support?'[10] The Shah requested that Kennedy meet the Deputy Iranian Prime Minister on the latter's upcoming trip to Washington, and suggested topics for discussion: the Communist danger; the insufficiency of US military aid; the necessity for more economic aid; and an increase in Iranian oil production. The attachment then stated: 'Without these actions, doubt may arise in public opinion about the utility of the present policy of Iran.'[11] The Shah wanted more military assistance in return for his support of containment.

The Kennedy administration faced the same conundrum that Eisenhower confronted for eight years; if not the Shah, then whom? The Iran Desk Officer John Bowling produced a pessimistic white paper on the potential for democratic government in Iran, stating: 'The term "political compromise" cannot be translated into everyday Persian without a connotation of "sell-out"'; 'The urban middle class has historically had no interest in or knowledge of financial realities'; and 'Democracy in the Western sense means nothing to the urban middle class'. He pointed out that the emergence of urban middle class leadership with political power might bring class war and retribution against the wealthy. Bowling concluded that the threat could only be halted by 'stopping the process of culture clash, and that is impossible in the world today'. The report also saw no 'competent' leadership emerging from the urban middle class, the military, or the traditional leaders, including the clergy, landlords, and very large merchants. It concluded: 'There is one potential leader who has the necessary ability, personality, and talent, and whose political capital is not yet quite exhausted. That is the Shah himself.'[12] Riots in January and February 1961 left the Shah increasingly dependent on the security forces, 'which are not, in our view, very dependable'. Washington feared an alliance between civilian and military dissidents to overthrow the Shah.[13] The Soviets also increased pressure for a neutral Iran. Fearing a Soviet-Iranian rapprochement, the NSC called for a reaffirmation of US support for Iran, saying: 'Given the psychological make-up of the man, it is always possible that he may move a considerable distance toward neutralism.'[14] The Iranian monarch had convinced Washington that non-alignment was a real option.

Just to make certain that the message was clear, the Shah sent General Teymour Bakhtiar, chief of SAVAK, to Washington to emphasize that the Shah was concerned about the sincerity of the United States. Bakhtiar and

Iranian Ambassador Ardeshi Zahedi contended that Soviet pressure might force the Shah to come to terms with Moscow. Just to make his point, in late February 1961 the Shah announced that the Soviet Union had agreed to accept a high-level Iranian delegation headed by the Prime Minister to explore avenues for lessening tensions between the two countries. In the Kennedy White House, concern mounted: 'The Shah believes that he has been grievously mistreated by the United States and that he has not received the aid, which he considers to be the rightful price of his adherence to CENTO. He may break up CENTO, out of pique or out of a calculated desire to go neutralist for its political, military, and economic benefits.' The report added: 'He sees no other substantive benefits in CENTO; he does not really trust his regional allies.'[15] Washington's perception of the Shah's 'troubled and confused mind' played again to the monarch's advantage.[16] A neutral Iran would have been a disaster for the US.

Doing something about Iran

Thoroughly alarmed, the President dispatched Special Presidential Envoy Averell Harriman to Iran in March 1961. Harriman explained to the Shah the budgetary constraints facing the new administration. The Ambassador's conclusions vis-à-vis the situation in Iran decisively affected the new administration and reflected Eisenhower's views. Harriman wrote the President saying that he was impressed with the improved standards of housing, the 'appearance of the people', the level of education, and 'substantially' reduced unemployment. Harriman also remarked that the professionalism of the army and bureaucracy were much improved, and offered the following analysis: 'On the one hand, Mullahs and large landowners oppose progress, and on the other, national front (Mossadequists) are rabble-rousers and give little promise of stable government, and are probably infiltrated by Tudeh influence. Shah is at the moment our only hope of stability with pro-West policy. Neutrality in Iran would today mean Communist takeover.' Harriman went on to say: 'I believe Shah should be supported, dealt with frankly, and not treated as an unwanted stepchild.' He concluded that the Shah wanted social, economic, and political reform including the 'development of democratic institutions'. Citing natural resources, under-population, and a 'close association with the West', Harriman stated: 'Iran is a good bet if social advance and political stability can be achieved.'[17] The Ambassador's message mirrored the Shah's own arguments in the 26 January letter to Kennedy and the views of the previous administration.

At the NSC, Komer reacted to the Harriman report by fuming at George McGhee about the 'old refrain' from the State Department. In a memorandum entitled 'Do-Nothingism in Iran', Komer ranted to McGeorge Bundy and Walt Rostow: 'Sure, says State, the real threat to Iran is internal rather than external. Sure the Shah is a vacillating weakling who cannot be pressed too hard. Sure we must still rely on him as our chosen instrument until we get something better. But are we still debarred from anything more than further "delicate inferences" by our ambassador, plus giving him some more Baksheesh?' Komer went on to say that all the State Department had to offer was a view of 'what we should have been doing for the last five years'. Wanting the US to act, Komer argued: 'One of the key reasons why the Shah thinks as he does is that we have not made enough of high level effort to educate him. For my money, Harriman did more in a few hours than Wailes in three years.' Pontificating, Komer stated: 'Hence, with authority of "New Frontier" behind us is not now the time for frank re-orientation of our efforts and greater pressure if necessary?' He concluded that the Shah needed to be told that it was in his 'own best interest' to face up to the 'stark realities of life'.[18] It remained to be seen who would 'educate' whom on these stark realities.

Citing Iranian 'determination to carry out the necessary stabilization measures', Kennedy advisors concluded that 'crucial elements', including timely US aid and rapid steps toward a Third Development Plan, would determine Iran's success or failure.[19] On 27 March, Thomas E. Morgan, Vice-Chairman of the Policy Planning Council, concluded: 'It would appear preferable that the United States would be best advised to continue its present policy of reassurance to the Shah of United States sympathy and support, along with persistent but delicate inferences by our Ambassador to the effect that the Shah should devote his attention to his internal political problems.' Morgan added that the United States needed to monitor the Shah's dealings with the Soviet Union closely.[20] Morgan's memo contributed to the cumulative frustration and concern in the White House and provoked an explosion of sorts on the part of Walt Rostow.

Scoffing at 'delicate inferences', Rostow irascibly asked: 'Can't we get more specific in the matter of "Inducing" the Shah to win the confidence of the urban middle class?' Exasperation rising, Rostow bombarded McGhee at State with questions:

> Should we not back, for example the notion of the Senior Development Corps, which, I understand, is incorporated in the Third Iranian Five-Year Plan? ... Should we not support the proposal in the Third Iranian Five-Year Plan, which would allocate increased resources to the private sector where a new class of acquisitive businessmen of some competence is emerging? ... Is it really out of the question to establish contact with, and perhaps – in appropriate ways – to induce the Shah to bring into his administration a limited number of able and reasonably reliable new men rising in Iranian society? ... Should we not strain the capacity of our staff work resources in Washington to clarify the direction we should like his [US Ambassador to Iran Julius C. Holmes] 'delicate inferences' to take? ... Should we not make a fresh try to come to a more solid understanding with the Shah on the nature of our security commitment to him and concerning the purposes his military establishment should fulfill? If joining CENTO is impossible, is there not some way to increase his sense of security about American support?[21]

Rostow saw the looming impasses that faced the Eisenhower administration, and he could not accept that they were insurmountable. Worse, he feared that the inability of the Shah to control the situation might result in another 1953, something the new administration wanted to avoid at all costs. For Rostow and the administration, the notion that a solution to social and economic problems could not be engineered in a pro-Western country with ample natural resources was simply unacceptable. The possibility flew in the face of everything that Rostow believed about economics and nation-building. Rising to the challenge, Rostow went to Professor T. Cuyler Young at Princeton University with a series of questions. How does the United States get the Shah to deal effectively with the unrest in the urban middle class without creating in him an 'intolerable sense of personal insecurity'? Rostow wanted a formula to reconcile the irreconcilable. He wanted the Shah to liberalize and give the urban middle class, who hated him, a stake in the government. He wanted the urban middle class co-opted into the Pahlavi state, and he wanted to alleviate Iranian xenophobia toward outside help and influence.[22]

Professor Young told Rostow that the Shah based his support on the army, security services, and upper classes, and that any step taken that detracted from their power and wealth would probably bring his downfall. The professor also questioned whether or not the Shah had any real intention of political liberalization: 'The difficulty was that the Shah was sold on the idea of creating a political situation, where there was no real political alternative to himself.' Young stated that the only way to get the Shah to seriously look at reform might be through some sort of 'shock treatment'.[23] In addition to his suggestion of 'shock treatment', two weeks later Young suggested an approach vaguely akin to nationalization of the Iranian oil industry, reduction of the army, and, the clincher, Iranian acceptance of Soviet aid and 'pro-Western neutralism'. The professor called this list his 'top ten suggestions' for change in Iran, Soviet aid and neutralism being the tenth.[24] Sound or not, the professor's ideas did not make the 'top ten' list at 1600 Pennsylvania Avenue. Iranian control of the oil industry and pro-Western neutrality were unacceptable. Rostow wanted to believe that the Iranian cloud had a silver lining but, like it or not, he and the president faced the same policy impasse that had plagued Eisenhower. Doing something about Iran might alienate or unseat the Shah, for whom they had no alternative.

The eleventh hour arrives?

May 1961 brought a conclusive demonstration that the Shah responded only to Iranian necessity, and not to pressure from the United States. On 4 May, Washington learned that a teachers' strike in Tehran involving more than 50,000 demonstrators had ended in a violent confrontation with security forces, with perhaps hundreds of casualties. The following day, Iranian Prime Minister Jafar Sharif Emami and his cabinet resigned. On 6 May, the Shah appointed the former Ambassador to Washington, Dr. Ali Amini, as Prime

Courtesy of National Archives
Chester Bowles and Phillips Talbot

Chester Bowles and newly-sworn-in Assistant Secretary for Near Eastern and South Asian Affairs, Phillips Talbot. Talbot's realistic support for Pakistan caused Bowles, a former and future Ambassador to India, to regret Talbot's appointment. Bowles had wanted to be Secretary of State but lost a power struggle with Dean Rusk and became Under Secretary.

Minister. Amini was a favorite of those in Washington advocating reform. Amini accepted the position on the condition that the Shah dissolve the Majlis (not exactly a democratic move), create a special court to try cases of corruption, and give him the right to name the cabinet, with the exception of Minister of Defense. The Shah agreed, and on 9 May Amini presented his new government to the Shah. The new Prime Minister, not particularly politically liberal himself, quickly banned demonstrations and began a series of meetings with the striking teachers to discuss their problems.[25]

Within the US administration, the turmoil in Tehran brought the arguments about Iranian policy to a head. At the 5 May NSC meeting President Kennedy expressed concern that he was not closely enough informed on the situation in Iran.[26] An intelligence report entitled 'Tehran Situation Critical' contributed to the sense of urgency. The report stated that the teachers' strike incited by the National Front 'may start a chain reaction with undetermined results.' The report added: 'The court is very much alarmed, particularly so as it is the feeling that none of the troops in Tehran would fire against striking teachers. ... Tomorrow is a critical day for the regime should major demonstrations reoccur and should security forces refuse to fire in the event of need, the outcome may gravely threaten the Shah's regime.'[27] Concerned, Kennedy instructed Secretary Rusk to set up a crisis task force on Iran. Rusk tasked Talbot with putting a task-force plan together.[28] The manner in which the Iranian Task Force came into being provides some insight into the power struggle over Iranian policy in Washington. Rostow and Komer, among others in the White House, wanted to take the policy formulation portfolio for Iran out of the State Department. It was Rusk's rice bowl, and he was an experienced Washington bureaucrat. To head off the power play, Rusk appointed Talbot to head the Task Force. Talbot and Rusk had a history that went back to World War II and India.[29] Rusk could not be certain how the Talbot move would work, but the risk with Talbot was preferable to the certain knowledge of trouble if someone like Komer took over. By appointing Talbot, Rusk appeased the White House staff with an 'outsider', while maintaining control through a State Department official that he knew.

On 7 May, Talbot responded with a lengthy document that included the plan for a task force and a series of options and recommendations for dealing with Iran. The options ran the gamut from 'Full Support of the Shah' to 'Support of the Mosadeqists [*sic*]', to 'Replacing the Shah by Military Leadership', and finally to 'Limited Support of the Shah'. The position paper argued that 'Full Support of the Shah' was the weakest option for the long term and predicted that an 'eventual explosion, when it came, would be directed as much or more against the United States as against the Shah.' In addition, the report argued that the 'successor regime would be virulently anti-Western and proportionally open to communist penetration.' This prediction was a vision truly through a 'dark glass dimly': Talbot, in effect, saw what would happen 18 years later, minus the Communist takeover he had envisaged. The Task Force's 'second extreme alternative' was to support a Musaddiqist takeover by peaceful means or coup, and allow 'the United States to roll with the punch of history'. Talbot described the immediate cost as 'immense', including Soviet aid for Iran, abandonment of CENTO, heavy pressure on American oil interests, and anti-Western agitation by 'communist demagogues'. Talbot added: 'The prospects for Communist penetration of the nation would, for the short run, be greatly enhanced.' This option was a non-starter. Talbot and the Task Force dismissed military leadership as a deadend, arguing that no military leader had sufficient stature to replace the Shah. The more extreme solutions were out.

This left only one option. Talbot and his group recommended 'Limited Support for the Shah', the same position taken over eight years before by the Eisenhower administration. This support included the economic and financial aid to prevent a collapse, 'a reasonable minimum of military assistance', and 'advice to the Shah' about placating or winning over his 'Mosadeqist opposition'. The report went on to state that while the 'Middle ground between the regime and the Mosadeqists is narrow and shaky', the Task Force believed that Amini's emergence as Prime Minister improved the chances of a successful compromise. In the end, Talbot concluded that the Shah's view of US support was so closely tied to military aid that it had to continue. The hope existed that as only a potential goal, the other forms of aid might eventually lessen the Shah's focus on the military. Talbot stated that the US should 'continue to adhere to the basic policy of Eisenhower's July 1958 letter to the Shah which focused attention on improving the operational proficiency of existing forces.' The key foreign policy makers in the Kennedy administration concluded that the Shah was a temporary alternative for American interests in Iran and that his collapse would be viewed as an US failure.[30] This interpretation of the US predicament in Iran was almost identical to that of the Eisenhower administration, with one exception: the Kennedy administration intended to use the Amini government as a new 'alternative'.

Support for Amini

The tenure of the Amini government would be inextricably tied to the White House's hopes and support for reform in Iran. As Komer, underlining for emphasis, stated on 18 May: '<u>The gut issue was how far we should really go in supporting Amini</u>.' He added: 'All Task Force members agree that Amini's moderate reformist program offers the only good alternative to an unpopular military dictatorship or a Mosadeqist revolution.'[31] The program's survival would be a litmus test for liberalization within a pro-Western framework. The US Embassy in Tehran had a different take on the Amini government. Ambassador Wailes wrote to Washington, arguing that the United States should not 'publicly' support or oppose Amini because his appointment reflected the Shah's 'perturbation over deterioration political and economic situation'. Wailes went on to say that, while Amini might have initial powers greater than those of previous Prime Ministers, 'it remains to be seen how much authority Amini can retain' if the 'Shah as expected' could refrain from interfering in government operations. The Embassy argued that it did not see Musaddiqists as an immediate threat and believed that the United States should refrain from offering 'advice' where there was no chance that the advice would be taken. Ambassador Wailes absolutely opposed support for local government, arguing that it would cause political chaos.[32]

Washington ignored the advice from Tehran. At the NSC meeting on 19 May 1961, Kennedy, acting on recommendations from the Iran Task Force, decided to 'make a major effort' to back the Amini government.[33] The recommendation read: 'Amini appears to be the best, and maybe the last, hope of averting political chaos and the possible loss of Iran to the West. The U.S. should take vigorous action to assist him in stabilizing the situation and in building a new political synthesis through a broad program of moderate reform.'³⁴ While the Task Force feverishly worked to quell the crisis and avert the imminent collapse of the Pahlavi regime, the Shah was vacationing in Norway. He obviously had a different take on the gravity of the situation at home. The Shah also had a different take on Amini. On 13 May, the Shah stated that Amini was only popular due to the fact that he had been out of the public eye. The Shah knew that Amini's popularity would fade as soon as his followers understood that he could not meet their 'demands'. As for neutralism, the Shah stated that he would rather abdicate than countenance a neutralist policy on the part of the new government. 'Such a policy would lead to (an) eventual Communist takeover, and was totally contrary to his personal convictions.'³⁵ On 23 May, an SNIE concluded: 'Should Amini be able to stabilize the situation sufficiently to enable the Shah to recover from his present fright, the latter will move to resume the dominant position.'³⁶ The prognosis squarely hit the mark.

Amini: 'the last hope'

The appointment of Ali Amini as Prime Minister was a shrewd move on the part of the Shah. Amini was an American favorite with the image of a pragmatic reformer, but the Shah knew his man. Quasi-liberal reformist sentiments were one thing; ruling in Tehran was quite another. Amini had an authoritarian streak that would emerge. By saddling him with the problems of government, the Shah undermined him as an alternative power center. No head of government in Tehran could please the competing factions; Amini would prove no different. The new Prime Minister would have to pursue a balancing act that would isolate him politically and make him increasingly dependent on the Shah for support. Amini's appointment offered another advantage. The Shah saw Amini as a potential lever on the United States. The Shah could claim to be supporting a reform candidate, and Amini could take the lead in demanding more military and economic aid. As things would develop, Amini's appointment gave the Shah even more leverage than he could have hoped for. Against the advice of Ambassador Wailes and the Iran experts in the State Department, the Kennedy administration, urged on by Komer and others, moved to directly support the Amini government. Komer and others in the administration simply could not get it through their collective heads that the National Front was not the primary threat to the Shah and that Amini was not the key to controlling the National Front. They could not grasp, or perhaps admit, that the Shah, not Amini, was the ultimate arbiter of things Persian, and that Amini was merely the Shah's latest creature. Ambassador Julius Holmes, Kennedy's appointment to replace Wailes and his unwelcome advice, understood this almost immediately and focused his attention on the Shah, but the White House staff continued attempting to solve the problem of Iran by using a flawed set of assumptions.

Amini takes the reins

From May until late July 1961, the Amini regime doggedly tried to drive reform. Amini's anti-corruption campaign even included the arrest of a handful of generals.[37] Amini managed to negotiate a settlement of the teachers' strike by giving in to the strikers' demands, which eventually put additional stress on the government budget.[38] In addition, he appointed Muhammad Derakhshesh, the rabble-rousing leader of the *Jame'eh-ye Mo'alleman-e Iran* ('Iran Teachers Association'), as Minister of Education.[39] As the financial crisis continued, the US provided a series of grants and loans to alleviate the immediate fiscal pressure.[40] By June, Amini had garnered some additional political support from the Shah and there was hope that the Shah might acquiesce in a 'more ceremonial role'.[41] US support for Amini created a 'breathing space', and the Shah's support for the time being appeared genuine. The situation on the financial front improved as well. The immediate budgetary crisis passed, and the long-discussed land-reform programs got underway.[42] Along with improvement came signs that the Shah might reassert himself. Commenting to the diplomatic community, the monarch stated: 'If Amini's objectives were not [mine], Amini would not be Prime Minister.'[43] Washington hoped that Amini could avoid a direct confrontation with the Shah over reform measures and security issues.[44]

Optimism was short-lived. In August 1961, frustration in the White House once again approached boiling point. Washington had made an unprecedented commitment to Amini's success, and there was nothing dramatic to show for it. The Iranian Task Force bombarded Amini with a plethora of well-meaning but often confusing or useless advice. Land reform was a case in point. The administration became concerned that it was proceeding too quickly and that the focus should be on 'land tenure', not 'land distribution'. Other suggestions included: 'Any approach to land reform should be in the context of the Third Development Plan', or 'attention should be paid to the prerequisite measures which are called for in the so-called 'Consolidation Program'.[45] Fearing chaos, the British worried, as related by the Indian Ambassador, that Amini and Minister of Agriculture Hassan Arsanjani 'had burned their boats' by pushing too far, too fast.[46] Arsanjani had been an outspoken advocate of land reform in Iran since the early 1950s.[47] When Arsanjani's ideas found their way into law, the British argued that it was basically 'illegal' and only succeeded in alienating most of the landowning class.[48] The British cautioned that US support for reform would actually undermine the regime.

In a contradictory approach, Washington overtly pushed for land reform, and simultaneously counseled Ambassador Holmes to talk to Amini about putting the brakes on his program. Arsanjani made no secret that he wanted a sweeping land-reform program that would start a genuine revolution by 'lighting land reform fires in the countryside ... which would eventually become a conflagration'. The Shah was experimenting as well. Land reform extended the control of the central government into rural areas at the expense of the landowning classes, and could serve to bolster his popularity by creating a new base of support among the peasant classes.⁴⁹ The fact that Amini and Arsanjani were leading the effort also provided an opportunity for the Shah to shift the blame, if things did not go well.

Despite all the initial concern and trepidation about the instability in Iran, by August 1961, the Kennedy administration realized that a lack of progress on reform had not brought a collapse. It had become apparent that Kennedy and his advisors had underestimated the resiliency of the Shah and his ability to deal with the situation. Just as former Ambassador Wailes had predicted, instead of Amini pushing the Shah toward the National Front and political reform, the Shah actually pulled Amini into his camp. To maintain power, Amini now had to accommodate the Shah and suppress the National Front, the very group whose support Washington had believed Amini would attract. In short, the Shah had subverted the 'American' Prime Minister and engineered his isolation from alternate power bases, simply by making Amini the instrument of the regime's escalating attacks on the National Front. This transformed Amini into just another political creature of the palace dependent on the Shah for support.⁵⁰ This outcome was exactly the opposite of what the Iranian Task Force had had in mind when it decided to support 'last chance' Amini the previous May.⁵¹

Amini, reform, and the reaction in Washington

The reaction in Washington to the lack of progress by Amini was as entertaining as it was instructive. At the NSC, 'Blowtorch' Bob Komer, in a 4 March memorandum to the President, pointed out that since the administration's anointment on 19 May of the Amini government 'as the best, and perhaps last chance of averting political chaos and possible loss of Iran to the West ... the situation has gotten worse instead of better.'⁵² Obviously frustrated, Komer stated that while Amini had announced a 'vigorous reform program', execution was difficult, 'especially in a gimcrack country like Iran'. A thoroughly alarmed, and alarmist, Komer stated that Iran was 'treading on the thin edge of potential disaster'. 'Desperate times call for desperate measures', he intoned. He argued for: 'Treat[ing] Iran as a real crisis situation by using Iran Task Force (on Vietnam model) as an operating mechanism, largely as a means of keeping pressure on State.' Asserting that 'This is no time for too much haggling', he also believed that the US had to keep Iran financially 'afloat'. Amazingly, Komer concluded that should Amini fail, the United States should prepare a contingency plan for a military or National Front government.⁵³ It seemed not to occur to the President's principal NSC advisor that the Shah would just name a new government.

Komer's memo did raise President Kennedy's level of aggravation. On 5 August, Bundy requested an update on the situation in Iran. The Iranian Task Force forwarded a memo with the analysis from its 2 August meeting. Eisenhower's NSC could have written it. Amini and Shah were 'firmly resisting neutralist pressures from right and left'. Amini 'has not been able to capture the imagination of large sectors of the population while at same time adjusting to the political and legal realities of the situation.' Komer went on to state: 'It appears inevitable that the Iranian Government will soon request a considerable budget grant from the United States in order to avoid breaching its economic stabilization agreement with the IMF and losing drawing rights under that agreement.' The report also pointed out that the threat of mass unemployment loomed larger, and the Shah continued to press for more military assistance and support.[54] Under Amini, nothing had changed.

Reacting to the discouraging news, Kennedy pressed the bureaucracy for action. Through Bundy, Kennedy expressed his concern that the Amini regime had 'lost much of its initial momentum' and lacked a political base. The President was also concerned about the additional costs associated with propping up the Amini government. He asked: 'If the situation seems to be deteriorating rather than improving, are there any further steps which the US could profitably undertake?' The memo included the usual questions about whether or not the Iran situation was a crisis that should be given the same 'treatment' as South Vietnam. The President queried: 'Can we ... glamorize the new "Third Plan" and get the Iranian population to enthusiastically support it?' He wanted to know how the US could help Amini 'generate a political base', 'get a more competent cabinet', 'split the National Front', or get more support from the Shah.[55] A note of desperation had begun to creep into the administration's internal dialogue. It appeared that the President had signed up to support Amini's sinking ship.

Kennedy wanted additional options from the State Department. Komer, who viewed the reply as too pessimistic and non-activist, sent it back for them to 'completely redo'. Given the 'can-do' atmosphere of the White House, Komer wanted action. The option paper went back for a more palatable version, namely one that agreed with Komer's preconceived notions. Describing the attitude among the 'Old Persian hands', including Peyton Kerr and John Bowling, as 'fatal resignation', Komer concluded that the US 'would have to live sooner or later with a chaotic Mosadeqist regime.' Komer stated that he had reassured State that the White House was not going to 'push the panic button' and potentially make things worse.[56] As a consequence of the White House attention, Armin Meyer in NEA asked Ambassador Holmes in Tehran for his opinion. The letter discussed 'anxiety at the highest levels' and requested an assessment and prognosis of the political situation. In short, they wanted Holmes' view on Amini's survivability and their theory about creating a 'bridge' between the Shah and his National Front opposition. Nervous, Meyer also wanted some confirmation that he had been correct to argue that Iran did not face the danger of immediate revolution.[57]

Ambassador Holmes responded on 27 August 1961. Holmes argued in effect for institutionalizing the primacy of the Shah in US foreign policy. He hammered home the point that there were no current or foreseeable alternatives to the Shah and that he deserved the full support of the United States. Holmes made it clear that Amini had the critical support of the Shah, the military, and conservative elements of Iranian society, but the Ambassador pointedly added that without the Shah's support, the Amini government would not survive. Holmes sought to educate the administration to the fact that no government survived without the blessing of the Shah. Second, he predicted that if the Shah's support continued, the Amini government would survive for 'some time'. Holmes also chided Washington for expecting too much too soon.

> I do not now fully share the apparent deep concern reflected in your letter. For one reason, I do not see how anybody, and particularly a Persian dealing with Persians, could have begun to make significant progress towards this goal in the chaotic situation in which the Amini regime came into office and in the short time it has been in power. ... I strongly believe that it is unreasonable to expect notable progress towards so difficult a future.

Holmes also stated that he saw no real threat of 'immediate or crucial political crises'.[58] The Ambassador saw problems, but not a crisis. Lewis Jones in the NEA Bureau concurred: 'The situation in Iran could never really be called good. Iran was somewhat like an individual ... consistently subject to a low-grade fever. ... There was no clear evidence of crisis but sometimes the temperature was down a little ... and sometimes it was up a little.' Jones added matter of factly that 'sometimes the fever went up and the patient died.'[59] NEA had a far better grasp of the situation than the Kennedy brain trust.

Holmes also debunked the perceived threat posed by the National Front, stating that they 'possess no unity' and 'cannot agree on a political program.' Holmes argued that for this reason the National Front, or 'neo-Mosadeqist elements' as he termed them, should not be included in the government. The Ambassador asserted that the National Front would merely form a disruptive element and 'have a profoundly negative effect on the stability of Iran and on our interests here.' Aware of the activist bent of the administration and their rejection of Wailes' appeal not to take a more direct role in supporting Amini, Holmes admitted that he risked being labeled as supporting the *status quo*, but he believed that change would occur at an Iranian pace and 'not by dramatic or violent action'.[60] Holmes' analysis poured cold water on Komer and the NSC. He minimized anti-American agitation, stating that it fluctuated wildly and could not be used as a barometer of US relations. He dismissed fear of Iranian neutralist sentiment, believing that it was overstated. Like Wailes before him, he counseled patience.

Talbot chooses sides

During this period, in one of the most important internal developments, Talbot began to support Holmes. Talbot visited Iran in August 1961. On 7 September 1961, he reported Amini to be a competent administrator, but one who did not 'seem to possess the characteristics of a charismatic popular leader.' He found the Shah 'ebullient and articulate', but almost entirely focused on military issues as opposed to the economy. Talbot noted that the National Front opposition was disorganized and unable to mount an effective challenge to the Shah or the Amini government. The evaluation of the economy was dismal, with 'no panaceas' or 'grand slam solutions' to Iran's 'deeply rooted problems' in sight. He told the Iran Task Force that there could be 'no sudden quick solution'. Talbot also stated that he saw no immediate threat to either the Shah or to Amini's government as long as Amini maintained good relations with the monarch.[61] The Talbot trip and report squelched talk of an immediate emergency and reoriented Washington's focus to the coming financial crisis. Ambassador Holmes also emerged as the least pessimistic US senior official on the future of Shah and as his greatest supporter.[62]

Tied to a policy of direct support for Amini, but believing that the Shah was the real power in Iran, Holmes gradually transitioned US policy toward direct support of the Shah. The catalyst for this transition would be the failure of the Amini government. Having publicly supported Amini, the US government could hardly revert to an Eisenhower-like distancing vis-à-vis the Shah. Kennedy had let the 'genie' out of the proverbial bottle. It was now abundantly clear that the only means of reform that included a pro-Western government lay through the Shah's rule. Playing a key role, Holmes increasingly took the Shah's side on military assistance, in part to maintain his own relationship with the monarch and to some degree in hopes of furthering reform. Thus the Kennedy administration would not only fail to establish an alternative to the Shah or to improve his relationship with the National Front, but it would, in fact, permanently establish the personal rule of the Shah as the only real option for US policy.

The outcome of the August 'mini-crisis' in Washington enhanced Holmes' influence. Quick to take advantage, he forwarded a request for military assistance to Rusk who had asked for a 'Check List for Iran'. On 13 September, Holmes responded with what would become his standard position. Holmes stated that while a reduction in military expenditures was desirable and would free up financial resources for economic development, the adverse effects would 'outweigh [the] benefits'. The Ambassador argued that the internal social and economic weaknesses and the requirement for reform made military assistance a critical element, stating: 'At the moment, and I venture to say for the next five years anyway, the Shah and the armed forces hold the key to the stability of this country.' He argued that without modernization, a disgruntled military might be tempted to stage a coup, bringing any benefits accruing from Amini's reform programs to naught. Holmes then laid out his military-assistance plan for Iran; this called for a reduction in Iranian standing forces, but a significant upgrade in equipment and training for the remaining units. Holmes estimated the cost savings at $50 million, and he believed that the modernization would bring the Shah around to Washington's views on reducing military manpower.[63] When the Pentagon balked at supplying modern arms, Holmes countered that the United States 'must back the Shah to the hilt as our 'chosen instrument' in Iran.

The Ambassador also managed to wrest some control of Iranian affairs away from the Task Force and the NSC. Komer and Bundy, of course, opposed this move, but their recent, somewhat unfounded alarms about Iran had undermined their credibility. The White House had begun to wonder whether the Task Force was worth the effort, and whether it should just be reconstituted for the next crisis. Even Komer had some doubts: 'Changing situations may periodically alter the value of task forces. They are more useful in a clear crisis situation than in an episodic one – during hiatus between action problems they're often a nuisance.'[64] Circumventing the foreign policy apparatus had its complications.

Amini on the slippery slope

While this jockeying occurred within the US bureaucracy, in Iran the Shah was under growing pressure from some of his closest supporters to get rid of

Courtesy of National Archives
Chester Bowles and Julius Holmes
Chester Bowles and the new Ambassador to Iran, Julius Holmes. Bowles had saved Holmes' State Department career by securing him this post, but later regretted it because of Holmes' stalwart support of the Shah's ambitions over reform in Iran.

Amini.⁶⁵ It was not a coincidence that the pressure and threats aimed at Amini paralleled discussions in Washington about the new military-assistance package (MAP) for Iran. The Shah knew that Holmes and the MAP officers in Iran supported a program that reduced the Iranian military from 200,000 to 150,000 men over three to five years, while substantially increasing the number of modern weapons and amount of training. The Defense Department opposed the plan, and wanted a more severe reduction. The Shah let Holmes know that he would not agree to reductions without significant modernization.⁶⁶

At the Shah's insistence, Holmes raised the issue of an official visit to Washington. Talbot rejected the request, arguing that Iran was 'now near the bottom of the trough into which it has slid'. The White House was concerned about the reception that the Shah might receive and about the potential political fallout from a visit in which the Iranian monarch made exorbitant demands for military aid. In a stinging letter to Talbot on 7 December, Holmes countered: 'I should be less than frank if I did not convey to you my deep sense of disappointment on receiving your letter.' Holmes pointed out to Talbot that a visit to Washington was not a 'reward for good conduct' but rather an 'instrumentality for <u>ensuring</u> good conduct'. Holmes argued that the Shah had committed himself to reform and to the support of the Amini government, and to let the opportunity pass for President Kennedy to reinforce that progress would be a mistake. 'We should leave no stone unturned to make sure that the momentum toward these goals does not falter.' Holmes then asked why no one questioned a visit by Nehru or Sukarno, and yet a visit by a 'proven friend' came under scrutiny. 'We have only to contemplate the damage to our prestige and our position in the Middle East which would result from Iran's defection from the Free World to realize how great a return we are getting for our money.' Holmes then attacked the assumptions made by the Iran Task Force with regard to the potential of the National Front and 'rising urban middle class'. He concluded his blistering retort by saying: 'Your letter surprises me. To my mind we should not seek to offer the Shah courtesies that may give him satisfaction ... but rather to take action to cause him to do the things we want him to do in the interest of the United States, and Iran too for that matter.'⁶⁷

Chapter 12: The Shah Ascendant

1962 introduced a new phase in US-Iranian relations. In 1961, although supporting the Shah, the Kennedy administration introduced the new element of American 'personal support' for an Iranian politician, Prime Minister Amini. During that same period, the Shah concluded that to preserve his position against Iranian and foreign detractors, including those in Washington, he needed to cultivate advocates to further his goals. The US Ambassador in Tehran, Julius C. Holmes, became one of these advocates. By January 1962, the Shah had become more sophisticated about getting his message through to Washington. Because Prime Minister Amini had become the Kennedy administration's 'chosen instrument' for reform, the Shah steadily increased Amini's dependence on the palace for support, thoroughly co-opting the Prime Minister. By December 1961, the Shah had enough control over Amini to use the Prime Minister to advocate both his military and his economic priorities with Washington.

On 3 January 1962, in a meeting with Deputy Chief of Mission Stuart W. Rockwell, Amini raised the Shah's unhappiness with the levels of military aid. Amini stated that his 'deep concern' matched that of the Shah. He explained that his government and the Shah were coming under increased pressure from 'old fashioned, neutralist politicians'. These politicians wanted Iran to move toward a neutralist stance as quickly as possible to avoid being diplomatically abandoned. Because of US overtures to the Soviet Union, Amini argued that Washington sought improved relations with Moscow and that inadequate funding of economic and military aid to Iran had been the price. According to Amini, these neutralists supported a pre-emptive Iranian move to neutrality before the US could totally abandon the regime in a new arrangement with the Soviets based on 'sphere(s) of influence'. Rockwell defended the US position, pointing to past aid and to the military aid currently under consideration. To this, Amini replied that the Shah had a 'legitimate concern about military assistance'. Amini added that the Shah would undoubtedly feel better about the entire situation, including a reduction of forces, if 'the quality and quantity of his military equipment substantially improved'.[1] Now Amini, the Kennedy administration's chosen instrument for creating an alternate political power center to the Shah and for driving a program of social and economic reform, was lobbying for the Shah's agenda.

The Shah, military assistance, and Julius Holmes

The developing alliance between the palace and the US Embassy in Tehran became more apparent in a letter from Holmes to Secretary Rusk on 22 January 1962 about proposed defense aid for Iran. Rusk liked the new-found leverage that Holmes' aggressive advocacy of the Shah's position gave the State Department; it kept Komer and the White House staff on the defensive. Holmes argued that the recommendations of the 'Defense Steering Group' in the Iran Annex had given inadequate weight to four factors:

(1) Although the key to drastic reduction in military aid without serious political repercussion is to persuade the Shah that U.S. forces will help him in Iran if he gets into difficulties, we know he knows, and the report likewise asserts, that this is not possible.
(2) It is the judgment of all of us here [in Tehran] that the Shah will not cut his forces from 205,000 to 150,000 if offered no more modernization than envisaged in the Steering Group's recommended level of aid.
(3) A further probability is that such a level of aid will impel the Shah to draw more heavily on Iran's oil revenues for his armed forces – to the detriment of the country's development programs.
(4) There is a further problem involved in talking to the Shah about additional economic aid accompanying reduced military aid in that our own procedures make advance commitments of greater economic aid extremely difficult.

Holmes stated that since the Steering Group admitted that 'it has not been able to obtain a clear cut picture of what the long term shape of economic programs is likely to be', it would be less than 'realistic' to expect the Iranians to put much faith in it.

Using a litany of arguments, the Ambassador stated: 'The concept held in some quarters that the Shah has no place to turn but to the United States is erroneous'; the Steering Group 'seems totally to disregard' the impact of US military assistance to Iran on the Middle East; no commitment to defend Iran in lieu of a robust Iranian military force is 'believable'; and finally, the talk of 'glamour' equipment instead of real force modernization reflects a complete lack of understanding of the Shah's position. Holmes passionately argued that military assistance was not a 'quid pro quo' for 'preserving the current direction of Iranian foreign policy'. Holmes underlined 'quid pro quo' and went on to say: 'I would hate to see Iran, by turning to neutralism and accommodation with the USSR, demonstrate to us that there are points beyond which the needs and desires of an ally cannot be ignored. The catastrophic nature in that event of the consequences to U.S. interests need not be elaborated.' Labeling the Steering Group report 'a retrograde course', Holmes contended that 'the risks entailed by such a course would be too great', and he implored Washington to adopt his recommendations on military aid to Iran for the fiscal years 1962-1967.[2] The administration's plan to 'personally' support Amini and reform had now dissolved into Holmes' all-out support for the Shah.

Holmes: the Shah's ambassador

The Shah's tactics and Ambassador Holmes' outspoken support benefited the Iranian ruler in another way – it brought a steady stream of high-level dignitaries to Tehran. These visits stroked, or stoked as the case may have been, the Shah's ego and subjected key policy-makers to the pomp and arm-twisting of the palace and the Embassy. The Shah still faced skeptics concerning his official visit. Komer, still disgruntled over the 'optimism' of Holmes and still insisting that things were 'going to hell in a hack in Iran', complained that the two immediate questions were 'how much military baksheesh to give the Shah and whether to have him here for a visit'. Komer was fixated on an 'NF government', as he called it. Komer, once hostile to State, was now gratified that the reports of John Bowling, the Iran Desk officer 'reeked with pessimism'. The White House also resurrected Professor Young, who advocated pushing the Shah harder and justified his support of a tougher policy on the basis that the US was 'damned if we do and damned if we don't.'[3] Tehran became a popular place for US officials to visit, so that they could see the situation at first hand and weigh in on what needed to be done.

In the meantime, much to Komer's frustration, Holmes won his argument for the Shah's official visit. On 10 February, Chester Bowles, the Under Secretary of State, arrived in Tehran for a four-day visit to evaluate the situation in Iran and to invite the Shah to Washington on a visit to be arranged for September. In the past, Bowles had supported economic versus military aid. As a result, Ambassador Holmes sent an evaluation of the visit to Washington on 13 February, before the Under Secretary had even departed Tehran. Holmes' report was to preempt any criticism of the Shah that might emanate from Bowles' report. The next day, from Cairo, Bowles sent his own evaluation. Bowles stated: 'The Shah's prestige and presence is essential in holding the country together.' He also stated that he subscribed to the Ambassador's 'urgent plea' that a sound aid package would be put in place as soon as possible: 'Speed is of the essence.' At the same time, Bowles argued that the MAP package for military modernization should follow the recommendations of the 'MAP Steering Group' and not that of the Ambassador.[4]

On 18 February, Holmes read the Bowles' airgram, and sent a response directly to President Kennedy and Secretary Rusk, stating: 'I do not believe that the MAP Steering group recommendations for military aid to Iran are sound.' Holmes also raised Washington's intention to ask the Shah for 'two more special facilities' for monitoring Soviet missile development, and pointed out that the enhanced military-assistance program was a small price to insure a positive answer.⁵ In connection with the Shah's visit, Holmes wrote to Talbot on 4 March. He thanked Talbot, whom Holmes had castigated and bulldozed as a result of the first rejection of the Shah's visit, for 'describing the complications of Iranian Affairs in Washington'. He then quickly added that while pleased with the decision to invite the Shah, the late September date was disappointing. Holmes wanted the visit moved up to April.

The Ambassador used the 4 March letter to Talbot to lobby again for his version of the military-assistance plan: 'Perhaps I should not say anything more about my proposal for a Military Program because I have been pretty insistent about it and I don't want to get shrill.' Then came the 'however', and a long argument that the Embassy program was the minimum that the Shah would accept in order for him to seriously contemplate a reduction in his armed forces.⁶ Holmes' letter to Talbot brought in a fresh round of meetings and memoranda. Lucius Battle, Executive Secretary to Dean Rusk, wrote Bundy at the White House, restating the contents of Holmes' letter. The memorandum began with the well-established preamble: 'the Shah of Iran is depressed and resentful over allegedly inadequate United States military assistance. ... The Shah may be considering abdication.' Then came the traditional punch line: 'His abdication would result in political chaos in Iran which could only benefit the Soviet Union.'⁷ Since the decision had been made to offer only the lower amount of assistance, approved by the MAP Steering Group, State sought ways to soften the blow.

Battle strongly suggested to the White House that the date of the Shah's official visit be moved forward in an attempt to limit his 'brooding' over the military aid. They reasoned that prompt notification would allow the Shah to 'absorb' the blow before arriving in Washington. Under no circumstances did the State Department want to give the Shah the bad news about military aid when he arrived in Washington.⁸ The 'final decision' to stick with the MAP Steering Group resulted in the dispatch of General Maxwell Taylor to Tehran to break the news to the Shah.⁹ On 9 March 1961, Talbot informed Holmes that the decision on military aid was 'final'. He mentioned 'the tendency in some quarters to regard the Shah's tactics as sheer blackmail'. Talbot told Holmes that $290 million was all the Shah would get, and that he was lucky to get that. The President also wanted the Shah to implement a force reduction plan as well, or face 'a flat negative [sic]'on assistance in the coming year. The letter went on to say that Holmes could expect instructions to break this news to the Shah as quickly as possible, in light of plans to advance the Shah's official visit to April or June. In an effort to prevent further telegrams to the President, Talbot asserted that 'Presidential interest' in a resolution 'made it impossible' to consider additional arguments from Tehran for the larger program.¹⁰

While Talbot probably enjoyed being the bearer of bad tidings, the setback for the ever-tenacious Holmes was only temporary. On 13 March, Secretary of

State Rusk met with Iranian Prime Minister Amini in Geneva. Amini told Rusk that the Shah would only agree to reduce the size of the armed forces if they were substantially modernized. Amini stated that he could not finish the planning for the development and economic programs until he knew the answer to the military-aid situation. The Prime Minister also warned that in order to support the military the Shah had in the past transferred civilian funds. Rusk, hoping to preview the bad news to come, stated that Congress had cut back military-aid programs and that Holmes would soon brief Amini and the Shah on the implications for Iran.[11]

The Shah comes to Washington

The complaints from the Pahlavi palace and Ambassador Holmes not only secured the Shah's visit, but also advanced it to 10-16 April 1961. The administration viewed the Shah's visit as an opportunity to secure a 'double-barreled objective'. Facing the 'annual budget blackmail exercise' with Iran, Komer described the Shah as 'volatile', having an 'unstable temperament', 'fearing for his throne', 'jealous of competitors for power', and given to 'periodic moods of depression'. Komer also pointed out that the Shah felt that both Pakistan and Turkey received better treatment than Iran through CENTO. Thus, the first objective was to 'calm the Shah's concerns'. Uncontrolled, Washington believed that these 'concerns' might lead to the Shah's sacking of Ali Amini. At the same time, the White House feared, as bizarre as this may seem, that the Shah might, in a fit of pique, resign. The Kennedy administration, even the ardent Shah-bashers like Komer, now realized that the Shah was the essential element of stability in Iran, and that an alternate power center around Amini had simply not materialized. Komer grudgingly admitted: 'Hence, we regard [the Shah's] continued presence and support of the Amini [or like] government as indispensable to Iranian stability over the next several years. There is no feasible alternative that would serve US interests as well.'[12] The second point was to convince the Shah that economic development should be the Iranian priority over military aid. Like Eisenhower, Kennedy wanted to 'convince the Shah that accelerated reform and development is the best guarantee of Iranian security and of his own future.'[13]

Single-handedly, Holmes had put Iranian policy back in traditional channels. This was no mean feat. He had successfully wrested control of Iranian policy from Talbot's Iran Task Force and limited the NSC's options to grousing. The Ambassador had made a cogent argument that the National Front was a grossly overstated threat and, thereby, had laid the foundation for discrediting the NSC view of impending doom. He had managed to co-opt several major administration figures to his view that the Shah was indispensable to the pro-Western future of Iran. The fact that Chester Bowles, an official with a typically jaundiced view of the Shah, announced that the Shah was the key to Iranian stability was just one of the conversions for which Holmes could take credit. Holmes' success laid the groundwork for the Shah's future maneuvering that in turn would seal the fate of the Pahlavi dynasty and the United States in Iran.

In Washington, fear of the Shah's instability drove much of the planning for the visit. In daily Embassy reports, the fluctuating mood of the monarch had become the major policy issue. It resembled a weather forecast as Holmes contrived to make the royal humor a critical issue for decision-making. On good days, Holmes reported: 'The Shah appears to be in good spirits', and the Shah expressed his 'gratitude at the President's "assurances" with regard to military and economic aid for Iran'.[14] On bad days, the Shah would be depressed if he could not address Congress. Ambassador Holmes, like any good advance man, suggested that not only should Congress invite the Shah to speak, but also that Congressional leaders should 'persuade, by whatever means, members to attend'. Just to make his point crystal clear, the Ambassador stated: 'I recognize problem this presents for executive branch but there is no repeat no doubt in my mind about adverse effects on our interests if this part of program is eliminated.'[15] Again, Secretary Rusk called the Senate Majority Leader Mike Mansfield to secure the Congressional address and attendance.[16]

In order to further demonstrate that persistence pays, neither the Shah nor Holmes allowed the MAP issue to die. The Shah took the position that the MAP appropriation was still open for the discussion. Fearing that Kennedy would be caught flat-footed by one of the Shah's recitations of shabby treatment, administration officials subjected the President to a barrage of advice and briefing papers. Komer advised the President to let Secretary of Defense McNamara give the Shah the bad news about the reduced military assistance.[17] The White House staff wanted to avoid the potential for a personal confrontation between Kennedy and the Shah. The concern over the Shah's reaction to the MAP figure of $300 million became so acute that the administration 'found' another $30 million to bring the total to $330 million, just to placate the Shah.[18] Indications were that this might not be sufficient. On 9 April, the day before the visit was to begin, Komer wrote President Kennedy warning that Ambassador Holmes 'still holds out for about $424 million package, despite his talks in State, AID, and Defense.' Fearing Holmes might persuade Kennedy to add funding, Komer 'urged' the president to hold firm at $330 million.[19] On 10 April, Kenneth Hansen furnished a paper comparing and justifying US MAP and economic assistance to Pakistan and Turkey in relation to that of Iran.[20] Also on 10 April, Bowles weighed in with a memorandum about the Shah's fixation on military aid. Arguing for the $330-million cap, Bowles urged the President to 'resist pressures to increase' military assistance.[21] Given the similarities in language and views, Komer and Bowles undoubtedly coordinated their appeals.

During the actual visit, the discussions went reasonably well. In meetings with President Kennedy, the Shah made his arguments for increased military aid to Iran. In response, President Kennedy presented the US case for reduced Iranian military expenditures and increased focus on economic development.

Kennedy congratulated the Shah on his excellent choice for Prime Minister and committed the US to 'help within our resources'. He also assured the Shah that the administration believed Iran would collapse without his leadership: 'The President wanted the Shah to know that he had the support of the President.' As expected, the Shah presented Kennedy with an extensive shopping list. In addition to the military assistance, the Iranian ruler raised the possibility of 'Civic Action' programs for the military, increased shipments of surplus grains, and additional aid to assist in reorganizing the Iranian military.

The Iranian monarch also took the opportunity to raise the issue of Nasserist agitation against his regime. Stymied in one area, the Shah merely shifted to another, resembling a day in an Iranian bazaar. He made one point clear: he believed that 'a first-class, honest Army, with decent living standards, was a pre-requisite for time and security, the two things most needed to allow Iran's economic development.' The Shah refused to commit himself to cutting the size of the Iranian armed forces until their 'mobility and mechanization' had been addressed.[22] The Shah also raised the issue of two frigates that had been deleted from the assistance plan, and insisted that those be reinstated.[23] The mobility, mechanization, and frigate requests were the difference between the $330 million budget and the $424 million supported by himself and Ambassador Holmes. During the visit, the Shah showed a reasonable amount of interest in economic development and reform, no doubt to offset his focus on the military. On 13 April, he told Averell Harriman that he was most unhappy with the outcome of his talks at the Pentagon.[24] It was a clear indication that Kennedy had not heard the end of the MAP issue.

The end of the Amini era

The official visit to Washington and the commitments made during that visit effectively started the clock ticking on the Amini government. Amini had served his purpose; the Shah had wrung every possible advantage from his tenure. Amini had delivered on emergency economic aid in 1961, and his appointment had cleared the way for the Shah's visit to Washington. American support for Amini had also exceeded historical boundaries in that the Kennedy administration had thrown its weight openly behind his government. In the Shah's eyes, Amini had failed in two respects: he had failed to maintain direct budgetary support for the Iranian government, and he had failed to gain the military modernization-program funds advocated by Ambassador Holmes and the Shah. As long as Washington was willing to contribute materially to Amini's survival, then the Shah supported the Prime Minister, but the benefits of US material support determined the length of Amini's tenure. Both of these factors were nearing an end.[25]

Following his talks with President Kennedy, the Shah hoped that the additional aid requested might yet materialize. Amini had one more opportunity to deliver. As noted, the Shah had never agreed to reduce the military budget. This constituted, in effect, his trump card in dealing with Washington over military assistance, budgetary support, and development aid.

The Shah had a modernization program for the Iranian army that more or less conformed to the higher total of $424 million over five years. The US refusal to fund above $330 million, plus the possibility of two patrol frigates, disappointed the Iranian monarch. The Shah's solution was simple: at his direction, Amini informed the US government that the 'military budget could not be cut and in fact might have to be increased in view of the requirements of modernization to be undertaken with U.S. assistance.' Necessary or not, the Shah was determined to have his modernized military, even at the cost of starving development programs and reform. The Shah could also divert more financial resources from increasing oil revenues. Amini understood that this would be the outcome if the Shah did not get the larger MAP amount.[26]

In Washington, the Kennedy administration reacted with consternation: 'In discussion this question between Shah and highest U.S. official ... it was made clear that ... new overall military budget could in fact be decreased.'[27] Kennedy and other administration officials mistakenly assumed that the Shah, with his ego massaged, having been wined and dined at the White House and charmed by the President, would accept the US view of the military aid package. They could not have been more mistaken. The Iranian budget that finally emerged astonished Washington. The Shah acted as if the larger MAP amount, or something approximating it, had been agreed upon. In addition, the civilian side of the budget was so large that it would require either a postponement of many of its provisions or a 'big US loan'. The White House and Komer in particular, along with the State Department, expressed concern and concluded: 'We may be heading for another crisis in Iran.' Komer added: 'State is trying to find out if situation as bad as feared. And I've been arguing we should run scared nonetheless. A stitch in time, you know.' True to form, Holmes expressed his doubts that the situation was really that serious. The President's personal diplomacy also had a downside. The Shah took advantage of the exchanges to argue that Kennedy had promised to 'underwrite a 2,000-man commando brigade for Tehran riot control'. The Shah also believed he was promised a 500-watt transmitter for the propaganda campaign against Nasser. These claims sent official Washington scurrying to determine what exactly had been promised. Exasperated with trying to track down the alleged 'commitments', Komer complained: 'Shah will just queer himself with everybody here if he keeps translating small talk into firm commitments.'

In Tehran, Amini was worn out, the Prime Minister finding himself unable to exert any control over the situation, a reality not lost on Washington.[28] Upon taking office, Amini had promised that Iran would have a balanced budget in fiscal year 1962 (April to April). It was now clear that the deficit would total between $100 and $200 million. In addition, the Director and Deputy Director of the CPO resigned in protest, partly from 'annoyance' over corruption investigations and partly from concern that allocations for development would be severely cut.[29] No matter the cause, the situation 'threatened seriously the structure of confidence' on which Iran and the US were hoping to build an 'international effort to help Iran's Third Plan'. The odds had always been against Amini's bold promise to end the deficit. In fact, the reform programs contributed significantly to the renewed financial crisis. The series of contributing factors included problems in tax collection, resumption of building programs, an economic depression that lowered the tax base, the military budget, salary-raises for teachers, land reform, large allocations to the Plan Organization, and finally, unpaid bills from the previous budget year. In effect, the pressures of modernization and reform, bad luck, and reduced direct financial support in both the military and civilian areas caused a chain reaction that ballooned the budget, and Amini was left holding the bag.

As government revenues fell, Amini himself admitted that he had been 'remiss in the business of eliminating waste and duplication'. The high expectations for increased administrative efficiency and improving tax collection had gone unrealized. The zealous supporters of reform in the Kennedy administration had failed to reckon with the problems associated with the arcane Iranian tax system and with Persian creativity in avoiding the government collectors. In addition, the IMF, with the blessing of both the Eisenhower and Kennedy administrations, had imposed a stabilization program on Iran to fight inflation. It succeeded too well and caused a 'first-class' depression. As a result, the tax base degenerated, further reducing government revenues. Increasing taxes or implementing 'quick-return new taxation measures' was not an option. Neither the Shah nor Amini could face the political fallout associated with raising taxes in the middle of a depression. The possibility of floating bonds offered little promise of raising any significant amount of revenue. It was unlikely that the IMF would have approved a credit expansion with the necessary scope to offset the deficit and, even in the event of approval, Washington speculated that it 'would start a wild inflationary spiral' with totally unpredictable political and economic consequences.

In reality, the military budget, the usual culprit cited by the Shah's detractors, constituted only a part of the problem. Other factors were cited as the principal contributors. Amini had managed to shoot himself in the foot as well. The pay increases that Amini had given to teachers in order to end the riots of May 1961 had contributed significantly to budget growth. To delay, reduce, or renege on them would alienate 'Amini's last beachhead among the intellectuals' and cause the Minister of Education, Mohammad Derakhshesh, to resign.[30] The Prime Minister could ill-afford to alienate Darakhshesh, a key strike-leader, or his followers.[31] Amini had also approved the completion of all construction projects that were 80 per cent finished. This created critical jobs during a depression, but it also added to the government deficit. Land reform also created a drain on the budget. Simply put, it cost money to cancel or alter it, and would have brought the resignation of the Minister of Agriculture, Hasan Arsanjani; it would also have damaged relations with the US. The Kennedy administration had declared land reform, 'the regime's brightest long-

Courtesy of National Archives
Shah of Iran Publicizing Land Reform

The Shah presents land to a farmer. Land reform became the Holy Grail of modernization programs in Iran. Strongly supported by both the Eisenhower and Kennedy administrations, it reduced tax revenues, damaged agricultural production, and undermined traditional support for the regime. The Shah supported it because he saw land reform as a means to reduce his reliance on the traditional elites, who often opposed modernization.

range prospect for political strength'. Amini had the option of cutting funding for the CPO, but this in turn would bring 'an irretrievable loss of momentum for long-range and comprehensive economic planning'. Because this would not have an immediate 'catastrophic political' effect, Washington viewed it as the best option for Amini: 'A delayed or truncated Plan would be better than no Plan at all, and a neglect of political factors could easily mean no Plan at all.'

The military budget, separate from the MAP, continued to be an issue. Because of US reductions in direct budgetary support, just to maintain the military budget at the previous year's level required an additional expenditure of $15 million. While Komer and others had argued that the US had intended for the Iranians to reduce the military budget, such a move was unlikely even had the Shah been predisposed to do it. The Embassy in Tehran, the Iranian Desk at State, and the CIA recognized that rising discontent and serious 'grumblings' in the army over housing, facilities, and pay posed a threat not only to reform but also to the regime itself. The US and Prime Minister Amini feared that holding the line on military spending might bring not just a political parting of the ways with the Shah but possibly 'military subversion'. Washington recognized the Iranian military represented the 'key to the security situation'. Cutting the military was not an option.

The situation really had only one possible solution, namely, grants in emergency aid from the United States. Emergency grants and budgetary support were simply no longer available. Washington faced its own budgetary problem. Kennedy gave everything that he could to the Shah, but the fact was that US commitments were outstripping the ability to pay, and cuts had to be made somewhere. Promises to 'bear any burden' had their limitations. The administration had made it clear that additional budgetary support for Iran would not be forthcoming. Contrary to other interpretations that argue that the Kennedy administration used cuts in the military-assistance program to push the Shah toward reform, the cuts were across the board and included civilian subsidies. The reductions in support of the civilian government and its related reform efforts were in fact much more severe. Military support lost $15 million, while civilian lost $30 million. The cumulative effect of cuts in civilian and military budget support created a situation in which Amini could not achieve his promised goals. Washington cajoled, prodded, and pushed the Shah and Amini regime toward reform, but balked at the bill. The very reform efforts that were to transform Iran into a modern, progressive state had created a financial drain that threatened Iran's political stability. Bowling saw it clearly: 'Something will have to give.'[32]

On 24 June 1962, Amini appealed to Ambassador Holmes for additional aid. The Prime Minister listed the measures that he had taken to increase revenues and reduce expenditures. The government had tried to cut the ministry budget by at least 15 per cent, but Amini explained that the military budget would not be cut given the regional political and security issues. He followed with a special plea to restore the $15 million cut from the military assistance. Holmes stated: 'He [Amini] was making a desperate try in a belief, possibly shared by the Shah, that if we could be convinced of the critical character of the existing situation, that it was worth a try to get us to do one more rescue mission.' Holmes reminded Amini that both he and the Shah had received notification months before that they could depend on continued support. The Ambassador then restated that 'there were no funds available for this purpose.' Disappointed, Amini stated that he would ask the Shah to make a public statement of support endorsing the direction that the government had chosen for the coming five years. Amini did not appear to be contemplating resignation, and although tired and harassed, he believed that the Shah would support him. According to Holmes: 'It may be that events will prove that he is a "spent force" but it is very evident that he does not think so.'[33] Within weeks, Holmes had his answer.

On 17 July 1962, Amini presented his resignation to the Shah. According to intelligence reports, after 14 months in office Amini's resignation was 'welcomed by nearly all political elements in Iran'. Amini's efforts, aimed at gradual change in Iranian social and economic processes, had created more resentment than results. Land reform, anti-corruption campaigns, and the economic stabilization-program had managed to alienate large segments of the most influential political groups in Iran. Reform had garnered little support from more radical nationalists in the National Front. The landlord-merchant classes saw his reforms as a political and economic threat to their position of influence. His refusal to hold parliamentary elections and his 'gradual' approach to reform undermined any potential support from the radical nationalists. Amini's controls over credit and the money supply, while temporarily stabilizing Iran's finances and foreign-exchange crisis, brought on an economic depression.[34]

The aftermath of Amini

Amini, the Kennedy administration's 'last hope', blamed Washington's reductions in economic and military-budget assistance for the ongoing financial crisis and record budget deficits. The Prime Minister told all who would listen that the United States 'let him down'.[35] In attempting to reduce the deficit, the 15 per cent program had met stiff opposition from the ministers of education and defense.[36] Rumors circulated in Tehran that Derakhshesh, whose education ministry had the largest civilian budget in the government, had threatened strikes if the education budget were cut.[37] The Shah refused to intervene in this deadlock, and for good reason. He obviously supported the military budget and, like Washington, feared growing unhappiness in the army. At the same time, cuts in education threatened a renewal of the teachers' strikes and student rioting that had originally brought Amini to power. The Shah wanted to avoid a repetition of May 1961. Both he and Amini believed that Washington's personal commitment to the Amini government would translate into a belated reversal of the US decision not to supply the required budgetary aid.[38] The realization that the aid would not be forthcoming proved a bitter disappointment for both, but particularly for Amini. The Prime Minister believed that he had Kennedy's support and had tried diligently to follow Washington's 'advice'. To Amini, Kennedy and his advisors were heaving his regime overboard to lighten Washington's financial and political load. Kennedy had done this despite the fact that the very programs advocated by Washington had significantly contributed to the problems Iran now faced.

In a last ditch effort, Komer urged Kennedy to save Amini 'despite his wild charges about lack of US aid'. When the rumor first circulated that Amini would resign, a thoroughly alarmed Komer told President Kennedy: 'We've got to back Amini's hand.'[39] After the resignation, Komer argued: 'Our aim should be to get Amini back in, with such backing from the Shah. Instead of Holmes' policy of standing back and letting Iranians come to us, we ought to go tell them.'[40] Realizing that the Amini effort had run its course, the President ignored Komer. Holmes and the traditional foreign policy establishment had wrested control of Iranian policy from the activism of the New Frontier. Anticipating the questions from Washington on the course of action that the US should pursue in the wake of the Amini resignation, Holmes wrote: 'I see no useful initiative which could be taken by US. In essence only thing Shah, Amini or anyone else who might assume responsibility for affairs here wants to hear from US government is that we will provide enough money to ease budgetary situation which clearly has not yet been squarely met by Iranians.' Believing that the Shah and Amini might yet attempt to get the United States to make up the difference, estimated by one Iranian official at $80 million for the civilian government and $20 million for the military, Holmes suggested that Washington wait for the dust to settle before contemplating any action. Squarely in the Shah's camp, Holmes also warned against attempting to find either another Amini to support or a 'Shah-equal'.[41] In reporting that the current head of the Pahlavi Foundation, Asadollah Alam, would become Prime Minister, the Ambassador pointed out that under Alam that there would be 'no question of independence': 'Alam will be a graceful scapegoat for any matters which do not go well.'[42] The Ambassador informed Washington that the reform programs of Amini would go forward, but that progress would depend on the Shah.[43] Holmes had now passed Amini's reformist mantel to the Shah, making him not only the undisputed Iranian political focal point, but also the only vehicle through which the Kennedy administration might hope to see reform.

The appointment of Alam left little doubt that the Shah would actively run the government and Iranians would hold him directly responsible for the outcome.[44] On 21 July, the Shah reinforced this view of personal control by offering 'faint praise' of Alam for being 'young, loyal, and energetic'. In speaking to Holmes, the Shah insisted that the program of reforms and the anti-corruption campaign would continue, as would the pro-Western orientation of Iran. The Shah then took occasion to raise the issue of 'loans' to help the Iranian budget crisis in lieu of the grant program that had ended.[45] He made it clear that some form of financial assistance remained on his agenda with the Kennedy administration. The CIA reported: 'Some means must be devised to permit urgent economic aid of a type that will stimulate economic life and create the means for combating the serious unemployment which now exists and which poses a grave political threat.' There was also a realization that the 'stabilization program' had done more damage than good and that 'less conservative economic policies' might be required. Former opponents of the

Amini regime were now praising the ex-Prime Minister and the policies that they had assisted in toppling. From Washington, it appeared that Alam, and thus the Shah, would not aggressively pursue reform, leaving them vulnerable to National Front elements.[46]

In his final assessment of the Amini tenure, Holmes pointed out that most of the 'organized groups' opposed him and that his only real support had come from the Shah himself. Holmes argued that Amini became a prisoner of men like Derakshesh, and did not insist on putting the best available men in his cabinet. In addition, the Shah had believed that, contrary to what he was repeatedly told, Washington would ultimately bail him out of his predicament. For that reason 'he kept putting off the day of reckoning.' Amini's resignation had political fallout in Washington. Talbot wrote to Holmes relating a lunch with Senator Stuart Symington of Washington in which the Senator accused the administration of 'wasting money on those who oppose us while letting our friends go down the drain for lack of even small sums of the support that they deserve.' Talbot counseled that, despite the problems, the US government needed to see the current course through. He argued: 'We have already accepted major costs [Amini's fall] to carry forward the difficult process of weaning a client away from budget support.' Talbot compared it to 'the weaning of a baby in spite of fretting and crying' but commented: 'Proper weaning does not mean the inducement of starvation.'[47]

Kennedy and the Iranian reality

The Kennedy administration now had an epiphany on Iran. At the White House, Brubeck wrote to Bundy stating that Amini, 'on whom we had pinned great hopes for economic and social reform in Iran', resigned because of problems with the Iranian budget. He went on to state: 'The termination of U.S. budgetary support contributed to his difficulties.' Brubeck reaffirmed the administration's position on refusing budgetary support, and then added a caveat: 'Should it appear that alignment with the Free World is seriously and immediately jeopardized, we would reconsider this policy. ... With Prime Minister Amini out of the picture, the Shah is the principal bastion of pro-Western strength and even of political stability in Iran.' As a result, Washington had to retain the Shah's 'confidence and goodwill'.[48] In an intelligence estimate on 17 August 1962, the CIA reported no apparent immediate threats to the Shah's rule. The agency stated that his return to the position of 'single focal point' in Iranian politics meant that future unrest would be directed at him. The fact that the Shah would have to face the mounting problems alone created the possibility that instability might lead to his overthrow or abdication.[49] The Shah seemed to know exactly what Washington was thinking. Playing on tried and proven methods of getting Washington's attention, the Shah made certain that the Kennedy administration heard that if the Alam government failed and there was little chance of a similar government succeeding, he would abdicate and leave Iran.[50] The CIA evaluation expressed Washington's view of the situation best: 'Once again then, storm warnings appear to be in order.'[51]

These warnings gave added importance to Vice President Lyndon Johnson's upcoming visit to Tehran.[52] Johnson was first to 'reassure the Shah of United States support, understanding, and encourage him toward responsible and progressive leadership'; second, to assure the Iranian people that the United States would 'protect them from aggression', help them 'modernize themselves', and respect and appreciate their 'achievements and culture'; and third, to encourage Iranian officials, including the Prime Minister, to use 'self-help measures' toward 'national unity and progress'. The paper went on to warn that the Shah believed that military assistance lacked the necessary 'quality and quantity'. It warned against getting into any discussion with the Shah on specifics issues of budgetary support or military aid, pointing out that the conversation would undoubtedly be 'misinterpreted' as commitments. This was obviously an oblique reference to the President's 'personal diplomacy' during the Shah's official visit to Washington and the claims that the Shah made with regard to promised military aid. Given the end of US budgetary support, it was suggested that the Vice President 'persuade the Iranians to face up to their own problems and to take the responsibility for the failure and success of their own actions.'[53]

Johnson followed his instructions to the letter. He pressed the Shah on reforms, the economy, and reductions in the military. The Vice President made it clear to the Shah exactly where the administration stood. 'We realize the extent to which our views and those of your farsighted leaders are parallel. We all agree on the necessity for programs of responsible change. We have seen that the status quo alone provides no safeguard for freedom.'[54] He reported to Kennedy that the Shah had accepted the reduction in his defense support and the termination of his budgetary support, as well as the admonition not to make new demands for any resumption. Johnson concluded that despite his 'shortcomings', the Shah was a 'valuable asset', and 'since we have no acceptable alternative', the United States must 'cooperate' and 'influence' him 'as best we can'.[55]

By mid-September 1962, after over a year of debate and controversy, Ambassador Holmes and Major General John C. Hayden prepared to present the final five-year military assistance plan to the Shah. Almost on the eve of the presentation, Holmes cabled Washington and asked to be allowed to include the two frigates eliminated from the plan. He argued that aside from whatever military benefits might accrue, it would reassure the Shah of US good intentions and support.[56] When Komer saw the request, he immediately fired off a memorandum to Bundy stating: 'I am just firmly opposed to our giving Holmes and Shah their way on frigates.' For Komer, the struggle with the State Department had now become as important as the issues with the Shah. Discredited but still ranting, Komer argued: 'I wish we could convince Ambassador of this too, and get him to spend half the energy on pressing Shah domestically that he does on military problems. In fact, Holmes is beefing before he even tries out on Shah. ... Admittedly, this is only a $5 million item but where do we draw the line? I'd like to tell Bill and Phil that President personally says "hell no".'⁵⁷ Komer lost again. The Secretaries of Defense and State obtained permission to include the two frigates, as a personal gesture from the President, with the understanding that Washington had nothing else to give.⁵⁸ On 19 September 1962, Holmes and General Hayden presented the MAP package to the Shah. After some discussion, the Shah accepted, leaving the door open for more military assistance. The Shah had three conditions: first, that his request for more tank units was noted, and that consideration of their supply would be given if resources allowed; second, that two early-warning radar stations would be better than one; and third, that if the security situation changed and unforeseen threats arose, discussions would be reopened.⁵⁹ Komer concluded from the Shah's conditions that Holmes had not been explicit enough with the Shah about additional aid requests. Komer stated: 'We can expect more pleas from Pahlevi [sic] all too soon.'⁶⁰

Crisis over – almost

Despite unhappiness at the NSC, the collapse of Amini, and rumors of continued instability, Tehran's 'acceptance' of the MAP ended hopes that an alternative to the Shah might exist. It also constituted the Kennedy administration's categorical return to Eisenhower's policies – with one exception: the Kennedy administration had tied itself absolutely to the Shah's dynastic fortunes. NEA and CIA representatives on the Iran Task Force recommended that Iran be removed from the 'Critical Country List', and the other Task Force members agreed. Iran continued to be unstable, and the situation 'could change completely tomorrow'; however, the overall situation had improved.⁶¹ Iran would continue to have problems and crises, but the Kennedy administration's experiment with the Task Force had added little to the situation, while inviting considerable interference from the White House and NSC. Those charged with policy in NEA now wanted these outside irritants removed; they wanted to manage relations with the Shah and Iran in a traditional manner, as they had been managed under Eisenhower.

The subsiding crisis mentality also allowed the State Department to focus on more mundane issues that had languished during the tumultuous Amini period. One of those issues, the 'status of forces' agreement, would evolve into something far more serious than anyone anticipated. Congress wanted an agreement on US jurisdiction over US military personnel in Iran.⁶² On 26 September, John Armitage, First Secretary at the US Embassy in Tehran, wrote to Jack Miklos, the new Iranian Affairs officer: 'Now that the ambassador has so neatly dispatched the MAP negotiations, I will turn my attention to your favorite problem, jurisdiction and immunities.'⁶³ In July 1962, the Chief of the American Affairs Section in the Political Division of the Iranian Foreign Ministry, Ali Fouthi, warned that an agreement on immunity would be impossible to get and that the US and the Iranian governments would 'regret it one day'. Fouthi explained that sooner or later there would be a new Majlis and the agreement would come under strong attack by nationalists; he urged the US Embassy to drop consideration of a formal agreement.[64]

The Embassy was attempting to explore some reciprocal agreement with the Iranians that would keep US servicemen out of Iranian courts, while allowing the Iranians to save face. On 12 October 1962, Washington responded: 'It is our view here that we should not seek to solve the jurisdictional problems in Iran through negotiating a treaty with Iran, but we much prefer the less complicated process of an executive agreement.'[65] On 5 November, the Deputy Chief of Mission, Stuart Rockwell, raised the issue with Foreign Minister Abbas Aram. Aram gave some indication of sympathy for the US concern and added that Amini had 'forbidden him to give sympathetic consideration' to the US position.[66] Rockwell put brackets around the statement about the Amini government as if to indicate concern over possible Iranian resistance to the American position. Fouthi's warning foreshadowed the controversy that would grow into a hurricane over immunity for US servicemen in Iran. This issue would ultimately become the principal catalyst around which opposition to the Shah and the US role in Iran would coalesce, but that lay in the future. By the end of 1962, despite all the effort and the creation of a special task force, Kennedy and his advisors found themselves tethered to Eisenhower's approach and enduring the carping about military assistance not only from the Shah but also from their own Ambassador in Tehran.

Chapter 13: Pakistan, India, and Priorities

The outcome of the US presidential election of 1960 raised several questions about the future direction of US policy toward Pakistan and India. It appeared that Kennedy's election might shift US containment policy toward an economic posture as opposed to military aid. This had serious implications for Pakistan. Kennedy, as a candidate, took the position that the US's commitment to 'northern tier' defense – Turkey, Iran, and Pakistan – had undermined the possibility of a more balanced policy across the Greater Middle East. The Indians and the Pakistanis concluded that a Kennedy administration might in fact be serious about reducing military aid and pressing forward with a greater focus on economic aid and development aid in the region. It also appeared that a new emphasis on democratic government and reform might emerge, and favor democratic India over authoritarian Pakistan. Also troubling for Karachi were indications of a more positive and tolerant US approach to non-alignment. As if to emphasize the point, Kennedy appointed Chester Bowles, the former US Ambassador to India during the Truman administration, as one of his principle foreign policy advisors. The fact that Bowles had once written 'Jawaharlal Nehru *is* the politics of Asia' was not lost on Ayub Khan. Bowles believed that the US should emphasize economic development and political reform, and viewed Eisenhower's pro-Pakistani tilt as counter-productive for US interests.[1] Bowles made no secret of his desire to see a major US policy reorientation and a more pro-Indian stance. Ayub saw Bowles as an old adversary. His presence as a Kennedy advisor, coupled with the Senator's statements, was disquieting. Ayub, like the Shah, had discreetly supported Nixon's candidacy and looked with foreboding on Kennedy's election.

In New Delhi, a cautiously optimistic Nehru viewed with interest the arrival of the Kennedy administration. Kennedy had argued that India was the key to Western policy in Asia and that its 'economic and political leadership of the East' had to be a primary US goal.[2] If other statements during the campaign were taken at face value, India might receive more economic and development assistance, as well as the possibility of a shift in US relations with Pakistan. Kennedy's intention to reduce tensions with the Soviet Union might also bring a commensurate reduction in the value of the US relationship with Karachi. In addition, Kennedy had fought for 'massive economic aid' for India and gone out of his way to flatter Nehru. In his inaugural address, Kennedy referred to the 'soaring idealism' of Nehru. The administration named well-known economist John Kenneth Galbraith as Ambassador to India.[3] Nehru probably hoped that Washington would renege on its arms commitments to Ayub. Shrewd, well-educated, and perceptive, Ayub also took note of how candidate Kennedy's ideas on foreign policy might affect US-Pakistan relations and specifically arms shipments to Pakistan. He was sensitive to arguments that arms for Pakistan forced India to divert much-needed funds for economic development into arms purchases.[4] Ayub feared that the new American administration might not be as enamored of 'controlled democracy' as the old had been.[5]

In addition, Ayub believed that increased US economic aid to India would merely allow Nehru to divert other funds to a military build-up.[6] Ayub found himself in much the same position as his CENTO partner, the Shah of Iran. Ayub feared that Kennedy might not value its relationship with Pakistan.[7] Ayub concluded that just in case the new administration actually contemplated serious shifts, he needed to reeducate Kennedy and his advisors about the realities of US defense needs and containment policy in the Greater Middle East and Asia. Pakistan was the lynch-pin in both CENTO and SEATO, making it imperative that a pro-Western and pro-US regime maintained control in Karachi.[8] Given the coup in Iraq and the perceived instability of Iran, Pakistan under Ayub had become the most stable of the critical 'northern tier' states. Both Turkey and Pakistan had military governments. In Turkey, the army had intervened on 27 May 1960 and overthrown the government of Prime Minister Adnan Menderes.[9] In Pakistan, Ayub appeared to have stabilized both the political and the economic situation. Ayub's call for a joint Indo-Pakistani defense policy had gained him a sizeable political following in the US Congress, while Nehru's rebuff damaged India's image with conservatives.[10] How the Kennedy administration would handle this situation remained the only outstanding question.

Nothing new under the sun

In 1961, Kennedy and his advisors found that Eisenhower's last foreign-aid budget represented a 'huge increase' over what had gone before, and required no additional funding.[11] The plan allotted India approximately $1 billion over the first two years of the Third Five-Year Plan, excluding shipments of PL 480 grain. Washington slated $250 million for Pakistan, with the same exclusion.[12] The administration also sent out a series of fact-finding missions, not only to obtain an independent view of the situation between India and Pakistan, but also to assess rumors of Ayub's discontent.[13] Karachi opened a two-front campaign designed to get Kennedy's attention. Pakistani Foreign Minister Bhutto advocated conclusion of an oil- and gas-exploration agreement with the Soviet Union. Arguing that the agreement was not a change in policy, Bhutto believed that Western oil companies 'left to themselves, will not allow themselves to find oil in Pakistan … because of the world glut in that commodity' and that the Soviets lacked 'inhibitions' in that regard. Any Pakistani agreement with Moscow was cause for alarm in Washington. Simultaneously, editorials appeared in several Pakistani newspapers comparing the merits of alignment and non-alignment. One editorial stated that Pakistan was 'putting the new American Administration "on notice"' over the direction of any new policies.[14] For good measure, Ayub told the US Ambassador in Karachi that he had serious concerns about US attitudes toward the Kashmir issue.[15]

On 21 February 1961, the Indian Ambassador in Washington, Braj Kumar (B.K.) Nehru, met with Averell Harriman. Harriman told him that he had been asked to go to Europe, Iran, Pakistan, and New Delhi to consult with the various leaders. Harriman stated:

> The foreign policy of the new administration would … present a sharp break from that of its predecessors. The President's position in Congress, however, was a difficult one. Due to the narrowness of [Kennedy's] electoral victory and lack of support by the Southern Democrats, the President could not afford to offend the Republican vote in Congress by announcing in words a drastic change in foreign policy. His [Kennedy's] deeds would gradually show in which direction he was going and they had to date been clear.

Harriman stated: 'India, in spite of its being an uncommitted nation, was the greatest ally the United States had – much more so than its vaunted military allies of SEATO [because] … under the leadership of Mr. Nehru, the values of India were the same as the values of the United States.' Harriman asked the Ambassador if, based on this common foundation, Prime Minister Nehru would participate in regular 'consultations' with President Kennedy on foreign policy.[16]

The Harriman mission

In March 1961, Averell Harriman went to the region to assess the situation. He visited Karachi in hopes of putting Ayub's concerns about Kennedy to rest. Harriman reaffirmed US commitments to Pakistan and delivered personal letters from the President. He also reconfirmed Ayub's state visit to Washington scheduled for November 1963. In a cordial but straightforward manner, Ayub stated that he knew that the 'US needed Pakistan as Pakistan needed the US' because the only way to combat Communism was for the 'free world' to remain united. Ayub expressed concern over Soviet adventures in Afghanistan, and discussed Pakistan's defense requirements to combat this threat. He then brought up the issue of Kashmir and the need for the US to put its weight behind a UN plebiscite.[17] Ayub took a positive stance with Harriman, but delegated others to make certain that the Special Envoy understood what was at stake in Pakistan. On 22 March, Harriman faced a grueling news conference in which he was bombarded with questions on foreign aid, Kashmir, and non-alignment. One reporter bluntly asked: 'What is the approach of the new American Government towards implementing the UN resolution about holding a plebiscite in Kashmir?' Another wanted to know: 'Is the new administration to pay more attention to neutral countries than to America's allies?'[18] The questions would never have been asked had Ayub not approved them. Harriman got the message.

In London, Harriman's trip raised questions. The British took exception to Harriman telling Ayub that the Kennedy administration did not 'regard neutrality as necessarily immoral'. The Foreign Office wondered: 'May not remarks such as these also encourage the tendency in Pakistan to ask what tangible benefits are to be derived from membership of CENTO and SEATO?'[19] Harriman tried to explain that he had emphasized the importance of CENTO and SEATO, but justified Western support for neutrals, stating that the US needed to assist them in maintaining their independence. He asserted that there was a distinction between committed 'allies' and the uncommitted, and he included Afghanistan and India among the latter.[20] Unimpressed, London concluded: 'Pakistan-U.S. relations may remain in rather a delicate state until the Kennedy Administration has settled down.'[21]

In India, Nehru lectured Harriman on the aggressive designs of the Chinese and the unreasonable Pakistani position on Kashmir, insisting 'on the boundaries as they now are'.[22] In the background, the Indian Defense Minister, Krishna Menon, called Pakistan a 'remnant of imperialism ... an imperialist stooge, tied to the United States through SEATO, CENTO, and large-scale military aid'.[23] The Indians also emphasized that since the signing of the Indus Waters agreement Ayub had exhibited a 'hostile' attitude. Apparently, during a recent Asian tour, Ayub had on several occasions referred to India as 'Pakistan's real enemy'. The Indians pointed out that Ayub and *Dawn* had blamed India for the Jabalpur communal riots and for making numerous 'provocative statements'. In addition, Pakistan now seemed intent on negotiating its northern border with China, an area occupied by Pakistan but claimed by India.[24] The Harriman visit produced a clear picture of what Eisenhower had dealt with from 1953 onwards.

Many in Washington believed that the resolution of the Indus dispute would be a first step toward the settlement of other outstanding issues, including the impasse over Kashmir. Of course, everything depended on the willingness of India and Nehru to compromise. To show sensitivity to the India position, Kennedy appointed officials with well-known Indian sympathies to key positions. In Chester Bowles, the Under Secretary of State, and John Kenneth Galbraith, the new US Ambassador to New Delhi, the administration had two staunch advocates of a pro-India point of view. Galbraith viewed military aid to Pakistan as an 'evil', if an understandable one.[25] More to the point, Bowles fumed that the intelligence installations at Peshawar were simply not worth the resulting loss of US 'influence' in India.[26]

The possibility of Pakistani-Chinese collusion with regard to India created another problem for the Kennedy administration's relationship with New Delhi, because, at Menon's urging, Nehru sought additional insurance by increasingly viewing the Soviets as a counterbalance to China, to Pakistan, and to pressure from the United States. In Pakistan, the Soviet influence in Afghanistan, Indian intransigence over Kashmir, and presumed Indo-Afghan agitation in Pushtunistan constituted an ongoing threat.[27] For Karachi, China offered additional leverage. Kennedy found himself forced to wink at the dictatorship in Pakistan and the 'hoax' of a Communist threat to justify military aid clearly aimed at India. Following Eisenhower's example, Kennedy tried to divert attention away from the confrontation with India toward economic development. In India, economic-development aid continued, while New Delhi's non-alignment, and congressional perceptions that New Delhi had ignored warnings about Soviet influence in India, prevented meaningful military aid.[28]

The Johnson mission to South Asia

In May 1961, on his Asia trip, Vice President Lyndon Johnson visited India and, in meetings with Nehru, pushed for economic development. Having just visited Southeast Asia, Johnson raised the issue of Communist aggression in Laos and South Vietnam.[29] Johnson asked Nehru to speak out 'in stirring and ringing tones against the Communist tactics' in Southeast Asia, and pointed to Laos as an example of the 'moral force' that India could exert. Nehru stated that he understood the US desire for him to take a position, but refused to do so.[30] In a pointed reference to Southeast Asia and Pakistan, Nehru told Johnson that he agreed that economic development was the principal guarantee against totalitarianism, not arms.[31] Johnson came away from these meetings optimistic that Nehru would consider taking a more pro-American stance on the situation in Southeast Asia.[32] Johnson's group then traveled to Karachi. Ayub pressed Johnson about economic aid to India. He stated: 'Nehru would not listen if he did not feel compelled to.'[33] Ayub made it clear that he believed that US economic aid, the refusal of Washington to put real pressure on Nehru, and the pro-Indian sentiments emanating from the administration were the primary impediments to a settlement on Kashmir. Contrary to Washington's protestations, Ayub insisted that Washington 'did have the power to influence him [Nehru].' Ayub argued that the dangerous situation with China left Nehru with no choice but to listen.[34]

In contrast to Nehru's cautionary advice on Southeast Asia, Ayub wholeheartedly supported the US position and offered Pakistani troops to confront the Laotian Communists and their North Vietnamese masters.[35] Reporting to the President, Johnson described an 'intellectual affinity' and an 'affinity of spirit' with the Indians. With regard to Pakistan, Johnson stated:

'President Ayub of Pakistan is the singularly most impressive and, in his way, responsible head of state encountered on this trip.' The Vice President argued that while it was 'impossible' and 'probably unnecessary' to convince India to drop its non-aligned status, Pakistan's strategic position deserved full consideration for military and economic modernization. Ayub's views that 'open representative' government would invite chaos and 'Communist infiltration' making it impossible to 'eradicate poverty, ignorance, and disease' resonated with the administration. Fundamentally, Kennedy and his advisors shared the same conviction with Eisenhower that only in a controlled political environment could Pakistan and Iran safely modernize.[36] Kennedy did not want to be remembered as the 'man who lost Pakistan'.

Nehru apparently hoped that improved US-Soviet relations would help India. As Krishna Menon stated, Nehru wanted the 'Kennedy regime' to respond favorably to Russia's new 'liberalized' outlook.[37] It appears that Nehru viewed rapprochement between the Soviet Union and the United States as an additional guarantee against aggressive Chinese moves in the north.[38] As Nehru observed, it was in 'the strange twist of destiny' during this lifting of the 'clouds of cold war' that India and China moved closer to open hostilities.[39] The Indian Prime Minister may also have viewed the meetings between Khrushchev and Kennedy as something of test for the new American administration. In a follow-up report on the meetings and the Soviet reaction to them, Arthur Lall borrowed a Russian saying from the Soviet Ambassador: 'A credulous fool is more dangerous than an open enemy.' Lall concluded: 'The Russians would therefore rather have Dulles than Kennedy.'[40] Nehru saw the situation with regard to Berlin as the 'real crisis' because of Moscow's fears of a resurgent Germany.[41] The fact that Kennedy reaffirmed Eisenehower's and Truman's position on access to West Berlin served notice on Nehru that the new administration would be much like the old in its approach to the Soviet Union and Communism.

Mending fences with Ayub

As Ayub increased his complaints about US policy, fears grew in Washington that relations with Pakistan were slipping dangerously. In reaction, Washington advanced President Ayub's official visit to July 1961 from its original date in November 1963.[42] To counter the impression of being 'enamored with non-alignment', the White House added an 'unrivalled occasion', a dinner at Mount Vernon.[43] The change in dates moved Ayub's visit ahead of one planned for Nehru in November. On his way to Washington, Ayub gave Kennedy a preview of what was to come. He stopped in London and told British Prime Minister Macmillan that the inability of the US to bring stability to the subcontinent called into question Pakistan's decision to join the Western alliance system. Ayub pointed out that the proposed new constitution of 1962 might force a neutralist course. Ayub knew that Macmillan would pass the substance of the conversation to Kennedy. He calculated that having just muddled through the Bay of Pigs crisis and a failed

Vienna summit with the Soviets, Kennedy would appease Pakistan.⁴⁴ He was right.

Like Eisenhower, Kennedy wanted to avoid the Kashmir issue and to discourage Pakistani action in the UN Security Council. The administration believed that: 'Given the present Indian and Pakistan positions, there is no immediate possibility for a formal solution to the Kashmir problem.' The official US position argued that only bilateral contacts could resolve the issue and that Pakistan should cultivate broad relations with India as a starting point in settling the dispute.⁴⁵ The administration anticipated a 'major effort to demonstrate Pakistan's loyalty and to win increased US aid'.⁴⁶ Fundamentally, nothing had changed: Washington needed Pakistan for its collective security alliances, CENTO and SEATO, and the relationship required arms. These

Corbis

Ayub, Eisenhower, and Kennedy

Ayub Khan, President of Pakistan, Eisenhower, and Kennedy at a state dinner during Ayub's official visit to Washington in July 1961. This picture symbolizes the close relationship between Eisenhower and Kennedy policy. Pro-Indian pronouncements raised fears of Pakistan's defection to the neutral camp, prompting Kennedy to advance the date of Ayub's visit by more than two years and resulting in an outpouring of reassurances to Pakistan.

same arms threatened good relations with India.

During the July 1961 visit, despite efforts to the contrary, discussions with Ayub always found their way back to Kashmir. Ayub used Soviet involvement in Afghanistan to highlight Pakistan's lack of military capability to defend itself. Ayub disagreed with US aid to India, stating that the purpose of US aid to India was 'not with the expectation that India would support US policies' but to prevent an Indian economic collapse. Ayub maintained that this approach only made India more difficult to deal with on Kashmir, and freed other funds for military use. Ayub asked for American help with Nehru and told Kennedy that the Kashmir situation had reached a point where the 'Pakistani people' had to see some sort of progress, which contributed to demands for a closer relationship between Beijing and Karachi. Kennedy asked Ayub to wait until after Nehru's visit that fall to contemplate additional action at the UN. Ayub made it clear that if Kennedy failed to make progress with Nehru, Pakistan would have no alternative but to raise the Kashmir issue again in the UN Security Council.[47]

Ayub believed that he and President Kennedy saw eye-to-eye on most issues.[48] Ayub had obtained Kennedy's promise to support the Pakistani position on UN resolutions on Kashmir, should it come to that. Kennedy also promised a 'major effort' with Nehru during his US visit, stating: 'It was in the vital interest of the United States that this issue [Kashmir] be solved.'[49] The comments made during Ayub's visit were also noted in New Delhi. Nehru called them 'aggressive and even offensive' with regard to Kashmir. Terming it 'India baiting' and a 'revelation,' Nehru stated: 'The kind of language he used even on State occasions was the essence of bitterness against India.'[50] The prospect of any pro-Pakistan shift in US policy, coupled with the Chinese threat, had increased Indian insecurities.

The trip also had significant long-term ramifications for US-Pakistani relations. Pressed on Kashmir, President Kennedy made some injudiciously vague statements. Kennedy reassured Ayub that the US had 'no intention now' of giving military aid to India and, in the event of some important change in the situation like a war with China, 'President Kennedy would talk with Ayub first.'[51] A 'vigorous, frank military man', Ayub took the statement at face value.[52] At the conclusion of the meeting, Kennedy reaffirmed that the United States would continue economic aid to India to stave off economic collapse and the resulting political chaos, but that Pakistan was the principal US ally in the region. Kennedy also agreed to talk to Ayub prior to any change in that policy. US officials knew that they had misled Ayub about the nature of the 'talk' that would occur between Pakistan and the United States. Should it come to that, Kennedy would inform, not consult with Ayub. Talbot saw the problem coming and commented that the conversation left an 'uncertain taste in the mouth'.[53] Personal diplomacy tended to leave a trail of misunderstandings, and President Kennedy certainly left Ayub with the wrong impression.

Following Ayub's visit, Kennedy sent Bowles ostensibly on a tour of South Asia, but with the expressed purpose of reassuring Prime Minister Nehru. During the meetings, to everyone's surprise, the issue of India-Pakistan relations never came up.[54] This was unusual given the recent aggravations in US-India relations. For example, Galbraith in New Delhi requested that Washington allow him to notify Nehru of the type and number of F-104s to be delivered to Pakistan. Karachi objected, and Washington ordered the New Delhi Embassy not to inform the Indians.[55] In a letter to President Kennedy in August 1961, Ambassador Galbraith opined:

> If the State Department drives you crazy you might calm yourself by contemplating its effect on me. The other night I woke with a blissful feeling and discovered I had been dreaming that the whole Goddamn place had burned down. I dozed off again hoping for a headline saying no survivors. ... The touchiest issue here is the shipment of military hardware to Pakistan – arming the present rival and foe and the ancient enemy and rulers of the Hindus. A few weeks ago one of our aircraft carriers brought twelve supersonic jets (F-104s) to Karachi where they were unloaded in all the secrecy that would attend mass sodomy on the B.M.T. at rush hour.

Galbraith complained that in placating the Pakistanis, the United States allowed the Indian intelligence service to report the unloading of between 50 and 75 aircraft. The Ambassador 'threatened physical violence' to get permission to explain the transfer to the Indians, causing Pakistan to complain that the US had not kept it a secret. Galbraith was beginning to understand what he viewed as the unpleasant realities of Kennedy policy.[56] Pakistan provided key support to US strategic interests, and was a member of various alliances qualifying it for military aid. Non-aligned India was not.

Problems with India

Between Ayub's visit in July and Nehru's in November, events placed additional strain on US-Indian relations. From 1 to 6 September 1961, a Non-Aligned Conference met in Belgrade, Yugoslavia, with Nehru in attendance.[57] The Conference communiqué condemned both the Soviet Union and the US equally for the resumption of nuclear testing.[58] The Soviets had actually broken the moratorium, not Washington. As a result of a meeting on 26 August with Galbraith, Desai suggested to Nehru that 'there is a lot of justification for the attitude taken by the United States' on nuclear testing and promised to recommend a modification.[59] At the end of the conference, the non-aligned states produced a statement that 'put the US and the USSR on the same level and blamed both for the crisis.'[60] Galbraith, who thought that he had an understanding with the Indians, was perturbed.[61] The Ambassador accused Desai and Nehru of undermining the ability of the 'Kennedy administration to push through their liberal policies' by providing ammunition to the US domestic opponents of closer ties with India.[62]

With regard to Southeast Asia, the Indian position was also problematic. Averell Harriman, who was responsible for the Geneva negotiations over Laos, detested Arthur Lall, who headed the India contingent.[63] Lall was a long-time protégé of Krishna Menon, or, as Lall described the relationship, Menon's 'closest aide'.[64] Galbraith complained to Desai that the Indian delegation led by Lall, and undoubtedly influenced by Menon, supported the most radical views of the Chinese and North Vietnamese in the negotiations, even when the United States and Soviet Union agreed. In commenting on the Indian role as Chair of the ICC on Indochina, Chester Cooper, a member of the US delegation, described Krishna Menon as the 'wordy, windy, and exasperatingly oratorical' 'Super Star of the Geneva Follies'. Cooper stated that while the Indians 'provided an occasional oasis of amusement in a desert of dull speeches ... more often than not they sent most of the long-suffering delegates into spasms of frustration and irritation.' In the US view, the Indians were 'more interested in discussing broad international profundities' than in making the ICC work effectively.[65] Desai, an opponent of Krishna Menon and therefore a Lall detractor, reported to Nehru: 'I do not see why we should come in the way of their coming together and support the Chinese and North Vietnamese who always take an extremist line at Geneva.'[66] In a minute on 28 August, Nehru concurred: 'I agree with you. ... We need not be more royalist than the King.'[67] Despite Nehru's views, nothing changed in Geneva.

On 8 September, Galbraith informed Desai that Lall continued to be an impediment. According to Galbraith: 'Harriman maintains that Arthur Lall is never helpful in any way and continues to damage the American position even when the Americans are able to get the agreement of the Russians on some issues.'[68] Even though the Indians had supported a move to take the neutralization issue and that of the infiltration of Laos by North Vietnam directly to the ICC, India refused to condemn the North Vietnamese.[69] At every opportunity, Galbraith harped on the need for a solution in Laos in which neither rightist or leftist extremist elements took over.[70] He implored the Indians to assist in a solution that would preserve the credibility of the Kennedy administration by preventing a 'communist takeover of Laos under the guise of neutrality'.[71] Useful Indian diplomatic assistance, however, never materialized.[72]

Nehru: 'the worst official visit'

These issues formed the backdrop for Prime Minister Nehru's November 1961 Washington visit. Disappointingly, Nehru either lectured Kennedy or gave him the renowned 'silent treatment'.[73] For Nehru's part, Kennedy's narrow election victory, the Bay of Pigs fiasco, and official American concerns that the liberal policies proclaimed during the election were not in fact being implemented raised doubts about whether or not 'the untroubled certainty of

Courtesy of National Archives

Nehru and Kennedy

Kennedy and Nehru during Nehru's 1961 official visit to Washington. Kennedy remarked that it was the 'worst official visit' of his presidency. Unimpressed by the new President, Nehru gave Kennedy his famed silent treatment.

judgments at the White House' were reliable.[74] Second, the visit demonstrated the lengths to which the Kennedy administration was willing to go to get India to counterbalance China in Asia, a competition Eisenhower had pointedly avoided. Washington gave all the appearance of preferring that India be embroiled in a conflict with China. Third, Krishna Menon would not go away. The US suggestion that Lall be removed certainly did not sit well; Nehru reacted negatively to any hint of external coercion. Finally, there was the issue of Galbraith's use of the American right-wing bogey man in an attempt to apply leverage to India policy. It raised doubts about the administration's ability to conduct pro-India policies championed by Galbraith and Bowles. From the Indian perspective, either the administration was too weak to change Eisenhower's policies, or too duplicitous to be trusted.

On 7 November, Nehru arrived at the White House. At the beginning of the meeting, Kennedy asked for Indian support 'on those occasions when [the United States] might be right'. Nehru responded that he attached weight not only to the merits of an issue, but to the 'manner of approach as well'.[75] It could not have helped that Kennedy told Nehru directly that Krishna Menon was an impediment to any American administration that wanted closer cooperation with India.[76] Kennedy offered an interesting explanation of US support for non-democratic regimes: 'The foreign policy of the United States [is] to support countries with democratic systems, but even more basically to support national sovereignty.' Nehru countered that weak regimes propped up by outside military forces merely resulted in 'weaker' dependent regimes and invited outside subversion. In a pointed reference, Nehru then opined that if the countries involved had abided by the terms of the 1954 agreements on Indochina, there would be no problem of infiltration in Laos, nor would there be any need for intervention in South Vietnam.[77] The exchanges were friendly, but the Kennedy charm was getting nowhere.

At this point, as he had promised Ayub, Kennedy brought up the issue of Kashmir. Kennedy observed that this flashpoint issue hindered the ability of both Pakistan and India to focus resources on economic development. Nehru pointedly countered that India could only consider a settlement based on the *status quo*. He went on to say that neither he nor the Congress Party could accept Pakistan's argument for a plebiscite in Kashmir because Muslim communalism formed the basis of and motivation for that effort. Nehru stated that a plebiscite recognized the efficacy of communalism, something that he had long rejected, and thus the possibility of partition threatened the fundamental basis of the Indian secular state. To recognize the Pakistani claim and their communal argument would invite a never-ending cycle of agitation among minorities and threaten the existence of the state itself. Nehru pointed out that general elections in India, something that Pakistan did not have, would occur in three months' time, and to raise this issue would cause 'huge troubles'. The President's probing indicated that no room for compromise existed on the Indian side.[78] The meetings were not productive for several reasons. As Talbot commented: 'Nehru's style was not of a sort calculated to stir or fully engage the President's interest.'[79]

Kennedy's problem in dealing with Nehru was more fundamental. Nehru's attitude was that of a senior statesman advising a young, inexperienced American President. As one observer commented: 'He was like a tremendous nanny, talking to Khrushchev and Kennedy as if they were naughty nephews, hoping they wouldn't get into war.' Nehru saw Kennedy as 'brash, aggressive, and inexperienced'. Nehru had gotten along well with Eisenhower, in part because he viewed him as an equal.[80] The much-anticipated visit also left Washington unimpressed. For an administration obsessed with youth, vigor, and action, Nehru's demeanor in the meetings caused Kennedy and his advisors to conclude that: 'Nehru had aged and was a tired old man who had stayed around too long.'[81] Kennedy later described Nehru's visit, 'as the worst head of state visit I have had'.[82]

Menon and Goa

Before returning home, Nehru added insult to injury. He asked Kennedy to meet with the Indian Defense Minister.[83] The purpose of this meeting was a mystery. Menon was broadly despised, and his irascibility and rudeness were legendary.[84] Yet Nehru prevailed upon Kennedy to discuss the situation in Vietnam and Laos with Menon. On 21 November, the President met with Menon, who, while staying on what was for him his very best behavior, still managed to disagree with Kennedy on every point of substance in the conversation. Menon was blind to North Vietnamese infiltration and violations of Laotian neutrality. He lectured Kennedy on Washington's need to get along with the Soviets.[85] It was neither a productive nor a pleasant meeting, and given what was about to transpire it was embarrassing.

Three weeks later, on 17 December 1961, Nehru gave Menon the green light to occupy the Portuguese enclave of Goa. Founded in 1510, it was the last vestige of colonial presence in India. The occupation was over in 26 hours and almost bloodless. Nevertheless, it brought a stinging condemnation from Britain, France, and the United States. Embarrassed, Kennedy admonished Nehru stating: 'All countries including, of course, the United States, have a great capacity for convincing themselves of the full righteousness of their particular cause. No country ever uses force for reasons it considers unjust.'[86] UN Ambassador Adlai Stevenson accused India of having 'killed the UN' and termed the attack a 'stab in the back', referring to US attempts to improve relations with India.[87] US officials accused Nehru of taking action on Goa to improve the sagging position of the Congress Party and his friend Krishna Menon, and to distract public opinion from their inaction in confronting the Chinese in the north. Nehru virtually admitted as much to Galbraith: 'Failure to react to the Portuguese would I feel sure, be disastrous both for the people of Goa, who would have to suffer terribly, and our own people round about the border, the position of India generally in regard to other problems that we face, including other borders.'[88] The move was wildly popular in India. It not only bolstered the political standing of Nehru's Congress Party, but also appeared to assure a solid political future for his protégé, Krishna Menon. Menon, Kennedy's guest just weeks before, dismissed US opposition as a 'vestige of Western imperialism' and 'British influence'.[89] Nehru also hoped that it would serve as a warning to both Pakistan and China and demonstrate independence from the West.[90]

Pakistan reacts to Goa

Reacting to the Indian occupation of Goa, Ayub Khan demanded UN action on Kashmir, something Washington and London wanted to avoid. Galbraith hurriedly met with Nehru and argued that a 'slugging match between Zafrullah Khan and Krishna Menon' at the UN would revive the Goa issue and have a negative impact on India's position in the US. Nehru agreed to consider inviting Pakistani General Burki for preliminary talks leading to a potential meeting between himself and Ayub.[91] Galbraith reported this to Washington, only to have Nehru undermine the effort by stating: 'Our view has been that we should start with the acceptance of things as they are.'[92] The proposed talks collapsed into the usual finger-pointing between New Delhi and

Karachi.[93] The British Foreign Office summed up the situation: 'We hope that it will be possible for Minister to avoid being drawn on Kashmir issue in both India and Pakistan, particularly if matter is currently under discussion in Security Council.'[94] Ayub insisted that Kennedy stand by his commitment to support Pakistan at the UN. Just as in 1957, the US attempted to 'avoid a brawl'.[95] Then Ayub made it clear that a failure by the West to support Pakistan would lead to 'a reappraisal of Pakistan's present friendships'. Kennedy understood this to mean that US intelligence sites might be in jeopardy as well as the possibility of improved Pakistani-Chinese relations.[96]

Fearing that an embarrassing debate at the UN would harden India's stance, the US tried to prevent the confrontation: 'Our (US) efforts should be directed at forestalling bitter and highly emotional public debate and at behind-the-scenes encouragement of both parties to refrain from taking positions from which there can be no withdrawal or no compromise.'[97] The White House decided to engage in another round of 'personal diplomacy'.[98] Kennedy wrote letters to Prime Minister Nehru and General Ayub arguing for bilateral talks. After reading the letter, B.K. Nehru, the Indian Ambassador in Washington, offered his view of personal diplomacy and observed: 'If I may say so, this was not a wise thing to do. However, it is an interesting démarche.'[99] Kennedy's letter made acceptance of the US proposal for bilateral talks contingent upon the suspension of the Pakistani action in the United Nations.

Pakistan accepted Kennedy's proposal but refused to delay its UN effort, for three reasons: first, the press in Pakistan had already blamed US pressure for the delays in utilizing the Security Council; second, the Indians would delay on bilateral talks unless the 'heat [was] kept on them' at the UN; and third, the Kashmir situation was heating up as a result of major Indian military deployments in Kashmir.[100] Kennedy appealed directly to Ayub to forego the Security Council debate and pressured Nehru to accept bilateral ministerial discussions. When Galbraith interpreted a non-committal Nehru response as a commitment to talks, Kennedy was encouraged. Instead, the Indians responded with a vague invitation that did not meet the Pakistani criteria for real talks on Kashmir. India would not allow 'mediation' over her sovereign territory.[101] Ambassador Rountree in Karachi commented: 'We are, of course, greatly discouraged by report of meeting. ... What we had assumed would be important Indian initiative to bring about discussions of Kashmir seems to have ended.'[102] Rountree was 'discouraged' but not surprised.

More concerned than ever, Kennedy proposed that Eugene Black, President of the World Bank, act as a mediator in discussions between India and Pakistan.[103] Ayub accepted, but as one Pakistani official put it: 'The Indians would not negotiate except under strong and continued pressure from some outside source.' He added that Nehru would 'wriggle' and 'wheedle' in an attempt to escape his tight situation. Ayub and his advisors were convinced that the Americans did not 'understand the Hindu mentality and the Indians were taking full advantage of this.'[104] In New Delhi, Desai was also pessimistic because the 'Kashmir dispute was one of sovereignty', and he thought Black a poor choice. The British commented: 'It will need all Galbraith's skill and persuasion to bring Indians to accept this.'[105] On 23 January, Galbraith met with Nehru, who stated that he would discuss the matter with Desai.[106] Ayub took the position that the entire episode was a test of the American government and 'whether the USG insists on a definite, repeat definite, answer from the Indian Government this week'. The root of Ayub's position was his fundamental distrust of the Nehru-Menon axis and his fear that Menon might actually manage to succeed the ailing Nehru. The British were concerned that if the Indians offered an indefinite answer and Washington accepted it, 'there may be an explosion.'[107]

In an attempt to forestall that explosion, Kennedy accelleraterd aid programs for Pakistan: 'A failure to provide what competent analysts have determined to be Pakistan's needs would seriously weaken the image of the United States and the West as determined to advance the development of our staunchest partners.'[108] The Pakistanis dusted off the SEATO agreements and reminded Washington that 'the United States would promptly and effectively come to the assistance of Pakistan if it were subjected to armed aggression.' The State Department concluded that under the Note of 15 April 1959 'the assurances undertaken by the United States ... pertained to a case of armed aggression "against Pakistan" without any limitation as to the place of attack.' The provision in the treaty could be interpreted to include an attack on Pakistani forces in Kashmir. Kennedy reaffirmed in writing to Ayub that 'my government most certainly stands by these assurances.' The United States had made similar guarantees to India in the event of an attack by Pakistan.[109]

Nehru's 'doubts and misgivings'

On 29 January, Nehru replied in writing to Kennedy on the Black proposal. He stated that he had no confidence in 'third party' approaches and that 'direct talks between the two countries [was the] 'only possible way.' Nehru pointed his finger at Washington, stating: 'We have had the feeling that a certain measure of support that Pakistan got from other countries made it much more rigid in this matter.' Just to make sure that Kennedy understood, Nehru added sharply: 'There is no lack of confidence in Mr. Black, but we have certain doubts and misgivings about your proposal.'[110] The Indian government clearly lacked confidence in the White House. In Washington, Ambassador Nehru told Phillips Talbot that: 'President to Prime Minister correspondence of this nature because of the consequences if India were forced to say "No" to the President was undesirable.'[111] Within the administration, the pro-India optimists, Komer, Bowles, and Galbraith, believed that improved relations with India coupled with Chinese pressure had created an opportunity to reassess US policy on the subcontinent. In addition, the Pakistani démarches of January 1962 had ruffled feathers. Questions arose about whether the US should be 'more interested in a Western-oriented weak ally or a strong neutralist India able to defend its own national interests (which happen to broadly coincide with ours).'[112] The pro-India elements wanted to eliminate

Pakistan as the US's 'chosen instrument on the subcontinent with a veto on our Indian policy'.[113]

Often led by Talbot, traditionalists successfully countered that, no matter how frustrating, the US needed both relationships. India carried more weight in international affairs, but the relationship with Pakistan directly affected US security. Pakistan's position in the alliance system contributed to containment and supplied 'certain special facilities' to the US. Pakistan also supported US initiatives at the UN. India and Pakistan were too important for the US to choose between them.[114] Putting the best face on a difficult situation, Talbot argued that India and Pakistan had negotiated an end to the Indus water dispute. Furthermore, there were indications that influential people on both sides were 'fed up' with the dispute: 'There is reason to believe that to get a settlement some of the top Pakistani leadership too would be prepared to make very substantial compromises of existing demands.'[115] They argued that after the Indian elections, a window of opportunity for negotiations would open.

During early 1962, the Kennedy administration attempted to produce alternatives to Pakistani efforts to bring the Kashmir dispute to the UN Security Council. The US continued to hope that the parties might yet be amenable to 'bilateral talks' or a mediation effort. Ayub had a better grasp of the situation, however, and made it abundantly clear that he expected little or no progress with Nehru.[116] In March, Under Secretary of State Ball informed Pakistani Ambassador Ahmad that the Security Council effort was premature and damaging to the potential for 'direct negotiations', and that Pakistan should not 'overestimate potential support' in the Security Council. Ball then pointed out that any resolution would face a Soviet veto, leaving Pakistan only the option of going to a less sympathetic UNGA.[117] Concern about an impasse was well founded. Despite the Congress Party's gains, Nehru understood that, even were he so inclined, any move toward a compromise with Pakistan would jeopardize its hold on power. In addition, Menon, the hero of Goa, had gained considerable stature. 'He now emerges as one of the very few Congress Party figures who can be considered national in character.'[118] Menon's increased influence fed Nehru's natural inclination to maintain an uncompromising stance on Kashmir.

There were problems in Pakistan as well. Pakistan's 1959 land-reform program attempted to reduce the influence of the 'landed gentry' while increasing the support of the mid-sized landowners for the government. It had run into difficulties.[119] In addition, Pakistan was about to inaugurate a new constitution, which had been in the works since 27 October 1959. Despite the ultimate authority residing in the presidency, the new constitution would give political voice to elements of Pakistani society that would react negatively to any reduction of pressure on India over Kashmir.[120] Introduced on 1 March 1962, some Indians described the 'Ayub Constitution' as 'a government of the President, by the President, and for the President'.[121] Nevertheless, Ayub wanted the new constitution to be at least a propaganda success, and the Kashmir campaign partially served to insure this outcome.[122] Washington's reluctance to press the Kashmir issue at the UN convinced Ayub that he had been misled. On 12 April, Talbot met with Sir Zafrullah Khan, the Pakistani UN Representative, and Aziz Ahmad, Karachi's Ambassador in Washington. They accused the Kennedy administration of dragging its feet on pressing India for negotiations, the Black mission, Kashmir, and Goa. Pakistan intended to bring the issue of Kashmir to the Security Council on 27 April, a move for which they expected US support.[123]

To reinforce this message, Ayub Khan wrote to President Kennedy, explaining Pakistan's 14 years of patience and Kennedy's promise to support the Pakistanis.[124] Ayub stated that he understood that current US policy would not bring any positive results for Pakistan with regard to Kashmir, but he wanted the US to take a public stand. The White House concluded that it had no alternative but to support the resolution calling for bilateral talks between Pakistan and India over Kashmir.[125] In the end, the 'fierce diplomatic onslaught' led by Krishna Menon left only the United States and Ireland co-sponsoring the resolution, which the Soviet Union killed with a veto on 22 June 1962.[126] Kennedy had fulfilled his commitment to Ayub but had nothing to show for it. Ayub became more disenchanted with Kennedy, and India now decided to pursue closer ties with Moscow.

Nehru explores the Soviet option

In May 1962, the Indians concluded that they needed modern arms for protection against the Pakistanis and Chinese. The Soviets were happy to accommodate them. In Washington, the moment of truth had arrived. Rumors of the arms deal rumbled around the bureaucracy for months, but most of the pro-India faction dismissed the possibility.[127] Then the Indians announced the purchase of MIG-21 aircraft. The US Senate reacted sharply, with a drastic reduction in aid.[128] New Delhi balked and delayed the agreement. A quick analysis at the White House concluded that if the price of stopping the Soviet arms purchase was the supply of F-104 Starfighters like those provided to Pakistan, then it was simply not worth it.[129] The administration concluded that the best approach would be to argue that the arms purchase would severely damage India's economic development, not only by diverting funding but also because of aid that India would lose.[130]

Both the State Department and the NSC concluded that the cost in political and financial terms of supplanting the Soviets was just too high, and little would be gained. Krishna Menon, the architect of the Soviet deal, would get credit for having forced Washington's hand. The Pakistanis would be enraged, and CENTO and SEATO would be damaged, undermining US influence in the region.[131] 'The value of our special relationship with Pakistan, particularly in the military field, is such that we cannot contemplate withdrawal. Also, the U.S. cannot yet accept the dissolution of CENTO and SEATO, which might follow if Pakistan withdrew. ... [E]qual treatment for India would be interpreted in Pakistan as a U.S. decision to change fundamentally the relative role of Pakistan and could adversely affect our interests in Pakistan.' The US policy statement went on to say that it was imperative to strengthen ties with Pakistan 'in order to obtain the additional freedom of action to take the steps necessary to deal with India in the light of our national interests. An improvement in Pak-Indian relations is an essential element in gaining this additional flexibility.'[132] The decisive issue appeared in a CIA memorandum for the national intelligence board: 'US provision of F-104 fighter aircraft to India would draw a sharply adverse reaction from Pakistan. ... Pakistan would almost certainly not permit expansion of the special US facilities and would probably seek to impose new restriction on them.'[133] Those intelligence facilities were simply too important.

Simultaneously, Ambassador Galbraith confronted Krishna Menon about the possibility of US aid subsidizing Soviet arms; Menon denied this, and claimed that India was paying cash for them. Galbraith, who detested Menon, retorted that given the state of the rupee, it was military aid pure and simple. Having temporarily delayed significant Soviet military assistance, Galbraith, Bowles, and to a lesser degree, Komer argued that the lack of meaningful US military assistance for India had opened the door to the Soviets and undermined pro-Western elements in the Indian military. Galbraith further pointed out Nehru's poor health and the fact that the Soviet arms deal enhanced the reputation and influence of Krishna Menon, the pro-Soviet and anti-American Minister of Defense. At a minimum, Galbraith wanted to offer India C-130 transports to stave off the MIG transaction. He failed, and in bitterness commented: 'Yesterday an incredible telegram came from the Department washing out the C-130 offer. ... And, likewise any suggestion of military aid. All in craven reaction to Congress and, I fear, to the President's displeasure with India.'[134] In frustration, Galbraith decided to resign.[135]

On 24 September 1962, Ayub stopped in the US on his way to a Commonwealth Conference in Canada. He visited Hammersmith Farm, Jacqueline Kennedy's family farm at Newport, Rhode Island. There he met with President Kennedy for several hours. He argued doggedly that large-scale US economic aid allowed India to divert resources into the purchase of increasingly sophisticated weapons systems. Ayub made it clear that he viewed the US reluctance to use economic aid to pressure India as the principal obstruction to progress on Kashmir. Frustrations were growing.[136]

In the final analysis, despite campaign rhetoric and hopes for closer ties, US policy continued along the same track established by the Eisenhower administration. The attempt to improve the situation with India had complicated the relationship with Pakistan.[137] Military and economic aid to Pakistan continued at the same levels as those during the Eisenhower administration. Ayub remained popular at DOD, in the CIA, and on Capitol Hill. When it came to the fundamental US policy of containment, Pakistan, not India, was more important. In this environment of distrust and dissatisfaction, the Chinese provided a catalyst that permanently altered the dynamic of US relations with both New Delhi and Karachi.

Part IV: Frustrations of the Fall – JFK and 1963

In the fall of 1962, the Cuban missile crisis and its potential for Armageddon with the Soviet Union consumed the Kennedy administration. Nevertheless, two smaller crises, the beginning of the Yemen civil war and the Sino-Indian border war, significantly altered the direction of the administration's policy in the Greater Middle East. These two events complicated US relations with pro-Western states and Britain, and chilled relations with the UAR and India. The Kennedy administration brought to Washington an intellectual acceptance of the principle of non-alignment. Implicit in this acceptance was a belief that the Eisenhower administration had mismanaged relations with the developing world and that a more sophisticated application of 'personal diplomacy' and economic aid could bring the non-aligned countries to a more pro-Western orientation. As with Eisenhower, the Kennedy administration viewed Nasser's Egypt as the key to the Arab world and to any Arab-Israeli peace. By the late 1950s, Nehru's India had become a potential counterbalance to growing Chinese power. While Eisenhower had shied away from encouraging this competition, many in the new administration, including President Kennedy, believed that if the dispute with Pakistan over Kashmir could be solved, non-aligned India would move into a more pro-Western posture and potentially counterbalance Chinese influence in Asia. Like Eisenhower, Kennedy's ultimate goal was the containment of Soviet and Chinese Communism, and, if anything, Kennedy was even more aggressive and less risk-averse in pursuing that goal.

During 1961 and 1962, cooperation and building a working relationship with Nasser and Nehru had not gone well, and the attempt to cultivate better relations with these non-aligned states, to one degree or another, had antagonized US allies in the region. In the fall of 1962, a series of shocks began the process of exorcising Kennedy's intellectual flirtation with non-alignment and of placing US policy goals back on the pragmatic footing developed by

Eisenhower between 1958 and 1960. To grasp the complexity of events during the fall of 1962, one need only examine a single page in the Melbourne, Australia, newspaper *The Age*. The 28 October edition provided a snapshot of the chaotic fall of 1962. Column one discussed a 'new ray of hope' in the Cuban missile crisis. The next column described fresh Indian troops moving up to stem the Chinese attack along the northern border. Yet another announced the arrival of Jordanian and Saudi Arabian forces along the northern border of Yemen to support royalist elements battling the UAR-sponsored republican government in Sanaa.[1] In retrospect, Cuba was the beginning of the end for Khrushchev's regime, and in the same vein, the Yemen civil war and the Sino-Indian border conflict would crush Kennedy's hopes for improved relations with the two key non-aligned states in the Greater Middle East. The crises also undermined the efficacy of White House 'personal diplomacy'. Given the pressures of the Cuban situation, of necessity the handling of Yemen and India devolved to more traditional channels within the foreign policy establishment, but Kennedy still played an active role in policy formulation.[2] He wanted personal credit for any breakthroughs on the non-aligned diplomatic front. Unfortunately, by December 1962 events forced President Kennedy to conclude that his 'personal diplomacy' had done little to alter the situation. In fact, the inability of the President to affect substantive changes in the Arab-Israeli dispute or the Indo-Pakistani conflict over Kashmir placed the onus of failure squarely on the White House. In terms of diplomacy, presidential correspondence, personal statements, and initiatives often diminished Kennedy's stature, while at the same time compromising his goals.

As 1963 began, the Kennedy administration faced a growing number of frustrations and disappointments in the Middle East. The White House had attempted to juggle traditional US security interests and simultaneously broaden relations with key non-aligned states. Kennedy found that he faced the same constraints confronted almost a decade earlier by the Eisenhower administration. Kennedy also learned that these constraints were less a matter of choice and more a matter of necessity dictated by the requirements of containment. Kennedy, like Eisenhower, had no choice but to support US regional allies. Also like Eisenhower, the Kennedy administration believed that economic development and reform were the best long-term guarantors of containment, but reality often made security and stability for the traditional allies the more immediate priority. As a result, Kennedy, the erstwhile progressive, drove the UAR and India into closer cooperation with the Soviet Union, the absolute opposite of what he had originally intended. He also alienated Pakistan, and left the United States unambiguously dependent on the fortunes of the Pahlavi dynasty in Iran, a goal diametrically opposed to what the administration had planned in 1961. The United States found itself tied to Saudi Arabia, Jordan, Libya, and other traditional or conservative authoritarian states. Labeled as imperialist, the White House found itself alienated from most secular revolutionary states. In addition, policy toward Israel set Washington on a path toward massive arms and economic subsidies to the Jewish state.

Sensing the lack of progress in relations with the UAR and India, Kennedy returned to the more conservative, less activist foreign policy established by Eisenhower and Dulles between 1958 and 1960. Ultimately, Kennedy bet the future of the United States in the Greater Middle East on Iran, Saudi Arabia, Pakistan, and Israel.

Chapter 14: The Best Laid Plans

The spring and summer of 1962 had not gone well for 'personal diplomacy'. Nehru stoutly refused to consider the 'Black mediation plan' for Kashmir, pointedly citing 'confidence' in Black but a lack thereof in President Kennedy's proposal. Nasser publicly rebuffed Kennedy over the Johnson Plan, much to the relief of the Israelis, who were only too happy to lay the onus for failure on Cairo. Kennedy and his advisors had adopted Eisenhower's view that Nasser was the key to the Arab Middle East and to a solution of the Arab-Israeli dispute, yet they had no more progress to show for their efforts than Dulles had had. Kennedy also believed, using a phrase borrowed from Eisenhower, that the new revolutionary nationalist leaders were the 'wave of the future', but the White House found itself increasingly committed to the traditional 'feudal regimes'. John Badeau, Kennedy's Ambassador in Cairo, could have been speaking for the Eisenhower administration when he stated that US support for traditional monarchies 'played into the Russian hands as they ... depict [the US] to the Middle East as the supporters of the vanishing order', 'that the traditional order is doomed', and that 'radical change' was the 'wave of the future'.[1] As Komer stated, it was 'hard to imagine any alternative to Egypt and Cairo as the center of this movement'.[2] The difference was that Kennedy believed that he could succeed on the Nile where Eisenhower and Dulles had failed. Kennedy believed that he was different because initially he had failed to understand the complexity of the situation; it was lack of experience, pure and simple.

On the whole, the Kennedy administration had a faulty understanding of what had occurred between 1953 and 1956. Eisenhower and his advisors had five brutal years of policy experience that tempered their views. Kennedy and his advisors really believed that the situation in the Middle East was due to ineptitude on the part of Eisenhower and John Foster Dulles. In addition, they believed their own high-minded rhetoric about managing change. They would overcome the mismanagement and insensitivity to regional aspirations that had alienated key regional leaders, and their superior management would enable them to succeed where Eisenhower had failed. In addition, Kennedy's advisors were process-oriented technocrats. They tended to see developmental stages in economics and politics, and they believed that Nasser had already passed through his revolutionary stage. The administration believed that with the proper incentives and handling 'radical change' would occur in terms of economic development and cooperation in the region. This change would relegate political differences to history's dustbin, as economic development drove the dynamic in the region.

September surprise: Egypt and the Yemen coup

Policy differences had always existed between Washington and Cairo, but the Syrian coup and dissolution of the union with Egypt further complicated the relationship. Now Nasser faced the combined verbal abuse of Damascus and Baghdad, and rather then helping, Washington's attempt to move closer to Nasser merely added to the voices assailing him. Simply put, the relationship with Washington was increasingly becoming a liability: Nasser could not afford to act in concert with the US for fear of further damaging his revolutionary Arab nationalist credentials. To the contrary, the Egyptians needed to openly challenge the US on some key issues to demonstrate their independence. Cairo decided that accusations from various Arab capitals, particularly Baghdad and Damascus, suggesting that the UAR would sell out to Israel over Palestine in return for US economic aid needed to be demonstrably discredited. Kennedy's personal correspondence with Nasser proved too tempting to pass up. Kennedy had proposed a settlement with Israel in return for increased economic aid and development assistance. Referring to Kennedy's proposals as 'foolish', the Egyptian government published the contents of the President's correspondence with Nasser. The public rebuke caused considerable embarrassment in Washington, and also created a major problem for Ambassador Badeau and those advocating more understanding in dealing with Nasser.[3] The flare-up in US-UAR relations occurred in early September 1962.

On 18 September 1962 in Sanaa, Imam Ahmad died and Crown Prince Badr declared himself Imam. The Crown Prince had supported close ties with Cairo and had long been viewed as pro-Nasserist and pro-Soviet. Badr had no sooner taken the reins than Egyptian-trained army officers staged a coup. The coup began in the early hours of 26 September 1962, led by a group of Yemeni army officers headed by Colonel Abdullah al-Sallal. Using Soviet-supplied tanks, the rebels surrounded key government installations, and after a pitched battle in Sanaa's 'Old City' around the Imam's palace, the coup leaders announced the death of the Imam and the creation of the Yemen Arab Republic. Unfortunately for the plotters and the UAR, to paraphrase Samuel Clemens, rumors of the Imam's demise had been greatly exaggerated.[4] The Yemen coup contrasted sharply with that of Iraq 1958. In Iraq, despite early suspicions to the contrary, homegrown revolutionaries overthrew the Hashemite government. The coup in Yemen had Nasser's fingerprints all over it. Despite alliances with the Mutawakkals, Cairo had supported and harbored in Cairo the anti-monarchist Yemeni Union led by Ahmad Muhammad Numan and Muhammad Mahmud Zubayri. In December 1961, Nasser asserted control over the opposition movement by replacing both Numan and Zubayri with a new leader, Abd-al-Rahman Baydani. Apparently Numan and Zubayri had displeased Nasser by conferring too closely with Ba'thist party elements and by refusing to work with Baydani.[5] Nasser and Baydani set about plotting a coup against Imam Ahmad. As fate would have it, before the coup could be mounted, Imam Ahmad conveniently died, more or less of natural causes. The coup actually succeeded against his successor, Badr.

Cairo, along with several Arab states and the Eastern bloc, immediately recognized the YAR.[6] Egyptian paratroopers were airlifted to the Yemeni capital to support the new government.[7] Initially, the Kennedy administration was positively predisposed to the plotters. Working with the Imam and Crown Prince had always been difficult, and Yemen was one of the most backward places on the planet. It was difficult to understand how the coup could have a negative impact on US interests and, as Komer colorfully pointed out: 'it could be a head-hunter fight in the depths of New Guinea. As long as it didn't impinge on our interests, no problem.'[8] Against this backdrop, Ambassador Badeau, in Cairo, received a friendly 'word of advice' from Anwar Sadat. Sadat's influence had grown in the Nasser entourage. He was now the 'presidential watch-dog' for political organizations. He bluntly told Badeau: '90 per cent of [Yemen's] intelligentsia support the coup and republic' and warned the US not to succumb to the expected Saudi pressure and support the royalists. Sadat also informed Badeau that Free Yemeni officials wanted to meet with him in Cairo, and asked Badeau to oblige them. The Egyptians obviously had a vested interest in the new Yemeni regime. With regard to support for the royalists, Badeau dutifully responded that unless the situation in Yemen endangered 'vital US interests', Washington would not intervene.[9]

Naturally, Nasser feigned surprise at the coup, and in the next breath announced his pleasure at the triumph of anti-feudalist and anti-imperialist forces.[10] Yemen hardly compensated for the loss of Syria, but it was better than nothing – perhaps. Given the vagaries of Yemeni planning, Nasser might not have known the coup's exact timing, but his involvement was clear. By 9 October, journalists reported that Sanaa was 'crawling' with Egyptian troops.[11] Be that as it may, the US carefully avoided pointing the finger at Nasser while attempting to understand what was going on and what position the US should take. Predictably, Badeau strongly favored US recognition. He advised Washington: 'Our evaluation of UAR intentions and capabilities persuades us that the time has come for US recognition of the new Yemen regime.' Badeau argued that the Imamate was a 'paragon of anachronism' and that the US needed to identify with progressive forces. Rejecting Saudi and British arguments against recognition, Badeau maintained that UAR-US cooperation in Yemen against future Soviet influence could result from early US recognition of the Sallal regime.[12] Badeau accepted YAR Foreign Minister Al-

Ayni's and Anwar Sadat's assurances that neither the YAR nor the UAR had designs on destabilizing Saudi Arabia; he also emphasized the problems associated with delayed recognition.[13] To increase the pressure, the YAR government threatened to bring in Soviet assistance and advisors if US recognition were not forthcoming. In an effort to spur recognition, Badeau suggested from Cairo that the US trade YAR recognition for an UAR agreement to guarantee Saudi stability.[14]

Kennedy and other key administration officials were not yet ready to give up on their attempt to co-opt the Egyptian leader. The Cuban missile crisis also reduced the role of the White House in the early stages of the Yemen affair. Preoccupation with Cuba, the Soviet Union, and the possibility of nuclear war allowed the handling of the Yemen coup to revert to Talbot, Badeau, and the foreign policy apparatus. All were inclined to follow through with rapid recognition. Kennedy wanted to avoid a confrontation with Nasser by minimizing the conflict and putting recognition for the new regime on the fast track.[15]

The allies react

Reporting from Yemen indicated that the Republican government had broad support and, in Washington, recognition appeared to be only a formality. In Cairo, the Egyptians arranged multiple Yemeni testimonials to further the republic's claim to legitimacy.[16] As Komer explained it, recognition appeared to be readily forthcoming had not 'this little crisis, of no importance in itself, [become] a sort of vortex' for other regional issues.[17] Saudi Arabia's security lay at the heart of that vortex. When the coup occurred, Crown Prince Feisal happened to be in Washington. Feisal told Phillips Talbot that US aid to Nasser did not moderate the UAR's activities, but rather freed other funds for propaganda and subversion. Arguing against recognition, Feisal stated that the new regime in Yemen would not only be bad for Yemen, but also would threaten other governments in the region.[18] Jordan and Britain also argued strongly against US recognition. Washington was now in a real quandary. If its UAR policies were to be salvaged then recognition was unavoidable, but such a course now appeared to have repercussions for US relations with the British and other traditional US allies in the region.

In Jidda, Amman, and London, concern grew. While the White House viewed the coup as a minor event in an insignificant place, the British in Aden, the Jordanians, and the Saudis saw the coup as evidence of resurgent aggressive revolutionary nationalism. In Damascus, events in Yemen revived fears of additional attempts by Nasser to reclaim Syria as a part of the UAR. In Amman, King Hussein and his advisors predicted a renewal of Egyptian subversion.[19] Then, just to add chaos to confusion, rumors spread that the Imam was very much alive and organizing the northern tribes of the Bakil confederation to retake the capital and destroy the YAR government. The Jordanians, dedicated Nasser-bashers and distant relatives of the Mutawakkals, began to send military advisors to Saudi Arabia and offered a Jordanian brigade to support Riyadh. Both monarchies began to support the Royalists.[20]

Despite the long list of outstanding problems between the Saudi regime and the Imamate, the destruction of a fellow monarchy that inconveniently left Nasser and an Egyptian army ensconced immediately next door was unnerving. To calm Saudi fears, Kennedy offered Feisal a series of 'small scale' proposals and the president's assurances of US support for the Kingdom. The White House was attempting to avoid upsetting Nasser.[21] That particular horse had already departed the barn. Komer put it this way: 'Unfortunately, the Yemen revolt has brought to a boil all Saudi fears of Nasserism (the house of Saud well knows it might be next).' The fact that Radio Cairo said the same thing did not help the situation. Trying to avoid openly taking sides, the US position remained that 'deliberate, controlled internal reform is the best antidote to Nasserism.'[22] On 5 October, Feisal asked Kennedy to use his influence with Nasser to prevent subversive Egyptian activities. The President responded by saying that the US, despite its aid programs, lacked that kind of influence with the Egyptian leader.[23] The Saudis believed that the US had a close enough relationship with Nasser to control his activities, therefore unfortunately making the US responsible for something over which it in fact had no control. The Crown Prince then criticized what he viewed as the shortsighted 'belief that Nasser is the natural and inevitable leader' and complained that Nasser appeared to be the 'chosen US instrument' in the region. Feisal warned Kennedy that he was making a serious mistake.[24]

During the 5 October 1962 meeting, Feisal informed Kennedy that King Saud had not been well and was no longer participating in the details of government.[25] This was the first solid indication that the power struggle in Riyadh between the Crown Prince and King Saud had concluded. The Yemen coup had initially stunned Riyadh. In response to an appeal from Yemeni Prince Hassan, Saudi Arabia pledged covert support for the royalist cause. When the King ordered the Saudi Air Force to begin ferrying supplies to advanced bases on the Yemen border, three aircrews defected and took their planes and cargo to Egypt – so much for covert support. The Saudis immediately grounded the air force, fearing more defections.[26] The coup, the air-force defections, pro-Feisal elements in the royal family, and pro-Nasserist elements in the government brought King Saud to the point of physical and mental collapse. On 17 October, Saud gave Crown Prince Feisal unfettered authority.[27] Although not immediately apparent, the Yemen coup and Egyptian intervention did as much to stabilize the situation in Saudi Arabia as any other single event. It permanently removed King Saud from power and brought the decline of Prince Talal's 'Free Princes' or 'Young Nejd' movement with its pro-Nasserist sentiments.[28] It also placed a competent leader at the head of the Saudi state. Radio Mecca announced the change on 18 October 1962. Predictably, Radio Cairo called it a desperate move to shore up a collapsing regime.[29] An immediate change in the level and sophistication of SAG activity occurred – Feisal announcing plans to accelerate reform, while pressuring the

US about the threat posed by Nasser.³⁰ While Feisal's presence in Washington had, in some ways, been fortuitous, the confusion at the top of the government in Riyadh created an opportunity for the new YAR government to steal a march on its opponents.

YAR-UAR diplomatic offensive

Fearing the combination of British, Saudi Arabian, and Jordanian influence in Washington, the UAR orchestrated a diplomatic campaign to gain US recognition of the YAR. On 19 October, the YAR government invited the US Consul General in Ta'iz to Sanaa. The Consul met with Sallal and several influential, well-known pro-Western and pro-American Yemenis. Ahmad Muhammad Numan and his US-educated son Abd-al-Rahman Numan were present, along with Abdul Ghani Nagi. The elder Numan was purported to be an 'influential political advisor' to Sallal. In convincing terms, Numan insisted that Sallal wanted 'cordial relations' with the US. As a result of the meeting, the Consul reported favorably that the YAR met the dual criteria for US recognition, i.e., popular support and effective control of the country.³¹

In Jidda, Ambassador Hart reacted positively as well. Mentioning Saudi confusion in Riyadh, Hart recommended immediate recognition of the YAR regime. Hart also asked permission to inform his contacts in the Saudi government that the Yemen revolution was 'succeeding and counter-revolution [could not] succeed' because the 'Imamate had acquired too evil and backward reputation' which it had 'richly earned' that attempts at a 'restoration' would 'drain SA's resources and injure its position' in the Arab world. The Ambassador believed that Yemen intended to steer a 'neutralist' course and had no intention of becoming a 'tool of the UAR, USSR or anyone else'. He argued that given the fact that 'several Cabinet members [were] pro-Western', the Yemeni leadership 'could be much worse'. Hart concluded: 'An independent YAR no longer under pressure to accept UAR military help for survival can be no threat to SA', and interjected that the revolution might offer an opportunity to reverse the 'unacknowledged but universally known' Saudi interference in Yemen. In Hart's view, Feisal, a 'progressive reformer', would 'welcome' just such a policy because it removed 'the threat from the north' and acted to inhibit Soviet inroads in Sanaa.³² Of course, Hart was very wrong indeed about Feisal's support, but the position of the US Embassy in Jidda, supported by the reports from Ta'iz, resonated with Badeau in Cairo and the desk in Washington. By the time the Saudis had reorganized and lodged a dissenting view, senior US officials in the region had spoken out in favor of YAR recognition.

On 6 November, aware of planned UAR air raids against tribal resistance in northern Yemen and southern Saudi Arabia, the YAR government summoned the American Consul General in Ta'iz once again to Sanaa. Claiming a 'Saudi invasion', Baydani stated that the YAR would be justified in retaking Najran and Asir, lost to King Abdul Aziz Ibn Saud in 1933. Invoking the 1956 defense pact with Egypt, which had ironically been signed by the Imam, Baydani stated that the YAR, with UAR assistance, would attack airfields at Jidda, Riyadh, and Jizan. Baydani also accused the US of supplying arms and pilots for the Saudi and Yemeni royalist efforts.[33] Wasting no time, the Egyptians began to bomb villages in southern Saudi Arabia. Alarmed, Washington instructed the Consulate in Ta'iz to make it clear to the YAR government that the 'USG is morally committed to support maintenance of integrity of reformist Feisal regime and cannot stand idly by in the face of such attacks.' The administration offered assurances that Saudi forces were not active in Yemen – a reassurance of questionable value in Sanaa and Cairo. The attacks delayed US recognition of the YAR and brought a threat to forego it altogether.[34] Riyadh demanded additional US military assistance, and broke diplomatic relations with Cairo.[35] Like it or not, the Kennedy administration found itself involved in the Yemen conflict.

The advice of friends

In the middle of this confusion, the State Department concluded that recognition of the YAR government would prevent a further escalation of the conflict, limit UAR influence, and undermine Soviet influence. Washington also feared that Saudi Arabia and Jordan might face a rebellion by internal dissidents as a result of their participation in the Yemen conflict. On 12 November, despite the UAR air raids on Saudi border areas, Secretary Rusk recommended to Kennedy that the United States recognize the new republican government in Sanaa. The administration felt that the delayed recognition, coupled with assurances to Feisal in the form of 'Operation Hard Surface', the dispatch of US combat aircraft to Dhahran, would soften the blow and make both the Saudis and Egyptians more agreeable to a compromise. The Secretary also pointed out that the United States would seek assurances from the Egyptians that no further attacks on Saudi Arabia would occur and that neither they nor the Yemenis had any territorial designs on Saudi Arabia or Aden.[36]

News of the US intentions presented the British with a problem. On the one hand, they had no desire to be left out of the recognition cavalcade, but on the other, London had real concerns about the 'Federal Rulers in the Aden Protectorate'. The federation was a British creation designed to support the British presence in Aden. London believed that recognition of the Yemen republic would undermine Adeni confidence and, ultimately, their position there.[37] Anti-UAR and anti-YAR elements had an irrepressible British champion, none other than the Nasser-hating, American-baiting Sir Charles Johnston, former Ambassador to Jordan and now the Governor-General in Aden. Sir Charles wasted little time in expressing himself: 'We had a difficult enough time combating Yemeni subversion in the 1950s when there was not a vestige of Yemeni irredentism toward Aden or the Protectorate. The task might well prove impossible if a strong Egyptian type republic now emerges in the Yemen.'[38] Warming to his task, Sir Charles lobbed another well-placed shot at London on 8 November:

We do not wish to challenge H.M.G.'s view. We would, however, remind you that in this matter H.M.G. is handling the Federation's foreign affairs in terms of the treaty and that H.M.G. therefore has an obligation to consider the question of recognition from the point of view of the Federation's interests. In these circumstances, if H.M.G. intends to recognize the Yemeni Republican regime in its conduct of the Federation's foreign affairs, we must ask that I should only do so after the Yemeni Republican regime has first given a formal public undertaking to recognize the existence of the Federation as an Arab Government under the United Kingdom's protection and to respect its integrity. Clearly, it would be unreasonable for H.M.G. to oblige the Federation to acquiesce in the recognition of a regime within a neighbouring state, which has refused to give such an undertaking.[39]

Johnston's barrage had the desired affect. Whitehall concluded: 'British recognition is unlikely in the very near future, even if Royalist make no Progress.' Fearing that they would be the odd man out, the CRO sent a circular telegram aimed primarily at the governments in Ottawa, Canberra, and Wellington: 'we therefore still hope that there will be no rush to recognize, especially by members of the Commonwealth.'[40]

On 14 November, Macmillan wrote to Kennedy explaining the British position and the potentially 'disastrous effect' that the loss of Aden would have on 'the Anglo-American position in the Gulf'. He suggested that Kennedy needed to withhold recognition in order to make sure that he got something concrete in return from Nasser. Macmillan stated: 'I therefore feel that you should get something more than words before you give recognition and money. I quite recognize that the loyalists will probably not win in Yemen in the end but it would not suit us too badly if the new Yemeni regime were occupied with their own internal affairs during the next few years.' The Prime Minister pointed out that Sallal's public call for a revolt against the British in Aden made recognition impossible. On 15 November, Macmillan reiterated opposition to recognition and suggested that the US should use economic aid as leverage against Nasser and the Egyptians. The Prime Minister warned that recognition 'would spread consternation among our friends throughout Arabia.' Macmillan concluded by stating: 'I very much hope that you will accept this view for I am sure that it would have great dangers for our position in Arabia if recognition was accorded without a precise plan for Egyptian withdrawal and evidence that they were carrying it out.'[41] The issue was apparently not cut and dried in London. The British Ambassador in Cairo, Sir Harold Beeley, supported recognition and believed that Sir Charles and the Colonial Office had not yet recognized that *Pax Britannia* was a thing of the past.

By early November, Feisal was officially in charge in Saudi Arabia. He informed Ambassador Hart that he was moving forward with social reforms, infrastructure improvements, the abolition of slavery, and improved financial controls. Using these reforms and the ever-present issue of oil as leverage, Dr. Rashal Fir'awn, Feisal's chief advisor, pressed the US for support against Nasser in Yemen and a delay in recognizing the YAR government.[42] In an unsettling note, the royal family faced more defections to Cairo by ministers whom Feisal had removed.[43] These events heightened concerns in Washington about the viability of the new government under Feisal.[44] Fearing revolutionary instability in the Kingdom, the Kennedy administration continued to hedge in its support for Feisal, expecting a renewed power struggle with the reformist princes or with King Saud at any time with an unforeseeable outcome.

Recognition of the YAR

US hedging did not go unnoticed in Riyadh. As Feisal became more secure, he flexed his diplomatic and economic muscle. Feisal told Ambassador Hart: 'The US considered relations with its sincere friends, like SAG, as less important than helping Nasser.' He instructed Hart to inform Washington to stay out of SAG policy vis-à-vis Yemen. At the same time, Feisal became increasingly aggressive in his demands for US support against the UAR bombing campaigns. He believed that the war had become a grinding stalemate and that he could economically crush Egypt. Feisal had no intention of backing down in the face of UAR attempts to intimidate him. He calculated that a UAR invasion of Saudi Arabia would bring US intervention and that, short of an invasion, the Kingdom had the resources to undermine the UAR in Yemen and at home.[45] Washington could not ignore Saudi oil. The White House authorized Feisal's publication of an October letter from President Kennedy that promised 'full United States support for the maintenance of Saudi Arabia's integrity'. The letter got Cairo's attention.[46] When the Egyptians raised this letter with Badeau, he downplayed the warning, calling it only a pledge of support for Saudi internal reforms. Despite Badeau's rationalization, Nasser correctly saw the letter as full US support for Feisal 'come what may.'[47] Increasing problems in US-UAR relations spurred Badeau to redouble his efforts for YAR recognition.

As US recognition of the YAR became more likely, opposition intensified. The British cited Royalists' gains and the potential impact of their defeat on the regime in Saudi Arabia. In response, the US attempted to reassure the British that it had extracted non-interference pledges from the UAR regarding Saudi Arabia and Aden.[48] On 27 November, the Jordanians urged a further delay in US recognition for the YAR, stating that most of the people of Yemen did not support the YAR government. Amman also pointed out that the Royalists were gaining ground and would be disheartened. The Jordanian government requested that the US await the report of a British parliamentary delegation currently visiting Yemen. The Jordanians questioned US reliability, stating that Washington would recognize any splinter group, including ones in Saudi Arabia or Jordan that might gain temporary power. With three key US allies, Britain, Jordan, and Saudi Arabia, in opposition, Badeau had his work cut out for him. At Badeau's prodding, the White House finally concluded: 'US recognition will be the necessary catalyst which will bring about a gradual disengagement.'[49]

Having made the decision to recognize the YAR, the administration began a damage-control effort, addressing letters to both Feisal and King Hussein. Washington informed both Riyadh and Amman that US recognition was in the interest of both Jordan and Saudi Arabia. In a personal letter to King Hussein, Kennedy wrote: 'I believe that my proposal [withdrawal of all foreign forces] is the one most likely in the long run to assure the independence of Yemen, to abate the conflict now raging in the country, and to offer the Yemeni people the opportunity to determine their future.' It also warned against Jordanian 'diversions' that might undermine domestic development goals.[50] Jordan had already dispatched aircraft to Saudi Arabia and advisors to the border regions of Yemen, and shipped large amounts of rifles and ammunition to the Royalist forces. While these moves caused internal dissatisfaction, including the defection of the commander of the Jordanian air force and two other pilots with their aircraft to Egypt, the embarrassed monarch was not dissuaded from supporting the Royalist cause.[51]

The pro-Western states and Britain lectured the Kennedy administration on the folly of trusting Nasser and on YAR instability.[52] At the eleventh hour, Feisal warned the US that formal relations with the YAR would 'backfire against (the US) in the region'.[53] Ratcheting up the pressure, Wasfi Tal, the Jordanian Prime Minister, castigated Kennedy, stating: 'The sole purpose of the US recognition action was to save UAR President Gamal ABDUL-NASSER [*sic*] from the consequences of the difficulties into which he had gotten himself in Yemen.' King Hussein added: 'Why is Cuba considered a matter different from Yemen?'[54] Recognizing that withdrawal in the short term was unlikely, in early November Badeau began to argue that the UAR could not withdraw from Yemen in the 'absence of something resembling victory'. He stated further: 'In sum, success in Yemen of major importance to UAR regime in its aspirations towards Arab world.' The Yemen desk in Washington highlighted that passage in the margin; they had gotten the message.[55] In early December, Badeau traveled to Washington to personally argue for recognition. Relaying messages through the Chargé in Cairo, the administration attempted through Nasser to get agreements out of the Sanaa government.

The US wanted the YAR to acknowledge the Sanaa Treaty of 1934, to recognize British rights in Aden, and to recognize the rights and status of the US Agency for International Development mission in Ta'iz.[56] The YAR government flatly refused. Undeterred, Badeau and Talbot recommended: 'We believe it is imperative that we recognize the Yemen Arab Republic as soon as possible in order to (a) avert an escalation of the conflict endangering the stability of the whole Arabian Peninsula; [and] (b) prevent the termination of an American presence in Yemen which would likely lead to a considerable increase in Soviet influence.'[57] On 20 December 1962, the United States recognized Yemen. US recognition received a mixed review. In Cairo, *Al-Juhuriya* attributed it to Ambassador Badeau's consultations in Washington. *Al-*

Ahram sarcastically described it as 'Recognition Number 39', and stated the US had been 'forced to face up to reality'.[58] The *Egyptian Gazette* heralded it as 'a significant development [which] wouldn't have made much difference.' The same article also described the US as the 'main prop' for reactionaries.[59]

In Jordan, Prime Minister Wafsi Tal called the recognition of the YAR a 'sell out' and 'totally immoral', stating that Jordan would reconsider its dealings with the US. King Hussein also expressed indignation from London, where he was meeting with his 'British allies'.[60] These allies viewed US recognition as a mistake because Yemen would become another base from which Nasser would stir up trouble. There was one exception – British Ambassador Beeley, in Cairo, saw the Yemeni chaos as an opportunity for Britain to get its South Arabian Federation organized.[61] Nevertheless, the increasingly violent tone of Nasser's pronouncements on the 'forthcoming liberation' of Aden left Whitehall more convinced than ever that US recognition had been a mistake.[62] Kennedy had once criticized the Eisenhower administration for demonstrating to the developing world that 'the shortest route to Washington was through Moscow.'[63] To Arab observers, a new route lay through Cairo. Yemen provided a final context for Nasser's evaluation of Kennedy. The Egyptian President concluded that the US had little positive to offer. Komer tried to put the best face on it, stating: 'I would say that U.S.-U.A.R. relations did not slide backward during the Yemen episode up to October 1963.' In the same conversation, he took a different angle: 'The significant thing is that our relations did not slide backward despite the existence of this highly disruptive peanut crisis in which we played quite a significant role.'[64] In fact, the Yemen civil war was the beginning of the end of any real attempt to seek a real accommodation with Nasser. Kennedy found himself relearning the lessons of 1954-1955. A fundamental shift in attitude took shape within the Kennedy administration. The Yemen coup and civil war demonstrated to the White House that economic development usually took a back seat to political considerations in the Middle East.

Chapter 15: India, Pakistan, and China – Eastern Opportunities?

The looming confrontation between China and India had long been a topic of speculation in Washington, but familiarity had bred complacency. In addition, the problem with Yemen and the UAR, not to mention the mounting concerns about Soviet missiles in Cuba, also distracted the Kennedy administration. As a result, the responsibility for watching the situation fell heavily on the US Embassy in New Delhi and Ambassador Galbraith. The responsibility for monitoring the Embassy and Galbraith fell on Talbot at NEA and Komer at the NSC. The idea that conflict would erupt simply did not fit Galbraith's preconceived notions about non-alignment. His lack of insight also resulted from his dependence on senior Indian officials, whose heads were firmly buried in the sand, for information. Nehru certainly did not see the dispute erupting into a major border war. Even the Chinese may not have believed that it would escalate, but they were prepared just in case. The success of the Goa operation served as a catalyst that made Nehru and Menon over-confident, significantly increasing their capacity for self-deception and miscalculation. In Washington, the foreign policy apparatus understood that India could not successfully challenge China and believed that Nehru understood it as well. They were wrong.

Galbraith believed that a war would not occur because India was militarily unprepared and because Nehru was ideologically predisposed against the use of force. The Ambassador chose to ignore the Goa adventure as an aberration. The intellectual association of India with non-alignment, and non-violence, coupled with the leftist leanings of Nehru himself, placed the potential for hostilities outside Galbraith's preconceived realm of possibilities. In addition, Galbraith's well-known hubris made it easy for him to discount any opinions contrary to his own. The situation with the UAR magnified the impact of his lack of appreciation of the potential for conflict. The Yemen conflict distracted Talbot at the State Department and Komer at the NSC, despite the fact that

Talbot, in particular, lacked confidence in Galbraith's judgment. Talbot was not alone in this sentiment; it was shared by other senior officials in the administration. However, they were totally absorbed in the Cuban crisis.[1] As a result, Washington deferred to Galbraith's judgment much more than it might otherwise have done.

Nehru's miscalculation

By the fall of 1962, Nehru had backed himself into a corner with the Chinese, and extrication, no matter in what way, promised to be painful. Nehru and Menon had placed unprepared India on a military collision course with China. To complicate the situation, the 'stepmotherly attitude' of the Congress Party toward the military during the 1950s made military readiness a low priority. The politicians resented the military, because many of the senior officers had served the Raj. In addition, Nehru argued that Indian security was based on the concept of 'mutual rivalry. ... No country will tolerate the idea of another acquiring the commanding position [over India], which England occupied for so long. If any power were covetous enough to make the attempt, all the others would combine to trounce the intruder. This mutual rivalry would in itself be the surest guarantee against an attack on India.'[2] Viewing American-armed Pakistan as the primary threat, the Indian government refused to allow the military to draw up even a contingency plan for the Chinese border areas. This prohibition continued even after Beijing began to make aggressive moves in the late 1950s. In 1957, Krishna Menon's appointment as Minister of Defense further undermined the professional military. Menon had favorites and created a 'promotion crisis,' which severely damaged army morale. With an under-equipped army, a demoralized chain of command, and a leftist Defense Minister who was roundly despised by most of his subordinates, India faced an experienced, tough, stubborn adversary in the Chinese.

The only bright spot for the Indian military, the Goa operation, had in fact created more problems than solutions. As a result of Goa, surging popular support in India for the government provided a seductive brew that lowered the threshold for aggressive military posturing. Nehru had opposed the military option in settling disputes, but the muddled decision to go ahead with the Goa operation provided a rationalization that was soon applied to China, namely: 'to drive out an intruder who is in illegal occupation of part of out territory is not aggression.'[3] This so-called 'forward policy' vis-à-vis China became an integral part of the January 1962 election campaign. Campaigning for Menon in Bombay, Nehru declared that the Indian army was prepared to repel any threat to Indian territory. Nehru added that the boundary dispute with China was 'more important that a hundred Goas'. More significantly, he managed to convince himself that the Indian military could actually defeat the Chinese.[4] He also underestimated the lack of ideological synergy between India and China. In reality, Maoist Beijing possessed a fundamental ideological antipathy toward India. The Chinese resented India's close ties with Washington, as well as its growing ties with Moscow. India had become a Chinese target that would allow Beijing to demonstrate that it, not New Delhi, was the real power in Asia.[5]

Blind to these realities, Nehru pushed his 'forward policy'. Unwilling or unable to offer more realistic advice, Menon and General B.M. Kaul stoked Nehru's intransigence by assuring him that the Indian military could handle the Chinese. They 'brow-beat' local Indian commanders, stifled dissent, and placed Indian army units in untenable positions. In September 1962, the Chinese responded to the Indian aggressiveness with a forward policy of its own. New Delhi concluded that the Chinese moves, particularly at Thag La Ridge, would be the trip-line for Indian action. When the Indian press reported Chinese advances in the vicinity of Thag La Ridge, a violation of the McMahon Line, which had been the established boundary of British India, failure to act would have undermined public support for the government.[6] Nehru's personal control over foreign policy significantly increased the potential for a serious Indian miscalculation. The aging Prime Minister lacked the energy, the basic information, and the focus to deal with the situation. In addition, there was no dissent. Nehru controlled the foreign policy apparatus personally, and those who disagreed with him were ignored or marginalized.

To complicate matters, the Indians lacked basic information and intelligence to accurately evaluate the situation. B.N. Mullik, a former police official, headed the so-called intelligence service.[7] He was obsequious and totally unsuited for the job, owing his tenure in the Intelligence Bureau to Krishna Menon.[8] The intelligence chief simply lacked either the experience or the personal fortitude to provide Nehru with accurate and objective assessments. Nehru might not have listened, but with Mullik in charge, there was almost no information of substance on which to rely. On 9 September, Krishna Menon convened a meeting of a handful of Defense Ministry officials. At the meeting, the Defense Minister declared that the Chinese must be evicted immediately from the Thag La Ridge area. Menon then took a strong public position on ejecting the Chinese. Nehru immediately supported the decision. Neither Nehru nor Menon saw the possibility of military disaster, only a quick Indian victory and political gain.

Indian military commanders on Thag La ridge took a different view. They protested that their troops were unprepared only to have Menon browbeat the area commanders. Resignations followed and morale plummeted further. On 3 October, Nehru appointed his own protégé, as well as that of Menon, General B.M. Kaul, to command Operation Leghorn, the expulsion of the Chinese. The Prime Minister told him in no uncertain terms that India had tolerated the Chinese incursions for too long and that Beijing would be given the choice of withdrawing its troops or facing forceful removal.[9] At the same time, the Indians intensified their campaign for diplomatic support. On 4 October, Secretary of State Rusk met with Indira Gandhi at the UNGA. He reassured her of US support for India. Rusk pointed out that the US had no influence with China, but was willing to be of assistance should the situation warrant it.[10] On 13 October, Nehru, in Colombo for a conference, fueled the fire by making particularly belligerent statements to the press about Indian intentions to drive the Chinese out.[11] The Kennedy administration actually welcomed increased tensions between India and China. The situation promised to translate into New Delhi's support on Cuba and in Southeast Asia. Finally, Washington hoped that the confrontation with Beijing would create problems in Indian relations with Moscow.

In Beijing, the Chinese, decidedly unimpressed by Indian demands, called for negotiations. On 6 October, the Indians not only rejected the Chinese overture, but also announced New Delhi's withdrawal from discussions planned for 15 October. India's refusal to negotiate was 'categorical as well as explicit', even though the note blamed China for refusing to negotiate.[12] The Kennedy administration found Indian feelers about military assistance encouraging.[13] Washington clearly understood that it was New Delhi that had refused to negotiate and welcomed Indian belligerence. No matter how foolhardy for Nehru and his government, the prospect of a clash, diplomatic or military, between China and India could be a windfall for Washington. Although concerned about the condition of the Indian army, both Washington and London believed that the difficult terrain in the border regions would lead to either a military stalemate or a localized Chinese victory and then a move by India toward a Western alliance. On 12 October 1962, given the hype in the press, public expectations, and the approaching date for convening the next Parliament, Nehru issued instructions to remove the Chinese from the Thag La Ridge by 1 November. Well aware of Indian intentions, the Chinese prepared to teach the Indians and their American and Soviet backers an object lesson.

The Chinese teach Nehru a lesson

On the morning of 20 October 1962, concentrated Chinese mortar and artillery shredded the vulnerable, poorly-deployed Indian front-line units. The onslaught that followed left the Indian army in total disarray.[14] The Chinese had attacked in force along the Thag La Ridge in the North-East Frontier Agency and also in Ladakh, and the Indians collapsed. Casualties were staggering. Shocked by the setbacks, the Indian press, public, and government blamed Krishna Menon. Questions arose about India's unwillingness to accept Western military aid. A thoroughly-shaken Nehru immediately called on London and Washington for help. Having predicted 'no war', Galbraith was in London on vacation when the war broke out. Making frantic arrangements, he returned to New Delhi and met with Nehru and M.J. Desai. The Indians were in shock. Their Soviet friends told them that they could not restrain the Chinese and advised New Delhi to agree to the Chinese terms.[15] From the beginning, Washington viewed the war as an opportunity to gain influence in New Delhi. To test its leverage, the US requested in a blatant *quid pro quo* that India support a call at the UN for inspectors in Cuba. Concerned, Galbraith viewed this tactic as counter-productive, and even asked for permission to change the content of a letter from President Kennedy to Nehru because it 'lacked tact'. In meetings with Nehru, Galbraith took a swipe at Menon, blaming him for the lack of US support and the poorly prepared Indian Army.[16]

In Washington, Komer wrote to Talbot: 'Though we still see through a glass darkly, we may have a golden opportunity for a major gain in our relations with India.' Komer briefly acknowledged 'delicate tactical problems', including Pakistan, but added that Washington 'ought to be prepared to move fast.' Kennedy and his advisors hoped that the Soviet inability to pressure the Chinese would sour Indo-Soviet relations.[17] On 26 October, Nehru's letter to President Kennedy reinforced White House excitement concerning the possibility of a major policy breakthrough with India. Disingenuously, Nehru stated that in its zeal for peace, India had decided against taking 'immediate action to resist' the Chinese: 'Being wedded to ways of peace, we combined our effort to persuade Chinese to end this aggression by withdrawing from our territory.' Nehru asked for US support to protect its territorial integrity.[18] Knowing full well that Nehru had provoked the crisis, Kennedy pragmatically accepted the Prime Minister's explanation, and promised support. On 28 October, having just castigated Nehru over the Goa operation, Kennedy, with tongue no doubt in cheek, stated that he understood how Nehru had tried to 'put into practice what all great religious teachers have urged', but 'alas, this teaching seems to be effective only when it is shared by both sides in a dispute.'[19] Talbot's characterization of the potential for a military assistance program to India as a 'revolutionary development with far-reaching effects' reflected the administration's overall optimistic and opportunistic view of the situation.[20]

The British assessment more or less agreed with that of Washington. On 12 November 1962, key Kennedy administration officials met with British officials in London to discuss the Sino-India conflict. The British believed 'there was a chance that India's external policies might be realigned as a result of the Communist Chinese attack.' The British understood that Krishna Menon had not been solely responsible for the Indian collapse, but welcomed his political demise as a bonus for the West. London and Washington quickly agreed to focus on arms for an entrée into the Indian military establishment, to counter Soviet influence, and to contain the conflict. The ultimate goal was the 'preservation of a strong, stable and effective democracy in India'.[21] The British also saw potential for increased Indian support in Southeast Asia and the possibility that New Delhi might move to settle the Kashmir issue with Pakistan.[22]

Washington attempts to take advantage

The success of the Chinese attack appeared to knock India off the Cold War fence. Hope soared that Nehru's 'panicky appeal' for military aid would end 'all pretense of non-alignment'. For those advocating the primacy of India over Pakistan, the border war was a godsend. Chester Bowles, Galbraith, and Komer believed that 'a whole new chapter in the relations with the subcontinent' had begun. The real question was how to take advantage of it. If it was only a limited border incursion, as most thought, then how long would the Indian panic last, and what would the follow-on reaction be? The confusion was apparent. Komer called the border war the end of 'nonalignment' and then, in almost the same breath, he asserted that it did not affect India's non-aligned status. He stated: 'While not compromising India's position of nonalignment, we have now moved into being their prime suppliers, both in the military and the economic field. In turn, Pakistan is no longer our chosen instrument on the subcontinent with a veto on our Indian policy.' Far more skeptical, the realists at the State Department, the Pentagon, and the CIA saw a solution to Kashmir as an unlikely outcome. President Kennedy sided with the realists and for good reason. He was again under pressure from Ayub. The Pakistanis insisted that the United States withhold all aid until India compromised on Kashmir.[23]

The pro-India faction in the administration focused their short-term strategy on emergency military aid to India and on immediate pressure to restrain the Pakistanis. Galbraith, Komer, and Bowles wanted Pakistan neutralized. Galbraith's assessment of the situation showed the depth of division within the administration: 'These [Pakistani activities] continue to poison feelings here, and McConaughy in Karachi and Talbot in Washington have both made approaches to the Pakistanis. Unfortunately, both men are exceedingly soft. The Pakistanis would not be aware that either had talked to them.' Criticize as he might, Galbraith had been outmaneuvered. The State Department and CIA emphatically argued that when the shooting stopped, the chances of a settlement on Kashmir would be remote. They saw immediate negotiations and concessions from Nehru and Ayub as the only hope for progress. Galbraith resisted arguing that the Indians would interpret this as the Pakistanis and Americans attempting to obtain territorial concessions 'just as the Chinese were grabbing land'. As an alternative, Galbraith obtained permission to ask Prime Minister Nehru to meet with Ayub and discuss their problems. In an obvious delaying tactic, Nehru halfheartedly agreed to do so 'on some appropriate occasion'. The Pakistanis were demanding immediate action on Kashmir, arguing that 'the Chinese have very limited intentions and that the Indians are using the dust-up as a way of getting military aid.' Ayub also predicted that when the dust settled and the crisis was over, Nehru would be as intransigent as ever on Kashmir.[24]

Ayub understood India well, and urged that the US stop pressuring its 'friends' for policy concessions. He stated that Washington should encourage India to establish normal relations with its neighbors and 'court peace' by following up on its international obligations under the 1947 and 1948 agreements for a plebiscite in Kashmir. He pointed out that Pakistan was the 'aggrieved party', and yet Pakistan had been far more willing to compromise than India.[25] On 13 November 1962, Galbraith noted: 'We are facing a serious problem as to what arms we should give the Indians for their protection. Until now, it has been a few million dollars' worth of items for immediate use by their infantry. But they are about to come in with requests for arms manufacturing capacity, most of the raw materials to run it, tanks and other armored equipment and an air force. Pakistan will want similar amounts; we will then have the absurdity of arming both sides partly against each other.' He concluded that the US would provide military aid to India, but only as part of a general settlement of disputes with Pakistan.[26]

Problems with Pakistan

Recognizing the growing problem with Pakistan, Kennedy wrote Ayub on 27 November, stating that the United States intended to provide India with the help it needed. He assured Ayub that any military assistance would not be used against Pakistan. Kennedy also asked Pakistan not to take advantage of the situation. Kennedy speculated that 'the painful moments which India is now experiencing will teach them how much more important the threat from the North is to the whole of the subcontinent than any regional quarrels within it.'[27] Suspicious, Ayub laid the blame for the current situation squarely on New Delhi: 'This is the direct outcome of distorted and fallacious thinking on the part of Mr. Nehru and his associates and consequence of a baseless foreign policy.' Ayub then described his view of Indian foreign policy:

(a) bend backwards to appease Communism; (b) hoist the white flag of Neutralism to appease Communism and get other wavering nations to join him; (c) intimidate and threaten Pakistan in order to politically isolate it and economically weaken it; and (d) abuse the West, and especially the U.S.A., in season and out of season. ... No Mr. President, the answer to this problem lies elsewhere. It lies in creating a situation whereby we are free from the Indian threat, and the Indians are free from any apprehension about us. This can only be done if there is a settlement of the question of Kashmir.

Ayub sarcastically rejected Kennedy's assurances that arms to India would not be used against Pakistan: 'This is very generous of you, but knowing the sort of people you are dealing with, whose history is a continuous tale of broken pledges, I would not ask a friend like you to place yourself in an embarrassing situation.' Ayub went on to assure Kennedy that the Chinese incursion was limited and that the US arms would be turned on Pakistan 'at the first opportunity'.[28]

Worse yet, Ayub believed that Kennedy had broken his word about consulting with Pakistan on arms for India, and could no longer be trusted. Ayub stated: 'The U.S. attitude, in fact, was that India should have all sympathy and support and that Pakistan would be well advised not to raise any difficulties.'[29] Ayub had hit the nail on the head. In Washington those supporting closer alignment with India urged the President not to compromise nor to apologize to Ayub. Leading the pack, Komer stated: 'We're in for a long and painful dialogue with Ayub, but one which was essential at some point and which from our standpoint could hardly be conducted under better cover than now. The Chicom attack in effect justifies a long needed readjustment in our policy.'[30] They believed that the long-sought conditions for 'a basic reorientation of Indian foreign policy' with 'far-reaching implications for the non-aligned states' had arrived, along with the 'best opportunity yet' for solving the Indo-Pakistani dispute.[31] Komer, Galbraith, and Bowles wanted no compromises with Pakistan that might jeopardize their goals in New Delhi.

Ayub's barbs with regard to US military aid to India and the 'failure' of the US to consult with Pakistan added to White House anxiety. Kennedy understood that Ayub had strong backers in the Congress, including Senator Stuart Symington of Washington. No matter how large the potential opportunity with India, the President could not allow the lid to blow off the relationship with Pakistan. On 18 November, Secretary of State Rusk sent an 'eyes only' cable to Galbraith to make certain that he understood the situation: 'Pakistan is now a central problem for India affecting its own vital security and national existence. India must understand the limits upon our capacity to influence Karachi. We ourselves cannot prevent a Pakistan-Peiping side deal and a withdrawal of Pakistan from CENTO and SEATO.' The Pakistanis had 'whipped themselves into a near hysterical state', and the administration had to defuse the situation. Pakistan had to be convinced that its 'basic long-range interests' lay in continued close relations with the United States and improved relations with India.[32]

Another Harriman mission

Once again, Kennedy dispatched Averell Harriman to Karachi and New Delhi. As a result of his talks, Harriman concluded that the war with China had brought 'fundamental changes in Indian thinking'. He believed that the Indians now viewed China, not Pakistan, as the primary military threat. Quoting Nehru, who had said that India had been 'living in a dream world', Harriman believed that the possibility of a compromise settlement of the Kashmir situation existed, but he did not underestimate the challenge. Harriman quoted Desai, who had stated that he preferred 'defeat at the hands of the Chinese to humiliation by Pakistan'. Apparently some important officials had not changed their views on Pakistan as the primary enemy. Harriman also pointed out that the Indian refusal to blame Communism indicated a desire to maintain its ties with the Soviet Union, in the hope that Moscow would restrain the Chinese. Despite Menon's resignation, Harriman saw no Indian inclination to abandon non-alignment. Harriman voiced his concern that despite the need for quick movement, Nehru was moving 'dangerously slowly' because he was 'emotionally' unable to cross the 'great chasm' between 'intellectual conviction' and 'meaningful negotiations'.[33]

Meanwhile, Galbraith, Komer, and Bowles complained bitterly because aid to India was moving so slowly. On 23 November, Komer wrote to Bundy: 'Forgive my verbosity, but here's a really big problem on which I can't get movement and which I think rates thought by you and indeed JFK. Making all due allowance for Komer activism, State's bureaucratic inertia is a more besetting sin. Major crises create opportunities for movement, which it would be folly to neglect.'[34] In likely coordination, the next day Galbraith compared 'the State Department's reaction time ... [with] the rate at which the Chinese can walk'.[35] On 27 November, President Kennedy decided to send a high-level military mission to India to assess the situation and provide transport aircraft and spare parts.[36] The same day, the CIA reported that a unilateral Chinese ceasefire was holding and that the Chinese objectives continued to be 'essentially local and limited'. Changing its tune somewhat, the agency now concluded: 'Indian leaders, shocked by their recent military defeats, are likely to give serious thought to the possibility of a rapprochement with Pakistan.'[37]

Prior to his talks with Ayub, Harriman received a telegram from the President emphasizing that the 'moment of truth' had arrived in relations with Pakistan, but he cautioned Harriman not to 'push' Ayub too hard.[38] Harriman commented that most Pakistanis viewed India as their sworn enemy, 'with the notable exception of Ayub and some of his immediate entourage'. US military aid to India had been a 'shock', magnified by the lack of 'prior consultation' with Karachi. The report stated that politicians of all stripes had exploited the situation, and Ayub himself had 'permitted' and 'encouraged' the political and press outcry. Harriman stated that Ayub believed that only a settlement of the Kashmir issue on 'acceptable terms' could correct the problems and rehabilitate Washington's image. Domestically, Harriman also saw signs of increased political pressure on Ayub. Harriman warned: 'Progress on Kashmir settlement may be crucial to [Ayub's] continued ability to control the government.'[39] Ayub told Harriman that new constitutional procedures limited his freedom of action, and that he expected Western assistance in 'getting a fair settlement' with India.[40]

In a meeting with British Commonwealth Secretary Duncan Sandys and Harriman, Ayub agreed to meet with Nehru. Using shuttle diplomacy, Sandys returned to New Delhi and met with Nehru, Desai, and Gundevia. After some modifications, they agreed, in a vaguely-worded joint communiqué, to talks.[41] Steadily a consensus began to emerge that military assistance for India required, if not a settlement, major progress toward a solution on Kashmir. Prior to Kennedy's upcoming Nassau meetings with Macmillan, Talbot summed up his recommendations: 'India's new anti-Chinese Communist and pro-West (especially pro-U.S.) turn can give us a major breakthrough in Asia, provided we can find ways to help India stand firm against the Chinese without disrupting our relationships with Pakistan. India can become an important asset in our confrontation with China.'[42] The possibility of a major reorientation of Indian foreign policy was simply too tantalizing to pass up, but Washington could not afford to see the relationship with Pakistan disrupted.

New tactics for the pro-India faction

Having gotten the message about the importance of Pakistan, the pro-India faction began to voice support for 'ministerial level talks' between India and Pakistan. More realistically, Talbot predicted: '[Ayub's] position is not sufficiently secure for him to face this prospect without anxiety.'⁴³ Problems arose from the outset. The Indian government released the communiqué on Kashmir talks with Pakistan on 29 November 1962. The following day, the Indian opposition attacked Nehru in Parliament, demanding a clarification of the Kashmir issue.⁴⁴ Nehru indicated that he was 'prepared to talk but not budge'. On 2 December, Lal Bahadur Shastri publically commented: '[N]egotiations could not lead to any further division of the country.' While Kennedy hoped for a breakthrough, US diplomats closer to the problem had become increasingly pessimistic. The political officer in New Delhi, Carol C. Laise, stated: 'Pressure must be maintained on Mr. Nehru if the talks are to contribute to any improvement of Indo-Pak relations.' Laise believed that unless key Congress Party members, influenced by 'strong' US economic and military aid, could convince Nehru of the necessity of a settlement, Nehru would not compromise. Laise also pointed out that the 'bouleversement' of the Chinese experience had reinforced the Indian government's 'notable lack of logic and inability to relate phenomena'. Laise warned:

> In this confused state of mind and humiliated posture, haunted by fear of communal strife and without any real willingness to resolve the central problem of Indo-Pak relations – Kashmir – except on India's terms of an adjustment of the cease-fire line, Indian opinion is likely to rely entirely upon Nehru's lead as far as Pakistan is concerned. ... All signs point to continued unwillingness of the Prime Minister to trust us or to confide in us, especially as regards Pakistan.

Laise insisted that in India, there would be 'no retreat from the status quo in Kashmir'.⁴⁵ Although prophetically accurate, these views did not fit Ambassador Galbraith's agenda, and were relegated to internal memoranda that were never sent to Washington.

On 7 December 1962, the same day as the Laise memoranda in New Delhi, Komer wrote to Bundy at the White House expressing his concern about the improving situation in the Sino-Indian conflict. In a memorandum entitled 'Where do we go from here?' Komer stated: 'There are some real disadvantages, from the US viewpoint, in the already pronounced trend toward petering out of the Sino/Indian affair.' Komer stated that limiting escalation in the border war worked against US goals of getting India to side with the West or to compromise on Kashmir. Komer also pointed out that the end of the Chinese incursion undermined the justification for arms to India. He wanted to press Ayub to show restrain and limit pressure on Nehru while hoping for continued Chinese pressure on India. Komer advised: 'If we can only manage to continue using Peiping's adventurism against it, we have the greatest chance of making major gains.' Komer suggested, 'to put it crudely', that the US needed to convince the Indians to be 'pugnacious' with the Chinese so that the crisis would continue.⁴⁶

A solution to Kashmir

The Kennedy administration believed that the Chinese invasion had a 'very deep' impact on India, moving it from a 'first generation nationalism (anti-imperialism) to a second generation concept of the independent state in need of protection'.[47] Ironically, this view echoed those on Nasser having moved from a 'revolutionary' to a 'nationalist' stage, with about the same degree of misunderstanding. Having committed to a serious attempt to encourage Indian-Pakistani talks on Kashmir, the administration predictably set up a 'Kashmir Working Group'. As with the other 'working groups', Washington had an agenda – emergency military aid, air defense, Kashmir, and a military assistance program. There was concern about Ambassador Galbraith; as Komer put it: '[the] subcommittee will have a hard time trying to keep up with our distinguished delegate from Delhi. ... We ought to decide now how to handle Galbraith's consultation back here, because only WH will be able to control him.'[48] Despite concerns, Komer supported Galbraith's view that military aid to India should not be linked to progress on Kashmir and that Washington should supplant the British role in the joint effort. Komer did not want concerns over Kashmir or Pakistani to 'become too great a bar to doing what may be necessary to keep India's anti-Chinese nationalism at full tide'.[49]

On 10 December, President Kennedy issued NSAM No. 209. The President ordered the NSC Subcommittee on South Asia to come up with a plan of action that would encourage a Kashmir settlement. Two days later, Talbot clarified the fundamental problem: 'The operational question is how the U.S. and the U.K. can translate Nehru's present reluctant agreement and Ayub's eagerness to talk about Kashmir into effective negotiations.' Talbot concluded that only continued diplomatic pressure from Washington and London could cause Nehru to conclude that a settlement was to his advantage. Talbot pointed out that 'in the absence of further frightening Chinese military successes' progress would be 'difficult and slow'.[50] By 17 December, there were further indications that the initial scare in New Delhi had worn off. In Washington, Ambassador Nehru requested a meeting with President Kennedy, and complained about Pakistani efforts to use its relationship with the United States to pressure India into an unfair settlement. The Ambassador promised 'good faith' on Prime Minister Nehru's part but stated: 'The Prime Minister hopes that the president will realize progress may be slow and unspectacular, even if the Pakistanis show more willingness to cooperate than they have done until now.' Kennedy stated straight out: 'The question of Kashmir is inescapably linked to what we can do to assist India militarily.' Kennedy also told the Indian Ambassador: 'The best posture would be to enter seriously in the discussions and show the world that India is determined to reach some sort of settlement.'[51]

On 17 December 1962, in a memo to President Kennedy, Secretary of State Rusk pointed out that essentially the US faced a no-win situation. He told the President: 'We're heading for trouble.' Rusk believed that Ayub had overplayed his hand and that the US had encouraged him to do so. The Secretary believed that just by getting talks started, the US had performed its service to Ayub. Rusk believed that Ayub saw US responsibility extending to the point of actually leveraging a settlement. It was the Secretary's view that a common front against China and not a settlement on Kashmir should be the primary goal: 'Any realistic Kashmir settlement must reflect the actual balance of power between India and Pakistan and will thus give less to Pindi than it might expect.' Rusk feared that Ayub's unrealistic expectations would bring serious instability there and the US 'may even lose Ayub.' He wanted pressure applied to bring Ayub back to a more realistic position.[52]

Growing misgivings about the early optimism concerning an Indo-Pakistani rapprochement gave way to confusion within the administration about how to rescue the effort. By 19 December, Komer described a policy picture that largely contradicted his view of only a week before. In a memorandum to Bundy, Komer stated that Harriman and the Department of Defense opposed any aid, beyond the $120 million in emergency military aid and the air defense assistance, without progress on Kashmir. Komer added that Talbot and Galbraith wanted no linkage between aid and Kashmir for fear of hardening Nehru's views. Underlining for emphasis, Komer then argued that he supported 'Harriman' because without the hint of 'longer term buildup dependent on Pak-Indian reconciliation Nehru will see no incentive to compromise.'[53] Komer misrepresented both his own position and that of Talbot from only a week before. At that time, Komer had strongly supported Galbraith's contention that aid should not be linked to progress on Kashmir and that Pakistani concerns should not 'bar' military aid to India. Ever the realist, Talbot's admonition about pressure on Nehru merely reflected what he knew to be the Indian Prime Minister's aversion to such tactics. Talbot had always understood and valued what was at stake in intelligence sites in Pakistan far more than Komer.

Just for good measure, Komer also reversed himself on the issue of India as a counterweight to China in Asia. Having consistently supported Galbraith's view of India's value to American policy in Southeast Asia, Komer now ascribed this position entirely to Galbraith and labeled it 'nonsense – Indians can't defend India, much less SEA.' In another memorandum to Bundy on 19 December, Komer hinted that Galbraith had gone off the diplomatic reservation: 'Ken [Galbraith] must also stop talking about his ideas on Kashmir settlement. Indians have already picked them up with ill-concealed satisfaction, seeing in them a means of retaining Kashmir sovereignty while accepting a little 'European-type' window dressing. This may be all we can get in the end, but to float it now will only outrage the Paks and confirm Indian feeling they've got us in tow.' In the same memo, Komer expressed the opposite concern that the Indians now viewed US involvement as problematic. Given the reduced pressure on New Delhi resulting from the unilateral Chinese cease fire and continued US pressure for a Kashmir settlement, Komer colorfully concluded: 'While the Chinks lie doggo, the Indians are already beginning to fear we won't help them any further unless Kashmir settled.' With their hopes collapsing, Komer and other key administration officials called for immediate military aid to India and for pressure to keep the talks going between Karachi and New Delhi in the hope of avoiding an 'explosion' in Pakistan.[54] Now the unilateral Chinese ceasefire had undermined US leverage in New Delhi and hopes for an Indian policy realignment.

Administration concerns were well-founded. The British agreed that hopes for real negotiations had significantly 'deteriorated'. In New Delhi, reduced Chinese pressure removed any sense of 'urgency' on the part of the Indians with regard to Kashmir. Even among political figures that had supported such a settlement, the reality of what it would cost had taken a toll. Krishna Menon may have been out of power officially, but he and his leftist supporters agitated against any deal with the West that involved Kashmir. Their argument was simple: the Soviet Union would supply the necessary arms and aid without strings. Non-leftists presented a corollary to this theme, arguing that because of the Soviets, the West would provide military support with or without progress on Kashmir. The net result was that the Indians convinced themselves progress on Kashmir was not vital to their national security.

Then there was the problem of Nehru. In London's view, Nehru's 'restless garrulity' in front of the media had severely damaged prospects for a settlement; he called pressure to negotiate a settlement on Kashmir 'opportunistic blackmail'.[55] On 20 December, Nehru told *Washington Post* reporter Selig Harrison that the United States and Britain had better not use 'pressure tactics' on Kashmir. Just for good measure, the Prime Minister accused the Pakistanis of an 'attitude of blackmail'.[56] In Pakistan, Nehru's public statements merely served to underscore skepticism about his good faith. In addition, talks of a 'condominium' or other solutions short of a plebiscite were viewed as part of an Anglo-American conspiracy aimed at the 'murder [of] Pakistani freedom' and an attempt to embroil Pakistan in a conflict with China.[57] A settlement of the Kashmir dispute rested on the willingness of Nehru to use his prestige to drive a settlement, and Nehru would not deliver.

On 20 December, President Kennedy and British Prime Minister Macmillan met in Nassau, and discussed the pros and cons of providing military support to India, and the possible ramifications of this in Pakistan. Macmillan and Commonwealth Secretary Sandys proposed that the Anglo-American effort go slowly. Macmillan supported Averell Harriman's concern for the impact on Pakistan. Concerned that Pakistan might abandon CENTO and SEATO, Macmillan commented: 'We support people who are troublesome, such as Nehru and Krishna Menon, and abandon the people who support us.' The British were concerned that massive arms aid to India without progress on Kashmir would leave such a taste of betrayal in Ayub's mouth that Pakistan might abandon its Western ties.

There was also the fear of Soviet arms deliveries to India. When asked about potential MIG deliveries, Ambassador Galbraith, the man who had dismissed the possibility of war with China, minimized the potential and stated that any deliveries would only be 'a symbolic gesture'. The British Foreign Minister,

Lord Home, believed that Nehru would not compromise on Kashmir and that nothing short of another Chinese attack would make a settlement possible.[58] Kennedy questioned the impact of Pakistan leaving CENTO and SEATO. At that point, Sandys, Home, and Macmillan reminded him that it would be a major psychological victory for the Communist bloc and that Iran would doubtless quickly follow suit. The President and Prime Minister concluded that they would continue with plans to provide air defense for India while pressuring both Ayub and Nehru to come to an agreement on Kashmir.[59]

On 26 December, the first ministerial-level meetings took place between the Pakistanis and an Indian delegation headed by Sardar Swaran Singh, in Rawalpindi, Pakistan. In the middle of the meetings, Pakistan announced an agreement with China to negotiate a settlement of its northern border with Tibet. The Indians debated using the announcement of negotiations as a pretext for breaking off the talks but decided against it.[60] In the talks, the Pakistani Foreign Minister, Bhutto, made it clear that Pakistan could not accept the *status quo*. In response to a question by Swaran Singh, Bhutto stated that Pakistan would consider a proposal to redraw the boundary line through Kashmir, but that Karachi still supported a plebiscite. The Indians intended to propose a redrawn boundary line that essentially confirmed the current ceasefire line. This, of course, was entirely unacceptable.[61]

On 27 December, while the talks with the Indians in Rawalpindi were in progress, Ayub told US Ambassador McConaughy that he believed the crisis between China and India was basically over and that only significant US and British pressure would bring any modification in India's position on Kashmir. Ayub bluntly told McConaughy that he would tolerate the current levels of military aid to India on condition that the US pressure India about Kashmir. If that did not occur then Washington could expect his attitude to 'harden'.[62] Reporting to Rusk on the situation, Talbot stated: 'There is a sense of an inescapable relationship between Kashmir and the extent to which we can aid India militarily on the long run.'[63] So began the effort to achieve a compromise over Kashmir and hopefully to draw India into a closer alignment with the West, without jeopardizing the alliance structure in which Pakistan participated.

The Kennedy administration had clutched at the Chinese border war as a way to reorder the entire political map of South Asia, but had at first underplayed and then later overplayed its hand. Galbraith, Komer, and Bowles, the pro-India faction, had prevented massive pressure on Nehru at the beginning of the crisis, and once the crisis abated there was no chance that Nehru would compromise. To be sure, Nehru wanted military assistance and diplomatic support, but the question remained: would he sacrifice a lifetime of political conviction with regard to non-alignment and Kashmir? Quite simply, if the Chinese incursion and the sound military defeat that Beijing administered to the Indians did not fundamentally change the orientation of India, then nothing would. In addition, if the United States and its Western allies supported India in its moment of crisis and had nothing to show for it, then the Kennedy administration's assumptions about a more Western orientation on the part of New Delhi were fundamentally flawed. Supporting and courting India at the expense of Ayub's Pakistan had been a major mistake. From Karachi's point of view, military aid to India and Kennedy's promises left the US with only one option. Washington could attempt to pressure India into a settlement of the Kashmir dispute that was acceptable to Pakistan, or Washington could expect Karachi to take a very dim view of US policy and a very skeptical view of US promises. The Kennedy administration's entire policy structure toward the non-aligned world hung in the balance in 1963.

Chapter 16: 1963 – The New Frontier in Tatters

With the arrival of 1963 came the realization that in Dulles' Greater Middle East the policy 'innovations' of the New Frontier had either failed or were teetering on the brink of failure. The Arab-Israel peace initiative was stillborn. Neither side had the inclination or much incentive to compromise, and Kennedy's concern over domestic political repercussions prevented any dramatic initiatives that might alienate Israel and its supporters. Israel demanded more military aid, refused to cooperate on any plan involving a settlement with the Palestinians, and refused any meaningful inspection of its 'peaceful' nuclear program. Nasser's Yemen adventure underscored his intention to pursue a more radical revolutionary course and his growing conviction that Washington had little to offer that would enhance his standing in the Arab world. The border war between India and China, which seemed to promise a major reorientation in Indian foreign policy, ended in a Chinese-dictated truce. Bitterly disappointed and broken by the Chinese inflicted humiliation inflicted, Nehru deeply resented US attempts to use the war to leverage a compromise with Pakistan over Kashmir. As a consequence, Nehru moved ever closer to cooperation with the Soviet Union.[1] The Kennedy administration's plan to co-opt non-aligned Egypt and India was on life support, leaving its advocates within the administration struggling to salvage what was left of their hopes for a new US role in the region.

The unhappiness of US allies with the administration was perhaps more alarming. Kennedy's initiatives with the non-aligned states threatened to wreck containment. In Iran, the Amini experiment to 'save' Iran had collapsed. Having given its support for the first time to a specific Iranian politician, Washington now had little choice but to make a similar commitment to the Shah. Thus, the long-standing Eisenhower policy of supporting Iran, but not necessarily the Pahlavi regime, vanished in Kennedy's effort to establish an alternative to the Shah. The fortunes of the United States in Iran were now unambiguously tied to the Shah. In Pakistan, US military assistance for India, Kennedy's unwillingness to use economic aid to pressure New Delhi, and Nehru's refusal to compromise on Kashmir alienated President Ayub. This development threatened Pakistani participation in CENTO and SEATO, as well as US strategic intelligence interests. Ayub believed that President Kennedy had intentionally misled him with regard to Pakistan's role as Washington's principal partner in South Asia. Britain, Saudi Arabia, and Jordan were all at odds with US policy in the Arabian Peninsula to one degree or another. Nothing had gone well.

Searching for a balance: Saudi Arabia, Yemen, and the UAR

In addition to straining relations with its allies, the Yemen conflict had placed US-UAR relations under considerable stress. Having recognized the YAR, Washington now faced pressure from its allies to secure a UAR withdrawal.[2] US Ambassador Badeau in Cairo sought Nasser's agreement to outside mediation. Recognizing the difficulty of this task, Badeau and the administration attempted to put the onus for the Yemeni disengagement on Saudi Arabia and Crown Prince Feisal. Badeau argued that by prolonging the conflict, the Saudi government raised the specter of instability and revolt.[3] Feisal's supporters pointed out that not only was Saudi Arabia pursuing the reforms that Washington had long sought, but, also under Feisal, the government in Riyadh was more stable that it had been since the death of Abd-al-Aziz al-Saud in 1953. These realists also argued that Western Europe and potentially the United States needed Saudi oil significantly more than they needed good relations with Cairo.[4] Realizing this, the administration tried to 'leave the UAR with an honorable line of retreat'.[5] In Washington's view, the easiest way to secure an 'honorable' way out for Nasser was to pressure Feisal to stop arms shipments to the Yemeni Royalists.[6] The assumption was that the collapse of the Royalist cause would bring a UAR withdrawal.

Writing to Feisal, President Kennedy called on Riyadh to end its support to the Royalists. Feisal responded by accusing Kennedy of selecting Nasser as the 'chosen instrument' of the US in the Arab world. An old charge dating from the Eisenhower administration, it was doubly effective. It put Kennedy on the defensive and put pressure on Nasser to demonstrate his independence from Washington. Addressing Feisal's accusations, he denied the existence of a special relationship with Nasser, stating: 'We avoid preferential relationships and have no "chosen instrument" in the Near East.' Defensively, Kennedy stated that the United States had close relations 'with monarchies around the world, as well as with republics'. Kennedy referred to the 'backward rule' and 'isolation' of the Imamate, and then added: 'It is with Saudi Arabia's welfare in mind – as with the peace and prosperity of the Near East as a whole – that in December I sought to find a formula for disengagement of outside forces from the Yemen, in order that this society, so long isolated and beset by poverty and backward rule, might find its own true way.'[7] Undoubtedly, Feisal thought that it was he, not the President, who had Saudi Arabia's 'welfare' most 'in mind'. It appeared that Kennedy and his advisors failed to appreciate that while the frail Crown Prince might have been born in what was then the dusty village of Riyadh in the Najd, he was a shrewd politician, highly sophisticated in assessing his political and economic leverage, and the politics of Arabia.

The British had a better appreciation of Feisal. When Prime Minister Macmillan shared his response to a letter from Kennedy on the Saudi-UAR situation, the indefatigable Sir Charles Johnston loosed an anti-American salvo from Aden: 'The Saudi regime is unstable at all times and could blow up tomorrow. But Faisal is after all not a fool and is capable of judging his own interest. ... The State Department are assuming a heavy responsibility in claiming to understand Faisal's interests – and King Hussein's – better than those Princes do themselves.' Always at the head of the line to give Washington a good bashing, Sir Charles stated that US policy was predicated on two things: the Americans 'wish to save Nasser from the consequences of his adventure', and 'The American theory that an Arab Republic has something inherently more stable about it than an Arab monarchy seems to me to be more derived from ideology than fact.' Obviously warming to the subject, Johnston pointed out that Jordan, with everything going against it, had been more stable than either Iraq or Syria. In conclusion, Johnston argued: 'With all respect I think that the Americans' policy about Nasser is a menace both to our interests and their own.'[8] Sir Charles obviously believed that it was Kennedy who needed the lecture on national interests from Feisal.

On 19 January 1963, Kennedy wrote to Nasser complaining that UAR and YAR activities were the cause of Saudi and British alarm and intensified their opposition to the revolutionary government in Sanaa. In a backhanded rebuke, Nasser responded on 3 March chiding Kennedy. Nasser stated that his willingness to discuss Arab matters with outsiders was in and of itself a 'significant concession'.[9] With calls for Arab unity in Syria and Iraq once again ringing in everyone's ears, Nasser told Kennedy that he 'had to respond to [Kennedy's] great concern owing to my knowledge – and the confirmations made to me by the American ambassador to Cairo Dr. John Badeau – of your strong ties with the Saudi Arabian Kingdom.' Nasser mentioned mounting 'doubts' about US 'endeavours in the Yemen problem'. He pointed to the fact that 'the United States was tied up with powers hostile to Arab nationalism and the Arab Revolution' and that these 'ties ... cannot be overlooked.' Laying the problem at Kennedy's door, Nasser stated that Saudi intervention had been made possible by American assistance. He pointed out that the defecting Saudi air force pilots did so in 'American made [aircraft] and the cargo of arms on board was still in the American aid cases'. He then informed Kennedy that the UAR had documentary proof that American pilots in the employ of Saudi Arabian Airlines were ferrying arms to the Yemen front'. Referring to the Imamate, Jordan, and Saudi Arabia as the 'remnants and residue of the past', the Egyptian leader asserted that his differences were 'imbedded in the depths of the social condition prevailing in the Arab World' and his 'hope' for the future.[10]

Badeau firmly believed that experience of the Syrian breakup and Nasser's new foreign policy direction, *wahdat al-hadaf* ('unity of goals'), drove his support of the YAR government, and not some plot against Saudi Arabia or US interests in the region.[11] Seeing potential for a serious collision of interests, Badeau attached his own summary to Nasser's letter. He argued that the YAR and UAR had acted with restraint given the magnitude of Saudi interference. The Ambassador wondered: 'How much concern expressed in reference telegram stems from objective judgments USA interests and how much represents drive by well known critics recent USA-UAR policy who seize upon Yemen situations as effective instrument to consolidate their view.'[12] Because of Soviet gains and Washington's 'failure ... effectively to influence Feisel', Badeau pointed out: 'If we decide Yemen conflict justifies radical policy change take decision with eyes fully open to its implication.' Badeau effectively argued that the Egyptians were not going to change their policies without some concrete response from Riyadh.[13] Badeau discussed 'Yemen's relative unimportance', as compared to further Soviet inroads with the UAR or to a flashpoint for enlarged Arab conflict.[14] Ba'thists coups in Syria and Iraq, and various reports that a new expanded UAR might be in the offing, also gave pause for thought. Kennedy wanted to avoid alienating Nasser and other Arab nationalist leaders, while at the same time placating pro-Western states by urging 'moderation, restraint and statesmanship'.[15]

In March 1963, Kennedy sent Ambassador Ellsworth Bunker on a mediation misison to Egypt and Saudi Arabia. Bunker's effort paralleled another mission by Dr. Ralph Bunche, UN Under-Secretary for Special Political Affairs. Bunche and Bunker performed shuttle diplomacy between Cairo, Sanaa, and Riyadh.[16] Kennedy wanted the Bunker mission to: '(a) reassure Faysal of US interest in Saudi Arabia; (b) convince him of the importance of his disengaging from Yemen; (c) explain to him how we think this can be done without loss of face.' Cannily, Feisal refused to compromise without concrete guarantees from the US. In return for the 'temporary' basing of US fighters at Dhahran, Feisal finally agreed to end his support for the Yemeni Royalists. Kennedy also promised to assist 'at Saudi expense' in building up the Kingdom's air defenses including a new airbase near the Yemeni border at Najran. The cessation of Saudi support for the Royalists was conditional pending an 'initial' withdrawal of Egyptian forces from Yemen.[17]

Feisal also provided a long list of caveats associated with Saudi security that made achievement of an agreement with the UAR virtually impossible unless the US demonstrated its commitment to defend Saudi Arabia.[18] Feisal got what he wanted in the form of 'Operation Hard Surface'.[19] On 6 March, Bunker offered to place US fighter aircraft at Dhahran air base in return for Feisal's compliance with a ceasefire in Yemen. On 7 April, after signing the Yemen disengagement agreement, Feisal accepted the Bunker offer. On 13 April, Radio Cairo announced that the UAR had agreed to a ceasefire, followed by a similar announcement from Radio Mecca on 15 April.[20] On 17 April, Ambassador Badeau informed Nasser that this US 'training mission' would conduct exercises near the Saudi-Yemeni border. In a thinly-veiled threat, Badeau expressed concern that 'grave consequences ... would arise from a confrontation' between US and UAR aircraft.[21]

On 18 April, the day after the announcement of Hard Surface, Kennedy reassured the UAR leadership that 'United States policy has not changed, nor do I see any current reason to change it.'[22] Despite Kennedy's reassurances, Nasser, through his intelligence chief, Zakaria Muhyi al-Din, knew that Saudi activities and Feisal's support for the Yemeni opposition continued. This created a credibility problem for Bunker, who was trying to obtain a UAR commitment to withdraw its forces. In discussions with Nasser, Bunker finally agreed to a token withdrawal of as little as half a company of troops.[23] The Kennedy administration continued to believe that relations with the UAR might yet blossom. Kennedy believed that the US and the UAR had always been able 'to find escapes from difficult impasses and to point the way toward solution of problems that might at first glance have seemed impossible'. Uncertain about the prospects for an expanded UAR, Kennedy congratulated Nasser and his 'Iraqi and Syrian collaborators ... on the formation of a new and enlarged United Arab Republic'.[24]

On 2 May 1963, in spite of solid evidence that the Saudis continued to support the Yemeni Royalists, the US dispatched a Hard Surface advance team to Dhahran with non-combat aircraft. Internal memoranda from Komer to the President indicated that both were well aware of the commitments made to Nasser that the squadron would not be sent until Saudi support for the rebels had stopped, and they were also aware that Feisal had not lived up to his side of the bargain.[25] From Cairo's perspective, the arrival of US Air Force components at Dhahran and the Saudi's continued support to the Yemeni rebels constituted a breach of faith. In trying to steer a middle course, the Kennedy administration had damaged its credibility. The relationship with Nasser was further complicated when Washington announced the sale of Hawk missiles to Israel. According to Heikal, Nasser concluded that Kennedy's informing him of the Hawk transaction with Israel had been a 'deceitful maneuver' and that the President 'had double crossed him.' This suspicion undermined any attempts by Kennedy to gain Nasser's cooperation with regard to the situation in Yemen.[26] The Hawk deal with Israel, Israel's perceived veto over US policy, and the pressure on Nasser to accept the Johnson plan destroyed Nasser's confidence in Kennedy. For Nasser and the Egyptian leadership, Kennedy had become little more than a rerun of the disappointments from a decade earlier with the Eisenhower administration – John Foster Dulles in a more urbane package.

A new dynamic: changes in Iraq and Syria

As the Yemen crisis threatened to boil over, coups in Syria and Baghdad once again changed Washington's perspective on Nasser's utility and influence in the region. On 8 February 1963, in Baghdad, Ba'thist, nationalist, and Nasserist army officers overthrew Qasim's regime. From a Western perspective, the destruction of the Iraqi Communist Party and the subsequent damage to Soviet influence was the single most important outcome. Prior to the coup, the ICP held positions of substantial influence and 'advantage' in Iraq. Nasser had no influence. Qasim's isolation created a situation in which the ICP had become his most faithful supporter and the Soviet Union the principal benefactor of his regime. Soviet military aid, economic support, and technical assistance dominated Iraqi development. In return, Iraqi foreign policy, diplomacy, and propaganda followed the Soviet line. The Iraqi government regularly referred to the Soviets as 'friendly people' and the British and Americans as 'imperialists'.

The 8 February coup appeared to change the situation dramatically. By the next day, Qasim was dead, executed 'after a short trial', along with the Communist commander of the Iraqi air force, Brigadier Jalal Awqati, and other Qasim supporters.[27] Radio Baghdad announced the formation of yet another RCC and called on the 'masses to descend to the streets to see the body of Qasim'.[28] The Communists knew the score. They would receive the same consideration that they had meted out when they hung Ba'thists and Nasserists from lampposts in Mosul in 1959. Just to make certain that there was no ambiguity, the RCC issued Proclamation 13. It called for the 'annihilation of anyone that disturbs the peace' and exhorted the people to inform against 'the agent – Communists – the partners in crime of the enemy of God'.[29] Washington welcomed the news that thousands of Communists were either dead or in jail and that the shops in Baghdad were doing a booming business in portraits of the new President, Abd-al-Salaam al-Aref, Qasim's pro-Nasserist co-conspirator in 1958.[30]

Neither Washington nor London knew exactly what the coup meant, but both believed that it had to be an improvement over the Qasim regime. Ironically, the broadly-held assumption that the coup resulted from US-UAR cooperation created the biggest stir among the pro-Western states in the region.[31] In Washington, administration officials told the Saudi Arabian Ambassador, Sheikh Abdullah al-Khayyal, that the Iraqi coup coming on top of the Yemen situation made it imperative for the Kingdom to cease its involvement in Yemen for fear that 'emboldened ... nationalist elements' might move against the monarchy.[32] From the Saudi perspective, the coup and the message appeared to be a US warning issued on behalf of the UAR. To compound this speculation, both the Syrians and Jordanians openly discussed the danger posed by the US's 'chosen instrument', Nasser and resurgent Pan-Arab nationalism.[33] The Arabs simply refused to believe that the Kennedy administration and Nasser were not working hand-in-glove.

The Kennedy administration's initial analysis concluded that Iraq would continue to chart an independent course as a 'separate pole of alignment' in the Arab world. In this vein, Washington intended to be 'as responsive as possible to the new government so that we may have the maximum amount of influence with the new regime at an early stage.'[34] Early predictions of 'no lasting gain for the UAR' were encouraging.[35] Washington believed that the same forces that had driven a wedge between Nasser and, respectively, Nuri Sa'id and then Qasim, would separate the new regime from Cairo. The potential downside was that the Ba'thists in Iraq might succeed in overthrowing the monarchies in both Saudi Arabia and Jordan, possibly with UAR complicity.[36] Kennedy and his advisors wanted an Iraq friendly to the West and independent of Nasser. The administration now feared a coalescence of interests between the Iraqi Ba'thists and Nasser that might overpower the weaker pro-Western monarchies. There was also the outside possibility of another Nasserist unification movement.

Given the problems over Yemen with Nasser, the possibility of an Iraq cleansed of Communists and friendly to the West presented Washington with an inviting potential for Baghdad to reclaim its traditional role as a counterbalance to Cairo. In Cairo, the triumph of the Ba'th Party in Iraq caused a shift in policy that brought condemnation of the Syrian Ba'thists and proferred an olive branch to the Iraqis. On 15 February, in *Al-Ahram*, the ever-creative Heikal pointed out that it was necessary to differentiate 'between the real Ba'th and the opportunists and profiteers' in the party, the latter obviously referring to the Syrian secessionists. Heikal stated that the UAR looked forward to the possibility of fresh approaches that the Iraqi Ba'thists might have with regard to furthering Arab unity. Nasser may have been disappointed by the Iraqi Ba'th's refusal to side with the UAR against its Syrian branch, but he carefully left the door open for cooperation.[37]

British assessments had a slightly different interpretation of the coup. London concurred that the new regime would be domestically anti-Communist and nationalist, but they believed that it would maintain correct relations with the Soviet Union. There was too much Soviet military hardware laying around for it not to be on speaking terms with Moscow. Because of their support for Qasim, the British were concerned that their lack of connections with the new government, the Nasserist influence, and the imposition of austerity programs might effect Britain's commercial position. They also worried about Kuwait.[38] The British also predicted good relations between Cairo and Baghdad but 'no attempt to establish joint institutions'. Sir Howard Beeley, the British Ambassador in Cairo, commented that these 'loose arrangements' for propaganda purposes would include the UAR, Iraq, Algeria, and the YAR.[39]

Immediately following the coup, the new Iraqi Foreign Minister, Talib Shabib, outlined the foreign policy of the regime. On the matter of Yemen, the Iraqi government supported the YAR and UAR position. Baghdad made it clear that the culprits standing in the way of progress and peace in the region were the Saudis, who were subsidizing and supplying the Royalists, and the British, who were creating problems on the southern border. Feisal and Hussein were 'going against the tide'. Officially the Iraqi government intended to stay out of it but it 'could not control' the 45 newly-licensed Iraqi publications. Shabib also stated Iraq's intention to cooperate closely, but not federate, with the UAR, YAR, and Algeria. As for Syria, Baghdad expressed specific concerns in light of reports that fugitive Iraqi officials had fled there. Shabib stated that while Iraq did not plan direct action against Syria, he left no doubt that Baghdad would welcome a more 'congenial' government there at the earliest possible date. The wait was short.

The Baghdad coup left the Syrian government of President Nazim al-Qudsi in an impossible position. In a desperate bid for political survival, Qudsi resorted to what could only be described as a kind of policy schizophrenia. He needed friends and could not afford to be too choosy. Following Syria's secession from the UAR, the US faced incessant Syrian media and propaganda attacks, predicated on the proposition that Cairo and Washington were working in consort to undermine Syria. In January 1963, the Syrian government suddenly reversed itself and began to question US support for Saudi Arabia in the Yemen conflict. High-level Syrian officials warned the US that 'overt US support' could be the 'kiss of death' for the Saudi regime.[40] It was a clumsy attempt to placate Nasser. Facing mounting problems with Syrian Ba'thists, and believing that the US had the influence to put in a good word with Nasser, Qudsi attempted to enlist US help against his Syrian Ba'thist and Nasserist opposition. On 19 February, with the Iraqi coup as backdrop, President Qudsi responded to a letter from Kennedy in which Kennedy protested that Syrian accusations against US officials for allegedly supporting UAR subversion in Syria were false. In a more or less friendly response, Qudsi lodged an obligatory complaint about Israel, but agreed that the charges against the US officials were unfounded. He also wrote that US-Syrian relations were better than 'they have been in the last decade'.[41] Isolated, with internal opposition surging, the Damascus regime was simply flailing about in a futile attempt to save itself.

On 8 March 1963, Ba'thist military and party elements overthrew the Syrian government and announced a policy that supported Arab unity with Iraq, the UAR, the YAR, and Algeria. The new regime also declared its opposition to indigenous Communism.[42] In Syria, Michael Aflaq's Ba'th of old had fractured. His credibility undermined by his agreement with Nasser in 1958 to dissolve the Ba'th party, Aflaq was no longer the dominant power in the new Syrian Ba'th. Instead, a group of military officers, refered to as the 'Military Committee', ran the show. This secretive cabal, composed of Muhammad 'Umran, Salah Jadid, Hafiz al-Assad, Abd-al-Karim Jundi, and Ahmad al-Mir, resented Aflaq and Bitar because of their agreement in 1958 to dissolve the Ba'th. All were members of minor sectarian groups. 'Umran, Jadid, and Assad were Alawi; Jundi and Mir were Ismaili. Now the military Ba'thists no longer needed the civilians in order to grab power. In addition, Nasser, not Aflaq, remained the most visible symbol of Arab nationalism and unity. These factors, along with the arrival in Damascus of exiled Syrian Nasserists, resulted in a call on 14 March for 'tripartite unity' between the UAR, Syria, and Iraq.[43]

Negotiations ensued in Cairo in March and April 1963 between Syria, Iraq, and the UAR, paralleling the Yemen mediations. The Iraqis and Syrians arrived in Cairo expecting to conclude a quick arrangement with Nasser. Remembering 1958 and 1961, Nasser put them off. He explained that before negotiations could begin, he had to clear the air between the Syrian delegation and the UAR with regard to the creation of the UAR and Syria's secession. Nasser wanted his pound of flesh in terms of an admission by the Syrian Ba'th of their past sins, and submission to Egypt's 'Charter of National Action' and 'revolutionary experience' for inspiration. In short, unity required the humiliation of the Syrian Ba'th. Nasser used his stature to intimidate the delegates.[44] The meetings became an inquisition for the Syrian Ba'thists. Nasser set the tone early and recorded the meetings. He opened with a question: 'Are we asked to unite with the Ba'th Party or with Syria? If the Ba'th party is ruling Syria and we are supposed to unite with it, then I am not at all prepared to continue these discussions. Union with Syria would be welcome, but to union with the Ba'th my answer would, no thank you.' The Ba'thists were taken aback. Nasser pressed them: 'Is the regime in Syria Ba'thist?' One Ba'thist participant said: 'No, a National Front.' Another Abd-al-Karim Zuhur said: 'It is not Ba'thist, Sir, but the Ba'th is a partner', and so it went on.[45] Nasser intended to string out the talks, either obtaining the total supplication of both the Syrian and Iraqi Ba'thists or gaining time for his own supporters to grab power in Damascus and Baghdad. As the unity talks progressed, pro-Nasserist pressure in the form of riots and demonstrations grew in Syria. On 17 April, Nasser appeared to have triumphed when it was announced that Iraq, Syria, and Egypt would unite in a federal state to be called the 'United Arab Republic'.[46]

Despite prognostications from the CIA and the State Department that Iraq would maintain its independence from the UAR, Kennedy wanted to hedge his bets. As long as the potential existed for Nasser to head a federated Iraq, Syria, and Egypt, the White House intended to tread lightly on the Yemen issue. Like Dulles and Eisenhower in 1958, the administration feared finding itself confronted by a hostile Arab super-state. Kennedy's conciliatory letter to Nasser on 18 April reflected the uncertainty created by the tripartite negotiations. He congratulated Nasser on the formation of the new UAR and argued for restraint in Yemen.[47] Kennedy wanted to preserve his options with the UAR while defusing the Yemen situation. To accomplish this, he preferred that the Saudis simply to withdraw support from the politically odious Yemeni Royalists. This would allow the US to avoid a confrontation with Nasser, but now with Iraq and Syria, Kennedy saw the possibility that Nasser might pull another rabbit from his political hat.

Soured relations with the UAR

After Nasser's unification talks, Jordan and Saudi Arabia once again became the focus of concern. On 27 March, in Amman, the coups in Iraq and Syria and internal dissatisfaction brought the fall of the Tal government. The King called on the venerable Samir Rifa'i to form his last government. Regime instability and domestic opposition to Hussein's rule created the possibility, or in minds of some, the probability of a Hashemite collapse. In such an event the

Israelis would occupy all or part of the West Bank. In addition, the Macmillan government made it clear that it was 'not wedded to the status quo in Jordan'. There would be no repeat of the 1958 military rescue of the Jordanian Hashemites. Quite simply, the potential damage of such a rescue to British petroleum interests in the Arab world was now unacceptable.[48] The rhetoric from Damascus fueled more concern. Leading Syrian Ba'thist Saladin al-Bitar told the US officials that the 'Hussein regime' in Jordan was 'entirely unacceptable' to the 'Arab National Movement' and to a majority of the Jordanian people. As a result, it was 'doomed to go'.[49] Pro-union demonstrations in various Jordanian and West Bank towns resulted in Parliament passing a no-confidence vote in the government. Annoyed, King Hussein dismissed Parliament. On 20 April, Rifa'i's government fell, but instead of backing down, the King appointed his uncle, Sharif Hussein ibn Nasir, Prime Minister on 27 April.[50]

The combination of Syrian rhetoric and Israeli threats from the ever-irascible Ben-Gurion raised the Kennedy administration's concern over the Jordanian situation to new heights. On 25 April 1963, Ben-Gurion sent President Kennedy a note citing the unification of Iraq, Syria, and Egypt and their promise to liberate Palestine. While pointing out that Israel 'can defeat all three', the Prime Minister lobbied for new weapons, because now 'the Hawk alone is not a deterrent.'[51] The Ben-Gurion letter also coincided with attacks on Assistant Secretary Talbot's statement on 22 April 1963 to the National Foreign Policy Conference of Editors and Broadcasters that the administration did not believe that the proposed UAR federation 'measurably affected' Israel's security situation.[52]

On 26 April, the Israeli Ambassador met with State Department officials to discuss the Ben-Gurion note. During the meeting, the Israelis stated that an attempt to overthrow the Jordanian government would occur 'within a few hours or days'. The Israelis stated that they would not sit idly by and have a hostile regime replace the Hashemites. When US officials expressed their doubts about Nasser's involvement, the Israelis stated that they believed that the anti-Hashemite propaganda broadcasts were coming from Cairo and that they feared a repeat of the Yemen scenario. Using the UAR unification announcement, the Israelis expressed concern about the difference between that possibility and the initial US view that the Syrian and Iraqi coups would form a 'counterpoise' to Nasserist ambitions. Warning against Israeli action, US officials pointed out that Israeli actions had a tendency to unify the Arabs. As James Grant, the Acting Assistant Secretary in NEA, put it: 'Left to themselves, the Arabs have a very considerable capacity to decentralize and neutralize themselves.' The Israelis returned the next day with visiting minister Modechai Gazit in tow. They were now complaining that Jordan was not the 'major problem' and pointing to the 'declaration of a war of destruction' against Israel by the UAR. The Israelis wanted to know how the US justified economic and military aid in light of this. Department officials cautioned the Israelis not to overreact to the situation.[53]

Ben-Gurion's letters and the meetings in Washington had their desired affect. The administration sent Ambassador Badeau scurrying to Egyptian officials on 27 April with another warning about intervention in Jordan. Badeau met first with Sami Sharaf, one of Nasser's aides and a direct pipeline to the Egyptian President, to warn about the situation in Jordan and to complain about Egyptian propaganda emanating from the Voice of the Arab Nation radio. Sharaf denied any knowledge of the station even when confronted by Badeau with its exact location.[54] As a result of the démarche, Nasser summoned Badeau to a meeting the next day, when he stated that Sharaf's report about the situation in Jordan 'kept him awake most of the previous evening' because his sources showed no indication of 'imminent action in Jordan'. Nasser was concerned that action might be taken based on information unavailable to him and asked Badeau to keep him informed.

Acknowledging that any move against Hussein would be laid at his 'doorstep', Nasser stated that at the beginning of the unification talks he had personally squelched a Syrian initiative to undermine the Hashemite regime. He added that the overthrow of Hussein was inevitable and could happen at any time, given the level of discontent in the officer corps, but he had no information of an imminent threat. He warned the US that an Israeli move against Jordan would provoke an Egyptian move against Israel and 'nobody knows where it will end.' Badeau ended the conversation by telling Nasser that Washington would attempt to restrain Israel but that the UAR needed to stand clear of any appearance or real involvement in the Jordanian crisis. In his comments on the meeting, Badeau attempted to preempt any further demands on Nasser for assurances, stating that guarantees would not be forthcoming.[55] Badeau also pointed out that Nasser was already under Arab pressure for taking US aid in return for turning a blind eye to Israel. Concerned about Nasser's reaction to continuing pressure from Washington for UAR guarantees on everything from Yemen to Jordan to Israel, and now the current move by pro-Israeli elements in the US Senate to cut off aid to Egypt, Badeau worried that Nasser would finally conclude that the 'US will never support any genuine Arab cause.'[56]

Just to make certain that Nasser understood who was behind the US warning, no doubt in hopes of further complicating US-UAR relations, Ben-Gurion gave interviews to several newspapers, warning that any takeover of Jordan by the UAR would be 'viewed by Israel as a grave action which would endanger its security'. To add fuel to the fire, the Israeli newspaper *Haaretz* reported from Washington that 'Authoritative US Sources' had made it clear that 'Nasser fully understands' the US warning not to intervene in Jordan.[57] Ever adaptive, Israeli Ambassador Harman once again met with US officials and changed the Israeli position on the UAR threat. Harman explained to Averell Harriman that the perceived Egyptian threat really had nothing to do with Jordan or UAR unity 'at the moment', but that Ben-Gurion was actually concerned about Nasser and the 'constant military threat' posed by Egypt. This was the same military threat that Ben-Gurion had earlier assured Kennedy in writing that Israel could handle. The Israelis pushed the US to once again tell Nasser: 'There is a firm line.'[58] US approaches to Nasser, followed by Israeli public pronouncements and press reports, followed by more Israeli demands for US approaches to Nasser, created the impression in Cairo and other Arab capitals that Kennedy had become Ben-Gurion's errand boy. The Israelis no doubt calculated that Congressional pressure on the White House over aid to the UAR, and the looming elections of 1964, put Kennedy in a position where he could not ignore Israeli demands. In addition, there was always the possibility of an added bonus that an irritated Nasser might break with Washington.

In Cairo, with Arab unity again perhaps within his grasp, Nasser needed to demonstrate his independence from US pressure. US moves to 'show military interest in Jordan' made this demonstration even more critical. The Kennedy administration had dispatched a small joint exercise Air Force team with two aircraft. The administration also concluded that, regardless of other considerations, the maintenance of Jordan as an independent, pro-Western state served US interests.[59] This was a major shift from the preceding year when Washington cut all categories of aid to King Hussein. Now, in July 1963, fearing a 'crisis of confidence' in Amman and the 'cost to us if it folded', an alarmed White House brought Ambassador Macomber to Washington to talk to the President.[60] Just to provide added impetus to the debate, Jordan established diplomatic relations with Moscow and moved to improve relations with the UAR. To improve his Arab credentials, Hussein asserted his position vis-à-vis Israel by allowing Jordanian border guards in Jerusalem to fire on an Israeli military patrol in a disputed zone. He also promised to support Syria in its clashes with Israel.[61] The additional leverage earned King Hussein an invitation to make an 'informal' call at the White House in early 1964 to 'clear the air' on Arab issues and on problems in US-Jordanian relations.[62]

Nasser had additional frustrations. The Ba'thists in Syria and Iraq had become even more reluctant to enter into the kind of union proposed by Nasser. Nasser wanted a plebiscite to be held on the question of whether rule of the united UAR should be by committee or a single president. Remembering 1958, the Syrian Ba'thists and government rejected the plebiscite. This resulted in the resignation of the five Nasserist ministers.[63] On 18 July 1963, Syrian Nasserists attempted to displace the Ba'thists in a coup led by Jaim 'Alwan. The coup failed and, rather than the usual exile, the coup ringleaders were tried and executed. The coup and the subsequent suppression effectively ended Nasserism in Syria. In addition to this defeat, Nasser correctly concluded that US policy had favored the Ba'thists in Syria and Iraq as a counterweight to a resurgent UAR.[64] In August 1963, Nasser withdrew from the agreement of 17 April, and with a straight face accused the Ba'th of attempting to use it for 'their own political ends'. He also attacked the Ba'th Party as an agent of Zionism and imperialism, claiming that he, not the Ba'thists, was determined 'to restore the rights of the Palestinian people'.[65] As a result of these setbacks, the US and Britain braced for Nasser's policies to 'swing to the left'.[66]

The split with Nasser pushed the Syrian and Iraqi Ba'th parties into closer alignment. On 26 August, Abd-al-Salaam Aref, Nasser's old supporter and now President of Iraq, agreed to unity talks with the Syrian Ba'th. On 8 October 1963, Iraq and Syria signed the 'Military Unity Charter' as an initial step toward full unification. Despite outward signs of progress, relations between the two Ba'th party branches had already begun to unravel. Basically, the strong Nasserist element in Iraq and staunch Iraqi nationalists would not reconcile themselves to Syrian Ba'thist domination. Nasser's refusal to consider an alliance with any government in which the Ba'thists were a member increased the pressure. On 18 November, Aref displaced the Iraqi Ba'thists in a coup.[67] Aref, however, did not purge the Iraqi government of all Ba'thists, but rather controlled their access to power.[68] In Cairo, Nasser waited for events to settle down, assuming that the Ba'th in Iraq was finished.[69] Aref acted quickly and outlawed the Ba'th, established a non-party nationalist leadership, and invited Nasser to Baghdad for a state visit. With Syria isolated, it looked like Nasser might regain his status as the 'the guide and guardian of modern Arab Nationalism'.[70]

To protect his flank from Arab criticism over Washington's perceived influence in Cairo, Nasser sought a pretext for an attack on US policy. It was not hard to find. In response to anti-Nasserist pressure from the Israeli lobby and from the pro-Western Arab states, the US Congress amended the foreign aid bill, threatening to end PL 480 wheat grants to Egypt. Nasser now had to face the prospect of losing US aid altogether if he did not toe the US policy line. In addition, Kennedy sent Nasser a pointed verbal message via Badeau expressing his 'concern' that Egyptian troop withdrawals from Yemen were 'inconsistent' with the terms of the UN agreement.[71] Fed up with US pressure, Nasser bitterly attacked the administration, stating that the UAR's experience in 1956 left him convinced that the West was an unreliable partner and, despite hopes to the contrary, now 'it seemed clear that [he] must "go back" to 1957.'[72] Nasser concluded that even when relations were good, US policy would change course without regard to clear US interests in the region.[73] The use of aid as a 'club' to alter UAR policy, particularly its Arab policies, had always been a non-starter.[74] As Bundy pointed out to Senator J. William Fulbright on 11 November: 'Dispatches from Cairo make it clear that the Gruening Amendment has had a strong impact there, but unfortunately the effect is the opposite of what supporters of the Amendment must have intended. ... We make people more, and not less, nationalistic by action which seem to them to be "neo-colonial pressure".'[75]

Iran: another year, another crisis or two

Just as Kennedy's policy initiatives with Cairo had collapsed, the administration faced setbacks with allied states as well. By late 1962, with the Amini government behind him, the Shah told Washington that he intended to carry through with the reform program. So there would be no doubt that he was in charge, the Shah appointed Asadollah Alam, former head the Pahlavi Foundation and a palace creature, as Prime Minister. During the fall of 1962, a lull fell over Iranian politics. Never happy with the Shah, Komer at the NSC stated: 'Anyone familiar with this feeble country knows this as just another lull before the storm.' Komer went on to comment that the Amini period had been 'instructive'. Although running scared, the Tehran regime had opted for a new approach, but 'once the Shah and his entourage realized the crisis was over, they resumed the perennial game of cutting the new boy down to size. We too relapsed into our usual preoccupation with the military rather than internal problems.'[76] While accurate as far as it went, Komer's view failed to consider that the US had no real alternatives, and that his own view of Amini as the 'last hope' had been badly flawed and had failed. Nevertheless, activist elements in the administration continued to want to do something about the Shah, and Komer even mused about encouraging the Iranian opposition. Returning to reality, and underlining for emphasis, Komer wrote: <u>'But there is no presently foreseeable alternative better than some combination of the Shah and a reformist cabinet with his full backing or at least acquiescence</u>.' Grudgingly, Komer admitted: 'I'm persuaded of one thing – the Shah does mean something in Iran. He's more than a symbol; with all his weaknesses he's the chief existing source of power in a country with few if any competing power centers.'[77] Like it or not, the Shah provided the only viable pro-Western source of power.

In addition, no matter how misguided or half-hearted his efforts, the Shah really did want to reform Iran, albeit in a manner acceptable to him. In December 1962, borrowing an idea from King Hassan II of Morocco, he toyed with the notion of holding a national referendum on his reform programs. The Shah and Prime Minister Alam wanted to hold an up-or-down vote on land reform, the sale of government factories, profit-sharing for workers, a national literacy corps, a new election law including women's suffrage, and the nationalization of forests.[78] Feeling confident that land reform was 'a fact of life', the Shah indicated that he planned to hold Majlis elections in 1963.[79] The problem was that the Shah's land-reform program had alienated support among rural landowners and the religious establishment.[80] The Shah held his referendum, and the Iranian public, despite a boycott by the National Front, approved the goals of what now became known as the 'White Revolution'.[81] The Shah's move to break with the past and with the 'traditional moneyed, land-owning, and religious elites' received strong support in Washington.[82] Komer stated: 'It's been a long time since we last massaged the Shah, so his reform program and referendum provide a first-class occasion for JFK to do so (and remind him that big brother is watching).'[83] In a more sober assessment, Roger Hillsman in INR cited the landowner, religious, and nationalist opposition to the Shah's program, and warned that 'grave problems' remained.[84]

On March 14, 1963, having just authorized the new military-assistance program for the Shah, President Kennedy ordered a full policy review for Iran to answer the question: 'Is the thrust of existing U.S. policy toward Iran still basically valid?' As expected, Holmes in Tehran painted a generally positive picture, but with one sobering note: the Shah 'has aroused the animosity of the dispossessed elite and the fanatical clergy, and having not yet consolidated the support of the emancipated peasantry, he is dependent in the immediate future to a greater degree than ever on the support of the military and security forces.'[85] With regard to elections, on 29 May the British Ambassador in Tehran suggested that elections might undermine the opposition to the Shah's reform program.[86]

Unfortunately, trouble with the clergy had already begun. An associate of Ayatollah Borujerdi of Qom, the Ayatollah Ruhollah Khomeini, had been preaching openly against the referendum and the reforms. The message first attacked land reform and then later, women's suffrage under the planned election law. There was only one consistent theme: the Shah was the puppet of the Americans. To support this claim, Khomeini and other nationalists pointed to the status of force agreement being imposed on the Shah by the Kennedy administration and the US Congress. In return for military aid, the Iranian government had to give up the right to try US military and aid personnel in Iranian courts for crimes committed in Iran. This smacked of the old concession system practiced by various and sundry colonial powers in Qajjar Persia and Pahlavi Iran and, perhaps as much as any other issue, branded the US a colonial power. It was an issue tailor-made for the Shah's opposition.

In March 1963, in retaliation, Iranian paratroopers broke into the *madrasa* where Khomeini preached and arrested him. Several students were killed in the process. Khomeini was released a short time later but resumed his attacks. Sporadic outbreaks incited by disaffected clergy continued during the spring.[87] Then, on 3 June 1963, Khomeini launched a violent attack on the Shah and US influence in Iran. He was arrested the next morning on Muharram, the day of Husayn's martyrdom. When word got out, chaos erupted. In several major cities, Muharram crowds, already massed and emotionally charged, rioted, calling for the overthrown of the regime. The uprising went on for several days, but was finally suppressed by security and military units, with heavy loss of life. The cooperation between religious opponents of the regime and nationalists began with the rioting of June 1963, and a little-known cleric from Qom became a widely-known and influential opponent of the regime.[88]

Following the June 1963 uprising, the assessment by the Kennedy administration was virtually unanimous. The Shah's White Revolution had challenged the traditional foundations of Iranian society. As a result, the monarch's survival rested on the loyalty and efficiency of the military and his security services. In addition, land reform had reduced the focus on long-term development, with the probable outcome being immediate and mid-term economic problems.[89] Finally, taking US advice, the Shah was attempting to restructure Iranian society and focus on economic development. As a result, the opposition labeled him an American puppet. It was the reform program that had served as the catalyst for the uprising. Military assistance contributed to the problem, but it was the Shah's attempt to modernize Iran and his White Revolution that sparked the revolt. Kennedy's advisors now realized that the Shah, with Washington's encouragement, had alienated the traditional centers of support for the monarchy. For the Shah to succeed or even to survive, the military and security services would be the key. The June eruption dampened carping in Washington about liberalization and complaints that the Shah had not sufficiently reduced the armed forces.[90] On 20 June, Kennedy, in a personal message, commended the Shah for 'surmounting the disturbances' and encouraged him to improve the economic situation to ensure the success of his reforms. Kennedy also cautioned the Shah about the stresses that reform put on a society.[91] Kennedy, the progressive reformer, was cautioning against rapid reform; he wanted reform in Iran, but not if it resulted in the collapse of the Shah's regime. The administration had returned to its Eisenhower roots in Iran. As for the Shah, he now had the long-sought, undivided attention of the Kennedy administration and felt reasonably sure that Washington saw no real alternatives to his rule.

India and Pakistan

The situations in India and Pakistan also defied the Kennedy touch. On 4 January 1963, the British expressed their reservations about the Kashmir situation. Lord Home, the Foreign Secretary, stated categorically: 'H.M.G. should avoid becoming involved at this stage either in details of the negotiations between Pakistan and India on Kashmir, or in any capacity of "honest broker".'[92] Kennedy hoped that the Chinese threat would cause India to reach a settlement with Pakistan, stating that a 'Kashmir settlement is our chief goal.' He also wanted Nehru to understand that significant US military assistance against China required a compromise with Pakistan over Kashmir and Indian help against the Chinese elsewhere in Asia.[93] Komer cynically made the US position abundantly clear: 'Whatever we can do behind the scenes to keep this [Chinese] threat visibly evident will serve our long-term ends.'[94] On 16 February, Nehru wrote to Kennedy, stating that he could not offer Pakistan more than he had offered India – in effect nothing – without creating 'an uproar in India and put[ting] our Government in a very difficult position'. Nehru added: 'The talks had as good as broken down.'[95]

Reaching the same conclusion, Ayub was simply unwilling to accept the limited adjustments that Nehru might offer.[96] As the Kashmir talks simmered on, a downturn in the Pakistani economy emboldened Ayub's internal opposition. There was a rising sense that Ayub's rule had run its course and a belief that Pakistan was descending into yet another period of political instability and economic stagnation. In addition, senior government officials and army officers felt that Washington had sided with India and that support for the West counted for little in terms of military and economic aid. Fear existed among Pakistani officials that India would take over the subcontinent while the US stood by and watched.[97] Embassy reporting from Pakistan indicated a building crisis on domestic issues and discussion of taking Kashmir by force. These rumors resulted in what Pakistan perceived as its abandonment by the US.[98]

By April 1963, the bilateral talks on Kashmir had yielded nothing, and comments by Pakistani Foreign Minister Bhutto and Nehru were discouraging.[99] Predicting a major crisis in the negotiations, Walt Rostow called the obstruction an insurmountable 'psychological [and] political ... stone wall' that the participants anticipated from the very beginning.[100] On 15 April, in a meeting with Galbraith, Nehru's 'vehement' anger left no doubt that his 'antipathy' for Pakistan simply would not allow any meaningful compromise.[101] In addition, the Chinese repatriated 3,000 Indian prisoners of war, indicating that there would be no more pressure on Nehru from that quarter.[102] India only stayed in the talks hoping for military aid from the West. Sandys, the British facilitator, believed that once India obtained military aid, all hope for a compromise on Kashmir would evaporate. As a result, both the US and Britain took the position that while a settlement on Kashmir was not a precondition to arms aid, India should not 'expect arms aid in advance of a settlement'.[103]

No matter what support existed in the Indian Government for a compromise and settlement – and the rumors varied – Nehru categorically opposed any agreement that potentially meant the loss of Kashmir. Having spent a lifetime arguing for a secular, united India, he could not bring himself to compromise.[104] As the negotiations deteriorated, the Kennedy administration began to consider any option that promised the slightest chance of success.[105] On 21 April, Nehru sent another letter to Kennedy, in which he stated: 'Pressurizing Governments ... can hardly be useful.' He added: 'Ill-considered and ill-conceived initiatives ... made it impossible to reach any settlement.'[106] By June, the bilateral talks between India and Pakistani had failed completely.[107] Despite this obvious failure, Kennedy was willing to go ahead with an arms package to India. Then the situation changed.

During the summer of 1963, a series of developments further undermined a compromise on Kashmir. First, Prime Minister Nehru, in increasing ill-health, suffered a series of internal political setbacks. Historically, Nehru had used Krishna Menon and K.D. Malaviya (both leftists) to balance the conservative wing of the Congress Party. Menon was gone, and in July 1963, conservatives in Congress forced Malaviya from power. Nehru, himself a leftist, found his power and prestige reduced, leaving him little room to maneuver on the Kashmir issue, even were he so inclined.[108] Second, in Pakistan a general review of foreign policy began. Karachi criticized the joint communiqué issued by Kennedy and Macmillan following the Nassau meeting on 30 June, saying the guarantees for Pakistani security were 'meaningless'. In addition, the 'opposition' in the Pakistani National Assembly argued that CENTO and SEATO membership, as well as the alliance with the US, had brought greater – not reduced – insecurity. Pakistani politicians of every stripe recommended that serious consideration be given to nonaligned status in the future.[109] In addition, Pakistani disillusionment created a groundswell for closer ties and even a mutual-defense arrangement with Beijing. This development would indeed represent a serious setback for US containment policy in the region.[110] Lastly, the Soviet Union, through Czechoslovakia, offered the Indians a massive arms deal on highly-favorable payment terms.[111] The US realized India really wanted its own modern air force, with a manufacturing capability. If an arms deal with the West did not offer this, then Soviet-Indian cooperation was highly likely.[112] The cost of providing a Western-style aircraft industry was prohibitive. Kennedy summed it up well: 'if we give too little we might lose India and ... if we give too much we might lose Pakistan.'[113]

The Pakistanis pressed Washington citing their reluctance to seek other allies in the region, meaning the Chinese, while making the case that leftist influence in India and cheaper weaponry made closer ties with the Soviet Union almost inevitable.[114] The most disturbing issue to those supporting military aid to India was the attitude of President Kennedy; he stated that he understood Ayub's concerns. John McCone, Director of the CIA, reiterated the vital importance of the 'Peshawar facility' and the need for its now stalled expansion.[115] In a September meeting with George Ball, Ayub pointed out that Nehru showed no inclination to negotiate on Kashmir, and he reminded the administration that both Truman and Eisenhower had attempted to work with India over the Kashmir issue and failed; given the situation, 'Pakistan saw no alternative but to proceed toward normalization of relations with Communist China and ultimately with the Soviet Union.'[116] Ayub had concluded that the defense arrangements with the United States were worthless in the event of an attack by India and that continued isolation from China and the Soviet Union was unwise.[117]

Chester Bowles, now the new Ambassador to India, had already begun to formulate an alternative approach that might avoid Soviet military assistance to India and a total collapse in US-Pakistan relations. Knowing that the administration would ultimately decide that it had too much at stake in Pakistan to risk military aid to India, Bowles asked: 'Does anyone believe that there are any predispositions on the part of the Indians and Pakistanis to reach a settlement at this time, or indeed to do anything more than attempt to secure a tactical advantage enabling one to embarrass the other? My conversations ... lead me to conclude that it would be futile for us to proceed with this venture now.'[118] Wanting to avoid further bad press for Nehru, Bowles urged that the mediation be dropped, while the pro-Pakistani contingent argued that giving up showed bad faith toward Pakistan and played into India's hands.[119] The offer went forward. Pakistan accepted and India rejected it.[120]

Bowles then urged a dual-track policy, whereby both countries received defensive weapons on an equal footing. Bowles, now the principal spokesman for the pro-India group, realized that concern over Pakistani overtures to the Chinese would wreck any chance for military aid to India. Knowing that he had little time, he pushed hard for this approach, arguing that India was 'not only friendly democratic power but most outspoken Asia enemy of Chicoms'.[121] In a separate evaluation, the State Department concluded that efforts to supply India with US weapons had severely undermined the relationship with Pakistan, which would now attempt to build relations with the Chinese and to curry favor with the Soviets.[122] Washington was convinced that despite flirtations with China and the Soviets, US economic and military aid placed an effective 'limitation' on how far these relationships with Pakistan could go.[123]

During the fall of 1963, Bowles continued to push for a major US military aid program for India to counter the threat of a major Soviet arms deal with New Delhi. Talbot, Rusk, and McNamara opposed him, discounting Soviet assistance. According to Bowles, Kennedy asked him to work something out. Bowles returned in November 1963 with a plan to provide arms to India that he believed would not upset the Pakistanis. He managed to get Komer's attention, and the latter coordinated a meeting with the President. Komer explained: 'Chet Bowles is very anxious to get some flavor of your current thinking about India-Pakistan tomorrow. He's putting up a brave front but actually feeling a bit low, and wondering whether we're still signed on to moving ahead with India. The important thing to do with Bowles is to reassure him that we intend to go forward with India, while getting him to set his sights a little lower and more realistically.'[124] Bowles presented his plan to Kennedy. The President believed that it only had a '50-50 chance of success' because it only amounted to $50–75 million per year and did not create a modern air force. With reference to the plan, Komer asked: 'If Bowles turns out to be over-optimistic, have we really lost very much?'[125] Rusk, Talbot, and McNamara continued to oppose Bowles, and Kennedy set a follow-on meeting for Tuesday, 26 November to discuss modifications and alternatives. The meeting never happened.[126]

The day after Kennedy's assassination, Bowles pressed for a positive decision on the Indian military-assistance program. Komer relayed the message and requested that President Johnson approve it. In his memo to Bundy, Komer stated that Johnson was known to be pro-Pakistani and the plan for India needed a sign-off before a potential change of heart occurred. Komer referred to Talbot's alleged fears that the Pakistanis would take 'great heart from LBJ's advent' and be more difficult than ever about arms for India. He also stated that the Indians were very nervous. He asked that Bowles be given five minutes of LBJ's time so that he could take a personal message back to Nehru about the arms.[127] This exercise marked a last-ditch effort on the part of Bowles and Komer to salvage arms for India. In fact, Komer's statement that this was Kennedy's policy was something of an overstatement. Kennedy only authorized Bowles to explore his plan with New Delhi. Given the record and Bowles' belief that Talbot had undermined the pro-India policy, it is unlikely that Talbot had been a party to this effort to slip the India arms deal by the new President. Bowles knew that he had lacked the clear-cut support of Kennedy and that McNamara, Rusk, and Talbot actively opposed him; therefore, he tried to use a quick meeting with President Johnson to commit him to the India arms deal.

On 30 November, the meeting on aid to India finally occurred, but without Bowles; Johnson met rather with Bundy and CIA Director McCone. McCone insisted that the intelligence relationship with Pakistan was of the 'greatest importance' to the security of the United States. McCone couched this argument not in terms of the Middle East, but in terms of the hard-intelligence collection sites that directly affected US security. They reviewed with President Johnson the commitments made to Pakistan with regard to an attack by India and the recent deterioration in US-Pakistan relations. Johnson responded, expressing the 'greatest of confidence in Ayub' but also stating that the US 'had not been forceful enough ... and had not given him a feeling of confidence in our motives and he had drifted into the thought that we would abandon him in favor of India.' Johnson then instructed Bundy and McCone to 'correct' this situation 'in the most positive manner'.[128]

The legacy of 1963

The Kennedy administration attempted a transformation of US foreign policy. From top to bottom, Kennedy and his advisors believed that they could bring significant improvement to the baseline foreign policy handed them by Eisenhower. By 1963, it had become apparent that they had nothing to show for their efforts. The administration had failed to give proper consideration to or to try and understand exactly what the Eisenhower experience had been. Kennedy found himself pursuing policies that had failed eight years before. The relationship with Nasser provides a good example. Kennedy's early approach to Nasser had almost all of the goals and attributes of early Eisenhower efforts. As in the 1950s, Nasser and the UAR continued to pursue their goal of pan-Arab revolution. The UAR could not be enticed to make further compromises with Israel or to withdraw its forces from Yemen for any amount of aid. When pressured by the US to follow a certain policy, they defied Washington and ignored threats to cut off aid. In Iran, Kennedy's attempts to find an alternative to the Shah failed, and left the US identified more than ever with the Pahlavi regime. With US encouragement, the Shah then charged ahead with reform at such a frightening pace that it appeared to threaten his own survival. This situation left the reform-pushing Kennedy administration counseling caution and emphasizing the critical need for loyal military and security forces. With regard to India and Pakistan, the opportunity posed by the Sino-Indian border war turned into a mirage and worse. US pressure on India coupled with Washington's unwillingness to provide New Delhi with an indigenous manufacturing capability for advanced arms, resulted in a broad program of military cooperation between New Delhi and Moscow. In Pakistan, the limited arms that India did receive angered and frustrated Ayub Khan. To show his displeasure, Ayub opened relations with Communist China and accused President Kennedy of bad faith. For Kennedy and his advisors, 1963 saw virtually all of their ideas and hopes for the Greater Middle East unravel. The planned great opening to the non-aligned world collapsed with the down-turn in relations with India and the UAR. The situation in which the Kennedy administration found itself in 1963 was a far cry from where it had confidently assumed that it would be three years earlier. In fact, Kennedy found himself struggling just to maintain the more conservative policy positions established by Eisenhower between 1958 and 1960.

Conclusion: Reform and the Primacy of Containment

Global containment of the Soviet Union, China and indigenous Communist movements dominated US foreign policy for more than 40 years. The Truman administration created the first manifestation of this policy in its commitment to the defense of Western Europe and Japan coupled with strong support for economic development and reconstruction as a means of undermining Communism's political influence. This commitment to military confrontation, for example in Korea, or containment through deterrence represented by alliances like NATO and parallel programs for economic development and reconstruction like the Marshall Plan became the model for US Cold War policy. Although it was clear what this meant in terms of Western Europe and Japan, the exact form and substance of containment in the developing world was far more undefined.

The natural reaction of the Truman and later American administrations was to take the model for Europe, modify it and apply it to Latin America, Africa, the Far East, and the Greater Middle East. Remarkably, echoes of this same approach could be heard from neo-conservatives in the 21st century as they used the post-1945 experiences of Japan and Germany to justify their democratic "nation-building" in Iraq. With respect to the Truman years, historians have argued that this lack of policy definition sparked the Korean War and created a muddled situation in Indochina that led from the French to the American war in Vietnam. For more then 40 years, American administrations took the Truman model for Western Europe and Japan, used it as a baseline and, for better and worse, attempted to construct a Cold War policy paradigm for the developing world. Arguably, this policy transposition has continued with the blend of military force and economic assistance to combat the global asymmetric threats of the post-Cold War era. In the immediate post-World War II environment, it was an *ad hoc* learning process that reflected all the pitfalls of 'real-time', 'on-the-job' policy development and

CONCLUSION: REFORM AND THE PRIMACY OF CONTAINMENT 315

execution in cultural and political environments where Washington's politcial, cultural and social understanding of the situation was, to put it mildly, limited. Truman created a containment policy that held the line against Communist expansion in Western Europe and Japan, but he bequeathed to his successors the unenviable and complex task of creating a workable formula for containment in the developing world.

It would be the Eisenhower administration, through trial and error, that would develop and, to a large degree, institutionalize containment in Latin America, Africa, and the Greater Middle East. Later administrations might embellish or at times peripherally modify the policy approach, but attempts to substantially deviate from the course set by Eisenhower have not gone well. Almost universally, one of three results have occurred: a corrective return to Eisenhower's cautious policy course, as in Kennedy's experiences with Ayub, Nasser, and Nehru; a lasting policy complication, like Kennedy's policy shifts with regard to Israel and the Shah; or a outright disaster like that in Indochina.

In 1953, the Eisenhower administration arrived in Washington believing that long-term political stability and staunch anti-Communism could come only from economic development and political reform. Eisenhower believed that the new nationalisms of the Middle East and developing world had to be encouraged or, in some cases, tolerated and supported through economic-assistance programs and, if need be, military assistance. The initial emphasis lay clearly on the economic development. Eisenhower and Dulles believed that military assistance should conform to the requirements of internal security and order. This primacy of economic development and political reform as the best guarantor of containment and Western interests in the Middle East had strong support from White House advisors like Walt W. Rostow, who first served the Eisenhower administration and then became a key policy-maker in the Kennedy and Johnson administrations. Eisenhower clearly understood the limits of military power in shaping not only the struggle with the Soviet Union and global Communism but also the character of the developing world.

Between 1953 and 1955, the Eisenhower administration tried to implement this vision of containment. The administration attempted to use economic assistance to entice Egypt into the Middle East Defense Organization, obtain a solution to the Arab-Israeli problem, bring an end to the Kashmir dispute between India and Pakistan, and stymie Soviet attempts to penetrate the region. The United States pressured the Shah of Iran to reorient his focus from military expansion to developing the economy and on bringing social reform and political liberalization to Iran. Eisenhower and his advisors fundamentally accepted the idea that traditional regimes in the region would ultimately succumb to nationalist revolutions. Despite India's non-aligned status and antagonism with US policy, the administration strongly supported economic assistance and Nehru's focus on development. Eisenhower pushed Pakistan toward democracy, economic development, and social reform. In the developing world, adherence to a Western defensive organization represented more of a political commitment than a military one. Military aid to regional non-NATO allies was niggardly compared to economic assistance. Military aid was to pacify the various officer corps in order to maintain their political identification with the West and to encourage their support for economic and political development. The litany of complaints from members of the Baghdad Pact concerning the lack of military aid dominated the history of the organization through 1958. Even the crisis of 1956 failed to garner significantly more military aid for western aligned states. Initially, in Eisenhower's view, containment first required economic development, followed by political and social reform, and only enough military assistance to maintain internal stability.

The Baghdad Coup of July 1958 shifted the paradigm. A key pro-Western regime in the process of instituting reforms collapsed in revolution. Worse yet, what was thought to be a Nasserist revolution instead turned out to be a nationalist revolt strongly supported by the Iraqi Communist Party and the Soviet Union. Suddenly, short-term stability and a pro-Western political posture took priority over the longer-term theoretical benefits offered by economic development and the uncertainties of reform. This re-prioritization brought a shift in Washington's thinking about the importance of stability in the quest of reform. The maintenance of pro-Western stability became the baseline for economic development and political reform. This shift began a process in which the United States found itself increasingly identified with authoritarian monarchical or military regimes. In terms of military and economic aid, Iran and Pakistan were the greatest beneficiaries of 1958, but Jordan, Saudi Arabia, Kuwait, and others benefited as well. Fearing another Baghdad-style coup, the Eisenhower administration raised the priority of shoring up military loyalty and internal-security forces. Despite this, the administration continued to press for economic development: fear of unrest and instability brought a very cautious approach to reform. In 1959 and 1960, the Eisenhower administration adopted a more flexible approach to both the non-aligned and aligned states. Relations improved and economic assistance to the UAR and India increased, as did economic and military aid to aligned Pakistan, Iran, and Jordan. It was this proportionally greater and, therefore, much more visible increase in military aid that resulted in the Eisenhower administration being unfairly characterized as weak on economic development. The military aid constituted a pragmatic reaction to the events of 1958; it did not end Eisenhower's focus on economic development, but was instead a means to provide internal security and stability for the very economic development that Washington believed would maintain pro-Western regimes. It became an instrument for top-down reform and economic growth.

In 1961, when Kennedy took office, he inherited a pragmatic, functioning foreign policy, which he largely adopted. While Kennedy had run for office on a foreign policy platform that attacked Eisenhower and Dulles for their alleged blunders between 1955 and 1958, the adjustments made by the Eisenhower White House between 1958 and 1960 restored stability and direction to US policy in the Middle East. Containment remained the centerpiece of the US policy thrust, but the administration adjusted the application of those policies

CONCLUSION: REFORM AND THE PRIMACY OF CONTAINMENT 317

to meet the challenges of non-alignment and revolutionary nationalism. Despite these improvements, Kennedy and his advisors, including Rostow, believed that through superior management and sophisticated application of economics they could attain results that would far exceed those of Eisenhower and Dulles.

Instead of objectively assessing Eisenhower's policies of 1953 to 1955 and its failures, Kennedy and his advisors concluded that Eisenhower and Dulles had been too doctrinaire and lacked the creativity to achieve key US policy goals. As a result, the major Kennedy administration goals in the Middle East reflected those that had been tried by Eisenhower and had failed. Kennedy made the UAR the center of its efforts to achieve an Arab-Israeli peace, and attempted to dampen radical Arab nationalism by encouraging Cairo to focus on economic development. It was vintage Eisenhower *circa* 1953. Pushing the Shah toward economic development and away from his fixation on military assistance paralleled similar Eisenhower efforts. Kennedy, like Eisenhower, attempted to identify an alternative to the Shah's rule. The Kennedy administration also attempted to foster better relations with India and a more pro-Western orientation through economic assistance and the promise of military aid in return for a settlement of the Kashmir dispute with Pakistan. Eisenhower had entertained the same proposition. Kennedy, no less than Eisenhower, found himself tied to Ayub's regime in Karachi because of its key position in the Western alliance structure and because of intelligence sites critical to the strategic defense of the United States.

Given the similarities, what were the real differences between Eisenhower and Kennedy? Initially, Kennedy was over confident and lacked an appreciation for the degree of change that had occurred in the Middle East during the 1950s. As a result, he failed to learn from Eisenhower's setbacks. In one sense, Kennedy had the luxury of inheriting a set of relatively stable, functioning policies that Eisenhower had acquired by trial and error; but in another, Kennedy failed to apprehend the magnitude of the difficulties encountered during the 1950s, and as a result blamed Eisenhower and Dulles for policy shortcomings. This lack of objectivity and perspective condemned Kennedy and his administration to repeat many of Eisenhower's early mistakes.

The activist bent of the Kennedy administration also created problems. Eisenhower had learned through bitter experience that the Middle East often required a wait-and-see approach to developments. Kennedy's can-do attitude created an imperative to take a proactive approach to developments and issues. In addition, Kennedy attempted to become his own Secretary of State. He did not trust the foreign policy establishment and in a series of moves attempted to personalize foreign policy within the confines of the White House. In pronouncements that have a ring of George W. Bush, Kennedy and his advisors believed that the President's charisma and intelligence would win over other foreign leaders where traditional diplomacy and foreign policy give and take had failed. Kennedy did his best to remove foreign policy making from the State Department. He created a very tight-knit group of advisors. He reduced the NSC staff from 120 to 12 people in an attempt to centralize control in the Oval Office. While it must be noted that in sharp contrast to the second Bush, Kennedy's pragmatic flexibility and intense intellectual engagement allowed for much more timely shifts in policy, some of the initial similarities are striking. Against strong advice, Kennedy wanted to look Khrushchev "in the eye" in Vienna in 1961, a confrontation for which the president clearly was not prepared. In the end, it encouraged Khrushchev to gamble on putting missiles in Cuba with near disastrous results for all concerned. In his adroit handling of the crisis Kennedy was both brilliant and fortunate, but under Eisenhower, odds are that neither the Vienna meetings nor the Cuban Crisis would have occurred.

This personalized approach to foreign policy coupled with aggressive administration pronouncements and policies often brought exactly the opposite results from what was intended. Pressing Nasser on the issue of a settlement with Israel made the Egyptian leader vulnerable to criticism from his Arab rivals, including pro-Western Arab states. In 1961, despite warnings from Ambassador Wailes about supporting individual Iranian politicians, the US attempt to inflate the importance of Prime Minister Amini at the expense of the Shah left the US even more firmly identified with and dependent on the Pahlavi dynasty. Campaign rhetoric concerning support for India created a situation in which Kennedy had to demonstrate the importance of Pakistan to US interests. This, in turn, discredited Washington in Nehru's eyes. This credibility problem was further complicated by overt, even crude, attempts to leverage the border war with China into an Indian compromise on Kashmir. The overwhelming desire for action, to get something done, caused a series of miscalculations that actually undermined US stature and influence vis-à-vis the gains made by Eisenhower between 1958 and 1960. Arguably, by late 1963 the US position in the Greater Middle East had taken a clear step backward from its position in 1960 at the end of the Eisenhower era.

Lessons in containment and economic development, 1953-1958

The events of 1953 to 1958 underscored the prophetic accuracy of Eisenhower's 6 January 1953 conversation with then Prime Minister Winston Churchill. Eisenhower told the Prime Minister:

> Nationalism is on the march and world Communism is taking advantage of that spirit of nationalism to cause dissention in the free world. Moscow leads many misguided people to believe that they can count on Communist help to achieve and sustain nationalistic ambitions.

Eisenhower and Dulles recognized the problems associated with rising nationalism, British imperial baggage, and the Soviet threat. The administration believed that through astute policy management the US could successfully

CONCLUSION: REFORM AND THE PRIMACY OF CONTAINMENT

contain, and perhaps even undermine, Soviet influence. The key to long-term stability and a pro-Western political posture was economic development. The Eisenhower administration shared the views of Walt Rostow and others that economic assistance would foster economic self-sufficiency, which in turn would bring a pro-Western political orientation and hopefully stable democratic institutions. Eisenhower added: 'with our experience and power, [the US] will be required to support and carry the heavy burdens of decent international plans, as well as to aid infant nations towards self-dependence.' Eisenhower went on to say that this leadership required 'persuasion and example', 'patient negotiation, understanding and equality of treatment', and not a 'take it or leave it' approach.[1] Both he and Secretary Dulles viewed economic development as the most viable path to stability and a pro-Western orientation.

If economic development constituted the principal thrust of Eisenhower's containment policy, then why did the administration pressure states in the Middle East to join Western defensive alliances and provide military assistance? It has been on this point that Eisenhower's policies have been most misunderstood, misrepresented, and criticized. Whether the Baghdad Pact or SEATO, Western defensive alliances constituted political rather than military organizations. Adherence to the Western alliances represented a statement of pro-Western political orientation and solidarity. No one in Washington, and certainly not President Eisenhower, believed that any of the members of the pro-Western defense pacts, either alone or collectively, could stand up to the Soviet Union. For this reason, military aid was limited. For example, the members of the Baghdad Pact continually complained about the lack of military assistance, the lack of a command structure, and the utter ineffectiveness of the organization as a real military alliance. Washington quite simply saw little or no military value-added in the pacts. Military aid was either intended to placate the various military establishments or provide for internal security, or both. Between 1953 and 1958, Eisenhower avoided large-scale military assistance that provided any real offensive capability. Military assistance was to provide enough internal stability and control to allow for economic development, the real guarantor of long-term stability and containment.

The situation with Egypt represented a clear case in point. It was the unwillingness of the Eisenhower administration to provide sufficient military assistance to Egypt – in order that Cairo might challenge Israel – that brought on the Czech arms deal. This precipitated a crisis in relations with the West that ultimately led to the nationalization of the Suez Canal and the resulting Anglo-French-Israeli debacle of 1956. Historians have often credited Nasser's unwillingness to join a Western defense pact as the Eisenhower administration's primary reason for not supplying arms to Egypt. In reality, had Nasser joined a Western pact, Egypt would not have received either the quality or quantity of arms that it sought to confront Israel. Eisenhower intended to limit arms and military assistance to the essentials required for internal security.

Between 1953 and 1958, no country in the Western alliance system in the Greater Middle East was satisfied with the level of military assistance provided by Washington; Egypt would have been no different. The Eisenhower administration steadfastly refused to contribute to an arms race in the region, preferring instead to offer economic aid and to encourage economic development. Nasser could not get what he wanted, so he turned to the Soviet Union.

Nasser's realization that sufficient arms would not be forthcoming from the West provided an additional impetus toward non-alignment. The situation became more complicated when the Turko-Iraq Pact of 1955 led to the creation of the Baghdad Pact. Now the West had refused to arm Egypt while arming its Iraqi rival. The Israeli raid on Gaza in February 1955 merely iced Nasser's cake. Now he faced an immediate threat to his rule from Western-supported Israel, while Washington was unwilling to provide arms for Egypt's defense. The Soviets were the natural choice to provide what the West would not. In Nehru's case, the US arms for Pakistan under the 1954 Turko-Pakistan alliance placed him squarely at odds with the Eisenhower administration. No matter how limited in scope, Washington had not only armed India's bitter enemy, but had also attacked the very ideological foundations of Nehru's view of the developing world's place in the Cold War environment. Ultimately, Nehru too would turn to the Soviets as a counter-balance. In a real sense, the pro-Western northern-tier alliance linked Indian and Egyptian interests at a critical historical moment. The governments in Cairo and New Delhi were attempting to consolidate internal political power in the face of potentially serious opposition, while at the same time facing what they viewed as external threats funded by Washington. No amount of economic aid could compensate for the political pressure created by insufficient arms for Egypt and any amount of arms for Pakistan. For Nasser, the *quid pro quo* for cooperation with the West would not be what he needed in the way of arms, and would probably cost him the support of the Egyptian military, a potentially fatal political development. For Nehru, US military aid for Pakistan and the Kashmir problem, threatened India's very integrity. Despite their differing political practices and ideological proclivities, Nehru's and Nasser's confluence of political interest at the 1955 Bandung conference produced a revolution in Middle East politics. Bandung provided the crowning blow to the Eisenhower administration's initial plans for the defense of the Greater Middle East. Egypt provided India with an effective counter-balance to Pakistani influence in the Islamic and Arab states, and Nehru provided Nasser with global stature and, most of all, a Chinese mid-wife in the form of Chou En-Lai for the delivery of Soviet arms.

Egyptian-Indian policy also profoundly affected Western allies in the region. Countries like Iran, Pakistan, Jordan, and Saudi Arabia learned to barter their allegiance in ever-escalating demands for economic and military aid from the United States. While Washington continued to push economic development and reform, its allies pressed for arms to compete with their non-aligned neighbors or with the Soviet threat. Ultimately, Washington found that influencing even its allies became increasingly difficult as it attempted to maintain a balance between the demands of its erstwhile allies and their actual needs. US parsimony generated threats to quit the Baghdad Pact from Iraq, Iran, and Pakistan. Eisenhower's good intentions in 1953 for economic development and an Arab-Israeli peace had degenerated into confrontations with Nehru and Nasser, the leaders of what Eisenhower and Dulles believed to be the two most important states in the region. Eisenhower moved, from faith in the power of economic development to influence not only the political process but also the political orientation of states in the Middle East, to a more realistic view that took into account the balance between economic development and political considerations generated by regional rivalries.

Containment revamped 1958-1960

Despite these problems, Eisenhower and Dulles never lost sight of their goals in the Middle East. In the post-Suez, Eisenhower Doctrine environment, with expectations scaled back, they sought to regenerate working relationships with Nehru and Nasser. Military aid was out of the question. As a result, the administration once again focused on economic development. Eisenhower and his advisors hoped to correct the inability of the US to project the good intentions of its policies properly, and thereby gain greater acceptance from non-aligned and nationalist movements. By late 1957, Nasser's rejection of the Eisenhower Doctrine, Nehru's refusal to compromise with the US over Kashmir, and widespread instability among the pro-Western regimes in the Greater Middle East forced a major re-evaluation of US policy.

In February 1958, the union between Syria and Egypt and the formation of the United Arab Republic accelerated the process. Washington might have arrived at the same policy course in its own good time, but Nasser's diplomatic coup brought an immediate shift in US policy toward the new UAR. Believing that it was only a matter of time before pro-Western regimes in the region collapsed and joined the UAR or defected to the neutralist camp, Eisenhower decided to resurrect a working relationship with Cairo, using economic and financial incentives. Eisenhower and Dulles were still conflicted about working with Nasser. On the one hand, Washington courted him, while on the other it encouraged Iraq, Saudi Arabia, Lebanon, and Jordan to resist UAR pressure. This desire for improved relations with the UAR realistically adopted a case-by-case approach. Based on his experience over the previous five years, Eisenhower had decided on a more flexible but conservative course that allowed the US to improve ties with Egypt and India while pursuing its strategic Cold War objectives in the region. The administration had no expectation of major breakthroughs with regard to Nasser's revolutionary activities, the Arab-Israeli dispute, Nehru's non-alignment, or the Kashmir dispute, but it hoped to garner limited influence from economic and financial aid.

Then, on 14 July 1958, Brigadier Qasim's detour through Baghdad destroyed the Hashemite regime and most of what remained of British prestige in the Middle East. If Iraq's entry into the Western security system had sent tremors through the region, its exit was an earthquake. The British were more than willing to settle for a new arrangement with Qasim that protected their oil interests. In the confusion that followed, Eisenhower, assuming Nasser was behind the coup, ordered a military operation to support the Lebanese government against intervention from the Syrian part of the UAR. The US also pressed the British to provide similar support to Jordan. Fearing US intervention in Syria, Nasser sought immediate Soviet support and lambasted Anglo-American intervention. This situation threatened to wreck improved ties between Cairo and Washington as the effects of the Iraqi coup rippled across the northern tier, undermining improving US-Indian relations.

Fearing the collapse of the Western alliance system and of containment, the White House immediately increased the flow of military and economic aid to what remained of the Baghdad Pact. The administration continued to believe that economic development and reform held the key to long-term, pro-Western stability, but Washington's focus shifted dramatically to the short-term perspective, namely the survival of pro-Western regimes. As a result, Eisenhower put a priority on stability, economic development, and controlled reform, in that order. Economic and military aid to Pakistan and Iran increased dramatically. The aversion to engendering New Delhi's ill will largely disappeared; Pakistan was simply too important to US security and intelligence interests. In October 1958, Pakistan became even more attractive as an ally when General Ayub Khan replaced the dysfunctional civilian government in a military coup. Military rule stabilized the situation in Karachi, providing what the White House hoped would be a stable environment conducive to economic development and safe reform. Unfortunately for Nehru, he could ill-afford to risk a break with the US. Not only did India need US aid, but it also faced an increasingly threatening dispute with Beijing along its northern border. In Cairo, Nasser was also obliged to look the other way, given the increasing enmity between the Qasim regime in Baghdad and the UAR.

For Iran, the collapse of Iraq was a transformational experience. Bouts of depression and vacillation aside, the Shah had become the real center of political gravity for containment. Survival of a pro-Western regime, if not the Pahlavi dynasty, became an absolute priority in Washington. As a part of its conservative approach to Iran, the Eisenhower administration assiduously avoided direct commitments to either the Shah or his dynasty. Washington wanted to maintain the option of supporting a more broadly based pro-Western ruler, on the off chance that such an alternative might arise. As a result, the White House assured Tehran that the United States was committed to the 'independence' and 'territorial integrity' of Iran, not the Pahlavi dynasty. The inability or unwillingness of the Shah to bring constructive change frustrated the administration. As a result, the US provided the minimum amount of aid necessary to maintain the Tehran regime. The Shah deeply resented and vigorously complained about the niggardly dole from Washington, particularly for the military. The Iraqi coup was a godsend for the Peacock Throne. The Shah recognized the opportunity immediately, and began to demand additional military and economic support. He interspersed these demands with random soliloquies about the virtues of non-alignment and accommodations with Moscow. Bluff or not, the Eisenhower administration was in no position to take a chance, dramatically increasing economic and military aid.

In addition, the Iraqi coup had an unexpectedly positive impact on US-UAR relations. Within weeks of the coup, Qasim and his Communist allies began to undermine Nasserist elements in the government. As disagreements escalated, Nasser found himself under increasing attack from Baghdad, while his supporters in Iraq found themselves in prison or worse. Strong Communist support for the Qasim government also brought strong Soviet support and military aid from Moscow. From Khrushchev's perspective, he finally had an Arab client who did not hang Communists as an avocation. In the ensuing Arab Cold War, the hostility between Nasser and Qasim spread to the UAR's relations with the Soviet Union. Much to the delight of the Eisenhower administration, Nasser finally shared Washington's concern about the threat of Communism. Ironically, the British once again faced a situation in which Nasser, with the encouragement and assistance of the Eisenhower administration, was bent on undermining Qasim, whose fall would threaten British petroleum interests in Iraq. The US and UAR found themselves on even better terms because of the political synergy created by their joint aversion to Qasim's Iraq. The Eisenhower administration suffered no misconceptions about the depth of cooperation. Washington and Cairo had a mutual problem in Iraq, but there was no expectation that cooperation on Iraq or compromises over the situation in Lebanon would translate into solutions for more vexing regional problems like the Arab-Israeli dispute.

Between 1958 and 1960, the Eisenhower administration constructed a pragmatic Middle East policy based on lowered expectations and cooperation with India and Egypt. The White House really believed that, no matter how problematic it might at times become, a working relationship with Nasser and Nehru was critical to US interests in the region. This realization was in fact an acknowledgement that the region had undergone a fundamentally revolutionary change. In 1953, both the President and Dulles had recognized the nature of the coming change, but their strategies were overwhelmed by its complexity. Between 1958 and 1960, they reconstructed US relations in the Middle East based on new political realities and more limited goals. At the same time, they managed to maintain the fundamentals of their containment strategy with regard to the Soviet Union. By December 1960, with the knowledge that things could have been far worse, Eisenhower could look back with satisfaction on the progress that had been made since 1958, particularly in US relations with Egypt and India. The policies of 1958 to 1960 did not include dramatic breakthroughs, but they were balanced and workable.

Through eight very tough years of policy ups and downs, the Eisenhower administration had learned that some regional problems were simply insoluble, that the situation was usually neither as bad nor as promising as it appeared, and that the US had little leverage, economic or otherwise, to force solutions. Thus, tactical muddling-through usually provided the only option. January 1961 would bring a new administration and its own understanding of the lessons of the Eisenhower years.

Kennedy's Middle East and the Eisenhower legacy

In January 1961, the Kennedy administration had the options of continuing with Eisenhower's conservative but workable foreign policy in the Middle East, or embarking on the series of activist initiatives proposed during the presidential campaign, or both. In an almost exact reflection of Eisenhower's attitudes about Truman in 1953, the Kennedy administration arrived in Washington determined to replace what they considered the lethargy and mismanagement of the Eisenhower administration with activist programs. Kennedy and his team intended to get things done. Just as Eisenhower and Dulles had believed that their ability to manage foreign policy would immeasurably enhance US interests, so Kennedy believed that his technocrats and intellectuals would correct the shortsighted policies of the past and open a new era of US influence in the developing world – the 'pay any price, bear any burden' approach. In an intellectually selective way, the new administration viewed US Middle East policy in terms of the turmoil of 1955 to 1958, rather than over the continuum of the entire Eisenhower period. They also ignored the fact that the junior senator from Massachusetts had often supported Eisenhower's policies when the majority of Democrats had opposed them. Here again was a rough parallel with the Eisenhower administration's arrival in 1953. Eisenhower criticized the very Truman policies that he had helped create as NATO Supreme Commander.

Given the close election, no one could expect Kennedy and his advisors to compliment Eisenhower on the improving situation in the Middle East after 1958, but once in power, a more even-handed evaluation of US policy from a broader context would have provided the White House with a better understanding of how that policy had arrived at its current juncture. Instead, Kennedy took office committed to correcting what he viewed as the mistakes of the past. He wanted to translate into policy his campaign rhetoric about the importance of India, the UAR, an Arab-Israeli settlement, and an accommodation with non-alignment. Distrusting the traditional channels of foreign policy development, Kennedy brought with him a cadre of experts and technocrats who believed that they had the answers. Using these outsiders, Kennedy sought to bypass the bureaucracy and put his personal stamp on US foreign policy. Thus, a small group of 'experts' attempted to reshape policy largely without the benefit of an objective evaluation of what had gone before. In the Middle East, the quiescence of the Arab-Israeli dispute, the shared views of Nasser and Eisenhower on Iraq, and growing Indian preoccupation with

China tended to mask the chronic nature of regional conflicts. The situation created the illusion that key states in the region were actually moving toward more moderate positions and away from confrontation or revolutionary agitation.

As a result, Kennedy and his foreign policy advisors concluded that more activist policies could result in major gains. For example, Kennedy advocated more aid to India, criticizing Eisenhower for ignoring the importance of Indian economic development. The new administration arrived to find an extensive aid program in place, which Rostow and other Kennedy advisors believed required no additional funding.[2] During the campaign Kennedy had advocated economic aid to the UAR in an attempt to turn Egypt away from revolutionary activity and toward economic development. The new administration arrived in office to find aid programs already in place, including a large Public Law 480 wheat-purchase program. Kennedy pronouncements about a new opening to the non-aligned countries had raised the expectations of both Nasser and Nehru. When Washington deemed the existing programs sufficient, there was a sense of disappointment and a feeling that the New Frontier largely represented a continuation of Eisenhower policies.

This is not to say that Kennedy's activism had no impact. It did, but usually not the impact desired. The Eisenhower administration had learned from bitter experience between 1953 and 1955 that aid often translated into only limited leverage in the Middle East, and the new administration failed to learn from that experience. Like Eisenhower and Dulles in 1953, Kennedy was far too optimistic about economic aid generating a political *quid pro quo*. For example, Kennedy concluded that US aid and an increased Egyptian focus on economic development would open the door to an Arab-Israeli peace settlement. He failed to consider that funding for Aswan had not altered Nasser's arms deal with the Soviet Union or his Arab nationalist policies. Aid had little effect on Ben-Gurion, who was even more opposed to a settlement. The new foreign policy team also saw positive potential in escalating problems between India and China. With increasing aggressiveness, the administration attempted to exploit the growing rift and later the border war itself. First, Washington attempted to gain Indian support in opposing North Vietnamese and Chinese policy in Laos and Vietnam, and then attempted to use the border war itself to leverage a settlement of the Kashmir issue with Pakistan. This effort only succeeded in worsening relations with New Delhi. Across the board, the administration's efforts to find solutions to chronic regional problems failed.

These same activist policies that were to improve relations with non-aligned India and the UAR precipitated a series of problems between Washington and its allies in the region. Neither the Shah nor Ayub Khan were particularly enamored of Kennedy's campaign pronouncements about increased support for non-aligned states. In Pakistan, pro-India statements by candidate Kennedy necessitated an immediate campaign to reassure Iran and Pakistan of continued US support. Kennedy was no less committed as a Cold Warrior than Eisenhower, and he had every intention of keeping Pakistan and Iran in the

Western camp. In fact, Kennedy had to be even more circumspect about maintaining the Western alliance system than Eisenhower. The latter's stature as a famous military figure provided him with a latitude vis-à-vis security issues that Kennedy did not enjoy. Thus a move by any significant US ally in the Greater Middle East toward neutrality or accommodation with the Soviet Union constituted a major credibility problem for the Kennedy administration.

With regard to Pakistan, word of Ayub's unhappiness with Washington prompted high-level reassurances from Washington that US policy had not changed. Kennedy could ill-afford to lose the hinge between CENTO and SEATO. Worried, Kennedy's effusive assurances of support in 1961 for Pakistan and for a compromise settlement of the Kashmir dispute did little to endear the administration to Nehru. In Iran, the Kennedy administration, like Eisenhower's before it, started off with a crisis. Where Eisenhower and Churchill toppled the Musaddiq government, unrest resulted in Kennedy's open support for Prime Minister Ali Amini. This move in favor of a specific Iranian politician departed significantly from past policy. Despite Eisenhower and Dulles' role in placing the Shah back on the throne in 1953, the US had refused to provide specific support to any politician in Iran, including the Shah. Under Eisenhower, Washington supported only the independence and territorial integrity of Iran. The administration believed that it needed options, given the political instability of the regime and its disappointing track record with regard to reform. Having removed the day-to-day management of the Iranian crisis from the State Department and placed it under a special Iran Task Force, the more limited group concluded that Amini was the 'last hope' and that his survival required direct US support. As a result, the administration committed to supporting a particular Iranian politician, who, as it turned out, was totally reliant on the Shah for survival. When Amini fell, the administration found itself tied even more firmly to the Shah. Now US interests in Iran were irrevocably tied to the Pahlavi dynasty.

The Kennedy administration's failure to appreciate the parallels between its plans and those that had failed during the Eisenhower administration two years earlier constituted a clear case of political myopia. Kennedy's desire to influence India and Egypt through economic aid mimicked that of Eisenhower and Dulles, as did his conspicuous lack of success. The plan to bring about an Arab-Israeli peace was stillborn. In Iran, crises greeted both administrations. Eisenhower put the Shah back on his throne because he lacked another realistic option. In the end, Kennedy's direct support for Amini backfired, and tied US fortunes directly to the Pahlavi dynasty. The collapse of the Syrian union ushered in a revolutionary surge on Nasser's part that ultimately led to the Yemen revolution and strained US relations with the UAR and its allies, Saudi Arabia, Jordan, and Britain. The 1963 Ba'thist coups in Iraq and Syria created regimes less objectionable to Washington and independent of UAR control. Resenting Western support for the new Iraqi regime, and suspecting that the US and Britain had attempted to undermine Arab unity talks in March and April 1963, UAR policy gravitated toward a renewal of closer relations with Moscow. With regard to India, the euphoria created in Washington by the border war with China dissipated rapidly. The thinly-veiled attempt to force an agreement over Pakistan angered Nehru, and when the threat passed, drove India into the close military relationship with Moscow that continues to this day. The modest provision of US arms to India and Washington's failure to pressure New Delhi successfully during the China crisis sparked simmering resentment in Karachi, and soured US-Pakistani relations.

By November 1963, the US position was weaker than when Kennedy took office. The realities of US Cold War commitments came into conflict with the same regional political realities that had plagued Eisenhower and Dulles. The US position with the key non-aligned states of the region, India and the UAR, was in tatters. New Delhi and Cairo had turned to broad military assistance and economic cooperation programs with the Soviet Union. Following the Chinese border war, undisguised US pressure to compromise on Kashmir in return for arms had pushed New Delhi into an arrangement with the Soviets. Upset by limited US military aid to India, Pakistan now pursued closer relations with Beijing. Nasser concluded that the combination of Saudi Arabian oil and increasing Israeli domestic political pressure on Kennedy left little to be gained in better relations with Washington. In the Arab Middle East, the traditional regimes of Jordan and Saudi Arabia and the clients of the British were now the principal US allies. Ties with Israel had strengthened, further isolating the US from Lebanon, Syria, and Iraq. In Iran, the fortunes of the Shah would now determine those of the US as well.

Convinced of their intellectual and management superiority, Kennedy and his advisors misunderstood the broader political context in the region. Often relying on personal diplomacy, Kennedy and his advisors seemed oblivious to the fact that their initiatives were almost identical to the failed Eisenhower initiatives of 1953 through 1955. Like Eisenhower in 1953, the Kennedy administration imagined itself to be fundamentally different from and superior to its predecessor. In reality, Kennedy was bound by Eisenhower's policies emphasizing economic development, coupled with the necessity of military assistance for internal security.

Eisenhower, Dulles, and Herter weathered the turmoil of the Greater Middle East during the 1950s, and emerged on the other side of Macmillan's 'tempest' with the Western alliance system largely intact. Eisenhower successfully blunted Soviet expansion and, after 1958, maintained reasonable working relationships with India and the UAR. In the process, the United States largely displaced the British as the guardians of Western interests in the Middle East, and did so with relatively little political or economic dislocation. They pushed for change in Iran, Saudi Arabia, and Pakistan, and settled on a policy of top-down reform. Kennedy inherited the Eisenhower policies. Where Kennedy maintained Eisenhower's limited goals, things went well. Where he pushed for more activist approaches, he usually repeated Eisenhower's failures. Kennedy learned that pressure on Nehru and Nasser brought negative results. He learned that neither the Arabs nor Israel really wanted a peace settlement.

He learned that personal diplomacy put the prestige of the presidency on the line, and often backfired. And by November 1963, Kennedy learned, as Eisenhower had in 1953-1956, that chronic regional problems were largely unsolvable and that no amount of economic or military aid could force a settlement. Kennedy learned that the maintenance of US containment strategy in the Middle East required a pragmatic, deliberate approach, tempered by limited expectations. Political conflicts and regional rivalries took precedence over any amount of economic or military aid. As his initiatives failed or personal diplomacy faltered, Kennedy had the ultimate foreign policy establishment insider there to re-engage the issues, namely Secretary of State Dean Rusk. Presidential interest in personal diplomacy receded in parallel with the potential for spectacular success. President Kennedy was still very much engaged but Rusk and the traditional bureaucracy had been restored to its position of influence. Kennedy's death in November 1963 served to accelerate this trend under Johnson. With no pretensions about personal diplomacy, Johnson relinquished the everyday control of foreign policy to his hold-over Kennedy advisors who now controlled the traditional bureaucracy. In the Greater Middle East, the Kennedy experience and Vietnam resulted in a more conservative set of policies that focused on allies in the region and that held a narrower view of US interests. This would eventually evolve into the so-called pillar policy, the remnants of which have continued into the 21st century.

NOTES

1 Rostow, Walt W. and Max F. Millikan, *A Proposal: Key to an Effective Foreign Policy*. New York: Harper, 1957, pp. 140-141.
2 Ibid, pp. 44-48.
3 Klaus Larres, in *Churchill's Cold War: The Politics of Personal Diplomacy* (New Haven: Yale University Press, 2002), pp. 200-210, 254, argues that it was Eisenhower and not Churchill that took the initiative in attempting to exploit Stalin's death in March 1953. He paints the Eisenhower administration as the real hardcore anti-Communists. In reality Churchill's anti-Communism was selective. Larres manages to avoid mentioning the fact that it was Churchill, in 1953 and 1954, who advocated getting rid of Musaddiq in Iran and the Egyptian government, Neguib or Nasser, because of the opening that, in his view, both provided to the Communists. Larres makes it clear that while John Foster Dulles and Charles E. Wilson, the strongly anti-Communism Secretary of Defense, argued that the use of 'liberation rhetoric' could have dangerous repercussions and urged caution, others in the administration, including Rostow, saw Stalin's death as 'the really first big propaganda opportunity'. Fearing a Soviet peace initiative that might endanger French ratification of the European Defense Community (EDC), Rostow, who was serving as an *ad hoc* member of C.D. Jackson's Psychological Strategy Board (PSB), drafted a speech for Eisenhower designed to forestall any Soviet overtures. It called for free elections in Germany, a solution to the Austrian problem, and high-level talks on disarmament. It made any high-level meetings with the new Soviet leadership contingent on the Soviets ending the Korean War. Rostow was clearly in the hard-line camp, and played a key role in countering Soviet Premier Georgi Malenkov's 'peace campaign'. Larres describes Rostow and his boss in the PSB, C.D. Jackson, as 'Eisenhower's trusted associates' and the driving force behind 'plans for a psychological warfare offensive' aimed at Moscow. This underscores the fact that from the very beginning, Rostow was heavily involved, at the highest levels of the Eisenhower administration, with critical policy issues related to contaianment and anti-Soviet policies. Rostow's association with both the Eisenhower and Kennedy administrations also supports the contention that a strong relationship existed between the policies of both with regard to the relationship between economic development, political reform, and the over-arching strategy of containment. In *Europe After Stalin: Eisenhower's Three Decisions of March 11, 1953* (Austin: University of Texas Press, 1982), pp. 6-7, 55, 65, 69-83, Rostow's view of the PSB and its activities differs significantly from that of Larres. Rostow states that the PSB, including himself and C.D. Jackson, strongly supported a

summit conference with the Soviet leadership immediately following the death of Stalin. He argues that it would have headed off the Soviet 'peace initiative', and might have resulted in the unification of Germany on terms favorable to the West. Rostow emphasizes Eisenhower's inclination in April 1953 to seek a breakthrough with the Soviet Union, stating: 'We are in an arms race. Where will it lead us? At worst, to atomic warfare. At best, to robbing every people and nation on earth of the fruits of their own toil. ... Now, there can be another road before us – the road of disarmament. What does this mean? It means for everybody in the world: bread, butter, clothes, homes, hospitals, schools – all the good and necessary things for decent living. So let this be the choice we offer.' On March 11, Eisenhower made three decisions: he rejected a summit with the Soviets; he decided to give a speech to 'give the people of the world hope for peace'; and he called for a 'Western' summit to discuss what course of action to take. What happened to Eisenhower's sentiments for ending the arms race? Rostow provides several explanations. Churchill's intervention and suggestions were believed to be premature, and even Macmillan and Eden expressed concerns in that regard; Eisenhower functioned in staff mode and allowed controversial decisions to sort themselves out, thus precluding a decisive initiative from the top. The President, Dulles, and the State Department had all criticized 'summitry' in the form of Yalta and Potsdam and were afraid of domestic 'right-wing' Republican criticism and the rising influence of Senator Joseph McCarthy. Finally, there was concern that negotiations with the Soviet leadership might undermine Western European support for the EDC. These differences in interpretation notwithstanding, the fact remains that Rostow played an important part as a 'Cold Warrior' in the policy-formulation process in the Eisenhower administration. At times, he may have advocated a more aggressive approach to engaging the Soviets but it was always with the same strategic view of subverting the Soviet empire. This work is well worth reading for a well-documented perspective on the decisions of March 11 and a birds-eye view of Rostow's early involvement with Cold War policy and the Eisenhower administration. See also Rostow's *The Dynamics of Soviet Society* (New York: Norton, 1953) pp. 231-259. Rostow analyzed Soviet society in light of the expected departure of Stalin from the political scene. Completed just prior to Stalin's death, Rostow revised the last chapter after it. Entitled 'Post-Stalin', it was intended to 'take stock of the position within the Soviet union as of the interim date May 15, 1953'. The author cited five 'elements making for change' and, while warning that the regime continued to possess the levers of power necessary for control, he argued that 'conflict at the top of the Soviet structure' would potentially 'bring them into play' enhancing the potential for a 'more peaceful and stable world ... (in) accord with our interests'. Given the timing of this book and the views on Soviet society expressed therein, it is evident why he was selected to participate on the PSB. The work provides a useful glimpse into the thinking the drove policy advisors and the Eisenhower administration in the immediate aftermath of Stalin's death. Rostow's book *The Process of Economic Growth* (New York: Norton, 1952) also increased the level of his participation in early Eisenhower policy planning. Written from research generated in a graduate seminar at MIT in 1950-1951, the work includes a detailed discussion of 'The Take-off into Self-sustained Growth'. Rostow attempts to explain within a historical context the phenomenon of economic development. His discussions of stages of growth and the requirements for transition from one stage to another caught the attention initially of Eisenhower's and later of Kennedy's administration. The book provides insight into the importance of economic development as a policy pillar in both administrations. It was revised and reprinted in 1960 and 1962.

4 Iraq from 1958 to 1961 was the one exception to this rule. In an effort to preserve their oil interests, the British maintained a working relationship with Abd-al-Karim al-Qasim's regime, despite its reliance on Communist Party support, and pressed the US

to be more accommodating as well. When Iraq threatened to invade Kuwait in 1961, British policy shifted to an anti-Qasim stance closely in line with that of the US. Ideology and association with the Communists drove US policy, while economic interests drove the British.
5 'Muhammad Musaddiq, Man of the Year'. *Time*, 7 January 1952, p. 59.
6 Macmillan, Harold, *Tides of Fortune, 1945-1955*. New York: Harper & Row, 1969, p. 141.

Chapter 1

1 Eisenhower, Dwight D., *The White House Years: Mandate for Change 1953-1956*. New York: Doubleday, 1963, p. 142. In 1952, as Eisenhower was leaving his post at SHAPE, he stopped in London for talks with Churchill and Foreign Secretary Anthony Eden. With the Prime Minister's blessing, Eden had broached the subject of the new potential American Secretary of State and 'expressed the hope that [Eisenhower] might appoint someone other than Dulles.' Eisenhower informed them that 'he knew of no other American so well qualified' to become Secretary of State. Harold Macmillan, in *The Blast of War 1939-1945*, makes it plain that the British concerns about Dulles began with their contacts with him during the Second World War. In July 1942, in discussing the Caribbean situation as a part of the Anglo-American Caribbean Commission, Dulles told the Colonial Secretary that 'American public opinion regarding the British Colonial Empire' harbored a 'deeply embedded ... fundamental distrust of what they called 'British Imperialism'.' Dulles told the British that 'it was utterly futile' for London to try to convince the US public of the benefits of colonialism. Only through working in cooperation with the US to better the lot of developing nations could something positive be achieved. (See pp. 133-134.)
2 Ferrell, Robert H. (ed.), *The Eisenhower Diaries*. New York: Norton, 1981, p. 221. In 1951, Dulles worked on Far East issues for the Truman administration. British Foreign Minister Herbert Morrison believed that Dulles had acted duplicitously on a series of issues, including the trilateral ANZUS Pact with New Zealand and Australia that excluded Britain, a bilateral pact with Japan that did not (as Dulles had promised) allow Japan to make its own choice about recognizing one of the two Chinas, and a bilateral pact with the Phillipines that excluded Hong Kong and Malaya. (See Hoopes, Townsend *The Devil and John Foster Dulles*. Boston, MA: Little, Brown, 1973, pp. 107-109.) This lack of trust in Dulles reflected itself in Eden's relationships with him. On 13 November 1952, Eden met with Dulles, who asserted that the Western nations had to present a united front in dealing with non-Western problems in the developing world. Eden agreed, but he may have been alerted by Herbert Morrison that Dulles could not be trusted, undermining any real willingness on Eden's part to work with the Secretary of State. (See Ovendale, Richey, *Britain, the United States, and the Transfer of Power in the Middle East, 1945-1962*. London: Leicester University Press, 1996, p. 63.)
3 It should be noted that the British readily accepted Dulles' view of the Middle East as encompassing the Arabic-speaking states, Turkey, Iran and Pakistan, and stretching to the borders of India. In fact, in traditional British parlance, the 'Middle East' referred to the Persian Gulf and what is now referred to as Southwest Asia. Just as Britain worried about the political connectivity and the impact of events in the Arab Middle East on the situation in Iran, Afghanistan, and British India in the 19th and early 20th centuries, the Eisenhower and Kennedy administrations also treated the region as politically, economically, and culturally connected in the mid-20th century. Policy-makers then broke their responsibilities down by sub-regions and 'country desks'. This conceptualization varied between agencies, but even these variances tended to underscore the view of an overall cohesiveness of the broader region. As a case in point, the State Department lumped Greece together with the Middle East, in a desk that had responsibility for Greece, Turkey, and Iran. Because of the NATO connection,

the CIA placed Greece and Turkey in Europe and Iran in its Near East Division, which also included Pakistan and India. The State Department also placed Pakistan and India in the same bureau, that of Near Eastern and South Asian Affairs. The State Department placed North Africa, with the exception of Egypt and sometimes Libya, into the Africa bureau, while the CIA placed all the Arabic-speaking countries in the Near East Division. At the NSC level, these slight organizational differences were totally transparent because the same set of experts had responsibility for what amounted to the Muslim Middle East – Morocco to Pakistan and India, and often beyond to Southeast Asia. Thus the historical view of the region contributed not only to connectivity in policy formulation, but also to the bureaucratic organizational structure set up to deal with the region, which tended to reinforce this broader conceptualization of region. While there were peripheral organizational differences, a cohesive core existed based on Egypt, the Levant, Arabia, the Persian Gulf, Iran, Pakistan, and India. That is what principally concerns this study.

4 Louis, W. Roger, *The British Empire in the Middle East 1945-1951*. Oxford: Oxford University Press, 1984, pp. 54-102. Louis's work lays out the various schemes through which the British hoped to maintain their influence in the Arab Middle East and Persian Gulf under the Labour government of Clement Atlee, 1945-1951. He points out that Atlee's government had no desire to pull out of the Middle East or to allow independent states to pursue policies detrimental to British interests. Rather, the Labour government hoped to use regional collective security arrangements to maintain its influence and indirect control. Churchill's overarching foreign policy goals, namely British influence and control, were the same; Churchill was merely more willing to use coercive means to accomplish them. See 'Diary Entry by Eisenhower about a foreign policy meeting with Dulles, 10 January 1953'. DDEL, AWF, AWD Series, Box 9, p. 2. The entry, on a January 10 strategy meeting on foreign policy in the Middle East, indicates clear frustration with the British version of the 'northern tier'. Dulles and Eisenhower opposed the British plan to include Arab states and criticized London's ignoring of US advice on the dangers of 'pressuring' Jordan to join the 'Northern Tier Pact'. Eisenhower fumed that the British 'went blindly ahead', and domestic riots forced the Jordanians to withdraw, not only handing London a diplomatic defeat but also, clearly more annoying, making the United States, as well as Britain, the focus of local unrest.
5 'DDE Diary Entry, 8 February 1953'. DDEL, AWF, AWD Series, Box 9, p. 2.
6 'DDE Diary Entry, 6 January 1953'. DDEL, AWF, AWD, Box 9, pp. 4-6.
7 Interview with Walt Rostow, 12 June 2002. Rostow served as an advisor to the Eisenhower administration from 1953 to 1958. He stated that Eisenhower favored the use of economic aid and modernization as the best defense against Communist infiltration in the developing world, but that in the the first administration he never asserted himself with the 'right-wing' of the Republican Party, which, in Rostow's view, staunchly opposed them.
8 'DDE Diary Entry, 6 January 1953'. DDEL, AWF, AWD, Box 9, pp. 6-7.
9 Ibid, p. 7.
10 'DDE Diary Entry, 10 January 1953'. DDEL, AWF, AWD Series, Box 9, p. 2. See also 'DDE Diary Entry, 8 February 1953'. DDEL, AWF, AWD, Box 9, p. 2. On February 8, in talks with Anthony Eden, the British Foreign Secretary, Eisenhower recommended that the British attempt to settle the Buraimi Oasis issue with Saudi Arabia by direct high-level talks, and reaffirmed American support for the tripartite agreement of May 25, 1950 made by France, Britain, and the United States on controlling potential Arab-Israeli hostilities. The exchange leaves the impression that Eisenhower sought to warn the British against a more aggressive approach to its regional problems.
11 'Minutes 133rd NSC Meeting, 24 February 1953'. DDEL, AWF, NSC, Box 4, p. 2.

12 'Minutes 132nd NSC Meeting, 19 February 1953'. DDEL, AWF, NSC, Box 4, p. 2. See also Eisenhower's *Mandate for Change, 1953-1956*, pp. 159-166. Eisenhower's remembrance of events diverges somewhat from the historical record. In his memoirs, the President stated that he had 'confidence that the 'young Shah' would prove an effective leader of his people'. The Shah's failure to remove Musaddiq, followed by his abdication, shook official Washington to its core. Washington's real confidence centered on General Zahedi as he 'rumbled through the avenues of Tehran in a tank.' President Eisenhower's 1963 reflections on Musaddiq focused much more on the Iranian Prime Minister's 'stability' than did contemporary accounts. Apparently Musaddiq's habit of appearing in his pajamas perturbed the President – he mentioned it several times in his memoirs.
13 'Minutes 135th NSC Meeting, 5 March 1953'. DDEL, AWF, NSC Series, Box 4, p. 5.
14 'Communism in the Middle East, 20 October 1955'. DDEL, WHO, NSC Staff Papers 1948-1961, OCB, p. 9. The 1951 assassination of General Razmara became the feared model for what might happen to the Musaddiq government. Washington believed the National Society for Struggle Against the Anglo-Iranian Oil Company, the League of Peace Partisans, and numerous other organizations to be Communist-front organizations, and cited the August 1951 statement in the Cominform Journal that 'conditions are now maturing for building an anti-imperialist front capable of uniting the progressive national forces.'
15 'Minutes 136th NSC meeting, 12 March 1953'. DDEL, AWF, NSC, Box 4, p. 14.
16 'Summary of Reactions to PSB D-22, 'Psychological Strategy Program for the Middle East', Appendix A, May 1953'. DDEL, WHO, NSC, OCB, Box 77, p. 8.
17 Ferrier, Ronald 'The Anglo-Iranian Oil Dispute'. In Bill, James A. and William Roger Louis (eds.), *Musaddiq, Iranian Nationalism, and Oil*. London: Tauris, 1988, p. 190.
18 'Minutes 178th NSC Meeting, 30 December 1953'. DDEL, AWF, NSC, Box 5, pp. 3-6.
19 Afhavi, Shahrough 'The Role of the Clergy in Iranian Politics, 1949-1954' and Rajaee, Farhang 'Islam, Nationalism and Musaddiq's Era: Post-revolutionary Historiography in Iran'. In Bill, James A. and William Roger Louis (eds.) *Musaddiq, Iranian Nationalism, and Oil*. London: Tauris, 1988. These articles examine the role of the clergy in the coup of 1953. The Shi'a Ulama strongly opposed the Tudeh and secular nationalist forces in Iran, and played a significant role in the fall of Musaddiq. Opposition to the Shah would follow, but use of Islamic influence in the Cold War struggle against the Soviet Union and various Communist and Socialist groups became a standard feature of US policy, reaching its apogee in the Afghan War of the 1980s. See also Bill, James A., *The Eagle and the Lion: The Tragedy of American-Iranian Relations*, New Haven, CT: Yale University Press, 1988, pp. 51-72. Bill describes the defection of Ayatollah Abul Qassim Kashani from the Musaddiq coalition in early 1953 as 'the major blow' to the National Front government. The move forced Musaddiq into a position more dependent on the leftist parties and particularly the Tudeh.
20 'Eisenhower to Acting Secretary of State, April 23, 1953'. DDEL, AWF, Dulles-Herter Series, Box 1, p. 3.
21 Macmillan's diary, May 6, 1953. Macmillan Papers, Bodleian Library, Oxford University. Also quoted in Harold Macmillan's *Tides of Fortune*, pp. 502-503. It is interesting that Dulles' first major trip through the Middle East and South Asia coincided with a 'crisis' in Anglo-American relations that became the major topic of an NSC meeting even before the Secretary returned home. See also 'Who Likes Dulles – Who Doesn't'. *Newsweek* 27 January 1958, p. 28. The British dislike of Dulles reflected a difference in personal style. They saw him as 'too rigid' and detested his moralizing. Dulles liked to talk and he liked the limelight. Bridling at the competition, Churchill allegedly stated: 'I am told that on Mondays, Wednesdays and Fridays, Mr. Dulles makes a speech. And that on Tuesdays, Thursdays and Saturdays, he holds a press conference. And that on

Sundays he is a lay preacher. With such a regimen, there is bound to be a certain attenuation of thought.'
22 'Dulles in Baghdad to Eisenhower, May 17, 1953'. DDEL, AWF, Dulles-Herter Series, Box 1, p. 1. An interview with William C. Lakeland, in Berkeley, California, 23-24 September 2003, sheds additional light on British frustration with the situation in Cairo. Much to the chagrin of the British, the American Embassy in Cairo had imposed itself as the 'go-between' for Anglo-Egyptian negotiations. American Ambassador Jefferson Caffery used his relationship with British Ambassador Sir Roger Stevens and the relationship between his political officer William Lakeland, Muhammad Heikal, and Nasser himself to gain a bird's-eye view of the negotiations. Lakeland became the intermediary carrying versions of the agreement back and forth between the Egyptians and the British. Lakeland's role would have consequences later, when he was branded by key British officials in the Jordanian crisis of 1960 as too pro-Nasserist and willing to give up on the Hashemite regime.
23 'Dulles in Baghdad to Eisenhower, May 17, 1953'. Box 1, p. 1.
24 Heikal, Muhammad, *The Cairo Documents*. New York: Doubleday, 1972, pp. 48-51.
25 Interview with Lakeland. Lakeland stated that only the belief that significant 'economic and military aid' would be forthcoming from the US convinced the Egyptians to compromise on the departure date of the British, on issues related to British redeployment to the Canal Zone, and on the issue of independence for Sudan. Heikal stated that Nasser took Dulles at his word and sent Ali Sabry to Washington to negotiate for arms. At the same time, Nasser assured officers in the Egyptian army that the US would provide them with modern arms. As Heikal put it, all Nasser got back was Ali Sabry himself – an embarrassment to both Nasser and Sabry. The latter became an implacable foe of US interests in Egypt and the region.
26 'Dulles in Cairo to Eisenhower, May 12, 1953'. DDEL, AWF, Dulles-Herter, Box 1, p. 1.
27 'Dulles in Baghdad to Eisenhower, May 17, 1953'. Box 1, p. 3. Dulles rejected Syria and the Shishakli regime as 'very unpopular' and potentially unstable. 'No one can guarantee tenure or even life of dictator like Shishikli.'
28 'Australian High Commission, New Delhi [R.H. Birch] to DEA, 13 January 1954'. File No. 7/3/2/2, Memo No. 69, NAA, A1838/276, 169/11/148, Part 6, p. 1.
29 Podeh, Elie, *The Quest for Hegemony in the Arab World: The Struggle Over the Baghdad Pact*. Leiden: Brill, 1995, p. 69. This work provides a very good narrative of the process through which the Baghdad Pact came into being, and of the Egyptian struggle with Iraq for influence in the Arab world. It does not treat the ramifications of the Pact on India. In addition, in treating anti-American propaganda on the part of Egypt, Podeh appears to ignore, or is ignorant of, the CIA's role in supporting Nasser. During part of 1954, in order to protect Nasser from internal criticism, the CIA was actually assisting in creating anti-American propaganda.
30 Polk, William R., *The United States and the Arab World*. Cambridge, MA: Harvard University Press, 1969, p. 265.
31 'Minutes 145th NSC Meeting, May 23, 1953'. DDEL, AWD, NSC, Box 4, pp. 2-3.
32 'Churchill Letter to Eisenhower, 19 December 1953'. DDEL, AWD, Box 4, pp. 1-2.
33 'Eisenhower Letter to Churchill, 21 December 1953'. DDEL, AWD, Box 4, pp. 1-3.
34 Ibid. See also 'Memorandum Eisenhower-Churchill Conversation, Bermuda Conf, 4 December 1953'. DDEL, AWF, International Meetings, Box 1, p. 1.
35 'Churchill Letter to Eisenhower, 22 December 1953'. DDEL, AWD, Box 4, pp. 1-3.
36 Macmillan, Harold, *Tides of Fortune*, p. 504.
37 Nutting, Anthony, *Nasser*. New York: Dutton, 1972, pp. 70-73. In Egypt, various groups opposed the 1954 compromise agreement on two basic grounds. It allowed the British almost two years to complete their withdrawal from the Canal Zone, and it

provided for the 'reactivation' of the British bases in the event of war or a threat to the Canal. Neguib and his supporters, as well as the Muslim Brotherhood, attacked Nasser as a 'traitor'. When a member of the Brotherhood attempted to assassinate Nasser in October 1954, he used the incident as justification to crush the Brotherhood and his other political opponents

38 Copeland, Miles, *The Game Player*. London: Aurum, 1989, p. 167. Copeland states that the CIA brought in Paul Linebarger, 'perhaps the greatest 'black' propagandist who ever lived', to coach the Egyptians and that a 'goodly portion' of the anti-American propaganda coming out of Cairo was written with CIA help.
39 Nutting, *Nasser*, p. 69. Also, interview with Lakeland, 23-24 September 2003, supports this view.
40 Podeh,*Hegemony*, p. 97.
41 Ibid, pp. 69-70.
42 Ibid, pp. 107-122. See also Spain, James W., 'Middle East Defense: A New Approach'. *Middle East Journal*, Summer 1954, Volume 8, pp. 251-266. This article provides an interesting contemporary perspective on the 'northern tier' concept, and the difficulties faced by the Eisenhower administration in its early attempts to come up with a containment strategy for the Middle East.
43 'Eisenhower to the Acting Secretary of State, 23 April 1953'. DDEL, AWF, Dulles-Herter Series, Box 1, pp. 2-3.
44 'Dulles in Baghdad to Eisenhower, May 17, 1953'. p. 3.
45 'Discussion 207th NSC Meeting, 22 July 1954'. DDEL, AWF, NSC, Box 5, pp. 12-13. There was a long discussion of the role of the American Zionist lobby at the NSC meeting on July 22, 1954. Eisenhower's impression of Israel showed a remarkable lack of understanding of the nature of the Jewish state. Referring to a conversation with a visiting Israeli who told him 'that the government of Israel was thoroughly unreligious and materialistic', the President said he had been 'astounded by such a statement, since he had been of the opinion that a good many members of the Israeli Government were religious fanatics.' At the meeting, Nixon commented that decisions had to be made on the basis of 'national security' and not 'domestic political considerations'. 'Presidents Truman and Roosevelt had been obliged to assure themselves of the Jewish vote and they had largely secured this vote. The Republicans, on the other hand, do not require this vote and aren't likely to get it, no matter how hard they try.' In fact, Nixon went on to say that a sensible policy from the White House could actually gain support from 'moderate and wise Jews'.
46 'Outline of Suggested Program for Peace in the Near East, 1 December 1953'. DDEL, AWD, Box 4, pp. 1-3.
47 'NEA to Eisenhower, 7 October 1953'. NACPM, GRDOS-59, Johnston Mission, Box 1, p. 1-2. The State Department attempted to dampen optimistic expectations related to the Johnston effort stating: The refugees are an important key to the problem and agreement on the use of the Jordan waters offer[ing] the only opportunity to settle quickly a substantial number.' It was not anticipated that the Johnston Mission would bring back a clear-cut solution; it was intended as an exploratory step to determine whether a basis for agreement existed.
48 'Dulles in Baghdad to Eisenhower, May 17, 1953', p. 3.
49 'Discussion of Need for Early Diplomatic Initiative by Washington on Palestine Issues, 17 August 1953'. NACPM, GRDOS-59, Johnston Mission, Box 1, pp. 1-6.
50 'NEA to Johnston clarifying Presidential Letter of October 7, 1953, 13 October 1953'. NACPM, GRDOS-59, Johnston Mission, Box 1, pp. 1-3. President Eisenhower charged Eric Johnston with 'securing agreement of the states of Lebanon, Syria, Jordan and Israel to the division and use of the waters of the Jordan River Basin', instructing him to 'secure agreement from Jordan and Israel on plans that may be prepared for the

internationalization of Jerusalem.' As for Jerusalem, the NEA stated: 'The objective of the United States is to obtain the agreement of Israel and Jordan to a plan for the functional internationalization of Jerusalem which will also prove acceptable to the Catholic countries and command the necessary majority in the General Assembly. ... In the execution of your mission, you will receive the full backing of this Government.' See also 'Report to the President on NE Mission, Summary of Conclusions, 17 November 1953'. NACPM, Johnston Mission, Box 1, pp. coversheet, 1-8. The new administration saw the Jordan waters as 'a central element of American policy in the Near East. Decisions with respect to American political support and economic assistance should be conditioned upon the attitude displayed by the states concerned toward the United Nations proposals. ... With respect to the Arab-Israel conflict, generally, it is clear that we are not leaving the problems to solve itself. The peril of a policy drift, based on the assumption that time will iron out the difficulties, has been demonstrated by the recent outbreak of serious border incidents, the quarrel over water rights on the upper Jordan and other events. ... The impasse can be broken, in my opinion, only by the exertion of strong pressure from the outside, mainly by the United States, Britain, and France, on behalf of measures calculated to remove irritants and promote indirect cooperation between the parties on a practical rather than a political level.' See also 'Discussion of Need for Early Diplomatic Initiative, 17 August 1953', pp. 1-6. Incidentally, concerns about the influence of the Zionist lobby surfaced in discussions of the Johnston effort. 'If the U.S. is to win back a measure of confidence in its good will and impartiality in the Near East as well as broad domestic support for its new policy, it should take some action, however limited, to demonstrate its attitude before Israel seizes the diplomatic initiative and the initiative with American public opinion.'

51 'Report on Eric Johnston's Trip to the Near East, 7 May 1954', DDEL, AWF, Dulles-Herter Series, Box 3, p. 1.
52 'Bermuda Meeting, December 4-8, 1953, Unified Plan for Jordan Valley Development, 27 November 1953'. NACPM, Johnston Mission, Box 1, p. 4.
53 'Memcon Eisenhower and Johnston, 5 March 1956'. DDEL, AWD, Box 5, pp. 1-2.
54 'Ambassador Johnston's Statement to the Israeli Committee on Jordan Waters, 31 January 1955'. NACPM, Johnston Mission, Box 2, p. 3.
55 Neff, Donald, *Warriors at Suez: Eisenhower Takes America into the Middle East*. New York: Simon & Schuster, 1981, pp. 30-35. Neff makes an excellent case that the Gaza raid was the key event that ultimately drove Nasser to Moscow for the arms that the United States would not provide. The Egyptian Army comprised Nasser's political constituency and he had to deliver arms, and at least the appearance of military parity with the Israelis, if he was to survive. See also Stephens, Robert, *Nasser, A Political Biography*. New York: Simon & Schuster, 1971, pp. 151-155. The Gaza raid was as much the result of internal Israeli politics and the gross embarrassment caused by the Lavon Affair as it was about security-related issues on the border. In the Lavon Affair, the Egyptians had uncovered an Israeli covert operation in which Israeli agents in Egypt were to attack British and American consulates and embassies with explosives. The goal was to blame the attacks on the Egyptians and increase Anglo-American anti-Arab sentiment. When it was uncovered, the operation significantly embarrassed the Israeli military (IDF) and Pinhas Lavon, the Israeli Labor Party (Mapai) Defense Minister, resigned. Ben-Gurion returned to the government in his place. To restore morale in the IDF, Ben-Gurion pressed Moshe Sharett to authorize the raid. Ben-Gurion then made sure that the raid would have maximum impact by appointing a young paratrooper, Ariel Sharon, to carry it out. Sharon had previously carried out a violent raid against the Palestinian village of Qibya with numerous non-combatant deaths. The scale of the casualties not only horrified Sharett but also placed Nasser in potentially the same internal political

situation as that experienced by King Faruq following the failure of Egyptian forces in the 1948 war. Nasser told Sir Ralph Stevenson that he had to have arms to maintain his government, no matter what the source. (See Heikal, *Cairo Documents*, p. 53.) Nasser delivered the same message to US Ambassador Byroade in Cairo. See Neff, *Warriors*, p. 67 – Neff shares this view and quotes Nasser's comments to columnist Cyrus Sulzberger: 'Our revolution was stimulated in the Army by a lack of equipment. If our officers feel we still have no equipment, they will lose faith in the government.' Neff further cites Nasser's comments to his Central Intelligence Agency contact Miles Copeland when buzzing Israeli jets interrupted their Cairo conversation: 'I have to sit here and take this – and your government won't give me arms.' See Vatikiotis' *Modern Egypt* (New York: Praeger, 1969), p. 390. Vatikiotis also credits the combined impact of the Gaza Raid and the Baghdad Pact negotiations as the determining factors causing Nasser to embrace 'non-alignment' and seek arms from the Soviet Union. See Amam, Abdullah, *Nasir wa 'Amir* (al-qahira: nashir al-yulia, 1985), p. 56. Amam focuses primarily on justifying the demise of Egyptian Field Marshall Abd-al-Hakim al-Amir following the 1967 war. The author emphasizes the theme of the Egyptian military being out of step with Nasser's political goals and agenda. Amam's view, while something of a rationalization, fits closely with the views of Neff on the subject of Nasser's need to placate the military in general and Amer in particular.

56 Heikal, *Cairo Documents*, p. 54.
57 'OCB Progress Report on the Near East'. DDEL, WHO, NSC Staff Papers, OCB, Box 78, 5 April 1956, p. 6. In an assessment, the OCB and White House issued a summary stating: [T]he controversy over the Israeli proposal to divert Jordan River water threatened to erupt into war. With the dismissal of General Glubb from the Jordan Arab Legion, an incipient military struggle for power was added to the already volatile compound of refugees' hatred for Israel, and anti-British, anti-West, anti-Baghdad Pact sentiment. No progress was made towards the settlement of the Arab refugee problem, nor towards an agreed and equitable division of the waters of the Jordan River system.'
58 'Poem in Jordan Waters file, 23 September 1955'. NACPM, GRDOS-59, Johnston Mission, Box 2, p. 1.
59 'Congressional Presentation FY 1961 of Jordan Valley Development, March 1960'. NACPM, GRDOS-59, Johnston Mission, Box 3, p. 1.
60 Nutting, *Nasser*, pp. 144-156.
61 Nehru, Jawaharlal, 'Asia Finds Herself Again: A Speech Inaugurating the Asian Conference, New Delhi, 23 March 1947'. *Independence and After: A Collection of Speeches 1946-1949*. New York: Day, 1950, p. 298.
62 'Attachment, Memcon Eisenhower and Churchill, Bermuda Conference, 4 December 1953'. DDEL, AWF, International Meetings, Box 1, p. 1.
63 'Australian HC, New Delhi (Birch) to DEA, 13 January 1954'. 7/3/2/2, No. 69, NAA, DEA, A1838/276, 169/11/148, Part 6, p. 1.
64 Macmillan, Harold, *Riding the Storm 1956-1958*. New York: Harper & Row, 1971, p. 381. Macmillan took pride in his attempt to foster a climate of mediation and cooperation between India and Pakistan at the Commonwealth Conference, 1957. On July 5, he arranged a luncheon at No. 10 that 'was rather a risk'. It included himself, Nehru, and the Pakistani Foreign Minister, Husayn Shaheed Suhrawardy. Suhrawardy and Nehru had never met and were 'on the worst of terms'. At this meeting, Macmillan encouraged both to accept the International Bank's proposal to settle claims related to the Indus River waters. The Prime Minister believed that this might be the first step to a negotiated settlement on Kashmir. He viewed the eventual agreement in 1960 as 'an impressive reminder of the lost unity of the sub-continent following the disappearance of the British Raj'. This very British view is interesting in that it reflects the British view

that a unity existed on the subcontinent under the Raj – a contention that continues to be debated today.
65 'Bilateral Talks during December 1952 NATO Meeting – Kashmir from Christopher Van Hollen to Secretary of State [Marshall], Negotiating Paper, Kashmir, December 10, 1952'. NAPCM, GRDOS59, NEA, NEA/INC, Records on Kashmir, Entry 5252, Box 1, pp. 1-3. Also Interview with Christopher Van Hollen on 12 June 2003, Washington, DC; Van Hollen is the former Assistant Secretary of State for South Asian Affairs. He stated that neither the Truman nor Eisenhower administrations saw any real chance for compromise on India's part with regard to Kashmir. While some in the Kennedy administration believed that compromise actually might be possible, events would prove this to be an 'erroneous assumption'. 'Memocon US Ambassador Gross and UN Representative Bunche, New Delhi, February 26, 1953'. NACPM, Box 1, pp. 1-3. In February 1953, Dr. Ralph Bunche of the United Nations discussed Indian attitudes in general and Kashmir in particular with the US Ambassador to India, Ernest A. Gross, and his staff. Bunche stated that Nehru had no apparent successor, and in fact carried the Congress Party through his own charisma. He commented that the Indians had emphasized the military in a recent National Day celebration and that this was directed not toward Communism, but toward Pakistan. It also appeared that the Indian officials whom he had met were 'discouraged' by the prospect of years of economic struggle to get the country on its feet and deal just with the population and food problems. He reported that, in Pakistan, the military received even greater focus and that Kashmir remained the dominant theme in all discussions. The Pakistanis were deeply concerned that India wanted the situation to 'drift', and solidify into permanent Indian control.
66 'Eisenhower 'Personal and Confidential' Letter to Captain E.E. 'Swede' Hazlett, December 24, 1953'. DDEL, AWF, AWD, Box 4, p. 3.
67 'Discussion 176th NSC Meeting, 16 December 1953'. DDEL, AWF, NSC, Box 5, p. 6.
68 'Australian HC, New Delhi [Birch] to the DEA, 13 January 1954'. NAA, A1838/276, 169/11/148, Part 6, p. 1.
69 'President's Statement on Military Aid to Pakistan, 16 February 1954'. DDEL, AWF, Dulles-Herter Series, Box 2, p. 1.
70 'Discussion 176th NSC Meeting, 16 December 1953'. DDEL, AWF, NSC, Box 5, p. 6. Within the context of the discussion on Pakistan, Nixon commented that in his talks with the Shah and Prime Minister Zahedi in Iran, both focused on military aid. He clearly believed that stability in Iran depended on a strong military and that this model also applied to other countries in the region. He also supported direct immediate aid because he believed that the northern-tier organization would take too much time to unfold.
71 'Eisenhower to Nehru on Military Aid to Pakistan, 16 February 1954'. DDEL, AWF, Dulles-Herter Series, Box 2.
72 'Deputy Under Sec State Hoover to Eisenhower, 16 February 1954'. DDEL, AWF, Dulles-Herter Series, Box 2. See also 'Eisenhower to Dulles, 27 October 1953'. DDEL, AWF, Dulles-Herter Series, Box 2. Eisenhower had suggested in late October that the United States should wait until after Indian troops were disengaged from peacekeeping in Korea to 'say something publicly about our admiration of the whole India contingent'. The President wanted to wait because 'we might compromise – at least in Soviet propaganda – the neutrality of the Indian participants.' In *Prospects for Communist China* (Cambridge: MIT Press, 1954), pp. 88, 200, Walt Rostow commented that the Indian initiative on Korean in December 1952 was done with 'Chinese Communist knowledge and backing', including the 'prisoner of war resolution'. Rostow saw the Indians as surrogates for Chinese policy in Asia and also viewed Soviet opposition to the Indian resolution as an indication of 'Moscow-Peking differences'. Rostow points out later that 'deep undercurrents of raw nationalism set distinct limits within which

Moscow can control Peking without risking serious rupture.' Rostow should get credit for seeing early signs of a Soviet-Chinese split over national interests. He speculated that China would move to 'complete the conquest of Indo-China' and make other moves against Thailand, Burma, India, and Indonesia to 'pose as the leading power of Asia'. See also 'Suggested Message from President Eisenhower to Prime Minister Nehru, 16 February 1954'. DDEL, AWF, Dulles-Herter Series, Box 2. See also Ram, Janaki, *V.K. Krishna Menon: A Personal Memoir*. Delhi: Oxford University Press, 1997, pp. 86, 101, in which Ram discussed Menon's role in the Korean 'peace' process. Ram highlighted not only Western opposition to some of the content in Menon's plan for prisoner of war repatriation in Korea but also Soviet attacks on him at the United Nations. In these attacks, Soviet delegate Vishinsky called Menon, much to his shock and embarrassment, 'a lackey of the British'. Ram was something of an apologist for Menon and attempted to explain away many of his obvious shortcomings. Ram called the 'Jeep Scandal' a 'mistake' rather than malfeasance, and he appeared to be using the incident with the Soviets to portray Menon as something other than a Communist or Soviet agent of influence. Daluit Sen Adel in *Krishna Menon and Contemporary Politics*, (New Delhi: Institute for Socialist Education, 1997), pp. 124, 127, provides a clearly leftist interpretation of events, but stated that Menon was 'bitterly' surprised by the Soviet attack on his 17-point plan to solve the prisoner of war impasse in Korea. This comment is all the more significant when viewed in the context of Adel's interpretation of Korean events. 'On June 25, 1950, the South Korean army of Sygmund Rhee launched a surprise attack on the northern half of Korea along the entire 38th parallel. ... The situation became more explosive with the use of biological weapons by the United States of America which carried bacilli plague, cholera and other infectious diseases'. The point here is that even those holding radical leftist views of events found themselves taken aback by the vehemence of the Soviet attack on Menon.

73 Rostow, Walt, Prospects for Communist China, p. 310.
74 Talbot, Phillips and S.L. Poplai, *India and America, A Study of Their Relations*. New York: Harper, 1958, pp. 87-88. William Phillips Talbot published this work when he was the executive director of the American Universities Field Staff. Sources for the following biographical information include a personal letter from Phillips Talbot to Roby Barrett on July 3, 2002, an interview with Talbot by Roby Barrett at the Century Association in New York on May 31, 2002, and a reprinting of his letter to the Institute of Current World Affairs provided by the New India Digest Foundation, Pune, India at http://www.rediff.com/freedom/gandhi.htm. Educated at the University of Illinois, Talbot received a Crane Grant to study South Asian politics and history in 1938 in Britain, followed by a course of study at Aligarh College in India. When World War II broke out, Talbot served in naval liaison in the China-Burma-India theater, returning to India after the war as a foreign correspondent for the *Chicago Daily News* to cover the transfer of power in 1947. Talbot knew many of the leading figures of Indian politics personally, including Nehru, Gandhi, and Patel. The Institute of Current World Affairs published an account of his walk and conversation with Gandhi in the East Bengal district of Noakhali during the turmoil of 1947. Talbot returned to the United States and completed a doctorate in South Asian studies at the University of Chicago before joining the Field Staff. In 1961, Talbot became the Assistant Secretary of State for Near Eastern and South Asian Affairs and one of the key drivers of regional policy from Cairo to Calcutta. Days after the assassination of President John F. Kennedy, Talbot would play an instrumental role in the maintenance of the pro-Pakistani tilt in US foreign policy in South Asia under the administration of President Lyndon B. Johnson. For these reasons, Talbot's views on the situation in South Asia, often published in the Field Staff journals, are particularly germane to the story of continuity between the policies of Eisenhower and Kennedy through the region.

75 Talbot, *India and America*, p. 91. Talbot states: 'India feels that its security and other interests are best served by encouraging "neutralism", by cultivating extremely friendly relations with Egypt, and by befriending the Arab countries and cold-shouldering Israeli claims.'
76 Gopal, Sarvepalli, *Jawaharlal Nehru, A Biography*. Volume II: 1947-1956. New Delhi: Oxford University Press, 1979, p. 185. See also pp. 183-193, in which Gopal pointed out that Nehru was concerned as early as 1952 during the Truman administration about the possibility that Pakistan might join a Western defense structure. He viewed it as a mistake on the part of the United States and Britain to 'rely more and more on the military aspect' of alliances instead of focusing on economic development. Nehru noted on November 25, 1952: India counts for them and they will not easily adopt such a policy. But if military opinion is dominant, they might very well override political considerations.'
77 'Australian HC, New Delhi [Birch] to the DEA, 13 January 1954'. NAA, A1838/276, 169/11/148, Part 6, p. 1.
78 'Indian HC London [D.N. Chatterjee] to MEA New Delhi [Morari Desai], 27 February 1954'. NAI, MEA, United Kingdom, K/54/132/141, p. 6.
79 'NEA to Dulles on UN Observer Group in Kashmir, Washington, March 24, 1954'. NACPM, Kashmir, Entry 5252, Box 1, pp. 1-2. The US quickly complied with India's request 'so that US-Indian relations, already seriously impaired by our aid to Pakistan, not be further worsened'.
80 'Australian HC, New Delhi [Birch] to the DEA, 13 January 1954'. NAA, A1838/276, 169/11/148, Part 6, p. 1.
81 'Canadian HC New Delhi [Escot Reid] to DEA, Ottawa, 11 November 1954. No. 1298, NAA, A1838/272, 169/11/161 Part 4, pp. 2-3, 6-7.
82 Brown, Judith, *Nehru, A Political Life*. New Haven, CT: Yale University Press, 2003, p. 259. Brown struggles with balancing Nehru's political theory and its practical application. Pointing out that relations with the US deteriorated after the 1954 arms agreement with Pakistan, she state that Nehru really would have preferred to forego economic assistance from the US. There is just as sound an argument that the arms agreement provided Nehru with an 'out' vis-à-vis negotiations with Pakistan over Kashmir, and that he was more than happy to get that bonus along with his economic aid from Washington. Nehru was nothing if not a practical politician, and as such, principles were usually fine as long as the price was not too high.
83 'Brief *Economist* article, "India Progress and Plan, 22 January 1955", circulated to Dulles, Harold Stassen, Nelson Rockefeller from President Eisenhower'. DDEL, AWF, AWD Series, Box 5. This particular article came to the President's attention and he thought it important enough to have it circulated to senior administration officials with the notation to 'Stick this in our diary'.
84 'India: The Tea Fed Tiger'. *Time*, 2 February 1962, cover, p. 16. Menon made the cover of *Time*, with a snake charmer's pipe on one side and a menacing cobra on the other. The symbolism was clear. The article describes him as 'abusive, rude, and overbearing', pointing out: 'Nehru values Menon highly as a friend, confidant and traveling apostle.' The article goes on to say: 'Nehru admires his provocative intelligence, uses him as a shock absorber to take attacks that might otherwise be directed at him to his government.' The article quotes an Indian politician comparing Menon to a 'wind-up car'. 'Nehru sets its pace by winding it and watching go around. Whenever the car comes to an obstacle, Nehru removes the obstacle from its path and rewinds it.'
85 Adel, *Menon and Contemporary Politics*, pp. 1, 4, 42, 112-115. Menon had close contacts in the British Labor Party dating from the 1930s, and appeared to be the logical choice to represent India to the Atlee Labor government following independence. Appointed High Commissioner to Britain in 1947, scandals forced Menon to resign in 1952.

Menon paid over $300,000 for 15 British army surplus Jeeps, none of which would run or had spare parts. He also purchased a palatial mansion as the residence and a Rolls Royce for the High Commissioner. He did all of this at a time when the Indian government faced a monumental economic crisis. Adel, a sympathetic leftist himself, even states that 'Krishna Menon made a wrong start by accepting the office of High Commissioner in the United Kingdom' because it only served to make him a target of the Congress Party conservatives. See also Ram, Janaki, *V.K. Menon: A Personal Memoir*. New Delhi: Oxford University Press, 1997, p. 92. Ram, a nephew, wrote that the Jeep Scandal was an error of judgment in that Menon arranged the contrast privately and not through government channels. See also Arora, *Menon – A Biography*, p. 98. Another pro-Menon biographer explained the scandal in terms of a controversy centered on Sudir Gosh, who was Vallabahbhai Patel's candidate for the London post, and Menon. This account claims that the Gosh brought the Jeep scandal to light and Patel used it to discredit Menon. Interestingly, not even his most ardent supporters offered any explanation of what happened to the money.

86 Arora, *Menon – A Biography*, Foreword.
87 Lengyel, Emil, *Krishna Menon*. New York: Walker, 1962, p. 239.
88 Adel, *Menon and Contemporary Politics*, p. 131. Adel also asserts that Menon became the favorite target not only of the US Congress, but also of Indian Congress Party conservatives.
89 Akbar, M.J., *Nehru, The Making of India*. London: Viking, 1988, p. 491. Akbar criticized the US for 'sniping' the Control Commission into 'impotence', but at the same time he felt that the 'backlash' against Menon, because of his 'acerbic, and garrulous speeches', was detrimental to India and to Nehru personally. The author also argued that the foreign policies of Truman and Eisenhower were the 'same'. See also Gopal, *Nehru*, Volume III, pp. 191-192. Gopal stated that Nehru obtained a resolution calling for all 'Great Powers' to stay out of Vietnam and to let the Vietnamese settle their differences. In support of Nehru's arguments, Menon gave over 200 interviews, lasting an average of two hours each, in just three weeks. Gopal clearly believed that Menon made a positive contribution, and that the genesis of any difficulties lay in US support for leaders 'who to Nehru symbolized the most decadent aspects of Asia'.
90 Cooper, Chester L., *The Lost Crusade: America in Vietnam*. New York: Dodd, Mead, 1970, p. 186. Cooper commented that the best that could be said for the Indian predisposition to discuss 'broad international profundities' was that it 'provided an occasional oasis of amusement in a desert of dull speeches'. See also p. 75, where Cooper was almost as critical of John Foster Dulles, stating: 'Like Shakespeare's whining schoolboy, the American delegation 'crept like a snail unwillingly' to Geneva.' He lends credibility to Akbar's view of US 'sniping' stating: 'Eisenhower and Dulles had been fighting a rearguard action against the conference for months, hoping that somehow the whole unpleasant affair would go away.' Describing Dulles as 'hardly an ebullient personality even under the most salubrious circumstances', Cooper states that his arrival that 'gray April day lent little joy' to either the 'cheerless' surroundings or the 'oppressive mood' of the US delegation.
91 Arora, *Menon – A Biography*, p. 173.
92 Gopal, *Nehru*, Volume II, p. 189.
93 Interview of Walt Rostow by Roby Barrett on June 12, 2002 at LBJ Library in Austin, Texas. Walt W. Rostow, who served as a consultant to the Eisenhower Administration from 1953 to 1958 and then as National Security Advisor in the Kennedy and Johnson administrations, tersely summed up the majority American view of Krishna Menon: 'He was a slob.' Rostow repeated that assertion a second time for emphasis. Rostow explained that his comment referred not to Menon's physical appearance but rather to the fact that he was an untrustworthy, hypocritical, pro-Soviet example of the worst

form of cronyism. Rostow stated that Nehru also was anti-American and untrustworthy. See also Ram, *Menon: A Personal Memoir*, p. xv. Janaki Ram, Krishna Menon's nephew and a more sympathetic voice, states: 'He [Menon] was quite ineffectual at public relations and said rather optimistically that one's deeds were the best public relations. This might have been true, up to a point, in the British environment he was so familiar with, but in India, where he had no roots due to his long absence, he made no effort to publicize his sacrifices. ... Consequently he was treated as an upstart in politics depending on the Prime Minister, Jawaharlal Nehru, for support, patronage and sustenance. This is why he is so misunderstood.'

94 'Minute from Desai to Nehru, 25 January 1954'. NAI, MEA, United Kingdom, K/54/132/41, p. 5.
95 'Indian HC London [Chatterjee] to New Delhi [Desai], 14 January 1954'. NAI, MEA, UK, K/54/132/41, p. 1.
96 'Indian HC London [Chatterjee] to New Delhi [Desai], 9 March 1954'. NAI, MEA, UK, K/54/132/41, p. 24.
97 Mende, Tibor, *Conversations with Mr. Nehru*. London: Secker & Warburg, 1956, p. 94. This lengthy interview published in book form provides interesting first-hand responses by Nehru to a series of questions affecting policy in the mid-1950s. It is a part of a much larger collection of Indian government publications at the Australian National Library, Canberra.
98 'Biographic Report on the Delegates from India to the United Nations General Assembly, Ninth Session, 15 September 1954.' DOS, Office of Libraries and Intelligence Acquisition, Division of Biographic Information, CRES, CIA-RDP80-01446R000100170033-3, p. 10. The report contains a series of personality profiles from a 'controlled American source'. With regard to the Colombo incident, it stated that Ceylonese Prime Minister Sir John Kotelawala 'jumped up' and 'demanded' that Menon either apologize or 'leave the Conference' on the threat that Kotelawala would 'walk out' if Menon did not do one or the other. Menon backed down and apologized. The report credits Menon with being 'a brilliant orator of the rabble rousing type'.
99 'Message from the Australian High Commission Karachi [HC L.E. Beavis] to DEA, Canberra, 5 May 1954'. Memo No. 334/54, File No. 502/2, NAA, DEA, A1838/276, 169/11/148 Part 6, pp. 3-4.
100 'Telegram from US Consulate Singapore to WDC, 7 January 1955'. NACPM, GRDOS – 59, African Republics (AF), CDF, 670.901/1-655, p. 1.
101 'New Delhi [Flanagan] to WDC, 3 January 1955'. NACPM, 670.901/1-355, p. 1.
102 'Memcon on Afro-Asian Affairs [Dulles], Washington DC, 14 January 1955'. NACPM, 670.901/1-455, pp. 1, 2, 4. The participants in the meeting discussed the lack of a clear British position on the conference, citing a lack of any instructions on the matter from London. See also 'New Delhi to WDC, 11 January 1955'. NACPM, 670.901/1-1155, p. 1. The Embassy in New Delhi commented that the British attitude toward the conference was one of cautious welcome.
103 'The Asian-African Conference, Top Secret Eider, 6 April 1955'. NSA, CRES, CIA-RDP80R01443R000300300002-5, pp. 3, 12.
104 'Memcon Afro-Asian Affairs [Dulles], 14 January 1955'. pp. 3-4.
105 'New Delhi to WDC, 15 January 1955'. NACPM, 670.901/1-1555, p. 1. The particular article also called on the United States to 'urge friends to participate' in the effort because it was intended to avoid controversial topics and focus on 'economic cooperation'.
106 'New Delhi to WDC, 28 January 1955'. NACPM, AF, CDF, 670.901/1-2855, p. 1.
107 'New Delhi to WDC, 28 January 1955'. NACPM, 670.901/1-2855, p. 2.
108 'Memcon Asian Town Hall [Dulles], 27 April 1955'. NACPM, 670.901/4-2755, p. 1.

109 Stora, Benjamin, *Algeria 1830-2000: A Short History*. Ithaca, NY: Cornell University Press, 2001, pp. 67-68. Stora's history lives up to its billing: it is short, but useful. In three very short chapters on the Algerian war: 'The War of the Algerians 1954-1958,' 'De Gaulle and the War 1958-1959', and 'The Wars within the War 1960-1961', the author provides good summaries of the phases of the war and a snapshot of the broader political context in which it occurred. This raises a broader and perhaps in some quarters more controversial point about the Algerian conflict and the present work. Why is the Algerian war relegated, almost literally, to a footnote since it was an ongoing event in Dulles' geographic definition of the Middle East that chronologically duplicates the footprint of this work? There are two reasons for this exclusion: first, the Algerian conflict was a sideshow to the central theme of pan-Arab nationalism that dominated the Arab struggle between Baghdad and Cairo; second, Algeria was a civil war, and more European in many respects than Middle Eastern; and third, it was not central to the US policy of containment. In fact, remarkable unanimity existed between the Western powers, the Arab states, and the non-aligned states that the French needed to get out of Algeria. This unanimity did not always take the same form, but the basic premise was that self-determination should be the basis for the outcome of the struggle in Algeria. Despite Cairo's support for the FLN, the US never felt as threatened by Nasserism in Algeria because there was a fundamental recognition that the independence movement was indigenous and that the Algerian leadership was almost as concerned about maintaining its independence from Nasser as it was about gaining it from France. In addition, the Algerian movement had very strong critical support from pro-Western and anti-Nasserist political leaders in Tunisia and Morocco. Algeria was a special case, and only fit into the Middle East policy models pursued by Eisenhower and Kennedy from the standpoint that both administrations understood that colonialism in Africa and Middle East was coming to an end and both wanted to see independent non-Communist, if not pro-Western, states emerge. Algeria was a stumbling block to NATO policy in Europe and a problem for French political stability, posing bilateral problems for the US and France. The problem was more binary in nature, and revolved around decisions in Paris, not in Arab capitals. For these reasons Algeria is not central to this study.

110 'Memorandum from DOS South Asia Office to Far East [Robertson], 30 April 1955'. NACPM, 670.901/4-2755, p. 1. See also 'Memorandum from DOS South Asia Office (Allen) to NEA (Allen), 30 April 1955'. NACPM, 670.901/4-2755, p. 1. It should be noted that Washington was as yet unaware that Nehru's facilitation of a meeting between Chou En-lai and Nasser had resulted in a major Soviet coup in the Middle East: the Czech arms deal for Egypt. Within a matter of months, the importance of the conference and its impact on the Eisenhower administration's perception of Western interests in the region would become more apparent. See also 'Memorandum from NEA [Richard H. Sanger] to Office of South Asian Affairs (SOA) [Jones], 5 May 1955,' NACPM, 670.901/1-2855, pp. 1, 3. Adam Clayton Powell, the U.S. Congressman from Harlem who attended the Bandung Conference without the blessing of the administration, commented: 'Nehru was the greatest loser at the Conference. Part of the reason was because he now depends so much on Krishna Menon, who was with him all the time and went around in white robes and consciously posed as an Indian Holyman or saint. Menon made it clear he was anti-west and anti-U.S. Nehru had drifted far from Gandhi. Nehru's influence declined after the very first day. He became jumpy and irritable. In fact he suggested someone who was mentally ill.' This is a harsh judgment coming from a sympathetic advocate of the Civil Rights movement in the United States who was presumed sympathetic toward Gandhian ideas on non-violent protest. It is indicative of many American reactions to meeting with Nehru in person. Kennedy had a similar reaction at his first meeting with the Indian leader, a topic to be discussed later.

It is also interesting that when theState Department attempted to dissuade Powell from attending, officials described the US attitude toward Bandung as 'benevolent indifference'. In addition to Powell, Chester Bowles had discussed attending, but was convinced by the White House not to do so.

111 'Indian Permanent Mission to UN [Arthur Lall] to MEA [B.K. Nehru], 10 January 1955'. NAI, MEA, Asian-African Conference, 1(9) – AAC/55, p. 1.

112 'Memo Counselor DOS [Douglas MacArthur II] to Dulles, 21 January 1955'. NACPM, 670.901/1-2155, p. 1.

113 'New Delhi to WDC, 28 January 1955'. NACPM, 670.901/1-2855, p. 1.

114 Heikal, Muhammad, *Qasa al-Suisa*. Beirut: sharikat al-mutabua't li tawzia wa al-nashar, 1988, p. 51.

115 'Indian Embassy Jakarta to MEA, New Delhi, 31 January 1955'. NAI, MEA, Asian-African Conference, 1(2) – AAC/55, p. 1. See also Nehru, Jawaharlal, *Glimpses of World History*. New Delhi: Indraprastha, 1982, p. 736, in which Nehru compares the respective positions of India and Egypt in the British colonial system. Writing in 1933, Nehru stated: 'The nationalist movements of India and Egypt have adopted different methods, but, fundamentally, the urge to national freedom is the same and the objective is the same. And the way imperialism functions in its efforts to suppress these nationalist movements is also much the same. So each of us can learn much from the other's experiences.' He went on to elaborate: 'Among all these [Arab] countries the nationalist movement first took shape in Egypt, and it was thus natural for Egyptian nationalism to become a model for the other Arab countries.' Nehru had been thinking about the synergy between Egypt and India. It is hardly surprising that Nasser would become the focus of a campaign to bring Egypt into the non-aligned group. See also Nehru, Jawaharlal, *The Discovery of India*. New Delhi: Indraprastha, 1981, pp. 548-549, in which Nehru compares the Soviet Union and the United States, stating: 'All the evils of a purely political democracy are evident in the U.S.A.; the evils of the lack of political democracy are present in the U.S.S.R.' Nehru speculated that the clash between the two systems would lead to 'another era of imperialism' in which the 'moral urges of mankind and its sacrifices are used for base ends.' Nehru believed that the developing world had to find a middle way.

116 Abdel-Malek, Anouar, Egypt: Military Society – The Army Regime, the Left, and Social Change under Nasser. New York: Random House, 1968, p. 227.

117 Interview with Muhammad Hakki, Washington, DC, 8 August 2003. Muhammad Hakki graduated from Cairo University in 1954. In 1955, he became information officer at the Egyptian Embassy in Washington. He would later work for Muhammad Hussein Heikal at *Al-Ahram* during the height of the Nasserist era. According to Hakki, Bandung is the key to understanding Nasser and Nasserist Egypt. Bandung convinced Nasser that his ideas and vision transcended those of his comrades in the RCC. He now viewed himself as a world leader, not just an Egyptian one. This self-image of superiority and importance drove everything he did in the 1950s and 1960s. Bandung went completely to his head. Nehru and Sukarno told him that he was the leader of the Arab world and he believed it. 'He was convinced that the whole Arab world was his sphere of influence.'

118 'Observations on the Likely effect of Bandung on the UN from British UN Mission [Pierson Dixson] to FO and Whitehall [Macmillan], 7 May 1955'. NAA, DEA, A1838/278, 3002/1 Part 6, p. 6. See also 'Asian-African Conference Bandung 18-24 April 1955 [MEA R.G. Casey], 30 May 1955'. NAA, DEA, A10299/1, A3, pp. 1-12.

119 Nutting, *Nasser*, p. 101. Something of a consensus exists that Nasser, like many other world leaders, viewed dealing with Nehru as tedious. An intellectual with personal participation in many of the most momentous events of the 20th century, Nehru tended to deliver aggravatingly didactic lectures that were tests of endurance and patience.

120 Neff, *Warriors*, p.76.
121 Eveland, Wilbur Crane, *Ropes of Sand: America's Failure in the Middle East*. London: Norton, 1980, pp. 90-105. Eveland provides an excellent description of the arms negotiations with Nasser. The US was willing to provide $20 million in arms and equipment suitable for internal security purposes. Nasser wanted $100 million with which to confront Israel. Eveland commented that Mossad had organized the Zionist lobby in Washington to oppose the arms deal even before the exploratory delegation had departed Cairo. In addition, the CIA, represented by Copeland and Roosevelt, had no legal basis on which to negotiate a major arms agreement because it required Congressional approval. Eveland stated that Ambassador Jefferson Caffery and Deputy Chief of Mission G. Lewis Jones were concerned that Nasser's expectations had risen to the point that the likely failure of the CIA effort to broker an arms deal would have serious long-term consequences. Their concerns proved well-founded.
122 Interview with General Andrew Goodpaster, 7 August 2003, Washington, D.C. Goodpaster stated: 'In my own mind, I believe that President Eisenhower's heart attack was the catalyst for the Soviet move.' Goodpaster stated that the Soviets took advantage of what they perceived as a moment of 'weakness and confusion' in the US administration to renege on their agreements and move into the Middle East. He speculated that Moscow calculated that should Eisenhower die, the ensuing change in administration would offer additional opportunities to expand their influence. Goodpaster firmly believed that if Eisenhower had not had a heart attack, the Czech arms deal would never have happened.
123 'Indian Embassy Jakarta [Ambassador BFHB Tyabji] to Commonwealth Affairs Secretary [Dutt], New Delhi, on Bandung Conference, 28 April 1955'. NAI, MEA, Section: Asian-African Conference, 1(37)—AAC/55, p. 4. The Indians and Nehru viewed the conference as disappointing. The Indian Ambassador in Jakarta reported: 'Unfortunately, the Indian point of view did not get good local publicity. I have not seen the foreign reports. Partly, ... China stole the limelight from India because the Chinese and Indian views happened to coincide; and people are inclined to think when this happens, that India has yielded to China, rather than the other way around. And partly, it is due to the pro-West opposition parties who have made much of alleged Indian attempts and desire to dominate the Conference, and to deprive Indonesia of the credit in organizing it.' See also *Asian-African Conference, 18-24 April 1955: Prime Minister Jawaharlal Nehru's Speeches and the Final Communiqué from the Publications Division of the Ministry of Information and Broadcasting* (New Delhi: Government of India, 1955), found in the India collection at the Australian National Library, Canberra. This was published to counter the impression that India and Nehru had taken a back seat to other nations at the Bandung Conference.
124 'Memcon NEA [Jernegan and Hannah] and British Embassy [Scott and Morris], 13 September 1955'. NACPM, 788.00/9-1355, pp. 1-3.
125 'Dispatch Tehran [Seldan Chaplin] to WDC, Assessment of the Shah's Government, 21 April 1956'. NACPM, 788.00/4-2156, pp. 1-3.
126 'Dispatch Tehran to WDC, 4 June 1956'. NACPM, 788.11/6-456, pp. 1-3.
127 'US DefAtt Tehran to WDC, 27 December 1956'. NACPM, 788.00/12-2756, p. 1.
128 'Dispatch Tehran [Francis Stevens Chargé], to WDC, 29 January 1957'. NACPM, 788.00/1-2957, p. 5.
129 Srodes, James, *Allen Dulles, Master of Spies*. Washington, DC: Regency, 1999, pp. 460-461. In Washington, Kermit Roosevelt, the almost mythic hero of Tehran 1953, refused to participate in British-sponsored schemes to overthrow Nasser. CIA Director Allen Dulles stated that both his older brother John Foster Dulles and Eisenhower badgered Roosevelt into surveying the situation first-hand in Cairo. Upon returning, Roosevelt told the White House that the sole reason that Tehran had worked was because the

momentum against the Musaddiq regime already existed. In contrast, he pointed out that Nasser was actually popular and that a coup had no chance of success. 'I tried to tell them that these operations never work, if you are going against the grain of events. You have to have so much going your way before you dare undertake them. First and foremost, you have to have the vast majority of the people behind you. We did in Iran. And you have to have a leadership that is better than the one in power and one that can take control. We had in Iran in the army and the power structure; and the Shah himself was a very gentle and reasonable person, although later he turned into a tough customer.' Roosevelt advised the White House to get used to Nasser because an 'Iran option' simply did not exist. Roosevelt actually became so aggravated with the elder Dulles that he quit over persistent attempts to enlist him in attempts to overthrow Nasser. Srodes believes that Roosevelt's friendship for Nasser played a role in the decision. Roosevelt stated: 'Foster became too demanding. He had the idea that I could solve almost anything, anywhere. That just wasn't true. Allen was upset about it and recognized eventually that I couldn't take it any longer. Allen tried to protect me and he would try to reason with Foster as long as he thought he could, and then he would give up and go to ground.'

130 Nabih A. Faris, in *The Crescent of Crisis* (Lawrence: University of Kansas Press, 1955), pp. 102-103, argues that the Cold war placed the Middle East 'between two mill stones: the United States and Russia'. In addition, the US lacked 'a long-range and independent Arab policy ... [that did] not necessarily parallel those of her allies [the British, French, and Jewish pressure to support Israel] or subject to local political pressures.' 'In the absence of an independent American policy, these interests (petroleum and geopolitical presence) have led the United States to align itself with Britain and France, against whom the Arabs are continuing their struggle for independence. At the same time, the influence of the local American scene on American foreign policy has hoodwinked American policy-makers into espousing the cause of Israel, and has so far thwarted all efforts to disengage American Arab policy from that of Israel.' Faris was an American-educated Palestinian who had served as the Head of the Arab Desk in the Overseas Operations Branch of the Office of War Information. This work provides an interesting perspective on the growing perception that US policy in the 1953-1954 timeframe had fallen under British and Israeli influence. This was written prior to the Soviet arms deal with Nasser, and Faris predicted that Arab perceptions of US policy would result in major policy gains for the Soviet Union in the Arab Middle East.
131 Macmillan, *Riding the Storm*, p. 138.
132 Kyle, Keith, *Suez*. New York: St. Martin's, 1991, pp. 148-152, 278.
133 Kyle, *Suez*, pp. 157-158, 194, 259, 553. Interspersed throughout his narrative, Kyle provides a series of excellent snapshots of the Indian role. Despite a disagreement over tactics and concern in India that problems with the Canal would harm the Indian economy, Nehru supported Nasser's right to nationalize the Canal. Krishna Menon told the British that India could not come out publicly against Nasser, but that India would push for an international conference and encourage the Egyptian leader to attend. Menon attempted to get Nasser to the negotiating table, with no success because Nasser 'did not like or trust Krishna Menon, whom he suspected of having some link with the Russians.' Kyle concluded by saying that Nehru's solution of an international conference appealed to Eisenhower. The author blamed Menon as an 'unfortunate' choice as a mediator because he 'antagonized in turn everybody in sight'. Although something of a reach, Kyle infers that had Nehru taken a more personal role Suez might have been avoided. Najma Heptulla, in *Indo-West Asian Relations: The Nehru Era* (New Delhi: Allied, 1991) states that Menon's failure to carry out Nehru's policies in the Suez crisis successfully underscored Menon's limited utility at the UN. See also Lall, Arthur, *The Emergence of Modern India*. New York: Columbia, 1981, pp. 136-137. Lall, a

senior Indian diplomat and the self-described 'closest aide' to Krishna Menon for 17 years, related Nehru's disillusionment with Menon. The latter failed to gain acceptance of Nehru's plan for avoiding war over Suez, and then voted against the US resolution condemning the Soviet Union for its actions in Hungary. Lall provided a rationalization of these actions: 'Krishna Menon was highly intelligent but also impetuous. Moreover, his health played great tricks with him, and on a bad day his impetuosity was as swift as lightning.' As a result, Nehru telephoned Lall every morning with specific instructions for Menon to carry out in that day's UN session. Lall described Menon as 'galled' but obedient.

134 Heikal, *Qasa al-Suisa*, p. 56. Heikal argues that Suez underscored waning British influence and the beginning of real problems for the British in protecting their oil interests in the Middle East. In *Suez, 1956: A Personal Account* (London: Trinity, 1978), Selwyn Lloyd, the British Foreign Secretary, offered a systematic, if biased, assault on American policy, arguing that it was simply naive and wrong-headed. See also 'The 'Get Dulles' Campaign', *Newsweek*, 4 February 1958, p. 21. Following Suez, Dulles' credibility and competency came under attack. In January 1957, testifying before a joint session of the Senate Foreign Relations and Armed Services Committees in an attempt to get support for the Eisenhower Doctrine, Senator J. William Fulbright accused Dulles of 'wasting the fruits of billions in U.S. largesse showered on friendly nations and of precipitating a 'disastrous and remarkable collapse' in relations with our closest allies, British and France.' Fulbright stated: 'I've about decided that if support of the Mideast resolution is going to be considered as an expression of confidence in Dulles' conduct of foreign policy, them I will have to vote against it.' See also Mosley, *Dulles*, pp. 418-435. The author discusses the general confusion and disagreement among presidential advisors and military officers when it became apparent that the Anglo-French attack was under way. According to Admiral Arleigh Burke, Dulles ordered him to prepare to engage anyone in the Mediterranean, including the French and British. The Secretary of State then headed off to talk to Allen Dulles and the President. The direction to Burke would later be denied, as would the refusal to float the pound sterling unless the British troops were withdrawn. Mosley also points out that Dulles was preoccupied with Hungary, exhausted, and would be hospitalized within days for major cancer surgery. Nevertheless, there was an undercurrent in the administration that the US stance against intervention had been a mistake. In 1958, upon learning that the US would land troops in Beirut, Macmillan telephoned Eisenhower and said: 'You are doing a Suez on me!' The President is said to have 'laughed'. See Finer, Herman, *Dulles Over Suez*. Chicago: Quadrangle, 1964, p. 264. In less understanding accounts, Eisenhower and Dulles had a choice of 'Nasser or Eden' and they chose the 'assassin' over their old ally. See also Neff, *Warriors*, pp. 422, 293, 441, 425-426. The Democrats pounded both Dulles and Eisenhower for betraying allies. Adlai Stevenson stated: 'The Eisenhower Administration acquired for itself ... a reputation for unreliability which is about as damaging a reputation as a Great Power can have ... one question which arises irresistibly out of the Middle Eastern crisis is this: has the President of the United States really been in charge of our foreign policy?' On November 17, the *New York Times* commented that the United States had enabled Nasser to 'pull a political victory out of his military defeat'. Neff concludes: 'Eisenhower emerged from the crisis under severe criticism for opposing America's traditional allies, and historians since then have generally been critical of his actions during this period. In fact, his firm insistence that the rule of law be obeyed is one of the high points of his presidency.'

135 Trevelyan, Sir Humphrey, *The Middle East in Revolution*. London: Macmillan, 1970, pp. 105, 129, 130, 138. Trevelyan's account of the events leading up to the Suez Crisis is an interesting first-hand view of events and well worth reading. Later, the author was British Ambassador to Iraq following the July coup. Trevelyan stated that he never

supported intervention, either in Egypt in 1956 or Iraq in 1958, because both lacked any real chance of success given the post-World War II environment. No Arab government put in power by the West could survive. He stated: 'No Government set up by the occupying Forces would last.' About Iraq, he said: 'No Government established by British force could have lasted.' Trevelyan clearly viewed the post-1958 period as an 'epilogue' to British dominance in the Arab Middle East. See also Vernon Bogdanor's article 'Suez changed everything' in *The Times*, 29 October 2006, p. 21. In an article commemorating the 50th anniversary of Suez, Bogdanor argues that Suez 'ruined British foreign policy, destroying national self-confidence for 25 years until Margaret Thatcher regained the Falklands, and led to Harold Macmillan making Britain the 'junior partners in the Pax Americana'. He also pointed to later comments by Eisenhower regretting that the US had intervened as it had in the crisis. These views tend to reflect a British school of thought which was prevalent at the time in the Colonial Office that Suez was a net negative for Britain in the Middle East. To the contrary, with pretentions about prerogatives in the former colonial empire gone, the British government could focus on downsizing its commitments; London no longer had the ability to support the breadth of its former commitments in the Middle East, nor was it necessary to do so. British foreign policy was hardly 'ruined'; rather, it merely took a different and perhaps more effective and certainly more sophisticated form. Macmillan shifted the responsibility and the costs largely to the United States, and yet maintained a very effective program of influence over those policies through Washington. Eisenhower's decision was correct in 1956 and even more correct in the hindsight of 50 years. His lament about not supporting the British arguably had as much to do with wishing that the British, as opposed to the US, still had responsibility for the region than it did getting rid of Nasser. As for Bogdanor's comment on the Falklands, Thatcher knew that she required the support of the US, politically and with tactical and strategic US intelligence support, and she got it. She acted exactly as Macmillan would have with the cover of the 'Pax Americana'. Bogdanor also blames Suez for Britain's estrangement from Europe, and for the French commitment to Europe.

136 'OCB Report US Objectives and Policies Near East, 23 November 1956'. DDEL, NSC/OCB, Box 78, p. 7.
137 'The Middle East – How and Why the U.S. Aims to Fill the Vacuum'. *Newsweek* 7 January 1957, p. 24.
138 'Warsaw ... Cairo ... Moscow'. *Newsweek* 28 January 1957, pp. 41-42. The British privately voiced their concern that, given the unlikely possibility of a direct Soviet attack on the Middle East, the Eisenhower Doctrine was ill-advised and served only to inflame local nationalism and anti-Western sentiment.
139 Eveland, *Ropes of Sand*, p. 239. In November 1956, Ben-Gurion made withdrawal even more difficult by claiming in the Knesset that the Sinai was historically a part of Israel, and by asserting Israel's 'right' to expand beyond its 1956 borders. Although partly for domestic Israeli political consumption, his statements and intransigence confirmed in Arab minds the aggressive and expansionist aims of the Jewish state.
140 'OCB Memorandum of Meeting of the Ad Hoc Committee on Middle East Informational Activities, 18 January 1957'. DDEL, WHO, NSC, OCB, Box 77, p. 2.

Part I

1 Louis, The British Empire in the Middle East, p. 26.

Chapter 2

1 Copeland, Miles, *The Game of Nations: The Amorality of Power Politics*. New York: Simon & Schuster, 1969, pp. 214-218. Copeland offers an entertaining account of the various

reactions to the Eisenhower Doctrine. First, he quoted a member of the US Middle East Policy Planning Committee asking the CIA: 'Would you fellows like to send someone along on the mission that's going out to explain it to the Arab chiefs of state? We can't afford to associate ourselves with every lunatic scheme that comes along.' He quotes Nasser as saying: 'The genius of you Americans is that you never make clear-cut stupid moves, only complicated stupid moves which make us wonder at the possibility that there may be something to them we are missing.' Complicated or not, Copeland points out that Nasser understood that the Eisenhower Doctrine targeted his version of Arab unity and his influence in the region. At the same time, it encouraged his enemies, chief among them Nuri Sa'id and the Hashemites in Iraq.

2 Ferrell, Robert H. (ed.), *Eisenhower Diaries*, p. 350. See also Nutting, *Nasser*, p. 59. At their first meeting in October 1952, during a dinner, Nasser made it clear to Kermit Roosevelt that Neguib was a figurehead by dismissing or ignoring contemptuously everything that the General said. See Copeland, *Game*, pp. 74-77. Copeland credits William Lakeland, the Political Officer at the US Embassy in Cairo, with being the first official American to grasp that Nasser was the real power in the Revolutionary Command Council (RCC) and not Neguib. It was through Lakeland's friendship with Muhammad Heikal, then just a reporter in Cairo, that the primary early conduit for communication between the Embassy and the RCC was established.

3 Kerr, Malcolm, *The Arab Cold War, 1958-1967*. London: Oxford University Press, 1967, p. 1. Kerr commented on Arab nationalism, particularly the 20th-century version, stating that it was a 'mystery that neither Arab nor western historians have satisfactorily explained. ... (T)his obsession, whatever its causes, is an important psychological force, and therefore a political reality, which warring politicians seek to use against each other.'

4 Ismael, Tariq Y., *The Arab Left*. Syracuse, NY: Syracuse University Press, 1976, pp. 78-79. See also Mitchell, Richard P., *The Society of Muslim Brothers*. Oxford: Oxford University Press, 1993, pp. 105-164. Nasser's view of a 'sound democratic life' fell somewhat short of pluralistic democracy. He was suspicious of political parties, particularly after the Muslim Brotherhood attempted to assassinate him in 1954 and leftist elements strongly supported more radical measures and closer ties with the Soviet bloc. Arms from the Soviet Union were one thing, but political challenges from the Left were another. Nasser responded to both movements with brutal suppression. Richards' work is in large part a contemporary chronicle of events. Richards, an American student in Cairo in the early 1950s, knew many of the *Ikhwan* members personally. His narrative of events in the 1953-1954 timeframe presents an historical narrative that is also a first-hand street-level view of events.

5 Al-Atasi, Jamal, *Al-Thawra li Jamal Abd-al-Nasser wa ala Fikrihi al-Istratiji wa al-Tarikhi*. Beirut: Mahad Al-Agmaln Al-Arabi, p. 7. See also Shalaq, Al-Fadhi, 'Concepts of the Nation and State with Special Reference to the Sunnis in Lebanon'. In Choueiri, Youssef M. (ed.), *State and Society in Syria and Lebanon*. New York: St. Martins, 1993, pp. 122, 123. Nasser's *Philosophy of Revolution* was partly propaganda to establish ideological credentials and partly a reflection of his personal revolutionary nationalism. Nasser believed in the permanence of the revolutionary struggle, and would repeatedly return to revolutionary activities when moderate policies failed. In addition to his support for 'positive neutralism' and 'non-alignment', Nasser declared that Egypt stood ready to play a key role in 'three circles': Arab, African, and Islamic. See also Abd-al-Nassar, Jamal, 'The Principles that Guide Egypt's Political Life'. In Karpat, Kemal H. (ed.), *Political and Social Thought in the Contemporary Middle East*. New York: Praeger, 1963, p. 202. Here again, Nasser couched this ideology in terms of the 'elimination of imperialism', 'eradication of feudalism', and 'eradication of monopoly and the domination of capital'.

6 'Foreign Policy: On the Firing Line'. *Newsweek*, 21 January 1957, p. 25.

7 '352nd NSC Meeting, 22 January 1958'. DDEL, AWF, NSC, Box 9, pp. 7, 8, 12.
8 'Notes Cabinet Meeting, 6 February 1958'. DDEL, Dulles Papers, Smith Series, Box 3, pp. 1-4. Various calls for Arab unity over the years had anesthetized official Washington to the possibility of a real union. The degree of surprise associated with the Egyptian-Syrian union was attributed to a lack of adequate intelligence, and reflected itself in all manner of speculation, including the possibility of oil-sharing between Iraq and Egypt, the need to protect Kuwait and Iran, and Dulles' comment that if Jordan fell, a general Arab/Israeli war would result.
9 Nutting, *Nasser*, p. 215. See also, 'Telegram British Embassy WDC [Sir H. Caccia] to FO, 27 January 1958'. PRO, FO371/134386, p. 1. The Egyptian Chargé in Damascus told the American Ambassador 'the [Syrian] delegates burst into tears and fell on their knees before Nasser in order to get him to agree to help them out'.
10 Stephens, *Nasser*, p. 277. Taken from an article by Emile Bustani, 'Can Arab Unity Survive?' *New Statesman*, 5 January 1962, p. 48
11 Kerr, *Arab Cold War*, pp. 12-16.
12 Devlin, John, *The Ba'th Party: A History from Its Origins to 1966*. Stanford, CA: Hoover Institution Press, 1976, p. 115.
13 'Analysis Formation of the UAR [Lampton Berry, NEA] to Dulles'. NACPM, GRDOS – 59, CDF 55-59, NEA, 611.86B/2-758, Box 2555, February 7, 1958, pp. 1-3. See also Nutting, *Nasser*, p. 219. Nasser apparently confided in Raymond Hare, the US Ambassador in Cairo, that the union with Syria would become a 'great headache' and that most of the RCC actually opposed it. Zacharia Mohieddin described Nasser's reasoning by stating that the entire scheme 'would be an unnatural association built on sentiment and hampered by geography'. Most accounts of Nasser's reluctance to form the union came from a later period, after its collapse, and as a result ring somewhat false. There is little doubt that by 1962-3 Nasser regretted his decision but, in 1958, riding the crest of popularity and seeing a future full of promise, there is little doubt that he believed that he could manage the difficulties. See also Copeland, *Game*, p. 227. Copeland recounts the Egyptian optimism at the time: 'My Egyptian friends confidently predicted that during 1958 'Chamoun, Hussein, and Nuri will fall – and in that order'.' Clearly, in 1958, the Syrian adventure represented the welcomed first step on the road to Arab unity.
14 Kerr, *The Arab Cold War*, p. 21.
15 'The Middle East – Between Thunder & Sun'. *Time*, 31 March 1958, p. 17. When Nasser spoke in Cairo to announce the UAR, he linked himself with the legendary Arab leader Saladin: 'Always the Arab peoples were able to conquer invaders whenever they joined and stood together in one army – as in Saladin's day.' The crowd responded by proclaiming Nasser the new Saladin. Stage-managed or not, the crowd clearly reflected the mood in much of the Arab world.
16 'Egypt, Syria: Shotgun Wedding'. *Newsweek*, 10 February 1958, p. 52.
17 Copeland, *Game*, p. 224. Copeland points out that Nasser believed US assertions about Soviet designs on Syria, but he found American protestations of innocence in that regard somewhat disingenuous. Copeland states that with respect to Syria, circumstances drove Nasser to 'break one of his cardinal rules: take authority wherever you can get it, but avoid responsibility like the plague'.
18 'Telegram US Delegation, Baghdad Pact Meeting, Ankara, 25 January 1958'. *FRUS*, 1958-1960, Near East Region; Iraq; Iran; Arabian Peninsula, Volume XII, p. 408. See also 'Memorandum NEA [Lampton] to Dulles, 7 February 1958'. NACPM, GRDOS-59, NEA, CDF 1955-1959, 611.86B/2-758, pp. 1-4. Barry Lampton, the Egyptian desk officer in NEA, provided a briefing memorandum to the Secretary of State that included a background paper describing the sources for and development of the union. He traced the union effort back to a fundamental Egyptian and Syrian hostility to the

Baghdad Pact and the Syro-Egyptian military pact of October 20, 1955, which provided for a joint military command under an Egyptian general officer. He then cited Syrian activity in pushing for a political union during 1956 and 1957. In this interpretation, the Turko-Syrian crisis of September 1957 created the catalyst for a vote in both the Syrian and Egyptian parliaments on November 17, 1957 to explore political union. Lampton's argument followed the line of reasoning offered by Nasser, namely that the latter feared a Communist takeover. NEA also pointed out that the Syrians granted the Egyptian leader virtual dictatorial powers, making it an offer that Nasser could not refuse. See Nutting, *Nasser*, p. 213. Nutting provides an interesting evaluation of Abd-al-Hamid Sarraj, the head of the Syrian intelligence and security service or *muhabbarat*. According to Nutting, the American military attaché in Damascus approached Sarraj and told him that 'Washington had lost all faith in party politics government in the Arab World' and would be willing to back an army regime 'of good moral standing', if that regime declined 'to go all the way with Nasser'. True or not, the Eisenhower administration's frustration with civilian government throughout the Middle East-South Asia region had brought the US government to just such a conclusion. Military rule meant stability and was preferable to a civilian rule that invited plurality and Communist infiltration.

19 'Baghdad Pact Meeting Delegation Ankara to WDC, 25 January 1958'. *FRUS*, 1958-1960, Volume XII, p. 408.
20 'Memo NEA to Dulles, 7 February 1958'. NACPM, 611.86B/2-758, pp. 2-3.
21 Heikal, Muhammad, *The Sphinx and the Commissar: The Rise and Fall of the Soviet Influence in the Middle East*. New York: Harper & Row, 1978, pp. 88-93. Heikal comments that the Soviets 'were obliged to give the union their reluctant support', despite the arrest of Communist supporters. According to Heikal, it was the combination of the union and the suppression of Communist elements that made Nasser's April 28, 1958 visit to Moscow a top-priority item in the Kremlin. Washington was not the only Great Power attempting to gauge the potential for a relationship with the Egyptian leader. The Soviets had their own problems. Heikal believed that the Soviets not only were intent on impressing Nasser but also wanted to calibrate his relationship with the US, his views on the Arab-Israeli dispute, and their own long-term potential for a relationship. It was Nasser, not Khrushchev, who brought up the issue of UAR suppression of the Communist Party. According to Heikal, the Soviet leader responded that it was 'entirely your [an Egyptian] affair'. Interview with Muhammad Hakki, 8 August 2003. Hakki commented that Heikal's remembrances were often illuminating and always interesting; however, 'they must always be evaluated in the broader context.' According to Hakki: 'When Heikal quotes Nasser, one never knows whether it is what Nasser actually said, what Heikal thought Nasser should have said, or what Heikal would have said if he were Nasser.'
22 'Memorandum NEA [Lampton] to Dulles, 7 February 1958'. NACPM, GRDOS-59, NEA, CDF, 611.86B/2-758, Box 2555, p. 4. See also '353rd NSC Meeting, 30 January 1958'. DDEL, AWF, NSC, Box 9, p. 4. The report on the situation in Syria reflected Nasser's own explanation. 'Nasser had been reluctant to become involved in the Syrian picture and had been worried by Soviet opposition to the union, but had favored the union as a means of warding off Communism in Syria. The Syrians had been motivated by Pan-Arab nationalism, and by the Syrian Army's fear of eventual Communist control of Syria.' The popularity of the union with the Arab 'street' and its unpopularity in Saudi Arabia, Lebanon, Israel and among Syrian Communists was noted. Interestingly, there was no mention of Iraq or support for an alternative union.
23 'New Mideastern Gambit'. *Nation*, 15 February 1958, p. 129.
24 'Egypt, Syria: Shotgun Wedding'. *Newsweek*, 10 February 1958, p. 52. See also 'Mutual Security Problems, 15 June 1956'. *Executive Sessions of the Senate Foreign Relations Committee* (Historical Series), Volume VIII, Eighty-Fourth Congress Second Session, 1956.

Washington, DC: US Government Printing Office, 1978, pp. 409-432. In this session of the Committee, funding for the Baghdad Pact came under vociferous attack by Senator Wayne Morse, who opposed the aid on grounds that the US should 'do more for Israel'. Morse, in arguing with the other Senators, stated that the US should support 'free states', which in his view excluded most of the states in the Middle East and Africa. He pointedly stated: 'There is no individual liberty in these Arab States. They are police states, and Iraq is a good example. The individual has no freedom in Iraq, so we are going to pour our money in there.' When it was pointed out to Morse that he supported Turkey and Spain, the Senator tried unsuccessfully to separate out those authoritarian states that were not moving in 'a totalitarian direction'. In the same session several of the Senators expressed concern that Nasser was playing the US off against the Soviet Union on the issue of the Aswan Dam. Under Secretary of State Herbert Hoover, Jr. had made the case earlier that the dam at Aswan 'would be built'; it was just a question of whether it would be with Western or Soviet aid. Despite this, several Senators opposed supporting the project. Given the lack of support in Congress, whether the administration supported the dam or not may was probably irrelevant; there was considerable Congressional opposition. The debate was indicative of the difficulties that the administration had in getting the aid that it wanted to support containment policy in the Middle East and to maintain a balanced policy in the region that included support for allies, aid to the non-aligned, and placating the pro-Israeli lobby.
25 'Our Secretary of State, Americans Like Him – But…'. *Newsweek*, 27 January 1958, p. 33.
26 Tamer, A.M., 'Who Likes Dulles, Who Doesn't: The Arab States'. *Newsweek*, 27 January 1958, p. 29.
27 Copeland, *Game*, pp. 226-236. Copeland's description of the atmosphere in Beirut matches exactly the reality of double-dealing, so long a part of the Lebanese political landscape. While his descriptions of the camaraderie between competing intelligence services is to a degree exaggerated, there is some truth to it. His account of the 'Beirut Four' is entertaining. Sa'ib Salaam, Abdullah Yafi, Adnan Hakim, and Abdullah Mashnuq were pro-Nasserist operatives around whom the Egyptians built their strategy to mobilize the street mob. The Four were supported with money and weapons by Egyptian intelligence and Sarraj.
28 Copeland, *Game*, p. 234.
29 'Instructions, Dulles to Beirut, 3 February 1958'. NACPM, 611.83/2-358, pp. 1-3. In Muhammad H. Heikal's *Cutting the Lion's Tail: Suez through Egyptian Eyes* (London: André Deutsch, 1986), the author points out that within the framework of the Baghdad Pact, so-called 'free nations' were not allowed to address certain issues that were central to their own security. At the Baghdad Pact meeting on February 11, Zionism and Israel were, according to the American representative, topics that he had no authority to discuss with Pact members. Heikal comments (p. 228): 'These words, written almost on the eve of the pact's demise, could well serve as its epitaph.'
30 'British Embassy Ankara [Bowker] to the FO, 26 January 1958'. PRO, FO371/134386.
31 'Minutes on Syrian Situation, 28 January 1958'. PRO, FO371/134386.
32 'British Embassy Ankara [Bowker] to the FO, 28 January 1958'. PRO, FO371/134386.
33 'British Embassy, Ankara, 29 January 1958'. PRO, FO371/134386. See also 'British Embassy Amman [Mason] to FO, 3 March 1958'. PRO, FO371/134198, p. 1. At the time of the Syrian-Egyptian union, Sa'id was not the Prime Minister, although he represented Iraq at the Baghdad Pact conference in Ankara. Because of Sa'id's penchant for grandiose plans, Jordan's King Hussein, on March 3, 1958, learning that the Iraqi government had resigned, expressed the hope that Sa'id would not be asked to form a new one. His thinking was that Sa'id would cause an intensification of Egyptian and Syrian attacks and propaganda against both Jordan and Iraq. Hussein did not like Sa'id

on a personal level, and wanted his role limited to behind-the-scenes support for any new government.
34 'Minute UAR interference in Lebanon, 19 May 1958'. PRO, FO371/134118. The view that Nasser and the Soviets were in league in Lebanon persisted. As one supporter of stronger policy toward Nasser and the Soviets in region put it: 'The present unrest and rioting in Lebanon is – as no doubt you are well aware – due to Soviet-backed Nasserism.' See also 'Letter FO to Secretary of State, 16 May 1958'. PRO, FO371/134118. 'There is no need for any investigation into what has been quite obvious for some time past, viz: that the present trouble in Lebanon is due to Nasser's attempt to grab that country and incorporate it in his Arab Republic. Apart from Iraq and Jordan – Saudi Arabia continues to sit on the fence – there would then be no opposition to his plan of allowing Russia to establish herself in the Middle East in return for her acknowledgement of himself as head of the Arab States.' Although distorted, these views were widely held in 1958.
35 'British Emb Beirut [Middleton] to FO, 27 January 1958'. PRO, FO371/134386, p. 1.
36 'Minute [R.M. Hadow] FO on Egyptian/Syrian Union, 28 January 1958'. PRO, FO371/134386.
37 'British Emb WDC [Caccia] to FO, 30 January 1958'. PRO, FO371/134386, p. 2.
38 'British Embassy Ankara [Sir J. Bowker] to the FO, 28 January 1958'. PRO, FO371/134386, p. 1. Dulles' address to those present in this 'restricted meeting' of the Baghdad Pact, if rendered correctly by Bowker, was almost insulting to the delegates. 'Dulles noted that Nasser acted on the strength of Soviet backing, but he was not sure that any Arab State seemed prepared to act on the strength of United States backing; in fact, the only people who were prepared to take effective action in the area were Nasser and Ben-Gurion.' Perhaps this was a goad directed at Nuri Sa'id, since the initiator of any action had to be an Arab state and he represented the only Arab state present. Sa'id wanted a week to ten days to think about it. This was rejected, and discussions resumed the next day.
39 'British Embassy Ankara [Sir J. Bowker] to FO, 30 January 1958'. PRO, FO371/134386. See also 'British Embassy Baghdad to FO, 13 February 1958'. PRO, FO371/143197, in which Sir Michael Wright outlined the British view of a Jordanian-Iraqi union. Wright believed that union would strengthen the two weak Hashemite regimes and undermine UAR attempts to divide them. Wright feared that Nuri was overreaching in his plans, but that the US and Britain could hardly veto his activities for fear of demoralizing the anti-Nasser factions.
40 'Dulles to Baghdad, 8 February 1958'. *FRUS*, 1958-1960, Volume XIII, p. 420.
41 'Letter from Sir Charles Johnston Amman to FO, 8 April 1958'. PRO, FO371/133147. Johnston's report resulted from a meeting with none other than H.A.R. (Kim) Philby, used his erstwhile position as Middle East 'correspondent' for *The Observer* and *The Economist*, as a MI-6 cover while he really worked for the KGB. Johnston attached summaries of Egyptian news accounts to further illustrate the kind of pressure now confronting the Saudis. *Al-Ahram* made the most of the 'plot' and referred to calls by 'a large number of Saudi amirs' for an investigation; the paper further stated that the Saudi government maintained its grip on power only through repression, and used Prince Talal's 'stormy' meeting with King Saud as an example of the high-level unrest and dissatisfaction with the King's 'extreme policies'. See Page, Bruce, David Leitch, and Phillip Knightley, *The Philby Conspiracy*. New York: Ballantine, 1981, p. 272. Despite his 'kitchen Arabic', Philby used the reputation of his father (St. John Philby) as an eminent Arabist to mine information, particularly on Saudi Arabia and Yemen.
42 'British Embassy, Beirut, [Middleton] to FO, 7 March 1958 (No. 212)'. PRO, FO371/134390. This telegram included a complete listing of the positions and

appointees to the new UAR government. Sarraj was the deputy to Nasser as head of the Executive Council for the Syrian Province.
43 'U.A.R. – Father Ibrahim's Plot'. *Time*, 17 March 1958, p. 24. See also 'The Middle East: Undertow'. *Newsweek*,17 March 1958, p. 40, and 'British Embassy, Beirut, [Middleton] to FO, 7 March 1958, (No. 213A)'. PRO, FO371/134390.
44 Nutting, *Nasser*, p. 227.
45 'Letter, Johnston, Amman to FO, 8 April 1958'. PRO, FO371/133147. 'Between Thunder and Sun'. *Time*, 31 March 1958, p. 18. Contemporary analysis of the situation illustrates the degree of uncertainty and concern, particularly over Saudi Arabia. 'Whatever his sympathies Saud cannot afford to ignore Nasser's appeal to his impoverished subjects. Every Saudi Arabian village has radios tuned to Cairo's broadcasts. Egyptian technicians and teachers have deeply infiltrated the kingdom. For all his oil riches, Saud's financial position is so bad that world banks ceased several months ago to honor Saudi letters of credit. Educated Saudis almost to a man are disgusted. Said one: "The King is burning up our wealth wasting, wasting everywhere – palaces, women, bribes. He is destroying our country. It is a crime that cannot go on".'
46 'Minute [G. Lucas] FO on letter from Johnston Amman, 8 April 1958'. PRO, FO371/133147. The FO comments were signed off by A.R. Walmsley, and included the following comment: 'Mr. Philby's comments are, in my view, worth a good deal. … They also have the virtue of according with our own final assessment of these events.' This move on the part of Saudi Arabia represented a major setback for their perceived role in containing Nasser's ambitions. During much of 1957, many viewed King Saud as the most effective opposition to Nasser.
47 'Minute [Lucas] Foreign Office attached to Telegram Beirut to FO on Feisal policy statement, 21 April 1958'. PRO, FO371/133146. The British understood that the price of relations with Saudi Arabia required the British to withdraw support for Omani claims to the Buraimi Oasis. 'Minute [D.M.H. Riches] attached to an assessment: The Middle East and Communism, 29 January 1958'. PRO, FO371/133146. As Riches put it, the British 'could not abandon our friends', meaning the Sultan of Oman.
48 Eisenhower, Dwight D., *The White House Years: Waging Peace, 1956-1961*. Garden City, NY: Doubleday, 1965, p. 264.
49 'Discussion 358th NSC Meeting, 13 March 1958'. DDEL, AWF, NSC, Box 9, p. 13. Casting about for something positive to report, Dulles passed along rumors of a possible union between Tunisia and Morocco, commenting: 'Such a union would be anti-Nasser and, accordingly, advantageous to the United States if it were consummated.' This underscored the level of desperation for good news to which the administration had sunk.
50 Ibid. The administration faced growing pressure in the press on the Middle East, and it was an election year. Ernest K. Lindley, a conservative columnist, wrote an article entitled: 'How to save the Middle East'. *Newsweek*, 6 January 1958, p. 25. Lindley stated: 'Soviet imperialism is on the offensive and making gains. The free world is on the defensive and losing ground. Unless this trend is checked and reversed, the free world will eventually suffer a catastrophic rout.' He then provided nine actions that the administration should take and closed by stating: 'The Middle East can be saved. If it is lost, it will be basically for the same reasons that we lost the missile-satellite race.' Eisenhower was in a no-win situation. He had no control over events, but was being pilloried for doing nothing to reverse the situation.
51 Eisenhower, *Waging Peace*, p. 264. Describing Feisal as 'pro-Nasserist' emphasizes the unsophisticated view of the Middle East held at the highest levels. Saud was an incompetent and arguably a degenerate as well, but the administration had pinned its hopes on him for leadership. In contrast, Feisal would do more real damage to Nasser's position in the Arab world than any another Arab leader. Feisal was a realist who

understood that reforms had to be made in Saudi Arabia if the Kingdom were to survive. See 'British Embassy WDC [Benest] to FO [Walmsley], 23 May 1958'. PRO, FO371/133149; in May 1958, D.L. Benest wrote to A.R. Walmsley at the FO about his meeting with Feisal, who was in the States for medical treatment, stating: '[Feisal] seemed quite at ease, and he has apparently landed on his feet once more.' Feisal showed his interest in reforming the Kingdom, and explained what he was doing to reorganize the central administration of the government. He also speculated on Yemen and stated that he hoped there would be no outside interference in Lebanon.

52 'US Embassy, Cairo, to WDC, 17 April 1958'. *FRUS*, 1958-1960, Volume XIII, p. 441.

53 'Memcon US Consulate, Alexandria, 3 May 1958'. NACPM, GRDOS-59, NEA, CDF, 611.86/5-358, pp. 1-3. The Alexandria Consulate used Nicolas Rigos, a Greek businessman with excellent contacts in the Egyptian government, as a sounding board and information source. Rigos believed that the US's 'new policy' was so badly timed that much of the potential benefit was lost. Its close proximity to the Moscow trip made it appear that Nasser and the Egyptians were in the driver's seat. Rigos argued the US could not regain its position in Egypt because while Washington talked of aid, Russian factories were actually arriving in Egypt and Egyptian cotton was going to the USSR. He believed it was too little, too late. See also 'Dispatch US Consulate, Alexandria to WDC, 8 May 1958'. NACPM, 611.86/5-858, pp. 1-2. An article by Dana Adams Schmidt, 'Nasser Believed Warier of Soviet', in the *New York Times*, 9 May 1958, p. 5, quoted Assistant Secretary Rountree as stating that: 'encouraging signs of a growing realization of what constitutes true neutralism and of what wholesale Soviet offers of assistance are really worth' were emerging. Schmidt wrote that: 'Officials reject the idea that they United States is 'wooing' President Nasser', but that the US wanted to see normal relations develop with the UAR.

54 For a perspective on Nasserist activities in the Sudan, see 'Dispatch [Cole Chargé] Khartoum to WDC containing "Comments on the Pre-Election Period in the Sudan", February 8, 1958'. NACPM, 745W.00/2-858, pp. 2, 46. See also 'Dispatch [Cole] Khartoum to WDC on National Unionist Party reaction to Egyptian/Sudanese Border Dispute, March 8, 1958'. NACPM, 745W.00/3-858, pp. 1-7. In the Sudan, the Umma and Mahdist parties generally followed an anti-Nasserist line. The Peoples' Democratic Party (PDP) was essentially Nasserist, as were elements of the Nationalist Union Party (NUP). Both often cooperated with the Communists. Egypt's proximity to and historical involvement in Sudan made any form of 'union' with the UAR a bedrock point of political debate. Sudan had historically opposed Egyptian expansion, having experienced Egyptian rule first-hand. The British, having mid-wifed the creation of an independent Sudan, did not want to see it fall under Egyptian domination. Such an eventuality would have been embarrassing, all the more so if it occurred through the ballot box. The Nasserists had the problem of projecting a Sudanese nationalist image within the context of a pro-Nasserist program. A February 1958 border dispute with Egypt brought the issue of Sudanese nationalism to the forefront. The NUP took the position that Sudan should not surrender territory, while Nasserist elements argued that closer cooperation and coordination with Cairo would avoid such incidents in the future. Given the upcoming elections, the PDP and NUP recognized that support for formal union with Egypt would be political suicide. They announced their intention to work for a union between all the 'progressive' opponents of the Umma Party, branding it 'the only stumbling block in the way of an enlightened Sudan, "Nasser style"'. See also 'Dispatch Khartoum to WDC on Sudanese Elections, March 28, 1958'. NACPM, 745W.00/3-2858, pp. 1-2. Just prior to the election, the Nasserists announced that they would join with the Umma and Mahdist parties in return for an agreement affirming Sudan's non-alignment and adherence to 'positive neutrality'. The internal political situation quickly turned problematic when the PDP demanded half of the cabinet posts,

including the Ministry of the Interior for an ardent Nasserist, Ali Abdal al-Rahman. The Umma rejected both the demand for cabinet posts and Rahman's appointment, because of his 'leftist utterances and the strongly pro-Egyptian attitudes (that) made him singularly ill-suited to that sensitive post'. All involved anticipated additional Nasserist attempts to gain influence through the coalition government. See also 'Middle East: Our Edge in the Sudan'. *Newsweek*, 24 March 1958, p. 49. With pro-UAR elements now in the government, most Western observers believed Nasser and 'his Communist allies' would 'make mischief'.

55 Macmillan, *Riding the Storm*, p. 503. See also Leonard Moseley's *Dulles: A Biography of Eleanor, Allen, and John Foster Dulles and Their Family Network* (New York: Dial/James Wade, 1978), p. 412, an excellent analysis of the British view that Dulles had given the green light for the Suez operation.

56 Dresch, Paul, *A History of Modern Yemen*. Cambridge: Cambridge University Press, 2000, p. 81. Imam Ahmad had ruled Yemen since the 1948 assassination of his father, Imam Yahya. Imam Ahmad was quite the survivor, most probably because those closest to him were not. Colin Reid of the London *Daily Telegraph* compiled a list of Imam Yahya's fourteen sons that survived childbirth. The list was reprinted in 'And then there were only. . .'. *Newsweek*, 18 February 1958, p. 39. It is instructive on the nature of Yemeni internal politics, ordered from the oldest Ahmad to the youngest Abd-al-Rahman. Ahmad became the Imam; Muhammad drowned (not easy in Yemen, without assistance); Hassan was exiled; Hussein was murdered; Ali moved to Coventry (no doubt motivated by self-preservation); Abdullah was beheaded; Qazim exiled; Mutahir died in Cairo; Ibrahim disappeared; Ismail went 'abroad' and apparently stayed there; Abbas was beheaded; Yahya disappeared; Muhsin was assassinated; and the youngest, Abd-al-Rahman continued to live in Yemen. Interview with Lakeland, 23-24 September 2003. Following his tour in Cairo 1951-1955, Lakeland was given the post of Consul General in Aden and accredited to the Imamate in Yemen. In November 1955, he traveled to Ta'iz and then on to Hudaydah on the coast to meet with Imam Ahmad. There was at the time no real road from either Ta'iz or Hudaydah to the capital in Sanaa. Holding court in Hudaydah, the Imam, wearing a large turban, sat on a raised dais and took petitions from his subjects. He had a unique filing system. When an issue of importance came up, the Imam would jot down a few notes on a scrape of paper, take off the turban, put the note inside the turban, and put the turban back on. Lakeland missed Thanksgiving with his family in Aden that year because the Imam decided that he needed 'more exposure to Yemeni culture' and refused to allow him to depart until early December.

57 O'Ballance, Edgar, *The War in Yemen*. Hamden, CN: Archon, 1971, p. 59.

58 'British Legation Ta'iz, Yemen [Kemp] to FO [Riches], 31 December 1957'. PRO, FO371/132962. Looking for help, the British Consul in Ta'iz reported that King Saud had expressed his 'deep concern' over the presence of Soviet Communist in Yemen. See also 'Yemen: Grappling Demons'. *Newsweek*, 11 February 1957, pp. 45-46. Badr, in fact, believed that with Soviet arms and Egyptian assistance the British could be driven from Aden and the Protectorate. See also 'Yemen briefing provided to the members of the Baghdad Pact, 17 January 1958'. PRO, FO371/132955. For Badr, the arms had an additional purpose: distributed to his supporters, they would presumably ensure his accession to the crown

59 'Minute [Riches] on US attitudes in Yemen, 20 January 1958'. PRO, FO371/132962.

60 'British Legation Ta'iz [Kemp] to FO, 24 January 1958'. PRO, FO371/132950. See also 'British Legation Ta'iz [Kemp] to FO [Fretwell], 1 January 1958'. PRO, FO371/132950. The coup chronology is interesting and amusing. On December 28, 1957, Hadarani, identified as the 'Imam's Court Poet and Jester', appeared at the British Legation to tell Kemp about a 'plot to get rid of the Imam'. Also known as the Imam's 'spy and agent-

provocateur', Hadarani excited Kemp's concern that he and the British government were about to be blamed for something. Hadarani told Kemp that the coup would bring about 'the accession of someone more reasonable than the Imam and Crown Prince and would lead to the expulsion of the Communists and bring peace ... on the border of the (Aden) Protectorate.' Wary, Kemp told Hadarani: 'All [Britain is] interested in [is] the improvement of Anglo-Yemeni relations and ... the succession [is] the Yemenis' own affair.' This being Hadarani's third visit, Kemp knew that something was definitely up. Fretwell at the Eastern Department of the FO thought he knew Yemen well, and told Kemp that he saw no cause for concern. In Ta'iz, Kemp had developed that peculiar paranoia which comes from residing in Arabia Felix: the constant certainty that something bad is about to happen – because it usually does. 'British Legation Ta'iz [Kemp] to FO, 24 January 1958'. PRO, FO371/132950. One of the plotters allegedly had a letter on his person that implicated both the Americans and British.

61 'Minute [Fretwell] on coup report from Ta'iz, 28 January 1958'. PRO FO371/132950.
62 'Minute [Riches] on situation in Yemen, 9 January 1958'. PRO, FO371/132962.
63 'Minute [Riches] on US attitudes in Yemen, 20 January 1958'. PRO, FO371/132962. The attempted coup was peculiarly Yemeni. In making their way down the street to the palace in Ta'iz, the plotters were intercepted and arrested. The Yemenis of course believed that the British and their friends the Americans were behind the coup.
64 'Press release communicated by US Embassy Damascus to the FO on Badr's Syrian Speech, 29 January 1958'. PRO, FO371/132955
65 'Minute [Sir Frederick Hoyer-Millar] on Yemen and the Commonwealth, 24 March 1958'. PRO, FO371/132973.
66 'Memorandum Sir H.J.B. Lintcott to Hoyer-Millar, 24 March 1958'. PRO, FO371/132973. Lintcott wanted to inform the 'Old Dominions', get Canada, Australia, and New Zealand on board, and then later follow-up with the 'new' dominions of Pakistan and India, hoping that they would quietly acquiesce.
67 'Memo Eastern Dept FO [Riches] to Hayter, 30 April 1958'. PRO, FO371/132968.
68 'British Legation Ta'iz [Oldfield] to FO, 29 April 1958'. PRO, FO371/132952. This also covered a rumor about the imminent demise of the Imam and Crown Prince Badr's fall. It was the Yemeni rumor-mill at its best.
69 'Minute [Fretwell] on UN role in Yemen conflict, 6 May 1958'. PRO, FO371/132968. Fearing further pressure from Washington, and knowing the US contact to be Muhammad al-'Amri, the Deputy Foreign Minister, the British attempted to undermine his credibility. The British argued that 'Amri had consistently misrepresented their position in order to get the Imam's permission to talk to the British.
70 'British Legation Ta'iz [Oldfield] to FO, 18 June 1958'. PRO, FO371/132969.
71 'Minute [Fretwell], 23 June 1958'. PRO, FO371/132969.
72 'Letter Horace Phillips to Colonial Office [J.C. Morgan], 18 June 1958'. PRO, FO371/132969. See also Phillips, Horace, *Envoy Extraordinary: A Most Unlikely Ambassador*. London: Radcliffe, 1995; this is an interesting memoir on his career in the colonial service. Phillips was a particularly interesting character. Having previously served in Jidda, he became Ambassador to Saudi Arabia in 1968, at which point the *Jewish Chronicle* ran a story about his appointment, including the fact that he was born to a poor Jewish working-class family in Glasgow. At that point, King Feisal ordered his credentials withdrawn and Phillips left Saudi Arabia.
73 'Minute [Fretwell], 22 July 1958'. PRO, FO371/132970.
74 Macmillan, *Riding the Storm*, p. 505. See also 'Discussion 371st NSC Meeting, 3 July 1958'. DDEL, AWF, NSC, Box 10, p. 11. 'British Legation Ta'iz [Oldfield] to FO, 18 June 1958'. PRO, FO371/132969. In early July 1958, the Sultan of Lah'j, a member of the Aden Confederation, defected to the Imam. It was unfortunate timing, occurring

only two weeks before the Iraqi coup. At the regular NSC meeting, Dulles reported the incident saying: 'The British ... had suffered another reverse in the Aden area. Approximately one-half of the British-trained army of the Sultanate of Lah'j had defected to the Yemenis, taking with them valuable equipment.' This added to the US view that the British had lost their touch in the Middle East.

75 'Cairo [Hare] to WDC, 10 February 1958'. *FRUS*, 1958-1960, Volume XIII, p. 424.
76 'WDC to Baghdad, 21 February 1958'. *FRUS*, 1958-1960, Volume XIII, p. 431.
77 'Memcon with UAR Amb Ahmed Hussein, DOS, WDC, 3 March 1958'. *FRUS*, 1958-1960, Volume XIII, p. 433.
78 Cairo [Hare] to WDC, 20 March 1958'. *FRUS*, 1958-1960, Volume XIII, pp. 435-436.
79 'WDC to Cairo [Hare], 25 March 1958'. *FRUS*, 1958-1960, Volume XIII, pp. 437-438.
80 'Cairo, to WDC, 17 April 1958'. *FRUS*, 1958-1960, Volume XIII, pp. 442-446. Eisenhower, *Waging Peace*, pp. 262-263. In his memoirs, Eisenhower fails to mention the new policy toward Egypt. He refers to Nasser's political leanings as 'still something of a mystery' and briefly speaks of the 'troubled and confused atmosphere' at the close of the Baghdad summit. See also Macmillan, *Riding the Storm*, p. 502. Using similar words, Macmillan stated that 1958 'proved the signal for a period of confusion and even anarchy in which the Western powers were to become progressively involved'.
81 'Text of News Conference Held by Secretary Dulles'. *New York Times*, 9 April 1958, p. 10. Pressure had also been building in the press for a new policy approach to the Middle East. The day before the press conference, C.L. Sulzberger, in an article entitled 'Foreign Affairs: A Time for Diplomatic Calm' (*New York Times*, 7 April 1958, p. 20), had addressed the issue of Arab nationalism: 'There is no reason why the United States should oppose the principle of Arab unity. Indeed, we appear to support the recent Iraq-Jordan federation; we would not object to an eventual link between Morocco, Tunisia and Algeria; and we inferentially blessed the Syrian-Egyptian union when we recognized it. It might be wise for us once again to make some mild show of approval for Nasser's new state in order to demonstrate that it need not look only to Russia for help and psychological sympathy. But we cannot go too far. We cannot abandon our friends elsewhere now openly reviled by Cairo. What we must make plain is that while we have no objection to Nasser's confederation or to its extension through peaceful, voluntary adherence by other lands, we cannot tolerate moves to expand it by conspiracy or force. This need not be said by public declaration. We have tended to make too many such statements in the past. They have a hollow ring.'
82 'Letter Chairman Senate Foreign Relations Committee [Humphrey] to Rountree, 9 April 1958'. NACPM, 611.86/4-958, p. 1.
83 'Letter Rountree to Humphrey, 17 April 1958'. NACPM, 611.86/4-958, pp. 1-2.
84 'USIA Beirut, to WDC, 11 April 1958'. NACPM, 611.86/4-1158, pp. 1-2.
85 Caruthers, Osgood 'Nasser Calls a Halt to Attacks on U.S.'. *New York Times*, 15 April 1958, p. 1.
86 'WDC to London, 9 April 1958'. NACPM, 611.86/4-958, p. 2. See also 'WDC to Cairo, 16 April 1958'. *FRUS*, 1958-1960, Volume XIII, pp. 439-440 and footnote.
87 'Memo [Asst Sec NEA Rountree] to Dulles, 16 April 1958'. NACPM, 611.86/4-1658, p. 1. An article by Edward Weintal, 'Behind-Scenes in Washington: A Change Toward Nasser' (*Newsweek*, 21April 1958, p. 53) concluded that the new policy 'gamble' had a good chance of paying off with better relations and Egyptian gratitude for American assistance.
88 'WDC to US Embassies in the Middle East and Europe, 25 April 1958'. NACPM, 611.86/4-2558, pp. 1-2.
89 'Cairo, to WDC, 26 April 1958'. NACPM, GRDOS59, NEA, CDF, 611.86/4-2658, Section I, p. 2. The United States only released Egyptian assets after the British and French had done the same, but it was still viewed as a reaction to Nasser's Moscow trip.

90 Ibid, Section III, p. 2.
91 'Russia - Our Dear Guest'. *Time*, 12 May 1958, p. 26.
92 Seale, Patrick, *The Struggle for Syria: A Study of Post-War Arab Politics*. New Haven, CT: Yale University Press, 1965, pp. 70-71, 272-282. See also 'Record of Conversation between Dulles and Hammerskjold, 18 June 1958'. PRO, FO371/134125. Hammerskjold told Dulles that he believed that the Syrians really had more control over the operations in Lebanon than the Egyptians. Hammerskjold felt that Nasser 'was not happy with the situation' and wanted it to quiet down and wait for the elections, but that Sarraj and the Syrians had their own ideas about the disposition of Lebanon. He also felt that, left to their own devices, the Lebanese 'genius for compromise' would work things out. See also, Copeland, *Game*, p. 237. This is not to say that Nasser would have been unhappy with a pro-U.A.R. government in Beirut. To the contrary, it would have been a major plus, but having supplied the arms and encouraged his new Syrian partners to support the revolt, his control was probably limited at this point. Copeland makes an interesting point about Chamoun. Chamoun 'had been an "Arab" long before Nasser ever heard the word; at the American University of Beirut, where intellectual Arab nationalism was born, Chamoun had been an ardent advocate of Arab unity and united Arab resistance to the rise of Zionism.' In the 1950s, he became 'disenchanted' with the 'Moslem politicians of the worst type' who used Arab nationalism as a smoke screen for supporting Nasserist ambitions. While Nasser probably agreed with Chamoun's concern over linking Arab nationalism and Islam, the Lebanese President's support of the Eisenhower Doctrine and the West in general made him a target for subversion.
93 'Minute on UAR interference in Lebanon, 19 May 1958'. PRO, FO371/134118.
94 'Beirut to WDC, 7 May 1958'. *FRUS*, 1958-1960, Lebanon/Jordan, Volume XI, pp. 32-33.
95 'Beirut to WDC, 11 May 1958'. *FRUS*, 1958-1960, Volume XI, pp. 35-37 and 'Telegram Beirut [McClintock] to DOS, WDC, 11 May 1958'. *FRUS*, 1958-1960, Volume XI, pp. 38-40. Also see 'Minute on U.A.R. interference in Lebanon, 19 May 1958'. PRO, FO371/134118 for reference to the attack on the border post.
96 'Memo White House, WDC, 13 May 1958'. *FRUS*, 1958-1960, Volume XI, pp. 45-48.
97 'Minute FO [Rose] to British Embassy WDC, 20 May 1958'. PRO, FO371/134118.
98 'Amman to WDC, 30 June 1958'. *FRUS*, 1958-1960, Volume XI, pp. 294-296.
99 'British Embassy Beirut to the FO on US Ambassador in Cairo conversation with Nasser, 22 May 1958'. PRO, FO371/134118.
100 'British Embassy Beirut [Middleton] to FO, 22 May 1958'. PRO, FO371/134118.
101 Copeland, *Game*, p. 207.
102 'Cairo to WDC, 16 June 1958'. *FRUS*, 1958-1960, Volume XIII, p. 453.
103 'Cairo to WDC, 26 June 1958'. *FRUS*, 1958-1960, Volume XIII, pp. 456-457.
104 'British Embassy Beirut to FO, 22 May 1958'. PRO, FO371/134118.
105 'Minute [Riches] attached to an assessment: The Middle East and Communism, 29 January 1958'. PRO, FO371/133146. See also 'Memcon with Jordanian Ambassador, 28 March 1958'. PRO, FO371/133146. The Jordanian Ambassador complained to the FO about pro-Nasserist statements in the British press, one of which stated: 'the population in Iraq and Jordan were in the very large majority in favour of Nasser.' At the same time, the Ambassador argued that the press ignored the 'unanimous vote' in the Jordanian parliament for union with Iraq. Wanting at least to appear sympathetic, and perhaps also concerned, the FO concluded that *The Times*' diplomatic correspondent was irresponsible and 'one of Colonel Nasser's abler propagandists'.
106 'British Embassy [Caccia] WDC to the FO, 21 May 1958'. PRO, FO371/134118.

Chapter 3

1 Rubenstein, Alvin, *Red Star on the Nile*. Princeton, NJ: Princeton University Press, 1977, p. 5.
2 Pack, Chester J. and Elmo Richardson, *The Presidency of Dwight D. Eisenhower*. Lawrence: University of Kansas Press, 1991, p. 162. In light of pronouncements against Nasser, Pack and Richardson state that the Administration's position on Suez was hypocritical and inconsistent. Washington had overthrown the government of Iran, toyed with subverting Nasser's government, branded Nasser a 'Middle East variety of international Communism', denounced the illegal nationalization of the Suez Canal, and preached the dangers of radical nationalism in the Middle East to all who would listen. When the opportunity to get rid of Nasser's regime appeared, Eisenhower and Dulles failed to act, for presumably domestic political reasons related to the election of 1956, use of the Israelis, and personal pique at not being fully informed by the British and French.
3 'Minute FO [E.M. Rose] to British Embassy WDC, 20 May 1958'. PRO FO371/134118.
4 Macmillan, *Riding the Storm*, p. 511.
5 'Minister's meeting on Lebanon chaired by Prime Minister Macmillan, 14 May 1958'. PRO, FO371/134118.
6 Macmillan, *Riding the Storm*, p. 511.
7 Copeland, *Game*, pp. 231-233. Despite Chamoun's ever shriller calls for support, the US and Britain had managed to limit involvement to clandestine assistance. Then the assassination of Nasib Metni, an effective, anti-Chamoun, pro-Nasser journalist, elevated Chamoun to prime suspect. This set off an all-out revolt, fully aided and abetted by Sarraj, the Syrian security and intelligence chief, and various anti-Chamoun factions in Lebanon.
8 'FO and Whitehall to British Embassy WDC, 20 May 1958'. PRO, FO371/134118. The British wanted to make sure that Canada and Australia were on board should a military operation be mounted. Canberra and Ottawa wanted to bring in the UN, but London demurred because 'the State Department do not regard Lebanon's claims of large scale outside intervention as substantiated and doubt whether the Lebanon could make a case against the U.A.R. in the Security Council.' In other words, it was questionable whether Nasserist Syria was the source of the problem or merely supporting pro-Nasserist indigenous Lebanese.
9 'British Embassy WDC [Caccia] to FO, 21 May 1958'. PRO, FO371/134118.
10 'Discussion 366th NSC Meeting, 22 May 1958'. DDEL, AWF, NSC, Box 10, p. 3.
11 'Memcon Eisenhower and Macmillan, Washington, 9 June 1958'. DDEL, AWF, International Series (IS) Box 24, Section One, p. 1. See also 'WDC [Rountree] to Amman and Baghdad, 12 June 1958'. DDEL, AWF, IS, Box 35, pp. 1-2. Macmillan convinced Eisenhower to offer more support to Jordan and Iraq. This increased aid included $25 million to cover Jordan's entire share of the costs of Jordanian-Iraqi union and part of Iraq's share.
12 'Memocon Eisenhower and Prime Minister Macmillan, Washington, 9 June 1958'. DDEL, Section Two, pp. 1, 3. During this meeting, Assistant Secretary of State for NEA Rountree brought up the idea of replacing Chamoun with General Fuad Chehab, the Chief of Staff of the Lebanese Army. While those present complained that Chehab had 'recently shown a lack of political astuteness' – Chehab had made the West unhappy by playing both sides in the Lebanese struggle – they concluded that Chehab was one of the few acceptable candidates.
13 'Minute FO [Rose] on Lebanon, 16 June 1958'. PRO, FO371/134125.
14 'British Embassy WDC [Hayter] on Conversation with Dulles, 24 June 1958'. PRO, FO371/134125. See also 'Minute on Hayter Telegram by Hoyer-Millar, 25 June 1958'.

PRO, FO371/134125. Sir Frederick Hoyer-Millar, the Permanent Under-Secretary of State for Foreign Affairs, stated: 'It is, however, rather disquieting to see the rather wild ideas ventilated by Mr. Dulles.' See also 'British Embassy WDC [Caccia] to FO, 25 June 1958'. PRO, FO371/134125 in which the British were clearly aghast at Dulles' suggestion of getting the French, Turks, and even Pakistanis involved in any potential Lebanese operation. 'Memcon Selwyn Lloyd and Israeli Ambassador Elath, 2 May 1958'. PRO, FO371/134284. On May 2, 1958, Mr. Elath brought up the subject of Nasser with Selwyn Lloyd, the British Foreign Minister. Asked what he thought, Lloyd provided a revealing response: '[Nasser] suffered from schizophrenia: there was one side of him which would like to have an accommodation with the West but there was another which had dreams of a Middle Eastern and African Empire which could only be procured at the expense of Western interests. As with all schizophrenics, one did not know exactly what he was going to do, but on the whole one could assume that anything he did would be nasty.'
15 'Memcon Dulles and Hammerskjold, 18 June 1958'. PRO, FO371/134125. Hammerskjold warned Dulles that Charles Malik, the Lebanese Foreign Minister, was difficult and unreliable: 'At one moment screaming for action and the next wanting nothing done at all. At the moment, he seemed to be trying to force a crisis so that the Lebanese could call for Western intervention.'
16 'British Embassy Beirut [Middleton] to FO, 25 June 1958'. PRO, FO371/134125. In making a case for outside intervention, Chamoun accused the UAR of providing the funding and leadership for the Lebanese revolt. He argued that rebel forces in Lebanon were actually Egyptian, Syrian, and Palestinian 'volunteers'. In typical contradictory fashion, Chamoun stated that after Cairo's 1957 attempt to undermine Jordan, he knew Lebanon would be next; yet while he deplored Cairo's action, he had no intention of cutting off relations with the UAR.
17 'WDC to Cairo [Hare], 25 June 1958'. NACPM, NEA, 611.86/6-2458, pp. 1-2.
18 'Discussion 371st NSC Meeting, 3 July 1958'. DDEL, AWF, NSC Series, Box 10, p. 11.
19 'Beirut to WDC, 1 July 1958'. *FRUS*, 1958-1960, Volume XI, pp. 190-193.
20 'Memo Lord Hood and Rountree, 3 July 1958'. *FRUS*, 1958-1960, Volume XI, p. 198.
21 'Beirut to WDC, 10 July 1958'. *FRUS*, 1958-1960, Volume XI, p. 205. General Chehab had maintained strict neutrality in the civil conflict. As a result, the US administration had difficulty understanding where he stood in the conflict. Washington had assumed that Chehab, a Maronite Christian, would support Chamoun, but the Lebanese imbroglio was not that simple. See also 'Discussion 367th NSC meeting, 29 May 1958'. DDEL, AWF, NSC, Box 10, p. 3. Dulles believed that Chehab was 'sitting on his hands' and not prosecuting the war against the rebels and insurgents vigorously. He was afraid that Chehab's failure to act would necessitate intervention.
22 'Dispatch Baghdad to WDC, 18 March 1958'. NACPM, NEA, 787.00/3-1858, p. 1. In the Foreign Service cables are usually written so that the officer in question can always argue that they were with right, or at least partially right. No doubt, in July 1958, A. David Fritzlan, Counselor of the Embassy, would liked to have had this dispatch back so that he could better choose his wording.
23 'Telegram from British Embassy Baghdad [Wright] to FO [Lloyd], 11 February 1958'. PRO, FO371/134222.
24 Ibid.
25 'Minute FO [Rose] on Wright's telegram and analysis, 21 March 1958'. PRO, FO371/134222. See also 'Minute on Wright's telegram, 27 February 1958'. PRO, FO371/134222, that gives a more detailed analysis of Kuwait's role, including the fact that it kept keep France and Britain supplied with oil during the Suez crisis.
26 'Memcon Eisenhower and Macmillan, Washington, 9 June 1958'. DDEL, Section Three, pp. 1-2. Macmillan learned of Nuri's threat from Assistant Secretary of State

Richard Rountree during the 9 June meeting with Eisenhower. Sir Patrick Dean, a Macmillan advisor, quickly downplayed Sa'id's remarks: 'Nuri wants money more than he does Kuwait, which he can't really expect to have by this weekend.' See also 'Dispatch British Legation Consulate Basra [Judd] to Baghdad [Falle], 23 June 1958'. PRO, FO371/134199. Judd reported: 'Anti-Union [with Jordan] feeling, never very intense, seems to have given way to indifference as far as Jordan is concerned. Interest in the possibility of Kuwait's adhesion remains as strong as ever and any appearance of luke-warmness on the part of Her Majesty's Government in encouraging this would cause great resentment. ... The King, whether by good management or good luck, has appeared as one bearing gifts to a province which has long been deprived of the fruits of the oil it produces. The monarchy is probably more popular here than it has ever been.'

27 'British Embassy Baghdad [Wright] to FO [Lloyd], 11 February 1958'. PRO, FO371/134222. Sir Michael Wright recommended the consideration of a 'crash' program to build a pipeline from Kirkuk to the Persian Gulf and a deepwater offloading facility on the Fao Peninsula near Basra. He recommended that, as a stopgap measure, London issue a clear declaration stating that any move against the pipeline in Syria or Lebanon would be considered 'an aggressive act' and be met by 'any available means'.

28 'Briefing on the Middle East Situation, 22 July 1958'. *Executive Sessions of the Senate Foreign Relations Committee (Historical Series)*, Volume X, Eighty-Fifth Congress Second Session, 1958. Washington, DC: US Government Printing Office, 1980, p. 561.

29 Batatu, Hanna, The Old Social Classes and the Revolutionary Movement of Iraq: A Study of Iraq's Old Landed and Commercial Classes and of it Communists, Ba'thists and Free Officers. Princeton, NJ: Princeton University Press, 1978, p. 806. Batatu provides an outstanding analysis of social and political movements in Iraq and how these movements and individuals interacted to produce the July revolution of 1958. He suggests that 'one must take a wider view of things' in order to understand the importance of elements other than the military. The events of July 14 must be seen in their natural historical context. From this perspective, they are the climax of the struggle of a generation of the middle, lower-middle, and working classes. July 1958 was 'the culmination of an underlying, deeply embedded insurrectionary tendency of which the coup of 1936, the military movement of 1941, the Wathbah of 1948, the Intifadah of 1952, and the risings of 1956 were other manifestations'. The author believes that this class involvement is what made July 14th a true revolution and not just another coup. Batatu views the coup as the product of class struggle and irresistible historical forces; there is more than a little hindsight in this evaluation. The coup was hardly inevitable; arguably it was the result of bad luck and incompetence. It came as a big surprise, and it happened in an historical window that allowed it to survive – it endured. It could have easily been just another of the many failed Iraqi revolts.

30 Warner, Geoffrey, *Iraq and Syria 1941*. Newark, NJ: University of Delaware Press, 1974, p. 86. According to Warner, the British were able to reestablish control in Iraq because of the poor planning of the plotters, the lack of a solid military concept of operations, no Axis support, and the escape of the regent, Abd-al-'Ilah, Nuri Sa'id, and other key pro-British elements. Also, in 1941 there was never any doubt in London of what the course of action would be. Warner's short book on the coup in Iraq and the following campaigns in Iraq and Syria provides solid insight into the events in 1941 that returned Iraq to the British fold. In 1958, Qasim would argue that his 'revolution' was merely the fulfillment of 1941. See also Lyman, Robert, *Iraq 1941: The Battles for Basra, Habbaniyah, Fallujah, and Baghdad*. London: Osprey, 2006. This provides an excellent overview of the entire Iraqi campaign, including maps, diagrams, and pictures. The military analysis is first-rate and the political analysis, although more limited, is also very good.

31 'Diary Entry [Eisenhower] on meeting with Churchill'. DDEL, 6 January 1953, pp. 5-6. Eisenhower made his views clear on the British in the Middle East in his first meeting with Churchill after the election.
32 Phebe Marr, Email on the subject of the Baghdad Coup to Roby C. Barrett, 29 November 2008. Dr. Marr, who was in Iraq during the coup and for a year afterward, commented, 'Despite opposition to Nuri and the British most Iraqis who remember it--and most were in the streets then against Nuri--now wish they had done otherwise. The coup itself hung by a thread --and probably could have been stopped by replacing officers ahead of time--but Nuri et al were so involved in Arab politics they forgot to tend the store. A number of army units were waiting to see what foreigners would do and I always wondered what would have happened if foreigners had stepped in more forcefully. But I can't think what foreigners could have done then. But an occupation a year or two after--horrors. I found the British views on Kuwait very interesting. Of course, they turned out to be right about the Gulf and its oil, but Qasim, by that time, had already started to limit IPC with a resulting downward trend in Iraqi oil production for years after.'
33 'Minute FO [Wright] on Baghdad Coup, 26 July 1958'. PRO, FO371/133068. It should be noted that Qasim met with 'catastrophic success', to quote Donald Rumsfeld, but knew how to deal with it. See also 'Telegram Baghdad to WDC, 11 August 1958'. NACPM, 787.00/8-1158, p. 1. Qasim published a new series of laws: 23 articles divided into two sections. The first dealt with plotting against the security of the state, and the second with 'corrupting' the state. Plotting against the security of the state included: 'bringing the country nearer to the danger of war', 'using or threatening to use the armed forces against other Arab countries', 'plotting to overthrow existing regimes of Arab countries or interfering in their internal affairs', 'giving refuge to plotters against Arab governments', and 'attacking heads of Arab states through publications'. For added leverage against political enemies, the new regime made the law retroactive back to September 1 1939.
34 Macmillan, *Riding the Storm*, p. 510. See also 'Despatch Baghdad to WDC, 7 August 1958'. NACPM, GRDOS59, NEA, CDF, 787.00/8-758, pp. 1-8. This is an interesting analysis of what the US Embassy believed to be prearranged 'mob' action in the immediate aftermath of the coup. See also 'British Embassy Baghdad [Wright] to FO [Lloyd], 21 August 1958'. PRO, FO371/133068. Sir Michael Wright provided an excellent narrative of events on 14 and 15 July in Baghdad. See also 'British Embassy Baghdad [Wright] to FO, 26 August 1958'. PRO, FO371/133068. This telegram included a list of those being tried for crimes against the Iraqi people. These fell into four categories: first, members of the Iraqi and Arab Union cabinets and the internal security organizations; second, key military officers, including the Chief of Staff, his deputy and various division and brigade commanders; third, press figures responsible for attacks on Nasser; and fourth, supporters of the old regime in the Chamber of Deputies.
35 Macmillan, *Riding the Storm*, p. 511.
36 'Memcon Eisenhower and Dulles, Washington, 14 July 1958'. *FRUS*, 1958-1960, Volume XI, p. 209.
37 'Briefing on the Middle East Situation, 22 July 1958'. *Executive Sessions of the Senate Foreign Relations Committee* (Historical Series), Volume X, p. 572.
38 'Memo for Record, Washington, July 14, 1958'. *FRUS*, 1958-1960, Volume XI, pp. 210-211. The Pentagon suggested that planning also include also Jordan, Iraq, Syria, and the West Bank. General Twining wanted a coordinated approach that included British, Turkish, and Israeli participation. Cooler heads prevailed after Ambassador Frederick Reinhardt pointed out that the scale of Western intervention would probably determine the nature and scale of Soviet reaction.

39 Eisenhower, *Waging Peace*, p. 270.
40 'Conference with Eisenhower, 14 July 1958'. *FRUS*, 1958-1960, Volume XI, p. 212.
41 'Beirut [McClintock] to WDC, 14 July 1958'. *FRUS*, 1958-1960, Volume XI, p. 214.
42 Ibid, pp. 214-215. In the course of the conversation, Eisenhower mused: 'the most strategic move would be to attack Cairo in present circumstances, but of course this cannot be done.' During the meeting, Vice President Nixon, no doubt with an eye toward the 1960 elections, urged the President to consult Congress and the Democrats. Others present were reluctant to do this because they feared continued Democratic criticism.
43 Eisenhower, *Waging Peace*, p. 273. See also 'British Embassy Baghdad [Wright] to FO, 15 July 1958'. PRO, FO371/134199. In Baghdad, the Western embassies braced for more rioting on rumors of plans for intervention. Wright and US Ambassador Jernegan sought assurances from the Iraqi security chief, Brigadier Ahram Ahhad, that foreigners and foreign installations would be protected.
44 'Macmillan to Eisenhower, 14 July 1958'. DDEL, PPDDE, AWF, IS, Box 22, pp. 2-3.
45 'Eisenhower to Macmillan, 18 July 1958'. DDEL, Box 22, p. 2. Remembering 1954, Eisenhower commented that India would have issues with the US providing Pakistan with additional military aid.
46 'Memcon Dulles and Foreign Secretary Lloyd, Washington, 17 July 1958'. DDEL, Box 22, p. 1.
47 Nutting, *Nasser*, pp. 239-243. Murphy, Robert, *Diplomat among Warriors*. New York: Doubleday, 1964, p. 458. See also 'Briefing on the Middle East Situation, 29 July 1958'. *Executive Sessions of the Senate Foreign Relations Committee* (Historical Series), Volume X, pp. 645-651. In his testimony to the Senate Foreign Relations Committee, Allen Dulles, Director of the CIA, stated: 'Nasser was taken by surprise by the timing of the plot, but according to the reports we have, not by the fact that the plot existed.' Dulles provided a fairly accurate account of what actually happened, emphasizing the impromptu, now-or-never aspect of Qasim's move. He also added that the Iraqi government had been much more lax about security than the weaker governments in Jordan and Saudi Arabia, and this accounted for their survival. To his credit, Dulles told the senators: 'I do not foresee this movement so sweeping over this as to lead to any permanent United Arab world going from the Atlantic to the Tigris and Euphrates. ... There are elements of unity but there are great elements of divergence. You take Iraq. I do not believe for a minute, even the present government, which has many of Nasser's followers in it, has any idea of turning over its oil resources to Nasser.' This view undoubtedly was based on the British evaluation of the situation after it had filtered through the State Department and CIA.
48 'Minute FO [Riches] on Iraq, 14 July 1958,' PRO, FO371/132502.
49 Stephens, *Nasser*, pp. 293-295.
50 'Memo from Director INR Cummings], to Dulles, 5 November 1958'. NACPM, CDF, NEA, 787.00/11-558, p. 1.
51 'Memo INR [Cumming] to Dulles, 25 November 1958,' *FRUS*, 1958-1960, Volume XII, p. 353.
52 'Memo INR [Cummings] to Dulles, 5 November 1958'. NACPM, 787.00/11-558, p. 1.
53 'Memo Rountree NEA to Acting Secretary of State Dillon, 22 December 1958'. *FRUS*, 1958-1960, Volume XII, p. 370.
54 'Memo INR (Cummings) to Dulles, 5 November 1958'. *FRUS*, 1958-1960, Volume XII, p. 352.
55 Nutting, *Nasser*, p. 244.
56 'British Embassy Beirut to FO and Whitehall, 4 August 1958'. PRO, FO371/134313. Eisenhower's special envoy, Robert D. Murphy, related his conversation with Ben-Gurion to the British Ambassador in Beirut, Sir F.B.A. Randall. Murphy stated that he

believed that the Israeli 'provision' for the Arab population of the West Bank really meant that 'most of them would be driven out ahead of the Israeli army.' See also 'British Embassy Tel Aviv to FO, 19 August 1958'. PRO, FO371/134286. In this report on a conversation with Golda Mier, the Israeli Foreign Minister, the Embassy related Tel Aviv's intentions of moving into the West Bank in the event of a collapse in Jordan. Randall, the British Ambassador, stated that he believed that the Israelis might have second thoughts about such a move: 'The [Israeli] Government must realise that they cannot get away again with driving 800,000 Arabs into Transjordan nor control them if they stay.' Randall also discounted US fears that an Israeli seizure of the West Bank would bring a general Middle Eastern war, simply because Nasser was not ready.

57 'British Embassy Beirut to FO, 6 August 1958'. PRO, FO371/134313. Washington took the Ben-Gurion statements seriously, and informed the Israeli Ambassador in Washington that 'the Israel Government could not expect any support from the United States Government if they took such action.' The Israeli Embassy tried to explain that Ben-Gurion's remarks had been off-the-cuff, and did not represent a policy statement. Nevertheless, Nasser could not help but take heed of any Israeli threat and of the bellicose editorials in the Israeli press. See also 'British Embassy WDC [Hood] to FO and Whitehall, 8 August 1958'. PRO, FO371/134313. British discomfiture at not being taken into Washington's confidence on the initial approach to the Israelis was interesting. Also see 'British Embassy Tel Aviv to FO, 6 August 1958'. PRO, FO371/134313 and 'FO to British Embassy WDC, 7 August 1958'. PRO, FO371/134313, for more on their 'surprise' that 'the Americans should apparently be keeping us in the dark over a question which, since it was the subject of a personal letter from Mr. Dulles, is presumably of some importance.'

58 'FO to the British UN Mission, 18 August 1958'. PRO, FO371/134313. When questioned on the subject, Dulles stated that he refused to warn the Israelis formally against intervening in that he saw no reason to 'save Nasser any territory' in the event of a coup or revolution in Amman. Just the same, the US refused to be a party to any Israeli occupation. 'Memcon Armin Meyer, NEA, and Yohanan Meroz, Israeli Embassy, WDC, 7 November 1958, pp. 1-2. For months after the Ben-Gurion statement, the Israelis continued to try to clarify what he 'really meant'. 'Meroz stated that Israel's basic hope and expectation is that the status quo in Jordan can be preserved. If, however, there should be a "profound change" in Jordan or a change which could be termed a takeover of the country by outside forces, Israel has made clear that this would five rise to very acute problems for her.' Meroz wanted to know the US position on this. Meroz included the assassination of King Hussein or the establishment of a UAR republic. Meyer told Meroz that 'aggressive military action by Israel on the West Bank would not be in Israel's best interest.' Meroz had supported a hard line against the Arabs for his entire two-year tenure in Washington.

59 'Cabinet Meeting (Minnich), 18 July 1958'. DDEL, AWF, IS, Box 11, pp. 1-4. Quoting Lenin, Dulles discussed the Soviet use of nationalism and colonialism to influence the developing world. He stated that the Soviet Union had three great advantages in the Middle East. First, they had Israel as an issue to use with the Arabs. Second, the West needed oil and had to support the traditional regimes that owned most of it. Third, 'the USSR has a real asset in the personality of Nasser – who with great ability and fanaticism has given voice to the extreme pan-Arab movement. Nasser is the hero who has walked upon the stage which has been set …' presumably by the Russians. Dulles made the point that from 1953 to 1955, the US had 'tried to work with Nasser'.

60 'What Now?' (*Nation*, 2 August 1958, pp. 42-43) concluded that 'Anglo-American oil operations have been a prime cause of revolutionary ferment in the East' and that 'Arab nationalism has grown in more or less direct ratio to oil exports.' It cited the dangers of 'Nasserism' but stated that 'we should stop trying to force the Arab peoples to "choose

sides" in the cold war and that we should accept Arab neutrality.' See also Geoffrey Barraclough 'Anarchy of the Jungle' (*Nation*, 2 August 1958, pp. 44-45), which states: 'For the United States, the Iraq revolution was a question of heads you win, tails I lose.' Barraclough, Professor of International History in the University of London, added: 'Where there is no policy, there can be only expedients. Because Mr. Dulles squandered the unique opportunities to build up good relations with the Arab world which America enjoyed on the morrow of the Suez War.' The author equated intervention in Lebanon and Jordan with the Soviet intervention in Hungary, stating that in all three instances a 'tottering regime without popular support is being upheld by foreign arms. ... In all three cases, intervention was due not to considered policy but to blind fear and the lack of a viable policy; it stemmed from the failures of the preceding years and months.' The article argued that America had 'no conceivable grounds for conflict with Nasser' or with Arab nationalism. Barraclough represented a left-of-center view of the situation, but the views from right of center were hardly less critical. An article entitled 'Where Do We Go from Here?' (*Newsweek*, 28 July 1958, pp. 15-16) called the intervention a 'desperate risk' with 'not a moment to spare' to save Jordan and Lebanon, 'friendly nations which were being torn from their roots to be delivered into the eager hands of Egypt's empire-hungry Nasser'. The article advocated encouraging moderate Arab nationalism that did not threaten regional stability. In the same edition, 'The Clock Struck 2' (*Newsweek*, 28 July 1958, pp. 23-24) attacked Allen Dulles' management of the CIA. 'Not only was the news [from Iraq] momentous: the fact that it came as a surprise to Dulles and his CIA represented a sorry failure of U.S. intelligence'. See also Edward Weintal ('Intelligence Disaster in Iraq'. *Newsweek*, 4 August 1958, p. 20), lamenting the loss of Baghdad Pact intelligence files.
61 'London [Whitney] to Dulles, 16 July 1958'. NACPM, 787.00/7-1658, p. 2.
62 'Memcon Dulles and Lord Hood, 15 July 1958'. NACPM, 787.00/7-1658, p. 1. Dulles complained to Lord Hood about a 'great lack of information', revealing that the US was unclear about British intensions in Iraq and Jordan. Speculation was that the British might intervene.
63 'Australian Embassy WDC [Beale] to DEA Canberra [Menzies and Casey], 18 July 1958'. No. 1233, NNA, DEA, A1838/269, TS854/10/13/20 (Security Council Iraq), pp. 1-4. Selwyn Lloyd presented these views to Australian Ambassador Beale, Canadian External Affairs Minister Sidney Smith, Canadian Ambassador to Washington Norman Robertson, and Lord Hood, the British Chargé.
64 'Minute FO [Riches] to Hayter, 14 July 1958'. PRO, FO371/132502. Riches' career in the Middle East and Horn of Africa dated back to 1934.
65 'Aden [Luce] to Colonial Office [J.C. Morgan], 18 July 1958'. PRO, FO371/132502. Sir William Luce, the Governor General in Aden, endorsed these comments from two members of the Legislative Council in Aden, named Bashraheel and Bayoomi, and sent them on to London. Colonial Office officials saw this as evidence of 'another strain in Arab society which is not dazzled by the glory of Nasser, and realises where the true interests of the Arabs as a whole lie'. These two men were co-opted and supported by the British government in Aden, and were hardly unbiased observers.
66 'Minutes on Aden Telegram [Luce] dated 18 July to CO [Morgan], 24 July 1958'. PRO, FO371/132502. In reacting to Luce's views, the FO attempted to placate the Colonial Office by being 'as politic as possible without telling a straight lie'.
67 'Baghdad [Rockwell] to WDC, 16 July 1958,' NACPM, 787.00/7-1658, p. 2.
68 'Discussion 373rd NSC Meeting, 24 July 1958'. DDEL, AWF, NSC, Box 10, pp. 3-4, 9. Allen Dulles often failed to get justifiable credit for his long-term projections because of his pronouncements on near-term events. For example, to Dulles, meetings between the Emir of Kuwait and Nasser signaled that Kuwait might join the UAR, when in fact,

the Emir merely sought leverage against Iraq. See also Tripp, Charles, *A History of Iraq*. Cambridge: Cambridge University Press, 2000, p. 177.
69 '373rd NSC Meeting'. Box 10, p. 6. A debate took place about previous policy that not joining 'pacts with indigenous countries was a very undesirable concept'. The coup in Iraq sparked real concern that Iran might be next, and drove sentiment for the US to more closely align with Tehran as a further guarantee against just such an occurrence.
70 Weintal, Edward 'Intelligence Disaster in Iraq'. *Newsweek*, 4 August 1958, p. 20.
71 'Discussion 374th NSC Meeting, 1 August 1958'. DDEL, Box 10, pp. 6-10. This NSC meeting was a particularly interesting one. First, Dulles expressed his surprise that all the members of the Baghdad Pact encouraged the US to recognize the new regime in Iraq. Vice President Nixon went so far as to postulate that perhaps the United States should consider encouraging 'our friends not to align themselves too openly with the West; we may have to support independent national neutralism.' The frustration came through when Dulles referred to Nasser as being 'like Hitler' and when he described Nasser's ambitions as 'insatiable', despite the underlying desire to work something out with the Egyptian leader.
72 'Intelligence and State Department Synopsis of Events, 23 July 1958'. DDEL, AWF, Diary Series, Box 34, p. 1.
73 'British Embassy Amman [Johnston] to FO [Hadow], 30 October 1958'. PRO, FO371/134021. Sir Charles did not like Rifai' because Rifai' was pro-American and did not take Sir Charles into his confidence. Johnston believed that British Embassy in Washington and the FO were too affected by US pessimism regarding traditional regimes, and tended to overlook Washington's infatuation with Nasser. See also 'Letter from British Embassy WDC [Morris] to FO [Hadow], 13 October 1958'. PRO, FO371/134021, in which Willie Morris precipitated Johnston's rebuttal letter by stating that the US was more than happy to let Britain handle Jordanian affairs, until the Glubb dismissal and the termination of the Anglo-Jordanian Treaty. Morris believed that Dulles and Eisenhower viewed the survival of Jordan as not only important, but also a realistic possibility, while NEA believed that British military support for the Amman regime was only a 'reprieve' in the process that would lead 'inevitably' to collapse.
74 'Memcon with Eisenhower, 24 July 1958'. DDEL, AWF, Diary Series, Box 35, pp. 1-3. See also 'Telegram from British Embassy WDC to FO, 9 September 1958'. PRO, FO371/134279, in which the Eisenhower administration expressed its frustration at being handicapped by British colonialism and by Zionism. Dulles described Israel as a 'millstone around his neck', stating that 'except for Israel we could form a viable policy' in the Middle East. See 'Memcon with Eisenhower, 24 July 1958'. DDEL, Box 35, p. 1, in which Dulles commented: 'Israel is a hostage held against us.' In 'British Embassy Tel Aviv to FO, 19 July 1958'. PRO, FO371/134284, the British expressed concern that Ben-Gurion would use the Jordanian situation and British over-flights to extract new formal treaty arrangements from the West, guaranteeing Israel's frontiers and a supply of advanced weaponry. Fearing that Washington might agree, the British encouraged the US to resist Israeli demands for a guarantee of Israel's territorial integrity, and for a formal agreement recognizing Israel's unilateral claim to assistance. The British urged Washington to maintain a 'free hand' on the basis of its current relationship with Israel.
75 'British Emb Baghdad [Wright] to FO [Lloyd], 9 October 1958'. PRO, FO371/133070.
76 'Discussion 386th NSC Meeting , 13 November 1958'. DDEL, NSC, Box 10, p. 2.
77 'Discussion 384th NSC Meeting, 31 October 1958'. DDEL, Box 10, p. 13.
78 Ibid, pp. 16-17. The modifications included a statement on improving US-Yemen relations to counteract Soviet penetration there. In addition, there was an acknowledgement of the problem of the British in Aden. The US would 'seek to lend good offices to the extent possible to improve United Kingdom-Yemen relations.'
79 'Attachment Discussion 384th NSC Meeting, 31 October 1958'. DDEL, Box 10, p. 1.

80 'INR [Cummings] to Dulles on Iraq, 4 December 1958'. NACPM, GRDO59, NEA, CDF, 787.00/12-458, p. 2.
81 'Memo on Iraq to Cummings, 23 December 1958'. NACPM, 787.00/12-2358, pp. 1-2.
82 'Discussion 392nd NSC Meeting, 23 December 1958'. DDEL, Box 10, p. 2. See also 'British Embassy Baghdad [Crawford] to Consulate Kirkuk [Brown], 5 November 1958'. PRO, FO371/133073. In this message, Crawford discusses in detail the strong Communist opposition to any formal alignment with Cairo. In a communiqué, the Iraqi Communist Party stated: 'But the fact indicates day after day that those calling for the union did not give up their call, but on the contrary, they exploited their sharing in power using the press and radio as well as all the other capabilities for continuing in their call. We have received some confirmed information as we hear also different statements indicating that they are actually heading for measures to be taken preliminarily for the realization of the plan [union with the UAR]. ... They are working in isolation from the people in order to take the nationalist forces and the masses by surprise and place them before the fact within a short time.' The Communists went on to state that they viewed a 'federal union' like that between Yemen and the UAR as the proper relationship, and not unification. The declaration went on to argue that the union between Egypt and Syria had its problems as well.
83 'Memo NEA [Rountree] to Acting [Dillon], 22 December 1958'. *FRUS*, 1958-1960, Volume XII, p. 370. By the end of 1958, Nasser had concluded that the real threat to his leadership of the Arab nationalist movement and to his vision for the UAR lay in Baghdad. In discussions with Rountree, Nasser offered 'a scarcely-veiled invitation to collaborate on Iraq'. See also 'Discussion at the 39nd NSC Meeting, 23 December 1958'. *FRUS*, 1958-1960, Volume XII, pp. 372-374. In reporting on his visit to Baghdad, Rountree stated that the Communist-controlled press attacked with equal ferocity any hint of a Qasim-Nasser or Qasim-U.S. rapprochement. He also stated that Soviet aid to Egypt and the state of UAR-Iraq relations contributed to a real 'conflict of interests' for Nasser. Rountree also briefly discussed the widely-held belief in Baghdad, which the Communists fostered, that both the US and the UAR were plotting against the Qasim regime.
84 'London [Barbour] to Dulles, 15 December 1958'. NACPM, GRDOS59, NEA, CDF, 787.00/12-1558, p. 2.
85 'Statement of policy and options by Sir Roger Bentham Stevens, Deputy Under Sec FO, 9 December 1958'. PRO, FO371/133093.
86 'FO Statement of policy in the Middle East [C.A.E. Shuckburgh], 24 August 1958'. PRO, FO371/132545. The FO assumed that Washington had a contingency plan to take and hold Dhahran if necessary, and felt that Washington expected London to maintain its position in the Persian Gulf and Kuwait.
87 'British Embassy WDC [Morris] to FO [Hadow], 7 November 1958'. PRO, FO371/133086.
88 'FO Minute on Telegram from British Embassy WDC [Morris], 19 November 1958'. PRO, FO371/133086.

Chapter 4

1 Ranelagh, John, *The Agency: The Rise and Decline of the CIA*. New York: Simon & Schuster, 1986, pp. 316, 651.
2 Bill, *Eagle and the Lion*, pp. 113-116. Bill points out that during the Eisenhower years, the US provided over $1 billion in economic and military aid to the Shah's regime. This investment was critical to the Shah's survival. Bill faults this investment as misguided. He believes the aid allowed the US to control Iranian foreign policy and fostered corruption instead of progress. Along with others, Bill argues that this aid was the basis for the animosity of Iranian nationalists toward the US, and that this animosity led

directly to 1979. Bill sees US policy as the source for emphasis or imbalance in assistance toward military and security functions. This popularized view of Eisenhower's policy simply fails to give credit where credit is due. The Eisenhower administration was as concerned as the Kennedy administration and latter-day critics about the Shah's insecurities, his paranoia, and his preoccupation with military aid. Prior to 1958, Washington pressed for reforms, hoping to see the Shah's rule evolve into a stable constitutional monarchy. After 1958, the fear of another 'Baghdad' placed the initiative increasingly in the hands of the Shah, making it more difficult to ignore his priorities. Over the course of this study, we will see how the relationship between the Shah and the Eisenhower and Kennedy administrations evolved into one dominated by the Shah's preoccupation with military aid.

3 Interview with Walt Rostow, October 2001, Austin, Texas.
4 'Dispatch Consulate Meshed [Thomas Cassilly] to WDC, 26 July 1955'. NACPM, GRDOS59, NEA, CDF, 788.00/7-2655, p. 2. For evidence of Anglo-American pressure on the Shah for reform, see also 'WDC to Tehran, 9 July 1955'. NACPM, 788.00/7-955, p. 1. In this telegram, Washington instructed the Embassy to press the Shah over the 'ineffective manner Government handling task organizing economic program and general lack firmness in managing Government affairs'. The British made a parallel approach, and Washington cautioned the US Embassy not to leave the impression with the Shah that London and Washington were joining forces against him.
5 'Dispatch Tehran to WDC, 4 September 1955'. NACPM, 788.00/9-455, p. 1.
6 'Dispatch Tehran [Clock] to WDC, 23 January 1956'. NACPM, 788.00/1-2356, p. 1. The Iranian government arrested, tried, and executed members of the Fedayan-e-Islam, whom it believed had been responsible for the assassination of General Ali Razmara on March 7, 1951. Razamara's assassination led almost immediately to the assumption of power by the National Front under Musaddiq and to the nationalization of foreign oil assets. By early 1956, the Shah felt strong enough to open a broad investigation of events surrounding the assassination and to arrest those responsible. These arrests included that of Ayatollah Kashani, who had issued a *fatwah* calling Razmara an 'enemy of Islam'. Rumors floated around Tehran that the swift trials, the executions, and the death of one witness 'shot while trying to escape', were to cover up 'palace' contacts with the Fedayan prior to Razmara's assassination. This indicated the Shah's growing confidence, because the government had up to then been unwilling to tackle the problems associated with an investigation of the assassination, despite pressure from the military. See also Ladjevardi, Habib 'Constitutional government and reform under Musaddiq' and Akhavi, Shahrough, 'The role of the clergy in Iranian politics, 1949-1954'. In *Musaddiq, Iranian Nationalism, and Oil*, pp. 69-90, 91-117.
7 'Tehran [Chapin] to WDC, 23 August 1955'. NACPM, 788.00/8-2358, pp. 2-3.
8 'Discussion 296th NSC Meeting, 6 September 1956'. DDEL, Box 8, p. 1. NSC staff expressed concern that any British or French action against Nasser over Suez would lead to more Soviet pressure on Iran. In order to obtain more aid, the Shah busily stoked fear in Washington of Soviet efforts to 'neutralize' Iran.
9 'Dispatch Tehran [Clock] to WDC, 26 March 1956'. NACPM, 788.00/3-2656, pp. 3-4.
10 Dispatch Tehran [Clock] to WDC, 26 March 1956'. NACPM, 788.00/3-2656, pp. 4, 7. See also, 'Dispatch Tehran [Bowling] to WDC, 28 May 1956'. NACPM, 788.00/5-2856, p. 3. It should be noted here that Bowling would become a important figure in US-Iranian policy in the Kennedy administration. In this report, the Embassy discussed a growing list of complaints against the Shah's government, related to rising prices, free elections, and foreign influence. 'Both the Parliament and Cabinet are full of British stooges.' 'This is the government of the thousand families; the rich get richer and the poor get poorer.' 'We gave our oil back to the foreigners, but in return Ebtehaj is lining the pockets of the foreigners in return for things like strategic roads and airfields.'

Iranians also voiced strong criticism that the infrastructure improvements were aimed at projects useful to the Baghdad Pact and the military alliance with the West. See also, 'Dispatch Tehran [Bowling] to WDC, 11 September 1956'. NACPM, 788.13/9-1156, p. 4. In this discussion, Bowling viewed the end of martial law in Tehran and the establishment of a new security agency headed by General Bakhtiar as 'reform'.

11 'Dispatch Tehran [Campbell] to WDC, 15 August 1956'. NACPM, 788.13/8-1556, pp. 1-3, and 'Dispatch Tehran [Clock] to WDC, 1 September 1956'. NACPM, 788.13/9-156, p. 1-8. These dispatches contain detailed reports on the reforms in the Foreign Ministry, the Information Office, and the Justice Ministry. They point out that the old 'conservative' families would be hardest hit by these reforms.

12 'Dispatch Tehran [Clock] to WDC, 26 March 1956'. NACPM, 788.00/3-2656, p. 3.

13 'Dispatch from U.S. Embassy Tehran to WDC, 17 October 1956'. NACPM, GRDOS – 59, NEA, CDF 1955-1959, 888.00/10-1756 (Box 4963), p. 2.

14 'Dispatch Tehran [Clock] to WDC, 26 March 1956'. NACPM, 788.00/3-2656, p. 9.

15 'Tehran [Chapin] to WDC [Dulles], 25 July 1957'. NACPM, 788.00/7-2457, pp. 1-2. See also 'Memcon Grant E. Mouser [GTI] and Iranian Ambassador Dr. Ali Amini, 20 August 1957'. NACPM, 788.00/8-2057, p. 2. Many senior officials in the Iranian government shared this view of the Shah. Dr. Ali Amini, the Iranian Ambassador in Washington, stated that he had attempted to convince the Shah to work through his ministers so that they would take the blame for failures. The Shah refused. He was determined to take charge personally and to run the government himself. Dr. Amini attributed the Shah's refusal to take advice to the monarch's 'fear' of most prominent Iranians. In Amini's opinion, 'this was perhaps the basic flaw in the Shah's character.' In addition, Dr. Amini described the Plan Organization as being in 'chaos' and requiring 'drastic measures'. During his sojourn as Ambassador in Washington, Amini learned a great deal about what US officials wanted to hear vis-à-vis stability in Iran and the Shah's rule. To some degree, by telling official Washington what they wanted to hear, the Ambassador constructed his own American constituency. This would have very important future consequences.

16 'Dispatch from U.S. Embassy Tehran [Clock] to WDC, 20 July 1956'. NACPM, GRDOS – 59, NEA, CDF 1955-1959, 788.00/8-2057 (Box 3811), p. 1.

17 Ibid. Embassy reporting attributed the Shah's lack of confidence and lack of success to two factors: '(1) The Shah is indecisive to an alarming degree; he does not seem to have the ability to make up his own mind. The formidable image of Reza Shah dominates him and he seeks to imitate it; yet his personal characteristics inhibit. (2) The Shah is probably the most isolated man in this country. He has no personal staff he feels he can trust and his most frequent contacts are with a corrupt ineffective Court group, which seeks to influence him in its own personal behalf. The wide variety of opinions, rumors, and suggestions which pour in on him in this isolation combined with an innate tendency to intrigue continually probably leave him hopelessly confused and unsure of whom to trust.' Although these interpretations of the Shah became the standard fare of his Western detractors, the apparent vacillations and indecision, real and contrived, may in fact have worked in the monarch's favor. The Shah was attempting to placate political constituencies as diverse as the make-up of Iran itself. It was simply impossible. Whether by design or merely scrambling for survival, the Shah managed to keep his opposition divided and his foreign benefactors placated in what was a careening drive toward modernization. Even the end of the dynasty in 1979 was something of an accident, that could have gone in any direction, including that of the Peacock Throne's survival.

18 Ibid, p. 3.

19 'Memcon Mouser [GTI] and Ambassador Amini, 20 August 1957'. NACPM, 788.00/8-2057, pp. 1-3. Making a similar statement about economic aid, Amini stated that

NOTES

increasing oil revenue probably alleviated Iran's need for economic aid, but that the withdrawal of US aid would create a 'psychological and political problem'. See also 'Dispatch Tehran [Stelle] to WDC, 4 January 1958'. NACPM, 888.00/1-458, p. 5.

20 'Dispatch FO [Lloyd] to Dulles, 6 December 1957'. NACPM, GRDOS – 59, Office of GTI, Records of the Iranian Affairs Desk 1958-1963 (Iran Desk 1958-1963), 1958 Status of Forces thru 1960 – 3-A/1 Military Assistance (MilAsst), Box 1, pp. 2, 9. Pegov was Soviet Ambassador to Iran until 1963, and later became Soviet Ambassador to India during the Indo-Pakistani War of 1971.

21 'INR [Dreessen] to GTI [Mouser], 17 January 1958'. NACPM, GRDOS59, GTI, Iran, MilAsst, Box 1, p. 2.

22 Streit, Peggy and Streit, Pierre 'Close-Up of the Foreign Aid Dilemma'. *New York Times*, 13 April 1958, p. 10. The Streits evaluated a small, impoverished Iranian village where a USAID program had improved wheat production by 200 per cent. Because of the land-tenure system, the landlord who supplied the land, the seed, the water, and the 'beasts of burden' received 80 per cent of the proceeds while the laborers received only 20 per cent.

23 'British Emb Tehran [Stevens] to FO [Lloyd], 28 January 1958'. PRO, FO371/133013.

24 'Tehran [Dulles] to WDC, 26 January 1958,' NACPM, 888.00/1-2658, pp. 1-2.

25 'British Emb Tehran [Stevens] to FO [Lloyd], 27 January 1958'. PRO, FO371/133013.

26 'British Emb Tehran [Stevens] to FO [Lloyd], 28 January 1958'. PRO, FO371/133013.

27 'British Embassy Tehran [Stevens] to FO [Lloyd], 27 January 1958'. PRO, FO371/133013. See also 'British Embassy Tehran [Stevens] to FO [Lloyd], 28 January 1958'. PRO, FO371/133013.

28 'Tehran [Dulles] to WDC, 26 January 1958'. NACPM, 888.00/1-2658, pp. 1-2. See also 'Minute by David West FO on Dulles visit to Iran, 12 February 1958'. PRO, FO371/133013, in which the FO credits the Dulles visit to Tehran with heading off the Shah's 'dark hints' about withdrawing from the Baghdad Pact.

29 'WDC [Dulles] to Tehran [Chapin] Message for the Shah of Iran, 27 February 1958'. NACPM, 788.11/2-1758, p. 1. See also 'Memo White House [B.G A.J. Goodpaster] to DOS [Fisher Howe], 17 February 1958'. NACPM, 788.11/2-1758, p. 1. See also 'Letter from the Assistant Secretary of Defense [Irwin] to NEA [Rountree], 16 April 1958'. NACPM, 788.11/4-1658, p. 1. The Shah's schedule included visits to Taiwan and Japan prior to his arrival in Washington. This raised concerns that the large-scale military programs in those countries would bring more 'exorbitant' demands from Tehran for military assistance. The concern was so acute that the Pentagon asked for guidance from the State Department. The Acting Assistant Secretary, John Irwin, stated: 'I think it would be wise if we dispatched a joint State-Defense message to all U.S. civilian and military officials with whom the Shah might come in contact during this visit in the Pacific area, fully apprising them of our position regarding additional aid to Iran.' See also 'Letter NEA [Rountree] DOD [Irwin], 22 April 1958'. NACPM, 788.11/4-2258, p. 1. Rountree concurred that alerting civilian and military officials to 'the problem' of the Shah would be a good idea, but he added: 'While we want to avoid any ostentatious display of U.S. military aid in the countries through which the Shah will pass enroute to the United States, I do believe that it would be useful if we could find means of demonstrating to him the potential U.S. strength in the Pacific area and what it means to the protection of the Free World.' See also 'Letter Deputy Secretary of State [Murphy] to Assistant Secretary of Defense [Mansfield Sprague], 6 June 1958'. NACPM, 788.11/6-658, p. 1, in which a military program had been agreed upon for the Shah. It included naval demonstrations, Strategic Air Command briefings, and plane rides.

30 'Minute FO [D.J. West] to Selwyn Lloyd, 15 April 1958'. PRO, FO371/133006.

31 'Tehran [Wailes] to WDC, 8 June 1958'. NACPM, 788.11/4-1658, Section 2, p. 2.

32 'Memo Dulles to Eisenhower, 28 June 1958'. NACPM, 788.11/6-2858, p. 1. See also 'Tehran [Wailes] to WDC, 8 June 1958'. NACPM, 788.11/4-1658, p. 1. This telegram details some of the problems that the Eisenhower administration had with the Shah's unrealistic requests for military aid. A lack of trained personnel was the critical issue. For example, the Shah asked for two destroyers despite the fact that the commander of the Iranian Navy privately told the Embassy that he could not crew more than one corvette.
33 'Memo NEA to Eisenhower on visit by Shah of Iran, 23 June 1958'. NACPM, 788.11/6-2358, p. 2.
34 'Dulles to Tehran, 7 July 1958'. NACPM, 788.11/7-758, p. 1.
35 'Memcon Shah and Eisenhower, 1 July 1958'. *FRUS*, 1958-1960, Volume XII, p. 574.
36 'Dulles to Tehran, 7 July 1958'. NACPM, 788.11/7-758, p. 2. This message from Washington failed to quote the Shah exactly, calling his political philosophy 'positive nationalism' instead of 'constructive nationalism.'
37 'Memcon the Shah and Eisenhower, 1 July 1958'. *FRUS*, 1958-1960, Volume XII, pp. 572-573. The Shah commented that Nasser 'was essentially a conspirator and was motivated by "wrong doing"'. In the conversation, Dulles made a surprisingly sophisticated comparison between pan-Germanism and pan-Arabism: German romanticism had clearly influenced the pan-Arab movement. The Shah then began to talk about Nasser's *Philosophy of the Revolution* as a parallel to Hitler's *Mein Kampf.* Their processes in this regard were interesting, and Dulles' fascination with comparing Hitler and Nasser belied a more sophisticated grasp of Nasser's predicament. In fact, the impression emerges at times that Dulles' theories in conversations with other leaders were more the arguments of a lawyer attempting to sway a jury than they were his own personal view of the situation.
38 'Tehran to WDC, 15 July 1958'. *FRUS*, 1958-1960, Volume XII, p. 575 (footnote).
39 'WDC to Tehran with message from Eisenhower to Shah, 19 July 1958'. *FRUS*, 1958-1960, Volume XII, p. 576.
40 'Tehran [Wailes] to Dulles, 20 July 1958,' *FRUS*, 1958-1960, Volume XII, p. 578.
41 'Memo Special Assistant for Mutual Security Coordination [Barnes] to DOS [Dillon], 24 July 1958'. *FRUS*, 1958-1960, Volume XII, p. 581.
42 'Defense Attaché Tehran to WDC, 17 July 1958.' NACPM, 788.00/7-1758, pp. 1, 4. The Defense Attaché also reported that Reza Afshar, the President of Iranian Airlines, had alerted the American in charge of pilot scheduling to prepare a contingency plan for evacuating the royal household should the army revolt. Afshar stated that the army was not loyal to the Shah or its senior commanders, and that trouble from junior officers was anticipated. See also 'Minute on Telegram from British Embassy Tehran [Stevens] on loyalty of the Iranian Army, August 8, 1958'. PRO, FO371/133006. In London, the FO feared that another military coup might be in the offing, like that in Iraq or the attempted 1954 coup in Tehran. There was genuine concern that elements from the 1954 coup might be active again and that the Iranian security service might not know what was going on. In addition, the British were also concerned about Iranian army-unit distribution. They feared another opportunity like the one in Baghdad, in which no loyal units had been available to support the palace.
43 'Dispatch Tehran [Stelle] to WDC, 12 August 1958'. NACPM, 788.00/8-1258, pp. 1, 2. The Iranian government took the position that the Iraqi regime under Nuri Sa'id and the Hashemites was so unstable that a new regime with broad popular support would be welcomed and might 'settle down in peace with its neighbors, turning its attention to internal reform and economic development'. This view reflected more hope than expectation. In the short-term Tehran expected increased tensions and problems with the Qasim and with whatever government came after it.

44 'Tehran [Wailes] to WDC [Dulles], 14 August 1958'. *FRUS*, 1958-1960, Volume XII, p. 584. See also 'British Embassy Tehran [Stevens] to FO [Lloyd], 20 August 1958'. PRO, FO371/133006. Stevens began by stating: 'Sir, I have the honour to report that, for the last two weeks, Tehran has been the prey of rumours and disquieting talk of every kind.' Sir Roger then recited the rumors of dissatisfaction in the officer corps and the outspoken opposition to the regime on the street.
45 'Tehran [Wailes] to Dulles, 26 August 1958'. *FRUS*, 1958-1960, Volume XII, p. 586.
46 'Memo NEA [Rountree] to Dulles, 9 September 1958'. *FRUS*, 1958-1960, Volume XII, p. 590. See also 'Discussion 379th NSC Meeting, 18 September 1958'. DDEL, Box 10.
47 'Memcon on Iranian Budgetary Crisis, 9 December 1958'. *FRUS,* 1958-1960, Volume XII, p. 620.
48 'Dispatch British Embassy Tehran [Stevens] to FO [Lloyd], 7 August 1958'. PRO, FO371/133006, pp. 1-2, 9.
49 'British Embassy Tehran [Stevens] to FO [Lloyd], 21 August 1958'. PRO, FO371/133006, p. 2. This lengthy and alarming report reflected concerns, British and American alike, about the future for the regime. These concerns served to support further demands by the Shah for military and economic assistance.
50 'Memo Iranian Desk [Waggoner] to GTI [Jones], 30 July 1958'. NACPM, GRDOS59, NEA, GTI, Mil Asst, Box 1, pp. 1, 7, 8. This long memorandum on Kurdish issues and the lack of US knowledge and expertise in the region suggested that at least one Arabic- and Farsi-speaking Foreign Service officer be trained in Kurdish.
51 'Attachment to Memo Iranian Desk [Waggoner] to GTI [Jones], 30 July 1958'. NACPM, GRDOS59, NEA, GTI, Mil Asst, Box 1, pp. 1, 7, 8. The Baghdad broadcasts complemented broadcasts from the UAR designed to attract Kurds to a broader nationalist base.
52 'Dispatch Tabriz to WDC, 2 September 1958'. NACPM, 787.00/9-258, pp. 1, 3, 4.
53 'Memo NEA [Eagleton] to NEA [Lakeland], 14 November 1958'. NACPM, GRDOS59, NEA, GTI, Mil Asst, Box 1, p. 1. In a meeting with the Kurds in Baghdad, Eagleton pointed out that the word 'assimilation' should be avoided, even though the US wanted to point out to the Kurdish leadership, Mulla Mustafa, a Barzani leader, and Shaykh Latif of Sulaymaniya, that linkages with Iran were much more workable than those with Baghdad or Moscow. See also 'Memo NEA [Mouser] to Lakeland [GTI], 8 December 1958'. NACPM, GRDOS59, NEA, GTI, Mil Asst, Box 1, p. 1.
54 'Memo NEA [Lakeland] to GTI, 14 November 1958'. NACPM, GRDOS59, NEA, GTI, Mil Asst, Box 1, p. 1.
55 'Dispatch British Embassy Tehran [Russell] to FO [Lloyd], 27 October 1958'. PRO, FO371/133007, pp. 13-14.
56 'Dispatch London to WDC, 7 November 1958'. NACPM, 787.00/11-758, pp. 3-4.
57 'Dispatch British Embassy Tehran [Russell] to FO [Lloyd], 27 October 1958'. PRO, FO371/133007, p. 14.

Chapter 5

1 Heptulla, Najma, *Indo-west Asian Relations: The Nehru Era*. New Delhi: Allied, 1991, p. 187.
2 'Diary Eisenhower, 16 December 1956'. DDEL, AWF, IS, India, Box 29, and 'Diary Eisenhower, 18 December 1956'. DDEL, PPDDE, AWF, International Series, India, Box 29. These two entries form an amusing commentary on the meetings between President Eisenhower and Prime Minister Nehru. Apparently, State Department officials were concerned that Eisenhower would have difficulty engaging the notoriously difficult to-talk-to Nehru and that 'problems' might result. In briefings prior to a luncheon on 16 December, the President commented that he 'did not mind (the briefings) so much, except that the State Department was so afraid that he would say or

do the wrong thing.' The Department was properly 'berated'. On 18 December, Eisenhower acknowledged the difficulties in dealing with Nehru: 'It was difficult to be with someone you did not know for such a long period. ... sometimes Nehru would not speak, sometimes he would talk for an hour.' The entry writer commented that the President did not like the one-on-one: 'I think he [Eisenhower] missed us all.' Nehru was notorious for sitting silently for long periods even in one-on-one meetings. British Prime Minister Harold Macmillan referred to it as a 'silent conversation' with Nehru. When first encountered, it was disconcerting.

3 'Memcon Nehru and Eisenhower, 17-18 December 1956'. DDEL, Box 29, pp. 1-3. Nehru made some unintentionally amusing and at the same time 'disparaging' remarks about Nuri Sa'id and Iraq. Here again, the Indian aggravation with the Baghdad Pact and its implications for arms and Pakistan mirrored the Egyptian annoyance over Baghdad as a competing center of Arab power. Desptie Nehru's concern over the closing of the Suez Canal, ideologically and geopolitically he, like Nasser, had problems with the Western alliance system.

4 Ibid, p. 10. During the meeting, President Eisenhower attempted to get Nehru to bring up the subject of Krishna Menon. Menon had become a target of Western wrath after he voted against UN resolutions condemning the Soviet Union for the invasion of Hungary. Nehru knew the complaints that would follow any mention of Menon, and skillfully avoided the subject.

5 Ibid.

6 'Memo for Dulles, Karachi Conference, March 1956, on Kashmir Issue, February 23, 1956'. NACPM, GRDOS59, NEA, INC, Kashmir, Entry 5252, (Box 1), pp. 1-3.

7 'Memo NEA Rountree to Dulles on meeting with the Pakistani Foreign Minister, Firoz Khan Noon, June 19, 1957'. NACPM, (Box 1), pp. 1-2.

8 'UN Resolution on Kashmir attached to Memo [Frederic P. Bartlett] to NEA Rountree on the Kashmir Dispute, December 5, 1957'. NACPM, Box 1, p. 2. The US clearly wanted Britain to take the lead on the Kashmir issue, promising support in the UN Security Council. For a brief explanation of this relationship see 'Memo for Bermuda Meeting of March 21-23, 1957, March 14, 1957'. NACPM, Box 1, pp. 1-3. The British had pointed out early on to the US that the latter's 'role in the subcontinent should supplement and not supplant the UK'. See 'Problems of the Indo-Pakistan Subcontinent attached to Briefing Memorandum for George McGhee's Discussion with British Officials, London, September, 1950, April 25, 1950'. NACPM, Box 1, p. 1. See also 'UN Resolution, Commission for India and Pakistan on 13 August 1948'. NACPM, Box 1, pp. 1-8.

9 'Memcon NEA [Withers] and British Emb WDC [Bottomley], 12 April 1957'. NACPM, Box 1, p. 1.

10 'Memcon Pakistani Ambassador WDC [Muhammad Ali] and NEA [Rountree], 20 May 1957'. NACPM, Box 1, p. 2.

11 'Letter Ambassador Ellsworth Bunker New Delhi to NEA [J. Jefferson Jones III], March 14, 1957'. NACPM, GRDOS59, Records Relating to South Asia 1947-1959 (SA 1947-1959), Entry 1330 Miscellaneous Files, Lot file No. 62, D 43 (1 of 3) General Subject Files Relating to South Asian Affairs, 1957-1959, 790.00/3-1457, p. 1-3.

12 'Memcon NEA [Withers] and British Embassy WDC [Bottomley], 12 April 1957'. NACPM, GRDOS – 59, NEA, INC, Kashmir , Entry 5252, Box 1, p. 1.

13 'Memcon NEA [Withers] and British Embassy WDC [Bottomley], 7 June 1957'. NACPM, Box 1, p. 1.

14 'Letter Bunker, New Delhi to WDC, 6 May 1957'. NACPM, Lot file No. 62, D 43 (1 of 3) 790.00/5-657, p. 1.

15 'Memcon NEA [Withers] and British Embassy WDC [Bottomley], 7 June 1957'. NACPM, Box 1), p. 1. See also 'Memcon British Embassy WDC [Bottomley] and NEA

[J. Jefferson Jones III], 7 June 1957'. NACPM, Box 1, pp. 1-2; 'Memorandum from NEA/SOA [Jones] to NEA [Rountree], 6 June 1957'. NACPM, Box 1, pp. 1-2; 'Memcon British Embassy WDC [Bottomley] and NEA [Jones], 14 June 1957 (3 p.m.)'. NACPM, Box 1, pp. 1-2; 'Memo NEA/SOA [Jones] to NEA [Rountree], 14 June 1957' NACPM, Box 1, pp. 1-3; 'Memcon British Embassy WDC [Bottomley] and NEA [Jones], 14 June 1957, (6 p.m.)'. NACPM, Box 1, pp. 1-2; and 'Memcon British Embassy WDC [Bottomley] and NEA [Jones], 15 June 1957'. NACPM, Box 1, pp. 1-2.

16 'Briefing paper for Pakistani Foreign Minister Suhrawardy's Visit, 3 July 1957'. NACPM, Box 1, pp. 1-2.

17 Kux, Dennis, *The United States and Pakistan, 1947-2000*. Baltimore, MD: Johns Hopkins University Press, 2001, p. 91.

18 'Memorandum from NEA [Rountree] to Dulles, 18 October 1957'. NACPM, Box 1, pp. 1-2.

19 Gupta, Sisir, *Kashmir, A Study in India-Pakistan Relations*. New York: Asia/India Council of World Affairs, 1966, p. 322. See also 'Memo Rountree to Dulles on Meeting with Pakistani Foreign Minister Noon, Washington, June 17, 1957'. Box 1, p. 1. On the subject of a Soviet veto, the US recognized the certainty of it and discussed the matter with Pakistani Foreign Minister Noon during his June 1957 visit to the US. Noon came expressly to line up support for the Pakistani position on a plebiscite in Kashmir. See also 'Memcon Noon and Under Secretary of State Christian Herter, June 19, 1957'. NACPM, Box 1, pp. 1-3. Among other things, Noon, in what was supposed to be a brief courtesy call to Under Secretary Herter, launched into the Kashmir issue, claiming that the Indians were using a Nazi-trained officer, Allama Mashriqi, to train pro-Indian irregular troops in the region. See also 'Memcon British Embassy [Bottomley] and NEA/SOA [Withers], June 21, 1957'. NACPM, Box 1, p. 1. The British were eager to convince the US to take the lead in the UN. London viewed Washington's assessment and planned course of action as broadly similar to London's position, but the British saw no upside to leading the charge. Of London was 'anxious to know what happens in the meetings' so that they could influence US policy. 'Memcon [Bottomley] and NEA/SOA [Withers], June 21, 1957'. NACPM, Box 1, p. 1.

20 Arora, K.C., *V.K. Krishna Menon – A Biography*. New Delhi: Sanchar, 1998, p. 150.

21 'Memcon Eisenhower and Indian Finance Minister T.T. Krishnamachari, 9 October 1957'. DDEL, AWF, IS, India, Box 28, p. 3.

22 Talbot, Phillips 'Raising the Cry for Secession, the Ambitions of the "Political Dravidians". Letter from Tiruchirappalli, South India, May 22, 1957'. *American Universities Field Staff Reports*, South Asia Series, Volume II, No. 8. New York: AUSF, 1957pp. 2, 5. The cartoon appeared in *Murasoli*, a pro-DMK Tamil-language weekly, on May 10, 1957. It consisted of four block pictures. In the first, Gandhi predicted that Jinnah would drop his demand for Pakistan. In the second, Jinnah's image appeared next to a map of India showing an independent Pakistan. In the third, Madras Finance Minister Subramanyam predicted that C.N. Annadurai, the DMK leader, would drop his demand for a separate Dravidian state. The fourth displayed a map of India with a separate Pakistan and Tamilnad with Annadurai looking on. Talbot did not invent the comparison; rather, the Tamil Madrasis saw a parallel with Jinnah and the Muslims.

23 Ibid, pp. 3-7.

24 'Karachi [James M. Langley] to Dulles, January 31, 1958'. *FRUS*, 1958-1960, Volume XV, p. 620. Ambassador Langley emphasized his excellent rapport with President Mirza and the latter's willingness to listen to the his advice. Washington's response provides an even more instructive view of the trepidation in the US government concerning the situation in Pakistan. The Department instructed Langley not to become involved with Mirza to the point of giving advice: '(B)elieve that the USG must as a matter of principle avoid any semblance tutelage of Pakistani leadership.' Because of the unstable

situation, a close Embassy relationship with any particular politician or group could place the US on the wrong side if the government changed. 'Telegram from John Foster Dulles, Secretary of State, to Langley, Washington, February 4, 1958'. *FRUS*, 1958-1960, Volume XV, p. 622.

25 Talbot, Phillips 'A Glimpse of Pakistan: First Impressions of a Returning Visitor, Lahore, October 31, 1956'. *AUFS-SAS*, Vol. I, No. 1, p. 1-4. Talbot, Phillips 'Pakistan Doesn't Like It: Reactions to the Egyptian Crisis, Lahore, November 8, 1956'. *AUFS-SAS*, Vol. 1, No. 2, p. 5. Anti-British attitudes in Pakistan resulting from partition manifested themselves during the Suez crisis. First the populace wanted the Pakistani government to do something substantive to show solidarity with Egypt. Second, they demanded a withdrawal from the British Commonwealth. Lastly, they demanded a withdrawal from the Baghdad Pact, or the ejection of Britain. American demands that the French, British, and Israelis withdraw temporarily raised the US image. Although Talbot anticipated no overt action by Pakistan, he believed that the rise in 'Pan-Islamic feeling' foreshadowed more animosity toward Britain and new challenges to Pakistan's pro-Western foreign policy. Campbell-Johnson, Alan, *Mission with Mountbatten*. New York: Atheneum, 1986, p. 242. The issue of impartiality on the part of Mountbatten continued as a hotly-debated subject. Nehru had better and more frequent access than Jinnah. Particularly over Kashmir, Nehru's relationship with Montbatten's wife allowed him more immediate influence. In November 1947 *The Pakistani Times* claimed that Mountbatten was in 'active command' of Indian troops confronting Pakistani and Muslim tribal forces in Kashmir. As Campbell-Johnson put it: 'the bolder the lie the wider the credence.'

26 Talbot, 'A Glimpse of Pakistan', pp. 3, 8, 9. The 'writ' of the government running through the country was no doubt something of an exaggeration if the Pashtun tribal areas along the Afghanistan border are taken into account; tribal law prevailed there. This assessment was optimistic given the circumstances, and the overall tone tended to reflect an interest or perhaps even a bias on the part of Talbot.

27 'Letter British Embassy Karachi [Symon] to Lord Home, 14 April 1958'. PRO, FO371/136187, pp. 6-7, 10.

28 Talbot, Phillips 'A Note on India and Pakistan, New York, September 12, 1957'. *AUFS-SAS*, Vol. II, No. 9, p. 16. The characterization was important, since within a few years Talbot would be Assistant Secretary for NEA.

29 'Reuters news bulletin from CIA/FBIS on Nehru's statements on Kashmir, 9 April 1958'. DDEL, AWF, IS, India, Box 29.

30 'Memo from Dulles to Eisenhower, 17 April 1958'. DDEL, Box 29.

31 'Memo from Eisenhower to Dulles, 21 April 1958'. DDEL, Box 29.

32 'Letter from Eisenhower to Nehru, 14 May 1958'. DDEL, Box 29.

33 'New Delhi [Bunker] to WDC [Dulles], 2 June 1958'. DDEL, Box 29, p. 1.

34 'New Delhi [Bunker] to WDC [Dulles], 8 June 1958'. DDEL, Box 29, Section 2, p. 3.

35 'New Delhi [Bunker] to WDC [Dulles], 11 June 1958'. DDEL, Box 29, p. 1.

36 'WDC to Karachi, May 21, 1958'. *FRUS*, 1958-1960, Volume XV, p. 648.

37 'Letter Karachi (Langley) to NEA (Rountree), Karachi, July 1, 1958'. *FRUS*, 1958-1960,Volume XV, p. 651.

38 'Dacca to WDC, May 29, 1958'. *FRUS*, 1958-1960, Volume XV, pp. 649-650. The Consul General, William L.S. Williams, stated: 'If we should countenance a dictator in Pakistan, we would destroy our reputation as a democratic people with a democratic government, our strongest link with the populace and the vast majority of its leaders. ... [The] [p]ropaganda value to our enemies of Pakistan Army using US arms and equipment to quell rebellion against a dictatorship is inestimable.'

39 'Airgram Karachi to WDC, July 9, 1958'. *FRUS*, 1958-1960, Volume XV, p. 635.

40 Kux, *The United States and Pakistan*, pp. 93-95. US Ambassador Horace Hildreth, whose daughter was maried to Mirza's son, departed Pakistan in the summer of 1957. Hildreth had a real affection for Pakistan and avoided negative evaluations of the situation. When James Langley, a New Hampshire newspaperman with close ties to Sherman Adams, Eisenhower's Chief of Staff, took over, policy toward Pakistan got an unexpected scrubbing. Langley quickly concluded that policy toward Pakistan was largely based on 'wishful thinking' and that 'the present military program is based on a hoax, the hoax being that it is related to the Soviet threat.' During the same period, Ayub Khan, Chief of Staff of the Pakistani Armed Forces, worked with some success to convince Allen Dulles at the CIA and DOD officials that India threatened 'containment' policy, and that military aid was a small price to pay for the use of intelligence and U-2 facilities. Ambassador Langley may have had excellent access to the administration, but Ayub had his own Washington advocates.

41 'Karachi to WDC, July 24, 1958'. *FRUS*, 1958-1960, Volume XV, pp. 656-658.

42 'Memo for the File [Ambassador Langley], 17 September 1958,' *FRUS*, 1958-1960, Volume XV, p. 661.

43 'Karachi to WDC, October 5, 1958'. *FRUS*, 1958-1960, Volume XV, p. 665. See also 'WDC to Karachi, 6 October 1958'. *FRUS*, 1958-1960, Volume XV, p. 667.

44 'Karachi to WDC, October 15, 1958'. *FRUS*, 1958-1960, Volume XV, pp. 674-676.

45 'Memo Gleason on comments by Allen Dulles, CIA, 31 October 1958'. *FRUS*, 1958-1960, Volume XV, p. 679.

46 'Letter NEA Frederick Bartlett to Bunker New Delhi, Washington, October 27, 1958'. *FRUS*, 1958-1960, Volume XV, pp. 679-680. See also 'The Economic and Political Consequences of India's Financial Problems, Washington, September 2, 1958'. *FRUS*, 1958-1960, Volume XV, pp. 452-460. Given the anti-Western, pro-Soviet, and socialist elements in India, real concern existed about the problems India faced in its the Second Five-Year Plan. New Delhi had already reduced the plan's goals; without immediate additional foreign aid it would fail. Bunker made it clear what was a stake. He argued: 'The recent trend toward a weakening of the Congress party and toward an increase in Communist strength would almost certainly be intensified.' His report went on to state that if India got the aid that it needed, the reverse would happen and 'the prospects for maintaining an effective parliamentary system under moderate leadership will be strengthened.'

47 'Karachi to WDC, 31 October 1958'. *FRUS*, 1958-1960, Volume XV, p. 681.

48 'Annual Political Report for 1958, from Indian Embassy WDC [K.L. Dalal, First Secretary] to MEA New Delhi, 15 April 1959'. INA, MEA 50 (9) AMS/59.

49 'Letter, "Secret – Eyes Only" Bunker to Bartlett, 3 December 1958'. NACPM, Lot file No. 62, D 43 (1 of 3), Subject Files SA 1957-1959, 790.00/12-358, pp. 1-2.

50 'Letter from Bunker to Bartlett with attached Memcon betweeen Bunker and Nehru, Delhi, 19 July 1958'. NACPM, 790.00/7-1958, pp. cover letter, 1-6. This letter, with its attached memorandum, clearly underscored the nature of the relationship between the US and India. Bunker presented a letter from President Eisenhower to Prime Minister Nehru explaining US reasons for intervention in Lebanon on the heels of the coup in Iraq and asking for 'moderation' in Nehru's public comments on the situation. Nehru plainly told Bunker that he viewed the Iraqi coup a positive thing and that he had regarded the now dead Iraqi Prime Minister Nuri Said as 'a strange 19th-century feudal character … [who] had little concept of the changes, economic or social, which had come over the world in the last generation'. Nehru rejected the idea that Nasser was behind the coup in Iraq or instability in Lebanon. He stated that it appeared that the more direct cause of the Lebanese problem was a political breach of faith on the part of Lebanese Christian President Chamoun, who had attempted to amend the constitution

and succeed himself as President. Nehru bluntly stated that the important issue was to get American troops withdrawn as soon as possible.
51 'Letter, "Secret – Eyes Only", from Bunker to Bartlett, Delhi, December 3, 1958'. NACPM, Lot file No. 62, D 43 (1 of 3), 790.00/12-358, pp. 1-2.
52 'New Delhi to WDC, 8 January 1959'. *FRUS*, 1958-1960, Volume XV, pp. 474-475.
53 'Letter Bunker) to NEA/SOA Bartlett'. *FRUS*, 1958-1960, Volume XV, p. 473.
54 'Letter from US Ambassador Langley) to NEA Rountree, 27 December 1957,' NACPM, Lot file No. 62, D 43 (1 of 3), 790.00/12-2758, p. 13.
55 'Letter, 'Secret - Eyes Only' Bunker to Bartlett, 3 December 1958'. NACPM, Lot file No. 62, D 43 (1 of 3), p. 1.
56 Akbar, *Nehru*, pp. 486-487. See also, Gopal, *Nehru*, Vol. III, p. 57, in which he states that US support for Pakistan left Nehru with an 'uneasy mind' about the lengths to which the US would go in pursuit of its Cold War objectives.

Part II
1 Interview with General Andrew Goodpaster, 31 July 2003.

Chapter 6
1 Malcolm Kerr, in his excellent essay *The Arab Cold War* devotes a scant dozen pages to the discussion of the events of 1959 and 1960. He focuses instead on the revolutionary events of 1958, and then begins again with a more detailed narrative in 1961. To be sure, he hits the highpoints of 1959-1960, but his treatment skims over much of the complexity and confusion of the period. Kerr provides little detailed explanation of this or its longer-term consequences. Malik Mufti, in *Sovereign Creations: Pan-Arabism and Political Order in Syria and Iraq* (Ithaca, NY: Cornell University Press, 1996) covers the period in five pages, in his chapter entitled 'Nasser and Qasim'. Here, too, the complexity of the period is largely ignored. The author focuses primarily on the bilateral issues between Syria and Iraq, and particularly on the radically different mutations of their Ba'thist governments. Marion and Peter Sluglett in *Iraq since 1958: From Revolution to Dictatorship* (New York: Tauris, 2001) capture the situation in Iraq during the period by using the coup attempts against Qasim as the backdrop for their historical narrative, but here, too, the complexity and continually shifting nature of the overall situation is alluded to but largely missed. The story is much the same for Charles Tripp's *A History of Iraq*, although the author does provide limited additional insight into the external as well as the internal players. Although somewhat dated, Anthony Nutting's *Nasser* is the best biography. Nasser was at the center of the political storm, and thus a biography of the Egyptian leader touches most of the events of 1959-1960. Still, the Nutting book is a biography and thus, by definition, focuses on Nasser and not the overall situation in the region.
2 The term 'wave of the future' became synonymous with Nasser. In interviews with Phillips Talbot, General Andrew Goodpaster, William 'Bill' Lakeland and Walt Rostow, each used the term at one point or another to describe the US evaluation of Nasser and the Nasserist wave that seemed to be sweeping the Arab Middle East. It is interesting to note that in a recent television interview, when questioned about the viability of the Saudi monarchy, the then Crown Prince Abdullah ibn Abd-al-Aziz refered to the widespread belief in Nasser as the 'wave of the future' to state that the Saudi monarchy was still here in the 21st century and pointedly ask: 'Where is Nasserism?'
3 Tripp, *History of Iraq*, p. 153.
4 'Dispatch from the U.S. Embassy Baghdad [David Fritzlan] to WDC, 9 January 1959'. NACPM, GRDOS-59, CDF 1955-1959 (Box 3799), 787.00S/1-959, p. 1.
5 St. John, *The Boss*, pp. 299-300.

6 Roi, Yaacov (ed.) From Encroachment to Involvement: A Documentary Study of Soviet Policy in the Middle East, 1945-1973. Jerusalem: Israel Universities, 1974, p. 277.
7 'Radio Cairo 23 December 1958'. In Roi (ed.) *From Encroachment to Involvement*, p. 277.
8 Stephens, *Nasser*, p. 296.
9 Heikal, *Cairo Documents*, p. 141.
10 Nikita Khrushchev 'Opening Speech at the 21st Communist Party Congress in Moscow, 27 January 1959'. Reprinted from *Pravda*, 28 January 1958, III, pp. 59-60. In Roi (ed.) *From Encroachment to Involvement*, p. 279.
11 Heikal, *Sphinx*, p. 104. This work provides excellent detail on the ups and downs in the Egyptian-Soviet relationship. Heikal was certainly a witness over the years to this roller-coaster ride between Moscow and Cairo. Despite his prejudices, his views have to be taken seriously within the context of other official documents on exactly what transpired. Muhammad Hakki, who worked for Heikal at *Al-Ahram* during this period, stated (interview, 8 August 2003) that with regard to Nasser's statements and actions: 'One is never quite sure whether it is what Nasser said or did; what Heikal thought Nasser said or did; what Heikal thought Nasser should have said or done; or what Heikal would have said or done if he had been Nasser.' Nevertheless Heikal's views on the events of the period provide a quasi-official record of the positions of the Egyptian government and must be weighed and evaluated against what actually occurred, just as official US and British government records are evaluated.
12 Heikal, *Sphinx*, p. 104. Nasser chided Khrushchev pointing out that he had been a party to persecuting and executing numerous Communists, who he called 'very bad men' because they had deviated from an acceptable political course. Nasser listed Stalin, Beria, Malenkov, Kaganovich, Zhukov, Molotov, and Bulganin to make his point, and asked: 'What is Mr. Khrushchev trying to tell me? That it is not permissible to attack communists?'
13 St. John, *Boss*, p. 300.
14 Lacouture, Jean, *Nasser*. New York: Knopf, 1973, p. 201.
15 Interview with Muhammad Hakki, Washington, DC, 8 August 2003. Hakki was an Egyptian Information Service officer attached to the Egyptian Embassy in Washington, DC from 1957 to 1958. In early 1959, he joined the staff of *Al-Ahram*, where he worked closely with Muhammad Heikal. In 1973, Hakki stated that Anwar Sadat tapped him to head the Information Ministry, but the appointment was cancelled following Sadat's assassination.
16 Interview with Muhammad Hakki, Washington, DC, 8 August 2003. Qasim's failure to respond 'appropriately' and 'positively' to Nasser's overtures quickly found a rationalized explanation in private Egyptian leadership circles in the view that Qasim was an 'Iraqi' and exhibited the worst traits of an Iraqi. He was brutal – witness the slaughter of the Hashemites and mutilation of Nuri Said, as compared to King Farouk and General Neguib departing into comfortable exile. He was dependent on outside forces for his tenure, i.e., the Soviet Union by way of the ICP. He refused to be civilized by exchanging letters and holding talks. All of this reflected parochialism indicative of an Iraqi, the antithesis of progressive, Arab nationalist regimes. These differences, of course, would have been much easier to overlook had there been a political meeting of minds.
17 St. John, *Boss*, p. 301.
18 Heikal, Muhammad, *Matha Jara fi Suria*. Cairo: National, 1961, p. 103.
19 'Annual Political Report on Syria for 1959 from the Indian Consulate Damascus [A.N. Safrani] to MEA New Delhi, 5 January 1960'. INA, MEA 21-A (1) WANA/60, pp. 1-3. The Indian Consul had a pro-Iraqi bent. He stated that: 'Iraq gave promise of becoming a seat of democracy causing grave concern to the authorities in the U.A.R.' With regard to US-UAR relations, he stated that: 'The American were quick to realize that Nasser

20 Nutting, *Nasser*, p. 263. See also 'Report from the Indian Embassy Damascus to MEA, 27 May 1960'. INA, MEA 21A (24) WANA/60, pp. 4, 6. In evaluating the Syrian-Egyptian Union, Safrani, the Indian Consul in Damascus, provided a fair assessment of the situation. He posed the question: 'In what then are the Syrians disappointed and how does one explain the malaise that has crept in and is still growing in Syria?. The answer is simple. The Syrians opted for unity believing that they will be equal partners with Egypt and they joined the unity believing that their own surrender of freedom was but a prelude to the general realization of an Arab entity. In both these hopes they have been disappointed.' Safrani argued that Nasser relied too much on the Ba'thists; thus, when he removed them and replaced them with Egyptians, no Syrian party had a stake in the UAR. 'Henceforward there was to be no delegating of power to any Syrian. ... This constitutes the main grievance of the Syrians. No Syrian is in any position of power. ... For every small matter the Syrians have to go to Cairo.' In an attached minute dated 31 May 1960, Nehru commented that Safrani's 'broad appraisal of the situation in Syria is on the whole a good one'.

21 There has been a debate about whether Sarraj was acting on his own, i.e., without Nasser's knowledge, and whether Nasser really would have taken the risks associated with a coup attempt against Qasim. However, it strains credulity to believe that Nasser did not know and approve of Sarraj's preparations for the coup against the Qasim regime. Given Nasser's predisposition for intrigue and skullduggery, it absolutely lacks credibility that he did not know and approve of Sarraj's actions and plans at some level. Since the Iraqis in Mosul acted prematurely, obviously neither Nasser nor Sarraj knew the exact timing or exercised tactical control, but both were behind it. Nutting, in *Nasser*, p. 259, probably comes closest to the truth when he states that Nasser was furious with Sarraj not for supporting the coup, but for failing and thus embarrassing the UAR.

22 'Report on Iraq for the NSC Briefing, 24 Februrary 1959'. CIA, CIA Resource Extraction System (CRES), CIA-RDP79R00890A001100020006-7, pp. 1-2.

23 Sluglett and Sluglett, *Iraq since 1958*, pp. 66-68.

24 Nutting, *Nasser*, p. 257.

25 St. John, *Boss*, p. 301.

26 Nutting, *Nasser*, p. 259.

27 Sluglett and Sluglett, *Iraq since 1958*, p. 68.

28 'Baghdad [Jernegan] to WDC, 12 March 1959'. NACPM, 787.00/3-1259, p. 1.

29 St. John, *Boss*, p. 301.

30 'British Embassy Baghdad to FO, 25 March 1959'. (No. 261) (Eq1017/11) PRO, FO371/140711, p. 1.

31 'British Embassy Baghdad [Sir H. Trevelyan] to FO [Hoyer-Miller and Stevens], 24 March 1959'. (Eb10393/11) PRO, FO371/140711, p. 1. The Iraqi Foreign Minister stated that he believed that by leaving the Pact, relations with the members would improve 'since it would diminish the misunderstandings arising from their membership'. Although not stated, the withdrawal would also remove a major issue that Nasser could use in attacking the Qasim regime, while at the same time paving the way for more Soviet support. In March 1959, Britain still had troops and Royal Air Force personnel at Habbaniya Air Base in Iraq. On hearing the news, Ambassador Trevelyan immediately stated that Britain would now want to remove its military personnel as soon as possible.

32 'British Embassy Beirut [Crossthwaite] to British Embassy WDC [Ormsby-Gore] and FO, 21 March 1959,' No. 285, PRO, FO371/140398, p. 1.

33 'London [Whitney] to WDC, 10 February 1959,' NACPM, 787.56/2-1059, p. 1.

34 Nutting, *Nasser*, p. 257.
35 'SNIE, The Communist Threat to Iraq, 17 February 1959'. *FRUS*, 1958-1960, Volume XII, pp. 381-383.
36 'Baghdad to WDC, 26 March 1959'. No. 2758, Part 1, DDEL, Staff Secretary, Box 8, Section II, pp. 1-2.
37 'Telegram from WDC (Herter) to US Embassy Baghdad, 27 March 1959'. DDEL, Staff Secretary, Box 8, p. 2.
38 Interview with Lakeland, 23-24 September 2003.
39 'Discussion 398th NSC Meeting, 5 March 1959'. DDEL, NSC Series, Box 11, p. 2.
40 Interview with Andrew Goodpaster, 7 August 2003.
41 'Cabinet Paper entitled "Policy Towards Iraq", 25 June 1959'. PRO, CAB 21/5595, pp. 1-4, 5, 13.
42 'Baghdad to WDC, 3 April 1959'. DDEL, Office of the Staff Secretary, Box 8, Section 1, p. 1. See also 'Memcon Lloyd and Herter, WDC, 4 April 1959'. *FRUS*, 1958-1960, Volume XII, p. 41.
43 'Memo on Iraq, John A. Calhoun, Executive Sec, DOS, to Goodpaster, 15 April 1959'. DDEL, Box 8, pp. 8-9.
44 'British Embassy WDC [M.D. Weir] to FO [C.M. LeQuesne, Eastern Department), 1 May 1959'. (Eq10316/96) PRO, FO371/140940, p. 1.
45 'Baghdad to WDC, 3 April 1959'. DDEL, Box 8, Section III, p. 1. Secretary Herter reported on 20 April 1959 that: 'the relatively complacent British Government view of developments in Iraq had not significantly changed'. 'Discussion 403rd NSC Meeting, 23 April 1958'. DDEL, Box 11, p. 2.
46 'Memorandum from Calhoun to Goodpaster, 15 April 1959'. DDEL, Office of Staff Secretary, Box 8, pp. 2-3.
47 'Discussion 402nd NSC Meeting, 17 April 1959'. DDEL, Box 11, pp. 1, 8-11. At this meeting of the NSC, the resignation of John Foster Dulles was announced.
48 Ibid, pp. 4-11.
49 'Report on Iraq for Senate Briefing, 27 April 1959'. CIA, CIA Resource Extraction System (CRES), CIA-RDP82R00025R000100060023-4, pp. 1-3.
50 'Memo from Calhoun to Goodpaster, 15 April 1959'. DDEL, Staff Sec, Box 8, pp. 2-3.
51 Ibid.
52 Interview with Goodpaster, 7 August 2003.
53 Ibid, pp. 4-5.
54 'Discussion 404th NSC Meeting, 30 April 1959'. DDEL, Box 11, pp. 9-10.
55 'British Emb Baghdad [Trevelyan] to FO, 28 April 1959'. PRO, FO371/140957, p. 1. See also 'British Mission NATO [Roberts] to FO, 8 May 1959'. PRO, FO371/141011, p. 1.
56 'British Emb Baghdad [Trevelyan] to FO, 28 April 1959'. PRO, FO371/140957, p. 1.
57 Ibid. See also 'British Mission NATO [Roberts] to FO, 8 May 1959'. PRO, FO371/141011, p. 1.
58 'British Embassy Baghdad [Trevelyan] to FO [G.F. Hiller], 19 July 1959'. PRO, FO371/140948, p. 1.
59 St. John, *The Boss*, p. 302.
60 Nasser, Gamal Abdel 'Speech delivered in Damascus, 15 March 1959'. In Roi (ed.), *From Encroachment to Involvement*, pp. 296-302. Nasser also used the speech to cast doubt on Qasim's credentials as a revolutionary, crediting Abd-al-Salaam al-Aref as the leader of the 14 July coup and casting Qasim in the role of opportunist.
61 Khrushchev, Nikita 'Speech delivered at a reception for an Iraqi economic delegation, 16 March 1959'. In Roi (ed.), *From Encroachment to Involvement*, pp. 303-307.
62 Nasser, Gamal Abdel 'Speech delivered in Damascus, 20 March 1959'. In Roi (ed.), *From Encroachment to Involvement*, p. 308.

63 Stephens, *Nasser*, pp. 299, 309.
64 St. John, *Boss*, pp. 303-304. St. John states that during these escalating exchanges with Moscow, Egyptian Field Marshall Abd-al-Hakim al-Amer repeatedly made the point to Nasser: 'Spare parts, Gamal! Please remember we need spare parts.' This, of course, referred to Egyptian reliance on Soviet military hardware and spares. Whether or not the quote is accurate, it is easy to imagine the concern that must have existed in the Egyptian military about a total break with Moscow and the effect on its Soviet-supplied military establishment.
65 'Canada House Cairo to FO, 20 April 1959'. PRO, FO371/140940, p. 1.
66 'Discussion 404th NSC Meeting, 30 April 1959'. DDEL, Box 11, p. 10.
67 'Memo INR [H.W. Glidden] to INR Director [Cumming], 13 March 1959'. NACPM, 787.00/3-1359, pp. 1-2.
68 'Baghdad [Jernegan] to Dulles'. NACPM, 611.87/3-1859, Section II, p. 1. This telegram is a memorandum of aconversation between the US Ambassador in Iraq, Jernegan, and Qasim. In the conversation, Jernegan complained of the bad treatment of the US in the local press and that 'Iraqi press articles and statements by popular organizations sounded exactly as if they had been drafted in Moscow by PRAVDA'.
69 Tripp, *History of Iraq*, p. 157.
70 'British Embassy Baghdad [Trevelyan] to FO, 2 May 1959.' PRO, FO371/140915, p. 1.
71 'Memcon Profumo, Hoyer-Millar, and Nutting FO, 9 June 1959'. PRO, FO371/140953, p. 1. Nutting had just returned from Iraq and a round of meetings with various Iraqi officials. He met with Profumo and Hoyer-Millar at the FO to discuss his findings, and the memorandum of their conversation at that meeting was sent to Ormsby-Gore, Sir Roger Stevens and Lord Landsdowne.
72 'British Embassy Baghdad [Trevelyan] to FO, 9 June 1959'. PRO, FO371/140953, p. 1. See also 'Letter British Embassy Baghdad [Trevelyan] to FO [G.F. Hiller], 3 June 1959'. PRO, FO371/140960, p. 1. Jawad, the Iraqi Foreign Minister had raised this issue with Trevelyan, who discounted it. Jawad also raised it with the Pakistani Ambassador, who naturally blamed it on an Indian diplomat. Trevelyan believed that Jawad's concern was the end result of rumors emanating from the talk about a UAR/Lebanon/Jordan anti-Communist front.
73 'Memcon Profumo, Hoyer-Millar, and Nutting, FO, 9 June 1959'. PRO, FO371/140953, p. 1.
74 'Report on Iraq for the NSC Briefing, 17 June 1959'. CIA, CIA Resource Extraction System (CRES), CIA-RDP79R00890A001100060025-2, pp. 1-3.
75 Tripp, *History of Iraq*, p. 158. One of the assassins, 22-year-old Saddam Hussein, would flee to Cairo, where at UAR government expense he earned a university degree.
76 'Savingram Australian Embassy WDC to DEA, 27 November 1959'. NAA, DEA, A1838-250/10/5/6 Part 2, p. 1. The information on the current situation in Baghdad came from Australian Embassy discussions with William Lakeland, Jordan-Iraq desk at the State Department. Lakeland also updated the Australians on Qasim's condition following the attack, and described the Iraqi leader as 'even more rambling and lacking in lucidity than before'. 'The trouble was that as a leader he seemed completely bankrupt of ideas.' Lakeland downplayed Qasim's threats against the Syrian-UAR 'as no more than an attempt to pay Nasser back in the same coin for his interference in Iraq'. See also 'Cablegram Australian Embassy WDC to MEA Canberra, 5 November 1959'. NAA, DEA, A1838-250/10/5/6 Part 2, p. 1. See also 'Cablegram Australian Embassy WDC to MEA Canberra, 5 November 1959'. NAA, DEA, A1838-250/10/5/6 Part 2, p. 1. In a separate meeting, Lakeland pointed out that once responsibility for the assassination attempt had been firmly established there would be 'serious trouble' internally.

77 'Cablegram Australian Emb WDC to Canberra, 5 November 1959'. NAA, DEA, A1838-250/10/5/6 Part 2, p. 1.
78 'Dispatch Baghdad [Lee F. Dinsmore] to WDC, 12 January 1960'. NACPM, 787.00/1-1260, p. 1.
79 'Dispatch Baghdad [Jernegan] to WDC, 30 January 1960'. NACPM, 787.00/1-3060, p. 1.
80 'Comments by the Shah in a meeting with John Strachey in a memo from Geoffrey Harrison British Embassy Baghdad to Sir Roger Stevens, British Ambassador Baghdad, 25 January 1960.' PRO, FO371/149866, p. 1.
81 'Indian Embassy Baghdad [D.S. Kamtekar, First Secretary via I.S. Chopra, Ambassador] to the MEA New Delhi [V.H. Coelho, Joint Secretary] 3 January 1960.' INA, MEA, 6-A(2) – WANA/60, pp. 10-11. 'Indian Embassy Baghdad [D.S. Kamtekar, First Secretary via I.S. Chopra, Ambassador] to the MEA New Delhi [V.H. Coelho, Joint Secretary] 3 January 1960'. INA, MEA, 6-A(2) – WANA/60, p. 7. There is little doubt that most observers would have largely agreed with this assessment. The Indian Embassy in Baghdad at this time was decidedly anti-Qasim. In this lengthy report, they denigrate Qasim's contribution to the revolution, giving others including Abd-al-Salam Al-Aref, more credit. The Indians decribed Qasim as follows: 'sick mind', 'irrational search for power', 'the evil side of a split personality', 'absurd contradictions', and having the characteristics of 'mendacity and unreliability'.
82 'Baghdad [Jernegan] to WDC, 12 January 1960'. NACPM, 787.00/1-1260 CAA, p. 2.
83 Batatu, *The Old Social Classes*, pp. 936-931. Batatu's work is an unrivaled tome that deals in minute detail with the revolution and its aftermath. It is hard to imagine another work in more detail on any set of political events in recent Arab history. See also 'Baghdad [Jernegan] to WDC, 10 February 1960'. NACPM, 787.00/1-1060, p. 1. While Batatu carefully covered the internal political conflicts in Iraq, he did not have available at the time some of the documentation since declassified by the US and British governments. It is clear that Qasim authorized Foreign Minister Hashim Jawad to convey to the US Ambassador the message that he was bringing the mainline Iraqi Communists to heel. This lack of access hardly detracts from the internal political story, but more recently released sources place events in a broader context.
84 See 'Dispatch Baghdad [David Wilson, First Secretary] to WDC, 11 January 1960'. NACPM, 787.00/1-11-60, pp. 1-5, and 'Baghdad [Jernegan] to WDC, 19 January 1960'. NACPM, 787.00/1-1960, pp. 1-2.
85 'Baghdad [Jernegan] to WDC, 10 February 1960'. NACPM, 787.00/1-1060, p. 1. This telegram resulted from a conversation with Hashim Jawad, the Iraqi Foreign Minister, who was closely aligned with the National Democratic Party of Iraq. In *Old Social Classes*, p. 844, Batatu states that Jawad was a Sunni, born in 1911.
86 Batatu, *Old Social Classes*, p. 941.
87 'Dispatch Baghdad [Dinsmore] to WDC, 29 February 1960.' NACPM, 787.00/2-2960, p. 1 and enclosure. 'Savingram Australian Embassy WDC to Department of External Affairs (DEA) Canberra, 29 March 1960'. NAA, DEA, A1838-250/10/5/6 Part 2, p. 1. Speculation existed in relation to the Mahdawi's reaction to the commutation of the many of the conspirators' sentences. Mahdawi, the chief judge and Qasim's brother-in-law, refused any comment, and in fact reduced his own profile significantly. He had no intention of attempting to defy Qasim's order.
88 'Memcon with Ambassador Sulaiman, Iraqi Embassy WDC, with Turner B. Shelton, USIA, 7 March 1960'. NACPM, 787.00/3-760.
89 'Savingram Australian Embassy WDC to Department of External Affairs (DEA) Canberra, 16 March 1960'. NAA, DEA, A1838-250/10/5/6 Part 2, p. 1.
90 'Australian Embassy WDC to DEA Canberra, 21 April 1960'. NAA, DEA, A1838-250/10/5/6 Part 2, p. 1.

91 'Dispatch London to WDC attached *The Guardian* on 29 July 1960, 3 August 1960'. NACPM, 787.00/8-360, attachments.
92 'Baghdad [Jernegan] to WDC, 18 July 1960'. NACPM, 787.00/7-1860, pp. 1-2.
93 Kerr, *Arab Cold War*, p. 28.
94 Nutting, *Nasser*, pp. 250-251.
95 'British Mission Cairo [C.T. Crowe] to FO and Whitehall, 18 August 1960'. PRO, FO371/371/150903, p. 1. Nuruddin Khahala was Vice President; Fakher Kayyali was Minister of State; and Faid Zainuddin was Deputy Minister for Foreign Affairs.
96 Heikal, *Matha Jara fi Suria*, pp. 104-111. This work was the first attempt at a quasi-official explanation of the coup in Syria. Sarraj was in prison in Damascus, having had the misfortune to time his return from Cairo just before the 28 September coup. Heikal's book was an attempt to lay the blame at the feet of anyone but the Egyptian government and Nasser. Written in a typically Arab newspaper editorial style, the book presents series of questions and answers to explain the coup. With regard to Sarraj and his role as a catalyst for disaffection in Syria, Heikal debates the issue of Sarraj's alleged 'love of power'. He brings up the fact that King Saud attempted unsuccessfully to bribe Sarraj, and he points out that the power accumulated by Sarraj was not for personal gain but for the defense of Arab unity. The book explains the years 1959 and 1960 as ones in which Nasser and the loyal supporters of Arab nationalism and unity in Syria, of which Sarraj was the most prominent, attempted to preserve UAR unity against the forces of imperialism and reaction, which were strongly represented by Qasim, King Saud, and King Hussein. In Muhammad Abd-al-Aziz Ahmad and Wafiq Abd-al-Aziz al-Tahmi's *Tajraba al-Wahida bayn Misr wa Suria* (Cairo: National, 1962), pp. 56-62, the authors argue that the 'people of Syria' overwhelmingly approved of and support the union with Egypt. They then make the argument that the idea of Arab unity was part and parcel of the Syrian attempts to free itself from imperialism, and that the union with Egypt was a natural step in this progression. For support, these two authors quote voting returns on the various referendums on unity. In this section they particularly focused on 1960. This was an apparent attempt to combat criticism that the union showed signs of disintegration at a very early stage. They also recited the list of Syrian calls for unity, including 1955 and 1956. This work and Heikal's, although focused on explaining the split between Syria and Egypt and justifying the Egyptian position in this matter, provide an interesting insight into how the Egyptians chose to interpret the events of 1959 and 1960. These are period pieces providing a window on Egyptian attitudes toward Syria; they also reflect the inability of Egyptians to understand the problems that the UAR administration created for itself in Damascus. This also in some sense provides an insight into Nasser's own inability during this period to really understand Syrian resentment, and thus the dangers posed to the union, and into his failure to heed Sarraj's warnings. In Nutting's *Nasser*, p. 266, Sarraj probably had the most telling response of all. When asked if he had been too heavy-handed and repressive in his tactics as head of the *muhabbarat* in Syria during the 1959-1960 timeframe, he stated that 'allowed a free hand' the coup would never have occurred. Nutting states: 'Sarraj undoubtedly held the union together by the brutal efficiency of his intelligence network and by the sheer terror which his name exercised in the minds of any would-be secessionists.'
97 Nutting, *Nasser*, p. 265. 'Minute by John G.S. Beith, Levant Department, FO, 15 September 1960'. PRO, FO371/150901, pp. 1-2. On the jacket of Beith's minute someone speculated that Sarraj's appointment, as head of the Syrian Executive, was the means to eventually get rid of him, as a gesture to the 'will of the people'. As early as September 1959, rumors abounded that because of Sarraj's prickly relationship with Nasser and his clashes with Amer, he would be promoted to Vice President and moved

to Cairo. The conclusion was that the 'most critical of all factors in assessing the stresses in the Syro-Egyptian union is the Nasir[sic]-Sarraj rivalry.'
98 'British Embassy Beirut [Eden] to the FO, 12 September 1959'. No. 740 PRO FO371/150901, p. 1. Virtually all of the British information came through the American Consul Reams, in Damascus. This particular report came from the American Embassy via the Regional Information Officer in Beirut, who had visited Damascus.

Chapter 7

1 Salibi, Kamal, *The Modern History of Jordan*. London: Tauris, 1998, pp. 201-203. Given Jordan's precarious and highly vulnerable position, Salibi provides very little substance and even less analysis of the situation. Coverage of the 1959-1960 is spotty and disjointed. To the author's credit, he does state that the practice of laying all political unrest, plots and coup attempts at the feet of Nasser in Cairo was probably more politics than reality: 'Certainly, there were Nasserist involvements in a number of cases, but not necessarily in all. There were many in people in Jordan who felt hostile enough towards the regime, for one reason or another, to attempt acts of sabotage or terrorism.' That said, the author's presentation of what he calls 'The Difficult Years' overlooks Hussein's contributions to his own problems in the propaganda war with Nasser, and Jordanian concerns about the sincerity of US support for his regime. Influential elements in the US government viewed Jordan as a lost cause and a waste of aid money. This study will attempt to better place Jordan within the context of the Arab Cold War.
2 'British Embassy WDC [M.D. Weir] to FO [LeQuesne], 1 May 1959'. PRO, FO371/140940, p. 1. The situation in Jordan differed from that in Iraq in that the US Embassy in Amman took a more antagonistic line toward British pressure to support the Jordanian regime. In Iraq, the State Department actually informed the British Foreign Office that US Ambassador Jernegan 'reflected too closely' London's view of the situation in Baghdad. Jernegan's British view of the situation and, in general, his recommendations ran counter to the views and policy direction that the Eisenhower administration wanted to pursue.
3 Johnston will reemerge during the Kennedy administration as a persistent gadfly vis-à-vis US policy in South Arabia. Following his tenure in Amman, he was posted to Aden as Governor-General. This occurred during the border wars in which Yemen received Egyptian support. He was there during the Yemen Revolution of 1962 and the subsequent introduction of Egyptian troops into the Yemen civil war.
4 'Letter British Embassy WDC [Weir] to FO, 13 February 1959'. PRO, FO371/142117, p. 1. See also 'Minute attached to letter from British Embassy WDC [Weir] to FO, 13 February 1959'. PRO, FO371/142117, p. 1. The British were relieved when they learned that there would be no 'switch' in sources of supply. The Jordanian army was largely supplied with British arms, and both the British FO and the Ministry of Defence were concerned that the US government might insist that US military aid dollars be spent on US military equipment. J.D. Adams at the FO commented in a minute: 'It is satisfactory to have this re-assurance that there will be no switch from British to American sources of supply for the J.A.A.' 'Letter British Embassy WDC [Weir] to FO, 24 February 1959'. PRO, FO371/142117, p. 1. The British made a concerted effort to see what kinds of military equipment were on the list prepared by the Americans in order to protect orders for high-dollar equipment that the Jordanian had already made. They were very concerned that the US survey would not include radars. General Hart, the head of the US military mission, had stated that his primary goal was 'to keep down costs ... in view of the poverty of the country'. Jordan had placed an order for an expensive Marconi radar system, and intended to pay for it with the US aid. By deleting radar from the list, the US military mission placed the onus on the Jordanians to come

up with the money or the British to come up with the aid. Willie Morris, of the British Embassy in Washington, argued that in a country like Jordan: 'the army played an important educational and social role, as well as being the key political factor. It was therefore important that due weight should be given to the importance of maintaining the army's morale.' From London's point of view, maintaining morale was particularly important when it involved a large-scale sale of British radar purchased with US aid dollars.

5 'WDC to Amman, 4 February 1959'. *FRUS*, 1958-1960, Volume XI, pp. 670-681.
6 'Letter British Embassy WDC (Morris) to FO, 19 March 1959, (Vj10345/3)'. PRO, FO371/142117, p. 1.
7 'Letter from British Embassy WDC [Morris] to FO, 19 March 1959,') PRO, FO371/142117, p. 1. See also 'Letter from British Embassy WDC [Morris] to FO, 19 March 1959, (Vj10345/1)'. PRO, FO371/142117, p. 1. British concern about the rapprochement between Jordan and the UAR came from conversations in Washington with William Lakeland, the Iraqi desk officer. Lakeland's close relationship with Nasser and the Egyptians during the negotiation of the 1954 treaty for the removal of British troops from the Suez Canal Zone tended to raise British suspicions about Lakeland's presumed pro-Egyptian sentiments. During the period 1952-1954, Lakeland was on a first-name basis with Nasser, Amer, and Heikal, all of whom were guests at Lakeland's apartment on al-Gazira island from time to time. Interview with William Lakeland, 23-24 September 2003. The British were highly concerned because a link with Nasser would not only severely weaken their influence in Amman, but might, they believed, start a change of events that would result in the loss of their petroleum interests in Iraq. Morris informed London that Lakeland, speaking for himself and 'several of his colleagues ... felt that the sooner Jordan were associated with the U.A.S. [*sic* – UAR] the better'. Morris pointed out that Lakeland was sometimes 'out of line' with the powers-that-be in the State Department, but that clearly there was a debate going on about the degree of support that Nasser's anti-Communist campaign should receive.
8 'National Intelligence Estimate, The Outlook for Jordan, 10 March 1959'. *FRUS*, 1958-1960, Volume XI, pp. 681-687. Also see 'Memo Rountree to Herter, 14 March 1959'. *FRUS*, 1958-1960, Volume XI, pp. 687-690.
9 'British Emb Amman [Johnston] to FO, 16 March 1959'. PRO, FO371/142102, p. 1.
10 Ibid, p. 2. Johnston described a series of internal scenarios that he believed could occur in the absence of the King and Prime Minister. All centered on the Bedouin element in the army and the armored brigade that they controlled. Johnston feared that repression by Bedouin army units or the replacement of the al-Rifai' government with a military dictatorship would lead to a Nasserist revolt, or that the Jordanian army might take the Qasim route and overthrow both al-Rifai and the King. 'While the loyalty of the Bedouin rank and file is unquestionable, some of the senior Bedouin officers probably have their price.' See also 'British Embassy Amman [Johnston] to the FO, 16 March 1959'. PRO, FO371/142102, p. 1. In this follow-up telegram, Johnston informed London that: 'a fairly reliable Jordanian informant tells me that a pro-Nasserite coup is being plotted by elements in those who are usually believed to be loyal to King Hussein.' This informant stated that when approached by the group Nasser had offered his assistance. The coup itself had mutated from a movement against al-Rifai' to one that now included the monarchy itself.
11 'British Embassy Amman [Johnston] to the Foreign Office, 21 March 1959'. PRO, FO371/142102, p. 1. Johnston worried constantly about playing second fiddle to the Americans. He was well aware of who really paid the bills in Jordan, and saw every new development as a threat to British interests in Jordan. See also 'Amman to WDC, 11 July 1958'. *FRUS*, 1958-1960, Volume XI, p. 298.

12 'Amman [Lester Wright] to WDC, 21 April 1959'. NACPM, 611.85/4-2159, Section I, p. 2. Rifai' went so far as to state that if al-Shara was arrested or replaced that he (Rifai') would resign from the government. Informed speculation can make a very case for the possibility that Lakeland knew about Shara's plotting against the Hashemite regime through US intelligence. This information was undoubtedly available to MI6 through liaison contacts or its own sources within the Jordanian security services. Given the British views of where they wanted Jordanian policy to go vis-à-vis the UAR, it is not hard to imagine that the British had been encouraging the King to arrest Shara, and thus feared that Shara might escape the King's grasp by defecting while in the US.
13 Salibi, *Jordan*, p. 204.
14 'Memcon Hussein and Herter, 24 March 1959'. *FRUS*, 1958-1960, Volume XI, p. 694.
15 'Letter NE Affairs [Rockwell] to Amman [Wright], 2 April 1959'. *FRUS*, 1958-1960, Volume XI, pp. 707-709.
16 'Amman to WDC, 21 April 1959'. NACPM, 611.85/4-2159, Section III, pp. 12.
17 'British Embassy Amman [Johnston] to FO, 7 April 1959'. PRO, FO371/142117, p. 1.
18 'British Embassy Amman [Johnston] to FO, 7 April 1959'. PRO, FO371/142117, p. 2. This is a reference to Sulayman al-Nabulsi, the former pro-Nasserist Prime Minister in Jordan. See also 'Minute by R.M. Tesh on telegram Amman [Johnston] to FO, 7 April 1959'. PRO, FO371/142117, pp. 1-2. The FO minutes relative to the Johnston telegram suggest that the way to pressure the Americans was to get the Israelis involved, by pointing out to them that Iraq mightt be Communist it had no potential to occupy Jordan, while Nasser did. They believed that they could use the Israelis and Jewish organizations to guard against a change in US policy toward Jordan.
19 'FO to British Embassy WDC, 14 April 1959'. PRO, FO371/142117, p. 3. Johnston was extremely concerned about the British position in Jordan, particularly with reference to the Jordanian military. As an example of his sensitivity, at a dinner party in May 1959 the US military attaché accused the British of undermining Prime Minister Rifai' because he was too pro-American, and replacing him with the pro-British Majali. Additionally, Johnston reported that the American military attaché stated that he was sick of paying the bills in Jordan while the British got the credit. Johnston stated that he was concerned that the Americans were saying these things to the Jordanians, and perhaps even to the press, and asked for instructions on any action the he might take. See also 'Minute attached to a Letter from Amman [Johnston] to FO, PRO, FO371/142130, pp. 1-2. In this minute to Johnston's letter, the FO commented: 'Irresponsible and inexperienced [vis-à-vis the Arabs] as the Americans may be, it does not follow to my mind that a remark made at dinner in a colleague's house would necessarily be passed to the Jordanians – or the international press.' London had an almost full-time job keeping Johnston on an even keel. His paranoia about growing American influence and his fundamental dislike of any who disagreed with him, particularly if they were American, would also emerge in the Kennedy administration.
20 'British Embassy Amman [Johnston] to FO [Stevens] 16 September 1959'. No. 781, PRO FO371/142131, p. 1.
21 'FO [Stevens] to British Embassy Jordan [Johnston], 18 September 1959'. No. 1115, PRO FO371/142131, p. 1.
22 'British Emb Amman [Johnston] to FO [Stevens] 16 September 1959'. No. 792, PRO FO371/142131, pp.1-2.
23 'FO [Beith] to British Embassy Amman [Johnston], 22 September 1959'. No. 4122, PRO FO371/142131, p. 1.
24 'British Embassy Amman [Johnston] to FO [Stevens] 22 September 1959'. No. 781, PRO FO371/142131, p. 1.
25 'FO [Stevens] to British Embassy Jordan [Johnston], 24 September 1959'. No. 1147, PRO FO371/142131, p. 1. See also 'British Embassy WDC [Weir] to FO [LeQuesne], 1

May 1959'. PRO, FO371/140940, p. 1. A few months before, London had had its fingers burned with regard to the situation in Iraq when the American Ambassador's judgments had been called into question because they were too optimistic and tended to echo those of the British Ambassador and the Foreign Office.

26 'British Embassy Baghdad [Trevelyan] to FO, 24 September 1959'. PRO FO371/142131, p. 2.

27 'Dispatch British Embassy WDC [Weir] to FO [Rothnie], 26 September 1959'. PRO FO371/142131, p. 1, attached minute, attached article.

28 'Dispatch Amman [Andrew I. Kilgore] to WDC, 18 May 1960'. NACPM, 785.11/5-1960, pp. 1-2. See also 'Memo from C.M. Anderson, British High Commission, New Delhi to Y.K. Puri, MEA, New Delhi, 7 March 1960'. INA, MEA, 8/A(3) – WANA/60, p. 1. Instability in Jordan had become a widely-followed regional topic; so widely-followed that the British Embassy in New Delhi felt obliged to explain to the Indian government the nature of proposed British and American aid to the Hashemite kingdom.

29 'Amman [Mills] to WDC, 7 January 1960'. NACPM, 785.13/1-660, Section I, pp. 1-2.

30 'British Embassy Amman [Johnston] to the Foreign Office, 15 March 1960'. PRO, FO371/151058, p. 2.

31 'Letter from British Embassy Amman [Johnston] to the Foreign Office [J.G.S. Beith, Levant Department], 19 May 1960'. PRO, FO371/151058, p. 2.

32 'FO Minutes on Telegram from Amman [Johnston] to FO, 18 June 1960'. PRO, FO371/151058, p. 2.

33 'Minute by P.H. Moberly British Emb Cairo, 6 July 1960'. PRO FO371/151058, p. 1.

34 'Letter British Embassy Amman [L.C.W. Figg] to FO, 15 March 1960'. PRO, FO371/151058, p. 2.

35 'FO to the British Embassy Amman, 6 July 1960'. PRO FO371/151058, p. 2.

36 'WDC to Amman, 16 August 1960'. NACPM, 785.11/8-1660, p. 1.

37 'Letter British Emb Amman [Morris] to FO, 8 July 1960'. PRO FO371/151058, p. 1.

38 'Amman to WDC NIACT Immediate, 29 August 1960'. NACPM, 785.11/8-2960, p. 1.

39 'Amman [Kocher] to WDC, 2 September 1960'. NACPM, 785.13/9-260 HBS, p. 1.

40 'Amman [Kocher] to WDC, 30 August 1960'. NACPM, 785.13/8-3060 HBS, pp. 1-4. The issue of Majali's 'liberal nature' centered on the fact that the two perpetrators of the bombing plot apparently had known anti-government views and had previously participated in anti-government activities. Despite this Majali 'himself had suggested their employment as part of his general policy to attempt [to] rehabilitate those Jordanians whom he considered unjustly suspected'. The view was that, given the apparent result, the release of political prisoners would cease while 'interrogation, round-ups, arrests [were] all likely to increase'.

41 Interview with William C. Lakeland, 23-24 September 2003. BOGHAKYPU was the acronym for 'be of good heart and keep your pecker up'. William 'Bill' Lakeland was the Iraq-Jordan Desk Officer from the summer of 1958 to the summer of 1960 when he became the political officer in Baghdad. Lakeland viewed the Jordanian regime as a nuisance and a waste of foreign aid, a widely-held view in the foreign policy establishment.

42 Nutting, *Nasser*, pp. 280-281.

43 'Amman [Kocher] to WDC, 2 September 1960'. NACPM, 785.13/9-260 HBS, p. 1.

44 'Amman [Kocher] to WDC, 30 August 1960'. NACPM, 785.13/8-3060 HBS, p. 4.

45 'Memcon Melih Esenbel, Turkish Ambassador to the US and G. Lewis Jones, NEA, 29 September 1960'. NACPM, 785.11/9-2960, pp. 1-2. The US desire for good relations with Nasser had not gone unnoticed in Amman. The Turkish Ambassador to the United States, Melih Esenbel, told G. Lewis Jones, NEA, that many Jordanians blamed the US for the assassination of Majali. They believed that only the US had the actual

influence in Cairo to deter Nasser's aggressive intentions toward Jordan. As a result, they surmised that the US had condoned Nasser's activities. Jones responded that while the allegations were absurd, the US would do everything in its power to calm the differences between Jordan and the United Arab Republic. Jones hoped that a meeting might be arranged between Nasser and King Hussein since both had elected to attend the UNGA meeting in New York. In response to Esenbel's concerns over the reception accorded King Hussein, Jones stated that the US intended to give Jordan every indication of its continuing support.

46 'CRO to Commonwealth members, 10 September 1960'. PRO FO371/151045, p. 1.
47 'Telegram from the CRO to Commonwealth members, 13 September 1960'. No. 428, PRO FO371/151045, p. 1.
48 'British Embassy Amman [Johnston] to FO [Hoyer-Miller and Stevens], 12 September 1960'. No. 808, PRO FO371/151048, pp. 1-2. Additionally, Johnston pointed out that Fawaz Haher, a Circassian commanding the divisional headquarters, Majali's own Chief of Staff, another Circassian, Izzat Hassan, and Kasim Ohan, the Armenian Director of Military Training were all opposed to the adventure, but 'their protests are being ignored'.
49 'British Embassy Amman [Johnston] to FO, 12 September 1960'. No. 804, PRO FO371/151048, p. 1.
50 'Minute by Sir Roger Stevens on Cabinet Brief for Prime Minister Macmillan, 14 September 1960'. PRO FO371/151048, Cover Sheet. See also, 'British Embassy Tehran [Millard] to FO and Amman, 27 September 1960'. PRO 371/151061, p. 1. The concern had reached such a high point that the Americans and British asked the Shah of Iran to use his influence with King Hussein. In this vein, the Iranian Ambassador in Amman, Afshar, delivered a message from the Shah that sympathized with the King but urged 'him not to embark on a military adventure, which would be likely to prove disastrous'.
51 'British Embassy Amman [Johnston] to FO, 15 September 1960'. PRO FO371/151048, p. 2.
52 'Amman [Kocher] to WDC, 2 September 1960'. NACPM, 785.13/9-260 HBS, p. 2.
53 'London [Whitney] to WDC, 8 September 1960'. NACPM, 785.13/9-860 CAA, p. 1.
54 'British Embassy Amman [Johnston] to FO, 27 September 1960'. PRO FO371/151061, p. 1. The fact that Talal, Hussein's father, was certifiably mad was a point lost on few in the Arab world, and almost no one in Jordan.
55 Eisenhower, *Waging Peace*, pp. 584-585. President Eisenhower's memoirs describe the meeting with Nasser as 'a highly interesting experience', while not even mentioning a meeting with King Hussein that occurred at the White House after the UNGA on October 7, 1960.
56 'Herter to Amman, 12 October 1960'. NACPM, 785.11/10-1260, pp. 1-2.
57 'Amman [Kocher] to Herter, 8 October 1960'. NACPM, 785.11/10-860, p. 1.
58 'Minute by R.K. Nehru to F.S. Dutt and Prime Minister Nehru, 1 November 1960'. INA, 8A (2) WANA/60.
59 'Memcon Roger Stevens and US Under Secretary Dillon, 10 December 1959'. PRO, FO371/142141, pp. 1-3. This entire file is an excellent source for the early phases of what would become an ongoing battle over who had to pay for propping up Jordan. The British had managed to get the US committed to the idea of maintaining the Jordanian state, and now they wanted to limit their exposure. For London, despite its old ties to the regime, Jordan had never been the real issue; the heart of the matter was Iraq, the IPC and Kuwait.
60 'Memcon Selwyn Lloyd and Acting Secretary of State Dillon, 26 September 1960'. NACPM, 785.11/9-2660, pp. 1-2. See also 'Operations Memorandum "Basic Data on Jordan" from US Embassy Amman to WDC, 28 July 1961'. NACPM, 785.5 MSP/7-2861, p. 8. Total US aid to Jordan from 1951 to 1960 totaled $188 million. Of this

amount, $119 million was in direct budgetary support, with $20 million in PL 480 grain and $49 million in economic and technical aid. The British contributions since 1951 was considerably less.

61 'Operations Memo "Basic Data on Jordan" from Amman to WDC, 28 July 1961'. NACPM, 785.5 MSP/7-2861, p. 3. See also 'Memcon Finance Minister Erhard of West Germany, and Acting Secretary of State Dillon, 26 September 1960'. NACPM, 785.5 MSP-/9-2660, p. 1. Erhard attended a dinner on the same evening as the Dillon-Lloyd meeting. Both took this opportunity to press the Germans on the issue of aid, pointing out that West Germany had become the largest commercial supplier to Jordan. Erhard replied that he 'thought something would be possible' along the lines of $5 to $7 million in direct aid. The Chairman of the Deutsche Bank, Karl Blessing, who was also present, concurred that they could probably manage the problem.

62 'Memcon Selwyn Lloyd and Dillon, 26 September 1960'. NACPM, 785.11/9-2660, pp. 1-2.

63 Lacy, Robert, *The Kingdom: Arabia and the House of Saud.* New York: Harcourt, Brace, Jovanovich, 1981, pp. 310-371. The author offers a set of chapters that provides a well-organized domestic and international context for the period of the Arab Cold War. Although brief, the chapter on 'Colonel Nasser's New Way' gives an overview of the impact of Nasserism on the Saudi world. The book makes two particularly important points. First, it briefly discusses the role of Egyptian teachers in Saudi Arabia and the grassroots influence that they exerted on the Kingdom. Second, Lacey discusses the impact of Nasser's July 1956 visit to Dhahran and Riyadh, and the humiliation of the Saudi royal family: 'There could be no face-saving rationalizations of the hysteria that swamped the Egyptian leader when he arrived. ... Riyadh had never seen anything like it. No member of the house of Saud had ever inspired such spontaneous displays of passion.' Lacy also takes a look at the exact circumstances in which the decision to place Feisal in charge of the government occurred. In the chapter entitled 'Enter the Crown Prince', Lacy states that the meeting occurred immediately after Nasser's radio broadcast announcing Saud's attempt to bribe Sarraj and wreck the Syrian union (p. 320). No reference is made to an Arab Cold War, but the substance of these two chapters, and to a degree also the 'OPEC' chapter, place the internal situation in Saudi Arabia in the broader context of the Arab Cold War period. See also Holden, David and Richard Johns, *The House of Saud: The Rise and Rule of the Most Powerful Dynasty in the Arab World.* New York: Holt, Rinehart, Winston, 1981, pp. 203-205. *The House of Saud* is a popular history of the Saudi Kingdom. It deals with the period of the Arab Cold War in terms of the problems besetting the Saudi royal family, during the transition from Saud to Feisal. The book also provides a useful outline of the controversy surrounding Tallal ibn Saud and his attempts to secularize the Saudi state along Nasserist lines. The original author David Holden, a correspondent of *The Sunday Times* was shot and killed by unknown assailants on a trip to Cairo on December 7, 1977. Richard Johns then took over the partially-finished manuscript and completed the work. The authors treat the 1959-1960 period, in a chapter entitled 'A House Divided', as the beginning of more disciplined rule by Feisal following the erratic actions of King Saud in 1957 and 1958. They pointed out that Feisal's rapprochement with Nasser sharply reduced the shock of the Iraqi coup of 1958. 'Amidst the furor, [Feisal] believed, rightly, that the safest policy for the kingdom was one of non-alignment.' After an August 1958 visit to Cairo and nine hours of talks with Nasser, Feisal allegedly commented: 'Thank God our relations are so good now that if there was a cloud in the sky it has passed by.' The book provides a useful look at the transition of authority in Saud Arabia during the late 1950s and early 1960s, but not much analysis of the broader context that drove these events. The book is after all a history of the Saudi family.

64 'Discussion 406th NSC Meeting, 13 May 1959'. DDEL, Box 11, p. 2.

65 'Annual Political Report on Saudi Arabia 1959 from Indian Embassy Jidda [M.K. Kidwai] to MEA New Delhi and Nehru, 12 October 1960'. INA, MEA, 15-A (9) WANA/60, pp. 1-2.
66 Lacy, *Kingdom*, p. 338.
67 'Jidda [Heath] to WDC, 25 July 1958'. *FRUS*, 1958-1960, Volume XII, pp. 730-732.
68 Salibi, *History of Jordan*, p. 201. See also 'Jidda [Heath] to WDC, 25 July 1958'. *FRUS*, 1958-1960, Volume XII, pp. 730-732. US Ambassador Heath met with Crown Prince Feisal and 'For nearly an hour, listened to an almost unadulterated Nasserian exposition of the situation in the Arab Near East'. Like Nasser prior to his falling out with Qasim, Feisal defended the revolution in Iraq. After the Egyptian-Iraqi break, Feisal mirrored UAR rhetoric and attacked Qasim. Heath commented: 'I have the impression that while Faisal is fully conscious of the danger Nasser represents to the monarchical regime in Saudi Arabia he is determined on reconciliation with Nasser in order to buy temporary relief from radio attacks and, he hopes, defer an Egyptian plot to overthrow the Saudi regime. I believe in order to buy time and possibly temporary security against an Egyptian-guided coup he is willing to put Saudi Arabia, like Yemen, into the UAR.' See also 'SNIE: The Outlook in Saudi Arabia, 9 September 1958'. *FRUS*, 1958-1960, Volume XII, p. 735.
69 'Minute by Sir Roger Stevens on Anglo-Saudi Relations, 13 September 1960'. PRO, FO371/149244, pp. 1-9. This particular file contains a very good record of the various disputes between Saudi Arabia and Britain, the obstacles to settling those disputes, and to the reestablishment of formal diplomatic relations.
70 'Memo Australian High Commission London to Canberra, 8 December 1959'. NAA, MEA, A1838 67/1/4/35, Part 1, p. 1. The connection between Saudi Arabia and the UAR was strong enough for *The Times* to argue that diplomatic relations with Egypt would bring diplomatic relations with Saudi Arabia. The Saudis' retention of Azzam Pasha, the former Secretary General of the Arab League, reinforced this view. The suggestion that Saudi Arabia would follow the UAR lead was so strong that the Saudis felt compelled to deny it, stating: 'Diplomatic relations between the United Kingdom and the U.A.R. [were] not irrelevant to the Saudi attitude.'
71 'Brief on Saudi-British Relations prepared by FO for President Ayub's visit to Riyadh, 21 October 1960'. PRO, FO371/149247, p. 2. See also 'Minute FO on Ayub discussions with Saudi leaders on issue of British relations, 5 and 20 October 1960'. PRO, FO371/149244, p. 1-2. In minutes between Walmsley and others, FO officials discussed how an upcoming visit of President Ayub of Pakistan might be used to further the cause of diplomatic relations between London and Riyadh. An effort through the UN was underway to find a compromise on the issue of Buraimi. R.A. Beaumont at the FO felt that an approach by Ayub might complicate DeRibbing's UN effort. Beaumont finally decided that Ayub could assure the Saudis of Macmillan's desire to see a settlement, but London wanted Ayub to point out the process of solving this problem was a long one, and one that had proven intractable for over eight years. For additional background on the UN role in the negotiations, see also the documents in 'Saudi Dispute with the United Kingdom, 1959'. PRO, FO371/140367.
72 'Annual Political Report on Saudi Arabia 1959 from Indian Embassy Jidda [M.K. Kidwai] to MEA New Delhi and Prime Minister [Nehru], 12 October 1960'. INA, MEA, 15-A (9) WANA/60, p. 4.
73 'British Embassy Amman [Johnston] to FO [Stevens], 16 September 1959'. PRO, FO371/142131, p. 1.
74 'Annual Political Report on Saudi Arabia 1959 from Indian Embassy Jidda to MEA and Nehru, 12 October 1960'. INA, MEA, 15-A (9) WANA/60, p. 4. Kidwai, the Indian Ambassador in Jidda, stated that the Saudi Arabia 'loudly proclaims that she will have

no truck with Britain until the Bopurimi [*sic* – Buraimi] question was settled to her satisfaction'.
75 'NIE Outlook for Saudi Arabia, 19 April 1960'. *FRUS*, 1958-1960, Volume XII, p. 759.
76 Ball, George W. and Douglas B. Ball, *The Passionate Attachment: America's Involvement with Israel, 1947 to the Present*. New York: Norton, 1992), pp. 47, 42-49. George Ball was Undersecretary of State in the Johnson and Kennedy administrations, as well as Ambassador to the United Nations. The authors entitled the chapter on the period 1952 to 1960 'The Eisenhower Administration Halts the Retreat'. They were referring to the propensity for the Truman administration to enunciate a position on the Middle East, and then to back away from it under Israeli-orchestrated pressure. This work argues that Eisenhower, who was elected by a landslide with the vast majority of Jewish voters supporting the Democratic candidate, Adlai Stevenson, faced no such handicap in pursuing Middle East policy. In reaction to Suez, Eisenhower embargoed $26 million in aid to Israel and threatened to end the tax exemption for contributions to American Zionist organizations, in order to pressure Israel to accept UN observers. The authors take a highly negative view of Israel's ability to influence US policy. They describe Israeli explanations for the Kibya raid on the West Bank of 14-15 October 1953 on the West Bank in the following manner: 'Here again – as was to happen so often in the future – America was subjected to a mirage of untruths and bureaucratic obfuscation.' Both give Eisenhower high marks for his unwillingness to budge in the face of Israeli and American Zionist pressure, and for his television address to the nation in 1957, in which he issued an ultimatum to Israel to either withdraw from Sinai or face a total cut-off of US monetary and aid support. The authors present a picture of frantic and fanatical American Zionist political efforts to force the President to back down, and laud his refusal. The Balls argue that the major failing of the Eisenhower administration was fixation on Communist influence, and its inability to understand that a comprehensive Middle East peace was the only real protection against Soviet inroads. Additionally, the authors state that the death of John Foster Dulles weakened the drive for a solution in the region. This work is largely an indictment of Israeli and American Zionist influence on the policies of the United States toward the Middle East. It argues that, fundamentally, Israel used Holocaust politics and the cry of anti-Semitism to deflect any real attempts to solve the problems in the region. The authors quote Dulles' statement on the subject: 'I am aware how almost impossible it is in this country to carry out a foreign policy not approved by the Jews. Marshall and Forestall learned that. I am going to have a try. That does not mean I am anti-Jewish, but I believe in what George Washington said in his Farewell address that an emotional attachment to another country should not interfere.' Dulles added: 'We cannot have our policies made in Jerusalem.' While critical of Arab missteps, the authors view Eisenhower as the last American president to pursue US national interests in the Middle East. Many of the quotes used in this short chapter came from Neff's *Warriors at Suez*. Neff obtained them from the notes and minutes of meetings made by Eisenhower's chief of staff Brigadier General Andrew Goodpaster. The overall work is clearly anti-Zionist, anti-Israeli and highly concerned with what it views as the undue influence of Israel and the American Jewish community over American foreign policy. Mark Tessler, in *A History of the Israeli-Palestinian Conflict* (Bloomington: University of Indiana Press, 1994) makes little mention of the 1959-1960 period except to argue that despite Israel's military performance during the Suez war, it was Nasser that reaped political gains in the region. Other than brief comments about the impact of the Syro-Egyptian union on Israel, and the fact that Tel Aviv always continued to view Nasser as the primary threat, the period is hardly mentioned.
77 'Analysis of the Nasserist Movement in its Relations with East and West attached to Memo from Australian Legation Tel Aviv [B.C. Ballard] to Canberra, 25 November

1958'. NAA, A1838/2 175/11/20 Part 9, pp. 1, 6-7. These papers included a list of all Nasser's transgressions in the region. The Ministry of Foreign Affairs prepared the paper for a visiting representative of the Italian Prime Minister. The Ministry liked it so much that they handed it out to other Western embassies and legations. From its very inception, the Israelis viewed the UAR as the primary threat. They could only thrive in the disunity of the Arab world, and the union of Syria and Egypt suggested that Arab nationalism might be strong enough to unite it. The Israelis predicted that Syria was only the first step, and that attempts to include Lebanon and Jordan would surely follow.
78 Alteras, Isaac, *Eisenhower and Israel: U.S.–Israeli Relations, 1953-1960*. Gainesville: University of Florida Press, 1993, pp. 311-312. Alteras's work is a good narrative, examining the complicated relationship between the Eisenhower administration and Israel. Hoever, it does not discuss the last two years of that administration, and the author makes sweeping judgments that are in fact incorrect in that regard. Based on US funding for purchases of British tanks, electronic equipment and '1,000 recoilless guns', Alteras concludes that: 'Israel's role in stemming Nasserite and Soviet influence had not won the whole-hearted support and recognition of the United States.' This is simply not the case. As we have seen, Nasser and not Israel was the chosen vehicle for stemming the Communist tide in 1958-1960. While useful from time to time, Washington viewed Israel as a policy albatross, an impediment to Western interests in the Middle East. Between 1959 and 1960, the Israelis gained something of a break from violent Nasserist attacks, but Israel saw its principal benefactor as what the British called the United States, 'the rich uncle', encouraging and supporting Nasser's policies in the region. Additionally, Alteras fails to ask hard questions about issues like Ben-Gurion's fear of a Soviet attack. The high probability, almost a certainty, is that Israel had little or no fear of a Soviet attack, and merely used Soviet bluster in an attempt to gain a policy goal – namely a security guarantee from the United States. This is an interesting work that is reasonably good on facts up to 1958, but woefully short on analysis.
79 Alteras, *Eisenhower and Israel*, p. 312.
80 'FO Comment [Hadow] on Correspondence on Arab-Israeli Relations, 13 January 1959'. (Vr1052/10) PRO, FO371/142304, pp. 2, 4.
81 'Minute by Hoyer-Millar FO Comment [Hadow] on Correspondence on Arab-Israeli Relations, 23 January 1959'. PRO, FO371/142304, p. 5.
82 'Letter British Embassy Tel Aviv [Rundall] to the FO, 20 April 1959'. PRO, FO371/142293, pp. 1-2. The antipathy that the Israelis and Zionist organizations held for Byroad was pronounced, primarily because he outspokenly supported a solution to the Palestinian refugee problem and refused to criticize Arab efforts to use the refugees as a political issue against Israel. Byroad saw no difference between Zionists using the stateless-person argument to justify the founding of Israel and Arab leaders using the plight of Palestinian refugees for their political ends. Byroad's position on the refugees is summed up in the following: 'A breath of fresh air would be given the world if all concerned would simply admit the fundamental facts that these people are homeless, are in desperate want and are uncompensated for their property and other losses that they have suffered. Can anyone benefit by the continued compression of these people in tiny areas and in other circumstances that make for moral degeneration and the making of a new generation fed on bitterness and hate?' Lilienthal, Alfred M., *There Goes the Middle East*. New York: Devin-Adair, 1957, p. 38.
83 'Letter British Embassy WDC [Weir] to the FO [Rothnie], 29 April 1959'. PRO, FO371/142293, p. 1.
84 Cohen, Avner, *Israel and the Bomb*. New York: Columbia University Press, 1998, pp. 78, 81-84. Cohen's book is an excellent look at the Israeli nuclear program. While the early years remain sketchy due to the non-availability of documentation, Cohen does a solid

job of outlining the highpoints in the decision process that made Israel a nuclear power. In his short chapter 'Dimona Revealed', Cohen relates the story of how the US intelligence community had the information that could have led them to discover Israel's intent in the 1958-1960 timeframe, but failed to put it all together. Cohen use of interviews provides an interesting dimension to the story. His discussion of the Kennedy period is considerably more detailed because by 1960 the US government was both alarmed and aware that Israel was probably intent on creating a nuclear-weapons capability. The book is well-written, well-researched, and a fascinating read. It is particularly useful in understanding the process by which intelligence organizations seem to overlook the obvious due to an imperfect intelligence 'fusion' process. Cohen points out the evidence offered by NPIC consisted of a large site with a security fence around it, a large road network, significant provision for electrical power and, most suspiciously, what appeared to be an attempt to 'hide the dirt' from the excavation. While it had all the earmarks of a nuclear site, there was no way of telling what the exact nature, scope and purpose of the site would be. Additionally, NPIC personnel briefing senior government officials tended to be very conservative in their presentations. They presented only the facts and offered little speculation about a given site. Saying that it was a 'probable' nuclear site was going about as far as NPIC personnel would go in a senior briefing. Had the President or Strauss been privy to the private conversations at NPIC then their concerns would have no doubt been heightened considerably. In any case, the information received in early 1958 from all sources did result in a focused attempt to get an answer from the Israelis.

85 'Memcon Scientific Counselor Israeli Embassy WDC [Lahav] and DOS Atomic Energy Bureau [Farley], 11 May 1959'. NACPM, 611.84A97/5-1159 CS/B, pp. 1-2.
86 'Proposed Note attached to Memcon Lahav and DOS Atomic Energy Bureau [Farley and Johnson], 11 May 1959'. NACPM, 611.84A97/5-1159 CS/B, p. 2.
87 'Statement to Israel attached to Letter from Philip J. Farley, Special Assistant to the Secretary for Atomic Energy, to the Scientific Counselor Israeli Embassy WDC [Lahav] 17 June 1959'. NACPM, 611.84A97/7-2759 CS/B, p. 2. When questioned by Senator Clinton P. Anderson, Chairman of the Joint Committee on Atomic Energy, about the 'exception' the administration used the 'Arab on the inspection team argument' to explain Israeli concerns and provided the Senator with a portion of the official statement provided to Tel Aviv and cited above. Charles A. Sullivan, the Acting Special Assistant to the Secretary for Atomic Energy stated: 'The memorandum was phrased to make plain our continuing strong support for the International Atomic Energy Agency.' He then added, just to make sure that everyone understood: 'In view of the sensitive nature of Israeli-Arab relations and the delicacy of the United States position vis-à-vis this situation, the memorandum has been classified "confidential".' 'Letter Farley, Special Assistant to the Secretary for Atomic Energy, to Senator Anderson, Chairman, Joint Committee on Atomic Energy, 2 September 1959'. NACPM, 611.84A97/9-259 CS/TU, p. 2.
88 Cohen, *Israel and the Bomb*, p. 84. James Jesus Angleton was one of the primary reasons that the 'dots' went unconnected. Cohen describes Angleton as the head of the Israeli desk at the CIA. Angleton was much more than that. He was the chief of counterintelligence for the entire agency. An orchid-growing, bizarre figure given to regular mole hunts and counter-intelligence theories so convoluted that many thought him mad, Angleton wielded enormous power in the agency. He carried compartmentalization to the point that it was virtually impossible to share information. He also saw himself as the ultimate authority on counter-intelligence and on the Israelis. In the former persona, he failed miserably in detecting one of the greatest double agents of that period, Kim Philby. Philby was stationed at the British Embassy in Washington and was Angleton's British counter-intelligence contact. He was also a Soviet spy – a

minor detail that Angleton never suspected. In the case of the Israelis, Angleton believed that his contacts were so solid that Israel could not undertake a major effort in any national security area without him knowing about it. This leaves an interesting quandary. Either Angleton knew about the nuclear weapons program and did not tell anyone in Washington, or once again, he was fooled by his own secretive arrogance. The latter conclusion is the best bet.

89 'Letter British Embassy WDC [Weir] to FO [Rothnie], 30 September 1959'. PRO, FO371/142293, p. 1.

90 'Minute [Rothnie] on Letter from British Embassy WDC to FO, 30 September 1959'. PRO, FO371/142293, p. 1.

91 'Dispatch Tel Aviv [William B. Lockling] to WDC, 25 August 1960'. NACPM, 784A.00/8-2560, CAA, p. 2

92 Cohen, *Israel and the Bomb*, pp. 86, 94.

93 Shlaim, Avi, *The Iron Wall: Israel and the Arab World*. London: Penguin, 2000, p. 208. Shlaim's work provides an objective look at the Arab Israeli conflict. Its objectivity has made his work something of a lightning-rod for Israeli government criticism because it debunks many of the myths about the Jewish state. In fact, *The Iron Wall*, despite being an excellent and well-researched piece of scholarship, had not been published in Hebrew because of the challenge that it represented to official history. It was in effect politically incorrect to publish the Shlaim book. Recently, a private individual paid for the translation and publication. Because it is a very broad work, it provides an overview of the period 1959 to 1960, but Shlaim does not go into depth in discussing the Isreali nuclear weapons. This is unlike the detailed account of the program in the Alteras book.

94 'WDC [Jones] to Tel Aviv, 21 December 1960'. DDEL, Office of the Staff Secretary [Goodpaster], Box 8, p. 2.

95 'WDC [Jones] to Tel Aviv, 29 December 1960'. DDEL, Box 8, p. 2, and 'WDC [Jones] to Tel Aviv, 31 December 1960'. DDEL, Box 8, p. 2.

96 'DOD to Tel Aviv on Israeli Nuclear Program, 6 January 1961'. DDEL, Box 8, p. 2.

97 'Memcon Meeting with Eisenhower, 12 January 1961'. DDEL, Box 8, pp. 2-3.

Chapter 8

1 See Zürcher, Eric, *Turkey: A Modern History*. London: Tauris, 1998, pp. 245-249, for an overview of Turkish foreign policy, including its 'Atlantic' view. Turkey joined NATO on February 18, 1952. Membership placed Turkey on a level that none of the other countries in the Middle East or South Asia could match. NATO was a real military alliance designed to fight a war with the Soviet Union. The Baghdad Pact, CENTO, and SEATO were organizations intended to maintain the pro-Western orientation of their members at a minimum cost in economic and military aid. In contrast, Turkey's membership of NATO provided vast quantities of military aid and arms. Turkey may have abutted the Middle East, but it focused on Europe.

2 Eisenhower, *Waging Peace*, pp. 206, 389-390. Since the Sputnik coup of 1957, Khrushchev had periodically crowed about Soviet missile superiority and the Soviets' ability to attack the United States. The administration took this threat seriously, particularly when political opponents capitalized on it. Senators Stuart Symington and Henry Jackson bombarded the administration with accusations of Soviet superiority. While their concerns were largely exaggerated, the Eisenhower administration used every available means of collecting information on Soviet missile development and capabilities. Two sites in north-eastern Iran and the two in Pakistan, including U-2 operations, provided vital information Soviet test facilities in Central Asia and on missile deployment. These sites collected telemetry data and optical information on Soviet missile capability and thus contributed directly to the defense of the continental United States. The airfield at Peshawar in Pakistan was also a center for U-2 operations.

Given the limited technology of the day, the US government felt that those sites were critical to national security, and much of its policy toward Iran and Pakistan was predicated on the sites.
3 Arora, *Menon – A Biography*, p. 203. Arora states that Krishna Menon supported the move to modernize the Indian armed forces with Soviet arms because he feared a coup. According to Aurora, Menon believed that without new arms to confront the Pakistanis arms from the US, the Indian military might have staged an Ayub-like coup. While this was no doubt a rationalization in large part, there is some indication that Menon may have genuinely feared the military because senior commanders detested him and many had served the British.
4 'Memo Board of National Estimates to CIA Director Dulles, 10 November 1958'. *FRUS*, 1958-1960, Volume XII, pp. 597-600. The intelligence estimates, concerning the Shah, reflected the administration-wide overreaction to perceived intelligence failures, of which Iraq was viewed as a massive example. Many also feared that the Badhdad Pact intelligence files lost to the Qasim government provided a bonanza for the opponents of Western interests in the region. See also Weintal, Edward 'Intelligence Disaster in Iraq'. *Newsweek*, 4 August 1958, p. 20. In the aftermath of Iraq 1958, Iran logically became the next concern. The intelligence estimates lurched in the opposite direction, taking a more pessimistic view of the situation. Should Iran succumb to a revolution or coup, the intelligence community wanted to be able to say that the administration had been warned. Thus as 1959 arrived, warning of disaster and listing all the potential reasons for impending implosion in Iran were in vogue.
5 'Discussion 386th NSC Meeting, 13 November 1958'. *FRUS*, 1958-1960, Volume XII, pp. 600-604.
6 'NSC Report, 15 November 1958'. *FRUS*, 1958-1960, Volume XII, pp. 607, 612, 614.
7 'Memcon on Iranian Budgetary Situation, 9 December 1958'. *FRUS*, 1958-1960, Volume XII, pp. 619-621.
8 'Letter Robert Murphy, Deputy Undersecretary of State John H. Irwin II, AsstSecDef, 16 January 1959'. NACPM, Iran Desk, A/1 Military Assistance, (Box 1), p. 1.
9 'WDC to Tehran, 16 January 1959'. *FRUS*, 1958-1960, Volume XII, p. 622.
10 Yapp, M.E., Strategies of British India: Britain, Iran, and Afghanistan, 1798-1850. Oxford: Clarendon, 1980, p. 124.
11 'Letter Murphy DOS to Irwin, DOD, 16 January 1959'. NACPM, Iran Desk, A/1 Military Asst, Box 1, p. 1.
12 'WDC to Tehran, 16 January 1959'. *FRUS*, 1958-1960, Volume XII, pp. 622, 624.
13 'Tehran [Wailes] to WDC [Rountree], 17 January 1959'. *FRUS*, 1958-1960, Volume XII, Footnote No. 6, p. 624
14 'Discussion 394th NSC Meeting, 22 January 1959'. *FRUS*, 1958-1960, Volume XII, Editorial Note, p. 626.
15 'Minute on Telegram British Embassy Tel Aviv to FO, 12 June 1959'. PRO, FO371/142289, pp. 1-2. On June 4, Ambassador Rundall, in Tel Aviv, cabled that the Israelis were once again asking for British help in getting Tehran to recognize Israel. The British viewed such a move as 'ill-advised'. 'In Nuri's time [the British had opposed Iranian recognition] because it would embarrass [Nuri] in his dual role as Arab patriot and member of the Baghdad Pact, and after the Iraqi revolution because it would give more ammunition to anti-Western members of the Qasim regime.' They left the matter up to the Iranians, who had to date always in the end rejected it. Apparently the Israelis viewed the Shah's negotiations with the Soviets in January and February as an indication of Iranian insecurity and isolation, and were preparing another attempt at recognition. D.T. West at the Foreign Office commented: 'Neither country would derive any material benefit, and the furore likely to result from such a step, besides providing grist to the anti-Western mills in Baghdad and Cairo, who would for one be united on an

issue, might well imperil the supply of Iranian crude to the Haifa refinery.' In 'Letter British Embassy Tehran to British Embassy Baghdad [Hiller], 14 July 1959'. PRO, FO371/142289, p. 1, the British in Tehran took the view that such a move by the Shah could happen and might be a positive thing. The Iranians 'on the rebound from traditional dislike of the Arabs' might want relations with the Israelis just to demonstrate their independence to 'an ungrateful and unfriendly Arab world'. With its eye on Iraqi petroleum and not wanting this line of reasoning to get out of hand, A.K. Rothnie in the Foreign Officer responded in 'Letter FO [Rothnie] to Baghdad, Tehran and Washington, 27 July 1959'. PRO, FO371/142289, p. 1. 'What is much more important however from our point of view is the stability of Iran. Recognition by Iran of Israel will obviously not contribute to that; and if we thought it was imminent, any influence that we felt could be exerted would probably be against it.' Gestures of 'independence' were one thing; oil was distinctly another.

16 'Letter Eisenhower to Shah, 30 January 1959'. DDEL, International Series, Iran, Box 31, pp. 1-4.

17 'Ankara to WDC, 9 February 1959'. NACPM, 787.00/2-559, p. 1.

18 'Tehran [Wailes] to WDC, 9 February 1959'. NACPM, 787.00/2-559, p. 1. See also 'Baghdad to WDC, 14 March 1959'. NACPM, 787.00/3-1459, p. 1. Trevelyan, the British Ambassador in Baghdad, informed US Ambassador Jernegan that despite a downturn in relations between Qasim and London, he intended to recommend the sale of arms to Iraq. Trevelyan stated that the Iraqi army constituted the only stable, reliable force, and the arms might cultivate pro-Western sentiment. Trevelyan argued that because the actual delivery dates were well into the future, the arms agreement could always be broken if the situation in Baghdad worsened. 'Tehran to WDC, 19 March 1959'. NACPM, 787.00/3-1459, p. 1. In an effort to reduce the potential for an angry reaction, Ambassador Wailes wanted the British to approach the Shah, as a courtesy, before the official announcement of arms sales to Iraq. Wailes expressed this concern after Iranian talks on a non-aggression treaty with the Soviets had collapsed. Wailes was no doubt concerned that arms sales to Iraq would spark even greater demands for arms from the Shah. In a 'Circular Telegram, 24 February 1959'. NACPM, 787.00/3-1459, p. 1, Washington informed all posts in the region that Prime Minister Macmillan and President Eisenhower had talked and that the US concurred with the British plan to sell additional arms to Iraq. The circular stated that the US had no intention at this time of selling further arms to Baghdad, and that Baghdad had not raised the issue of previously-approved military assistance. See also 'SNIE: Consequences of a Soviet-Iranian Non aggression Pact, 3 February 1959'. FRUS, 1958-1960, Volume XII, pp. 632-635. This SNIE stated that the overthrow of Nuri Said, Soviet aid to Afghanistan, Soviet influence with Qasim, and the fear that the US was moving toward an 'accommodation' with Nasser had heightened the Shah's predisposition toward 'insecurity'. The report stated that the Shah was probably trying to get a limited agreement with the Soviet Union to reduce pressure on his regime from that quarter while not rupturing his relations with the United States. The SNIE concluded that an agreement with the Soviets would be a major propaganda coup, but that they only real casualty would be the Baghdad Pact arrangement.

19 'Recent Trends in Iranian-Soviet Relations, July, 1959'. NACPM, Iran Desk, A/1 Military Assistance, Box 1, pp. 8-9. Although not dated, this document offered the best blow-by-blow account of what actually transpired between the Soviets and the Iranians in February 1959. On 29 January 1959, a Soviet delegation led by A.P. Semeonov arrived in Tehran to negotiate the agreement. The talks quickly ran into trouble over two points: the Soviets wanted Iran to withdraw from the Baghdad Pact; and the Iranians wanted to cancel Articles V and VI of the Soviet-Iranian Treaty of 1921. The reason for the Soviet position on the Baghdad Pact is obvious. The Iranian position

however was linked to two articles in the 1921 agreement that under the Soviets' interpretation allowed 'them the right to dispatch troops to Iran in the event forces of third power are present on Iranian territory for the purposes of aggression against the USSR which Iran was unable to prevent'. At this point pressure from the Western powers and Baghdad Pact allies forced the Shah to reconsider. The Shah, who was 'surprised' by the Western reaction, now hoped that the Soviets would reject his original position and leave him a way out of the situation. In a surprise move, the Soviet delegation contacted Moscow and on the specific orders of Chairman Khrushchev gave in on both points. The pact was ready to be signed, at which point the Iranians changed the rules and stated that they wanted the right to conclude a bilateral defense arrangement with the US. 'Since there had been a clear understanding on both sides at the beginning of the negotiations that Iran would not go through with the bilateral agreement, the changed Iranian position introduced a new element.' This action resulted in a heated exchange on February 10 in which Semeonov became 'bellicose and insulting'. The Russian pointed out the 'dangerous consequences of Iran's actions', accused the Shah of 'bad faith', and left for Moscow the next day.

20 'Letter Murphy DOS to Irwin DOD, 16 January 1959'. NACPM, Iran Desk, A/1 Military Asst, Box 1, pp. 1-2. The Kurdish situation was of particular concern in both Iran and Iraq. Washington feared a 'Kurdish land-bridge' from the Soviet Union across Turkey and Iran into Iraq. The Iraq Desk concluded that the immediate target of any instability fomented by the Soviets would be Iran. See 'Joint Memo Iraq Desk [Lakeland] and Iranian Desk [Harrison Symmes] to NEA [Armin H. Meyer], 24 April 1959'. NACPM, Iran Desk, A/1 Military Asst, Box 1, p. 1. See also in 'Memo Iraq Desk, 27 May 1959'. NACPM, Iran Desk, A/1 Military Asst, Box 1, p. 5. The Iraq Desk followed up with a report on the Kurds that outlined a brief history of the issues and conflicts. The report did not have an addressee on it, but given the content, it probably resulted from a request at the Secretariat level. It provides an interesting overview and assessment of the situation in Iran as well as that in Iraq. It stated that the Kurds of Iran were 'quiescent at present' and 'still entertain a traditional loyalty to the institution of the monarchy' for the most part. But, the report added that the poor quality of Iranian administration coupled with endemic corruption had bred resentment. 'The Iranian Government is now showing a belated awareness of the importance of the Kurds to the internal stability of the country and, in the last year, has taken some positive steps toward winning their support. Efforts are being made to improve the quality of officials and army officers assigned to Iranian Kurdistan.'
21 'Recent Trends in Iranian-Soviet Relations, July 1959'. NACPM, Iran Desk, A/1 Military Asst, Box 1, p. 13.
22 'Memo Herter to Eisenhower, 23 February 1959'. DDEL, International Series, Iran, Box 31, pp. 1-4. Herter also mentioned that there were issues yet to be ironed out with regard to the wording of the bilateral agreements. Iran wanted the agreement to state that the US would deal with an attack on Iran as if it were an attack on US territory; Washington, of course, declined such wording. Most interestingly, Pakistan wanted to include any attack upon Pakistan. It was an obvious attempt to enlist US aid in the event of an Indian attack. That wording was also rejected, but it clearly demonstrates the linkage between Iraq 1958 and relations on the subcontinent.
23 'NIE: The Outlook for Iran, 3 March 1959'. *FRUS*, 1958-1960, Volume XII, p. 643.
24 'Discussion 413th NSC Meeting, 16 July 1959'. *FRUS*, 1958-1960, Volume XII, Editorial Note, p. 645.
25 'Recent Trends in Iranian-Soviet Relations, 1959'. NACPM, Iran Desk, A/1 Military Assistance, Box 1, p. 17.
26 'The Soviet Propaganda Campaign Against Iran'. In Roi (ed.), *From Encroachment to Involvement*, pp. 326-327.

27 'Memo Iran Desk to NEA [Jones] – Radio Moscow Persian Language Broadcasts to Iran, 21 July 1959'. NACPM, Iran Desk, A/1 Military Assistance, Box 1, p. 2.
28 'Karachi [Langley] to WDC, 27 July 1959'. NACPM, 788.00/7-2459, p. 1. Turkey, Iran, and Pakistan wanted to see the Baghdad Pact adopt a formal military command-structure. The Shah wanted to be appointed Commander-in-Chief. While his often-cited militaristic megalomania no doubt fed this proposal, there is also an argument to be made that the Shah felt slighted by the Americans in the aftermath of his turning down of the Soviet overtures about non-aggression pact and his rejection of non-alignment. The Shah wanted something to show for his cooperation that included increasing his own stature in the region and at home.
29 'Karachi [Langley] to WDC, 27 July 1959'. NACPM, 788.00/7-2459, p. 2. Ayub also pointed out that, in his view, British opinions vis-à-vis Baghdad Pact policy were suspect. He argued that the British were merely using the Pact to maintain their dwindling influence in the region and to manipulate the US. He added: 'Why can't you fellows see it?' Ayub obviously saw British involvement at the policy level as an impediment to greater US military support for Pakistan. London wanted to protect its economic and commercial interests in India, and arming Pakistan through the Baghdad Pact was not the way to do it.
30 'Tel Aviv [Reid] to WDC, 9 August 1959'. FRUS, 1958-1960, Volume XII, p. 648.
31 'Memo NEA (Jones) to Acting Sec State (Dillon), 23 July 1959'. FRUS, 1958-1960, Volume XII, p. 646.
32 'Letter British Embassy Tehran [Russell] to FO [Hiller], 23 July 1959'. PRO, FO371/140814, pp. 1-5.
33 'British Embassy Tehran [Russell] to FO [Hoyer-Miller], 25 July 1959'. PRO, FO371/140814, p. 1.
34 'Memcon Audience with the Shah on 25 July 1959, 3 August 1959'. PRO, FO371/140814, p. 1.
35 'British Emb Tehran [Harrison] to FO, 8 August 1959'. PRO, FO371/140814, pp. 1-3.
36 'Dispatch Tehran to WDC, 5 September 1959'. NACPM, 788.00/9-559, pp. 1-2. The interview actually occurred on August 26 1959 at Hekmat's home. The capital letters reflect those in the actual telegram.
37 'Memo Iran Desk to NEA – Analysis of Khrushchev's Remarks to the Iranian Ambassador in Moscow on September 2, 1959, 18 September 1959'. NACPM, Iran Desk, A/1 Military Asst, Box 1, p. 1.
38 Eisenhower, *Waging Peace*, p. 433.
39 'Memo Iran Desk to NEA [Jones], 25 September 1959'. NACPM, Iran Desk, A/1 Military Asst, Box 1, p. 1.
40 'Memcon Eisenhower and Iranian PM Eqbal, 9 October 1959'. FRUS, 1958-1960, Volume XII, p. 657.
41 'Memo Iran Desk to NEA (Jones), 25 September 1959'. NACPM, Iran Desk, A/1 Military Asst, Box 1, p. 1.
42 'Paris [Goodpaster] to WDC [Herter], 20 December 1959'. DDEL, Staff Secretary, International Trips and Meetings, Box 9, pp. 1-3.
43 'Memo Herter to Eisenhower, 31 December 1959'. FRUS, 1958-1960, Volume XII, p. 660. See also 'Letter DOD [Irwin)] to Under Secretary of State for Political Affairs [Merchant], 20 February 1960'. FRUS, 1958-1960, Volume XII, p. 667. DOD reported that the Shah had greatly overstated his requirements and the potential threats from Afghanistan and Iraq. The report added that the cost of the Shah's proposed military aid would exceed $600 million. Defense concluded that any significant increase in the size of the Iranian military establishment 'could be counterproductive' and 'would complicate our relations with other countries in the area increasing their demands for U.S. aid'.

44 'Editorial Note on Eisenhower's Letter to the Shah, 2 January 1960'. *FRUS*, 1958-1960, Volume XII, p. 662.
45 'Official-Informal Letter Economic Counselor [Taylor] Tehran to WDC Iran Desk [Mouser], 16 January 1960'. NACPM, Iran Desk, A/1 Military Assistance, Box 1, p. 1.
46 'NIE: The Outlook for Iran, 16 February 1960'. *FRUS*, 1958-1960, Volume XII, pp. 664-665.
47 'Tehran to WDC, 7 June 1960'. NACPM, 788.00/6-760, p. 1.
48 'Dispatch Tehran to WDC, 6 June 1960'. 788.00/6-760, p. 1. This dispatch contains a very detailed look at both parties and the principal politicians in each.
49 'Airgram Tehran to WDC, 21 June 1960'. NACPM, 788.00/6-2160, p. 1.
50 'Report on Land Reform in Iran from British Embassy Tehran [Harrison] to FO [Lloyd], 4 July 1960'. PRO, FO248/1580, pp. 1-2. The assessment in Washington and at the US Embassy in Tehran agreed that land reform had only succeeded in alienating the landowners in Iran. 'Discussion 440th NSC Meeting, 7 April 1960'. *FRUS*, 1958-1960, Volume XII, p. 671. See also the files contained in FO371/140856; these chronicle the impressive British study and tracking of land-reform efforts in Iran and the practical effects of the program. It charts the demise of fundamental reform as the Shah faced increasing pressure from many of his most loyal supporters.
51 'CIA Staff Memorandum No. 54-60 – Warning Flag on Iran, 10 August 1960'. DDEL, National Security Staff, NSC Registry Series 47-62, Box 3, pp. 1-2. See also 'Discussion 440th NSC Meeting, 7 April 1960'. *FRUS*, 1958-1960, Volume XII, p. 671, in which Acting CIA Director, General Cabell reported that General Bakhtiar was preparing a contingency plan in the event of the disappearance of the Shah from the political scene. Some argued that Bakhtiar's plan in fact constituted preparations for a coup.
52 'Dispatch Tehran to WDC, 24 September 1960'. NACPM, 788.00/9-2460, p. 1. Just that fact that the Shah survived the turmoil of the failed election surprised some. The CIA had predicted that unrest during the election could trigger a coup from within the military and the security services: 'If any mass agitation got underway, the Shah would probably not survive it.'
53 'Dispatch Tehran to WDC, 11 October 1960'. NACPM, 788.00/6-760, p. 1.
54 'Dispatch Tehran to WDC, 15 October 1960'. NACPM, 788.13/10-1560, pp. 1-2, 8.
55 'NSC Report: U.S. Policy Toward Iran, 6 July 1960'. *FRUS*, 1958-1960, Volume XII, pp. 681-684.
56 'Memo – The Financial Outlook for Iran – from Iran Desk [Mickles] to NEA, 7 September 1960'. NACPM, Iran Desk, A/1 Military Assistance, Box 2, pp. 1-4.
57 'Editorial note on the 453rd NSC Meeting, 25 July 1960'. *FRUS*, 1958-1960, Volume XII, p. 691.
58 'Memo Herter to Eisenhower, 19 September 1960'. *FRUS*, 1958-1960, Volume XII, p. 701.
59 'Memcon British Embassy WDC [Weir and Speares] and NEA Iran Affairs [Bowling], 19 July 1960'. NACPM, Iran Desk, A/1 Military Assistance, Box 2, p. 1.
60 'Partial British Telegram from Foreign Office attached to Memcon British Embassy WDC [Weir and Speares] and NEA Iran Affairs [Bowling], 19 July 1960'. NACPM, Iran Desk, A/1 Military Assistance, Box 1, p. 2. See also 'Memcon British Embassy WDC [Speares] and DOS Iranian Desk [Bowling], 3 October 1960'. NACPM, Iran Desk, A/1 Military Asst, Box 1, p. 1. The Soviets made another proposal for a 'demilitarized zone' on the Iranian border, and the United States and Britain were trying to come up with an argument against such an arrangement. The Soviets kept Washington and London on edge with a barrage of proposals to the Shah. He, quite naturally, made certain that the Western allies knew about them.
61 'Memo Iran Desk [Bowling] to NEA, 22 September 1960'. NACPM, Iran Desk, A/1 Military Assist, Box 2, p. 1.

62 'Memo NEA [Jones] to Acting Sec State [Dillon], 20 September 1960'. *FRUS*, 1958-1960, Volume XII, p. 702.
63 'Memo Iran Desk [Bowling] to NEA [Hart], 21 November 1960'. *FRUS*, 1958-1960, Volume XII, pp. 707, 710. Bowling concluded that to bring Iranian military forces up to the same level as the Turkish forces would take $500 million per year for five to ten years. He also saw little to be gained: 'Even a 400,000 man army with a billion dollars in new equipment would (little) more than delay the Soviets for a few days.'
64 'Memo Iran Desk [Miklos] to GTI [Miner] on Economic Factors in the Iranian Political Equation, 28 December 1960'. NACPM, Iran Desk, A/1 Military Asst, Box 2, p. 1.
65 'Memo Iran Desk [Bowling] to NEA, 22 November 1960'. NACPM, Iran Desk, A/1 MilitaryAsst, Box 1, p. 2.
66 'Revisions to the Mil Asst Plan for Iran, 2 December 1960'. NACPM, Iran Desk, A/1 Military Asst, Box 2, p. 1.
67 'Memo Iran Desk [Bowling] to NEA [Hart], 21 November 1960'. *FRUS*, 1958-1960, Volume XII, p. 711.
68 Kux in *The United States and Pakistan*, pp. 98-100, argues that the US attempted to prevent the coup in October 1958. He cites instructions from Washington to Ambassador Langley to tell Mirza 'there was insufficient cause for abandoning the democratic path'. Kux most likely misapprehends what occurred. Langley was well aware of the plotting. He had asked that his name not be put on Mirza's calendar because local newspapers published the calendar, and Langley was in Mirza's office almost every day. In addition, other US agencies, not under the control of the Ambassador, were quietly reassuring Mirza and Ayub of US government support come what may. The threat of collapse in Pakistan and of a virtual secessionist movement on the frontier with Soviet-influenced Afghanistan by Abdul Qayyum Khan, the leader of the Muslim League, met what Kux described as the criteria for Rountree's 'last resort.' Despite some misgivings in Washington, the Ayub takeover obtained quick American support.
69 'Letter Karachi [Langley] to NEA [Rountree], Karachi, December 27, 1957'. NACPM, 790.00/12-2758, pp. 1-3.
70 Bhargava, G.S., *Pakistan in Crisis*. New Delhi: Vikas, 1971, pp. 69, 89. Bhargava provides a useful overview of the development of Pakistani politics, in particular an interesting analysis of the linkage between the 'controlled democracy' of the Ayub regime and the outright military dictatorship of later regimes. His analysis also explains the development of Ayub's concept of political participation. In Bhargava's presentation, Ayub had an approach to political parties that was similar to Nasser's, i.e., it progressed from no political parties to officially-sanctioned ones that could be controlled. Ayesha Jalal makes the same point in *The State of Martial Rule: The Origins of Pakistan's Political Economy of Defense* (Cambridge: Cambridge University Press, 1990), p. 303: 'Ayub hoped to bolster central authority without being constrained by parties and politicians with provincial bases of support. This was part of a grand strategy to industrialize and militarize Pakistan in the quickest possible time; the general had lost no time negotiating a multi-million dollar agreement with the United States to help finance the rural development program and give a fillip to his basic democracies system.'
71 Interview of General Andrew Goodpaster, 7 August 2003. According to Goodpaster, 'Eisenhower saw Ayub as the hope for Pakistan.' Goodpaster stated that in the same vein the Iranian military was viewed as the key not only to the Shah's rule but also to continued pro-Western policies in Iran. In fact, should the Shah no longer be able to govern effectively, then military rule would become perhaps the only viable option. See also 'Dispatch Tehran [Bowling] to WDC, 11 September 1956'. NACPM, 788.13/9-1156, p. 2, in which Bowling argued that many elements in Iran viewed the army as an instrument of 'greater justice' than the civilian authorities: 'Most poor men would rather

take their complaints to a military government official than to a civilian official.' The report added: 'The great landlords and merchants, the conservatives of Iran, have long tended to regard the Army as a real or potential enemy, since, to the extent that it is able, it often cuts across the traditional conservative lines of influence.' This is only one of numerous reports supporting the view of the army as a potentially progressive alternative in the region. See also Shaw, Stanford J. and Ezel Kural Shaw, *History of the Ottoman Empire and Modern Turkey: Reform, Revolution, and Republic, 1808-1975*. Cambridge: Cambridge University Press, 1977, pp. 413-414. The military coup in Turkey on 27 May 1960 fell into the same category as had Ayub's. Given the paralysis and political chaos created by the Turkish Democratic Party and the Menderes regime, the army, under the leadership of General Cemal Gürsel and the National Unity Committee (NUC), took temporary control of the government. In effect, the military became a political watchdog, ensuring that the politicians acted 'responsibly'. See also Zürcher, *Turkey*, p. 253. Zürcher points out that military elements had planned the coup for years. A group of 'radical' mid-level officers had decided to 'extricate the parties from the irreconcilable situation into which they had fallen.' The author states that while General Gürsel headed the government, Colonel Alpaslan Türkes was initially the most influential member of the NUC. Türkes had no confidence in the politicians or the political process, and demanded reforms in the shape of curbs on political activities. From the US point of view, key Cold War allies could not be allowed to succumb or be incapacitated by irresponsible political elements, and in such an event 'temporary' military rule was both acceptable and desirable. See also 'Discussion 402nd NSC Meeting, 17 April 1959'. DDEL, DDEL, Box 11, pp. 1, 8-11. In the discussion of what to do about Iraq, Nixon wanted a 'Mossadegh type operation' to overthrow Qasim and put pro-Western military officers in power. Military rule had become a favored option.

72 'Special International Report: Pakistan – A Leader Gets Things Done'. *Newsweek*, 18 April 1960, p. 57.
73 'Letter, "Secret - Eyes Only" from Bunker to Bartlett, Delhi, December 3, 1958'. NACPM, Lot file No. 62, D 43 (1 of 3), 790.00/12-358, p. 2.
74 'Dispatch Karachi to WDC, February 26, 1959'. *FRUS*, 1958-1960, Volume XV, p. 702.
75 'New Delhi [Bunker] to WDC, April 17, 1959'. *FRUS*, 1958-1960, Volume XV, pp. 709-711. Ambassador Bunker in New Delhi quickly weighed with the view that US furnishing of 'more modern aircraft or "Sidewinders"' (heat seeking air-to-air missiles) to Pakistan would be met with 'consternation' in India and be viewed as an 'unfriendly act'. Because the US had agreed not to increase aid to Pakistan above the levels of the 1954 agreement, the Indians would view modern weapons as a serious breach of faith. See also 'Memo Assistant Sec State for Policy Planning [Smith] to Herter, April 23, 1959'. *FRUS*, 1958-1960, Volume XV, pp. 711-12.
76 'Memo US Delegation to SEATO Conference in Wellington, New Zealand on April 8-10, 1959, March 25, 1959'. Records relating to Kashmir, Box 1, 59-150-69-22-7/3-2659, p. 1.
77 'Karachi to WDC, October 31, 1958,' *FRUS*, 1958-1960, Volume XV, p. 682.
78 Dupree, Louis 'West Pakistan Revisited, August 27, 1959'. *AUFS-SAS*, Vol. III, No. 1, p. 6. This is a lengthy report to the AUFS on the situation in Pakistan. It glorifies Ayub as 'a strong ruler' and the leader of a 'revolution'. The use of 'revolution' to describe the coup was more sleight-of-hand to improve Ayub's image. It should be noted that when Dupree wrote this article, he was working for Phillips Talbot, Executive Secretary of AUFS and soon to be Assistant Secretary of State for NEA in the Kennedy administration.
79 'NIE, The Outlook for Pakistan, Washington, May 5, 1959'. *FRUS*, 1958-1960, Volume XV, pp. 713-714.

80 'Memo NEA [Rountree] to Dillon, Washington, July 2, 1959'. *FRUS*, 1958-1960, Volume XV, p. 737.
81 'Airgram Karachi to WDC, September 23, 1959'. *FRUS*, 1958-1960, Volume XV, p. 776.
82 'Memo NEAA [Rountree] to Herter, January 30, 1959,' NACPM, 786b.11/1-3059. See also 'Policy toward the Near East, August 19, 1958'. *FRUS*, 1958-1960, Volume XII, p. 149, and 'NSC Report – 5820/1, U.S. Policy toward the Middle East'. *FRUS*, 1958-1960, Volume XII, p. 195.
83 'Karachi [Langley] to WDC, 24 July 1959'. NACPM, 788.00/7-2459, p. 2.
84 Kux, The United States and Pakistan, p. 103.
85 'Minute by Borthwick dated 30 September 1959 on a Letter from Australian High Commission Karachi [A.R. Butler] to Canberra, 16 September 1959'. NAA, Series No. A1838/2, Control No. 169/11/148, Part 9, p. 1. See also 'Minute by Assistant Division Secretary dated 29 September 1959 on a Letter from Australian High Commission Karachi [A.R. Butler] to DEA, Canberra, 16 September 1959'. NAA, Series No. A1838/2, Control No. 169/11/148 Part 9, p 1. In response to the suggestion that Australia offer some private encouragement for a gesture on the part of Nehru to Ayub, the DEA in Canberra flatly stated: 'With respect, ... the relations between India and Pakistan touch upon interests and emotions altogether too sensitive for there to be room for any useful Australian intervention, however benign our intentions.'
86 'Memcon Eisenhower and Pakistani Foreign Minister, Manzur Qadir, 9 October 1959'. DDEL, IS, Pakistan, Box 62, p. 3.
87 'Memo Herter to the White House, President's Trip, Itinerary, November 25, 1959, attached Memo from Frederick F. Bartlett, SAO, November 19, 1959'. NACPM, Lot file No. 62, D 43 (3 of 3), 790.00/11-2559, p. 1.
88 'Bartlett Memo, November 19, 1959'. NACPM, Lot file No. 62, D 43 (3 of 3), 790.00/11-1959 p. 2.
89 'Memcon Eisenhower and Ayub, December 8, 1959'. *FRUS*, 1958-1960, Volume XV, pp. 781-795.
90 Discussion with Rostow, November 6, 2001, Lyndon Baines Johnson (LBJ) Library, Austin, Texas. This conversation between President Eisenhower and Walt Rostow apparently occurred after the latter had begun to work with the Kennedy campaign. It seems to provide another indication of the interchangeability of key Eisenhower and Kennedy advisors and policies.
91 'WDC to Karachi, February 19, 1960'. *FRUS*, 1958-1960, Volume XV, p. 799.
92 'WDC to Karachi, 3 March 1960'. DDEL, Staff Secretary, Box 13, p. 1.
93 'Karachi to WDC, 8 March 1960'. No. 2095, DDEL, Staff Secretary – Goodpaster, Box 13, p. 1.
94 Kux, United States and Pakistan, p. 112.
95 'Australian High Commission Karachi to Canberra, 29 July 1960,' NAA, Series No. A1838/2, Control No. 914/3 Part 2, p. 1. See also 'Memo Australian High Commission Karachi to Canberra, 14 March 1960'. NAA, Series No. A1838/1, Control No. 175/11/148, p. 1. Ayub argued that Pakistan could only maintain *de facto* neutrality with regard to Israel by continuing its policy of non-recognition. Pakistan's official position was that Israel was a foreign provocation that exacerbated Arab problems, and as such should not be recognized by Pakistan.
96 'Telegram on CENTO from Indian Embassy Jidda to MEA New Delhi, 6 November 1960'. INA, MEA, 23-A (21) WANA/60, p. 1.
97 'Letter British Embassy Baghdad [P.T. Hayman)] to FO [Hiller, 12 July 1960'. PRO, FO371/149874, p. 1.
98 Jalal, State of Martial Rule, p. 305.

99 'Letter British Embassy WDC [H.S.H. Stanley] to FO [F.A. Warner], 4 August 1960'. PRO, FO371/152225, p. 1. The Afghan government, with Soviet and perhaps even Indian collusion, supported the creation of a 'Pushtunistan State'. This was directed at weakening the government of Pakistan and creating leverage in the border areas. The situation was so acute that the United States and Britain discussed the possibility of tripartite talks with Pakistan on the Pushtunistan issue. The British were very wary of such an approach, fearing that it would drive the Afghan government into closer alignment with the Russians. See 'Minute by B.C.J. Warnes on Afghan-Pakistan Relations'. 18 March 1960'. PRO, FO371/152215, p. 5. Khrushchev viewed the Pushtunistan issue as a means of pressuring and punishing the Karachi regime for its cooperation with Washington. The Soviets called for a referendum by the tribes in the border region on the creation of a state. This Russian pressure on Ayub had the side benefit of generating pro-Soviet sentiment in New Delhi. See also 'Memcon Eisenhower and Prince Sardar Muhammad Naim, Foreign Minister of Afghanistan, 5 October 1960'. DDEL, Diary, Box 53, pp. 1-3. The border flare-ups between Pakistan and Afghanistan evolved into an issue that was addressed in a meeting between President Eisenhower and Prince Naim, the Foreign Minister of Afghanistan. The President encouraged Naim to seek an agreement with Ayub and to align Afghanistan more closely with Pakistan and Iran. See 'Telegram from US Embassy Karachi to WDC, 6 October 1960'. DDEL, IS, Afghanistan, Box 1, Section I, p. 1. There was particular concern about a widened border war. Recent defeats of Afghan *Lashkara* by Pushtun tribesmen loyal to Karachi had raised the possibility of a wider war, perhaps involving the regular armies. Washington feared that attempting to remain neutral in the dispute had hurt its relations with Pakistan, and wanted to avoid that development by not making any moves that would appear to legitimize the Pushtunistan claims.

100 'Airgram Karachi to WDC, December 3, 1960'. *FRUS*, 1958-1960, Volume XV, p. 822-823. See also 'Memo NEA [Jones] to Hare, December 2, 1960'. *FRUS*, 1958-1960, Volume XV, pp. 819-821.

101 'Memcon Eisenhower and Nehru, 10 December 1959'. DDEL, Staff Secretary, Goodpaster, Box 9, pp. 2-3.

102 'Athens [Eisenhower] to Herter, 15 December 1959'. DDEL, Staff Secretary – Goodpaster, Box 13, p. 3.

103 'Karachi [Rountree] to WDC Eyes Only White House [Eisenhower], 23 December 1959'. DDEL, IS, Pakistan, Section II, pp. 2-3.

104 Gopal, *Nehru*, p. 104.

105 'NIE: The Economic and Political Consequences of India's Financial Problems, 2 September 1958'. *FRUS*, 1958-1960, Volume XV, p. 460. See also 'New Delhi to WDC, 8 January 1959'. *FRUS*, 1958-1960, Volume XV, p. 475. Washington feared that a Soviet aid offensive in India, targeting high-visibility projects, would be a propaganda bonanza for Moscow. As a result, the aid situation came under review in an attempt to identify 'useful' but 'more visible' development projects for which the United States could get more political credit. Concern existed that the diffusion of US aid throughout the Indian economy reduced the ability of the Embassy to 'get across' the extent of US aid to the average Indian.

106 'Nehru on Communism: An Awakening, December 1958'. CIA, CRES, CIA-RDP78-02771R000400010002-2, pp. 1-15. See also 'New Delhi to WDC, 28 May 1959'. *FRUS*, 1958-1960, Volume XV, pp. 494-496. See also 'Letter New Delhi [Bunker] to WDC [Bartlett, SOA], 9 December 1959'. *FRUS*, 1958-1960, Volume XV, p. 473.

107 'Discussion 408th NSC Meeting, 28 May 1959'. DDEL, Box 11, pp. 6-10.

108 Neville, Maxwell, *India's China War*. New York: Pantheon, 1970, p. 96. Neville's work on the Sino-India border dispute that led to the border war in 1962 is the most comprehensive and best-balanced on the subject. As the author points out, the Indians

and Chinese, specifically Nehru and Chou En-Lai, exchanged significant correspondence and discussed the matter on more than one occasion. Neville quotes Nehru's 1950 statement: 'All the maps of China for the last thirty years have shown a certain portion of that north-east frontier which is now part of India as not part of India.' Neville also cites the 1954 discussion in which Nehru raised the issue of the currency of Chinese maps of the area, and suggested that the Chinese change their maps to reflect India's view that the McMahon Line accurately represented the border. Chou's replied that the Chinese intended to resurvey the border at the first opportunity and then any differences could be negotiated bilaterally between Beijing and New Delhi. In short, the Chinese were ceding nothing unilaterally, and expected negotiations prior to a confirmation of borders. The idea of negotiation over territory flew directly in the face of the Indian policy since 1950. The northern borders 'must not be opened to negotiation'. The obvious specific implication of negotiations with the Chinese would set a precedent and provide Pakistan ammunition on the issue of Kashmir.

109 Mullik, B.N., *The Chinese Betrayal: My Years with Nehru*. Bombay: Allied, 1971, pp. 190-208. Mullik was the director of the Indian Intelligence Bureau from 1950 to 1964. While obviously colored by his own interests and opinions, this work provides an excellent insight into not only the actual events and relationships leading up to the Chinese War, but also the Indian governmental processes. For example, the lack of any real border-monitoring in the regions adjacent to Tibet in the mid-1950s resulted in New Delhi learning of the Chinese penetration through the local rumor mill. Additionally, it took almost 18 months, from the confirmation of the Chinese presence to March 1958, for a formal report with recommendations to be issued by the Bureau.

110 Ibid, p. 214.

111 'Letter British High Commission New Delhi [Anderson] to CRO [H.A. Twist], 21 August 1959'. PRO, FO371/141264, p. 1.

112 Neville, *India's Chinese War*, p. 103. See also Mullik, *Chinese Betrayal*, p. 224. Mullik states that Nehru was also motivated by the need to maintain security on the northern frontier, and particularly in the Ladkah area. The central government hoped that sympathy toward the Dalai Lama would in turn increase its support among Buddhists in Dikkim, Nepal and Bhutan.

113 Neville, *India's Chinese War*, p. 103. See also Nehru, Jawaharlal, 'Letter to Chief Ministers, 25 March 1959'. In Parthasarathi, C. (ed.), *Letters to Chief Ministers 1947-1964*. Delhi: Oxford University Press, 1989, p. 227. In what were planned to be 'fortnightly' letters, Nehru lays out his position on the revolt in Tibet. He states that while he is sympathetic with the Tibetans, the situation is fundamentally an internal Chinese matter and India has no case for direct involvement. He also states that the Indian government is not suppressing stories of the uprising to reduce the pressure on his government to get involved. It is a clear attempt to be viewed as sympathetic, while maintaining separation from the dispute.

114 Nehru, 'Letter to Chief Ministers, 26 October 1959', Parthasarathi (ed.), *Letters to Chief Ministers 1947-1964*, p. 307. See also 'British Embassy WDC [Caccia] to FO, 4 December 1959'. PRO, FO371/141264, p. 1, in which appears Eisenhower's answer to a question about the border dispute. The President replied that no one really knew where the border or the McMahon Line was. He added that the important issue was the settlement of disputes by 'negotiation': 'We must do it by negotiation.' Ironically the President appeared to agree with Chou En-Lai and Mao Tse-Tung.

115 'Minute by R.W. Benson attached to the Letter date 10 November 1959 from Chinese Prime Minister Chou En-lai to Nehru, 11 November 1959'. PRO, FO371/141273, p. 2. The date on this letter is somewhat confusing because Gopal (in *Nehru*, Volume III, p.127) refers to the letter dated 17 December from Chou in a footnote. The source of the British copy of the letter was the Chinese Chargé d'Affaires in London, raising the

116 Neville, *India's Chinese War*, p. 98. See also 'Letter Nehru to Macmillan, 30 November 1959'. PRO, FO371/141264, p. 1, Cover Sheet. Nehru clearly expected the Chinese rebuff; 'If we get a favourable reply to our proposals, then the question will arise of my meeting Chou En-lai. But I am by no means sure that Chou En-lai's reply to me will be such as leads to a meeting in the future.' Nehru was clearly shopping for support as well; 'It is heartening to us in India to know that we have your sympathetic understanding and the friendship of the people of Britain not only in our present troubles, but in our endeavours to build a better future for our people.' In the attached Minute, P.G.F. Dalton at the Foreign Office commented about the 'unusually warm tones' of the letter, which indicated: 'that Mr. Nehru does not, in fact, expect to get very far with Mr. Chou En-lai'. See also 'Memo CRO to the FO, 3 November 1959'. PRO, FO371/141273, pp. cover sheet, 1-5. In this letter and its cover sheet, the CRO is 'encouraged' by the Soviet attitude on the dispute and the fact that they have not automatically sided with China. The text of the memorandum pointed to the fact that the Indians were also pleased with the Soviet position. This foreshadowed the relationship to come.

Before the opening paragraph, which begins "possibility that the Chinese published the letter...":

possibility that the Chinese published the letter in advance of any Indian announcement that they had actually received it. This supports the Foreign Office's view that the letter was a 'clever move' designed to place China in a favorable light.

117 Neville, *India's Chinese War*, p. 101.
118 'Letter British High Commission New Delhi [Anderson] to CRO [H.A. Twist], 21 August 1959'. PRO, FO371/141264, p. 2.
119 Akbar, *Nehru*, pp. 533, 550-552. Akbar argues that the responsibility for the Chinese war and subsequent debacle lies squarely with Nehru. First, Nehru trusted the Chinese: 'Nehru described the China war as a stab in the back. He was wrong. It was a stab from the front. He had only closed his eyes.' Second, Nehru's appointment of Krishna Menon as Minister of Defense was an unmitigated disaster for the military command structure and for defense preparedness: 'Menon tried out his leftism in the ministry least suited to it.' See also 'Intelligence summary from the British Foreign Office, 29 September 1959'. PRO, FO371/141273, p. 1. The British concluded that both sides had 'dug in their heels and showed no indication of wishing to reach a compromise'. It is interesting that the perception from London failed to take into account the possibility of a Chinese ploy for bargaining purposes, while later Indian biographical accounts did. See also 'Memcon British Sec State for Foreign Affairs and the Indian Defense Minister, Krishna Menon, 10 November 1959'. PRO, FO371/144186, p. 1. This memorandum indicated that Menon was feeling the political pressure, and to some degree personal insecurity, from criticism leveled at him in New Delhi. He downplayed any differences with the Indian armed forces Chief of Staff, General Thimayya, stating that 'he could not understand the criticisms made of him' over his handling of the military. He also stated that he was willing to accept the Chinese incursion in the Ladakh area, but that the McMahon Line should be held everywhere else. He was highly concerned about his personal position, requesting that the British Secretary of State support his contention that British unwillingness to see him on his last trip was a result of scheduling problems and not British ire. The Secretary summed it up stating: 'I got the impression that the main reason for Mr. Menon insisting on my seeing him today and for his desire to see the Prime Minister was this Indian Parliamentary criticism that he had fallen out in some way with the British.'
120 Brown, *Nehru*, p. 321.
121 'Biweekly Propaganda Guidance – Significant India-Pakistan Accord, 26 September 1960'. CIA, CRES, CIA-RDP78-03061A000100020010-9, Item No. 293, p. 1.
122 Gopal, *Nehru*, Volume III, pp. 133-134, 139. Gopal described Nehru and Chou as 'the world's two most intellectual Prime Ministers'. The author added, however: 'But Zhou

had always a clearer idea than Nehru of where power and interest lay.' Gopal's view of the events leading to the Chinese war is highly critical of Nehru, and particularly of his faith in Krishna Menon and his theoretical views on Asian cooperation.

123 'Memcon Eisenhower and Bunker, 25 April 1960'. *FRUS*, 1958-1960, Volume XV, p. 536. It had yet to dawn on the administration that India might go to the Soviet Union for modern military equipment. The speculation was that if the United States did not sell the equipment to the Indians, then, they would buy it from the British.
124 'Memo Office of India, Ceylon and Nepal Affairs, 7 June 1960'. *FRUS*, 1958-1960, Volume XV, p. 542.
125 'Letter NEA (Lewis Jones) to New Delhi [Bunker], 13 June 1960'. *FRUS*, 1958-1960, Volume XV, p. 546.
126 Gopal, *Nehru*, Volume III, p. 131.
127 'Mem from the Joint Chiefs of Staff to the Secretary of Defense [Gates], November 15, 1960'. *FRUS*, 1958-1960, Volume XV, p. 577.
128 'Memcon Eisenhower and Nehru, New York, 26 September 1960'. DDEL, Diary Series, Box 53, p. 6.
129 'British Embassy New Delhi to FO, 14 October 1960'. PRO, FO371/153638, p. 3.

Chapter 9

1 Grose, Peter, *The Gentleman Spy: The Life of Allen Dulles*. New York: Houghton Mifflin, 1994, p. 508. Probably the most famous campaign issue in 1960 was the 'missile gap'. The Kennedy used the dubious claims of Soviet Premier Nikita Khrushchev about Soviet missile superiority over the United States and transformed them into a campaign issue. In reality, no such gap existed. In an interesting twist, Allen Dulles, Director of the CIA, flew to Hyannis, Massachusetts on July 30, 1960 to brief Kennedy on intelligence matters. Rather than putting the 'missile gap' issue to rest, as the Nixon camp wanted, Dulles referred Kennedy's questions to the Pentagon. The Nixon camp later charged that Dulles, an old friend of the Vice President, intentionally ducked the issue in an attempt to preserve his position at the CIA. The Democratic candidate even used the occasion to take a jab at the Eisenhower White House by asking Dulles in front of reporters as he was leaving: 'Haven't you got any good news in that black bag of yours?' Dulles and Kennedy independently commented later that the briefings include nothing that could not be found in *The New York Times*. From Nixon's perspective, his friend Allen Dulles had let him down, and the non-existent 'missile gap' lived on as a campaign issue. Attacks on Eisenhower policy in the Middle East and South Asia were of the same ilk, if not so prominent. All contributed to a strategy that painted the US as bogged down and strategy-less in world where the Communists were gaining on all fronts.
2 'Who Likes Dulles – Who Doesn't'. *Newsweek*, 27 January 1958, p. 28.
3 'Address delivered before the American Society of Newspaper Editors, Washington, D.C., 13 April 1960'. *Vital Speeches of the Day*, June 1, 1960, No. 26, p. 485.
4 'Memo DOS/LR [Louis A. Cherry] to GTI [Bolling], 26 July 1960'. NACPM, Iran Desk, 3-A/1 Military Assistance thru 1961/4 Internal Security, Box 2, p. 8. The Iran Desk requested excerpts from campaign speeches to use with the Shah of Iran to show that all the candidates were committed to confronting Soviet aggression. The Nixon quote came from *US News and World Report*, 13 June 1960, p. 51.
5 'Special National Report: Candidate Nixon's Insiders'. *Newsweek*, 13 June 1960, p. 37.
6 Interview with Walt Rostow, 12 June 2002. The Kennedy campaign carefully avoided mention of Eisenhower policy in the post-1958 environment, because the facts did not fit their campaign strategy. There was virtually no difference between the policies advocated for the Middle East and South Asia by Senator Kennedy and those that had been in effect, to one degree or another, since early 1958. Those post-1958 policies did

not make good campaign issues, and the new Secretary of State, Christian Herter, had a close association with a principal Kennedy foreign policy advisor, Chester Bowles. As a result, differences had to be almost manufactured, or the focus had to be kept on the turmoil of the 1955-1958 period.

7 'Memo Cherry to Bolling, 26 July 1960'. NACPM, Box 2, p. 4. This quote is an excerpt from a statement given by Senator Kennedy in *Democratic Digest*, May 1960, p. 4. Kennedy repeated this theme time and again. In a speech entitled 'Time of Decision', in the Congressional Record, June 14, 1960, p 11631, candidate Kennedy stated: 'We must, in collaboration with Western Europe and Japan, greatly increase the flow of capital to the underdeveloped areas of Asia, Africa, the Middle East, and Latin America – frustrating the Communist hopes for chaos in those nations – enabling emerging nations to achieve economic as well as political independence and closing the dangerous gap that is not widening between our living standards and theirs.' This almost quotes verbatim Eisenhower's statements in 1953.

8 Interview with Walt Rostow, 12 June 2002. Rostow was an important advisor to the Eisenhower administration on foreign economic development from 1953 to 1958. He stated that Eisenhower never went as far as he should have with foreign aid because 'the president was a captive of the Republican right.' Interestingly enough, Rostow stated that during Herter's tenure there was 'no difference' between Republican and Democratic foreign policy goals. In fact, Rostow stated, the amount of foreign aid included in the last Eisenhower budget was so substantial that the incoming Kennedy administration did not have to ask for more than Eisenhower had provided.

9 *Oral History* – Chester Bowles, Assistant Secretary of State. JFK Library. Interviewed by Robert Brooks in New Delhi, India, February 2, 1965, pp. 17-20. In this account, Bowles states that President Kennedy, in common with his brother Robert, 'had a rather deep sense of skepticism about the Foreign Service and the State Department. He wanted the Department to run efficiently but he wanted to do the foreign policy making.'

10 'Memo Herter to Eisenhower on Arab-Israel Problem and US Presidential Campaign, 6 July 1960'. NACPM, UAR Policy, 59-786b.11/7-660.

11 Kennedy, John F. 'Remarks of Senator John F. Kennedy, University of Kentucky, Lexington, Kentucky, October 8, 1960'. Freedom of Communications – Final Report of the Committee on Commerce, U.S. Senate. Prepared by the subcommittee on communications, pursuant to S.R. 305, 86th Congress. Part I, 'The Speeches, Remarks, Press Conferences, and statements of Senator John F. Kennedy, August 1 through November 7, 1960', p. 522.

12 Lenczowski, George, *American Presidents and the Middle East*. Durham, NC: Duke University Press, 1990, p. 73.

13 Kennedy, John F. 'Question and Answer Session, Statewide TV Appearance of Senator John F. Kennedy, Civic Auditorium, Seattle, Washington, September 6, 1960'. *Kennedy Speeches*, Part 1, p. 141.

14 Kennedy, John F. 'Remarks of Senator John F. Kennedy, Roosevelt Field, Norristown, Pa., October 29, 1960'. *Kennedy Speeches*, Part 1, p. 813.

15 Kennedy, John F. 'Speech of Senator John F. Kennedy, Fieldhouse, University of Wisconsin, Madison, Wisconsin, October 23, 1960'. *Kennedy Speeches*, Part I, p. 715.

16 Kennedy, John F. 'Speech, Madison, Wisconsin, October 23, 1960'. *Kennedy Speeches*, Part I, pp. 714-716.

17 Kennedy, John F. 'Remarks of Senator John F. Kennedy, Luncheon, Denver Hilton Hotel, Denver, Colorado, September 23, 1960'. *Kennedy Speeches*, Part 1, p. 345.

18 Judith Brown, in *Nehru: A Political Life*, p. 248, provides an unflattering picture of Krishna Menon's eccentricities and erratic behavior. 'Menon was undoubtedly intellectually able, and devoted to what he saw as India's cause, and to Nehru

personally. But he was psychologically unstable, very difficult to work with, incapable of delegating, self-willed and self-opinionated and thus liable to disastrous misjudgments.' She attributes his appointment to the lack of sophistication in the Indian Foreign Service, to a lack of suitable alternatives, and to Nehru's 'isolation at the apex of India's political world'. While this was true, Brown's explanation smacks more of a rationalization for Nehru's lapse in judgment. Nehru knew Menon was unstable, but his desire to find a job for an old friend – a job far away from his political detractors in New Delhi – overrode his judgment. It also overrode Nehru's personal political interests, and ultimately the interests of India. Brown points out that Menon 'did much to alienate American opinion'.

19 Lall, *Emergence of Modern India*, pp. 136-137. According to Lall, Menon's statements and the vote against the US resolution on Hungary gave 'the impression that he favored the Soviet action in Hungary'. Lall claimed that as a result of Menon's vote, Nehru called Lall every morning between three and four o'clock with the 'latest instructions on the Hungarian situation'. Lall, in turn, passed these instructions on to Menon, 'much to his displeasure'. 'Galled by the instructions from Nehru conveyed via me [Lall], he nevertheless carried them out faithfully. But he continued to defend his vote on the first resolution on Hungary, which rubbed salt into the wound of the Americans.' Michael Brecher, in *India and World Politics: Krishna Menon's View of the World* (London: Oxford University Press, 1968), pp. 85-91, quoted Menon as saying that the presence of US and British forces in West Germany was the equivalent of the Soviet occupation of Hungary: 'In the Hungary Question the United States – the U.K. too – was most shamefacedly using the U.N. as an instrument of the Cold War.' Menon argued that a compromise between the Hungarians and the Soviets might have been possible except for the fact that Hungarian resistance 'stiffened'. Menon blamed this on American influence. He then complained that by standing up to the Western powers he was labeled a 'Communist'.

20 Emil Lengyel, *Krishna Menon*, p. 229-231. Lengyel's short, superficial biography of Krishna Menon was published in 1962, and thus forms something of a ground-level view of him. It also contains a brief but explanation of Menon as the focal point of media ire, particularly in the United States. Lengyel states: 'When writing about him [Menon], American newspapers tend to lose their manners, if not their objectivity. The *Time-Life-Fortune* combine, particularly, does not seen to be able to utter his name without hissing.' Lengyel then provides some quotes: 'Mouthpiece Extraordinary, Trouble-maker Plenipotentiary', 'Krishna Menon: Wasp of New Delhi', and the 'Great I Am.' Other quotes included: 'He has an unfortunate personality ... He is evasive ... He is rude ... He meddles.' The author quotes A.M. Rosenthal, *The New York Times* correspondent in New Delhi, as being typical of media views of Menon. 'He [Menon] is a disaster, I tell you, that man. Why does Panditji (Nehru) keep him? What does he see in that man?' Lengyel also quoted the Indian press. At the time of the Chinese border war, *The Hindustani Times* stated: 'Mr. Menon must go.' *The Times of India* correspondent A.G. Gorwala plainly stated that Menon was a Communist, and even some more moderate voices stated that although he at times served India well he should be removed from his diplomatic post because of his 'warped personality'. Lengyel's description of Menon's relations with the press continued with further observations on the British press as well, but the point well made is that Menon was a public-relations disaster of the first order for India and Nehru during the mid-1950s. In this regard, Ram Janaki, a nephew, wrote in *V.K. Krishna Menon: A Personal Memoir* (Delhi: Oxford University Press, 1997), p. xv: 'He was quite ineffectual at public relations and said rather optimistically that one's deeds were the best public relations. This might have been true up to a point, in the British environment he was so familiar with, but in India, where he had no roots due to his long absence, he made no effort to publicize' his

accomplishments. Janaki argues that as a result, Menon was treated as a 'political upstart' totally dependent on Nehru's 'patronage' for support. 'This is why he is so misunderstood.' Of course, he was dependent on Nehru's patronage, and did lack a political base in India.

21 Brown, *Nehru*, p. 248. Brecher, in *Krishna Menon's View*, attempted to map Menon's 'hostility statements' in a piece of 1960s-esque social science research. It is interesting to note that Menon's most frequent target was the United States (p. 362). Brecher also states makes the following observation about Menon's antipathy toward the United States: 'Menon was never an unqualified adherent of the Marxist creed; it was, rather, Laski's neo-Marxism of the thirties that shaped this part of his image. And, like all radical socialists of the contemporary era, he does not regard formal colonial rule as necessary to the policy of "Imperialism" or "Colonialism". The characteristics of "Capitalist" and "Interventionist", whether overt or covert, direct or indirect, political, economic, cultural or military, justify in Menon's eyes the designation "Imperialist" for the United States. Similar patterns of intervention by the Soviet Union escaped this condemnation, though not the substance of criticism.' (p. 301)

22 George, T.J.S., *Krishna Menon: A Biography*. London: Cape, 1964, pp. 218. George's book, while overstating Menon's accomplishments as Defense Minister, provides some interesting insight into what may have been Nehru's motivation in returning Menon to New Delhi. George acknowledges that Menon at the United Nations found himself under attack not only from the Western media but also at home: 'Sentiment against him grew in the process. Powerful business interests, which meant also powerful sections of the Press, became more and more vicious in their attacks.' His election in 1957 to the Indian Parliament gave Nehru the opportunity to bring him into the government as Minister of Defense. George states: 'Ideologically Menon brought a new element into the Cabinet. The Congress as a party was committed to s socialistic pattern of society, but the Cabinet contained no one, barring of course the Prime Minister, who was in earnest about it. Menon was articulate and influential enough to make socialism felt. On the one hand he gave Nehru the ideological support he needed. He provided a natural rallying point to those socialists in the Congress Party who had been languishing for want of leadership.'

23 Brown, *Nehru*, p. 248.

24 Gopal, *Nehru*, Vol. III, p. 129. Gopal states that Menon 'was ineffective and an embarrassment to Nehru and it was therefore not right that he should continue in office'. In a magnificent understatement, the author added that entrusting Menon with the Defense ministry 'proved one of Nehru's less fortunate decisions'. Brown commented, in *Nehru: A Political Life*, p. 248, that as Minister of Defense Menon would become 'Nehru's nemesis in 1962'.

25 'Letter Australian High Commission Karachi [Butler] to Canberra, 15 April 1959'. No. 537/59, NAA, 1838A/2, 169/11/148 Part 9, p. 1.

26 'Karachi to WDC, March 22, 1961'. *FRUS*, 1961-1963, Volume XIX, pp. 26-27. Kennedy's team did not diverge significantly from that of Eisenhower's on the respective aid packages for India and Pakistan. As pointed out earlier, Rostow stated that the last Eisenhower foreign aid budget needed no additional funding. Interview with Walt Rostow, 12 June 2001. The plan allotted India approximately $1 billion over the first two years of the Third Five-Year Plan, excluding PL 480 grain. A substantial amount of the US grant required that India use it to purchase US goods and products. Washington slated $250 million for Pakistan, excluding grain.

27 Bill, *Eagle and the Lion*, pp. 130-132. Bill draws several conclusions about differences between Kennedy's and Eisenhower's policies that are just not supported by the facts. Both administrations supported and encouraged 'peaceful reform from above'. Both administrations believed that ultimately the Shah had to have a powerful military and

security apparatus to ensure his continuation in power. The tendency to see differences between Kennedy's and Eisenhower's policies results primarily from giving too much weight to Kennedy image-building and not enough scrutiny of the differences between the 1958-1960 period and that of the Kennedy administration. The Eisenhower administration faced what it perceived to be the immediate emergency of the post-Iraq period. The initial part of this period focused on security and military issues. As the situation became clearer and stabilized, Dulles and later Herter, with the President directly involved, pushed 'reform from above' as a fundamental part of American policy toward Iran. In fact, in 1963 the Kennedy administration's stand on the status-of-forces agreement for US advisors in Iran and the fiery opposition to it would result in a little-known cleric, Ayatollah Ruhollah Khomeini, becoming the symbol of opposition to the Shah's regime and to the US presence in Iran. Khomeini's imprisonment and exile to Iraq would lead in the end to the Shah's fall in 1979.

28 Particularly in the 1956-1959 period, popular magazines like *Time* and *Newsweek*, in addition to many newspapers, carried editorial and cartoon attacks leveled against the Eisenhower administration. These included maps showing the spread of Soviet influence in the Middle East and caricatures of Dulles, the lightning rod for criticism of the administration. An article and map in *Newsweek* of May 5, 1958 is an excellent example of the criticism.

29 'President's Proposal on the Middle East, 30 January 1957'. *Executive Sessions of the Senate Foreign Relations Committee* (Historical Series), Volume XIX, Eighty-Fifth Congress First Session, 1957. Washington, DC: US Government Printing Office, 1979, pp. 174-179.

30 'President's Proposal on the Middle East, 7 February 1957'. *Executive Sessions of the Senate Foreign Relations Committee*, Volume XIX, 1957, p. 321.

31 Lenczowski, American Presidents and the Middle East, p. 73.

32 'Memcon Rockwell NEA, and George Ferris, President of Raymond International, and Dewey Thompson, Raymond International concerning Ferris's Meeting with Nasser'. NACPM, UAR Policy, 59-786b.11/12-160.

33 *Oral History* – Chester Bowles. JFK Library, pp. 17-20.

34 'Memo G. Lewis Jones to Herter on "Arab – Israeli Problem and the United States Presidential Campaign, 6 July 1960"'. NACPM, UAR Policy, 59-786b.11/7-660. In this memo, NEA informed Christian Herter, the Secretary of State, that the overall situation in the Middle East had improved but that the improvement was precarious. Jones cited both UAR and Iraqi relations as evidence of the improvement, and pointed out that the US had adhered to 'a policy of impartiality and friendship with both sides'. He pointed out that if the Arab-Israeli dispute became an open campaign issue then efforts to solve the refugee problem and achieve progress on other issues could be compromised. Interestingly he alluded to an informal understanding with the Democratic Platform Committee about avoiding references to the Arab-Israeli problem. Jones also recommended that the issue be kept out of the campaign. In a side note, apparently written by Herter, the Secretary stated: 'It will be difficult to keep it from being a major factor if there are any serious incidents in the area during the campaign.' 'Memo Herter to Eisenhower on "Arab-Israel Problem and the United States Presidential Campaign, 6 July 1960"'. NACPM, UAR Policy, 59-786b.11/7-660. In a memo to President Eisenhower, Herter reiterates his desire to avoid 'specific actions or statements which might harm United States' relations with one or more of the states of the Near East'. In his view this is a necessity given the relative 'quiet since the events of mid-1958'.

35 Bass, Warren, *Support Any Friend: Kennedy's Middle East and the Making of the U.S.-Israel Alliance*. Oxford: Oxford University Press, 2003, p. 56. Bass does his best to make the case that the Zionist lobby in the United States lacked the clout to influence policy, and that Republican claims that Kennedy found himself pressured to take a pro-Israeli stance was unsupportable. While Israeli influence in Washington was not what it is

today, Israel and its supporters carried enough clout for President Eisenhower to have to go on national television to explain his reasons for demanding that Israelis withdraw from the Sinai in 1957. Because Eisenhower took a courageously independent stand and refused to bow to political expediency should not be used to understate Israeli political pressure and influence peddling. In contrast, Kennedy had no choice, as he told Phillips Talbot when he blocked plans for a state visit by Nasser. *Oral History* – Phillips Talbot, Assistant Secretary of State, NEA. JFK Library, pp. 2324. As Talbot stated: 'As a consummate politician he understood the importance in our domestic politics, and to the Democratic Party, of that body of Americans roughly categorized as friends of Israel. These political considerations were constantly put to him ....' On Israel, Kennedy told Talbot: 'The trouble with you, Phil, is that you've never had to collect votes to get yourself elected to anything.' Interview with Phillips Talbot, 31 May 2002. In a later interview, Talbot also stated that Feldman used Israeli and Zionist influence to block pressure on Ben-Gurion over the Johnson Plan for a solution to the Palestinian refugee problem, and to prevent a state visit by Nasser. In this same interview, Talbot commented that Ed Bayne, a would be biographer of Ben-Gurion, stated that the latter had described the private session between him and Kennedy, at the Waldorf-Astoria during the UNGA in September 1961, as a meeting in which Kennedy had thanked him profusely for Israeli and Zionist support in the 1960 election. Allegedly Kennedy also stated that he recognized that without support from Israel and the Zionist community Nixon would have won. According to Ben-Gurion, via Bayne, Kennedy promised that he would not forget that debt in the future. Because of the importance of Jewish votes, Kennedy felt obliged to have Feldman in the White House and to adjust his Middle East policy, including the state visits of Arab leaders, to placate the American Zionist community. In light of this, Bass's attempt to argue a minimal Jewish influence in the Kennedy White House seems misguided.

36   Theodore Sorenson, Speech on foreign policy during the Kennedy years, Arlington, Virginia, November 2008.
37   Hoopes, *Devil and John Foster Dulles*, p. 486. During this turmoil, in 1957, Eisenhower had a major heart attack, the seriousness of which was kept from all but a few close aides, and in May 1959 Dulles died of cancer.
38   Hughes, Joseph V. and Holly O. Hughes, Shaping and Signaling Presidential Policy: The National Security decision Making of Eisenhower and Kennedy. College Station: Texas A&M Press, 1998, p. 49.
39   Kennedy, John F., 'Speech to the Zionists of America Convention, Statler Hilton Hotel, New York, N.Y., August 26, 1960'. *Kennedy Speeches*, Part 1, p. 48.
40   '7 Democrats Aid G.O.P. on Mideast'. *New York Times*, 2 March 1957, p. 1.
41   Kennedy, John F., 'Partial Text of a Speech delivered by Senator John F. Kennedy in Alexandria, VA on August 24, 1960'. *Kennedy Speeches*, Part 1, pp. 44-45.
42   Kennedy, John F., 'Speech to the Zionists'. *Kennedy Speeches*, Part 1, p. 48-49.
43   Kennedy, John F., 'Letter to Rabbi Israel Goldstein by Senator John F. Kennedy, August 10, 1960'. *Kennedy Speeches*, Part 1, pp. 962-963.
44   Senator John F. Kennedy, 'Speech by Senator John F. Kennedy, Zionists of America Convention, Statler Hilton Hotel, New York, N.Y., August 26, 1960'. *Kennedy Speeches*, Part 1, pp 48-49.
45   *Oral History* – Phillips Talbot. JFK Library, December 5, 1964, pp. 23-26. Talbot states: 'In the Senate and in his campaign speeches in 1960 he had made a number of bold statements about seeking peace in the Near East.' Kennedy 'saw the greatest challenge in the problem of developing a relationship with Nasser'.
46   *Oral History* – Robert W. Komer, Staff Member, National Security Council. JFK Library. Introductory Statement, Part I, June 18, 1964, Falls Church, VA, pp. 1-2. Komer recalled a conversation with Phillips Talbot the night after Kennedy's assassination that

accurately summarized the formulation of US Middle East policy under Kennedy. Talbot stated: 'You know, one of the great things about the New Frontier was the President's own personal handling of the affairs in which you and I, Bob, were involved. He really was the Secretary of State. We didn't have to deal with the Seventh Floor on Middle East Policy very much. We dealt directly with the White House.'

47 *Oral History* – Phillips Talbot. JFK Library, December 5, 1964, pp. 23-26.
48 Nolte, Richard 'Getting Tough in the Middle East, A Letter from Richard H. Nolte, Beirut, Lebanon, October 8, 1956'. *AUFS*, Northeast Africa Series, Volume II, No. 1, pp. 8-10, 14.
49 'When I was just about to get something done, on Indo-Pakistan relations, [Talbot] would do it in.' *Oral History* – Chester Bowles. JFK Library, July 1, 1970, pp. 83-84. The brief section on the Middle East is interesting for its impressions of personalities and relations. Bowles thought that Badeau was confident but 'afraid of Nasser'. Probably Badeau, the local academic, i.e., President of the American University at Cairo, was somewhat awed by having direct access to the most discussed man in the Middle East. Concerning Talbot, Bowles stated that it was he who had brought him into the administration, and that he viewed this as a mistake. Bowles preferred an approach that placed the priority on India and Talbot 'took the Pakistan view'.
50 *Oral History* – John S. Badeau, Ambassador to the UAR. JFK Library, interviewed by Dennis O'Brien in New York City, February 25, 1969, pp. 1-2, 9. In this account, Badeau emphasizes his distaste for Dulles' policy in the Middle East and Kennedy's desire to bring 'new blood' into the diplomatic corps. In another response, Badeau stated that Kennedy, during their first meeting before he left for Cairo, stated that Kennedy told him that he did not 'know what his policy would be'. In light of policy statements and commitments in speeches this is curious, but it reflects the President's intention, confirmed by Chester Bowles, to conduct his own personal foreign policy and use his Ambassadors and the State Department as implementation tools.
51 Al-Atasi, Jamal, *Al-Thawra li Jamal Abd-al-Nasser wa ala Fikrihi al-Istratiji wa al-Tarikhi*. Beirut: Mahad Al-Agmaln Al-Arabi, p.7.
52 Al-Fadhi Shalaq, Al-Fadhi 'Concepts of the Nation and State with Special Reference to the Sunnis in Lebanon'. In Choueiri (ed.), *State and Society in Syria and Lebanon*, pp. 122, 123.
53 Abd-al-Nassar, Jamal, 'The Principles that Guide Egypt's Political Life'. In Karpat, (ed.), *Political and Social Thought in the Contemporary Middle East*, p. 202.
54 'Addis Abba [Chester Bowles] to Rusk, 21 February 1962'. JFK Library, Papers of President John F. Kennedy (PPJFK) – President's Office Files (POF), United Arab Republic (UAR) Security, 1962, Box 127, p. 5. On this point, Chester Bowles wrote an assessment of Nasser and relations with Egypt on February 21, 1962, following a five-day visit to Cairo when he met with Nasser and several key members of the UAR government. In the telegram to Dean Rusk, Bowles describes the context in which Nasser and the leadership function as one of a 'colonial past, scarred by deep-seated suspicions, frustrations, and plagued by a sense of weakness and inferiority'. Bowles added: 'All this leads me to believe that the current US view of Nasser and his colleagues is oversimplified and defective. We have underestimated the basically revolutionary character of the regime.' The campaign and later the administration ignored the ideological warning indicated by past behavior and later by Bowles' telegram. They did not recognize it as a serious motivating factor.
55 'Memcon Senator Hubert Humphrey and Nasser, 22 October 1961'. NACPM, 786b.00/10-2261, pp. 13-15, 21-22. Hubert Humphrey's visit to the UAR and meeting with Nasser illustrated Badeau's attempts from Cairo to manage Nasser's image. Nasser told Humphrey: 'I am not a Communist, I am a leftist' and 'I am not a Marxist in the true sense.' He also strongly defended African socialist leaders whom the US had

branded as Communist. The Embassy chose to emphasize this aspect of Nasser, stating: 'On Communism, described Arab Communists as "traitors". He was aware Communists, directed and backed by Moscow, reviving popular front technique in Near East and Africa.' This was just after the Syrian coup, for which Nasser blamed his intelligence service and the fact that unlike in Egypt, where he locked up the capitalists whose property he confiscated, he had not done that in Syria and they had forced the coup against him. In effect, Nasser stated that he should have been more ruthless in locking up 'capitalist' and 'reactionary' elements in Syria. He also predicted another coup within six months in Syria – which did in fact occur, backed by Nasserist Syrians. Undeterred, Humphrey briefly discussed the political prisoners and then, following the administration line, brought up the possibility of an official visit to the US.

56 'Cairo, to WDC, 25 October 1961'. NACPM, 59-786b.11/10-2561, pp. 1-4. The Embassy chose to emphasize this aspect of Nasser, stating: 'On Communism, described Arab Communists as "traitors". He was aware Communists, directed and backed by Moscow, reviving popular front technique in Near East and Africa.'

57 *Oral History* – Phillips Talbot. JFKL, August 13, 1970, pp. 37-38. Talbot acknowledged this in an off-hand manner: 'He [Nasser] just couldn't avoid the temptation to respond to people who were coming to him from other Arab countries and saying, "Look, with a little help from you, we can really take over this place".'

58 Lenczowski, American Presidents and the Middle East, p. 69.

59 Grose, *Gentleman Spy*, p. 431.

60 The relationship between Jewish organizations and the Kennedy campaign had not gone unnoticed in Cairo. Nasser, like Ayub in Pakistan, was concerned about the political rhetoric and the perceived influence of the Israeli lobby. This is evidenced by the UAR reaction to the appointments, following the election, of Averell Harriman and Chester Bowles. These appointments encouraged Cairo to believe that a balanced policy would continue, and that the real question would be how the aid dollars would be split between Tel Aviv and Cairo. The one lingering issue troubling Nasser centered on Kennedy's pronouncements about 'opening Suez Canal transit for all nations'. 'Report from Indian Embassy Cairo [A.K. Dar] to MEA New Delhi, 24 January 1961'. INA, MEA, 6(5) R&I/60, p. 7.

61 'New Zealand Embassy WDC to MEA Wellington, 18 November 1960'. New Zealand National Archives (NZNA), ABHS, 950-206-3-12, Box 4059 – USA Presidents November 1960, p. 9.

Part III

1 Interview with Rostow, 12 June 2002. When questioned about this issue, Rostow, who worked as a consultant to the Eisenhower administration during this period, stated that he saw the policies of the administrations as 'completely different'. In explaining, he stated that Eisenhower failed to follow through on his policy instincts, with the exception of nuclear disarmament, because he was a 'captive of the Republican right wing'. When asked if he had recommended funding of the Aswan Dam following the announcement of the Soviet-Czech arms deal, he stated that he had not been consulted directly but that it was politically untenable. On the issue of the Herter State Department, Rostow stated: 'There was no difference between the foreign policy of the liberal Republicans like Herter and that of the Democrats like Kennedy.' At one level, key advisors like Rostow who were well-acquainted with both administrations understood the similarities between Eisenhower and Kennedy policy; on another level, Kennedy's administration, like Eisenhower's, simply could not bring itself to give their predecessors credit for having pursued what they themselves viewed as sound policies. In dealing with the apparent contradictions, Rostow stated that he believed that Eisenhower was simply unwilling to make 'command decisions' on foreign aid in the

Chapter 10

1 Ismael, Tariq Y., *The Arab Left*. Syracuse, NY: Syracuse University Press, 1976, pp. 78-79.
2 Al-Atasi, Al-Thawra li Jamal Abd-al-Nasser wa ala Fikrihi al-Istratiji wa al-Tarikhi, p.7.
3 Shalaq, Al-Fahdi, 'Concepts of the Nation and State with Special Reference to the Sunnis in Lebanon'. Choueiri (ed.), *State and Society in Syria and Lebanon*, pp. 122-123. In an interview on August 8, 2003, Muhammad Hakki stated that was almost impossible to overstate the impact of Bandung on Nasser: 'When he left Egypt, he was first among comrades, when he returned he was a world figure and clearly superior in his own mind to his former comrades on the RCC.'
4 Abd-al-Nassar, Jamal, 'The Principles that Guide Egypt's Political Life'. Karpat (ed.), *Political and Social Thought in the Contemporary Middle East*, p. 202.
5 Interview with General Andrew Goodpaster, August 8, 2003. According to Goodpaster, Eisenhower once remarked that having to choose between Nasser and the Communists was 'like choosing between John Dillinger and Al Capone'.
6 'Letter British Mission Cairo to FO [Lord Home], 9 February 1961, No. 14'. PRO, FO371/158786, p. 4.
7 'Canadian Embassy Cairo to FO via Canadian High Commission London, 11 January 1961'. PRO, FO371/158786, p. 13.
8 'Letter British Mission Cairo to FO [Lord Home], 9 February 1961, No. 14'. PRO, FO371/158786, pp. 4, 10.
9 'Canadian Embassy Cairo to FO via Canadian High Commission London, 11 January 1961'. PRO, FO371/158786, pp. 2-5, 9-12.
10 'Memo Jones and Lee Metcalf, NEA, on "President Kennedy on the Middle East, 9 February 1961"'. NACPM, 59-786b.11/2-961, p. 1.
11 'WDC to Cairo, 11 May 1961'. *FRUS*, 1961-1962, Volume XVII, pp. 110-112. See also 'CIA Analysis: The Arab-Israeli Situation, 6 December 1961'. CIA, CRES, CIARDP79S00427A000400060002-8, p. 5, in which the Agency flatly states: 'Israel, which at one time was willing to accept token repatriation, now opposes the repatriation of the Arab refugees, a position that on November 6, 1961 was endorsed by a Knesset vote including opposition parties as well as those in the government.'
12 *Oral History* – Phillips Talbot. JFK Library, 5 December 1964, p. 24. Talbot had suggested to President Kennedy that despite 'pain to Israel', the President needed to take a more overtly pro-Arab stand to protect US interests in the Middle East. Interview with Phillips Talbot, 31 May 2002. Talbot blamed Myer Feldman, in his role as special counselor to the President on Jewish issues, for blocking the Johnson Plan and a solution to the refugee problem. Talbot stated that Feldman kept the Israeli embassy informed on everything that went on in the White House.
13 Heikal, *Cairo Documents*, p. 193.
14 'Memcon NEA Armin Meyer and UAR Ambassador Mustafa Kamel, 30 August 1961'. NACPM, 611.84a/8-3061 (M1855), p.1.
15 Interview with Walt Rostow, 12 June 2002. Rostow stated that he 'never understood Arabs' because they always seemed to make 'the worst choices'. As for Nasser, Rostow argued that just when he should have been focusing on economic development, his 'revolutionary tendencies' would get the best of him, and he would 'go off on a tangent'. In Rostow's view, the war in Yemen was a perfect example of this tendency. Rostow's frustration was real, and reflected the disappointment felt in the Kennedy administration concerning their UAR policy. They sincerely believed that Nasser had

passed through his revolutionary stage and was ready for an inward turn. They did not interpret the situation as one in which another cycle of heightened revolutionary activity was about to begin. When it occurred, it came as a major disappointment to Rostow, because he had suggested to Kennedy that the United States should make a real effort with Nasser.

16 Badeau, John S., *The American Approach to the Arab World*. New York: Harper Row, for the Council on Foreign Relations, 1968, pp. 112, 173.
17 *Oral History* – Phillips Talbot. JFK Library, December 5, 1964, pp. 23-26. Talbot states: 'In the Senate and in his campaign speeches in 1960 he [Kennedy] had made a number of bold statements about seeking peace in the Near East.' Kennedy 'saw the greatest challenge in the problem of developing a relationship with Nasser'.
18 *Oral History* – Robert W. Komer. JFK Library, June 18, 1964, pp. 1-2.
19 *Oral History* – Phillips Talbot. JFK Library, December 5, 1964, pp. 23-26.
20 'Memo Jordan Desk [Randall Williams] to NEA [Meyer], 13 March 1961'. NACPM, 841.0085/3-1361, p. 1. The Jordanian fiscal year ran from April 1 to March 31. The British offered an extra one million dollars. This boosted aid to Jordan from seven million to eight million dollars for Jordanian fiscal year 1962. US and British aid for fiscal year 1961 totaled $47.5 million. based on an agreement that the United States footed 85 per cent of the bill.
21 'Amman [Macomber] to WDC, 13 May 1961'. NACPM, 785.5-msp/5-1261, p. 1.
22 'Amman [Macomber] to WDC, 3 February 1962'. NACPM, 885.10/2-362, p. 1.
23 'Dispatch Amman to WDC, 31 January 1962'. NACPM, 785.521/1-3162, p. 1.
24 'Amman [Macomber] to WDC, 3 February 1962'. NACPM, 885.10/2-362, p. 1.
25 'Amman [Macomber] to WDC, 7 February 1962'. NACPM, 885.10/2-762, p. 1.
26 'Official Informal Letter from Macomber Amman to Rusk, 6 March 1962'. NACPM, 841.00.85/3-662, pp. 1-2.
27 'Dispatch Amman to WDC, 15 February 1962'. NACPM, 785.13/2-1462, p. 2. See also 'Airgram Amman to WDC, 14 March 1962'. NACPM, 785.13/3-1462, p. 1, in which the American Ambassador opines that Tal's attempts to include in the cabinet persons sympathetic to the Ba'th Party were sharply criticized by King Hussein and other conservative elements in Jordan.
28 'Dispatch Amman to WDC, 8 May 1962'. NACPM, 785.13/5-862, p.1. See also 'Dispatch Amman to WDC, 6 June 1962'. NACPM, 785.13/6-662, p.1.
29 'Airgram Amman to WDC, 29 August 1962'. NACPM, 785.13/8-2962, pp.1-6.
30 'British Embassy Amman [Major] to FO, 14 March 1961,' PRO, FO371/157526, p. 1. In February 1961, King Hussein sent a letter to Nasser suggesting that they meet and consider settling their differences. Nasser did not bother to reply until almost a month later. This was taken as an insult by the Jordanian government, and even some pro-Nasserist elements that had applauded the letter were unhappy that a more prompt, positive reply had not been forthcoming. See also, 'British Embassy Amman to FO, 27 March 1961'. PRO, FO371/157526, p. 1, 'British Embassy Cairo to FO, 4 April 1961'. PRO, FO371/157527, p. 1, and 'British Embassy Amman to FO, 5 April 1961'. PRO, FO371/157527, pp. 1-2. These telegrams raise concerns that Nasser would get the best of King Hussein in exchanges of letters. They also point to the concerns of anti-Nasserist elements in the Jordanian government who did not believe that the exchanges with Nasser were a good idea. See 'British Embassy Cairo to FO, 10 April 1961'. PRO, FO371/157527, p. 1, in which King Hussein expressed his chagrin over the fact that Nasser published the correspondence after being asked not to do so.
31 'Memcon Macomber and King Hussein, 10 April 1961'. NACPM, 785.11/4-1061 (M-1855), pp. 1-2.
32 'Airgram Amman to WDC, 3 July 1962'. NACPM, 785.13/7-362, p.1.

33 'British Embassy Baghdad [Trevelyan] to FO, 1 May 1961'. PRO, FO371/156833, p. 2. Trevelyan characterized Qasim's statements as 'a typically unconsidered outburst'. Trevelyan surmised that Qasim's statements had been a reaction to rumors that the new treaty between Britain and Kuwait would make the latter a part of the Commonwealth (p. 1). See also Badeau, John S., *The Middle East Remembered.* Washington, DC: Middle East Institute, 1983, pp. 205-206. On the subject of Iraq and Kuwait, Badeau related a conversation with Nasser, with Badeau speculating that the Iraqi move was to compensate for the lack of financial success resulting from the IPC nationalization. Nasser said: 'Yes, you are right, that is what people say, but I don't think that is ultimately what the reason was. I think that one morning Qasim was in the men's room and he met his Chief of Staff and one man said to the other: "Why don't we take Kuwait?" Then the other man said: "*Wallahi, billahi, tallahi*" [By God that's a good idea, let's do it]. That's the way we sometimes reach decisions.' Apparently, in more recent times, the Iraqis are not the only ones who use that decision-making process.

34 'British Embassy Baghdad [Trevelyan] to FO, 30 June 1961'. No. 690, PRO, FO371/156875, p. 1. The British Embassy reported that on the night of 30 June railway flatcars loaded with British-supplied Centurion tanks departed the Baghdad area along with various Iraqi army units for the Kuwaiti border. See also 'British Embassy Baghdad [Trevelyan] to FO, 30 June 1961'. No. 692, PRO, FO371/156875, pp. 2-4, in which Trevelyan attaches 'overriding importance' to the ability to deal effectively with an Iraqi attack, but warns that the fallout from a military confrontation with Iraq would once again excite anti-British sentiment throughout the Middle East.

35 'FO to Bahrain, 30 June 1961'. No. 848, PRO, FO371/156875, p. 1.

36 'Macmillan to Australian PM Menzies entitled "Threat to Kuwait", 30 June 1961'. NAA, A6706/1, 37, p. 1.

37 'British Emb Baghdad [Trevelyan] to FO [Hoyer-Millar], 30 June 1961,' No. 692, PRO, FO371/156875, p. 3.

38 'FO to British Embassy Kuwait, 30 June 1961'. No. 476, PRO, FO371/156875, p. 2.

39 'British Mission Cairo [Beeley] to FO, 30 June 1961'. No. 662, PRO, FO371/156875, pp. 1-2.

40 'British Mission Cairo [Beeley[to FO [Hoyer-Millar and Stephenson], 2 July 1961'. PRO, FO371/156875, p. 1. Aburish, Said K., *Nasser: The Last Arab* (New York: St. Martin's, 2004), pp. 203-204. The author claims that Nasser 'played an anti-union role'. Aburish, in one of several strange conclusions, argues that by opposing the annexation of Kuwait by Iraq, Nasser 'ceded his position as the advocate of Arab unity'. The implication is that Qasim's actions were motivated by the very Arab unity that he had always resisted. It completely ignores that the fact that Qasim's motivations vis-à-vis Kuwait had nothing to do with pan-Arabism and everything to do with his personal goals, the economic mess in Iraq, and Iraqi nationalism. Aburish goes on to insinuate that the UAR position was in some way part of an American plot against Arab unity rather than a grossly stupid misstep by Qasim. Aburish forgets that not only the Americans but also most of the Arab world ultimately applauded the UAR position on the dispute; thus, by the author's logic, they must have been a part of the plot also.

41 'British Mission Cairo [Beeley] to FO [Hoyer-Millar and Stephenson], 2 July 1961'. PRO, FO371/156875, p. 1.

42 'Letter British Embassy Kuwait [Rothnie] to FO, 8 November 1961'. PRO, FO371/156894, p. 4. The Egyptians also managed to send only two companies of troops, totaling 160 men, which compared poorly with the 1,550 British marines and over 1,000 Saudi troops dispatched. This situation caused additional damage to UAR prestige.

43 'Amman [Kocher] to WDC, 3 August 1961,' NACPM, 785.11/8-361, pp. 1-2. King Hussein's bizarre proposal was for a union between Jordan, Kuwait, Saudi Arabia, and

Iraq. It can only be described as a feeble, illogical attempt by the Hashemite monarch to isolate Egypt, which had made the decision to dispatch troops to Kuwait. Why Hussein attempted to include Iraq, the perpetrator of the crisis, puzzled everyone.
44 Tripp, *History of Iraq*, p. 167. The Iraqi government accomplished this through Law 80. This move tended to discourage foreign oil companies from investing in the new exploration because of political uncertainties. Additionally, the IPC retaliated by decreasing oil production and thus curtailing Iraqi government revenues. It was a trade-off for Qasim. He lost revenues that worsened Iraq's economic situation but gained some prestige lost in the Kuwaiti adventure.
45 'Dispatch British Embassy Kuwait [Rothnie] to FO, 8 November 1961'. PRO, FO371/156894, p. 13.
46 'Dispatch British Mission Cairo [Beeley] to FO [Lord Home], 18 July 1961'. PRO, FO371/158786, pp. 1-7.
47 'Letter Kennedy to Nasser on the Congo Crisis, 3 March 1961'. JFK Library, PPJFK, NSF, Country Series UAR, Nasser Correspondence, Box 169, pp. 1-4. On the other side of the Atlantic, the Kennedy administration attempted to contain Egypt's African adventures. On February 5, 1961, Nasser wrote to Kennedy complaining about the assassination of Lumumba and calling for a greater United Nations role in stabilizing the country. Nasser argued that the current recognized regime in the Congo was illegitimate, and propped up by foreign powers. He was pointedly referring to the Congolese regime backed by strongman Joseph Mobutu, and strongly supported by the United States. In response, Kennedy made a strong case for non-aligned support for the UN mission in the Congo as a means of averting civil war.
48 Warren Bass, *Support Any Friend*, pp. 1-14. To his credit, Bass identifies the Kennedy administration as the beginning of the special relationship between the US and Israel, but he misapprehends the significance of domestic politics and political pressure by Jewish groups in support of Israel. The author's statement that: 'It was hardly foreordained that the U.S.–Israeli friendship would strengthen so appreciably on Kennedy's watch' misses the point. It may not have been 'foreordained' but it was certainly highly predictable, given Jewish electoral support and the close election. For example, Bass cites Kennedy's concerns over Dimona and the exclusion of US Jewish soldiers from Saudi Arabia as examples of a lack of Jewish influence. These policies had long existed and continued into the 1980s. They were hardly indications of a lack of Jewish influence. Bass argues that the Israeli lobby during the Kennedy period was not strong enough to heavily impact US policy. He also states: 'Kennedy had tried to moderate the foremost Arab radical and failed, which meant that risking Nasser's friendship over deepening American special relationship with Israel was not risking much at all.' The author seems not to comprehend what had actually occurred during the late Eisenhower era. Kennedy believed that the Arab leader had 'moderated' because of the rapprochement with the Eisenhower administration. On this basis, Kennedy and some of his advisors made assumptions that were simply not based in reality. The Eisenhower administration pursued an even-handed policy out of principle; Kennedy pursued a pro-Israeli policy out of naïveté over Nasser's malleability with regard to a settlement with Israel, and with an eye to votes in Brooklyn. It was Eisenhower's policy of 1953, but with additional domestic political considerations. There are strong indications that indeed the Zionist support and Jewish votes figured prominently in Kennedy's policy decisions. Bass also attempts to portray the triangular relationship between the US and Egypt and the US and Israel as one of almost equals 'test[ing] the limits of what American friendship meant'. See also *Oral History* – Komer. Volume II, Part V, pp. 73-85. Kennedy appointed Myer Feldman as his Special Counsel to represent Jewish and Israeli interests in the White House. Komer states: 'Mike Feldman played the role of lawyer for the Israelis,' and 'Mike was the lawyer they [the

Israelis] wanted.' It begs the question of why Nasser did not also have a lawyer on the White House staff. Komer also states that Feldman was instrumental in propagating 'the great Egyptian rocket scare', a story fabricated by the Israelis that Egypt was developing rockets and nuclear weapons. According to Komer, Feldman would often have to be told: 'Mike, you know, you're just wrong.' See also *Oral History* – Talbot. Part II, pp. 24, 26-27. Talbot states: 'Feldman was being used as a pipeline not just by American Jewry but by the Israeli embassy, ... his contacts with the Israeli ambassador were considerably closer than either of them talked about in public.'

49 Abd-al-Nasser, Jamal, *President Gamal Abdel-Nasser's Speeches and Press Interviews, January-December 1963*. Cairo: UAR Information Department/Al-Shaab Printing House, 1964, pp. 24-25, 121.
50 Sayf al-Dawlah, 'Ismat, *Nazariat al-Thawrah al-Arabiyah,* Volume VI. Beirut: Dar Al-Musira, 1972, pp. 10, 11. The official Ba'thist position became that Nasser's destruction of the union through his policies was the first in a series of steps that ultimately separated Egypt from the 'Arab Nation.'
51 'Dispatch British Mission Cairo [Beeley] to FO [Lord Home], 31 October 1961'. PRO, FO371/158793, pp. 2-6.
52 'Dispatch British Mission Cairo [Beeley] to FO [Lord Home], 9 November 1961'. PRO, FO371/158793, p. 1.
53 'FO and Whitehall to British Embassy Amman, 2 October 1961'. PRO, FO371/158790, p. 1.
54 'British Emb WDC [Hood] to FO, 29 September 1961,' PRO, FO371/158790, p. 1.
55 *Oral History* – Komer, JFK Library, July 16, 1964, Part II, p. 5.
56 'Cairo [Badeau] to WDC, 27 March 1963'. NACPM, 611.83/3-2762 (M1855), p. 2.
57 'Damascus [Knight] to WDC, 30 April 1962,' NACPM, 611.83/3-2762 (M1855), p. 2.
58 'Airgram Amman [MacComber] to WDC on US Aid to the UAR and Current Rumors, 24 May 1962'. NACPM, 786h.02/5-2462, p. 1. The Commander in Chief of the Jordanian army, Lt. General Habes Majali, also denied rumors that the US was supporting Jordanian dissidents, but he was very concerned that the Arab Tahrir Party, a right-wing, anti-regime religious party was using US aid to the UAR to create problems.
59 'Memo McGeorge Bundy to Rusk on Policy toward Egypt and Syria, 16 October 1961'. JFK Library, National Security Action Memorandum (NSAM), Box 332, p. 1.
60 'Research Memo INR, RNA-8, October 30, 1961, Outlook for Nasser'. JFK Library, NSAM, Box 332, p. 1.
61 'Memo INR to Bundy Reference NSAM Number 105 of October 16, 1961, November 16, 1961'. JFK Library, NSAM, Box 332, p. 2.
62 'Memocon from Sen Humphrey on Nasser, 22 October 1961'. NACPM, 786b.00/10-2261, pp. 13-15, 21-22.
63 'Cairo [Badeau], to Washington, 25 October 1961'. NACPM, 786b.11/10-2561, p. 1.
64 'Memo Rusk to Kennedy on Action Program for UAR, January 10, 1962'. JFK Library, NSAM, Box 332, p. 1. See also 'Memo from Humphrey on Conversations with Nasser, 22 October 1961'. NACPM, 786b.00/10-2261, pp. 13-15, 21-22. See also 'Memo Talbot to McGhee on Action Program for the UAR: Rationale, January 10, 1962'. NACPM, 786b.11/1-362 p. 1. This is the basis for the Rusk memorandum to the President, and clearly shows who is pushing an aggressive UAR policy.
65 Memo George Ball to Kennedy, 31 January 1962'. NACPM, 786b.11/1-3162, p. 1.
66 Memo Robert Komer NSC to Kennedy, 5 March 1962, Nasser Correspondence'. JFK Library, NSF, Box 169, p. 1.
67 'Bowles in Addis Abba, Ethiopia, to Rusk, February 21, 1962'. JFK Library, POF, UAR Security, 1962, Box 127, p. 5.

68 'Memo Komer to Kennedy on Bowles' meeting with Nasser, February 28, 1962'. JKF Library, POF, UAR Security, 1962, Box 127, p. 5.
69 'Letter Official Informal Talbot to Bowles, 6 March 1962'. NACPM, 123-Bowles, Chester, Box 313, p. 1.
70 *Oral History* – Komer. JFK Library, July 16, 1964, Part II, p. 7.
71 'Letter Official Informal Talbot to Bowles, 6 March 1962'. NACPM, 123-Bowles, Chester, Box 313, p. 1.
72 *Oral History* – Komer. JFK Library, July 16, 1964, Part II, p. 7.
73 'Notes on Third Plenary Session – Athens Chiefs of Mission Conference, 13 June 1962'. NACPM, Chiefs of Mission Conferences, Lot 670457, Entry 5269, Box 1, p. 2.
74 Wall, Irwin M., *France, the United States, and the Algerian War*. Berkeley: University of California Press, 2001, pp. 251-252. This work has not focused on the Algerian war, because it was peripheral to the main thrust of this narrative; however, Nasser's role in support of the FLN was significant and pugnacious. The success of the FLN in forcing France to accept an independent Algeria no doubt influenced his decision to pursue the Yemen adventure and to take a more aggressive stance toward the US. See also Horne, Alistair, *A Savage War of Peace: Algeria 1954-1962*. New York: Penquin, 1979; this is the best history of the Algerian conflict. For a detailed explanation of the role of Tunisia and Habib Bourgiba in the outcome of the Algerian situation, see Connelly, Matthew, *A Diplomatic Revolution: Algeria's Fight for Independence and the Origins of the Post-Cold War Era*. London: Oxford University Press, 2002, pp. 249-275.
75 'Cairo [Badeau] to Kennedy concerning publication of Nasser to Kennedy correspondence, 10 September 1962' NACPM, 786b.11/9-1062, p. 1. To counter this, Nasser authorized Heikal to print that portion of his letter to Kennedy in which he laid out Egypt's support for the Palestinian cause. Heikal stated that Saudi Arabian and Jordanian actions required it; otherwise they would not print the excerpted letter. Heikal told Badeau that this was the equivalent of the US providing a courtesy warning on the Syrian recognition issue following the coup and the sale of Hawk missiles to Israel. It is clear that Badeau was seriously aggravated and concerned by this development because he sent his communication NIACT ('night action immediate') and Top Secret/Presidential Confidential.
76 'Memo Bruebeck to Bundy with attached FBIS transcript of UAR broadcast, 24 September 1962'. NACPM, 786b.00/9-2462, p. 1.
77 Interview with Talbot, 31 May 2003.
78 Ball, Passionate Attachment, p. 51.
79 Eban, Abba, *Personal Witness: Israel Through My Eyes*. New York: Putnam, 1992, p. 324.
80 'Memo Talbot to Rusk, 9 July 1962'. *FRUS*, 1962-1963, Volume XVIII, pp. 2-5.
81 'Letter William Bundy, DepSecDef, to NEA [Grant], 16 July 1962'. *FRUS*, 1962-1963, Volume XVIII, p. 8.
82 'Memo Rusk to Kennedy on Johnson Plan, 7 August 1962'. *FRUS*, 1962-1963, Volume XVIII, pp. 31, 33-50.
83 'Memo Talbot to Feldman – Hawks and Johnson Plan, 9 August 1962'. *FRUS*, 1962-1963, Volume XVIII, p. 51.
84 'Memo from Feldman to Kennedy, 10 August 1962'. *FRUS*, 1962-1963, Volume XVIII, pp. 53-54.
85 'Letter Kennedy to Ben-Gurion, 15 August 1962'. *FRUS*, 1962-1963, Volume XVIII, pp. 60-61.
86 'Memo Komer to Bundy, 14 September 1963'. *FRUS*, 1962-1963, Volume XVIII, p. 96. As an indication of what Feldman saw as his priorities, he told Jewish leaders 'in confidence' about the negotiations over the Hawk issue and the Johnson Plan. Komer expressed concern that the situation with the UAR over the Hawks could get out of hand as the news spread. Feldman wanted to abandon US support for the plan, but as

Komer pointed out, 'JFK has written Ben-Gurion, Nasser, and Hussein about it and to retreat now would be a real loss of face.'
87 'WDC to Tel Aviv – Eyes Only Feldman, 20 August 1963'. *FRUS*, 1962-1963, Volume XVIII, p. 67
88 'Cairo (Badeau) to WDC, 24 August 1963,' *FRUS*, 1962-1963, Volume XVIII, pp. 74-77.
89 'Ta'iz, Yemen, [Stoltzfus] to WDC, 16 November 1962'. NACPM, 786h.561/11-1660, p. 1. The US Consulate lodged a formal complaint with the Yemen government about the arrival of Soviet tanks in Ta'iz because their trip from Hudaydah on the coast had 'torn up' the American-built road between the two cities. The Consul also described Yemeni proficiency in driving, stating that one of the tanks had been driven over a cliff, killing the driver and reducing by one the number that participated in a military parade the next day. He also recounted rows of tanks, trucks, armored cars, and guns parked in a large field near Bajil.
90 'Dispatch Ta'iz [Stoltzfus] to WDC, 1 April 1961'. NACPM, 786h.11/4-161, p 1. 'Taiz to WDC, 3 June 1961,' NACPM, 786h.11/6-361, pp. 1-2. Stoltzfus opined on June 3 that the results of the current Yemen situation could 'only be chaos in country and possibly civil war'. No one really cared about Yemen for Yemen's sake. This was one of the great joys of serving in Yemen.
91 'Minute on the Soviet Penetration of Yemen from British Legation Ta'iz [R.W. Bailey] to FO [Walmsley], 1 July 1961'. PRO, FO371/156393, p. 2. The British found themselves quite frustrated with US progress on various aid projects, and concerned that Washington did not take the situation in Yemen and Soviet penetration seriously enough. The British frustration included what, in their view, was a lack of suitable US progress on its two major aid projects, the Ta'iz to Hudaydah road and the Ta'iz water project. To further illustrate that the Soviets were besting the Americans, the British Consul pointed out: 'It is interesting to note that whereas last year the American request to set up a small meteorological station was turned down on religious grounds ("keeping a watch on Allah"), the Russians have now been allowed to build them.'
92 'Memo Meyer, NE, to William Brewer, NE, 9 January 1961'. NACPM, 786h.11/1-96, p. 1. Also see 'Memo Meyer, NEA, to Lewis Jones, NEA, 30 January 1961'. NACPM, 786h.11/1-30-6. pp. 1-2.
93 *Oral History* – Badeau. JFK Library, February 25, 1969, pp. 24-25.
94 'British Mission Cairo [Beeley] to FO, 24 December 1961'. PRO, FO371/158796, p. 1.
95 *Oral History* – Komer. JFK Library, July 16, 1964, p. 2.
96 'Cairo [Badeau] to WDC, 12 October 1962'. NACPM, 786h.02/10-1262, p. 2.
97 Al-Rasheed, Madawi, *A History of Saudi Arabia*. Cambridge: Cambridge University Press, 2002, p. 109. Rasheed's work should be labeled a 'short' history. Despite this, it is useful as a concise reference that provides a chronological framework around which the researcher or reader can arrange anecdotal but often more detailed accounts of specific events found in Holden and Johns' *The House of Saud* and Lacey's *The Kingdom*. Rasheed's reference to the Sudayri Seven is a case in point. The author states that the Sudayri Seven were allied principally to Feisal in the power struggle of the late 1950s and early 1960s, but she provides little explanation. In contrast, Holden and Johns, in *The House of Saud*, pp. 268-269, explain that the term 'Sudayri Seven' refers to Fahd ibn Abd-al-Aziz and his six surviving full brothers, and that their cohesiveness proved instrumental in maintaining the stability of the Saudi regime during the 1960s. Holden and Johns point out that the term 'Sudayri Seven' is something of a misnomer in that it refers to the seven sons of Hassa bint Ahmed al-Sudayri, when in reality Ibn Abd-al-Aziz al-Saud had two other Sudayri wives, Jauharah bint Saad al-Sudayri and Haya bint Saad al-Sudayri, both of whom also contributed sons to the dynasty and half-brothers to the Fahd group labeled as the 'Sudayri Seven'.

98 'Memo to Bundy, The White House, from Lucius Battle, Executive Secretary Department of State, 7 February 1962'. JFK Library, NSF, Saudi Arabian General Files (SAGF), Box 156A.
99 'Memcon Kennedy and King Saud, 13 February 1962'. JFK Library, Box 156A, pp. 2-4.
100 'Dhahran [Talbott] to WDC, 18 February 1962'. JFK Library, Box 156A, p. 1. Feisal indicated that he had been Nasser's friend, but that Nasser had deceived him. He now believed that Nasser was a Communist or afflicted by 'a rabid madness or schizophrenia' and warned Talbot that US aid to and faith in Nasser were misplaced.
101 'Saudi Arabian Arms Request, NSAM No. 73, 20 August 1961'. JFK Library, NSAM, Box 331, p. 1. Slow deliveries of arms also concerned President Kennedy, and he sent a note to Secretary of Defense McNamara asking why it took so long for the US to deliver promised military aid. Kennedy told McNamara: 'Guevara said in Montevideo the other day that everything that the United States does is strangled in the Washington bureaucracy. It seems to me that we could speed this up.'
102 'Airgram Jidda [Kidder], to WDC, 15 August 1962'. NACPM, 786a.00/8-1562, p. 1.
103 'British Emb Cairo [Beeley] to FO, 18 July 1961'. PRO, FO371/158786, p. 12.
104 'Dispatch Tel Aviv to WDC on Political Economic Assessment of Israel January to July 1961, 17 August 1961'. NACPM, p. 1. Ben-Gurion refused to accept Pinhas Lavon in a government coalition between the Maipai and Histadrut parties. As a result, both parties refused to enter a coalition headed by Ben-Gurion because of his handling of the Lavon affair.
105 'Memo Rusk to Talbot, 1 May 1961'. NACPM, 611.84a/5-161 (M1855), pp. 1-2.
106 'Memo Bowles to Kennedy, 30 March 1961'. NACPM, 611.84A45/3-3061 (M1855), pp. 1-2.
107 'Minute by A. Brooke Turner on Letter from British Embassy Beirut [Crosswaithe] to FO [Hoyer-Millar], 23 June 1961'. PRO, FO371/157286 (IAE 4153/40), pp. 1-2.
108 'Attachment to Memo Talbot to Kennedy on visit of Israeli Foreign Minister Golda Mier, 9 October 1961'. NACPM, 611.84A/10-961 (M1855), pp. 1, 4.
109 Tessler, Mark, *A History of the Israeli-Palestinian Conflict*. Bloomington: University of Indiana Press, 1994, p. 313.
110 'WDC to Tel Aviv, 22 June 1961'. NACPM, 611.84A/6-2261 (M1855), p. 2.
111 'Tel Aviv to WDC, 27 June 1961'. NACPM, 611.84A/6-2761 (M1855), p. 1.
112 Shlaim, *The Iron Wall*, p. 211. As Abba Eban is rumored to have once commented: 'The Arabs never miss an opportunity to miss an opportunity.'
113 'CIA Report: The Arab-Israeli Situation, 6 December 1961'. CIA, CRES, CIA-RDP79S00427A000400060002-8 (No. 2050/61S), p. 5.
114 'Memo Talbot to Kennedy on visit of Meir, 9 October 1961'. NACPM,, 611.84A/10-961 (M1855), pp. 1-4.
115 'Memcon Dr. Joseph E. Johnson, of the UNPCC and NEA [William R. Crawford], 6 February 1962'. *FRUS*, 1961-1962, Volume XVII, pp. 460-465.
116 'Policy Directive: Jordan Waters, 26 February 1962'. JFK Library, Komer, Box 429, p. 1.
117 'Tel Aviv to WDC, 3 May 1962'. NACPM, 611.84A/5-362 (M1855), p. 1.

Chapter 11

1 *Oral History* – Bowles JFK Library, p. 18. Bowles noted that both President Kennedy and his brother Robert had 'a rather deep sense of skepticism about the Foreign Service and the State Department. ... President Kennedy was always determined to dominate ... foreign policy making.'
2 Summitt, April R., 'For a White Revolution: John F. Kennedy and the Shah of Iran'. *Middle East Journal*, Volume 58, No. 4, Autumn 2004, pp. 560-575. Summitt's article on Iran and the Kennedy administration deals better with the reality of the situation from

1961 to 1963. Summitt states, correctly, that the Shah manipulated the Kennedy administration into continued support for his regime. The author makes the argument that the Shah exaggerated external threats to his regime, and as a result Kennedy and the State Department, fearing Communism and instability, moved away from support for 'a fresh approach in American relations with Iran'. The author leaves the impression that she believes there was some real alternative. Summit is aware of the bureaucratic battles in Washington, but her understanding would be greatly enhanced by a closer examination of the Eisenhower years. Eisenhower, Dulles, Herter, and Kennedy knew that the Shah exaggerated external threats. They understood that he had serious faults that might bring regime collapse at any time. They wanted a reform-minded, more liberal alternative to the Shah, but they were dealing with Iran – no such alternative existed. In fact, Kennedy's ill-advised decision to identify the US with Prime Minister Ali Amini was a major shift in US policy. The Eisenhower administration had steadfastly avoided identification with any Iranian faction. In fact, Ambassador Wailes, a holdover from the Eisenhower years, lobbied strongly against the Kennedy decision. He urged that Washington go no further than Eisenhower's position, guaranteeing the territorial integrity and independence of Iran. Kennedy's decision to back Amini personally drastically altered the dynamic of US-Iran relations. It led Washington down a torturous path to making similar commitments to the Shah. It placed the interests of the US squarely in the Pahlavi basket. This decision lashed Johnson, Nixon, Ford, and later Carter to an inherently unstable regime and left the US with no alternatives in 1979. Summit states: 'If American diplomats had studied and understood both the Shah and the needs of the Iranian people, perhaps the 1978 revolution could have been avoided.' The problem is 'American diplomats' did study and understand, but they could see no alternative given the Cold War and the commitment to containment. In addition, the Shah, not the United States, should be viewed as the proactive driver in the equation. He really was in charge of his own destiny. It was the Shah's understanding of the Iranian situation that allowed him to survive until 1979, and it was the Shah's miscalculations that led to his downfall. The mullahs of 1979, who are still in charge in Iran, say that the Shah's regime fell because he was not harsh enough in his suppression of the opposition. To date, they have elected not to make that same mistake.

3 Fischer, Michael M.J., *Iran from Religious Dispute to Revolution*. Cambridge, MA: Harvard University Press, 1980, pp. 187-188. In describing the events of 1961 and 1962, Fischer points to the very reform programs supported by Washington as the catalyst for anti-Shah activities. He cites the election issues of 1960 and 1961, and nullification by the Shah because of corruption. He points out that Ayatollahs Behbahani and Borujerdi opposed land reform. In November 1962, the *ulama* launched a campaign against the Shah's attempt to create a grass-roots political movement through the Local Council Election Bill, because it allowed women to vote and did not mention the Koran. In effect, many of the liberalizing reforms that the US urged on the Shah became the catalyst for growing traditional and religious opposition to the regime.
4 'Official Informal Letter Amman [Macomber] to Rusk, 6 March 1962'. NACPM, 841.00.85/3-662, p. 1.
5 'Memo Iranian Desk [Bowling] to NEA [Hart], 22 September 1960'. NACPM, Iran Desk, A/1 Military Assistance, 1958 Status of Forces through 1960, Box 2, p. 1.
6 Interview with Phillips Talbot, New York City, 31 May 2002.
7 Lippmann, Walter, *The Coming Tests with Russia*. Boston, MA: Little, Brown, 1961, p. 16.
8 Interview with Talbot, 31 May 2003. See *Oral History* – Chester Bowles, JFK Library, p. 6, in which Bowles relates the views of Dean Acheson, former Secretary of State under Truman. Acheson believed that Kennedy was 'unqualified and simply the wrong man'

for the presidency. The new White House knew about these views in various quarters and was most sensitive about them.

9 Bill, *Eagle and the Lion*, pp. 113-116, 128, 131-132-153, 156-157. Bill criticizes the Eisenhower administration, stating that the large US subsidies for the Shah's regime resulted in Iranian resentment of US influence: 'It was in the 1950s that the Iranians began to view themselves as the underdog, confronted by an American imperial giant.' Bill argues that Kennedy in contrast pushed for reforms from above, the 'White Revolution'. In fact, Eisenhower's administration consistently pushed for reform from above, and attempted to limit the Shah's appetite for weapons and military expenditures. Bill's work on Iranian-US relations distorts the real relationship between Eisenhower and Kennedy's policies toward Iran. In particular, he borrows from the State Department memos and telegram traffic of John W. Bowling, the Iran desk officer in the NEA Bureau. Bowling wrote the same kinds of plans for Iran during the Eisenhower administration. In fact, during the Eisenhower administration, Bowling made the statement that no one wanted to push the Shah too far and become known 'as the man who lost Iran'. Virtually all of the points made by Bowling in the plan cited by Bill were, at one time, goals and policy plans of Eisenhower foreign policy, whether under Dulles' or Herter's management. A closer reading of Bowling's positions during the Eisenhower administration would have revealed that Bowling was a weak choice to use to support the idea that Kennedy's focus and plans for Iran was different from those of his predecessor. In the case of T. Cuyler Young, the Princeton University expert, Bill credits the professor with having alerted the Kennedy administration to the problems and to rising anti-Americanism in Iran. The problem with the Shah was only too well known to the Eisenhower administration, as were Young's views on the situation. Many if not most of his views on the situation in Iran were shared by the Eisenhower administration, which actively tried to push the Shah toward reform. Bill also cites Kennedy efforts to alter aid to the Shah from military to economic; the Eisenhower administration used the same tactics. None of Kennedy's policy analyses or strategies were new. They had all been tried before, between 1953 and 1958. Bill also laid the controversial 'Status of Forces Agreement' of October 1964 at Lyndon Johnson's doorstep when in fact the US positions on the agreement were clearly established on Kennedy's watch. Bill states: 'There is little doubt that during the Kennedy presidency the United States pressured the shah's regime to begin a program of dramatic selective and controlled reforms.' These conclusions may reflect the use of FRUS without examination of the actual archival materials. Be that as it may, this is misleading vis-à-vis what had gone before and what actually occurred during the Kennedy years. As in the Eisenhower years, pressure from the United States for social and economic reforms and political liberalization caused the Shah to go through the motions of reform, just as he had under Eisenhower. In reality, he worked assiduously to undermine any real attempt to alter the *status quo* or to liberalize the political system. Kennedy followed the same policy path trodden by Eisenhower and, like his predecessor, learned that reform in Iran could not be purchased at a price that threatened the stability of the country. The Shah was just as determined not to relinquish his power, and to use whatever means were available to extract the military aid that he desired for the regime. Kennedy ended up in the same situation that faced Eisenhower: a choice between alienating the Shah, with unknown consequences, and more or less going along with the Shah's approach to governance, which latter included significantly increased amounts of military assistance. In addition, US military support finally reached a crisis point during the Kennedy administration, in which the solution insisted upon by Washington would ultimately lead to 1979. The idea that the United States could have controlled the Shah smacks of 'salvationist' superiority. At a minimum, it infers that the Iranians were not responsible for their own actions. It

should be remembered that most Iranians, including the clerics, supported the 1953 coup against Musaddiq. It also infers that a better policy strategy existed, and that an improved situation would have emerged had the Shah fallen. In all likelihood, just another corrupt regime would have taken power, touting the interests of its supporters over the rest of the country. But, most of all, it insinuates that United States owed something to Iran. The Iranians understood the game from their support of the 1953 coup to the 1979 revolution. Without that support, the coup would never have succeeded, just as the United States was unable to prevent 1979.

10 'Letter Shah to Kennedy, 26 January 1961'. NACPM, 3-A/1 Military Asst., Internal Security (Box 2), p. 2.

11 'Memo attached to the Letter from the Shah to Kennedy, 26 January 1961'. NACPM, 3-A/1 Military Assistance thru 1961/4, Internal Security, Box 2, p. 2. This is the document on which Bill relied so heavily in his interpretation of Kennedy administration policy and the 'so-called' fourteen-point 'blueprint' for Iran by Bowling, the Iran desk officer. In fact, at State, desk officers do not have 'blueprints'. They may offer opinion papers to the branch chiefs, who then in turn may pass the documents to the Assistant Secretary level, but the Bowling document is not a 'blueprint'. It offered a shopping list of options, most of which had been tried under Eisenhower and all of which the Shah had managed to circumvent. The analysis that Bowling offered about the nature of Iranians and of Iranian society at that particular juncture was very interesting and perceptive. Bill also overlooks the fact that Bowling concluded that there was no element of Iranian society capable of leading the country and preventing chaos other than the Shah. Bill, *Eagle and the Lion*, p. 133.

12 'Memo on the Characteristics of the Iranian Urban Middle Class and Implications for U.S. Policy, 14 March 1961'. NACPM, 1962 Prime Minister–1962 Iranian Good Offices, Iran Desk, Box 5, pp. 5, 9, 11. In Washington, intelligence and foreign policy analysts had two anchors for political stability along the northern tier, Turkey and Pakistan. In both, unstable but democratic governments had succumbed to more reliable, benevolent military dictatorships. Analysts looked for patterns when practicing the 'art' of intelligence and foreign political prognostication. The military had become the vehicle for modernization. Fundamentally, the assumption was that the potential for a military takeover was not only possible but also likely. Therefore, if a military takeover was a foregone conclusion, then what kind was preferable? During this period, the new nationalist governments that came to power by military coup tended to be composed of younger officers with new radical nationalist ideas and ideals – Nasser and Qasim were examples. These types of military governments created problems for Western policy, particularly given their penchant for non-alignment or even left-of-center policies. These types of coups seemed to occur in countries where the higher echelons of the military had become closely associated with the ruling elite. In other words, the senior military leadership became as much of a target to be disposed of as the political regime itself. In countries where coups occurred and the political orientation remained largely pro-Western, it was usually the senior military leadership that took the initiative to change the government before the building pressure from below had reached critical mass. See also Kux, *United States and Pakistan*, pp. 95-101. For example, on October 27, 1958, after months of stewing, General Iskander Mirza, President of Pakistan, with the support of the Pakistani Chief of Staff Ayub Khan, overthrew the government of Prime Minister Noon. While ostensibly opposed by the US government, in reality this coup became something of a model for 'controlled democracy' in the region. See also Henderson, K.D.D., *Sudan Republic*. New York: Praeger, 1965, pp. 105-110. Later in the year, events in Sudan further reinforced this trend. On November 17, 1958 a military coup led by General Ibrahim Abboud prevented what appeared to be a pact between the Peoples Democratic Party (PDP), the National Unionist Party (NUP), and pro-

Nasserist elements to initiate a 'National Socialist revolution' in Khartoum. See also 'Khartoum [Moose] to WDC, 17 November 1958'. NACPM, 745W.00/11-1758, p. 1. Initial reporting on the coup quoted General Abboud as saying that the army had taken over the country because of 'corruption' and the fact that 'too many members of parties had been seen visiting foreign embassies'. 'Khartoum [Moose] to WDC, 17 November 1958'. NACPM, 745W.00/11-1758, pp. 1-2. The new Abboud government reinforced the idea that the pro-Nasserist plotters included mid-level officers in the military. On November 26, former Sudanese Prime Minister Abdulla Bey Khalil told newspaper reporters in Khartoum: 'General Abboud freed country from foreign interference ... they had bought press and delivered country to anarchy according to methods which have become classic since they have been adopted about everywhere in Arab world. ... And I shall not conceal fact there was subversive movement shaping up within fraction of army officers which if successful would have endangered independence of country.' When asked by a Lebanese reporter what 'interference' specifically meant, Khalil asked: 'Why are you asking that question? Such an obvious fact should not escape an Arab newsman like yourself. You have come from Lebanon, haven't you? You are in a better position than I to understand meaning of constant interference of a certain state in internal affairs of its neighbors. It suffices, in Middle East, simply to allude to this aggressor in order that everyone will point his finger at him.' The point learned in Washington was that coups by conservative general officers were preferable to those of their potentially more radical subordinates.

13 'Memo GTI Desk [Miner] to NEA [Jones], 8 February 1961'. NACPM, Task force on Iran 20, Box 3, p. 1. See also 'Dispatch Tehran to WDC, 11 February 1961'. NACPM, Box 2089, pp. 1-6, in which the Embassy in Tehran describes the unrest associated with the riots. Despite the alarm in Washington, it appeared that SAVAK had the situation well in hand: 'Throughout the disturbances the security authorities acted firmly and showed generally good discipline and restraint, though it is known that some students were beaten severely.' The Embassy concluded the situation was 'nearing equilibrium', despite leaving a 'residue of bitterness' that appeared to have 'detracted from the regime's standing'.

14 'Memo NSC [Halla] to Bundy, 8 February 1961'. JFK Library, NSF, Iran, Box 115A, p. 1.

15 'Briefing Paper on Iran for Ambassador Harriman, 23 February 1961'. NACPM, 1962 Prime Minister–1962 Iranian Good Offices, Iran Desk, Box 5, p. 3.

16 'Memo NSC [Belk] to Bundy Attached CIA Analysis, 24 February 1961'. JFK Library, NSF, Iran, Box 115A, p. 1.

17 'Karachi [Harriman] to Kennedy, 19 March 1961'. NACPM, 123 Harriman, Averell, Box 320, pp. 1-2.

18 'Memo Komer to Bundy and Rostow, 27 March 1961'. JFK Library, NSF, Meeting Series, Komer March 15-29, 1961, Box 321, p. 1.

19 'Memo – Notes on Iran from NSC [Hansen] to Bundy, 20 March 10, 1961'. JFK Library, NSF, Iran, Box 115A, p. 1.

20 'Memo from the Vice-Chair Policy Planning Council [Morgan] to Bundy, 27 March 1961'. FRUS, 1961-1962, Volume XVII, p. 65.

21 'Memo NSC [Rostow] to DOS [McGhee], 28 March 1961'. JFKL, NSF, Iran, Box 115A, pp. 1-2. See also Oral History Bowles, pp. 92-93, where Bowles took credit for 'rescuing' Holmes and 'rehabilitating' him by putting him in Tehran. Bowles stated that Holmes had been 'fired out of the department for some shipping deal in Taiwan'. Bowles lamented that Holmes had become an impediment to new policies with regard to the Shah because he 'wanted to bring all these planes in all the time to please the Shah. So we were on opposite sides again. But at least he was deservedly put back to work.' See also 'WDC [Bowling] to Tehran [Holmes], 17 May 1963'. JFK Library, NSF,

Iran, Box 116A, p. 1, in which an Iranian informer claimed to have photocopies of cancelled checks from the Pahlavi Foundation made out to a number of US officials, including Ambassador Holmes. Also included in the payments were Allen Dulles and three former Ambassadors to Iran. These were provided to the McClellan committee investigating the Foundation. When a *New York Times* reporter attempted to write an article accusing the committee of 'gullibility', the paper refused to print it.

22 'Iran: Discussion with Professor T. Cuyler Young, 3 April 1961'. JFK Library, NSF, Komer Series, Box 424, p. 1.
23 Ibid, pp. 1, 2.
24 'Letter Professor Young to Rostow, 19 April 1961'. JFK Library, NSF, Iran, Box 115A, pp. 1-6. See also 'Letter Orson Cox to Rostow on the Shah of Iran'. JFK Library, NSF, Komer Series, Box 424, p. 3. Rostow's search for answers netted responses that were just as unpalatable. Cox, an attorney with business interests in Iran, told Rostow: 'The present Shah is a disruptive rather than a unifying influence in Iran. ... The Shah should resign and a regency be established to govern for the Crown Prince as the Shah.'
25 'Editorial Note No. 41'. *FRUS*, 1961-1962, Volume XVII, pp. 98-99.
26 'Memo for Talbot, 5 May 1961'. NACPM, 1961 Task Force on Iran – 20, Iran Desk, Box 3, Cover Memo.
27 'Defense Attaché Tehran to WDC, 5 May 1961'. JFK Library, NSF, Iran, Box 115A, pp. 1-2.
28 'Memo for Talbot, 5 May 1961'. NACPM, 1961Task Force on Iran – 20, Iran Desk, Box 3, Cover Memo.
29 Interview with Talbot, 31 May 2002. Talbot was a naval liaison officer based in Bombay, India during the Second World War. His wife got a job in Calcutta at CBI headquarters. Her office was in the same building and near that of Dean Rusk, who was an OSS officer. Rusk and Talbot met from time to time when Talbot was in Calcutta visiting his wife. There was no lasting or close relationship that flowed from this prior to the Kennedy years, but they did know each other personally and by reputation.
30 'Report from Iran Task Force, 7 May 1961'. NACPM, Task Force Iran – 20, Iran Desk, Box 3, pp. 5, 23, 26, 29.
31 'Memo Komer to Kennedy, 18 May 1961'. JFK Library, NSF, Iran, Box 115A, p. 1. The underlining is Komer's.
32 'Tehran [Wailes] to WDC, 10 May 1961'. NACPM, Task Force Iran, Iran Desk, Box 3, Section I, pp. 2-3.
33 'Record of action No. 2427, 484th NSC Meeting, 19 May 1961'. *FRUS*, 1961-1962, Volume XVII, p. 120.
34 'Attached Report NSC Meeting Agenda, 19 May 1961'. NACPM, Task Force on Iran, Iran Desk, Box 3, p. 1.
35 'Tehran [Wailes] to WDC, 13 May 1961'. JFK Library, NSF, Iran, Box 115A, pp. 2-3.
36 'SNIE – Outlook for Iran, 23 May 1961'. *FRUS*, 1961-1962, Volume XVII, p. 123.
37 'Tehran [Wailes] to WDC, 16 May 1961'. JFK Library, NSF, Iran, Box 115A, p. 1.
38 'Airgram Tehran to WDC, 17 May 1961'. NACPM, 788.00/5-1761 HBS, p. 1.
39 Boroujerdi, Mehrzad, *Iranian Intellectuals and the West*. Syracuse, NY: University of Syracuse Press, 1996, pp. 67-68. The author argues that it was under Derakhshesh that systematic and implacable opposition to the West took root in the Iranian educational system. Following his appointment in May 1961, Derakhshesh formed the Commission on the Aim of Iranian Education. Jalal Al-e Ahmad, a polemicist, wrote a report for the Commission, which was reviewed in November 1961 and again in January 1962. It was a 'nativist', anti-regime, and anti-Western work, and the Commission decided against publishing it. Following this rejection, Al-e Ahmad managed to get it published under the title *Gharbzadegi*. It enunciated the 'nativist', 'ethnic', and 'national' responsibility for all Iranians vis-à-vis colonialism, and demanded that Iranian intellectuals reexamine

their 'passive and servile embrace of Western ideas and culture'. Boroujerdi describes *Gharbzadegi* as the first to seriously attack Western intellectual modes of thought and to offer an Iranian alternative. Al-e Ahmad viewed Western thought and culture as a pandemic that threatened 'the eradication of Iran's cultural authenticity, political sovereignty, and economic well-being'. The author states that because *Gharbzadegi* 'questioned the basic foundations of contemporary Iranian social and intellectual history' in 'blunt' style, it was an 'intellectual bombshell' 'transformed into the holy book for several generation of Iranian intellectuals'. This raises an interesting question: without Amini, would Derakhshesh have come to power, and without Derakhshesh would Al-e Ahmad and *Gharbzadegi* have had the impact that they did? In attempting to foster reform, did the Kennedy administration helped to plant the seeds that bore fruit in 1979? There is simply no way that any American administration could understand the variables in attempting to change the fundamental nature of Iranian society, and that is exactly what Kennedy and his White House hoped to do. In so doing, they failed to realize how limited US options were in this regard. They tied themselves directly to the programs and person of Amini, who was in turn just as tied to the Shah. When Amini failed, the only option was an even tighter relationship with the Shah or, at best, a neutralist, anti-Western Iran. At the same time, the events of 1961-1962 would set in motion the ultimate unraveling of the pro-Western regime in Tehran. *Gharbzadegi* is just one example.

40 'Tehran [Wailes] to WDC, 27 May 1961'. JFK Library, NSF, Iran, Box 115A, p. 1.
41 'Airgram Tehran [Wailes] to WDC, 8 June 1961'. NACPM, 788.13/6-861 HBS, p. 1.
42 'Tehran [Holmes] to WDC, 15 June 1961'. JFK Library, NSF, Iran, Box 115A, pp. 1-4. In early June 1961, Julius C. Holmes replaced Edward T. Wailes as Ambassador to Tehran.
43 'Tehran (Holmes) to WDC, 4 July 1961'. JFK Library, NSF, Iran, Box 115A, p. 1.
44 'Tehran (Rockwell) to WDC, 29 July 1961'. JFK Library, NSF, Iran, Box 115A, p. 1.
45 'Memo Hansen to Rostow, 13 June 1961'. JFK Library, NSF, Iran, Box 115A, p. 1.
46 'British Embassy Tehran [Harrison] to FO on Land Reform, 17 January 1962'. PRO, FO248/1588, p. 7.
47 Hooglund, Eric J., *Land and Revolution in Iran 1960-1980*. Austin: University of Texas Press, 1982, p. 43. Arsanjani had long been an advocate of land reform, calling for it in an article in Darya on January 15, 1951.
48 'British Embassy Tehran [Harrison] to FO on Land Reform, 17 January 1962'. PRO, FO248/1588, p. 7.
49 Hooglund, Land and Revolution in Iran 1960-1980, pp. 52, 50.
50 'Dispatch Tehran to WDC, 29 July 1961'. JFK Library, NSF, Iran, Box 115A, pp. 1-5.
51 'Memo from Komer to Talbot, 5 June 1961'. NACPM, Task Force on Iran – 20, Iran Desk, Box 3, p. 1.
52 'Memo Komer to Kennedy, 4 August 1961'. JFKL, NSF, Iran, Box 115A, p. 1. The administration used these 'special task forces' to circumvent the normal diplomatic and intelligence channels. This often resulted in 'hyper-active' reactions to anything resembling a crisis and in some less than balanced interpretations of various situations. The key to Vietnam may be found as much in the information-interpretation processes emanating from the 'task force syndrome' as from other sources.
53 'Memo Komer to Kennedy, 4 August 1961'. JFK Library, NSF, Iran, Box 115A, pp. 1, 2, 3.
54 'Memo – Task Force Recommendations [Peyton Kerr, Acting Chairman], 2 August 1961'. NACPM, Task Force on Iran, Iran Desk, Box 3, pp. 1-2.
55 'Memo Bundy to Rusk, 7 August 1961'. NACPM, Task Force on Iran, Iran Desk, Box 3, p. 1.

56 'Memo Komer to Bundy, 11 August 1961'. JFK Library, NSF, Iran, Box 116, pp. cover memo, 1.
57 'Letter Official Informal NEA (Meyer) to Holmes, 11 August 1961'. NACPM, 3 – A/1 Military Assst thru Internal Security, Box 2, p. 2.
58 'Letter Official Informal Holmes to Meyer, 27 August 1961'. NACPM, Task Force Iran, Iran Desk, Box 3, p. 1.
59 'Memo Discussion at the DOS – JCS Meeting, 31 March 1961'. *FRUS*, 1961-1962, Volume XVII, p. 75.
60 'Letter Official Informal Holmes to Meyer, 27 August 1961'. NACPM, Box 3, pp. 3, 5.
61 'Meeting of the Iran Task Force, 7 September 1961'. *FRUS*, 1961-1962, Volume XVII, pp. 245-253. See also 'Comments on Iran [Komer], 7 September 1961'. JFK Library, NSF, Komer Series, Box 425, pp. 1-2, in which Komer made it clear that he wanted a crisis no matter what Holmes and Talbot reported. 'Even if we accept the Embassy's somewhat reassuring estimate of the prospects, is there not still sufficient risk of a potentially damaging blow to US interests to justify a more than normal effort to assure Amini's success? Should we not consider measures, which under more normal circumstances we would hesitate to take? Can we afford in view of the risks inherent in failure of the Amini experiment, not to do everything possible to make it a success?'
62 'Comments on Iran (Komer), 7 September 1961'. JFK Library, NSF, Komer, Box 425, p. 1.
63 'Letter Official Informal Holmes to Rusk, 13 September 1961'. NACPM, 788.11/9-1361, pp. 1, 2, 4.
64 'Memo Komer to Bundy, 28 October 1961'. JFK Library, NSF, Iran, Box 116, pp. 1, 2.
65 'Letter Official Informal Holmes to Talbot, 31 October 1961'. NACPM, 3 – A/1 Military Asst., Box 2, p. 1.
66 'Memo Komer to Bundy on Cut in Military Assistance, 7 November 1961'. JFK Library, NSF, Iran, Box 116, p. 1.
67 'Letter Official Informal Holmes to Talbot, 7 December 1961'. NACPM, 3 – A/1 Military Asst, Box 2, pp. 1-5.

Chapter 12

1 'Airgram Tehran to WDC, 3 January 1962'. NACPM, 788.10/1-562, pp. 1-2.
2 'Letter Official Informal Holmes to Rusk, 22 January 1962,' NACPM, 788.10/1-562, pp. 3, 2, 6.
3 'Memo Komer to Kaysen, 19 January 1961,' JFKL, NSF, Komer, Box 424, pp. 1, 2.
4 'Airgram Tehran [Holmes] to Kennedy and Rusk, 13 February 1962'. JFKL, NSF, Iran, Box 116, p. 5. One cannot help but be impressed by Holmes' bureaucratic expertise. Holmes knew that Bowles would express a very positive view of Amini and complain about the Shah's focus on the military. By sending a telegram straight to the White House and Secretary, he made certain that they heard his version of the discussion with the Shah before Bowles had an opportunity to comment on it. In fact, it appears to have been sent while Bowles was in the air.
5 'Telegram Tehran [Holmes] to Kennedy and Rusk, 18 February 1962'. NACPM, 788.5/2-1862, pp. 1-2.
6 'Letter Official Informal Holmes to Talbot, 4 March 1962'. NACPM, 1962 Helman River – 1962 Oil and Petroleum., p. 2. On March 4, Holmes cited a conversation with General Pakravan in which the general stated that US praise for Amini had left the Shah in a state of 'depression'. Attempting to enlist Talbot in his efforts, Holmes stated: 'Quite frankly, I am fearful, from what I have been told by recent visitors, that some people in Washington might construe such suggestions as a ploy to get my way about the Military Program on which I have been so insistent.' He then went on to say that he needed Talbot's help in advancing the date of the Shah's visit, because that might

improve the situation at the palace. 'Until I have in hand a Military Program, or more usefully, combined military-economic one, I can do little to reassure the Shah. I have done this many times and, of course, can offer my shoulder again, but it has become pretty wet!' Holmes then warned that the Shah's mood could have 'dangerous consequences' for 'American diplomacy in Iran in the very near future'.

7 'Memo Lucius Battle, DOS to Bundy, 8 March 1962'. JFK Library, NSF, Komer, Box 425, p. 1. In effect, the MAP Steering Group had decided to offer Iran $300 million in military aid over the fiscal year 1962 through fiscal year 1967. This included training and logistics support, but not a thorough modernization program. Ambassador Holmes and Amini, most probably with the Shah's support, wanted a $424 million program. This program included a thorough modernization of the Iranian military accompanied by a reduction in overall force levels from 205,000 to 150,000 men.

8 'Memo Battle to Bundy, 8 March 1962'. JFK Library, NSF, Komer Series, Box 425, p. 2.

9 'Memo Talbot to McGhee, 28 February 1962'. NACPM, Political Files, Iran, Box 8, p. 1. On his way to Vietnam, Taylor attempted to convince the Shah of 'the growing capability of the U.S. to wage limited war and to support friendly nations against communist-based subversive and guerrilla aggression'.

10 'Letter Official Informal Talbot to Holmes, 9 March 1962'. NACPM, 1962 Helman River, Box 6, p. 1.

11 'Memcon Rusk and PM Amini, 13 March 1962'. NACPM, 788.5/3-1362, pp. 1-5.

12 'Memo Komer to NSC Staff, 20 March 1962'. JFK Library, NSF, Komer Series, Box 425, p. 1. See also 'Memo Komer on Visit of Shah of Iran, 27 March 1962'. JFKL, NSF, Iran/Iraq, Box 117, p. 1, in which Komer states: 'We support a reformist government in Iran in its effort to achieve sweeping change and progress and to forestall an uncontrolled revolution. The Shah's presence in Iran and his support – or at least tolerance – of a reformist government like the present one is essential. The immediate alternative would be chaos, leading at best to a weak, ineffectual, neutralist Iran which would be easy prey for the Soviets.' Holmes' message that the Shah was the essential element for reform had now taken root. Personal support had shifted from Amini to the Shah.

13 'Memo Komer to NSC Staff, 20 March 1962'. JFK Library, NSF, Komer, Box 425, p. 1.

14 'Memo Talbot to McGhee on NSC Mtg on Iran, 22 March 1962'. JFK Library, NSF, Meetings Series, Box 314, p.1.

15 'Tehran [Holmes] to Rusk, 30 March 1962'. NACPM, 788.11/3-3062, pp. 1, 2.

16 'Memo by Komer, 2 April 1962'. JFK Library, NSF, Komer Series, Box 425, p 1.

17 'Memo Komer to Kennedy, 9 April 1962'. JFK Library, NSF, Komer Series, Box 425, p 1.

18 'Memo Komer to Kennedy, 28 March 1962'. JFK Library, NSF, Iran-Iraq, Box 117, p 1.

19 'Memo Komer to Kennedy, 9 April 1962'. JFK Library, NSF, Komer Series, Box 425, p 1.

20 'Memo Hansen to Kennedy, 10 April 1962'. JFK Library, NSF, Komer Series, Box 425, p 2, in which Hansen, fearing the Shah would raise the issue of preferential treatment for Turkey and Pakistan, put together a comparison sheet of the MAP with the economic-assistance levels of each. The briefing memorandum points out that Turkey had a larger population, and as a member of NATO provided a potential staging-area for US troops and intermediate range ballistic-missile sites, and that this accounted for any differences in aid. Pakistan was much poorer than Iran, with a larger population. In addition, Pakistan had been able to absorb more modern weapons than Iran because it 'inherited a trained cadre of specialists from British India'.

21 'Memo Bowles to Kennedy, 10 April 1962'. JFK Library, NSF, Komer Series, Box 425, p 2.
22 'Memcon Kennedy, Rusk, McNamara and the Shah, 12-14 April 1962'. JFK Library, NSF, Iran, Box 116, pp. 4-5.
23 'Memcon McNamara and the Shah, 12 April 1962'. JFK Library, NSF, Komer Series, Box 425, pp. 4, 8. In talks with McNamara, the Shah made it clear that the 150,000-man force envisioned by the US was insufficient and that higher force-levels would be required. McNamara agreed that this could be discussed, and implied that a 10,000-man increase over that number might work. The Shah readily accepted a 'planning team' from the Pentagon proffered by McNamara.
24 'Memcon the Shah and Harriman, 13 April 1962'. NACPM, 788.11/4-1362, p 1.
25 Keddie, Nikki R., *Modern Iran*. New Haven, CT: Yale University Press, pp. 140-148. Keddie's work on Iran is a general history, but in a brief eight pages she attempts to provide detail on the relationship between Amini and the Shah. Most traditional interpretations of this period tie Amini's tenure to the Shah's jealousy over US support for Amini's reforms, and his clashes with the Shah over those reforms; and In reality, Amini was little different from the Prime Ministers that went before him. The Kennedy view that Amini was more independent was flawed. Amini was just as dependent on the Shah's support as those that went before him. . A careful examination of the source materials reveals considerably more calculation on the part of the Shah. Amini's ability to attract US aid was the key. The Shah is clearly in control of the situation with Amini from the very beginning. In fact, one could argue that he appointed Amini instead of Teymour Bakhtiar, the Chief of SAVAK, to the Prime Minister's position because he believed that more US aid would result.
26 'Tehran [Holmes], 25 May 1962'. JFK Library, NSF, Iran/Iraq, Box 116, p 1.
27 'WDC to Tehran [Holmes], 25 May 1962'. JFK Library, NSF, Iran/Iraq, Box 116, p 1.
28 'Memo Komer to Bundy, 1 June 1962'. JFK Library, NSF, Komer Series, Box 424, p 1. Presidential diplomacy often caused problems. The fact that Kennedy held one-on-one discussions with foreign leaders left the substance of the meetings open for discussion. It gave foreign leaders the opportunity to ascribe something personally to the President. As we shall see, something similar happened with President Ayub Khan.
29 'Memo on "Our Current Dilemma in Iran" from Iran Desk [Bowling] to DOS/GTI [Miner], 5 June 1962'. NACPM, NEA, Iran Desk, Iranian Prime Minister 1962, Box 5, p 1.
30 'Memo "Our Current Dilemma in Iran" Iran Desk [Bowling] to DOS/GTI [Miner], 5 June 1962'. NACPM, Iranian Good Offices – Prime Minister 1962, Box 5, pp. 1-2.
31 Keddie, *Modern Iran*, p. 143.
32 'Memo 'Our Current Dilemma in Iran' Bowling to Miner, 5 June 1962'. NACPM, Box 5, pp. 1-4.
33 'Tehran [Holmes] to WDC, 24 June 1962'. JFK Library, NSF, Iran, Box 116, Section 2, p 2.
34 'CIA Current Intelligence Memo: The Resignation of Amini, 18 July 1962'. JFK Library, NSF, Iran, Box 116, pp. 1-2. The report commented that the British were happy to see Amini go because they viewed him as 'too close to the Americans' and believed that his policies had 'cut into their political and commercial interests in Iran'.
35 'Tehran [Holmes] to WDC, 18 July 1962'. No. 76, JFK Library, NSF, Iran, Box 116, p 1.
36 'CIA: The Resignation of Amini, 18 July 1962'. JFK Library, Box 116, p 2.
37 'Tehran [Holmes] to WDC, 18 July 1962'. No. 74, JFK Library, Box 116, p 2.
38 'CIA: The Resignation of Amini, 18 July 1962'. JFK Library, Box 116, pp. 1-2.
39 'Memo Komer to Kennedy, 16 July 1962'. *FRUS*, 1962-1963, Volume XVIII, p 10.

40 'Memo from Komer to President Kennedy, 18 July 1962'. *FRUS*, 1962-1963, Near East, Volume XVIII, p 11. This memorandum from Komer to President Kennedy illustrates the problem in selecting documents for publication. Komer's suspicion that 'Amini had to turn to blaming the US' because of the 'Shah's refusal to back him in cutting the military and civil budget' contributes to the view that the Shah was entirely to blame for the situation. Broader reading in the archives indicates otherwise.
41 'Tehran [Holmes] to WDC, 18 July 1962'. No. 76, JFK Library, Box 116, p 2.
42 'Tehran [Holmes] to WDC, 19 July 1962'. No. 86, JFK Library, Box 116, pp. 1-2. On page two of the telegram, Holmes also quoted his earlier speculation that Amini was a 'spent force'. Amini was 'mentally exhausted and psychologically worn out'. Holmes, ever mindful of his prerogatives as Ambassador, made sure that Washington 'remembered' that he had predicted the possible fall of Amini two weeks earlier. He added that, given Amini's condition that: 'it would therefore be unproductive make any attempt resuscitate Amini now.' Holmes had believed almost from the beginning that the Shah, not the Prime Minister, was the right political horse to bet on in Iran.
43 'Tehran [Holmes] to WDC, 19 July 1962'. No. 90, JFK Library, Box 116, p 1.
44 'CIA Tehran to WDC Alam Appointed Iranian Prime Minister, 20 July 1962'. No. 90, Box 116, p 1.
45 'Tehran [Holmes] to WDC, 21 July 1962'. No. 96, JFK Library, Box 116, p 2.
46 'CIA Tehran to WDC Alam Appointed Iranian Prime Minister, 26 July 1962'. No. 90, JFKL, Box 116, pp. 1-4. This report also noted the criticism that Alam was pro-British. 'It is true that many of the personalities, including Alam, have or have had British connections and may have been under British influence. However, British influence is not what it used to be, and in any case if there is no important divergence between British and American policy, this should create no difficulties.'
47 'Letter Official Informal Talbot to Holmes, 7 August 1962'. NACPM, Helman River 1962, Box 6, pp. 1, 2.
48 'Memo Brubeck to Bundy on Letter to the Shah, 27 July 1962'. NACPM, Prime Minister 1962, Box 5, pp. 2-3.
49 'CIA SNIE 34-62 – Political Prospects Iran, 17 August 1962'. JFK Library, NSF, Komer Series, Box 424, pp. 1-9.
50 'Memcon the Shah and Colonel Gratian Yatsevitch, 6 August 1962'. NACPM, Prime Minister – 1962 Iranian Good Offices, Box 5, p. 3.
51 'CIA SNIE 34-62, 17 August 1962'. JFK Library, NSF, Komer Series, Box 424, p. 9.
52 Bill, *Eagle and the Lion*, pp. 139-141, 154-155, comments on the Vice President's visit. Bill portrays Johnson as 'particularly blunt' with the Shah over the need for reform, and quotes Ambassador Holmes as saying that progress toward economic and social justice was the only real insurance against subversion and the Communist threat. With regard to military reductions, Johnson pointed out that even the United States with its global commitments and the Berlin Crisis had to demobilize two army divisions because of budget considerations. According to Bill: 'Johnson left no doubt about the thrust of the American message to the shah's government. "We realize the extent to which our views and those of your farsighted leaders are parallel. We all agree on the necessity for programs of responsible change. We have seen that the status quo alone provides no safeguard for freedom."' However, in the next breath, Bill makes a series of 'Kennedy Legacy' statements, insinuating or stating outright that the Shah duped Eisenhower, Dulles, Herter, Johnson, and Nixon but not John Kennedy, a position at considerable variance with documentary evidence. Three statements by Bill underscore this view. Firstly: 'The Shah, on the other hand, took the measure of Johnson and, smothering him with Persian hospitality convinced Johnson that he was a firm, reliable, anticommunist ally.' The Shah had done this with every senior US official. In addition, Kennedy's personal support for Amini, aside from the fact that it involved the US more

deeply in internal Iranian politics than ever before, was out of concern that the Shah would fall and that the US would need a strong anti-Communist alternative. Once the hysteria in the NSC and White House subsided, the Shah became the 'indispensable' element for stability in Tehran. With regard to political repression, secondly, the author argues: 'With the death of John F. Kennedy, … the Shah of Iran began another period of entrenched and repressive political rule.' The Shah's rule, and for that matter, Amini's as well, always had used heavy doses of repression. Shortly after his government came to power, Amini banned demonstrations and authorized the use of force on university students. The Shah and Amini jointly agreed upon the tough anti-riot measures of January and June 1962, and it was Amini, with strong Kennedy backing, who ruled unconstitutionally by not calling for elections. Thirdly, and of most interest, is Bill's statement that: 'In the end, it was his relationship with the Shah and not his understanding of the Iranian people that determined Johnson's foreign policy toward Iran.' What else could it have been? Very few in Washington, or in the Tehran Embassy for that matter, could truthfully state that they had an 'understanding of the Iranian people'. Which Iranian people? The National Front? Which National Front? It was so divided. The Tudeh? The Shah's supporters? What group of supporters? The bottom line is that those American officials with an understanding of the Iranian people believed that the Shah's survival and ability to 'control' the situation were essential to stability. These included John Bowling of the Iran Desk. For a final example, Bill states: 'Johnson was deeply impressed by the supportive [sic] of every Asian dictator he met.' Eisenhower, Kennedy, and Johnson viewed the situation in the same way. Asian dictators were always preferable to instability or Communist expansion. In fact, there is a good argument to be made that at least one Asian dictator, Ngo Dinh Diem, would earn a bullet in the back of the head, with the knowledge of President Kennedy, for entertaining an arrangement with the National Liberation Front in Vietnam. We will also get around to discussing how impressed Kennedy was with Ayub Khan during his visit to Washington in 1961. See interview with Phillips Talbot, May 31, 2002. The point is that Kennedy, like his successors, was trapped within the confines of US interests. Kennedy's problems with the Shah were no different from those of Eisenhower or Johnson. The Shah served a purpose, and there was a price attached to that. Bill's work on Iranian-American relations is a classic, but in understanding the actual dynamics of the Eisenhower and Kennedy years, it tends to place too much responsibility on the US. In reality, the United States never had any real control over events in Iran. For 25 years everyone in Washington wanted an alternative to the Shah; the fact is that it took until 1979 for the Iranians to produce one.

53 'Scope Paper for Vice President's Visit to Iran August 24-26 1962 from NEA/GTI/Iran Desk [Bowling], August 1962'. NACPM, Helman River 1962 to Oil and Petroleum 1962, Box 6, pp. 1, 4.
54 Bill, The Lion and the Eagle, p. 141.
55 'Report VP Johnson to Kennedy on Shah of Iran, 28 September 1962'. *FRUS*, 1962-1963, Volume XVIII, p. 72.
56 "Personal' Holmes to Rusk, 14 September 1962'. JFK Library, NSF, Iran, Box 116, pp. 1-3.
57 'Memo Komer to Bundy, 15 September 1962'. JFK Library, NSF, Iran – Iraq, Box 116, p 1.
58 'Memo Brubeck to Bundy, 17 September 1962'. JFK Library, NSF, Iran – Iraq, Box 116, p 1, and 'Rusk to Holmes, 17 September 1962'. JFK Library, NSF, Iran – Iraq, Box 116, p 1.
59 'Memcon the Shah and Holmes, 19 September 1962'. *FRUS*, 1962-1963, Volume, XVIII, pp. 104-105.
60 'Memo Komer to Kennedy, 24 September 1962,' JFK Library, NSF, Iran, Box 116, p. 1.

61 'Memo NEA to Talbot, 21 September 1962'. NACP, Helman River to Oil and Petroleum 1962, Box 6, p 1.
62 'Background Paper on Special Problems for Visit of Shah of Iran to Washington, DC, 2 April 1962'. JFK Library, NSF, Iran – Iraq, Box 116, p. 4. See also 'Memo on Status of American Personnel in Iran from Alfred Rubin, DOS/International Affairs to M.D. Smith DOS/GTI, 23 February 1961'. NACPM, 3-A/1 Military Asst thru Internal Security (Box 2), pp. 1-2. This document is a history of the status of the US military personnel issue, including the informal arrangements for jurisdiction, and argues that the time had come for a more formal arrangement to be put in place.
63 'Letter Official Informal Tehran [Armitage] to WDC, 26 September 1962'. NACPM, Helman River 1962 to Oil and Petroleum 1962, Box 6, p. 1.
64 'Letter Official Informal Tehran [Harry H. Schwartz] to WDC, 26 July 1962'. NACPM, Helman River 1962 to Oil and Petroleum 1962, Box 6, p. 1.
65 'Letter Official Informal from DOS/GTI [Miklos] to Tehran [Armitage], 12 October 1962'. NACPM, Helman River 1962 to Oil and Petroleum 1962, Box 6, p 1.
66 'Memo for the Record by Stuart Rockwell, DCM, Tehran, 5 November 1962'. NACPM, Helman River 1962 to Oil and Petroleum 1962, Box 6, p 1.

Chapter 13

1 Bowles was well known for his pro-Indian views and sentiments. In his book, *Ambassador's Report* (New York: Harper, 1954), pp. 99, 111, 252, 320-321, 386-387, Bowles criticized everything from US aid to immigration policies. He made it clear that he believed that Nehru was the real influence in Asia. 'We must make no mistake about it, when Nehru speaks on world issues, right or wrong, he expresses not only his own convictions but also the yearning and attitudes of the vast majority in free Asia and in Africa.'
2 Kennedy, John F., *Strategy for Peace*. New York: Harper, 1960, p. 142.
3 Gopal, *Nehru*, Volume III, p. 187.
4 Wilber, Donald N., *Pakistan*. New Haven, CT: Human Relations Area Files, 1964, p. 320. See also Jalal, *State of Martial Rule*, pp. 299-301. Jalal argues that Pakistan's growing involvement in the American defense structure after 1954 severely hampered economic development efforts. The author states that maintenance and administrative costs placed a serious burden on already limited amounts of economic investment funds. He contends that the coup of 1958 was less reflective of the political chaos claimed by Generals Mirza and Ayub, and more indicative of an attempt by the Punjabi-dominated ruling groups to 'thwart the growth of organised political parties' and to 'depoliticise Pakistani society before it slipped into the era of mass mobilisation'. K.K. Aziz, in *Party Politics in Pakistan 1947-1958* (Islamabad: National Commission on Historical and Cultural Research, 1976), traces the development and programs of the principal Pakistani political parties. He argues that the nation did indeed face political chaos and paralysis, and that Ayub took the only course possible in abrogating the 1956 constitution. In fact, both Jalal and Aziz are probably correct in the sense that each man identified elements that contributed to the 1958 coup and 'controlled democracy', but each, having an individual axe to grind, over-simplified and excluded other contributory factors that might complicate their particular arguments.
5 Jalal, *State of Martial Rule*, p. 301. Apparently, Ayub had toyed with the idea of 'controlled democracy' as early as 1954 when he was Defense Minister in Bogra's cabinet. Jalal speculates that that the idea might have been prepared with the backing of senior Punjabi civilian bureaucrats.
6 Bhargava, G.S., *Pakistan in Crisis*. Delhi: Vikas, 1971, pp. 103, 110-115. Bhargava argues that the entire structure of Pakistani foreign policy revolved around a desire to obtain a military advantage over India, and the 'megalamaniacal [*sic*]' designs of the Pakistani

military. While the author is over-the-top in his accusations leveled at Ayub Khan, he is undoubtedly correct about the real purpose of Pakistani military programs and about Ayub's view of economic aid to India.
7 Interview with Phillips Talbot, 31 May 2002. Talbot was probably the most experienced and best prepared of all the Kennedy appointees to deal with the intractable problem of India and Pakistan. In addition, he displayed remarkable appreciation of the situation in both countries, while never forgetting that his primary mission was to act in the best interests of the United States. Despite his many ties to India and his sympathy for Indian nationalism, Talbot also understood and appreciated the conflicted emotions that drove Muslim separatism. In the late 1930s he had attended Aligarh College, also known as the Muhammadan Anglo-Oriental College, founded in 1870 by Sir Sayyid Ahmad Khan, a Muslim reformist. He also wrote a paper in 1956 entitled: 'I am a Pakistani'. The paper provided Talbot's view of the emerging Pakistani national identity and the motivations that had driven the creation of the Pakistani state. This included the author's view of Muslim reactions to the Congress Party, Nehru, and Hindu-dominated identity. See Phillips Talbot, 'I am a Pakistani'. *AUFS-South Asia Series*, 28 November 1956, found in the Ian Stephens Papers at the Archives of the Centre for South Asian Studies, Cambridge University. Surprisingly, Talbot consistently provided the policy balance missing among those who more blindly supported the pro-Indian position within the Kennedy administration.
8 Grafurov, B.G., *Politika USA na Blishchnem i Srednem Vostoke*. Moskva: Akademiya Nauk CCCP – Institut Narodov Azii, 1960, pp. 53-65, 299-313, 339-343. Grafurov's work provides a discussion from the Soviet perspective on the relationships between NATO, CENTO, and SEATO, and the key role of Pakistan in the alliance system directed at the Soviet Union. To emphasize the linkages, the author cites the February 1959 visit of McGhee and Admiral Radford to Karachi as an example of the close collaboration within the western alliance system. The author also points to the direct link between the situation in post-coup Iraq and the massive influx of US aid. The overall work, of course, is an indictment of Anglo-American imperialist designs on the region and of the Ayub regime's complicity in those efforts. Grafurov also argues that Anglo-American designs on the region and exploitation of economic need and military dictatorship flew in the face of the ideas embodied in the Colombo Plan.
9 Zürcher, *Turkey: A Modern History*, pp. 248-261. In effect, political unrest and economic dislocation created a situation in which the democratic government of Menderes found itself attempting political reforms and launching an anti-corruption campaign that included formerly influential army officers. These moves further alienated an increasingly estranged army, segments of which had been attempting to piece together a coup since 1955. It coalesced in May 1960, spurred by the anti-corruption campaign. Ironically, the coup occurred the day before a planned state visit by Indian Prime Minister Nehru.
10 Kux, United States and Pakistan, pp. 101-104.
11 Interview with Walt Rostow, 12 June 2002.
12 'Memo Ball to Kennedy, Washington, April 19, 1961'. *FRUS*, 1961-1963, Vol. XIX, p. 33.
13 'Reports from A.K. Dar, Consular Indian Embassy Cairo to MEA New Delhi, 24 January 1961'. INA, MEA, 6 (5) R&I/60, p. 7. 'Notes from the Meeting of the External Affairs Committee on the Afro-Asian Bloc, 25 October 1961'. NZNA, MEA, ABHS, Series: 950, Item: 56/2/3, Box 1407, p. 1.
14 'British High Commission, Karachi [L.B. Walsh Atkins] to CRO [Neil Prichard] on Pakistani Foreign Policy, 3 March 1961.' PRO, FO371/159703, pp. 2-5.
15 'CIA Intelligence Summary January-June 1961,' JFKL, Komer Series, NLK-01-429-7-6-4, Box 429, pp. 1-2.

16 'Letter B.K. Nehru, Indian Ambassador WDC regarding his talks with Averell Harriman on 21 February 1961 to New Delhi [L.K. Jha, Secretary for Economic Affairs], 22 February 1961'. INA, MEA, 73 (37) AMS/61, pp. 3-4.
17 'Karachi to WDC, March 22, 1961'. *FRUS*, 1961-1963, Volume XIX, pp. 26-27.
18 'Dispatch Lahore to WDC, 31 March 1961'. NACPM, Trips 123 – Harriman, Averell, Box 320, pp. 1-2.
19 'Letter CRO to FO referencing the Pritchard Letter of 3 March 1961 on Pakistan, 14 April 1961'. PRO, FO371/159703 (SEA 48/6/1), p. 1.
20 'Karachi [Harriman] to WDC, 22 March 1961'. *FRUS*, 1961-1963, Volume XIX, p. 29. See also 'Minute by G.F. Hiller, FO to Lord Landsdowne on Afghan-Pakistan Relations, 13 April 1961'. PRO, FO371/157415, pp. 1-2.
21 'Letter CRO to Karachi referencing Pritchard Letter, 3 March 1961, 14 April 1961'. PRO, FO371/159703, p. 1.
22 'New Delhi [Harriman] to WDC Eyes Only Kennedy and Rusk, March 24, 1961'. *FRUS*, 1961-1963, Volume XIX, p. 31. Never a fan of the Shah, Nehru refered to the US position in Iran by observing how 'unfortunate' it was that the US backed 'unpopular governments'.
23 Brecher, Michael 'Elite Images and Foreign Policy Choices: Krishna Menon's View of the World'. *Pacific Affairs*, Vol. 40, No.1/2, Spring-Summer 1967, pp. 60-92), p. 77. Brecher's article provides an excellent insight into Krishna Menon's highly anti-Western views. Brecher calls Menon the 'principal aid of Nehru in policy formulation from 1953 [perhaps earlier] until 1962' (p. 62). He argues that Menon saw problems with both power blocs, East and West, but that 'The Western bloc is invariably the greater culprit; this part of his image can be traced to his acceptance of the Leninist theory of Imperialism as a phenomenon of expansion liked to the stage of "Monopoly Capitalism"' (p. 63). 'The tone and sweep of Menon's derisive comment on "American Imperialism" suggest an intense emotional antipathy, as well as intellectual disdain' (p. 64). 'American Imperialism is unquestionably the pre-eminent evil force' (p. 66). Brecher provides a solid overview of the inconsistencies of Menon's views, and of how they influenced and in many cases drove Indian foreign policy in the 1950s and early 1960s.
24 'Memcon Harriman and Yezdezard Dinshaw Gundevia, Commonwealth Secretary, New Delhi, 18 March 1961'. NACPM, Trips 123 – Harriman, Averell, Box 320, p. 1.
25 Galbraith, John Kenneth, *Ambassador's Journal*. Boston, MA: Houghton Mifflin, 1969, p. 100.
26 *Oral History* – Bowles. JFK Library, p. 72. Bowles commented that 'the Pentagon and the more sterile members of the Foreign Service' forced the United States 'to pay this outrageous price for that base in Pakistan'.
27 Pazhwak, Rahman, *Pakhtunistan: A New State in Central Asia*. London: Royal Afghan Embassy, 1960, pp. 1-28. The Soviet Union supported the Pushtunistan national movement: 'The millions of people of Pakhtunistan who resisted the combined might of the British Empire in upholding their national freedom and entity, cannot be expected to acquiesce to the encroachments of Pakistan.'
28 'Letter Dep Sec Def Gilpatric to Bowles, June 12, 1961'. *FRUS*, 1961-1963, Volume XIX, pp. 57-58.
29 'Memcon VP Johnson and Nehru, 18 May 1961'. *FRUS*, 1961-1963, Volume XIX, p. 42.
30 'Athens (Berger) to WDC (Bowles), 22 May 1961'. JFK Library, Trips & Conferences, Box 242A, p. 1.
31 'Memcon Johnson and Nehru, 18 May 1961'. *FRUS*, 1961-1963, Volume XIX, p 42.
32 'Athens [Berger] to WDC [Bowles], 22 May 1961'. JFK Library, Trips & Conferences, Box 242A, p. 1.

33 'Memcon Johnson and Nehru, New Delhi, May 18, 1961'. *FRUS*, 1961-1963, Volume XIX, pp. 48-49.
34 'Karachi [Rountree] to WDC [Rusk], 22 May 1961.' JFK Library, Trips & Conferences, Box 242A, p. 1.
35 'Memcon Johnson and Nehru, May 18, 1961'. *FRUS*, 1961-1963, Volume XIX, pp. 48-49.
36 'Memo Johnson to Kennedy, 23 May 1961'. JFKL, Trips & Conferences, Box 242A, pp. 8-9.
37 Brecher, *Krishna Menon's View*, pp. 182-183. On the topic of détente with the Soviet Union, Menon commented: 'I think the contribution of the late President Kennedy will be found, historically, to have been much exaggerated.' Menon's comments and attitudes are important particularly in light of the fact that Nehru followed the June meetings very closely and that much of the reporting on the June meetings came from one of Menon's long-time protégés, Arthur Lall.
38 Gopal, in *Nehru*, Volume III, p. 101, argues: 'It was galling that, at the time when the United States and the Soviet Union were seeking to improve relations and Khrushchev had visited the United States, India's relations with China were deteriorating.'
39 Ibid.
40 'Telegram on Kennedy-Khrushchev meeting from Arthur Lall, Indian UN Delegation, to New Delhi [M.J. Desai], 8 June 1961'. INA, MEA, 73 (56) AMS/61, p. 1. This view of the situation was seconded in a Minute to Desai by Y.D. Gundevia in the Indian MEA on 19 June, which is attached to the same document. Gundevia, born in 1908, joined the Indian Civil Service in 1931. He served as Ambassador in Switzerland 1953-1954; High Commissioner in Sri Lanka, 1957-1960; Commonwealth Secretary, 1961-1964; and rose to become Foreign Secretary, 1964-1965.
41 Nehru, Jawaharlal, 'Letter to Chief Ministers, New Delhi, 27 June 1961'. In Parthasarathi (ed.), *Letters to Chief Ministers, 1947-1964*, Volume V, 1958-1964. New Delhi: Oxford University Press, 1989, p. 478.
42 'Karachi to WDC, 22 March 1961'. *FRUS*, 1961-1963, Volume XIX, pp. 26-27.
43 *Oral History* – Talbot. December 5, 1964, p. 19.
44 Kux, United States and Pakistan, p. 121.
45 'Memo NEA to Talbot, President Ayub's Bilateral Talks on Kashmir, July 7, 1961'. NACPM, Kashmir, Entry 5252, 150-69-22-7/7-761, Box 1, p. 3.
46 'SNIE on Pakistan'. *FRUS*, 1961-1963, Volume XIX, p. 65.
47 'Memcon Kennedy and Ayub, 11 July 1961'. *FRUS*, 1961-1963, Volume XIX, pp. 68, 71.
48 *Oral History* – Komer, Part V, JFK Library, p. 14.
49 'Memcon Kennedy and Ayub'. *FRUS*, 1961-1963, Volume XIX, p. 70.
50 Nehru, 'Letter to Chief Ministers, New Delhi, 23 July 1961', in Parthasarathi (ed.) *Letters to Chief Ministers*, p. 478.
51 'Memcon Kennedy and Ayub, 11 July 1962'. *FRUS*, 1961-1963, Volume XIX, p 74.
52 *Oral History* – Talbot, JFK Library, p. 20.
53 'Memcon Kennedy and Ayub, 11 July 1962'. *FRUS*, 1961-1963, Volume XIX, p. 74.
54 'Memcon Bowles and Nehru, 8-9 August 1961'. *FRUS*, 1961-1963, Volume XIX, pp. 81-86. See also *Oral History* – Komer, JFK Library, No. 5, p. 15, and 'Memcon Kennedy and the Afghani Ambassador Muhammad Hashim Maiwandwal, July 21, 1961'. *FRUS*, 1961-1963, Volume XIX, pp. 75-76. The problems between India and Pakistan appear to have entered an almost dormant stage at this point, and did not come to the fore again until 1962, but pressure was building. The Afghanis argued that because of Pakistani 'taunting' Pushtun tribes and Kabul, with US weapons barring military and economic aid from the US, they had no alternative but to turn to the Soviet Union.
55 'New Delhi to WDC, August 4, 1961'. *FRUS*, 1961-1963, Volume XIX, pp. 79-80.

56 Galbraith, *Ambassador's Journal*, pp. 187-188, 195-197.
57 Nehru, 'Letter to Chief Ministers, New Delhi, 27 June 1961', in Parthasarathi (ed.) *Letters to Chief Ministers*, p. 449.
58 'Memcon Galbraith and Desai, 8 September 1961'. INA, MEA, 73 (92) AMS/61, p. 1.
59 'Desai to Nehru attached to Memcon Galbraith and Desai, 26 August 1961'. INA, MEA, 73 (92) AMS/61, p. 1.
60 'Memcon Galbraith and Desai, 8 September 1961'. INA, MEA, 73 (92) AMS/61, p. 1.
61 Galbraith, *Ambassador's Journal*, p. 203.
62 'Memcon Galbraith and Desai, 8 September 1961'. INA, MEA, 73 (92) AMS/61, pp. 1, 6, 7. According to Desai, Galbraith's frustration was evident when: 'He stated that it sometimes seemed as if the opposition was running the government in the USA. The Ambassador did not elaborate on this point but he was referring to the press report that Washington would henceforward take a hard look at the attitude of neutral nations towards various world problems while considering their appeal for U.S. financial aid.' Desai then commented to Nehru: 'The Ambassador was with me for about an hour and he did appear rather disturbed. It appears that he has got urgent summons from Washington for consultations.' Desai's report on Galbraith's grousing about the political opposition in Washington provides insight into the Indian perception that the Kennedy administration found itself constrained by the Republican opposition in its dealings with India. Later, Desai described Galbraith's concern that Indian policy would 'discredit the liberal group in the United States'. as 'repeat[ing] his familiar theme'.
63 'Memocon Galbraith and Desai, 8 September 1961'. INA, MEA, 73 (92) AMS/61, pp. 1-5. See also Lall, *Emergence of Modern India*, p. 144, in which Lall, apparently oblivious to Harriman's total disdain, commented that there was 'excellent cooperation between Kennedy's representative Averell Harriman and myself'.
64 Lall, *Emergence of Modern India*, preface and p. 160. Lall also claimed that he had been selected to succeed Menon as Minister of Defense, when the Chinese War resulted in Menon's ouster, thus destroying Lall's opportunities as well.
65 Cooper, Chester L., *The Lost Crusade: America in Vietnam*. New York: Dodd, Mead, 1970, p. 186. Cooper's work on the Vietnam conflict provides some interesting, if limited, views of India's role and also of Ambassador Galbraith's early involvement on behalf of the administration. It also reinforces the view that Galbraith was a duck out of water as a diplomat. Just as his suggestions that the US allow the recognition of Communist China proved unpalatable, Galbraith suggested 'strong medicine' for the Diem regime in the form of a demand that they liberalize politically or face reduced US aid. Galbraith did suggest that a change in government might be in order, as long the United States did not initiate it.
66 'Comment by Desai on Memcon Galbraith and Desai, 26 August 1961'. INA, MEA, 73 (92) AMS/61, p. 1.
67 'Minute Nehru to Desai on Memcon Galbraith and Desai, 26 August 1961'. INA, MEA, 73 (92) AMS/61, p. 1.
68 'Memcon Galbraith and Desai, 8 September 1961'. INA, MEA, 73 (92) AMS/61, pp. 1-5.
69 SarDesai, D.R., *Indian Foreign Policy in Cambodia, Laos, and Vietnam, 1947-1964*. Berkeley: University of California Press, 1968, p. 205.
70 'Memcon Galbraith and Desai, 26 August 1961'. INA, MEA, 73 (92) AMS/61, p 1.
71 'Memcon Galbraith and Desai, 8 September 1961'. INA, MEA, 73 (92) AMS/61, p 5.
72 Galbraith, *Ambassador's Journal*, pp. 195-203. Galbraith's 'rather disturbed' demeanor, and what appeared to be transparent insecurity in requesting that Nehru not respond to Kennedy's letter until after Nehru and Galbraith, had talked caught Desai's attention. This was reflected in Desai's comments in 'Memcon Galbraith and Desai, 8 September 1961'. INA, MEA, 73 (92) AMS/61, p. 7. Some of this concern probably resulted from

the battering that Galbraith took over his suggestion to Kennedy on August 26 that the US should allow Beijing to be admitted to the UN. If Rusk, Talbot, and Rostow had been waiting for an opportunity to bring Galbraith down a notch or two, the latter could not have done a better job of offering himself up. Galbraith stated that to oppose the 'inevitable' would put the Kennedy administration in a position where 'The New Frontier will get credit only for continuing the Old Frontier policy with the difference that with use it failed.' Desai had managed to convince Galbraith that no matter what happened, the Chinese would be admitted to the United Nations, and Galbraith, in turn, advised the President: 'There is no happy solution to this problem but wise men have long been told ... the proper reaction to inevitable rape. We should take a passive attitude on the Chicoms, making a token vote against them but no impassioned pleas. Our prestige should not be put on the block.' On August 27, Galbraith noted in his journal: 'My China cable brought one of the rudest and certainly the promptest response in the history of the Department. "To the extent that your position has any merit it has been fully considered and rejected".' Interview with Phillips Talbot, 31 May 2002. Talbot stated that Galbraith never understood the bureaucracy or how to use it. Galbraith's views on China were simply unacceptable. Talbot believed that Galbraith over-estimated and over-stated his influence with the President and, when he became aware of this, he grew more frustrated with the situation and ultimately left India. Talbot also commented that Galbraith's personal behavior bordered on the bizarre at times. He cited one instance when the Ambassador left his post in India unannounced and turned up at a military installation in Hawaii, also unannounced. In *Oral History* – Talbot, pp. 67-68, when asked about Galbraith's 'special pipeline', Talbot stated: 'In fact, it amused me. Here was a man who regarded himself as very close in, who had obviously been put halfway around the world for a reason, who was subject to his great flights of prose.' Interview with Phillips Talbot, 31 May 2002. Talbot stated that Galbraith had an 'enormous ego' and was totally inept at managing the bureaucracy. As a result, he seldom achieved his goals because he alienated the very people with whom he needed to work. Interview with Walt Rostow on 12 June 2002. Rostow was even blunter in his assessment of Galbraith: 'Galbraith was not taken seriously.' 'His personal contacts with JFK were overrated.' Galbraith was viewed as a 'nuisance' with a massive ego. 'Rusk despised Galbraith almost as much as he despised Bowles.' 'Like Bowles, Galbraith would not listen.' In addition, he had some 'unproductive ideas' about how policy with India and China should be conducted. Rostow believed that his suggestion about allowing China into the UN was 'ludicrous', given Mao's domination and his policies at the time in Southeast Asia. Showing the level of mutual distaste, Galbraith stated in *Ambassador's Journal*, p. 199: 'It is hard in this job not to develop a morbid dislike for the State Department. It is remote, mindless, petty and, above all, pompous, overbearing and late' (p. 199).

73 Akbar, *Nehru*, p. 491. Akbar lays the blame for the failure of the talks with Kennedy squarely at Nehru's feet. The author, a Muslim who remained in India because of his commitment to the Congress Party, pointed out that Nehru's 1949 and 1956 visits had been ruined by external factors. He listed 'anti-communist hysteria', Dulles' pro-Pakistani policies, and 'the backlash against Krishna Menon's acerbic, and garrulous, speeches'. He laments: 'When the USA did get a President who admired Nehru, John Kennedy, Nehru himself spoiled the opportunity by lecturing the younger man rather than turning his sympathy to advantage.'
74 Gopal, *Nehru*, Volume III, p. 188.
75 'Memcon Kennedy and Nehru, 7 November 1961'. *FRUS*, 1961-1963, Volume XIX, p 129.
76 Brown, *Nehru*, p. 248.

77 'Memcon Kennedy and Nehru, 7 November 1961'. *FRUS*, 1961-1963, Volume XIX, pp. 129-130. See also Gopal, *Nehru*, Volume III, p. 189, who states that in the middle of Nehru's Washington visit, the Kennedy administration announced that it would expand the military advisory team in South Vietnam and that the United States would assume 'combat support roles'.
78 'Memcon Kennedy and Nehru, 7 November 1961'. *FRUS*, 1961-1963, Volume XIX, pp. 128-132, 134.
79 *Oral History* – Talbot, p. 18. The only animated conversation that the two men had pertained to religion, during a banquet at the Indian Embassy in Washington. See also *Oral History* – Komer, No. 5, p. 14.
80 Gopal, *Nehru*, Volume III, pp. 189-190. Gopal stated: 'It was, curiously, Eisenhower with whom Nehru got on best. Truman's vulgarity had grated on him; and so did the affluence and glitter with which Kennedy was surrounded. ... But Eisenhower's sincerity and goodwill, especially in contrast to the blinkered preachiness of Dulles, struck a chord.'
81 Schlesinger, Arthur, Jr., *A Thousand Days: John F. Kennedy in the White House*. Boston, MA: Houghton Mifflin, 1965, p. 526.
82 Gopal, *Nehru*, Volume III, p. 188.
83 'Memcon Kennedy and Menon, 21 November 1961'. *FRUS*, 1961-1963, Volume XIX, p. 139.
84 Interview with Walt Rostow, 12 June 2002. Judith Brown, in *Nehru: A Political Life*, p. 248, offers an interesting and probably fairly accurate view of Nehru's clinging to Menon: 'Nehru's support of Menon, despite so much evidence that he was often a political liability to his country, indicates not only his talent for personal loyalty, but also his isolation at the apex of India's political world, where few were his intellectual companions, as Menon was, and even fewer were prepared to confront him with possibly unpleasant truths.'
85 'Memcon Kennedy and Menon, 21 November 1961'. *FRUS*, 1961-1963, Volume XIX, pp. 139-142.
86 Gopal, *Nehru*, Volume III, p. 201.
87 'Memcon Talbot and B.K. Nehru, Indian Ambassador, WDC, 29 January 1962'. NACPM, NEA/INC, Kashmir, 59-150-69-22-7, Entry 5252 (Box 1), p. 1.
88 Gopal, *Nehru*, Volume III, p. 202.
89 'Memcon Henry Kissinger, NSC Staff, and Krishna Menon, 8 January 1962'. JFK Library, Komer Series, Box 418, pp. 2-3. Menon also launched into a tirade about the American press, American officials, and even President Kennedy, 'who he said were ether reporting about him invidiously or had treated him in a high handed fashion.' Because of US UN Ambassador Adlai Stevenson's attack on the Goa action, Menon described him as 'conceited and arrogant' and worse than Henry Cabot Lodge, Eisenhower's UN Ambassador. Menon made sure that Kissinger understood that Kennedy was not exempt, stating: 'This was particularly true of the President. ... The President's rude behavior to him had not been directed against him personally, but against the Prime Minister. People who were afraid to tackle Nehru tackled him.'
90 *Oral History* – Talbot, p. 66. Talbot points out that Galbraith thought that the Indians would not move on Goa. For his part, Galbraith provides a detailed account of a telegram from the State Department telling him that the Indians were about to move on Goa, and then of his rushing around trying to convince the Indian government to stay the operation. Of course, it was to no avail. Galbraith, *Ambassador's Journal*, pp. 280-285. On December 21, four days after the Goa operation, the Indians approached the United States about military aid. The timing was so bad that Galbraith believed Menon intentionally arranged it in order to justify the Indian plan to produce supersonic aircraft. *Ambassador's Journal*, p. 290. In reality, Menon probably proposed the military

purchases knowing that Washington would turn them down. He could then argue that the United States had refused military aid once again, and thus begin his planned campaign to find another source in Moscow.

91 'New Delhi [Galbraith] to WDC, 28 December 1961'. *FRUS*, 1961-1963, Volume XIX, pp. 164-166.
92 'CRO New Delhi to FO on Nehru's Press Conference, 29 December 1961'. PRO, F0371/166356, p. 1.
93 'British Embassy WDC [Ormsby-Gore] to FO, 3 January 1961'. PRO, FO371/166356, p. 1; 'British Embassy New Delhi to CRO, 8 January 1961'. PRO, FO371/166356, p. 1; and 'British Embassy New Delhi to FO, 5 January 1961'. PRO, FO371/166356, p. 1.
94 'FO to British Embassies in Karachi and New Delhi, 2 January 1961'. PRO, FO371/166356, p. 1.
95 'Memo Talbot to Rusk on Kashmir, January 6, 1962'. NACPM, NEA/INC, Kashmir, 59-150-69-22-7, Entry 5252 (Box 1), p. 1.
96 'British Embassy Karachi to CRO, 24 January 1962'. PRO, FO371/166357, p. 3. See Eisel, Braxton, 'The FOBS of War'. *Air Force Magazine*, June 2005, p. 74, for an explanation of one aspect of the value of the intelligence sites in Pakistan and Iran. Khrushchev threatened the US with missiles that would approach North America from the south, thus evading early warning radars directed toward the North Pole. Development of the Global Rocket No. 1 (GR-1) began in 1960, with development approvals in April 1962. It was a derivative of the SS-9 heavy-lift ICBM. These low-trajectory missiles armed with 2.2-megaton warhead could strike US command and control targets, with less than five minutes' warning from US-based space surveillance assets. The GR-1 was silo-based at Tyuratam in Soviet Central Asia. This is one example of the strategic US requirement for information-gathering and missile early warning across the 'northern tier' in Pakistan and Iran that directly contributed to the US strategic defensive posture.
97 'Memo T. Eliot Weil to Talbot, Washington, January 3, 1962'. NACPM, NEA/INC, Records Relating to Kashmir, 1952-1964, 59-150-69-22-7, Entry 5252, Box 1, p. 1.
98 'Memo Jackson NEA to India Desk [Ludlow], 10 January 1962'. NACPM, NEA/INC, Kashmir, 1952-1964, 59-150-69-22-7, Entry 5252, Box 1, p. 1.
99 'Memcon Talbot and B.K. Nehru, 17 January 1962'. NACPM, NEA/INC, Records Relating to Kashmir, 1952-1964, 59-150-69-22-7, Entry 5252, Box 1, p 2.
100 'Memo from NEA (Talbot) to White House (Ball), 22 January 1962'. NACPM, India, NEA/INC, Kashmir, 1952-1964, 59-150-69-22-7, Entry 5252, Box 1, p. 1.
101 'Memcon Ashoke Chib, Indian High Commission, and David Linebaugh, US Embassy, Karachi, 5 February 1962'. NACPM, NEA/INC, Kashmir, 59-150-69-22-7, Entry 5252, Box 1, p. 1. See also 'Attachment dated March 15, 1962 to Memo from Talbot to Ball, 16 March 1962'. NACPM, NEA/INC, Kashmir, Box 1, p 1.
102 'Karachi [Rountree] to WDC, 14 January 1962'. JFK Library, Komer Series, Box 429, p. 1. See also 'Memo from Kashmir Working Group to Talbot, 15 January 1962'. NACPM, NEA/INC, Records Relating to Kashmir, 1952-1964, 59-150-69-22-7, Entry 5252, Box 1, pp. 1-7. The Administration had formed another of its vaunted working groups, the Kashmir Working Group. The group viewed the potential for Security Council debate as damaging to India and Pakistan, as well as to the interests of the United States. The objective was to get an alternative proposal on the table before the Kashmir debate began at the United Nations.
103 'Letter CRO [Stanley Martin] to FO [Philip F. de Zuluete], 19 January 1962'. PRO, FO371/166357, p. 1.
104 'British Embassy Karachi [Snelling] to CRO, 24 January 1962'. FO371/166357, p. 2.

105 'British Embassy New Delhi to CRO, 20 January 1962'. PRO, FO371/166357, pp. 1-2. See also 'Letter from Ayub to Kennedy, 18 January 1962'. JFKL, Komer Series, Box 429, pp. 1-4.
106 'British Embassy New Delhi to CRO, 23 January 1962'. PRO, FO371/166357, p. 1.
107 'Karachi to CRO, 22 January 1962'. PRO, FO371/166357, p. 2.
108 'NSAM No. 125, 22 January 1962'. NACPM, NSAM 125, p. 1.
109 'Memo Abram Chayes to McGhee entitled "Undertaking of the United States Government Relating to Possible Armed Aggression Against Pakistan and India", 16 February 1962'. NACPM, GRDOS-59, Country Director for India, Ceylon, Nepal and Maldives Islands (NEA/INC), Records Relating to Kashmir, 1952-1964, 59-150-69-22-7, Entry 5252 (Box 1), pp. 4-6, 8. The report pointed out that it might be very difficult to determine who started the conflict and, therefore, whom the United States was obliged to support. Looking for a loophole, it concluded: 'None of our commitment, however, is such as to oblige us to take appropriate action without having full and adequate opportunity to investigate all the circumstances.' The report observed that the best course might be to side with the state that was willing to 'order a cease fire'.
110 'New Delhi to WDC, 29 January 1962'. JFK Library, Komer Series, Box 429, pp. 1-2.
111 'Memcon Talbot, NEA, and B.K. Nehru, Indian Ambassador WDC, 29 January 1962'. NACPM, NEA/INC, Records Relating to Kashmir, 1952-1964, 59-150-69-22-7, Entry 5252, Box 1, p. 2. Talbot met with the Indian Ambassador the same day that the letter arrived from Prime Minister Nehru. Ambassador B.K. Nehru, in an attempt to put the best face on matters, 'praised' the straightforward nature of the letter. Talbot told him that he hoped that 'straightforward communication' might salvage Indo-US relations 'which [were] in somewhat fragile condition now'.
112 'Memo Komer to Bundy, Washington, 6 January 1962'. *FRUS*, 1961-1963, Volume XIX, pp. 179-181.
113 *Oral History* – Komer, No. 5, p. 16.
114 'Paper Prepared by NEA, undated'. *FRUS*, 1961-1963, Volume XIX, p. 183.
115 'Memo Talbot to Rusk, Washington, 6 January 1962'. NACPM, Kashmir, Entry 5252, Box 1, p. 2.
116 'Telegram from US Embassy Karachi [Hall] to WDC, 5 March 1962'. NACPM, NEA, 123- Bowles, Chester, Box 313, p. 1.
117 'Memo Talbot to Ball, Washington, 27 March 1962'. NACPM, NEA/INC, Kashmir, 59-150-69-22-7, Entry 5252, Box 1, p 1.
118 'Research Memorandum (RNA-19) from Hilsman, INR, to Rusk, 6 April 1962'. JFK Library, Komer Series, Box 418, pp. 1, 11. INR speculated that Menon, perhaps for the first time, actually thought that succeeding Nehru might be possible. Only time would tell, but Hilsman speculated: 'However, one straw in the wind suggesting a new, and ostensibly more responsible, view of himself may lie in the manner in which his criticism of the West and its positions has been tempered in recent weeks.'
119 Jalal, *State of Martial Law*, p. 305.
120 Wilber, *Pakistan*, pp. 245-252. This is a collaborative survey that has little interpretive value; however, it is a period work and some of the commentary reflects contemporary evaluations of the situation.
121 Bhargava, *Pakistan in Crisis*, p. 89.
122 Ayub Khan, Muhammad, 'Pakistan Perspective'. *Foreign Affairs*, Volume 38, No. 4, July 1960, pp. 547-556. The constitutional experiment in Pakistan was a much-watched phenomenon in the US. Ayub appeared to have brought stability to a failing state, and his apparent success brought him much acclaim as a model military ruler. His article in *Foreign Affairs* portrayed his paternalistic approach as the only reasonable methodology for representative government in the region. He laid out four requisites for the success of democracy 'in a country like Pakistan': simplicity and low cost of maintenance were

paramount; voting had to be based on simple issues that the average uneducated Pakistani could understand 'without prompting'; participation had to be limited, based on intellectual and 'mental horizons'; and the system had to produce 'strong and stable governments'. Ayub's experiment was the model that the Kennedy administration pursued in Iran. It became a standard for 'controlled reform'.

123 'Memcon Talbot and Aziz Ahmad, Pakistani Ambassador WDC and Sir Zafrulla Khan, Pakistani Permanent Representative to the UN, 12 April 1962'. *FRUS*, 1961-1963, Volume XIX, pp. 230-233.
124 'Letter Ayub to Kennedy, 20 April 1962'. *FRUS*, 1961-1963, Volume XIX, pp. 234-236.
125 'Memo Brubeck to Bundy on Kashmir Resolution, 17 May 1962'. JFK Library, Komer Series, Box 429, p.p. 1-2.
126 Kux, *United States and Pakistan*, p. 126.
127 'New Delhi to WDC, May 8, 1962'. *FRUS*, 1961-1963, Volume XIX, pp. 240-242.
128 'CIA/FBIS Report on India Jet Plane Purchase, 21 May 1962'. JFK Library, Komer Series, Box 420, p. 1.
129 'Memo Rostow to Komer on MIG purchase, 29 May 1962'. JFK Library, Komer Series, Box 420, p. 1.
130 'Memo Komer to Bundy, 22 May 1962'. JFK Library, Komer Series, Box 420, p. 1.
131 'Memo from Talbot to Rusk, 5 June 1962'. JFK Library, Komer Series, Box 420, p. 1.
132 'Memo Talbot, NEA, 13 May 1962'. *FRUS*, 1961-1963, Volume XIX, pp. 243-245.
133 'CIA Memo for the National Intelligence Board, 5 June 1962'. JFKL, Komer Series, Box 420, p. 2.
134 Galbraith, *Ambassador's Journal*, p. 399.
135 'The Periscope'. *Newsweek*, 6 August 1962, p. 9. See also, Galbraith, *Ambassador's Journal*, p. 399. There is an argument that Galbraith had always intended to leave after two years, and that his resignation was not a direct result of the failed US arms deal for India. Given the frustration, not only with the policy issues but with the bureaucracy as a whole, Galbraith most likely was simply fed up and decided to quit. There is no record of anyone in the administration being upset to see him go.
136 Kux, *United States and Pakistan*, p. 128. It was during the visit to the farm that Ayub and the First Lady spent a well-publicized afternoon horseback-riding. Jacqueline Kennedy's horse was one presented to her by Ayub. See also 'Memcon Kennedy and Ayub at Newport, Rhode Island, 24 September 1962'. *FRUS*, 1961-1963, Volume XIX, pp. 326-331.
137 'Memo Komer to Kennedy, 26 September 1962'. *FRUS*, 1961-1963, Volume XIX, p. 332. In September 1962, Ayub stopped briefly in Washington on his way to a Commonwealth meeting in Canada. *Oral History* – Komer. Vol. V, p. 16. According to Komer, nothing really transpired during the meeting with the exception that Ayub accused the Indians of overstating their problems with China. This did not particularly help Ayub's credibility, because a border war broke out within a matter of months.

Part IV

1 See 'Mr. Kennedy is Ready to Negotiate', 'Indian Soldiers in Better Position Against Chinese,' and 'Forces on North Border of Yemen'. *The Age*, 28 October 1962, p. 1.
2 *Oral History* – Komer. 18 June 1964, Part 1, p. 1.

Chapter 14

1 *Oral History* – Badeau, pp. 24-25.
2 *Oral History* – Talbot, pp. 28-29.
3 'Cairo [Badeau] to Rusk and Kennedy on publication of Nasser-Kennedy correspondence, 10 September 1962'. NACPM, 786b.11/9-1062, p. 1. See also 'Memo

Brubeck to Bundy with attached FBIS transcript of UAR broadcast, 24 September 1962'. NACPM, 786b.00/9-2462, p. 1.

4 'Jidda to WDC, 27 September 1962'. NACPM, 786h.00/9-2762, p. 1. Yemen Radio told everyone to stay indoors because people on the streets 'will be shot immediately', and instructed the police and military to 'arrest them [members of the old regime] even if they are innocent'. See also 'Jidda to WDC, 27 September 1962'. NACPM, 786h.00/9-2762, p. 1.

5 Douglas, J. Leigh, *The Free Yemeni Movement 1935-1962*. Beirut: American University of Beirut, 1987), pp. 234-236. Baydani was born in Cairo, and his wife was a close friend of Anwar Sadat's wife. Thus Sadat became Baydani's friend and a powerful patron within the Egyptian regime. The Ba'thists had supported the September 1961 coup against Egyptian rule in Syria; thus Nasser could hardly be expected to look the other way when his Yemeni protégés took a Ba'thist tilt.

6 'Cairo [Badeau] to WDC, 5 October 1962'. NACPM, 786h.00/10-562, p. 1. Pressing for early YAR recognition, Badeau told Washington that the UAR, USSR, Algeria, Tunisia, Syria, Yugoslavia, Czechoslovakia, Lebanon, Sudan, Bulgaria and Hungary had recognized the YAR.

7 'Jidda [Hart] to WDC, 31 October 1962'. NACPM, 786h.00/10-162, p. 1. Jidda pointed out that the new YAR Prime Minister, Abdullah al-Sallal, could not have pulled it off without UAR support. The Embassy also suspected that the propaganda from Radio Sanaa was directed by the UAR because it was a 'slick professional job and not the usual humdrum programs normally sent out from Yemen'.

8 *Oral History* – Komer. July 16, 1964, Part II, pp. 9-10.

9 'Cairo [Badeau] to WDC, 27 September 1962'. NACPM, 786h.00/9-2762, p. 2.

10 Nasser, *Speeches and Press Interviews*, pp. 44-45. See also 'Memo from Harrison M. Symmes, NE, to Talbot, NEA, on Diefenbaker Report on Nasser Meeting, 30 September 1962'. NACPM, 786.02/9-3062, p. 1. In another meeting a year after the coup, Nasser stated that the revolution in Yemen was a historical necessity and that the 'feudal' regime could not be allowed to return.

11 'Consulate Aden to WDC, 9 October 1962.' NACPM, 786h.56/10-962, p. 1.

12 'Cairo [Badeau] to WDC, 12 October 1962'. NACPM, 786h.02/10-1262, p. 1.

13 'US Mission UN [Stevenson] to WDC on meeting with YAR foreign minister, 18 October 1962'. NACPM, 786h.00/10-1862, p. 1; and 'Cairo [Badeau] to Washington, 18 October 1962'. NACPM, 786h.00/10-1862, p. 1.

14 'Cairo [Badeau] to WDC, 22 October 1962.' NACPM, 786h.02/10-2262, pp. 1-2.

15 *Oral History* – Komer. Part II, pp. 9-10.

16 'Cairo to WDC, 2 October 1962'. NACPM, 786h.00/10-262, p. 2. A paratrooper officer who was a member of the prominent Yemeni Zabarah family stated that he supported the Republic despite the fact that they had shot some of his relatives. He believed that the revolution was a necessity, but perhaps all the executions were not. He also predicted that the Royalists would 'cause trouble' but that the YAR would survive. He urged US recognition of the YAR as a counterbalance to the Soviets and Chinese, a typical UAR argument. This was typical of numerous reports coming out of Yemen following the coup, and no doubt influenced Washington's view.

17 *Oral History* – Komer. July 16, 1964, Part II, pp. 9-10.

18 'Memcon Talbot and Feisal, 4 October 1962'. NACPM, 786a.11/10-462, pp. 1-3.

19 'British Embassy Amman [Willie Morris] to FO [Figg], 19 October 1962'. PRO, FO371/164094, p. 1. See also 'Airgram Amman [Houghton] to WDC, 24 October 1962'. NACPM, 785.13/10-2462, (Box 2063), pp. 1-2, 4, in which Jordanian Prime Minister Wafsi Tal made it clear that Jordan continued to recognize and support Imam Badr, because he 'was still alive and in control of a large section of his country'. Tal added: 'This decision is based on conviction and we don't care who recognizes [Yemeni

Republican Premier] Sallal or not.' Tal also pointed out that some 'republics' were 'no better than the old Yemeni Imamate'. The Jordanians threatened to act on behalf of the 'legitimate' government of Yemen against foreign intervention if asked to do so. Tal also tried to assuage the gap between government policies and 'local opinion'. Calling for reform in Yemen, he stated that the new government was opposed not because it promised reform but because of the 'large-scale outside intervention.' The US Embassy in Amman commented that most Jordanians believed that the government was backing the 'wrong horse' in Yemen.

20 'Army Attaché Amman to WDC, 5 October 1962'. NACPM, 786h.00/10-562, p 1. The Saudi Royal family must have shuddered at the thought of the Hashemite Arab Legion protecting the Holy Places. It was the Saudis who had driven the Hashemites, who were direct decendants of the Prophet, out of Mecca and Medina in the 1920s. The Hashemites still viewed themselves as the legitimate protectors of the Holy cities.
21 'Memo Komer to Kennedy, 4 October 1962'. JFK Library, SAGF, Box 157, pp. 1-2. See also 'Memo Brubeck to Bundy, October 1, 1962'. JFK Library, PPJFK, Box 157, p 1.
22 'Memo Komer to Kennedy, 4 October 1962'. JFK Library, Feisal Briefing Book, Box 157A, p 1.
23 'Memcon Crown Prince Feisal and Kennedy, October 5, 1962'. JFK Library, Box 157, pp. 1-4.
24 'Memo about Discussion: UAR – Saudi Relations, October 1962'. JFK Library, Box 157A, p 1.
25 'WDC to Jidda and London, October 6, 1962'. JFK Library, Box 157, p. 2.
26 Holden and Johns, *House of Saud*, p. 227.
27 Safran, Nadav, *Saudi Arabia: The Ceaseless Quest for Security*. Ithaca, NY: Cornell University Press, 1985, p. 95.
28 Holden and Johns, *House of Saud*, p. 227. Prince Talal, either on October 17 or the following day, renounced his royal title in protest. On October 23 he called for a 'revolt' in favor of a 'national democratic government', proclaiming the current government was 'steeped in backwardness, underdevelopment, reactionary individuals and tyranny'.
29 'Cairo [Badeau] to WDC, 18 October 1962'. NACPM, 786a.00/10-1862, p. 2.
30 'US Mission UN [Stevenson] to WDC, 18 October 1962'. NACPM, 786a.00/10-1862, pp. 1-2.
31 'Consulate Ta'iz to WDC, 22 October 1962'. NACPM, 786H.02/10-2262, (M-1855), p 1.
32 'Jidda to WDC, 22 October 1962'. NACPM, 611.86h/10-22-62, (M-1855), p 1.
33 'Consulate Ta'iz to WDC, 9 November 1962'. NACPM, 786h.00/11-762, (M-1855), p 1.
34 'WDC to Consulate Ta'iz, 9 November 1962'. NACPM, 686B.86H/11-762, (M-1855, 59/250/3/27/4), p. 1. Washington told Ta'iz to 'categorically assure' the Yemenis that the United States was in no way supporting Saudi efforts to assist Yemeni loyalists.
35 'Airgram Jidda [Hart] to WDC, 6 November 1962'. NACPM, 786a.00/11-662, p 2.
36 'Memo Rusk to Kennedy - YAR recognition, 12 November 1961'. NACPM, 611.86H/11-1262, (M-1855), p. 1.
37 'FO to the Political Office Middle East Command, 2 November 1962'. PRO, CO1015/2150, p. 1.
38 'Aden [Johnston] to Secretary of State for Colonies, 30 September 1962'. 713, CO1015/2150, p. 1.
39 'Aden [Johnston] to Secretary of State for Colonies, 8 November 1962'. PRO, CO1015/2153, pp. 1-2.
40 'CRO to British Embassies in Commonwealth Countries, 2 November 1962'. PRO, CO1015/2150, p. 1. See also Badeau, *Middle East Remembered*, p 202.

41 'FO [Macmillan] to British Embassy WDC for Kennedy, 15 November 1962'. PRO, CO1015/2153, pp. 1-2.
42 'Memcon Jidda [Hart] and Dr. Rashad Fir'awn, Advisor to Crown Prince Feisal, 3 November 1962'. JFKL, SAGF, Box 157, pp. 1-3. See also 'Jidda [Hart] to WDC, 15 November 1962'. JFK Library, Box 157, p 1. The SAG published a new series of laws and reforms, perhaps the most sweeping in history. See also 'Airgram Jidda [Thatcher] to WDC, 8 November 1962'. NACPM, 786a.00/11-862, p 1.
43 'Airgram from US Embassy Jidda [Hart] to WDC, 19 November 1962'. NACPM, GRDOS-59, NEA, CDF 1960-1963, 786a.00/11-1962, p. 1.
44 'Jidda [Thacher] to Kennedy – Letter from Crown Prince Feisal, 29 November 1962'. JFKL, Saudi Arabia Security, Box 123B, p. 1-4. This letter was responding to a letter from Kennedy on November 8, 1962 which strongly encouraged Feisal to continue with his program of reforms. Feisal's response stated that he intended to provide the Kingdom with modern institutions and more responsive government. He noted Kennedy's advice that Saudi Arabia should not contribute to the 'tense atmosphere' in the region, all the while supporting and supplying the tribal elements fighting the YAR government and the Egyptians.
45 'Jidda [Hart] to WDC, 30 December 1962'. NACPM, 786h.00/12-3062, p. 1.
46 'Memo Komer to Bundy, 5 January 1963'. JFK Library, SAGF, Box 157, p. 1.
47 'Cairo [Badeau] to WDC, 22 January 1963'. NACPM, 786h.00/1-2263, p. 1.
48 'Memcon Robert C. Strong, NEA, and British Embassy WDC Patrick Wright, 12 October 1962'. NACPM, 786h.00/10-1262, p. 2. See also 'London [Jones] to WDC "Conversation with Walmsley, FO Arabian Department, 27 September 1962"', NACPM, 786h.00/9-2762, pp. 1-2.
49 'Memocon Saad Jum'a, the Jordanian Ambassador, and Talbot, 27 November 1962'. NACPM, 786h.00/11-2762, p. 1.
50 'Letter Kennedy to King Hussein attached to Memorandum from Brubeck to Bundy, 30 November 1962'. JFK Library, Komer Series, Box 429, pp. 1-2.
51 'Memo Brubeck to Bundy and O'Donnell, 4 December 1962'. JFK Library, Komer Series, Box 429, p. 2.
52 'Jidda [Hart] to WDC, 20 November 1962'. NACPM, 786h.00/11-2062, p. 2.
53 'US Mission UN [Stevenson)] to WDC, 10 December 1962'. NACPM, 786h.00/12-1062, p. 1.
54 'Airgram Amman [Wrampelmeier] to WDC, 22 December 1962'. NACPM, 785.13/12-2262, p. 1.
55 'Cairo [Badeau] to WDC, 10 November 1962'. NACPM, 786h.00/11-1062, p. 1.
56 'Cairo [Boswell] to WDC, 8 December 1962'. NACPM, 786h.02/12-862, p. 2.
57 'Memo Strong to Talbot, NEA, 11 December 1962'. NACPM, 786h.00/12-1162, p 1. Ambassador Badeau was in Washington ostensibly on consultations but presumably pressing for just this recognition. He was figuratively, if not literally, at Strong's elbow when this memo was written. In addition, Badeau met with President Kennedy, so a direct appeal to the President was undoubtedly made. The rapidity of the YAR's recognition following this memo suggests very high-level involvement.
58 'Cairo [Boswell] to WDC, 20 December 1962'. NACPM, 786h.02/12-2062, p. 2. A cartoon in *Al-Ahram* showed Kennedy sitting with a worried British P.M. Macmillan with the latter musing: 'What do we do to get him to recognize Britain?'
59 'Cairo [Boswell] to WDC, 20 December 1962'. NACPM, 786h.02/12-2062, p. 2. The Administration obtained no guarantees from the YAR, and little in the way of Egyptian goodwill, but Badeau and Talbot, with the support of the President, pushed their Egyptian agenda forward.
60 'Amman [Macomber] to WDC, 21 December 1962'. NACPM, 786h.02/12-2162, p. 1.
61 *Oral History* – Komer, Part II, p. 11.

NOTES
447

62 'Letter Political Office, Middle East Command, Aden [J.C.W. Bushell] to FO [Walmsley], 27 December 1962'. PRO, FO371/168625, p. 1. In this letter, Aden requested that London mount a diplomatic campaign to counteract Egyptian propaganda about the RAF bombarding the 'peaceful population' in Yemen and Oman. Bushell wanted the various British missions to point out that the RAF had 'never dropped napalm on defenseless villagers as the Egyptians do' or 'explosive cigarettes'. From London, B.R. Pridham wryly commented: 'I wonder if Mr. Bushell is serious in making the point in para 2 around which his letter is built. We can scarcely reply to propaganda by saying that we kill Arabs in a much more genteel manner than the Egyptians.'

63 Kennedy, *Speeches of Senator Kennedy*, p. 48.
64 *Oral History* – Komer. Part II, p. 9.

Chapter 15

1 Interview with Phillips Talbot, 31 May 2002.
2 Maxwell, *India's China War*, p. 179. Maxwell's work on the border war is by far the best. His discussion of the role of Krishna Menon and Menon's army protégé, General Brij Mohn Kaul, and their roles in the war with China is particularly interesting. Perhaps most instructive is Maxwell's narrative of Kaul's relationship with Nehru and his rapid rise through the ranks. In addition, the author provides an excellent examination of Menon's support for Kaul that resulted in the 'promotion crisis'.
3 Maxwell, *India's China War*, p. 231. While there is some debate about Nehru's exact role in the decision-making process, Maxwell believes that General Kaul and Menon pushed Nehru into the occupation of Goa when he might have chosen a different option. Others, including Judith Brown in *Nehru: A Political Life*, debated this. Brown believes that Nehru had little option but to end the Portuguese anachronism. Whether Nehru decided on his own to take Goa or was maneuvered into doing so is immaterial; the fact is that, without consulting Parliament, Nehru acted. This created a surge in political support not only for the Congress Party, but also for his embattled friend, Krishna Menon. It also encouraged a similar position with regard to China. As a result, they saw no downside in taking a provocative position with the Chinese, believing that it would merely increase domestic support for the government.
4 Maxwell, *India's China War*, p. 231. Maxwell argues that General Kaul and Krishna Menon intentionally hid those deficiencies from the Prime Minister. This conclusion parallels a similar conclusion in Brown's *Nehru: A Political Biography*, pp. 296, 317, concerning diplomacy during the late 1950s and the 1960s. Nehru conducted Indian diplomacy without significant input from others, with the exception of Krishna Menon.
5 Maxwell, *India's China War*, p. 275. Maxwell states that Beijing used the argument that Ayub and the military dominance of Pakistan represented a more developed stage in the progression toward a Marxist state than that of India. As far as India was concerned, the Chinese viewed New Delhi as falling more and more under the influence of the United States. To add insult to injury, the Chinese concluded that Soviet policy actually favored India, and that Moscow approved of the Indian alignment with the United States.
6 Maxwell, *India's China War*, pp. 298-301. See also B.N. Mullik's *The Chinese Betrayal*, pp. 321-322, which defends the 'forward policy'. Mullik, the erstwhile 'intelligence chief', states that the policy was later criticized on the grounds that India was militarily weak. He objects to this, stating: 'Because a country is militarily weak, does it follow that it shall not defend itself?' Mullik also claims that the army leadership agreed with the policy and only criticized it after the defeat of 1962 became apparent. Mullik states that the real problem with regard to the Chinese was the fact that the policy had not been

implemented two years earlier, in October 1959. He believed that much of the lost territory could have been 'saved from the Dragon's clutches'.
7 Brown, *Nehru*, p. 319.
8 Mullik, *Chinese Betrayal*, pp. 362-366, 381-387. Mullik defended both himself and Menon against charges that they had 'caused' the Chinese debacle. He argued that Menon was not responsible for the state of the army at the time of the invasion, nor was he responsible for the 'forward policy' that precipitated the Chinese attack. Mullik also defended himself against ministerial level charges of failure. One unnamed senior minister confronted him saying: 'You have let down the country by being in league with the Defense Minister.' Mullik hotly denied this; he claimed that the minister was upset became Menon had had him watched by one of the security services. The minister assumed that it was the Intelligence Bureau when in fact it was Department of Military Intelligence (DMI).
9 Maxwell, *India's China War*, pp. 303, 323-325.
10 'Memcon Rusk and Indira Gandhi, UNGA, New York, 4 October 1962'. JFK Library, Komer Series, Box 418, p. 2. During the conversation, Rusk raised Krishna Menon as a major issue in US-Indian relations. Rusk stated that Menon had been the 'principal face and spokesman of India' in the United States for many years and that he was a considerable problem in obtaining aid for India. Mrs. Gandhi replied that she sympathized with the US position on Menon but that it was impossible for her father, Nehru, to 'handle' or 'dismiss' Menon given his visibility and the US criticism of him.
11 Mullik, *Chinese Betrayal*, p. 366.
12 Maxwell, *India's China War*, p. 328.
13 'Memo Brubeck to Bundy, 15 October 1962'. JFK Library, Komer Series, Box 429, p. 3.
14 Maxwell, *India's China War*, pp. 356-358.
15 Galbraith, *Ambassador's Journal*, p. 431. In an interview with Talbot on 31 May 2002, he stated that Galbraith allowed personal issues to affect his conduct of government business in New Delhi. Talbot commented that on one occasion, Galbraith absented himself from the Embassy in New Delhi without notifying Washington and turned up at an army hospital in Hawaii with some unspecified medical ailment. Talbot also commented that the Chinese victory in the border war left Nehru 'a broken man' and contributed to his rapid decline and death.
16 Galbraith, *Ambassador's Journal*, p. 430.
17 'Memo Komer to Talbot, 24 October 1962'. LBJ Library, NSF, NSC Histories, SA, 1962-66, Box 24, Tab A 1-7, p. 1.
18 'New Delhi, 28 October 1962'. LBJ Library, Box 24, Tab A 1-7, pp. 1, 5.
19 'Letter Kennedy to Nehru in Cable from Rusk to New Delhi, 28 October 1962'. LBJ Library, Box 24, Tab A 1-7, p. 1.
20 'WDC to US Embassy New Delhi, 29 October 1962'. LBJ Library, Box 24, Tab A 1-7, p 1.
21 'Memo Anglo-American meeting on Sino-Indian Conflict, 12 November 1962'. PRO, FO371/164929, pp. 1, 10.
22 'FO to British Embassy WDC, 20 November 1962'. No. 8466, PRO, FO371/164929, p. 1. See also 'Memo Rusk to President Kennedy entitled "Request for Approval of US-UK Recommendations Regarding Sino-Indian Conflict", 19 November 1962'. JFK Library, Komer Series, Box 429, pp. 1-8. This document provides the US assessment of the London meetings and is remarkably similar to the Foreign Office and CRO documents. It reflected the Anglo-American agreement to coordinate assistance to India and to work together to lessen the impact on Pakistan.
23 *Oral History* – Komer. No. 5, pp. 16-17.
24 Galbraith, *Ambassador's Journal*, pp. 437-441, 455, 460. Ambassador Galbraith had already received notice from sources in contact with the Second Secretary in the

Political Section, Albert Lakeland, Jr., that the Indian cabinet and had met and called for Krishna Menon's removal and that Nehru would ask for his resignation. In the Ambassador's view, something good had come out of the Chinese military efforts. Galbraith took some pleasure in meeting with Menon later and seeing him desperately fighting for his political life. Menon greeted Galbraith and said: 'I am still sitting in the Defense Ministry; nothing has changed.'

25 'Karachi to WDC, November 5, 1962'. *FRUS*, 1961-1963, Volume XIX, p. 370. See also 'Memo Komer to Kennedy, Washington, November 12, 1962'. *FRUS*, 1961-1963, Volume XIX, p. 375. Komer's memorandum describes the Pakistanis as 'going through a genuine emotional crisis as they see their cherished ambitions of using the US as a lever against India going up in the smoke because of the Chinese border war'.

26 Galbraith, *Ambassador's Journal*, p. 471.

27 'WDC to Karachi, 28 October 1962'. LBJ Library, NSC, SA, Box 24, Tab A 1-7, p. 3.

28 'Letter Ayub to Kennedy, 5 November 1962,' LBJ Library, NSC Histories, South Asia, Box 24, Tab A 1-7, p. 3.

29 Ayub Khan, Muhammad, *Friends not Masters: A Political Autobiography*. London: Oxford University Press, 1967, p. 146.

30 'Memo Komer to Bundy, 6 November 1962'. LBJ Library, NSC Histories, SA, Box 24, Tab A 1-7, p. 1. See also 'Memo Komer to Kennedy, 12 November 1962'. LBJ Library, NSC Histories, SA, Box 24, Tab A 1-7, p. 1, in which Komer urges the President not to compromise with Ayub and argues that 'our assets', meaning intelligence facilities in Pakistan, should survive if the situation was handled properly.

31 'Memo Komer to Kaysen, 16 November 1962'. LBJ Library, NSC, SA, Box 24, Tab A 1-7, p 1.

32 'WDC to New Delhi, 18 November 1962,' *FRUS*, 1961-1963, Volume XIX, pp. 390, 392.

33 'Report of the Harriman Mission, (undated)'. JFK Library, Komer Series, Box 424, pp. 5-11.

34 'Memo Komer to Bundy, 23 November 1962'. JFK Library, Komer Series, Box 422, p 1.

35 'Memo Komer to Bundy, 24 November 1962'. JFK Library, Komer Series, Box 429, p 1.

36 'Memo for Record from Komer concerning meeting on Sino-Indian conflict chaired by President Kennedy, 16 November 1962'. LBJ Library, NSC, SA, Box 24, Tab A 1-7, p. 3.

37 'CIA Report Sino-Indian Border Dispute, 27 November 1962'. JFK Library, Komer Series, Box 429, p. 1. See also 'CIA Memo from the Office of National Estimates on Sino-Indian Border Conflict, 27 November 1962'. JFK Library, Komer Series, Box 429, pp. 1, 10.

38 'Letter contained in Cable Kennedy to Harriman, 25 November 1962'. JFK Library, Komer Series, Box 422, p. 2. See also 'Memo Komer to Bundy, 26 November 1962'. JFK Library, Komer Series, Box 422, p. 1, in which Komer reacts to the Pakistani view that the Chinese offer to cease military operations was real and made US military aid to India unnecessary. The Pakistanis stated that there were 'high hopes that real cease fire can be negotiated and that arms aid to India therefore will be promptly terminated'. Fearing an end to military aid to India before it began, Komer wanted Harriman to make it clear to Ayub that the aid would continue even in the event of a ceasefire.

39 'Report Harriman Mission, (undated)'. JFK Library, Komer Series, Box 424, pp. 9-10.

40 'Memcon Ayub and Harriman, 29 November 1962'. NACPM, NEA/INC, Kashmir, Entry 5252, Box 1, pp. 1-2.

41 Gundevia, Yezdezard Dinshaw, *Outside the Archives*. Hyderabad: Sangam, 1984, pp. 252-255. Gundevia served in various capacities in the Indian Ministry of External Affairs

from independence to 1969. During the period of the Chinese Border War, he was the Commonwealth Secretary. *Outside the Archives* is a collection of memoirs of his service. He provides a particularly interesting description of the climate in the Indian government during the Chinese Border war. He is very complimentary about Duncan Sandys' efforts during the process of establishing a basis for further discussions on Kashmir. His description of Sandys' meeting with himself, Nehru, and Desai on 29 November 1962 is particularly entertaining. Gundevia described it as 'three-cornered pencil ding-dong', with Nehru looking on in amusement.

42 'Memo Talbot to NSC, Subject: Recommendations on South Asia for Nassau Talks, December 15, 1962'. NACPM, NEA/INC, Kashmir, Entry 5252, Box 1, p 1.
43 'Annex 1(a) to Memorandum from Talbot for Nassau Talks, December 15, 1962'. NACPM, NEA/INC, Kashmir, Entry 5252, Box 1, p. 1.
44 Gundevia, *Outside the Archives*. p. 254.
45 'Internal Memo US Embassy New Delhi from C.C. Laise to Galbraith, 4 December 1962'. NACPM, NEA/INC, Kashmir, Entry 5252, Box 1, pp. 1-4.
46 'Memo Komer to Bundy, 7 December 1962'. JFK Library, Komer Series, Box 429, pp. 1-3.
47 'Memcon Gunnar Jarring, Swedish Ambassador, and Talbot, 6 December 1962'. NACPM, NEA/INC, Kashmir, Entry 5252, Box 1, p. 2.
48 'Memo Talbot to Bundy, 10 December 1962'. JFK Library, Komer Series, Box 429, p 1.
49 'Memo Komer to Bundy, 13 December 1962'. JFK Library, Komer Series, Box 429, p 2. See also 'NSAM, No. 209, 10 December 1962'. *FRUS*, 1961-1963, Volume XIX, pp. 429-430.
50 'Memo "Next Steps on Kashmir" from Talbot to Subcommittee on South Asia, 12 December 1962'. NACPM, NEA/INC, Kashmir, Entry 5252, Box 1, pp. 1-2.
51 'Memcon Kennedy and Indian Amb Braj Kumar Nehru, December 17, 1962'. NACPM, NEA/INC, Kashmir, Entry 5252, Box 1, pp. 1-2. Also in *FRUS*, 1961-1963, Volume XIX, pp. 439-440.
52 'Memo Rusk to Kennedy, 17 December 1962'. JFK Library, Komer Series, Box 429, p 1.
53 'Memo Komer to Bundy, 19 December 1962'. JFK Library, Komer Series, Box 429, p 1.
54 'Memo Komer to Bundy, 19 December 1962'. JFK Library, Komer Series, Box 429, pp. 1, 2.
55 'British Emb New Delhi to CRO, 24 December 1962'. PRO, FO371/164877, pp. 1-2. See also 'British Emb New Delhi to CRO, 21 December 1962'. PRO, FO371/164877, p. 1, in which the Canadian Deputy High Commissioner in New Delhi provided information that India had submitted shopping lists of military hardware to the United States, Britain, and the Soviet Union: 'Russians had offered military assistance unconditionally and were encouraging India to stick to her guns on Kashmir.' According to the Indian source: 'Russia was only Great Power which really understood and sympathized with India on Kashmir. ... Americans were incapable of understanding feeling existing between Hindus and Muslims which was like attitude of Crusaders to Saracens.'
56 'British Emb New Delhi to CRO, 20 December 1962'. PRO, FO371/164877, pp. 1-2.
57 'British Emb Karachi to CRO, 26 December 1962,' PRO, FO371/164877, p 2.
58 'Memcon Kennedy and Macmillan, Nassau, December 20, 1962, 3 p.m.'. *FRUS*, 1961-1963, Volume XIX, pp. 448-455
59 'Memcon Kennedy and Macmillan, Nassau, December 20, 1962, 6 p.m.'. *FRUS*, 1961-1963, Volume XIX, pp. 455-458.
60 Gundevia, *Outside the Archives*, p. 257.
61 'British Embassy Karachi to CRO, 30 December 1962'. PRO, FO371/164877, pp. 1-2.

62 'Memcon Amb McConaughy and Ayub, 27 December 1962'. *FRUS*, 1961-1963, Volume XIX, p. 462.
63 'Memo Talbot to Rusk, 27 December 1962,' NACPM, NEA/INC, Kashmir, Entry 5252, Box 1, p. 1.

Chapter 16

1 Interview with Talbot, 31 May 2003.
2 'Memo from Brubeck to Bundy, 4 January 1963'. JFK Library, Yemen-YAR security 1961-1963, Box 128A, p. 1.
3 'Cairo [Badeau] to WDC, January 24, 1963'. NACPM, 786h.02/1-2463, p. 1.
4 'Jidda [Hart] to WDC, January 26, 1963'. NACPM, 786h.00/1-2663, p.1.
5 'Memo Talbot to Rusk, 7 March 1963'. NACPM, 786h.00/3-763, p. 1.
6 'Memo Brubeck to Bundy, 4 March 1963'. NACPM, 786h.00/3-463, p. 2.
7 'Letter Kennedy to Feisal Carried by Bunker, 27 February 1963'. JFK Library, Saudi Arabia, Box 128B, pp. 1-4.
8 'Aden, Sir Charles Johnston, to CO, 15 February 1963'. PRO, CO1055/3, pp. 1-3.
9 Heikal, *The Cairo Documents*, pp. 197-199.
10 'Letter Nasser to Kennedy, 3 March 1963'. JFK Library, UAR Security, Box 169, pp. 1-10.
11 Badeau, Middle East Remembered, p. 206.
12 'Cairo to WDC, 3 March 1963'. JFK Library, UAR Security, Box 169, Section I, p. 2.
13 'Cairo to WDC, 3 March 1963'. JFK Library, UAR Security, Box 169, Section II, p. 1. See also 'Cairo to WDC on Conversation with Muhammad Heikal, 9 March 1963'. NACPM, Jordan, File Pol 27 Yemen Pol 1 Jordan, p. 1. Heikal, who had just returned from Sanaa, told a US Embassy officer that the 'UAR [was] deeply concerned over possibility US-UAR military confrontation in Arabian peninsula', and that 'Faisal must stop killing Egyptian boys'.
14 'Guidelines of United States Policy and Operations – Yemen, March 1963'. JFK Library, Komer Series, Box 418, p. 6.
15 'WDC Eyes Only to Bunker, Badeau, and Hart, 18 March 1963'. No. 1958, JFKL, UAR, Box 169, p. 1.
16 O'Balance, Edgar, *The War in Yemen*. Hamden, CT: Archon, 1971, p. 101.
17 'Memo Bundy to Rusk and McNamara, 27 February 1963'. JFK Library, Saudi Arabia Security, Box 128B, pp. 1-2.
18 'Dhahran to WDC on Feisal Meetings, 8 March 1963'. JFK Library, Yemen Security 1961-1963, Box 128A, Sections II, pp. 1-3, Section III, pp. 1-2. Feisal not only wanted the UAR to withdraw to its bases immediately, but also wanted a withdrawal of all supplies, tanks, and ammunition that the UAR was supplying to the YAR government.
19 'Memo Talbot to Rusk, 28 March 1963'. NACPM, 786h.00/3-2863, p. 1.
20 O'Balance, *War in Yemen*, p. 101.
21 'Memo for Record by T.W. Seelye, NEA-NE, 24 October 1963'. NACPM, 786a.11/10-2463, p. 1. See also 'Message from Joint Chiefs of Staff to Strike Command, 10 June 1963'. NACPM, 786a.00/6-1063, p. 2. 'Hard Surface' would not become operational on July 5th, and the deployment actually provided little real protection. Under the rules of engagement, pilots were not authorized to shoot except in self-defense, and could not pursue UAR aircraft. Of course, the Egyptians were unaware of the restrictions and unwilling to press the issue to see what would happen. It did however constitute a highly visible symbol of US support for Saudi Arabia, and a tangible signal to Nasser that Washington would protect the Saudi regime.
22 'WDC to Cairo [Badeau] Letter from JFK to Nasser, 18 April 1963'. JFK Library, UAR Security, Box 169, p. 2. See also Badeau, *Middle East Remembered*, p. 195. Sabry became Nasser's 'alter ego' to deal with foreign missions and emissaries during the early 1960s.

See also Heikal, *Cairo Documents*, pp. 48-49. This is that same Ali Sabry who was humiliated in 1952 when, on a mission to the US for arms, he returned empty-handed. During the last months of the Truman administration, US officials told Sabry that the decision had to await the arrival of the new administration. During the intervening time, skeptical Egyptian officers joked that 'Ali Sabry himself will be the first shipment.' Dulles would ultimately reject arms for Egypt. Interview with Lakeland, 23-24 September 2003, in which Lakeland stated that Sabry carried a grudge against the US as a result of what he took as a personal affront.

23 Badeau, *Middle East Remembered*, pp. 212, 222.
24 'WDC to Cairo [Badeau] Letter JFK to Nasser, 18 April 1963'. JFK Library, No. 2474, UAR Security, Box 169, p. 2.
25 'Memo Komer to Kennedy, 2 May 1963'. JFK Library, Komer Series, Box 429, p. 1.
26 Heikal, *Cairo Documents*, pp. 200-201.
27 'Baghdad to WDC on Qasim's death, 8 February 1963'. JFK Library, Iran - Iraq, Box 117, p. 1. See also 'Telegram from OUARMA US Embassy Baghdad to WDC, 13 February 1963'. JFK Library, Iran – Iraq, Box 117, Section II, p. 1.
28 'Baghdad to WDC on RCC, 8 February 1963'. JFK Library, Iran – Iraq, Box 117, p. 1.
29 Batatu, *Old Social Classes*, pp. 982-987. Batatu commented: 'The Communists fought as only men could fight who knew that no mercy was to be looked for in defeat.' Batatu also put Communist dead between February 8 and 10 at more than 5,000, and quoted King Hussein of Jordan as stating that he knew 'for a certainty' that the coup had the support of US intelligence. With reference to this last statement, the entire US government supported the coup. Washington wanted to see Qasim and his Communist supporters removed, but that is a far cry from Batatu's inference that the US had somehow engineered the coup. The US lacked the operational capability to organize and carry out the coup, but certainly after it had occurred the US government preferred the Nasserists and Ba'thists in power, and provided encouragement and probably some peripheral assistance.
30 'Baghdad to WDC on RCC, 12 February 1963'. JFK Library, Iran – Iraq, Box 117, p. 1.
31 'Memcon Syrian Amb Abou Riche and Talbot, WDC, 12 February 1963'. NACPM, CFPF 1963, Pol Iran – Pol Iraq, Box 3943, pp. 1-3.
32 'Memcon Saudi Amb and Talbot, 13 February 1963'. NACPM, CFPF, Pol Iran – Pol Iraq, p. 1.
33 'Memcon Syrian Amb Abou Riche and Talbot, 12 February 1963'. NACPM, CFPF, Pol Iran – Pol Iraq, pp. 1-3.
34 'Memcon VP of Socony Mobil Oil, William Lindemuth and Talbot, WDC, 14 February 1963'. NACPM, CFPF, Pol Iraq, pp. 1-2. See also 'Memo Brubeck to Bundy, 15 February 1963'. JFK Library, Iran – Iraq, Box 117, p. 1.
35 'Research Memorandum RNA-8, "Inter-Arab Implications of the Iraqi Coup of February 8, 1962", 14 February 1963'. JFK Library, Iran – Iraq, Box 117, p. 1.
36 'Memo Brubeck for Bundy, 15 February 1963'. JFK Library, Iran – Iraq, Box 117, pp. 1-7.
37 'Dispatch Canadian Embassy Cairo to Ottawa, 18 February 1963'. PRO FO371/170452, p. 1.
38 'British Embassy Baghdad to FO and Emb WDC, 11 February 1963'. JFKL, Iran – Iraq, Box 117, pp. 1-2.
39 'British Embassy Cairo [Beeley] to FO, 28 February 1963'. PRO FO371/170452, p. 1.
40 'Damascus to WDC, 9 January 1963'. NACPM, 611.83/1-963 (M1855), p. 1.
41 'Letter Qudsi to Kennedy, 19 February 1963'. JFK Library, Syria, Box 124A, pp. 1-5. See also 'Letter Kennedy to Qudsi, 28 January 1963,' JFK Library, Syria, Box 124A, pp. 1-4.

NOTES 453

42 'Memo to Kennedy on Cover Sheet of Letter from Kennedy to Qudsi, 28 January 1963'. JFK Library, Syria General, Box 124A, p. 1. See also, Malik Mufti, *Sovereign Creations*, p. 141. Syrian Ba'thists had outmaneuvered their Nasserist allies by announcing the coup for March 7. They told their Nasserist counterparts that it had been postponed until March 10, and then executed it on March 8. The upshot was that the Ba'thists were in control before the Nasserists realized what had happened. Ba'thist unity talks between the Iraqi and Syrian branches of the party had already been under way, and these now picked up steam. In spite of their talk about unity with the UAR, the Syrian Ba'thists had one eye cocked over their shoulders, determined to prevent a repeat of their 1958-1961 debacles with Nasser and his supporters.
43 Mufti, *Sovereign Creations*, p. 148.
44 Kerr, *Arab Cold War*, p. 67. The Syrian delegates called Nasser 'Your Excellency' or 'Mr. President', while he called them by their first names. Nasser also had the discussions secretly taped so that at a later date he could publish the transcripts to further embarrass and discredit the Ba'thist leadership. The meeting was 'theater', planned by Nasser for public consumption without the knowledge of his Syrian counterparts.
45 Khalidi, Walid and Yusuf Ibish, *Arab Political Documents 1963*. Beirut: American University of Beirut, 1963, pp. 76, 80. This set of documents, transcripts of the meetings published by the Egyptians, was an obvious attempt to completely undermine the position of the Ba'th in Syria and the region as a whole. The transcripts were printed in Al-Ahram between 21 June and 22 July 1963 and broadcast over Radio Cairo.
46 Mufti, *Sovereign Creations*, pp. 151-153.
47 'WDC to Cairo [Badeau] Letter from JFK to Nasser, 18 April 1963'. JFK Library, UAR Security, Box 169, p. 2.
48 'Memcon Dennis Speares, British Embassy WDC, and NEA [Strong and Killgore], 27 March 1963'. NACPM, CFPF, Jordan POL 1963, p. 2.
49 'Damascus to WDC Memcon with Saladin Bitar, 28 April 1963'. NACPM, CFPF, Jordan POL 1963, p. 2.
50 'Airgram Amman to WDC, 30 April 1963.' NACPM, CFPF, Jordan POL 1963, p. 1.
51 'Memo Brubeck to Bundy: Ben-Gurion note, 25 April 1963'. *FRUS*, 1962-1963, Volume XVIII, p. 482.
52 'Circular Telegram to Middle East posts from NEA [Grant], 26 April 1963, 28 April 1963'. NACPM, CFPF, Jordan POL 1963, pp. 1-2. See also, 'Excerpt from Transcript of Talbot Remarks to National Foreign Policy Conference, 23 April 1963'. JFK Library, Komer Series, Box 429, pp. 1-3.
53 Memcon Israeli Amb Harman and Acting Sec State, 27 April 1963'. NACPM, CFPF, Jordan POL, pp. 1-4.
54 Badeau, *Middle East Remembered*, p. 229. Badeau had triangulation experts come to Cairo in order to pinpoint the exact location of Sawt al-Umma al-Arabiyya. He provided the following account of his meeting with Sharaf. 'I said, "Sami. Come off of it. It's the third spur to the right of the Muhammad Ali mosque, up on the Muqattam Hills".' In a meeting the next day, Nasser apologized to Badeau for Sharaf, citing his inexperience, and for his (Sharaf's) lie about the radio broadcasts, telling him that he had told Sharaf not to lie if the other side knew you were lying.
55 'Cairo to WDC, 29 April 1963'. JFK Library, UAR Security 1963, Box 169, Section I, pp. 1-2, Section II, pp. 1-2.
56 'Telegram Cairo [Badeau] to WDC, 3 May 1963'. JFK Library, POF, UAR Security 1963, Box 169, Sec. I, pp. 1-3, Sec. II, pp. 1-3. Badeau expressed his concerns in a thinly-veiled 'hypothetical telegram' to Moscow from the Soviet Ambassador. Badeau, writing as though he were the Soviet Ambassador, explained Soviet setbacks in the Middle East but then pointed out that the Kennedy administration was on the verge of throwing it all away because of support for 'bourgeois imperialist Zionism'. The

telegram ended with a hypothetical comment by the Soviet Ambassador: 'Again I urge we move immediately to take advantage of this situation which the Americans have so kindly presented to us.' It was a creative way for Badeau to make his point, and events would prove it to be remarkably accuarate.

57 'Tel Aviv to WDC, 1 May 1963'. NACPM, CFPF, Jordan POL 1963, p. 1.
58 'Memcon Harriman and Israeli Amb Harman, 10 May 1963'. NACPM, CFPF, Jordan POL 1963, p. 2.
59 'Letter Official-Informal Macomber to Talbot, 18 June 1963'. JFK Library, Komer Series, Box 429, pp. 1-6. In this letter, Ambassador Macomber laid out both the economic and political situation in Jordan. He argued that the US had a fundamental choice either to wholeheartedly become the benefactor for the Hashemite regime in Jordan or to allow political and economic forces to take their course and undermine the Jordanian government to the point of collapse. As a result of this discussion, President Kennedy asked for a meeting with Macomber. See also 'Air gram Amman [Macomber] to WDC, 10 July 1963'. NACPM, CFPF, NEA, Jordan POL Internal Security, Box 3960, pp. 1-2. Macomber identified the principle threat to Hussein as internal and non-Communist. He cited the likely possible sources in the following order: first, apolitical dissident army officers; second, Nasserists; third, Qawmiyiim al-Arab (nationalists); and fourth, Ba'thists. In arguments reminiscent of the Dulles years, Macomber made the case that the pro-Western orientation of the Jordanian army was the critical element for the stability of the regime. See 'Memo Brubeck to Bundy, 20 July 1963'. JFK Library, Komer Series, Box 429, pp. 1-2. It was indicative of the shifting policies in the region that Macomber, with his close ties to Allen Dulles through the Office of Strategic Services and the CIA, and to John Foster Dulles, as his erstwhile special assistant, became the single most influential voice on the situation in Jordan. See also Dann, Uriel, *King Hussein and the Challenge of Arab Radicalism: Jordan 1955-1967*. Oxford: Oxford University Press, 1989, pp. 130-133. Dann's work provides excellent insight into the period, but his view that the Kennedy administration was willing to see the Hashemite regime in Jordan collapse as long as Jordan retained its independence is somewhat misleading. The author uses Talbot's statements on the maintenance of the 'separate state' in Jordan as an indication that this did not necessarily mean the Hashemite state. Theoretically this may have been true, but the hard reality was that since the crisis of 1958 the US government had seen no real alternative to the Hashemites. The Kennedy administration had little choice but to follow the course laid out by Eisenhower, a course in large part determined by the efforts of Sir Charles Johnston, the British Ambassador.
60 'Memo Komer to NSC staff on Jordanian Policy Issues, August 1, 1963'. JFK Library, Komer Series, Box 429, pp. 1-2. See also 'Memo Komer to Bundy, 22 July 1963'. JFK Library, Komer Series, Box 429, p. 1.
61 'Airgram Amman to WDC, 28 August 1963'. NACPM, CFPF, Jordan POL Internal Security, pp. 1-4.
62 'Amman to WDC, 7 October 1963'. NACPM, CFPF, Jordan POL Internal Security, pp. 1-2. See also 'Memo Komer to Bundy, 30 October 1963'. JFK Library, Komer Series, Box 429, p. 1. King Hussein's visit was cleared through Myer Feldman, Kennedy's advisor on Israeli affairs. Komer stated: 'Mike [Myer] Feldman is not unduly concerned by a low-key visit by King Hussein next June. He agrees that of all the Arabs, Hussein is probably the most acceptable in 1964. Mike feels, however, that we ought seriously to consider a brief visit by Eshkol, which would also be low-key and informal. ... Certainly such a visit would be a domestic political plus.' Nasser's view of the internal political situation in the US was not far off the mark.
63 'Briefing Notes for DCIA, Attachment on "Ba'th Ideology and Practice", 30 December 1963'. CIA, CRES, CIA-RDP75-00001R000400380006-7, p. 28.

64 'Memo Komer to Bundy, 15 November 1963'. JFK Library, Iraq, Box 117A, p. 1. See also Mufti, *Sovereign Creations*, p. 157.
65 'British Embassy Cairo [Beeley] to FO, 14 August 1963'. PRO FO371/172901, p 2.
66 'Minute attached to British Embassy Cairo to FO, 14 August 1963'. PRO FO371/172901, coversheet, p. 2.
67 Mufti, *Sovereign Creations*, pp. 159-165. Mufti provides an interesting and detailed outline of the events of November 1963 that led to the Aref coup.
68 'Briefing Notes for DCIA, Iraq Situation, 30 December 1963'. CIA, CRES, CIA-RDP71T00730R000200020004-5, p. 7.
69 'Cairo to WDC, 30 November 1963'. NACPM, CFPF 1963, POL Iran – Iraq, POL 15 Iraq, p. 1.
70 Nutting, *Nasser*, p. 337.
71 'WDC to Cairo, 19 October 1963'. *FRUS*, 1962-1963, Volume XVIII, p. 752.
72 'Cairo to WDC, 9 November 1963'. JFK Library, UAR Security 1963, Box 127A, p. 1.
73 Badeau, John 'U.S.A. and U.A.R.: A Crisis in Confidence'. *Foreign Affairs*, Volume 43, No. 2, January 1965, pp. 285, 281-296
74 'Chiefs of Mission Conference in Istanbul, Second Plenary Session, 15-18 October 1963'. NACPM, Chiefs of Mission Conferences, Lot 670457, Box 1, Entry 5269, p. 4.
75 'Memo Bundy to Fulbright, 11 November 1963'. JFK Library, UAR Security, Box 127A, p. 1.
76 'Memo from Komer to Bundy, 20 October 1963'. JFK Library, Komer Series, Box 424, p. 1.
77 'Memo Komer to Bundy, 20 October 1963'. JFK Library, Komer Series, Box 424, pp. 3, 5. Komer was still convinced that the US had to force reform in Iran, but he lacked any workable specifics. His disdain for Holmes was apparent: 'Julius Holmes is one of the most tough-minded operators in the Foreign Service. His problem is that he's tough-minded about the wrong things; he's great on military aid and earthquake relief, but fails to understand what really ails Iran.' In fact, Holmes, shortly after his arrival, clued into the fact that Shah was the center of power and that the National Front was no longer a real threat to the throne. At the same time, Komer was calling Amini the 'last hope' and worrying about building 'bridges' to the National Front.
78 'Airgram Tehran to WDC, 20 December 1962'. NACPM, 788.11/12-20-62, pp. 1-3.
79 'Memo GTI [Bowling] to NEA, 21 December 1962'. NACPM, 788.11/12-2162, p. 1.
80 'Memo William Polk to Talbot, 18 December 1962'. NACPM, 788.11/12-20-62, p 2.
81 Keddie, *Modern Iran*, p. 145.
82 'Memo Brubeck to Bundy, 21 January 1963'. JFK Library, Komer Series, Box 424, p 1.
83 'Memo from Komer to Bundy, 29 January 1963'. JFK Library, PPJFK, NSF, Country Files, Iran, Box 116A, p. 1.
84 'Res Memo RNA-6, INR [Hillsman], Iranian Referendum, 11 February 1963'. JFK Library, Komer, Box 424, p. 1.
85 'Airgram Tehran to WDC, 4 April 1963'. NACPM, CFPF 1963, POL Iran, p. 2.
86 'Savingram British Embassy Tehran [Sir Denis Wright] to FO, 1 June 1963'. PRO FO248/1590, p. 5.
87 'CIA: OCI – Report on Counter-Insurgency in Iran, 23 April 1963'. JFK Library, Komer Series, Box 116A, p. 1.
88 Keddie, *Modern Iran*, p. 147.
89 'CIA SNIE No. 34-63, The Iranian Situation, 10 April 1963'. JFK Library, Meetings Series, Box 315, p. 3.
90 'Memo Komer to Bundy, 30 April 1963'. JFK Library, Iran, Box 116A, p. 1. See also 'Memo Hansen to Komer, 7 May 1963'. JFK Library, Komer Series, Box 424, p. 1.
91 'Memo Komer to Holmes: Message from Kennedy to Shah, 20 June 1963'. JFK Library, Komer Series, Box 424, p. 1.

92 'Briefing Memo for Lord Home Meeting with S.K. Dehlavi, 4 January 1963'. PRO FO371/170639, p. 1.
93 'Memo Bundy to Galbraith, 7 January 1963'. JFK Library, Komer Series, Box 418, p. 1.
94 'Memo Komer to Galbraith, 15 January 1963'. JFK Library, Komer Series, Box 429, p. 2. See also 'Memo Rusk to Kennedy on Kashmir, 20 February 1963'. NACPM, NEA/INC, Kashmir, Box 1, p. 2.
95 'Letter Nehru to Kennedy, 18 February 1963'. NACPM, NEA/INC, Kashmir, Box 1, p. 2.
96 'Memo Komer to Kennedy, 19 February 1963'. JFK Library, Komer Series, Box 429, pp. 2-3.
97 'Airgram Consulate Lahore to WDC, February 8, 1962'. NACPM, CFPF, Political Pakistan to Political No. 5 Laws Pakistan, 2/1/63, p. 2.
98 'Airgram Consulate Peshawar to WDC, 6 February 1962'. NACPM, CFPF, Political Pakistan to Political No. 5 Laws Pakistan, 2/1/63, pp. 1-2. See also, 'Airgram Consulate Lahore to WDC, 16 February 1963'. NACPM, CFPF, Political Pakistan to Political No. 5 Laws Pakistan, 2/1/63, pp. 1-2.
99 'Briefing Memo on Kashmir for Lord Home Meeting with Indian High Commissioner Muhammad Ali Currin Chagla, 19 April 1963'. PRO FO371/170639, p. 1.
100 'Memo Rostow to Talbot, 8 April 1963'. NACPM, NEA/INC, Kashmir, Box 1, p 1.
101 'British High Com New Delhi to FO, 16 April 1963'. PRO FO371/170638, p 1.
102 'Briefing Memo Lord Home and Chagla, 19 April 1963'. PRO FO371/170639, p. 1. See also 'NSAM, No. 22, Appraisal of Sino-Indian Situation from Bundy to Rusk, McNamara, and McCone, 26 February 1963' NACPM, NSAM 223, p. 1.
103 'Karachi to WDC, 30 April 1963'. NACPM, CFPF, Political 32-1 Territory & Boundary Disputes, Violations, Incidents India-Pak, 2/1/63-5/1/63, Box 3934, p 3.
104 'Attachment to a Memcon for Bundy, Conversation Between Rusk and Indian Ambassador, B.K. Nehru, 4 May 1963'. NACPM, CFPF, Political 32-1 Territory & Boundary Disputes, p. 2.
105 'Memo Rusk to Kennedy, 19 April 1962'. NACPM, Kashmir, Box 1, pp. 1-3.
106 'Letter Nehru to Kennedy, 21 April 1963'. JFK Library, Komer Series, Box 429, p. 2. See also Gopal, *Nehru*, Volume III, p. 261.
107 'Memo NEA to Kennedy for European Trip, 18 June 1963'. NACPM, Kashmir, Box 1, p. 2. See also 'New Delhi to WDC, 11 July 1963'. NACPM, CFPF, Pol 32-1 Territory & Boundary Disputes, p. 1.
108 'New Delhi to WDC, 5 July 1963'. NACPM,CFPF, 1963, Political 15-1 Head of State Executive Branch India, To: Pol 23 Internal Security India. Box 3931. 1963 Alpha Numeric Political and Defense, pp. 1-2, 4.
109 'Airgram Rawalpindi to WDC, 7 August 1963'. NACPM, CFPF 1963, pp. 1-5.
110 'Airgram Karachi to WDC, 29 August 1963'. NACPM, CFPF, pp. 1-4.
111 'Research Memo INR-26, Implications of Soviet Military Aid to India, 9 July 1963'. JFK Library, Komer Series, Box 422, pp. 1-6.
112 'Memo Rusk to Kennedy, 8 May 1963'. *FRUS*, 1961-1963, Volume XIX, pp. 579-583.
113 'Summary 514th NSC Meeting, 9 May 1963'. *FRUS*, 1961-1963, Volume XIX, p. 583.
114 'Karachi to WDC, 8 August 1963'. *FRUS*, 1961-1963, Volume XIX, pp. 629--630.
115 'Memo Meeting with Kennedy on Pakistan, 12 August 1963'. *FRUS*, 1961-1963, Volume XIX, p. 637.
116 'Tehran to WDC, 5 September 1963'. *FRUS*, 1961-1963, Volume XIX, p. 664.
117 Ayub Khan, *Friends Not Masters*, p. 153.
118 'New Delhi to WDC, 30 July 1963'. NACPM, CFPF, Pol 32-1 Territory & Boundary Disputes, p. 2.
119 'Karachi to WDC, 31 July 1963.' NACPM, CFPF, Pol 32-1 Territory & Boundary Disputes, p. 2.

120 'Karachi to WDC, 23 August 1963'. NACPM, CFPF, Pol 32-1 Territory & Boundary Disputes, pp. 1-4.
121 'New Delhi to WDC, 9 September 1963'. NACPM, CFPF, Pol 25 Territory & Boundary Disputes, pp. 1-2.
122 'Research Memo DOS/INR, 25 September 1963'. NACPM, CFPF, 1963, Political 6 Prominent Persons Pak to Political 14 Elections Pakistan, 2/1/63, p. 2.
123 'Memo Talbot to Under Sec State, 28 September 1963'. NACPM, CFPF, Political 6 Prom Persons, Box, p. 2.
124 'Memo Komer to Kennedy, 12 November 1963'. *FRUS*, 1961-1963, South Asia, Volume XIX, p. 689.
125 'Memo Komer to Dep Asst SecDef William Bundy, 14 November 1963'. *FRUS*, 1961-1963, Volume XIX, p. 689.
126 *Oral History* – Bowles. JFK Library, p. 26.
127 'Memo Komer to Bundy, Washington, 23 November 1963'. LBJ Library, NSC Histories, South Asia, 1962-66, Box 24, Tab B, 1-13, p. 1. See also, 'Memo from Komer to Bundy, Washington, 29 November 1963'. LBJ Library, Box 24, Tab B, 1-13, p. 1. Komer stated that despite the situation with Pakistan, the US intended to go ahead with the military assistance to India. He was wrong: Johnson cancelled it after a study.
128 'Memo McCone, Director CIA, WDC, 30 November 1963'. *FRUS*, 1961-1963, Volume XIX p. 693. When Bowles returned later to brief the effort, Johnson turned him down. *Oral History* – Bowles. JFK Library, p. 70. Bowles states that Johnson finally set a meeting to discuss the India military-aid plan in late May, but Nehru died three days before the meeting and the effort collapsed. In 1964, the Indians went to the Soviets.

Conclusion

1 'Diary Entry Eisenhower on conversation with Churchill, 6 January 1953'. DDEL, Diary Series, Box 9, pp. 5-6.
2 Interview Rostow, 12 June 2002.

Bibliography

Archives and Collections
American Research Center Library periodical collection, Cairo
Bodleian Library, Macmillan Papers, Oxford University
British Library, India Collection, London
British National Archives, Public Records Office, Kew
Centre Archives d'Outre-Mer, Aix-en-Provence
Churchill Archives, Selwyn Lloyd Collection, Cambridge University
Dwight D. Eisenhower Presidential Library, Abilene, Kansas
John F. Kennedy Presidential Library, Boston, Massachusetts
Library of Congress, Washington, DC
Lyndon Baines Johnson Presidential Library, Austin, Texas
Menzies Asian Library, Australian National University, Canberra
Middle East Archives, St. Anthony's College, Oxford University
New York City Public Library, Middle East Collection
National Archives of Australia, Canberra
National Archives of India, New Delhi
National Archives of the United Arab Republic, Cairo
National Archives of the United States, College Park, Maryland
National Library of Australia, Canberra
National Library of the United Arab Republic (*Dar al-Watha'iq*), Cairo
Nehru Library and Archives, New Delhi
New Zealand National Archives, Wellington
New Zealand National Library, Wellington
St. Anthony's College, Middle East Archive, Oxford
South Asian Library and Archives, Cambridge University

Published Document Collections
Abdullah Ibn Husayn, *awraq Abdullah ibn Husayn: al-alaqat al-urduniya – al-misriya, 1925-1951*. Amman: al-wathiq al-urduniya, 1998.
The Chinese Threat. New Delhi: Publications Division of the Ministry of Information and Broadcasting, January 1963.
Executive Sessions of the Senate Foreign Relations Committee (Historical Series), Volume VIII, Eighty-Fourth Congress Second Session, 1956. Washington, DC: US Government Printing Office, 1978.
Executive Sessions of the Senate Foreign Relations Committee (Historical Series), Volume XIX, Eighty-Fifth Congress First Session, 1957. Washington, DC: US Government Printing Office, 1979.
Executive Sessions of the Senate Foreign Relations Committee (Historical Series), Volume X, Eighty-Fifth Congress Second Session, 1958. Washington, DC: US Government Printing Office, 1980.

Executive Sessions of the Senate Foreign Relations Committee (Historical Series), Volume XIX, Eighty-Sixth Congress First Session, 1959. Washington, DC: US Government Printing Office, 1982.

Ferrell, Robert H. (ed.). *The Eisenhower Diaries*. New York: W.W. Norton, 1981.

Foreign Relations of the United States. Washington, D.C.: U.S. Government Printing Office.

'Ismat Sayf al-Dawlah *Nazariat al-Thawrah al-Arabiyah, Volume VI*. Beirut: Dar Al-Musira, 1972.

Kennedy, John F. *Freedom of Communications – Final Report of the Committee on Commerce, U.S. Senate*. Prepared by the subcommittee on communications, pursuant to S.R. 305, 86th Congress. Part I, The Speeches, Remarks, Press Conferences, and Statements of Senator John F. Kennedy, August 1 through November 7, 1960.

Nassar, Jamal Abd-al. *Address by President Gamal Abdel Nasser to the Arab Socialist Union, February 21, 1965*. Cairo: United Arab Republic Information Department, 1965.

Nasser, Jamal Abd al. *President Gamal Abdel Nasser on Consolidation of the Cause of World Peace*. Cairo: Ministry of National Guidance – State Information Service, 1965.

Nasser, Jamal Abd-al. *President Gamal Abdel-Nasser's Speeches and Press Interviews, January–December 1958*. Cairo: United Arab Republic Information Department – Al-Shaab Printing House, 1959.

Nasser, Jamal Abd-al. *President Gamal Abdel-Nasser's Speeches and Press Interviews, January–December 1963*. Cairo: United Arab Republic Information Department – Al-Shaab Printing House, 1964.

Nasser, Jamal Abd al. *Where I Stand and Why*. Cairo: United Arab Republic Ministry of National Guidance, 1959.

Nasser's Pattern of Aggression. New York: Israeli Office of Information, 1957.

Nasser's Terror Gangs: The Story of the Fedayun. Jerusalem: Israeli Ministry of Foreign Affairs, Information Division, 1957.

Nehru, Jawaharlal. *Asian-African Conference, 18–24 April 1955: Prime Minister Jawaharlal Nehru's Speeches and the Final Communiqué*. New Delhi: Publications Division of the Ministry of Information and Broadcasting, Government of India Press, 1955.

Nehru, Jawaharlal. *The Discovery of India*. New Delhi: Indraprastha Press, 1981.

Nehru, Jawaharlal. *Glimpses of History*. New Delhi: Indraprastha Press, 1982.

Nehru, Jawaharlal. *Independence and After: A Collection of Speeches 1946–1949*. New York: John Day, 1950.

Nehru, Jawaharlal. *India-China Relations: Speech Delivered in Lok Sabha, 27 November 1959*. New Delhi: Publications Division, Ministry of Information and Broadcasting, 1959.

Nehru, Jawaharlal. *India Refuses U.S. Military Aid – Why? Prime Minister's Statement in the House of People*. New Delhi: Publications Division, Ministry of Information and Broadcasting, 1954.

Nehru, Jawaharlal. *Indo-Pakistan Relations: Prime Minister's Speech in Srinagar, 19 July 1961*. New Delhi: External Publicity Division of the Ministry of External Affairs, 1961.

Nehru, Jawaharlal. *Letters to Chief Ministers 1947–1964*, ed. C. Parthasarathi. Delhi: Oxford University Press, 1989.

Nehru, Jawaharlal. *Military Alliances: Excerpts from Prime Minister Nehru's Speeches in Parliament: 1954–1956*. New Delhi: Lok Sabha Secretariat, April 1957.

Roi, Yaacov, *From Encroachment to Involvement: A Documentary Study of Soviet Policy in the Middle East, 1945–1973*. Jerusalem: Israel Universities Press, 1974.

Interviews
General Andrew Goodpaster
Muhammad Hakki
William C. Lakeland
Walt Rostow

Phillips Talbot
Christopher Van Hollen

Published Works

'7 Democrats Aid G.O.P. on Mideast'. *The New York Times*, 2 March 1957, p. 1.
Abdel-Malek, Anouar. *Egypt: Military Society – The Army Regime, the Left, and Social Change under Nasser.* New York: Random House, 1968.
Abduh, Samir. *al-tahalil al-nafsii li-shaqsia jamaal abd-al-nasir.* Al-Qahira: Dar al-Kitab al-arabi, 1992.
Abir, Mordechai. *Saudi Arabia in the Oil Era: Regime and Elites and Collaboration.* London: Croom Helm, 1988.
Abrahamian, Ervand. *Khomeinism: Essays on the Islamic Republic.* Berkeley: University of California Press, 1993.
Abu Izzeddin, Nejla M. *Nasser of the Arabs, An Arab Assessment.* London: The Third World Center for Research and Publishing, 1981.
Aburish, Sayid K. *A Brutal Friendship, The Arab Elite and the West.* New York: St. Martins, 1998.
Aburish, Sayid K. *Nasser: The Last Arab.* New York: St. Martin's, 2004.
Adel, Daluit Sen. *Krishna Menon and Contemporary Politics.* New Delhi: Institute for Socialist Education, 1997.
Ahmad, Feroz. *Turkey: The Quest for Identity.* Oxford: Oneworld, 2003
Ahmad, Muhammad Abd-al-Aziz, and Wafiq Abd-al-Aziz al-Tahmi's *Tajraba al-Wahida bayn Misr wa Suria.* Cairo: National Publishing House, 1962.
Ahmed, Akbar S. Jinnah, *Pakistan and Islamic Identity: The Search for Saladin.* London: Routledge, 1997.
Akbar, M.N. *Nehru: The Making of India.* London: Viking, 1988.
Alexandrov, A., Blatov, A., Grubyakov, V., Dobrynin, A., Zemskov, I., Israelyan, V., Kapitsa, M., Koblyakov, I., Kutakov, L., Roshchin, A., Sanakoyev, S., Falin, V., and Khovostov, V. *History of Soviet Foreign Policy, 1945–1970*, trans. from *Istoriya bneshnei politik SSSR (1945–1970).* Ed. B. Ponomaryov, A. Gromyko, V.Khvostov, trans. D. Skvirsky. Moscow: Progress, 1974.
Alridge, James. 'Nasser in Three Dimensions'. *The African Communist*, No. 44, 1971, pp. 21–30.
Alteras, Isaac. *Eisenhower and Israel: U.S.-Israeli Relations, 1953–1960.* Gainesville: University of Florida Press, 1993.
Al-Amam, Abdullah. *Nasir wa 'Amir.* Al-Qahira: nashir al-yulia, 1985.
Ambrose, Stephen E. *Eisenhower: Soldier and President.* New York: Simon & Schuster, 1990.
Amin, Shahid M. *Pakistan's Foreign Policy: A Reappraisal.* Oxford: Oxford University Press, 2000.
'The Arab 'Summit': Nasser and the Kings'. *Newsweek*, 4 March 1957, p. 40.
Anderson, Lisa. 'Policy-Making and Theory Building: American Political Science and the Islamic Middle East'. In Hisham Sharabi (ed.) *Theory and Politics in the Arab World: Critical Responses.* New York: Routledge, Chapman & Hall, in cooperation with the Center for Contemporary Arab Studies, Georgetown University, 1990.
'And then there were only. . .'. *Newsweek*, 18 February 1958, p. 39.
Anthony, John Duke. *Arab States of the Lower Gulf: People, Politics, Petroleum.* Washington, D.C.: Middle East Institute, 1975.
Arabadshyan, A.Z. *Iranskaya Revolustiya, 1978–1979.* Moskva: Akademiya Nauk SSSR, 1989.
Armstrong, Hamilton Fish. 'Neutrality: Varying Tunes.' *Foreign Affairs*, Volume 35, No. 1, October 1956, pp. 57–71.
Armstrong, Hamilton Fish. 'U.N. on Trial.' *Foreign Affairs*, Volume 39, No. 3, April 1961, pp. 388–415.

BIBLIOGRAPHY

Arora, K.C. *V.K. Krishna Menon – A Biography*. New Delhi: Sanchar, 1998.
Ashton, Nigel John. *Eisenhower, Macmillan, and the Problem of Nasser: Anglo-American Relations and Arab Nationalism, 1955–1959*. London: Macmillan, 1996.
Assiri, Abdul-Reda. *Kuwait's Foreign Policy: City-State in World Politics*. London: Westview, 1990.
Al-Atasi, Jamal. *Itlalah ala al-tajribat al-thawrijat li jamal abd-al-nasir wa ala fikratu istratiji wa al-tarikhi*. Beirut: Mahad al-Nama al-Arabi, 1981.
Al-Atasi, Jamal. *Al-Thawra li Jamal Abd-al-Nasser wa ala Fikrihi al-Istratiji wa al-Tarikh*. Beirut: Mahad Al-Agmaln Al-Arabi, 1979.
Avery, Peter. *Modern Iran*. New York: Praeger, 1965.
Ayub Khan, Muhammad. *Friends not Masters: A Political Autobiography*. London: Oxford University Press, 1967.
Ayub Khan, Muhammad. 'Pakistan Perspective'. *Foreign Affairs*, Volume 38, No. 4, July 1960, pp. 547–556.
Ayubi, Nazih. N. *Overstating the Arab State, Politics and Society in the Middle East*. New York: Tauris, 1995.
Ayubi, Shaheen. *Nasser & Sadat: Decision Making and Foreign Policy, 1970–1972*. Wakefield, N.H.: Longwood Academic, 1992.
Aziz, K.K. *Britain and Pakistan*. Islamabad: University of Islamabad Press, 1974.
Aziz, K.K. *Party Politics in Pakistan 1947–1958*. Islamabad: National Commission on Historical and Cultural Research, 1976.
Badeau, John S. *The American Approach to the Arab World*. New York: Harper & Row, for the Council on Foreign Relations, 1968.
Badeau, John S. 'The Arab Role in Islamic Culture'. In *The Genius of Arab Civilization*. Cairo: American University of Cairo Press, 1983.
Badeau, John S. and Georgiana G. Stevens. *Bread from Stones: Fifty Years of Technical Assistance*. Englewoods Cliffs, NJ: Prentice-Hal, 1966.
Badeau, John S. *East and West of Suez, the Story of the Modern Middle East*. New York: Foreign Policy Association, 1943.
Badeau, John S. *The Emergence of Modern Egypt*. New York: Foreign Policy Association, 1953.
Badeau, John S. 'The Middle East: Conflict in Priorities'. *Foreign Affairs*, Volume 36, No. 2, January 1958, pp. 232–240.
Badeau, John S. *The Middle East Remembered*. Washington, DC: Middle East Institute, 1983.
Badeau, John S. 'U.S.A. and U.A.R.: A Crisis in Confidence'. *Foreign Affairs*, Volume 43, No. 2, January 1965, pp. 281–296.
Badeau, John S. *U.S.A. & U.A.R., A Crisis in Confidence*. New York: Near and Middle East Institute, Columbia University Press, 1966.
Badeeb, Saeed M. *The Saudi-Egyptian Conflict over North Yemen, 1962–1970*. Boulder, CO: Westview, 1986.
Baker, Raymond William. *Egypt's Uncertain Revolution under Nasser and Sadat*. Cambridge, MA: Harvard University Press, 1978.
Ball, George W. and Douglas B. Ball. *The Passionate Attachment: America's Involvement with Israel 1947 to the Present*. New York: Norton, 1992.
Bass, Warren. *Support Any Friend: Kennedy's Middle East and the Making of the U.S.-Israel Alliance*. Oxford: Oxford University Press, 2003.
Bayley, David. *The Police and Political Development in India*. Princeton, NJ: Princeton University Press, 1969.
Batatu, Hanna. *The Old Social Classes and the Revolutionary Movement of Iraq: A Study of Iraq's Old Landed and Commercial Classes and of its Communists, Ba'thists and Free Officers*. Princeton: Princeton University Press, 1978.
Beal, John Robinson. *John Foster Dulles: A Biography*. New York: Harper Bros, 1957.
Becker, Julian. *The PLO*. New York: St. Martin's, 1984.
Behbehani, Hashim. *The Soviet Union and Arab Nationalism 1917-1966*. London: KPI, 1986.

Beinin, Joel. *Was the Red Flag Flying There? Marxist Politics and the Arab-Israeli Conflict in Egypt and Israel, 1948–1965.* Berkeley: University of California Press, 1990.
Bhargava, G.S. *Pakistan in Crisis.* New Delhi: Vikas, 1971.
Bidwell, Robin. *Dictionary of Modern Arab History.* London: Kegan Paul International, 1998.
Bill, James A. and William Roger Louis (Eds.). *Musaddiq, Iranian Nationalism, and Oil.* London: Tauris, 1988.
Bill, James A. *The Eagle and the Lion: The Tragedy of American-Iranian Relations.* New Haven, CT: Yale University Press, 1988.
Bogdanor, Vernon. 'Suez Changed Everything'. *The Times,* 29 October 2006, p. 21.
Boroujerdi, Mehrzad. *Iranian Intellectuals and the West.* Syracuse, NY: University of Syracuse Press, 1996.
Bowles, Chester. *Ambassador's Report.* New York: Harper & Brothers, 1954.
Bowles, Chester. *A View from New Delhi, Selected Speeches and Writings.* New Haven, CT: Yale University Press, 1969.
Bowles, Chester. *The Coming Political Breakthrough.* New York: Harper Bros, Publishers, 1959.
Bowles, Chester. 'Is Communist Ideology Becoming Irrelevant?' *Foreign Affairs,* Volume 40, No. 1, July 1962, pp. 551–565.
Bowles, Chester. 'Toward a New Diplomacy'. *Foreign Affairs,* Volume 40, No. 2, January 1962, pp. 244–251.
Brass, Paul R. *The New Cambridge History of India,* Volume IV: *The politics of India since Independence.* Cambridge: Cambridge University Press, 1991.
Brecher, Michael. *India and World Politics: Krishna Menon's View of the World.* London: Oxford University Press, 1968.
'Britain Faces Collapse of Whole Mid-East Position'. *The Age,* 16 July 1958, p. 2.
Bromwell, Herbert. *Advising Ike, The Memoirs of Attorney General Herbert Bromwell.* Lawrence: University of Kansas Press, 1993.
Brown, Judith. *Nehru: A Political Life.* New Haven, CT: Yale University Press, 2003.
Brown, L. Carl. *International Politics and the Middle East: Old Rules, Dangerous Game.* Princeton, NJ: Princeton University Press, 1984.
Burrowes, Robert D. *Historical Dictionary of Yemen.* London: Scarecrow, 1995.
Burrowes, Robert D. *The Yemen Arab Republic, The Politics of Development, 1962–1986.* London: Westview, 1987.
Calvocoressi, Peter. *Suez Ten Years After.* New York: Pantheon, 1967.
'The Camel Driver'. *Time,* 29 March 1963, pp. 22–26.
Campbell, John C. *Defense of the Middle East: Problems of American Policy.* New York: Harper Bros, for Council on Foreign Relations, 1960.
Campbell-Johnson, Alan. *Mission with Mountbatten.* New York: Atheneum, 1986.
'Can Arab Unity Survive?' *New Statesman,* 5 January 1962, p. 48.
Carapico, Sheila. *Civil Society in Yemen.* Cambridge: Cambridge University Press, 1998.
Catherwood, Christopher. *Churchill's Folly: How Winston Churchill Created Modern Iraq.* New York: Carroll & Graff, 2004
Childers, Erskine B. *The Road to Suez.* London: MacGibbon & Kee, 1962.
Choueiri, Youssef M. (ed.). *State & Society in Syria and Lebanon.* New York: St. Martin's, 1993.
'The Clock Struck 2'. *Newsweek,* 28 July 1958, pp. 23–24.
Cohen, Avner. *Israel and the Bomb.* New York: Columbia University Press, 1998.
Comfort, Mildred Houghton. *John Foster Dulles, Peacemaker.* Minneapolis, MN: T.S. Denison, 1960
Cooper, Chester L. *The Lion's Last Roar: Suez, 1956.* New York: Harper & Row, 1978.
Cooper, Chester L. *The Lost Crusade: America in Vietnam.* New York: Dodd, Mead, 1970.
Confino, Michael and Shimon Shamir. *The U.S.S.R. and the Middle East.* New York: Wiley, 1973.
Connelly, Matthew. *A Diplomatic Revolution: Algeria's Fight for Independence and the Origins of the Post-Cold War Era.* London: Oxford University Press, 2002.

Copeland, Miles. *The Game of Nations: The Amorality of Power Politics.* New York: Simon & Schuster, 1969.
Copeland, Miles. *The Game Player.* London: Aurum, 1989.
Cordesman, Anthony H. *Bahrain, Oman, Qatar, and the UAE.* Boulder, CO: Westview, 1997.
Cordesman, Anthony H. *Iraq.* Boulder, CO: Westview, 1997.
Choueiri, Youssef M. *Arab Nationalism: A History, Nation and State in the Arab World.* London: Blackwell, 2000.
Daniel, Norman. *Islam and the West: The Making of an Image.* Oxford: Oneworld, 1993.
Dann, Uriel. *Iraq Under Qassem: A Political History, 1958-1963.* New York: Praeger, 1969.
Dann, Uriel. *King Hussein and the Challenge of Arab Radicalism: Jordan 1955–1967.* Oxford: Oxford University Press, 1989.
Dawisha, Karen. 'The Soviet Union in the Middle East: Great Power in Search of a Leading Role'. In Feuchtwanger, E.J. and Peter Nailor (eds.) *The Soviet Union and the Third World.* New York: St. Martin's, 1981.
Dawson, Pauline. *The Peacekeepers of Kashmir.* London: Hurst, 1994.
DeGaury, Gerald. *Faisal: Kind of Saudi Arabia.* London: Arthur Barker, 1966.
Dekmejian, Hrair. *Egypt under Nasir, A Study in Political Dynamics.* Albany, NY: State University of New York Press, 1971.
Devlin, John. *The Ba'th Party: A History form Its Origins to 1966.* Stanford: Hoover Institution, 1976.
Doran, Michael. *Pan-Arabism before Nasser: Egyptian Power Politics and the Palestinian Question.* Oxford: Oxford University Press, 1999.
Donovan, Robert J. *Eisenhower: The Inside Story.* New York: Harper Bros, 1956.
Douglas, J. Leigh. *The Free Yemeni Movement 1935–1962.* Beirut: American University of Beirut, 1987.
Dresch, Paul. *A History of Modern Yemen.* Cambridge: Cambridge University Press, 2000.
Duccci, Roberto. 'The World Order in the Sixties'. *Foreign Affairs,* Volume 42, No. 3, April 1964, pp. 379–390.
Dulles, Allen. *The Craft of Intelligence.* New York: Harper & Row, 1963.
Dulles, John Foster. 'Text of State Department Transcript of News Conference Held by Secretary Dulles'. *The New York Times,* 9 April 1958, p. 10.
Dupree, Louis. 'West Pakistan Revisited, 27 August 1959'. *AUFS-SAS,* Series Volume III, No. 1.
Eban, Abba. *Abba Eban: An Autobiography.* New York: Random House, 1977.
Eban, Abba. *Personal Witness: Israel Through My Eyes.* New York: Putnam, 1992.
Eden, Anthony. *Full Circle: the Memoirs of Anthony Eden.* Boston, MA: Houghton Mifflin, 1960.
Eden, Anthony. *The Reckoning: the Memoirs of Anthony Eden.* Boston, MA: Houghton Mifflin, 1965.
Eden, Anthony. *The Suez Crisis of 1956.* London: Times, 1960.
'Egypt, Syria: Shotgun Wedding'. *Newsweek,* 10 February 1958, p. 52.
Eisel, Braxton. 'The FOBS of War'. *Air Force Magazine,* June 2005, pp. 72–75.
Eisenhower, Dwight D. *The White House Years: Mandate for Change 1953–1956.* New York: Doubleday, 1963.
Eisenhower, Dwight D. *The White House Years: Waging Peace, 1956–1961.* New York: Doubleday, 1965.
Epstein, Leon D. *British Politics in the Suez Crisis.* Urbana: University of Illinois Press, 1964.
Eveland, Wilbur Crane. *Ropes of Sand: America's Failure in the Middle East.* New York: Norton, 1980.
Faris, Nabih Amin, and Mohammed Tawfik Husayn. *The Crescent in Crisis.* Lawrence: University of Kansas Press, 1955.
Farrah, Ilyas. *Evolution of Arab Revolutionary Ideology.* Madrid: MINUESA, 1978.

Fischer, Michael M.J. *Iran from Religious Dispute to Revolution*. Cambridge, MA: Harvard University Press, 1980.
Feldman, Herbert. *From Crisis to Crisis: Pakistan 1962-1969*. London: Oxford University Press, 1972.
Feuchtwanger, E.J. and Peter Nailor. *The Soviet Union and the Third World*. New York: St. Martin's, 1981.
Finer, Herman. *Dulles Over Suez, The Theory and Practice of his Diplomacy*. Chicago: Quadrangle, 1971.
Forbes, Colin D. *Innocent in a Revolution*. Sussex: Book Guild, 1999.
'Forces on North Border of Yemen'. *The Age*, 28 October 1962, p. 1.
'Foreign Policy: On the Firing Line'. *Newsweek*, 21 January 1957, p. 25.
'France, Tunisia Agree to Peace Move'. *The Age*, 18 February 1958, p. 4.
Fry, Michael Graham. 'Decline, Sanctions, and the Suez Crisis, 1956–1957.' *Diplomatic History*, Volume 17, No.2, Spring 1993, pp. 323–329.
Galbraith, John Kenneth. *A Life in Our Times – Memoirs*. Boston, MA: Houghton Mifflin, 1981.
Galbraith, John Kenneth. *Ambassador's Journal*. Boston, MA: Houghton Mifflin, 1969.
Gause III, F. Gregory. *Saudi-Yemeni Relations Domestic Structures and Foreign Influences*. New York: Columbia University Press, 1990.
Gavin, R.J. *Aden under British Rule, 1839–1967*. London: Hurst, 1975.
George, T.J.S. *Krishna Menon: A Biography*. London: Cape, 1964.
George-Picot, Jacques. *The Real Suez Crisis*. New York: Harcourt Brace Jovanovich, 1975.
Gerges, Fawaz A. *The Superpowers and the Middle East, Regional and International Politics, 1955–1967*. London: Westview, 1994.
'The 'Get Dulles' Campaign'. *Newsweek*, 4 February 1958, p. 21.
Ginat, Rami. *Egypt's Incomplete Revolution: Lutfi al-Khuli and Nasser's Socialism in the 1960s*. London: Cass, 1997.
Gomaa, Ahmed M. *The Foundation of the League of Arab States*. London: Longman, 1977.
Good-Adams, Richard. *The Time of Power, A Reappraisal of John Foster Dulles*. London: Weidenfeld & Nicolson, 1962.
Gopal, Sarvepalli. *Jawaharlal Nehru: A Biography, 1956–1964*, Volume II. Delhi: Oxford University Press, 1979.
Gopal, Sarvepalli. *Jawaharlal Nehru: A Biography, 1956–1964*, Volume III. Delhi: Oxford University Press, 1984.
'Government Falls, Leaders Die in Irak Coup, Varied Reports on King's Safety'. *The Age*, 15 July 1958, p. 1.
Grafurov, B.G. *Politika USA na Blishchnem i Srednem Vostoke*. Moskva: Akademiya Nauk CCCP – Institut Narodov Azii, 1960.
Grose, Peter. *The Gentleman Spy*. Wilmington, MA: Houghton Mifflin, 1994.
Guhin, Michael A. *John Foster Dulles: A Statesman and his Times*. New York: Columbia University Press, 1972.
Gundevia, Yezdezard Dinshaw. *Outside the Archives*. Hyderabad: Sangam, 1984.
Gupta, Sisir. *Kashmir, A Study in India-Pakistan Relations*. New York: Asia Publishing and the India Council of World Affairs, 1966.
Hahn, Lorna. 'Last Chance in North Africa'. *Foreign Affairs*, Volume 36, No. 2, January 1958, pp. 302–314.
Hahn, Peter L. 'Containment and Egyptian Nationalism: The Unsuccessful Effort to Establish the Middle East Command, 1950–1953'. *Diplomatic History*, Volume 11, No. 1, Winter 1987, pp. 23–40.
Harrison, Selig. *India: The Most Dangerous Decades*. Princeton, NJ: Princeton University Press, 1960.
Hasuna, Husayn. *sanawat ma al-malik faruq*. al-qahira: dar al-shuruk, 2001.
Hawaidi, Amin. *ma' abd-al-nasir*. al-qahira: dar al-mustaqbal, 1980.

Hazony, Yoram. *The Jewish State: The Struggle for Israel's Soul*. New York. Basic Books, 2001.
Heikal, Muhammad Hussein. *Autumn of Fury: The Assasination of Sadat*. London: André Deutsch, 1983.
Heikal, Muhammad Hussein. *azma al-aurush sadma al-juyush*. Al-Qahira: dar al-shuruq, 2002.
Heikal, Muhammad Hussein. *1967 al-infajar: harb al-thalathin sana*. Nashar: markaz al-ahram liltarjima, 1990.
Heikal, Muhammad Hussein. *al-aurush wa al-juyush: kathalik infajar al-srah fi falistin, 1948–1998*. al-qahira: dar al-shuruq, 2003.
Heikal, Muhammad Hussein. *abd-al-nasir wa al-thaqafun was al-thaqafa*. al-qahira: dar al-shuruq, 2002.
Heikal, Muhammad Hussein. *The Cairo Documents*. New York: Doubleday, 1972.
Heikal, Muhammad Hussein. *Matha Jara fi Suria*. Cairo: National Publishing, 1961.
Heikal, Muhammad Hussein. *al-Mufawadat siria bayn al-arab wa israil*. al-qahira: dar al-shuruk, 2001.
Heikal, Muhammad Hussein. *muthakarat fi siyasat al-misrit*. al-qahira: dar al-muaraf, 1954.
Heikal, Muhammad Hussein. *Qadia al-Suwis*. Beirut: sharaikat al-muthbuat al-tawzia wa al-nashir, 1988.
Heikal, Muhammad Hussein. *Qasa al-Suisa*. Beirut: sharikat al-mutabua't li tawzia wa al-nashir, 1988.
Heikal, Muhammad Hussein. *The Road to Ramadan*. London: Collins, 1975.
Heikal, Muhammad Hussein. *saqut nitham!* al-qahira: dar al-shoruq, 2003.
Heikal, Muhammad Hussein. *Secret Channels*. London: Harper Collins, 1996.
Heikal, Muhammad Hussein. *The Sphinx and the Commissar: The Rise and Fall of the Soviet Influence in the Middle East*. New York: Harper & Row, 1978.
Heikal, Muhammad Hussein. *Cutting the Lion's Tail: Suez through Egyptian Eyes*. London: André Deutsch, 1986.
Heller, Deane and David Heller. *John Foster Dulles, Soldier for Peace*. New York: Holt, Rinehart & Winston, 1960.
Henderson, K.D.D. *Sudan Republic*. New York: Praeger, 1965.
Henriques, Robert. *100 Hours to Suez*. New York: Viking, 1957.
Heptulla, Najma. *Indo-West Asian Relations: The Nehru Era*. New Delhi: Allied, 1991.
Hersh, Seymour M. *The Samson Option: Israel's Nuclear Arsenal and American Foreign Policy*. New York: Vintage, 1991.
Heydemann, Steven. *Authoritarianism in Syria: Institutions and Social Conflict 1946–1970*. Ithaca, NY: Cornell University Press, 1999.
Hiro, Dilip. *The Essential Middle East*. New York: Carroll & Graff, 2003.
Hiro, Dilip. *Dictionary of the Middle East*. New York: St. Martin's, 1996.
Hirschmann, Ira. *Red Star over Bethlehem: Russia Drives for the Middle East*. New York: Simon & Schuster, 1971.
Holden, David. *Farewell to Arabia*. New York: Walker, 1966.
Holden, David, and Richard Johns. *The House of Saud: The Rise and Rule of the Most Powerful Dynasty in the Arab World*. New York: Holt, Rinehart & Winston, 1981.
Hooglund, Eric J. *Land and Revolution in Iran 1960–1980*. Austin: University of Texas Press, 1982.
Hoopes, Townsend. *The Devil and John Foster Dulles*. Boston, MA: Little, Brown, 1973.
Hopwood, Derek. *Egypt: Politics and Society 1945–1990*. London: Routledge, 3rd edition, 1991.
Hopwood, Derek. *Syria: Politics and Society, 1945–1986*. London: Unwin Hyman, 1988.
Horne, Alistair. *Harold Macmillan*. Volumes I and II. London: Penguin, 1989.
Horne, Alistair. *A Savage War of Peace, Algeria 1954–1962*. New York: Penguin, 1979.
Hourani, Albert. 'Near Eastern Nationalism Yesterday and Today'. *Foreign Affairs*, Volume 42, No. 1, October 1963, pp. 123–136.

Hudson, W.J. *Blind Loyalty: Australia and the Suez Crisis, 1956*. Melbourne: University of Melbourne Press, 1989.
Hughes, Joseph V. and Holly O. *Shaping and Signaling Presidential Policy: The National Security Decision Making of Eisenhower & Kennedy*. College Station: Texas A&M Press, 1998.
Hunter, Shireen T. *Iran and the World*. Bloomington: University of Indiana Press, 1990.
Hussein ibn Talal. *Uneasy Lies the Head: The Autobiography of His Majesty King Hussein I of the Hashemite Kingdom of Jordan*. New York: Random House, 1962.
Hussein, Mahmoud. *Class Conflict in Egypt: 1945–1970*. New York: Monthly Review, 1977.
Huxley, Elspeth. 'The Next-to-Last Act in Africa'. *Foreign Affairs*, Volume 39, No. 4, July 1961, pp. 655–669.
Immerman, Richard (ed.). *John Foster Dulles and the Diplomacy of the Cold War*. Princeton, NJ: Princeton University Press, 1990.
'India: The Tea Fed Tiger'. *Time*, 2 February 1962, pp. 16–20.
'Indian Soldiers in Better Position against Chinese'. *The Age*, 28 October 1962, p. 1.
'In a Common Cause'. *Newsweek*, 24 February 1958, pp. 41–42.
Ismael, Tariq Y. *The Arab Left*. Syracuse, NY: Syracuse University Press, 1976.
Jalal, Ayesha. *The State of Martial Rule: The Origins of Pakistan's Political Economy of Defense*. Cambridge: Cambridge University Press, 1990.
Jankowski, James, and Israel Gershoni (eds.). *Rethinking Nationalism in the Arab Middle East*. New York: Columbia University Press, 1997.
Jawaharlal Nehru in Soviet Perspective. New Delhi: Sterling, 1980.
Johnson, U. Alexis. *The Right Hand of Power: Memoirs of an American Diplomat*. Eglewood Cliffs, NJ: Prentice-Hall, 1984.
Kalb, Madeleine G. *The Congo Cables: The Cold War in Africa – from Eisenhower to Kennedy*. New York: Macmillan, 1982.
Kaplan, Robert D. *The Arabists: The Romance of an American Elite*. New York: Free Press, 1995.
Karpat, Kamal H. (ed.). *Thought in the Contemporary Political and Social Middle East*. New York: Praeger, 1968.
Katouzian, Homa. *Musaddiq and the Struggle for Power in Iran*. New York: Tauris, 1999.
Katz, Mark N. *Russia & Arabia: Soviet Foreign Policy toward the Arabian Peninsula*. Baltimore, MD: Johns Hopkins University Press, 1986.
Keddie, Nikki R. *Modern Iran*. New Haven, CT: Yale University Press, 1981.
Kedourie, Ellie. *Politics in the Middle East*. Oxford: Oxford University Press, 1992.
Kennan, George F. *Realities of American Foreign Policy*. New York: Norton, 1966.
Kennedy, John F. *The Strategy of Peace*. New York: Harper & Row, 1960.
Keppel, Gilles. *Muslim Extremism in Egypt: Prophet and Pharaoh*. Berkeley: University of California Press, 1984.
Kerr, Malcolm. *The Arab Cold War, 1958–1967*. London: Oxford University Press, 1967.
Kerr, Malcolm. 'The Emergence of a Socialist Ideology in Egypt'. *Middle East Journal*, Spring 1962, Volume 16, pp. 127–144.
Khalidi, Walid and Yusuf Ibish. *Arab Political Documents 1963*. Beirut: American University of Beirut, 1963.
Khuri, Fuad I. *Imams and Emirs: State, Religion and Sects in Islam*. Beirut: Saqi, 1990.
Kingseed, Cole C. *Eisenhower and the Suez Crisis of 1956*. Baton Rouge: Louisiana State University, 1995.
Kinzer, Stephen. *All the Shah's Men*. Hoboken, NY: Wiley, 2003.
Kolkowicz, Roman. 'Middle Eastern Policy'. In Cofino, Michael and Shimon Shamir (eds.) *The U.S.S.R. and the Middle East*. New York: Wiley, 1973.
Korany, Bahgat, and Ali E. Hilal Dessouki (eds.). *The Foreign Policy of the Arab States: The Challenge of Change*. Boulder, CO: Westview, 1991.
Kothari, Rajni. *India*. Boston, MA: Little, Brown, 1970.

Kuniholm, Bruce R. *The Origins of the Cold War in the Near East: Great Power Conflict and Diplomacy in Iran, Turkey, and Greece*. Princeton, NJ: Princeton University Press, 1980.
Kux, Dennis. *The United States and Pakistan 1947–2000*. Baltimore, MD: Johns Hopkins University Press, 2001.
Kyle, Keith. *Suez*. New York: St. Martin's, 1991.
Lacouture, Jean, and Simone Lacouture. *Egypt in Transition*. New York: Criterion, 1958.
Lackner, Helen. *P.D.R. Yemen: Outpost of Socialist Development in Arabia*. London: Ithaca, 1985.
Lacy, Robert. *The Kingdom: Arabia and the House of Saud*. New York: Harcourt, Brace, Jovanovich, 1981.
Lall, Arthur. *The Emergence of Modern India*. New York: Columbia, 1981.
Lall, Arthur. *How Communist China Negotiates*. New York: Columbia University Press, 1968.
Laqueur, Walter (ed.). *The Middle East in Transition*. New York: Praeger, 1958.
Laqueur, Walter. 'Russia Enters the Middle East'. *Foreign Affairs*, Volume 47, No. 2, January 1969, pp. 296–308.
Larres, Klaus. *Churchill's Cold War: The Politics of Personal Diplomacy*. New Haven, CT: Yale University Press, 2002.
'Lebanon Rebel Chief Orders 'Cease Fire' in Beirut'. *The Age*, 17 July 1958, p. 1.
Ledeen, Michael and William Lewis. *Debacle: The American Failure in Iran*. New York: Random House, 1982.
Lefebvre, Jeffrey A. 'The United States and Egypt: Confrontation and Accommodation in Northeast Africa, 1956–1960'. *Middle Eastern Studies*, Volume 29, No. 2, April 1993, pp. 321–338.
Legum, Colin. 'What Kind of Radicalism for Africa?' *Foreign Affairs*, Volume 43, No. 2, January 1965, pp. 237–250.
Lenczowski, George. *American Presidents in the Middle East*. Durham, NC: Duke University Press, 1990.
Lenczowski, George (ed.). *Iran Under the Pahlavi's*. Stanford, CA: Hoover Institute, 1978.
Lengyel, Emil. *Krishna Menon*. New York: Walker, 1962.
Lesch, David W. *Syria and the United States: Eisenhower's Cold War in the Middle East*. Oxford: Westview, 1992.
Lia, Brynjar. *The Society of Muslim Brothers in Egypt: The Rise of an Islamic Mass Movement 1928–1942*. London: Ithaca, 1998.
Lilienthal, Alfred M. *There Goes the Middle East*. New York: Devin-Adair, 1957.
Lippmann, Walter. *The Coming Tests with Russia*. Boston: Little, Brown, 1961.
Little, Douglas. *American Orientalism: The United States and the Middle East since 1945*. Chapel Hill: University of North Carolina Press, 2002.
Little, Douglas. 'A Fool's Errand: America and the Middle East, 1961-1969'. In Dianne Kunz (ed.) *The Diplomacy of the Crucial Decade: American Foreign Relations in the 1960s*. New York: Columbia University Press, 1994, pp. 283–319.
Little, Douglas. 'From Even-Handed to Empty-Handed: Seeking Order in the Middle East'. In Thomas G. Paterson (ed.) *Kennedy Quest for Victory: American Foreign Policy, 1961–1963*. Oxford: Oxford University Press, 1989, pp. 156–177.
Little, Douglas. 'Gideon's Band: America and the Middle East since 1945'. *Diplomatic History*, Volume 18, No. 4, Fall 1994, pp. 513–540.
Little, Douglas. 'The New Frontier on the Nile: JFK, Nasser, and Arab Nationalism'. *Journal of American History*, Volume 75, No. 2, September 1988, pp. 501–527.
Little, Tom. *South Arabia: Arena of Conflict*. New York: Praeger, 1968.
Lloyd, Selwyn. *Suez, 1956: A Personal Account*. London: Trinity, 1978.
Lorne, Kavic J. *India's Quest for Security*. Berkeley: University of California Press, 1967.
Louis, William Roger. *The British Empire in the Middle East 1945–1951*. Oxford: Oxford University Press, 1984.
Louis, William Roger. 'Dulles, Suez and the British'. In Richard Immerman (ed.) *John Foster Dulles and the Diplomacy of the Cold War*. Princeton: Princeton University Press, 1990.

Louis, William Roger and Roger Owen (eds.). *A Revolutionary Year – The Middle East in 1958*. London: I.B. Tauris, 2002.
Louis, William Roger and Roger Owen (eds.). *Suez 1956: The Crisis and its Consequences*. Oxford: Clarendon, 1991.
Love, Kenneth. *Suez: The Twice Fought War*. New York: McGraw-Hill, 1969.
Lunt, James. *Hussein of Jordan*. London: Macmillan, 1990.
Lyman, Robert. *Iraq 1941: The Battles for Basra, Habbaniyah, Fallujah, and Baghdad*. London: Osprey, 2006.
Mackey, Sandra. *The Saudis: Inside the Desert Kingdom*. London: Penguin, 1987.
Macmillan, Harold. *At the End of the Day, 1961–1965*. New York: Harper & Row, 1973.
Macmillan, Harold. *Pointing the Way, 1959–1961*. London: Macmillan, 1972.
Macmillan, Harold. *Riding the Storm, 1955–1958*. New York: Harper & Row, 1971.
Macmillan, Harold. *Tides of Fortune, 1945–1955*. New York: Harper & Row, 1969.
Mansfield, Peter. *The New Arabs*. Chicago, IL: Ferguson, 1981.
Mansingh, Surjit. *Historical Dictionary of India*. New Delhi: Vision, 1998.
Marash, Ahsan. *al-thawara al-dimuqratiya al-arabiya*. Beirut: Dar al-Hakanu, 1982.
Marks, Frederick W. III. *Power and Peace, The Diplomacy of John Foster Dulles*. Westport, CT: Praeger, 1993.
Marr, Phebe. *The Modern History of Iraq*. Boulder, CO: Westview, 2004.
Martin, Vanessa. *Creating an Islamic State: Khomeini and the Making of a New Iran*. London: Tauris, 2000.
McLean, Donald. *British Foreign Policy: The Years Since Suez*. New York: Stein & Day, 1970.
Mende, Tibor. *Conversations with Mr. Nehru*. London: Secker & Warburg, 1956.
Meyer, Gail E. *Egypt and the United States: The Formative Years*. Madison, WI: Fairleigh Dickinson University Press, 1980.
'The Middle East – Between Thunder & Sun'. *Time*, 31 March 1958, p 17.
'The Middle East – How and Why the U.S. Aims to Fill the Vacuum'. *Newsweek*, 7 January 1957, p. 24.
'Middle East: Our Edge in the Sudan'. *Newsweek*, 24 March 1958, p. 49.
'The Middle East: Undertow'. *Newsweek*, 17 March 1958, p. 40.
Mier, Golda. *My Life, by Golda Mier*. New York: Putman, 1975.
Miller, Von T.B. 'Der Streit um Kaschmir'. *Europa-Archiv*, Volume 17, 1966, pp. 625–634.
Mirza, Humayun. *From Plassey to Pakistan: The Family History of Iskander Mirza, the First President of Pakistan*. New York: University Press of America, 1999.
Mitchell, Richard P. *The Society of Muslim Brothers*. Oxford: Oxford University Press, 1993.
Monroe, Elizabeth. *Britain's Moment in the Middle East, 1914–1956*. London: Chatto & Windus, 1964.
Morris, James. *Islam Inflamed: A Middle East Picture*. New York: Pantheon, 1957.
Mosley, Leonard. *Dulles: A Biography of Eleanor, Allen, and John Foster Dulles and Their Family Network*. New York: Dial Press/James Wade, 1978.
Mosely, Philip E. 'Soviet Policy in the Developing World'. *Foreign Affairs*, Volume 43, No. 1, October 1964, pp. 87–98.
'Mr. Dulles in Bid to Avert Showdown on Tunisian Dispute'. *The Age*, 17 February 1958, p. 4.
Muntisar, Salah. *min urabi ila abd-al-nasir*. al-qahira: dar al-shuruk, 2003.
'Mr. Kennedy is Ready to Negotiate'. *The Age*, 28 October 1962, p. 1.
Mufti, Malik. *Sovereign Creations: Pan-Arabism and Political Order in Syria and Iraq*. Ithaca, NY: Cornell University Press, 1996.
Mullik, B.N. *The Chinese Betrayal: My Years with Nehru*. Bombay: Allied, 1971.
Murphy, Robert. *Diplomat among Warriors*. New York: Doubleday, 1964.
Nasser, Jamal Abd-al. 'The Principles that Guide Egypt's Political Life'. In Kemal H. Karpat (ed.) *Political and Social Thought in the Contemporary Middle East*. New York: Praeger, 1963.

Neff, Donald. *Warriors at Suez: Eisenhower Takes American into the Middle East.* New York: Simon & Schuster, 1981.
Neville, Maxwell. *India's China War.* New York: Pantheon, 1970.
'New Mideastern Gambit'. *Nation,* 15 February 1958, p. 129.
Nixon, Richard. 'Address delivered before the American Society of Newspaper Editors, Washington, D.C., 13 April 1960'. *Vital Speeches of the Day,* June 1, 1960, No. 26, p. 485.
Nixon, Richard M. *The Memoirs of Richard Nixon.* New York: Grosset & Dunlap, 1978.
Nizameddin, Talal. *Russia and the Middle East: Towards a New Foreign Policy.* New York: St. Martin's, 1999.
Nolte, Richard. 'Getting Tough in the Middle East: A Letter from Richard H. Nolte, Beirut, Lebanon, 8 October 1956'. *AUFS – Northeast Africa Series,* Volume II, No. 1, pp. 8–10, 14.
Nutting, Anthony. *Nasser.* New York: Dutton, 1972.
O'Ballance, Edgar. *The Kurdish Revolt: 1961–1970.* London: Archon, 1973.
O'Ballance, Edgar. *The War in Yemen.* Hamden, CT: Archon, 1971.
'Our Secretary of State, Americans Like Him – But…'. *Newsweek,* 27 January 1958, p. 33.
Pack, Chester A. and Elmo Richardson. *The Presidency of Dwight D. Eisenhower.* Lawrence: University of Kansas Press, 1991.
Page, Bruce, David Leitch, and Phillip Knightley. *The Philby Conspiracy.* New York: Ballantine, 1981.
Pahlavi, Muhammad Reza. *Answer to History.* New York: Stein and Day, 1980.
'The Painful Presidency of Egypt's Nasser'. *Time,* 16 May 1969, pp. 29–39.
Parker, Richard. *John Kennedy Galbraith: His Life, His Politics, His Economics.* New York: Farrar, Straus & Giroux, 2005.
Parmet, Herbert. *Eisenhower and the American Crusades.* New York: Macmillan, 1972.
Pazhwak, Rahman. *Pakhtunistan: A New State in Central Asia.* London: Royal Afghan Embassy, 1960.
Peres, Shimon. *David's Sling.* New York: Random House, 1970.
Perret, Geoffrey. *Eisenhower.* New York: Random House, 1999.
'The Periscope'. *Newsweek,* 6 August 1962, p. 9.
Phillips, Wendell. *Oman: A History.* London: Wendell Phillips, 1967.
Peterson, J.E. *Historical Dictionary of Saudi Arabia.* London: Scarecrow, 1993.
Phillips, Horace. *Envoy Extraordinary: A Most Unlikely Ambassador.* London: Radcliffe, 1995.
Pinckley, Virgil and James F. Scheer. *Eisenhower Declassified.* Old Tappen, NJ: Renell, 1979.
Pipes, Daniel. *Greater Syria: The History of Ambition.* Oxford: Oxford University Press, 1990.
Podeh, Elie. *The Quest for Hegemony in the Arab World: The Struggle Over the Baghdad Pact.* Leiden: Brill, 1995.
Polk, William R. *The United States and the Arab World.* Cambridge, MA: Harvard University Press, 1969.
Pollack, Kenneth. *The Persian Puzzle: The Conflict Between Iran and America.* New York: Random House, 2004.
Prados, John. *Presidents' Secret Wars.* New York: Morrow, 1996.
Pruessen, Ronald. *John Foster Dulles, The Road to Power.* New York: Free Press, 1982.
Rabinovich, Itamar. *Syria Under the Ba'th 1963–1966.* Jerusalem: Israel University Press, 1972.
Rahmy, Ali Abdel Rahman. *The Egyptian Policy in the Arab World: Intervention in Yemen 1962–1967.* Washington, DC: University Press of America, 1963.
Ramazani, R.K. *Revolutionary Iran: Challenge and Response in the Middle East.* Baltimore, MD: Johns Hopkins University Press, 1983.
Ram, Janaki. *V.K. Krishna Menon: A Personal Memoir.* Delhi: Oxford University Press, 1997.
Ranelagh, John. *The Agency: The Rise and Decline of the CIA.* New York: Simon & Schuster, 1986.
Rashid, H. 'Egypt's Workers Fight for Freedom', *African Communist,* No. 44, 1971, pp. 31–37.

Rasheed, Madawi. *A History of Saudi Arabia*. Cambridge: Cambridge University Press, 2002.
'The Revolutionary'. *Time*, 26 September 1955, pp. 25–28.
Rejwan, Nissim. *Nasserist Ideology: Its Exponents and Critics*. New Brunswick, NJ: Jerusalem University Press, 1974.
Rivkin, Arnold. 'Israel and the Afro-Asian World.' *Foreign Affairs*, Volume 37, No. 3, April 1959, pp. 486–495.
Rizvi, Hasan Askari. *The Military and Politics in Pakistan*. Lahore: Progressive, 1974.
Robins, Philip. *A History of Jordan*. Cambridge: Cambridge University Press, 2004.
Rostow, Walt W. *The Dynamics of Soviet Society*. New York: Norton, 1953.
Rostow, Walt W. *Europe After Stalin: Eisenhower's Three Decisions of March 11, 1953*. Austin: University of Texas Press, 1982.
Rostow, Walt W. *Politics and the Stages of Growth*. Cambridge: Cambridge University Press, 1971.
Rostow, Walt W. *The Process of Economic Growth*. New York: Norton, 1962.
Rostow, Walt W., and Max F. Millikan. *A Proposal: Key to Effective Foreign Policy*. New York: Harper, 1957.
Rostow, Walt W. *The Prospects for Communist China*. Cambridge, MA: MIT Press, 1954.
Rostow, Walt W. *The United States in the World Arena: An Essay in Recent History*. New York: Simon & Schuster, 1969.
Roy, Meenu. *Thousand Days of Indo-US Diplomacy: The Kennedy-Nehru Era*. New Delhi: Deep & Deep, 1993.
Rubenstein, Alvin Z. *Red Star on the Nile*. Princeton, NJ: Princeton University Press, 1977.
'Russia – Our Dear Guest'. *Time*, 12 May 1958, p. 26.
'Russians Call West to Crisis Conference'. *The Age*, 21 July 1958, p. 1.
Sachar, Howard M. *A History of Israel: From the Rise of Zionism to Our Time*. New York: Knopf, 1976.
Sadat, Anwar. *In Search of Identity: An Autobiography*. New York: Harper & Row, 1977.
Sadat, Anwar. *Revolt on the Nile*. London: Allan Wingate, 1957.
Safran, Nadav. *Saudi Arabia: The Ceaseless Quest for Security*. Ithaca, NY: Cornell University Press, 1988.
Said, Abdel Moghny. *Arab Socialism*. New York: Harper & Row, 1972.
Saikal, Amin. *The Rise and Fall of the Shah*. PrincetonNJ: Princeton University Press, 1980.
St. John, Robert. *The Boss: The Story of Gamal Abdul Nasser*. New York: McGraw Hill, 1960.
Salibi, Kamal. *The Modern History of Jordan*. London: Tauris, 1998.
Salinger, Pierre. *With Kennedy*. Garden City, KS: Doubleday, 1966.
Sanger, Clyde. 'Toward Unity in Africa'. *Foreign Affairs*, Volume 42, No. 2, January 1964, pp. 269–281.
SarDesai, D.R. *Indian Foreign Policy in Cambodia, Laos, and Vietnam, 1947–1964*. Berkeley: University of California Press, 1968.
Sarhan, Muhammad Samir (ed.). *Who's Who in Saudi Arabia, 1976–1977*. Jidda: Tihama, 1977.
Sayf al-Dawlah, 'Ismat. *nathria al-thawra al-arabia*. Volume V. Beirut: Dar al-Musira, 1979.
Sayf al-Dawlah, 'Ismat. *nathria al-thawra al-arabia*. Voume VI. Beirut: Dar al-Musira, 1979.
Schaffer, Howard B. *Chester Bowles, New Dealer in the Cold War*. Cambridge, MA: Harvard University Press, 1993.
Schlesinger, Arthur, Jr. *A Thousand Days: John F. Kennedy in the White House*, Boston,MA: Houghton Mifflin, 1965.
Schmidt, Dana Adams. 'Nasser Believed Warier of Soviet'. *New York Times*, 9 May 1958, p. 5
Schmidt, Dana Adams. 'U.S. Set to Free Egyptian Assets'. *New York Times*, 25 April 1958, p. 9.
Schmidt, Dana Adams. *Yemen: The Unknown War*. New York: Hold, Rinehart, Winston, 1968.
Seale, Patrick. *The Struggle for Syria, A Study of Post-War Arab Politics*. New Haven, CT: Yale University Press, 1965.

Shalaq, Al-Fadhi. 'Concepts of the Nation and State with Special Reference to the Sunnis in Lebanon'. In Youssef M. Choueiri (ed.) *State and Society in Syria and Lebanon*. New York: St. Martins, 1993.

Sharabi, Hisham. 'The Scholarly Point of View: Politics, Perspective, Paradigm'. In Hisham Sharaby (ed.) *Theory and Politics in the Arab World, Critical Responses*. New York: Routledge, Chapman & Hall, in cooperation with the Center for Contemporary Arab Studies, Georgetown University, 1990.

Shaw, Stanford J. and Ezel Kural Shaw. *History of the Ottoman Empire and Modern Turkey: Reform, Revolution, and Republic, 1808–1975*. Cambridge: Cambridge University Press, 1977.

Sheean, Vincent. 'King Faisal's First Year'. *Foreign Affairs* Volume 44, No. 2, January 1966, pp. 304–313.

Shean, Vincent. *Nehru: The Years of Power*. New York: Random House, 1960.

Sherrod, Robert. 'The Violent and Vital World of Nasser'. *Saturday Evening Post*, Volume 236, No. 20, 25 May 1963, pp. 17–23.

Shichor, Yitzhak. *The Middle East in China's Foreign Policy, 1949–1977*. Cambridge: Cambridge University Press, 1979.

Shlaim, Avi. *The Iron Wall: Israel and the Arab World*. London: Penguin, 2000.

Shuckburgh, Evelyn. *Descent to Suez: Foreign Office Diaries 1951–1956*. New York: Norton, 1986.

Sidney, Hugh. *John F. Kennedy, President*. New York: Atheneum, 1964.

Sinai, Anne and Allen Pollock (eds.). *The Hashemite Kingdom of Jordan and the West Bank*. New York: American Academic Association for Peace in the Middle East, 1977.

Sinai, Anne and Allen Pollock (eds.). *The Syrian Arab Republic: A Handbook*. New York: American Academic Association for Peace in the Middle East, 1976.

Sluglett, Peter and Marion Farouk-Sluglett. *Iraq since 1958: From Revolution to Dictatorship*. New York: Tauris, 2001.

Somerville-Large, Peter. *Tribes and Tribulations*. London: Hale, 1967.

Sorenson, Theodore. *Kennedy*. New York: Harper & Row, 1965.

'Special International Report: Pakistan – A Leader Gets Things Done'. *Newsweek*, 18 April 1960, pp. 54–58.

Spain, James W. 'Middle East Defense: A New Approach'. *Middle East Journal*, Volume 8, Summer 1954, pp. 251–266.

'Special National Report: Candidate Nixon's Insiders'. *Newsweek*, 13 June 1960, pp. 33–38.

Srodes, James. *Allen Dulles, Master of Spies*. Washington, DC: Regency, 1999.

Stassen, Harold and Marshall Houts. *Eisenhower: Turning the World toward Peace*. St. Paul, MN: Merrill/Magnus, 1990.

Stebbins, Richard. *The United States in World Affairs, 1956*. New York: Harper & Row, 1957.

Stebbins, Richard. *The United States in World Affairs, 1959*. New York: Harper & Row, 1960.

Stephens, Ian. *Pakistan: Old Country/New Nation*. Harlow: Penguin, 1963.

Stephens, Robert. *Nasser, A Political Biography*. New York: Simon & Schuster, 1971.

Stora, Benjamin. *Algeria 1830–2000: A Short History*. Ithaca, NY: Cornell University Press, 2001.

Streit, Peggy and Pierre. 'Close-Up of the Foreign Aid Dilemma'. *New York Times*, 13 April 1958, p. 10.

Sulzberger, C.L. 'Foreign Affairs: A Time for Diplomatic Calm'. *New York Times*, 7 April 1958, p. 20.

Summitt, April R. 'For a White Revolution: John F. Kennedy and the Shah of Iran'. *Middle East Journal*, Volume 58, No. 4, Autumn 2004, pp. 560–575.

Talbot, Phillips. 'A Glimpse of Pakistan: First Impressions of a Returning Visitor, Lahore, 31 October 1956'. *American Universities Field Staff Reports, South Asia Series (AUFS-SAS)*, Vol. I, No. 1, pp. 1–4.

Talbot, Phillips. 'I am a Pakistani'. *AUFS-SAS*, 28 November 1956, Ian Stephens Papers, Archives of Center for South Asian Studies, University of Cambridge.

Talbot, Phillips and S.L. Poplai. *India and America, A Study of Their Relations.* New York: Harper, 1958.
Talbot, Phillips. 'A Note on India and Pakistan, New York, 12 September 1957'. *AUFS-SAS*, Vol. II, No. 9, p. 16.
Talbot, Phillips. 'Pakistan Doesn't Like It, Reactions to the Egyptian Crisis, Lahore, 8 November 1956'. *AUFS-SAS*, Vol. 1, No. 2, pp. 1–8.
Talbot, Phillips. 'Raising the Cry for Secession, the Ambitions of the 'Political Dravidians', Letter from Tiruchirappalli, South India, May 22, 1957'. *AUFS-SAS*, Vol. II, No. 8, pp. 1–7.
Talbot, Phillips (ed.). *South Asia in the World Today.* Chicago, IL: University of Chicago Press, 1950.
Tamer, A.M. 'Who Likes Dulles, Who Doesn't, The Arab States'. *Newsweek* (Beirut Bureau) 27 January 1958, p. 29.
'The Tea-Fed Tiger'. *Time*, 2 February 1962, pp. 16–20.
Tessler, Mark. *A History of the Israeli-Palestinian Conflict.* Bloomington: University of Indiana Press, 1994.
Tibi, Bassam. *Arab Nationalism: A Critical Enquiry.* Trans. Marion Farouk-Sluglett and Peter Sluglett. New York: St. Martin's, 1990.
Tiblock, Tim (ed.). *State, Society and Economy in Saudi Arabia.* New York: St. Martin's, 1982.
Trevelyan, Sir Humphrey. *The Middle East in Revolution.* London: Macmillan, 1970.
Tripp, Charles. *A History of Iraq.* West Nyack, NY: Cambridge University Press, 2002.
Toulouse, Mark. *The Transformation of John Foster Dulles from Prophet of Realism to Priest of Nationalism.* New York: Mercer University Press, 1985.
'U.A.R. – Father Ibrahim's Plot'. *Time*, 17 March 1958, p. 24.
'U.K. Troops Land in Jordan'. *The Age*, 18 July 1958, p. 1.
Varkey, K.T. *V.K. Krishna Menon and India's Foreign Policy.* New Delhi: India, 2002.
Vassiliev, Alexei. *Russian Policy in the Middle East: From Messianism to Pragmatism.* Reading, PA: Ithaca, 1993.
Vatikiotis, P.J. *The Modern History of Egypt from Muhammad Ali to Mubarak.* Baltimore, MD: Johns Hopkins University Press, 1991.
Vats, Bhagat. *Foreign Intrigue Against India.* New Delhi: Aman, 1967.
Wall, Irwin M. *France, the United States, and the Algerian War.* Berkeley: University of California Press, 2001.
Warner, Geoffrey. *Iraq and Syria 1941.* Newark, NJ: University of Delaware Press, 1974.
'Warsaw ... Cairo ... Moscow'. *Newsweek*, 28 January 1957, pp. 41–42.
Waterbury, John. *The Egypt of Nasser and Sadat: The Political Economy of Two Regimes.* Princeton, NJ: Princeton University Press, 1983.
Weintal, Edward. 'Behind-Scenes in Washington: A Change Toward Nasser'. *Newsweek*, 21 April 1958, p. 53.
Weintal, Edward. 'Intelligence Disaster in Iraq'. *Newsweek*, 4 August 1958, p. 20.
'What Now?' *Nation*, 2 August 1958, p. 42.
'Where Do We Go from Here?' *Newsweek*, 28 July 1958, pp. 15–16.
'Who Likes Dulles – Who Doesn't.' *Newsweek*, 27 January 1958, p. 28.
Wilber, Donald N. *Pakistan.* New Haven: Human Relations Area Files, 1964.
Wilson, Peter W., and Douglas F. Graham. *Saudi Arabia: The Coming Storm.* Armonk, NY: Sharpe, 1994.
Wirsing, Robert G. *India, Pakistan, and the Kashmir Dispute: On Regional Conflict and Its Resolution.* New York: St. Martin's, 1998.
Wolpert, Stanley. *A New History of India.* Oxford: Oxford University Press, 1997.
Wynn, Wilton. *Nasser of Egypt: The Search for Dignity.* Cambridge, MA: Arlington Books, 1959.
Yapp, M.E. *Strategies of British India: Britain, Iran, and Afghanistan, 1798-1850.* Oxford: Clarendon, 1980.
Yapp, M.E. *The Near East since the First World War.* London: Longman, 1991.

'Yemen: Grappling Demons.' *Newsweek*, 11 February 1957, pp. 45–46.
Zahlan, Said Rosemarie. *The Making of the Modern Gulf States*. London: Ithaca, 1998.
Ziring, Lawrence. *The Ayub Khan Era: Politics in Pakistan, 1958-1969*. Syracuse, NY: Syracuse University Press, 1971.
Zürcher, Eric. *Turkey: A Modern History*. London: Tauris, 1998.

Dissertations

Ashur, George Arthur. The Kennedy-Nasir Correspondence: A Policy of Accommodation. Harvard University, 1991.
Beatty, Kirk James. Egypt, the Struggle for Hegemony, 1952–1981. University of Michigan, 1985.
Fallatah, Muhammad A.S. The Emergence of Pan-Arabism and its Impact on Egyptian Foreign Policy, 1945–1981. University of Idaho, 1986.
Kabbara, Mahmoud Farouk. Abd-al-Nasir's Egypt and the Soviet Union: An Egyptian View, 1952–1970 – the Impact of the Differences between Arab Socialism and Marxist-Leninist Ideologies. University of Arizona, 1981.
Kling, Daniel Richard. The Yemen Civil War and its International Aspects. University of Arizona, 1969.
Yaqub, Salim Clyde. Containing Arab Nationalism: The United States, the Arab Middle East, and the Eisenhower Doctrine, 1956–1959. New Haven: Yale University, 1999.

Index

Aden 54, 55, 57, 270, 273, 277, 357n74
Adenauer, Chancellor Konrad 196
Afghanistan 156, 158, 167, 168, 248, 250, 253, 402-3n99
Aflaq, Michael, Ba'th Party leader 46-7, 300
Age, The, Melbourne 265
Ahmad, Imam, Yemeni ruler 55, 206, 268, 269
Ahmad al-Sabah, Sheikh Jair al-, Kuwaiti ruler 199
Ahmed, Aziz, Pakistani Ambassador 261, 262
Al-Ahram, Cairo 111, 196, 200, 202, 204, 277, 299
Al-Juhuriya, Cairo 276
Al-Nahar, Beirut 59
Al-Thawra, Baghdad 123
Alaa, Husain, Iranian Minister 87, 156
Alam, Asadollah 241, 306
Alavi-Moghadam, Medi Qoli 159-60
Algeria: FLN insurrection 30, 142, 168, 200, 204, 342n109
Ali Khan, Liquat, former Pakistani Prime Minister 169
Ali Razmara, General Sephabod Haj 14
Allen, George 153

'Alwan, Jaim 303
Amer, Muhammad Abd-al-Hakim, Egyptian Field Marshal 124-5, 201
Amin, Majid 123
Amini, Dr Ali, Iranian Prime Minister: yields to teachers' strike 22; claims land reform is meaningless 159; supported by Kennedy 212; appointed by Shah 217-18; moderate reform program 220; used by Shah as lever on US 221; must suppress National Front 223; Kennedy's personal support 229-30; warns of Shah's insistence on military aid 233; last chance to deliver 235; admits failure to control budget 236-7; responsible for economic projects 237-8; forced to resign 240, 430n34
Anderson, Robert B, Treasury Secretary 54
Anglo-American alliance 5-6
Anglo-Egyptian Treaty 1954 18, 19, 23
Ansari, Masud, Ambassador 157
Aqaba, Gulf of 53
Arab Cold War 107, 127, 128, 180, 377n1

INDEX

Arab League: opposes any non-Arab defensive alliance 18; throws off last British influence 40; admits Kuwait 200

Arab Union, Jordan and Iraq 53

Arab-Israeli dispute 20-1, 334n47

Aram, Abbas 245

Aref, Colonel Abd-al-Salam al- 72, 73, 77, 109, 112, 298, 304

Armitage, John 244

Arsanjani, Hassan 222-3, 237

Assad, Hafiz al- 300

Aswan Dam Project 33, 49, 187, 324, 351n24

Atlee, Prime Minister Clement 328; regional collective security schemes 331n4

Awqati, Brigadier Jalal 298

Ayub Khan, General Muhammad 100, 105, 149, 150, 156; criticises British position in Baghdad Pact 156, 398n29; military rule succeeds 163; coup as revolution away from Communism 165, 321, 40178; proposed talks with Nehru rejected 166-7; impresses Eisenhower as anti-Communist 167, 172; diplomatic role a success 168, 402-3n99; refuses to renounce military force 169; Kennedy victory endangers US-Pakistan relations 178, 409n26; disquiet at Kennedy's advisors 246, 433n7; fears aid to India enables military build-up 247, 433n4, 433n6; needs to remind Kennedy of CENTO and SEATO 247, 433-4n8; proposes controlled democracy 247, 433n5; offers troops against Laotian Communists 250; US aid to India prevents Kashmir settlement 250, 253; visits London and US 251; accepts Eugene Black as mediator 259; insists Kennedy support him at the UN 259, 440n96; calls for Kennedy to honor promises 262; visits Kennedy for talks 263, 442n136, 442n137; demands India honor plebiscite agreements 283, 447n25; tells Kennedy India cannot be trusted 284; no alternative to relations with Communist China 310

Azerbaijan 154

Azodi, Yadollah 159

B-57 aircraft 167

Badaber intelligence site: monitors Soviet missiles 93, 105, 167

Badeau, John, Ambassador: Arabist, but no diplomat 185, 411n49; downplays ideological differences with Nasser 186; argues Israel pursues its own interests 196; expects Nasser verbal attacks on US 202; told not to protest attacks on Kennedy 204; support for monarchies plays into Soviet hands 206, 267; Feisal takeover will assist stability 207; urged to recognize Yemen Arab Republic 269-70, 272, 443n6; downplays Kennedy's support of Saudi Arabia 275; visits Kennedy to recommend recognition 276, 445n57; wants Feisal to withdraw from Yemen conflict 294; urges caution towards UAR 296, 450n13; informs Nasser US aircraft exercise near Yemen 297, 450n21; pro-Israeli attempts to cut aid to Egypt 303, 452n56; warns Egyptians against intervention in Jordan 303

Badr, Yemeni Crown Prince Muhammad al- 55, 56, 268, 269

Baghdad Pact: Turkey, Egypt and Iraq 19; Pakistan is eastern pillar 31; Iraq joins, supported by Britain 37; US Refuses to join 48; neutral response to Egypt-Syria union 52,

351n29; conference 55; Britain blocks Kuwait joining 68; if Iraq leaves, US will join 76, 365-6n70; India sees Pakistani's presence as threat 102; becomes Central Treaty Organization (CENTO) 105; Qasim withdraws Iraq 113, 379n31; Shah demands US commitment 152; needs military command structure 156, 397-8n28; a political, not military, organization 318

Bakhtiar, General Timur, SAVAK 91, 160-1, 214-15

Ball, George 203, 205, 261, 310

Bandung Conference 1955 28, 29, 31-3, 320

Bartlett, Fred 101

Baruch, Bernard 10

Battle, Lucius 232

Baydani, Abd-al-Rahman 269, 272-3

Beeley, Sir Harold 274, 277, 299

Beersheba 147

Ben-Gurion, David, Israeli Prime Minister: no intention of refugee return 21; threatens to occupy West Bank 73, 363-4n55; developing nuclear weapons 127; forced to withdraw from Sinai 142; uses Soviet threats to obtain US guarantee 143; nuclear weapons priority 144; announces reactor exclusively peaceful 147, 394n93; US is doing more for Nasser than Iran 156; puts conditions on Johnson Plan 205-6, 209; offers US access to Dimona reactor 208-9; vehemently opposes any repatriation 209; makes no concessions to Kennedy 210; lobbies for new weapons after UAR threat 302; warns of constant threat of Nasser 303

Bergmann, Ernst David 145

Bhutto, Pakistani Foreign Minister 248, 291, 309

Bitar, Salah al-Din al- 125, 298, 301

Bizri, General Afif al- 50

Black, Eugene, President of World Bank 259, 267

Borujerdi, Ayatollah of Qom 307

Bourgiba, President Habib, Tunisia 52-3, 194

Bowles: tries to get Johnson to agree aid plan 311, 456n127

Bowles, Congressman Chester: opposes aid to Pakistan 167, 411n48; tells Kennedy Eisenhower's policy is similar 173; champions economic aid 177; believes Dulles policy was mishandled 181; sees UAR as basically revolutionary 203-4; urges economic aid and reduced military 231; says Shah is key to stability 233; urges cap on military budget 234; foreign policy advisor to Kennedy 246, 431n1; deplores intelligence base in Pakistan 250, 435n26; sent to reassure Nehru 254, 436n54; pro-India policies 256; lack of aid to India opens door to Soviet 263; give both countries defensive weapons equally 310; plans aid to India without upsetting Pakistan 311

Bowling, John W 162, 163, 214, 224, 231

British: phased withdrawal from Canal Zone 18, 334n37; cautious attitude to Bandung Conference 30, 341n102; reject support for Iraqi expansion 50; predict failure of Egyptian-Syrian union 51-2; concern over Soviet presence in Yemen 56, 355n58; concern over US aid program to UAR 59; find Dulles' reasoning unconvincing 66, 360n14; anger at US policy on

Jordan 76, 366n72; pressing US to join Baghdad Pact 86; expect a coup in Iran to follow that in Iraq 90, 272n49; hopes of keeping the Shah in power 91; encourages US to desist from reform campaigns 92; follows US lead on important issues 104; oil interests in Iraq safeguarded 105; main concern is Iraqi oil supply 115; attempt to improve US relations with Qasim 119; continue arms sales to Baghdad 119; neither Qasim nor army will submit to Communists 122; view collapse of Jordan as potential disaster 128; undermine US plans for Jordan-UAR detente 130, 385n7; not unhappy with US-UAR anti-Communist front 132; soft pedal diplomatic win over US 134, 386n25; worry that Jordan may attack Syria 137; reluctance to blame Nasser for assassination 138; debate on funding Jordanian budget 139-40, 388n60; discuss Jordan-Israeli relations 143, 392n82; dispatch aircraft and marines to Kuwait 199, 200; wish to keep Yemen neutral 206, 420n91; skeptical about US inspection of Israel's reactor 209; treaty link to independent Kuwait 211; cautions US support for land reform undermines regime 222; concern at the Harriman Mission 249; against recognition of YAR 270; oppose recognition of YAR 275; recognition of YAR a mistake 277, 445n62; support US aim of a stable India 282, 4447n22; fear coup in Iraq will affect commercial position 299; avoid becoming involved in Kashmir 308

Brubeck, William 242

Brugioni, Dino A 145

Bunche, Dr Ralph 296

Bundy, McGeorge 202, 205, 215, 224, 305, 312

Bunker, Ellsworth, US Ambassador 95-6, 99, 101, 102, 103, 296, 297

Buraimi Oasis dispute 142, 390n69, 390n71

Burki, General, Minister of Health, Welfare, and Social Affairs 258

Byroadism 144

Caffery, Jefferson, US Ambassador to Egypt 16

Camp David talks 158

Canada 56, 209

CENTO (Central Treaty Organization) 105, 150, 162, 215, 248-9, 262

Chaing Kai-Shek, Taiwanese President 27

Chamoun, Camille Nimur, President of Lebanon 50, 61, 62, 65; appeals for US assistance 66, 360n16; pressured to drop second term 67

Charles River School of economic theory 181

Chatterjee, D N, Indian High Commissioner 28

Chehab, General Fuad 62, 67, 360n21

China: enters disputed areas on India's border 170, 403n108; aggressive moves on Indian border 251, 436n38; resents India's ties with US and Soviets 279-80, 446n5; unilateral ceasefire 286; agrees border settlement 291; repatriates 3,000 Indian prisoners of war 309

Chou En-lai: Chinese Chairman 29, 31, 33, 38, 170; argues Sino-Indian border is not delineated 170, 404-5n116; rebuffs Nehru's appeal 170, 404n115; meets Nehru 171

Churchill, Winston Spencer: re-elected Prime Minister 5, 10, 318; opposes economic aid to Egypt 17
Colombo Conference 1954 28, 341n98
Congo conflict 194, 200, 201, 204
Cooper, Chester 255
Copeland, Miles, CIA contact 33, 62
Cuban missile crisis 264, 265, 269, 279
Czech arms deal 33, 38

Dacca 99
Dalai Lama, Tenzin Gyatso 170
Dayan Plan 147
Derakhshesh, Muhammad 222, 237, 240, 242, 426-7n39
Desai, Shri Morarji 28, 254, 255, 259-60, 281, 285
Dhahran, US air base 54, 200, 273, 296, 297
Dillon, Douglas 139, 140
Dimona nuclear rector 208
Din, Zakaria Muhyi al- 297
Dravida Munnetra Kazhagam (DMK) Tamil party 97
Dulles, Allen, CIA Director: concern about Bandung 29; alarm after Baghdad coup 70; Arab self-interest will reject Nasserism 76; predicts rising against Qasim regime 112; fears Communist takeover in Iraq 114; emphasizes threat of Communist takeover 115, 118; uncertainty of Shah's intentions 155
Dulles, John Foster, Secretary of State: holistic view of Greater Middle East 5, 40, 330-1n3; anti-colonial bent 10, 330n1; talks with Egyptian leaders 16, 333n22; hopes to influence Bandung Conference 30; sees Arab-Israeli dispute as security problem 46; support for Iraqi expansion into Syria 50, 55, 351n33; fears collapse of Saudi regime 54, 353n49; denies opposing Arab unity 58, 357n81; reaffirms support for Iraq and Jordan 60; opposes intervention in Lebanon 61-2; concedes that intervention may be needed 63; wants Chamoun to compromise 65; warns Nasser to end support for rebels 67; calls for immediate aid to Chamoun 70; blames Iraqi coup on Baghdad Pact 74; revives 'northern tier' concept 76, 365n68; still believes Nasser behind Iraqi coup 76, 365n67; US will join Baghdad Pact 76; wishes Britain to leave Jordan 77, 366n73; refuses arms, offers increased aid 87, 370n28; visit to Iran is contentious 87; warns Eisenhower the Shah will press for arms 88, 370n32; urges Eisenhower to facilitate Kashmir problem 98; increasingly incapacitated 104, 115; resigns 118; accuses Israel of compliance with Soviets 143; bilateral agreement with Shah is unacceptable 153; British dislike of his style 332-3n21
Dutt, F S 139

Ebtehaj, Abol Hassan 83, 87, 89, 151
Eden, Anthony, Foreign Minister: concerns about Dulles 330n1
Egypt: demands British withdrawal from Canal Zone 15; bombs villages in southern Saudi Arabia 273
Egyptian Gazette 277
Egyptian-Syrian Union: surprise to everybody 46, 349n9
Eisenhower, President Dwight D: anti-colonial bent 10; concludes Pakistan stability outweighs political democracy 10; proposes 'northern tier' alliance 11; rejects

joint action with Churchill 11-12; criticizes Churchill's paternalistic approach 12; warns Eden against aggressive approach 13, 331-2n10; supports economic aid to Egypt 15; foresees clash with non-alignment 24; assures Nehru about aid to Pakistan 25; British calls for intervention is colonialism 35, 344-5n129; obsessed with containment of Soviets 35, 37; Eisenhower Doctrine speech 38, 347n138; calls Crown Prince Feisal pro-Nasserist 54, 354n51; more fears of Communism 54, 353n50; regrets not backing British at Suez 64, 358n2; will avoid intervention at any cost 65, 66, 359n7, 359n8; dismay at Iraqi coup 69; orders troops into Lebanon 71, 362n41, 363n42; briefs Macmillan on joint campaign 72, 363n44; expenditure will rehabilitate US position 74, 364n58; agrees limited military aid to Shah 87; discusses Kashmir with Nehru 94; talks with Nehru 94, 372n2; tells Suhrawardy he will support call for plebiscite 96; offers direct involvement in Kashmir dispute 99; sees support for Pakistan as expedient 103, 150, 394n2; undertakes personal diplomacy 104; grumbles at choice between Qasim and Nasser 114; reasons intervention in Iraq will undermine US 118; agrees to British arms sales 119; reaps benefit of non-intervention in Iraq 125; aid to Jordan helps relations with British 127; lacks confidence in Jordan or King Hussein 130-1; meets Nasser at UN 138, 388n55; meets King Hussein 139; forces Israel to withdraw from Sinai 142, 390-1n76; opposes Suez invasion 142; agrees Doctrine covers Israel 143; continues nuclear agreement with Israel 146, 393n87; Israel's reactor not for solely peaceful use 147; holds conference on Israel nuclear issue 148; no alternative to supporting the Shah 151, 395n4; warns Shah of Soviet perfidy 153; meets Iranian Prime Minister 158; visits Iran 158; goal is stability, even if military rule 164, 400-1n71; peace mission to India and Pakistan 167; agrees to Pakistan's weapons demands 168; rejects use of India as counter to China 169-70; alarmed by India's arms deal with Soviet 172; sees no alternative to arms supply to Ayub and Shah 172-3; foreign-policy crises handling criticised 179-80, 410n28; containment by use of economic aid 315; stability requirement means military aid 316; confidence in Shah's ability 332n12

Emami, Jafar Sharif 159, 217
Eqbal, Manuchehr, Iranian Prime Minister 87, 158, 159
Eveland, Wilbur 32

F-104 Starfighters 167, 171, 254, 262, 263
Farouk I, King of Egypt 8
Federation of Rulers in the Aden Protecorate 273, 274, 277
Feisal Ibn Abd-Al-Aziz, Crown Prince: reform policy 53, 353n45; progress in modernizing the kingdom 128-9; asserts 'positive neutrality' 140, 389n63; pressures Saud to step down 140, 207; anti-British credentials 141-2, 390n68; fiscal restraints 141; rumored support for constitutional government 141; pro-Nasser policies 142, 390n74; Nasser a

rabid madman 207, 420-1n100; against recognition of YAR 270; uses power to accelerate reform 271; warns Kennedy not to support Nasser 271; commences reform program 274-5, 444n42; knows Saudi oil is indispensable to US 275; a shrewd politician and a stable reformer 295; agrees to withdraw from Yemen 296; continues clandestine support for royalists 297

Feisal II, King of Iraq 53, 69
Feldman, Myer 182, 205, 208, 419n86
Fir'awn, Dr Rashal 275
Fouthi, Ali 244-5
frigates, for Iran 235, 236, 243, 244
Fulbright, Senator J William 70, 167, 305

Galbraith, John K: champions economic aid 177; appointed US Ambassador to India 247; views military aid to Pakistan as evil 249-50; accuses Nehru of undermining Kennedy 254-5, 436-7n62; attempts to brief Indians on aircraft shipment denied 254; Lall an impediment to Laos talks 255, 437n65, 437-8n72; attempts to arrange India-Pakistan talks on Kashmir 258; learns reasons for annexing Goa 258; offers C-130 transports to stop MIG purchase 263; resigns in frustration 263, 442n135; suggests US aid is financing Soviet arms 263; believes war with China impossible 278; blames Menon for army failure 281-2; on vacation when China attacks 281, 447n15; Indian arms request has dangers 283-4; tries to get Nehru to talk to Ayub 283, 447n24; India as a counterweight to China 289; says Soviet arms to India only symbolic 290

Galib, Abd-al-Hamid al-, Egyptian Ambasador 49
Gandhi, Indira 280
Gandhi, Mohandas Karamchand 97
Gates, Thomas S, Jr 148
Gaylani, Rashid Ali 77, 109, 112
Gaza, Israeli raid into 21, 31, 38, 335-6n55
Gazit, Modechai 302
Geneva Convention on Indochina 27, 340n90
Godstein, Rabbi Israel 184
Gomberg, Henry 147
Graham, Dr Frank, UN Mediator 98
Grant, James 302
Greater Middle East: definitions 5, 40, 330-1n3
Gromyko, Andrei 156, 158, 162
Guardian, The, London 124
Gulf Emirates 54
Gundevia, Yezdezard Dinshaw 286, 448n41

Haaretz 303
Hammerskjold, Dag, UN Secretary General 57, 66, 156, 360n15
Hannah, Norman B 33
Hansen, Kenneth 234
Hare, Raymond A, US Ambassador 57, 58, 60-1, 62, 67, 132, 144
Harman, Avrahm, Israeli Ambassador 147, 303
Harriman, Averell 178, 181, 215, 235, 248, 285, 286, 290, 302
Harrison, Selig 290
Harrison, Sir Geoffrey 156-7
Hart, US Ambassador 207, 272, 274, 275
Hassan II, King of Morocco 306
Hassan, Yemeni Prince 271
Hawk anti-aircraft missiles 205, 209, 297, 302

Hayden, Major General John C 243, 244
Hayter, Sir William 56, 75
Heikal, Muhammad Hussein 111, 114, 196, 200, 202, 204, 297, 299, 378n15
Hekmat, Sardar Fakher 157
Herter, Christian 69, 116, 138, 144, 146, 148, 155, 158
Hillsman, Roger 306
Hindustani Times 170
Holmes, Julius C, Ambassador: urges caution on land reform 22; hints to Shah on reform 216, 425n21; sees Shah's role as vital 221; no alternative to Shah 224-5; military assistance plan for Iran 226; urges Shah be invited to visit US 228; warns of danger of neutralism 230; enhanced military assistance program 232, 428n6, 428-9n7; masterminds Shah's visit 233-4; rejects Amini's appeal for funds 239-40; urges wait and see policy 241, 430-1n42; asks for frigates for Iran 243; warns that the Shah is dependent on the military 307; evaluates Shah's visit 428n4
Home, Lord, Foreign Secretary 291, 308
Hood, Viscount Samuel 67
Hourani, Akram 124
Hoyer-Millar, Sir Frederick 56, 143
Humphrey, Senator Hubert 58, 59, 181, 203
Hussein I, King of Jordan: assassination plot 62; faith in army's loyalty 72; requests British troops 72; faces plots in government and military 127; sustained by Bedouin loyalty 128, 194, 384n1; visit to US has mixed success 129-30, 384n4; plot fails during his absence 131, 385-6n12; informs Saud he cannot attend meeting 134; recognizes Qasim regime in Iraq 136; believes Jordan would win a war with UAR 137, 388n48; Father's madness 138, 388n54; denounces UAR at UN 139; appeals against subsidy cuts 197; attempts to improve popularity 198; wants improved relations with Nasser 198, 415n30; Syrian coup poses threat from Nasser 202; Yemen a renewal of Egyptian subversion 270, 276; indignant at US recognition of YAR 277; dismisses Rifa'i government 302; asserts his Arab credentials 303; invited to US 303, 453n62

IAEA (International Atomic Energy Agency) 145-6, 148
ibn Nasir, Sharif Hussein 302
Ilah, Abd al-, Iraqi Crown Prince 90
India: refuses to enter Western military alliance 23; disengagement operations in Korea 26, 337-8n72; faces challenge from separatist groups 96, 374n22; requests US economic aid 96; regionalism threatens national polity 97; relies on Soviet veto in UN 97; political problems 101, 376n46; US support for Pakistan dictator causes disappointment 102; criticises Qasim and Iraq 123-4, 382n81; will not intervene between Hussein and UAR 139; remains non-aligned 169; establishes military posts on China border 171; Harriman calls it the greatest ally 248; annexes Portuguese enclave of Goa 258; purchases MIG-21 fighters 262; under-equipped army with demoralized command 279; rejects Chinese call for negotiations 281; reduced Chinese pressure removes

Kashmir urgency 290; Soviet arms deal could lead to modern air force 310

Indus water agreement 167, 169, 249, 261

Iran: assassination of moderate Prime Minister 14; Communist Tudeh suppressed 14, 82; General Zahedi coup, August 1953 14; joins Baghdad Pact 34; US sites observing Soviet missile tests 80; land reform is contentious issue 81, 368n4; security agency SAVAK created 83; Soviet pressure to withdraw from Baghdad Pact 86, 369n20; US aid benefits landowners not peasants 87, 370n22; anti-Shah rumors widespread 89, 371n44; confidence in Pahlavi regime shaken by coup 89, 371n42; recognizes new Iraqi government 89, 371n43; US military support increases dramatically 105; rising dissatisfaction among population 157; Majlis elections fiasco 159, 399n52; security forces may depose the Shah 159, 399n51; economic collapse possible 161; anti-Shah riots 214, 424n13; Third Development Plan 216, 222; teachers' strike, cabinet resigns 217; land reform program 222; National Front opposition threat 223, 224, 225, 226; referendum approves White Revolution 306; clergy brand Shah an American puppet 307; religious opponents and nationalists rioting 307

Iraq: joins Baghdad Pact 37; Hashemite dynasty toppled 40; wishes to expand into Syria 50, 351-2n33; British analysis of situation 67-8, 360n22; Bastille Day coup against Hashemites 69, 321, 361n29; Rashid Ali coup 69, 361-2n30; internal debate isolates pro-Nasserists 73; opposition to Nasser grows 77; Communist influence demonises US and Nasser 78, 366-7n81; calls for Kurdish National rights 91, 372n51; Qasim dependent on Communists 105; Qasim uncovers revolutionary plot 109; Russian influence grows 110; Sarraj arranges coup against Qasim 112, 379n21; Syrian backed coup bloodily suppressed 112; Qasim resists Communist demands 121; accuses US of collaborating with Nasser 122, 381n68; power of Communists curbed 122; military courts try Ba'thists 123; military court shows leniency 124, 382n87; British sell additional arms 154, 396n18; Ba'thist officers overthrow Qasim 298; Communists hunted down and killed 298, 451n29; Aref displaces Iraqi Ba'thists in a coup 305; Aref invites Nasser to visit Iraq 305

Iraqi Communist Party 73, 77, 105, 109, 112, 124, 298

Iraqi Petroleum Company 79

Israel: a liability for US policy in the region 6; if Jordan collapses, will take West Bank 73-4, 363-4n55, 364n56, 364n57; diverts US aid into nuclear program 129; US forces withdrawal from Sinai 142; rejects any compromise with Nasser 143, 391-2n77; fury at US pro-Nasser policy 144; nuclear weapons program 144-5, 194, 392-3n84; demands exemption from nuclear inspection 146; requests conventional arms 146; French assist with nuclear weapons program 147; purchases Hawk anti-aircraft missiles 205, 209, 297;

seeks alternative sources of uranium 209; express concern over possible overthrow of Jordan 302

Jadid, Salah 300
Jarring, Gunar V, UN Security Council 95, 96
Jawad, Hashim, Iraqi Foreign Minister 113, 122, 124, 382n85
Jernegan, John D 33, 114, 117
Jinnah, Muhammad Ali 97
Johnson Plan: for Arab-Israeli peace 204, 205, 209, 210, 267, 297
Johnson, Vice-President Lyndon 243, 250-1, 311, 312, 327, 431-2n52, 456n128
Johnston, Eric 21
Johnston, Sir Charles 76-7, 366n72; disagrees with US policies 128, 131, 384n3, 385n11, 386n18; appalled at idea of Hussein-Nasser détente 130; fears instability in King Hussein's absence 131, 385n10; advises Hussein against meeting Saud and Nasser 133; dislikes reliance on US financial aid 133, 386n19; seeks to stop Hussein's military action 137; Aden protest makes recognition of YAR unlikely 273-4; castigates US policy in Arabia 295
Jones, G Lewis 195, 225
Jordan 54, 62, 63, 357n105; US advises rapprochement with UAR 129-30; Prime Minister Rifai' expresses Jordan's hatred of Nasser 131-2; dangers of Nasser takeover 132, 386n18; anti-Nasser propaganda campaign 134-5; internal power struggle 134, 386n28; foments trouble in Syria 135; Prime Minister Majali assassinated 135, 387n40; additional funding for regime 197, 415n20; US denies supporting Jordan dissidents 202, 418n58; against recognition of YAR 270, 275-6, 443n19; offers troops to assist Saudis 271, 443n20; supplies arms aid to Yemen royalists 275; three pilots defect to Cairo 276
Jordan River water use 20-1, 22, 207, 210, 334n47, 334-5n50, 336n57
Jundi, Abd-al-Karim 300

Kashmir dispute: Nehru's hard line 24, 337n65; US observers leave 26, 339n79; Nehru's position is status quo 94; India declares Kashmir part of India 95; India refuses plebiscite 95, 257; Pakistan threatens to cut ties with US 95; Pakistan wants UN Security Council mission 95, 253, 373n8; US stays out 165; Ayub's proposal rejected 166-7; Ayub has concerns 248; Ayub calls for UN plebiscite 249; Indian-Pakistani talks at Rawalpindi 291
Kaul, General B M 280
Kennedy, John Fitzgerald: policies mirror Eisenhower's early plan 4, 191, 210-11, 413n1; wins Presidential election 147; blamed for supporting India 167; missile gap campaign tactic 174, 406n1; accuses Eisenhower of insufficient aid 175, 407n8; claims policies are out of date 175, 323-4, 407n9; creates 'facts' for his campaign 175, 406n6; exaggerates neglect of aid for India 176-7; support for the Shah a necessity 179, 409-10n27; uses Arab Middle East as campaign ploy 180-1; blames Eisenhower for coolness to Nasser 181-2; ignores Eisenhower's hard-earned lessons 181, 188; attacks Eisenhower Doctrine 182; private talks with Jewish leaders 182, 410-11n35;

seeks support from Jewish and Zionist groups 182, 188, 410n34, 413n59; personal diplomacy 184, 259, 265, 411n45; promises Arab-Israeli peace negotiations 184, 196, 415n17; tries to charm Nasser 184, 411n45; hopes China threat will make India anti-Communist 191; A Strategy for Peace 195; writes to Arab Leaders 195; needs Zionist votes 196, 201, 414n12, 417-18n48; sells Hawk missiles to Israel 205; bored by correspondence with King Saud 207; finds no alternative to the Shah 211, 214, 421-2n2, 424-5n12; excludes Foreign Service from decisions 212, 421n1; ties US to support of the Shah 212-13, 325-6, 422n3; reform tactics similar to Eisenhower's 213, 422-3n9; still believes only reform can save Iran regime 213, 422n8; concern about Amini government in Iran 223; doubts about Iran Task Force 227; fails to charm Shah 236; makes in-person promises to visitors 236, 430n28; refuses to back Amini 240-1; sees India as key to foreign policy 246-7; foreign-aid budget, Five Year Plan 247; appoints pro-India officials 249; talks with Krushchev 251, 436n40; gives Ayub false impression of support 253; uses India to counterbalance China 256; tries personal approach to Nehru and Ayub 259; guarantees assistance to Pakistan if attacked 260, 440-1n109; concludes personal diplomacy a failure 265; drives UAR and India into Soviet camp 265; inclined to recognize YAR 270; tries to calm Saudis without upsetting Nasser 271; hedges in support for Feisal 275, 444-5n44; promises full support for Saudi Arabia's integrity 275; learns from Yemen civil war 277; welcomes increased tension between India and China 281; assures Ayub US will not be used against him 284; sends military mission to India 286; tells Harriman not to push Ayub too far 286, 448n38; believes Chinese invasion has changed India's attitudes 288; orders plan for Kashmir settlement 288; sets up Kashmir Working group 288; talks with Macmillan at Nassau 290; questions impact of Pakistan leaving CENTO 291; calls on Feisal to end support for royalists 294; denies special relationship with Nasser 294; accuses Nasser of destabilizing the region 295; promises to defend Saudi Arabia 296, 450n18; tells Nasser US policy is unchanged 297, 450n22; denies US officials support UAR subversion in Syria 300; congratulates Nasser on forming new UAR 301; wants Saudis to withdraw support from Yemeni royalists 301; sends two aircraft to Jordan on exercises 304; full policy review for Iran 307; realises Shah's White Revolution challenges Iranian society 307; cautions Shah against too rapid reform 308; hopes China threat will make India settle Kashmir 308; understands Ayub's concerns over India 310; assassination 311; all hopes for greater Middle East unravelled 312-13; failure to learn lessons of Eisenhower's setbacks 316-17; proactive approach causes miscalculations 317

Kerr, Malcolm 107, 377n1

Kerr, Peyton 24

INDEX

Khayyal, Sheikh Abdullah al- 298
Khomeini, Ayatollah Ruhollah 307
Khurshid, Muhammad 165
Kirkuk: oilfield pipelines 68, 117, 361n27; US forced to close Consulate 91; Communist rally suppressed 122
Kiselev, Evgeny, Soviet Ambassador 110
Knight, Ridgeway B 165
Kohler, Foy D 154
Komer, Robert 'Blowtorch Bob': Near East policy troika 184-5, 196; on recognition of Syrian coup 202; advises inviting Nasser to US 203; boring correspondence with King Saud 207; urges greater pressure on Shah 215-16; accepts Amini regime must be supported 220; unable to see Amini is only a front for the Shah 221; predicts Iran crisis 223-4, 231, 428n61; concedes Shah is indispensable to stability 233, 429n12; urges cap on Iran military aid 234; urges Kennedy to save Amini 241, 430n40; lack of aid to India opens door to Soviet 263; Cairo is key to new wave 267; Yemen no problem 269; Yemen a vortex for regional issues 270; Yemen crisis a peanut 277; sees opportunity to sour India-Soviet relations 282; US is now prime supplier of arms and economic aid 283; advises Kennedy not to compromise with Ayub 284-5; complains of slowness of aid to India 285-6; regrets the end of Chinese confrontation 287; wants to keep India's anti-Chinese tide flowing 288; Indians can't defend India, much less SEA 289; no aid without progress on Kashmir 289; no alternative to the Shah and reform cabinet 306, 454n27; keeps China threat visible to India 308; not much lost if Bowles aid plan fails 311
Krishnamachari, Tiruvallur Thattai, Indian Minister 96
Krushchev, Nikita, Soviet Premier: supports India against Pakistan 34; replies to UAR anti-Communism 110, 378n10; chagrined by Nasser's attacks on Iraq 120, 380n61; Shah's ending of negotiations an affront 154; propaganda attacks on Iran 156; continues propaganda attacks on Shah 157; attempts to improve relations with Shah 161; assures India of support 171; says Iran ripe for revolution 213; talks with Kennedy 251, 435-6n37; Qasim a client who does not hang communists 322
Kurdistan 90, 154, 397n20
Kuwait 54, 68, 75, 79, 198, 200, 202, 299, 360-1n25

Ladakh 281
Laise, Carol C 287
Lakeland, William 114, 123, 131
Lall, Arthur 251, 255, 256, 437n63, 437n64
Langley, James M, US Ambassador 99, 100, 156, 163
Laos 250, 255, 257, 258
Lavon Affair 208 421n104
Le Jour 49
Lebanon: impending crisis 48, 49, 351n27, 351n34; crisis grows 61, 357n92; unrest spreading 65
Lintcott, Sir H J B 56-7, 356n66
Lippmann, Walter 213
Lloyd, Selwyn, Foreign Secretary 74-5, 75, 88, 116, 139, 140, 365n61, 365n62
London Declaration, July 1958 153
Luce, Sir William Henry Tucker 75, 365n64, 365n65

Lumumba, President Patrice 201
Lundahl, Arthur C 145

McClintock, Robert Mills, US Ambassador 67
McConaughy, US Ambassador 283, 291
McCone, John A 148, 310, 312
McElroy, Neil 152
McMahon Line 170, 280
Macmillan, Harold, British Prime Minister 44; relationship with Eisenhower 5; Britain still a Great Power 8; views Nasser as threat 54; believes US will intervene in Lebanon 65; talks with Eisenhower 66, 115, 359n11; shocked that Nuri threatened Kuwait 68, 361n26; shock at Iraqi coup 69, 362n33; urges caution after the act 72; finds Qasim a bastion against Communists 79; warns Hussein of consequence of war 137, 388n50; gets support from US and Dominions 199; suggests neutralist course 251-2; urges Kennedy not to recognize YAR 274; concern at Pakistan's reaction to arms for India 290, 291
McNamara, Robert Secretary of Defense 234
Macomber, William B., US Ambassador 197-8, 213, 303, 452-3n59
Mahdawi, Colonel Fadhil Abbas al- 114, 123
Majali, General Habis al- 131, 137, 198
Majali, Hazza al-, Jordanian Prime Minister 133, 134, 135, 136, 137
Makins, Sir Roger, UK Ambassador in Washington 30
Malaviya, K D 309
Malik, Charles Habib, Lebanese delegate 32, 51, 66

Mansfield, Senator Mike 234
Marshall, George G: Secretary of State 19-20
MEDO (Middle East Defensive Organization) 4, 10-11
Meir, Golda, Israeli Foreign Minister 144, 146, 205
Menderes, Adnan, Turkish Prime Minister 247
Menon, Vengali Krishnan Krishna: Indian UN delegate 27, 339-40n85, 340-1n93; at Colombo Conference 28, 341n98; attacks Britain and US 39; diplomatic shortcomings 94, 373n4; categorically rejects report on Kashmir 96, 374n19; ponders military relationship with Soviet 150, 394-5n3; Minister of Defense 171, 177, 405n119, 407-8n18; initiates talks with Soviet 172; inexplicable actions at UN 177, 408n19; labels US imperialist 177, 408-9n21; pro-Soviet leanings 177, 250, 408n20; abuses Pakistan 249, 435n23; supports Chinese over Indochina 255; impediment to cooperation 256, 257; dismisses US criticism as imperialism 258, 439n89; meeting with Kennedy 258; increased influence prevents Kashmir compromise 261, 441n118; defeats Pakistani resolution in UN 262; on military collision course with China 279, 446n2; widely blamed for military failure 281; resigned but still anti-West 285, 290; no longer balances conservatives 309
Meyer, Armin 224
MIG-21 fighters 262, 290
Miklos, Jack 244
Mills, Sheldon T, US Ambassador 133
Mir, Ahmad al- 300
Mirza, General Iskander, Pakistani President 97, 99, 100, 101

modernization theory 2
Morgan, Thomas E 216
Morris, Willie: British Embassy 33, 135
Morrison, Herbert, Foreign Minister: deplores Indian non-alignment 28; lack of trust in Dulles 330n2
Mosul, Iraq 112
Mountbatten, Lord Louis 97
Muhammad Ali, Pakistani Prime Minister 28
Mullik, Bhola Nath 170, 280, 446n8
Murphy, Robert 72
Musaddiq, Muhammad, Iranian Prime Minister 7, 13-14, 149
Muslim Brotherhood: revolt over Canal treaty 18

Nachal Soreq 144, 147
Nagi, Abdul Ghani 272
Nasser, Gamal Abdel: controls Revolutionary Command Council 8; power behind Neguib 15; believes US will provide arms 16, 333n25; refuses to join MEDO 16; removes Neguib and takes control 18, 34n2; tries to isolate Iraq 19; attends Bandung Conference 31; returns as world leader 31, 343n117, 414n3; proclaims non-alignment 33; reaction to Eisenhower Doctrine 40, 43, 320, 348n1; obtains arms from Soviets 41, 319; becomes symbol of Arab nationalism 43, 348n3; ideological principles 43, 348n4; Philosophy of Revolution 43, 186, 193, 348n5; attempts control of United Arab Republic 47, 349n13; proclaimed the new Saladin 47, 349n15; declares Communist Party illegal 48, 350n21; propaganda attacks on King Saud 52, 352n41; forges Yemen-UAR alliance 55; official visit to Soviet Union 61; denies fomenting unrest in Lebanon 62; denied Soviet intervention 72; makes pact with new Iraqi regime 72, 363n46; agrees with US on Iraq 78, 367n82; asserting authority creates strain in the Arab world 105; confident that Iraq will become ally 108, 377n2; hostility to Qasim develops 109; challenges Khrushchev on Iraq 110, 378n11; relations with Soviet undermined 110; defends his right to suppress Communists 111, 378n12; sees Qasim as personal threat 111, 378n16; attacks British for aiding Communist Iraq 113; launches virulent attacks on Qasim 113; accuses Qasim of handing Iraq to Communists 120, 380n60; responds angrily to Krushchev criticism 120, 380-1n64; lumps British policy in with Soviets 121; removes Ba'thists from key positions 125; will renew relations with British 142, 390n70; ideology 186, 187, 193, 412n53, 413n56; consistent anti-Communist 187, 413n55; believes Israel is last vestige of colonialism 188; revolutionary policy losing momentum 194; domestic radicalization program 196, 414n15; has to support Kuwait against Qasim 200, 416n42; policy shifts to focus on Africa 200, 417n47; purges reactionary elements in Egypt 201-2; assures Kennedy and Humphrey he is not Communist 203; publishes abuse of Kennedy's correspondence 204, 419n75; US Hawks to Israel creates arms race 206; publishes Kennedy's offer of conditional aid 268; calls coup triumph of anti-feudal forces 269, 442n10; prepares

coup in Yemen 269, 442n5; supports Yemen Arab Republic 269, 270, 443n7, 443n16; accuses Kennedy of military intervention in Yemen 295; concludes Kennedy has double-crossed him 297; token withdrawal of troops from Yemen 297; announces new United Arab Republic 301, 320; humiliates Syrian Ba'thist delegation 301, 451-2n44, 452n45; attacks US policy 305; insufficient US arms to challenge Israel 319; support for FLN in Algeria 419n74

Nation, The 48, 74, 364-5n59

Neguib, General Muhammad 8, 15, 16

Nehru, Braj Kumar 248, 259, 260, 288, 441n111

Nehru, Jawaharlal, Indian Prime Minister: preaches neutralism 8; committed to non-alignment 23, 27; distrust of Great Powers 23; opposes US arms for Pakistan 25; attacks US actions 26, 338n74; emphasises independence from US 27, 28, 339n84; attends Bandung Conference 30, 32, 342-3n110; entices Nasser to Bandung 31, 343n115; aids Nasser with Czech arms deal 33; incites world opinion against Suez War 38, 345n133; pursues political priorities 40-1; antagonistic to US-Pakistan rapport 93; urges Eisenhower to support Nasser 94, 373n3; rejects meeting with Pakistani Prime Minister 98; stalls at Eisenhower's offer of talks 99; disagrees with US policy in Middle East 102, 376n50; uneasy about US support for Pakistan 103, 377n56; worried by conflict with China 104-5, 249; will not meddle in UAR-Jordan detente 139; ponders threat posed by Pakistan 150-1; rejects Ayub's proposals for talks 166, 402n85; tells Eisenhower of fears over Pakistan 168-9; attempts to avoid involvement in Tibet 170, 404n113; must support the Dalai Lama 170, 404n112; presses China to recognize McMahon Line 170, 404n114; could not believe conflict with China possible 171; meets Chou En-lai 171, 405n122; brings Menon back from UN 178, 409n22, 409n24; refuses to take a position on SE Asia 250; hopes for improved US-Soviet relations 251, 435-6n37; condemns Ayub's statements in US 253; attends Non-Aligned Conference 254; visits Washington 255, 438n73; asks Kennedy to meet Menon 257-8, 439n84; rejects plebiscite in Kashmir 257; hopes Goa demonstrates independence from West 258, 439n90; claims Kashmir as sovereign territory 259; rejects Eugene Black as mediator 260; mutual rivalry guarantee against attack 278; believes India can defeat China 279, 446n4; Goa annexation leads to parallel with China 279, 446n3; forward policy unchallenged 280, 446n6; claims withdrawal is desire for peace 282; India has been living in a dream 285; claims he is being blackmailed 290, 449n55; moves to closer cooperation with Soviet 293; can offer nothing in Kashmir 308; ill health and reduced power 309; opposes any compromise on Kashmir 309

New York Times 134, 178

Newsweek 48

Nike-Hercules anti-aircraft missiles 167

Nixon, Vice-President Richard M 20; defies domestic Jewish vote 20, 334n45; argues for arming Pakistan 25, 337n70; advocates intervention in Iraq 113, 115, 117-18, 125; believes British prefer a deal with Iraq Communists 119, 121; advocates continuing containment policy 174-5, 406n4; identifies with Nasser's policies 187, 412-13n54

Nkrumah, President Kwame 201

Non-Aligned Conference: condemns nuclear testing 254

Noon, Malik Firoz Khan, Pakistani Foreign Minister 87, 96, 97, 98, 100, 164

'northern tier' concept 4, 11, 24, 76, 365n68

Numan, Abd-al-Rahman 272

Numan, Ahmad Muhammad 269, 272

Nuri Sa'id, Iraqi Prime Minister 19, 55; desires union with Kuwait 55, 68; plans to detach Syria from Egypt 55; murdered 69

Nutting, Anthony H 122, 381n71

oil 6-7, 68, 72, 73, 105, 115, 117, 275, 361n27

Oman 142

Operation Hard Surface 273, 296, 297, 450n21

Operation Leghorn 280

Pakistan: US supplies arms 25, 26, 31; in Baghdad Pact 31, 93; in SEATO (South East Asia Treaty Organization) 31, 93; reopens Kashmir issue at United Nations 39, 259; US intelligence sites monitor Soviet missiles 93, 105, 167, 259, 440n96; US support damages relations with India 93; instability blamed on British 97-8, 375n25; political instability and corruption 98, 375n26; military takeover forecast 99-100, 375n38; Ayub Khan leads military coup 101; containment ensures US support for military government 150; instability and corruption 163; Ayub regime 'controlled democracy' 164, 400n70, 433n5; wants modern weapons 165, 167, 401n75; Kennedy on notice about policies 248; receives F-104 shipment 254; Ayub Constitution introduced 261, 441n122; sees India as sworn enemy 286; domestic economy downturn 308; questions CENTO and SEATO benefits 309

Palestinian refugees 139, 168, 195, 196, 207; right to return 20-1, 209, 414n11

Pegov, Nikolai Mikhailovitch, Soviet Ambassador 86, 158, 162

Peres, Shimon 205

Phillips, Horace 57, 356n72

PL 480 wheat grants 59, 187, 194, 247, 305, 324, 388n60, 409n26

PSB (Psychological Strategy Board) 328n3

Qasim, Brigadier Abd-al-Karim: leads Baghdad coup 69, 362n32; forms pact of support with Nasser 72; no intention of joining UAR 73; relies on Communist support 73, 78, 109; growing ties with Soviets 110; foments unrest in Syria 111; accuses Nasser of complicity in coup plot 113; resists Communist demands 122; assassination attempt by Ba'thists 123, 381n75; encourages anti-Communist movement 123, 381n76; isolated, but opposition weak 124; licences split in Communist Party 124, 382n83; revives claim to Kuwait 198, 415-16n33; moves army to

Kuwait border 199, 416n34; acts against foreign investors 200, 416-17n44; executed after coup 298
Qudsi, President Nazim 300
Quwatli, Shukri al-, Syrian President 46, 47

Radford, Admiral Arthur W 180, 181
Reza Shah 84, 161
Rhee, Sygmund, South Vietnam President 27
Riches, D M H 56, 75
Rifai', Samir al-, Jordanian Prime Minister 62, 130, 131-2, 134, 301, 302
Rockwell, Stuart W 229, 245
Rogers, Attorney General William P 175
Roosevelt, Kermit 31
Rostow, Walt W: economic and development aid thwarts Communism 3, 328-9n3; emphasises economic aid 12, 81, 175, 177, 181, 331n7, 406n7; discusses aid with Eisenhower 167, 402n90; frustration at lack of response in reforming 215, 216-17; Kashmir talks a stone wall 309; *Europe After Stalin: Eisenhower's Three Decisions* 328-9n3; rebuts Soviet peace campaign 328n3
Rountree, William M: resumption of aid to Egypt 58; rapprochement begins 59; complains about British action in Lebanon 67, 359n12; visits Baghdad and Cairo 78; covert encouragement of anti-Communist Nasser 117; opposes intervention in Iraq 118; replaced at NEA by Hare 144; reminds Shah that Russian guarantees are unreliable 153; warned that Russians are chagrined 154; asks Ayub to renounce military force 169; discouraged by Indian stance 259, 440n102
Rundall, Francis 144
Rusk, Dean, Secretary of State: queried on policy after Syrian coup 202; advocates systematic aid to UAR should continue 203; puts Johnson peace plan to Ben-Gurion 205-6, 419n86; submits Johnson Plan to Kennedy 205; deplores sale of Hawks without Johnson Plan 206; asks for Check List for Iran 226; tells Amini of reduced military aid 233; arranges Shah's address to Congress 234; recommends recognition of YAR 273; tells Galbraith to keep Pakistan onside 285; fears Ayub expects US to force India to settle 288-9; reassures US support for India 380, 44710
Russell, John W, US Chargée 91-2, 156

Sadat, Anwar 269
Sa'id, Nuri, Iraqi Prime Minister 50, 53
Sallal, Colonel Abdullah 268, 272
Samir 131
Sanaa Treaty, 1934 275
Sandys, Duncan 154, 286, 290, 291, 309
Sarraj, Abd-al-Hamid: Nasser's Syrian intelligence chief 49; Syrian intelligence chief 49; meets Nasser for Iraqi pact 72; head of security in Syria 111; plans plot against Qasim regime 112; Nasser blames him for failure 113; attempts to purge the military 125; fear he may try to destabilize Jordan 131; blamed for assassination of Jordan's Prime Minister 135; attempt to subvert him by King Saud 140

Saud, King ibn Abd-al-Aziz: told Nasser is saving Syria from Communists 50; opposes UAR union 52; plots to assassinate Nasser 52, 54; unable to intervene in Lebanon 63; dismisses Iraqi offer of union 68; demands Kuwait is saved from Iraqi coup 70; forms united Arab front against Communism 133; bungles attempt to subvert Sarraj 140; struggles to regain power 141, 207, 275;complains about US aid to Nasser 207; slowness of US aid 207, 421n101; visits Washington 207; collapses and hands over to Feisal 271; had taken Najran and Asir from Yemen 272

Saud, Prince Tallal ibn Abd-al-Aziz 141, 207, 271, 444n28

Saudi Arabia 75; anti-Communist alliance with Nasser 128; feudal institutions 140; moves troops to Kuwait-Iraq border 200; power struggle between King Saud and Feisal 207, 420n97; three air force planes defect to Cairo 271

SAVAK 91, 160-1, 214-15

Sawt al-Arab radio (see Voice of the Arab Nation)

Scott, Sir Robert, British Embassy 33

SEATO (South East Asia Treaty Organization) 31, 93, 150, 248-9, 260, 262

Shabib, Talib 299-300

Shah Pahlavi, Muhammad Reza: cannot face down National Front 13; exorbitant demands 33; cannot effect social reform 34; plays off US against Soviets 34, 150; visits Moscow 34; aspires to dominant military power in Persian Gulf 81, 151; receives internal security weaponry only 81; exacts high price for joining Baghdad Pact 82- 3, 368n8; moves to placate secular conservatives 82; represses religious factions 82, 368n6; central planning intensifies nationalism 83; his program creates widespread dissent 83, 368n10; attempts to create political support 84; personal involvement in projects risks survival 84-5, 369n17; visits US for talks 87, 370n29; Baghdad coup enhances his demands for arms 88; opposes US aid to Nasser 88, 371n37; leverage with US for aid increases 91; laments no assistance to Iraqi anti-communists 123, 382n80; presses for military aid 149; resists US pressure for reform 150 improves relations with Soviets 153, 395-6n15; talks with Soviets fail 154, 396-7n19; complains about British lack of support 156-7; plans for major military buildup 158, 398n43; announces two-party elections 159; land reform lacks credibility 159, 399n50; Soviet proposals renewed 161-2, 399n60; expects military parity with Turkey 162, 163, 399-40063; would prefer Nixon to win 179; plays neutralist hand to Kennedy 213-14, 424n11; makes overtures to Soviet Union 215; uses Prime Minister Amini as cat's paw 221; no reduction in military without modernization 228; exerts control over Amini 229; invited to visit US 231; presents shopping list to Kennedy 234-5, 429n23; gives Amini one more chance 235, 430n25; appoints Asadollah Alam Prime Minister 241, 431n46; lip service only to reform 242; threatens to abdicate 242; starts reform program 306

Shahab, Qudratullah 166

Shara, Major General Sadiq 131
Sharaf, Sami 303
Shastri, Lal Bahadur 287
Shatt al-Arab 156
Shawwaf, Colonel Abd-al-Wahhab al- 112
Shishakli, Adib, Syrian Prime Minister 16
Shoaib, Muhammad 167
Sidewinder air-to-air missiles 167, 171
Singh, Sardar Swaran 291
Solod, Daniel, Soviet Ambassador to Egypt 33
Soviet: breaches understanding with Czech arms deal 33, 344n122; demands Israel stop US overflights 143; reaction to failure of talks with Shah 154, 397n20; propaganda campaign against Shah 155; threat to Pakistan 250, 435n27; resumption of nuclear testing 254; vetoes Kashmir negotiations 262; offers India massive arms deal 310
Stevens, Sir Roger Bentham 86, 90, 91, 135
Stevenson, Adlai, Ambassador 258
Strauss, Lewis 145
Sudan 54, 354-5n54
Suez: British, French and Israeli attack 5, 38, 346n134
Suez Canal 8, 38
Suhrawardy, Huseyn, Pakistan Prime Minister 95, 96, 97
Sukarno, Achmad, Indonesian President 31, 32
Symington, Senator Stuart 242, 285
Symon, Sir Alexander 98
Syria: Ba'th Party agrees Union 46; creates trouble in Lebanon and Jordan 62, 63, 357n95; disillusioned with Egyptian rule 73; Ba'th quarrel with Nasser and lose office 111; Nasser fails to see Syrian discontent 111-12, 378- 9n20; quarrel with Qasim affects trade 111, 378n19; Ba'thist politicians resign 125; military officers will lead coup against union 125, 383n97; Sarraj starts purge of military 125; Viceroy Amer blocks Sarraj purge 125, 383n96; Ba'thists claim Nasser caused the split 201, 418n50; military coup dissolves UAR 201; Ba'thists overthrow government 300, 451n42; call for tripartite unity with UAR and Iraq 300; Military Committee in power 300; Nasserists attempt coup which fails 303

Talbot, Phillips, US Universities Field Staff: reports on Tamil separatists in India 96-7; Raising A Cry for Secession 97; NEA policy troika 184-5; Kennedy appointee controls diplomacy 186; believes Nasser problems due to Dulles' prejudice 196; explains cancellation of Nasser visit 204; opposes sale of Hawk missiles to Israel 205; visits Riyadh and discusses reform 207; chairs Iranian Task Force 213; produces options for dealing with Iran 219; visits Iran and defuses emergency 225-6; rejects Shah's visit to US 228; Holmes uses him to lobby for Shah's visit 232; says Kennedy not impressed by Nehru 257, 438-9n80; hopes for Indian-US relations 260; US needs both India and Pakistan 261; predicts Ayub not secure enough to talk on Kashmir 286-7; Kashmir talks will need diplomatic pressure 288; senses relation between Kashmir and military aid to India 291; thinks India can become an asset against China 296; states UAR no

threat to Israel 302; worried by Kennedy's personal diplomacy 353
Talhouni, Bahjat, Jordanian Prime Minister 135-6, 197
Taylor, General Maxwell 232, 429n9
Tell, Wasfi, Jordan Prime Minister 197, 198, 276, 277, 301
Thag La Ridge 280, 281
Tibet 170, 291
Time magazine 7
Times of India 178
Tito (Josip Broz) Yugoslav President 32, 119
Tolkovsky, Dan 145
Trevelyan, Sir Humphrey, British Ambassador: Suez costs Britain dominance in Middle East 38, 346-7n135; Iraq withdraws from Baghdad Pact 113; encourages US relations with Qasim 119-20; assures Qasim US is not creating hostile front 122, 381n72; plays down Qasim's threats to Kuwait 198; warns an Arab dispute may fuel anti-British mood 199
Truman, President Harry S 4, 8, 314
Turkey: military coup 190, 247, 433n9
Turkish-Iraqi defensive alliance 1955 19, 319
Turkish-Pakistani Pact 18, 25, 36-7, 394n1
Twining, General Nathan F 152

U Nu, Burmese Prime Minister 29
U-2 'Blackbird' surveillance flights 93, 145, 167
'Umran, Muhammad 300
United Nations: talks on Aden-Yemen border 57; Security Council peace initiatives 66; General assembly 138-9, 203, 261
US: intelligence failure Iraq 114-15
US intelligence sites in Pakistan 93, 105, 167, 259, 289, 312, 316, 440n96

US policy: British influence tilt towards monarchies 5, 330n4; concludes Pakistan needs political stability 10, 375-6n40; Eisenhower's priorities 13; fear of Communist take-over in Iran 13-14, 332n14; use of Islamic influence in the Cold War 15, 332n19; defensive military agreement with Pakistan 24-5; internal security arms only for Nasser 33, 344n121; sees economic aid as key to stability 34-5; abandons support for nationalism 35, 345n130; loyalty of security forces key to stability 37-8; condemns any coup against Nasser 38; continues economic aid to India 41; more modest targets for 1958 42; Egypt-Syria Union better than Communist takeover 47, 349n17, 349-50n18; refuses to join Baghdad Pact 48, 351n24; overtures to Egypt 49, 351n29; will not interfere in Syria 52, 352n38; moves to regain influence in Cairo 54, 354n53; intends to recognize UAR 57; renewed attempt at economic aid for leverage 58, 357n80; rapprochement with Nasser 59, 357n87; criticism leads to pressure to act 70, 362n37; concern about Nasserism recedes 77; will normalize relations with Nasser 77-8; return to containment of Communism 78, 366n77; economic aid to Iran, not military 80, 367-8n2; encourage reform for Iranian people 84; doubts Shah will survive xenophobia 85; relies on Iranian military to support reform 85, 369n19; fears disaffection in Iranian army 89; warns Tehran against using Kurds to upset Baghdad 90, 272n50; fears Soviet influence on Kurds 91, 372n53; split between pro-Indian and pro-Pakistani policy 102; aiding military rule in Pakistan is an exception 103; for containment, with security aid as well 104; flexible containment adjusts to regional issues 107; concern about Iraq becoming a Soviet satellite 114; considers working with Nasser 114; agree with British on non-intervention in Iraq 116-17, 380n45; approaches Nasser in joint anti-Communist effort 119; delight at Nasser's friction with Moscow 121; sees success of pragmatic policies 126; disagreement with British over Jordan 128, 384n2; presses Jordan to come to terms with UAR 129-30; tells Hussein to cease propaganda campaign 135; deplores Jordan's anti-Nasser propaganda 136, 387n41; pleased with Majali's departure 136, 387-8n45; will withdraw funding for aid to Jordan 139, 388n59; chooses containment over Arab-Israeli peace 142-3; welcomes Feisal's improvements in Saudi Arabia 142; ends grant-in-aid for Israel 144, 392n82; monitors Israeli nuclear program 146, 393n88; agrees military aid to Pakistan 150, 394n2; bilateral security agreement with Iran 154-5, 397n22; assessment of Shah's position 161; proposes Kennedy invite Shah for state visit 163; military rule is necessary 164, 400n68; Pakistan considered benevolent dictatorship 166; fears Soviet influence in India 169, 403n105; refuses modern fighters to India 171, 405n123; allows Nasser's visit to lapse 204; reform and change for Yemen without involvement 206; search for ways of galvanizing reform in Iran 217, 426n24; Iranian Task Force continues Eisenhower policy 219-20, 223, 427n52; Rusk sets up Iranian Task Force 219, 426n29; overt support for Iranian land reform 222; support of Amini creates breathing space 222; permanently tied to supporting the Shah 226; military assistance program to Iran 231-2; military aid to Turkey and Pakistan 234, 429n20; across the board cuts in grants to Iran 239; US jurisdiction over US military personnel 244-5, 432n62; solution to Kashmir problem not possible 252; to strengthen ties with Pakistan 263; assures YAR Saudi forces are not active in Yemen 273, 444n34; sends combat aircraft to Dhahran 273; recognizes Yemen Arab Republic 276-7, 445n58, 445n59; if Feisal withdraws from Yemen, so will UAR 294; maintenance of Jordan serves US interests 303, 452-3n59; threatens to end PL 480 wheat to Egypt 305; containment policy 314; poor intelligence over Egypt-Syria Union 349n8

Vietnam: North infiltrates Laos 255, 257, 258; US intervention in South 257, 438n77

Voice of the Arab Nation Radio, Cairo 55, 137, 138, 303, 452n54

Wailes, Edward T, US Ambassador 88, 152, 154, 220, 221, 223

Washington Post 290

West Berlin crisis 251

West Germany 140, 196, 338-9n61

Whitney, John Hay 'Jock', US Ambassador 74

Wilson, Charles E, Secretary of Defense 20
Wright, Edwin M, US Chargé 132
Wright, Sir Michael 68

Yapp, Malcolm E 152
Yemen: declines US aid package 54-5; threatens Aden 55, 355n56; plot to overthrow Imam Ahmad 56, 206, 356n60, 356n63, 420n90; places artillery on Aden border 57; claims to Aden 206; Soviets supply arms 206, 420n89; Jordan and Saudi Arabia back royalists 265, 294, 295; UAR sponsors republican government 265; coup creates Yemen Arab Republic 268, 442n4; new Iraqi regime supports UAR and YAR 299
Young, Professor T Cuyler 217, 231

Zafrullah Khan, Sir 258, 262
Zahedi, Ardeshi, Iranian Ambassador 215
Zahedi, General Fazlullah 14, 15
Zubayri, Muhammad Mahmud al- 55, 269
Zuhur, Abd-al-Karim 301